THE LOST ONE

THE
LOST ONE

A LIFE OF
PETER LORRE

❖

STEPHEN D. YOUNGKIN

THE UNIVERSITY PRESS OF KENTUCKY

Publication of this volume was made possible in part by a grant
from the National Endowment for the Humanities.

Scholarly publisher for the Commonwealth,
serving Bellarmine University, Berea College, Centre College of Kentucky, Eastern
Kentucky University, The Filson Historical Society, Georgetown College,
Kentucky Historical Society, Kentucky State University, Morehead State University,
Murray State University, Northern Kentucky University, Transylvania University,
University of Kentucky, University of Louisville, and Western Kentucky University.
All rights reserved.

Editorial and Sales Offices: The University Press of Kentucky
663 South Limestone Street, Lexington, Kentucky 40508-4008
www.kentuckypress.com

09 08 07 06 05   5 4 3 2 1

All illustrations are from the author's private collection unless otherwise noted.

Library of Congress Cataloging-in-Publication Data

Youngkin, Stephen D.
   The lost one : a life of Peter Lorre / Stephen D. Youngkin.
      p. cm.
   Includes bibliographical references and index.
   ISBN 0-8131-2360-7 (hardcover : alk. paper)
   1. Lorre, Peter. 2. Motion picture actors and actresses—United States—Biography.
I. Title.
   PN2287.L65Y64 2005
   791.4302'8'092—dc22   2005009206

Dedicated to

MEY

and

JMA

CONTENTS

Illustrations follow pages 106, 266, and 426.

ACKNOWLEDGMENTS

Dating from the late Curmudgeon Period, I am the most disgruntled detractor of those Academy Award recipients who shed glycerin crocodiles and name names I've never heard of (and don't care to): from a twice-removed aunt who sewed sequins on a grade school costume to a mechanic who lubed the Ferrari that got them there. However lonely the writing of a book, it is uniquely individual. Or so I told myself until I began crediting my many contributors. The list fast scrolled into a cast of thousands. Composition, it appears, is no less collaborative than film production.

For those who kept me company for most or all of the way, I am infinitely grateful, for without them I might well have steered off course. Raymond J. DeMallie midwifed the birth of the biography and babysat it through early drafts, exercising a maternal care that was deeply touching. Without his willingness to broach the idea of a book to Vincent Price, who kindly made himself available for countless questions and consultations, the project might not have survived its infancy. Mary Youngkin rode the roughest part of the journey and paid the highest fare, with few complaints. Her tendered support played many unsung roles. When the conveyance slowed to a crawl, my wife, Julia Alpert, got out and pushed, then pulled, and finally whipped it over the finish line. Never did she ask to get off, however long the ride or distant the destination. My debt of gratitude to her is greater than can be expressed.

I also owe a collective thanks to the Lorre family—brothers Francis and Andrew (Bundy), sister-in-law Zelma (Musia), daughter Catharine, nephew Lawrence, and niece Kathy (Vern-Barnett)—which weighs me down with "interest and interest's interest." By allowing me to go to the wellspring of memory as often as I liked, they helped quench my thirst for source materials. Though unrelated by blood, Celia Lovsky, Peter Lorre's first wife, qualifies as family. Friend, mother, and helpmate to Peter, she was all that and more to me. Understandably cautious, Robert Shutan invoked attorney-client privilege long enough to cross-examine me. Finding my motives just and honorable, he offered a hand in friendship and a memory keen with insight. James Lyon, the beacon of Brecht scholarship, inspired me to set my sights higher with his constructive criticism. I am also much indebted to James Bigwood and Raymond G. Cabana Jr., my coauthors on *The Films of Peter Lorre.* Our collaboration has fed a friendship that has not gone out of print. Cheryl Morris, who has contributed the most comprehensive list of Lorre's radio, television, and American stage credits to date, climbed aboard in the early stages of what stretched into a prolonged passage to the printed word. As she matured from enthusiast to expert, her proofing skills likewise developed into editorial expertise. Milena Hidatty and Ursula Gressenbauer, my Berlin and Vienna contacts, mopped up more errands than I thought possible during the push toward submission. Their patience and perseverance tested positive time and time again. Knowing there are no small details, Tom Weaver kept the east-west pipeline flowing with a steady stream of rare finds. To archivists, librarians, interviewees, and buttonholed co-workers who shared this adventure, I am equally thankful to them and for their contributions. University of Southern California archivist Ned Comstock comes first to mind. If all the acknowledgments paying tribute to his service above and beyond the call of duty were laid end to end, he would have a book to himself, which is as it should be. With feet on both continents, Lotte Guertler extended an old-world hospitality and a new-world common sense. How lucky to find a Hamburgian who told it like it was and tells it like it is. Dr. Ron Smelser, Department of History, University of Utah, kept his red phone free for emergency consultation on matters historical. Janet Smoak arbitrated disputes between me and my chronically contentious computer. Nancy Litz flew many fact-finding missions over the Internet. Ted and Martha Youngkin kept the lights on in Studio City. From New York, my agent, Adam Chromy, exercised careful patience and perseverance in placing my manuscript in the right hands. Leila Salisbury, David Cobb, and the staff of the University Press of Kentucky brought this long journey toward publication to a final destination. Lois Crum kept me on track, adding much without taking anything away. To these and countless others who bore tales of Lorre labors with polite forbearance, I give thanks.

Interviewees and other individuals: Robert Alda, Irwin Allen, Robert Allen, Jürgen von Alten, John Alvin, Eric Ambler, Leon Ames, Morey Amsterdam, Ken Annakin, Samuel Z. Arkoff, Fred Astaire, Frankie Avalon, Charles Barton, Pat Battle, Thomas Beck, Don Beddoe, Charles Bennett, Eric Bentley, Elisabeth

Bergner, D.A. Berryhill, Alvah Bessie, Gerhard Bienert, Henry Blanke, Edwin H. Blum, Richard Bojarski, Ronald V. Borst / Hollywood Movie Posters, Mort Briskin, Karl Brown, Joseph Buloff, Murray Burnett, David Butler, Red Buttons, Jeanne Cagney, Corinne Calvet, William Campbell, Frank Capra, John Carradine, Rudolph Cartier (Katscher), Chick Chandler, Ralph Clanton, Roger Corman, Hazel Court, Broderick Crawford, John Croydon, Robert Cummings, Delmer Daves, Ron Davis (Southern Methodist University), Irma Delson, William Demarest, Walter Doniger, Gary Dorst, Kirk Douglas, Frances Drake, Amanda Duff, Philip Dunne, Hal Eddy, Barbara Eden, Axel Eggebrecht, Lotte H. Eisner, Denholm Elliott, Terry Ellison, Julius J. Epstein, Paul Falkenberg, Harun Farocki, Rudi Fehr, Fritz Feld, Marta Feuchtwanger, Geraldine Fitzgerald, Richard Fleischer, Robert Florey, Norman Foster, Gustav Fröhlich, Suzanne Gargiulo, Tay Garnett, Rhonda Gaylord, Leonard Gershe, Julie Gibson (Barton), Sir John Gielgud, Harper Goff, Alex Gordon, Barry Alan Grael, Martin Grams Jr., Dr. Ralph Greenson, Daniel Haller, David Hamson, Mike Hawks, Paul Henreid, Gerald Hiken, Alfred Hitchcock, Felix Hofmann, John Houseman, John Huston, Andreas Hutter, Joe Hyams, Burl Ives, Lotte Jacobi, Sam Jaffe, Joyce Jameson, Paul Jarrico, Rudolph Joseph, Michael Kanin, Hal Kanter, Irvin Kerschner, Andrea King, Sidney Kingsley, Howard Koch, Paul Kohner, Walter Kohner, Ernst W. Korngold, Johanna Kortner-Hofer, Henry Koster, Ben Kranz, Buzz Kulik, Kay Kyser, Ilse Lahn, Inge Landgut-Oehlschlaeger, Fritz Lang, June Lang, Lilli Latté, Matthew Levins, Dr. William C. Link, Johnny Lockwood, Joan Lorring, Rouben Mamoulian, Marion Marsh, Tony Martin, James Mason, Richard Matheson, Victor Mature, Paul Mayer, Herb Meadow, Burgess Meredith, Marta Mierendorff, Ivor Montagu, Caroline Moorehead, Jacob and Zerka Moreno, Harry Morgan, Milton Moritz, Robert Morley, Oswald "Ossie" Morris, John Mueller (University of Rochester), Corinna Müller, Harold Nebenzahl, Jean Negulesco, Gerhard Nellhaus, Joseph M. Newman, Phillip Notarianni, Jan Oser, Marvin Paige, Hermes Pan, Harvey Parry, Lee Patrick, Lotte Pauli-Rausch, Alf Pearson, Joseph Pevney, Karlheinz Pilcz, Richard Pirodsky, James Powers, Fred Pressburger, Walter Reisch, Naomi Replansky, Rhoda Riker, Allan Rivkin, Cliff Robertson, Casey Robinson, Wolfgang Roth, Viktor Rotthaler, Jochen Ruge, Willy Saeger, Hans Sahl, Lester Salkow, Wendy Sanford, Tom Sawyer, Jürgen Schebera, Dan Seymour, Sidney Sheldon, Vincent Sherman, Armin Shimerman, Herman Shumlin, Don Siegel, Jonas and Beatrice Silverstone, Curt Siodmak, John Spalek (State University of New York at Albany), Milton Sperling, Sam Spiegel, Ellis St. Joseph, Michael Stock, Herbert Swope, Barbara Sykes, Paul Tiessen (Wilfred Laurier University), Michael Todd Jr., John Trayne, Gisela Trowe, Janell Tuttle, Ludwig Veigel, Hans Viertel, June Vincent, Ilse

Waldner, Joseph Warren, Lotte Lenya Weill, Billy Wilder, Bob William, Elmo Williams, Lucy Chase Williams, Bob Wood, Thomas Wood, Morton Wurtele, Margaret Tallichet Wyler, Keenan Wynn, Irving and Naomi Yergin, Alastair Young, and Paul Zastupnevich.

Archives, institutions, and organizations: Walter Huder, Akademie der Künste (Berlin); Krista Vogt and Hannelore Renk, Akademie der Künste der DDR (East Berlin); Phil Gries, Archival Television Audio Inc.; Archiv Dr. Karkosch (Munich); Associated Actors & Artistes of America; Carol Stuart, *Aufbau;* Bayerische Staatsbibliothek (Munich); Krystyna Rohozińska-Owczarek, Biblioteka Uniwersytecka, Uniwersytet Wrocławski (Wrocław, Poland); Bibliothèque du film (Paris); Marc Wanamaker, Bison Archives (Los Angeles); Elfriede Borodin, Brecht-Weigel-Gedenkstätte, Stiftung Archiv der Akademie der Künste; Brenner-Archiv (Innsbruck); James D'Arc, Special Collections and Manuscripts, Brigham Young University (Provo, Utah); Claire Thomas and Saffron Parker, British Film Institute National Library (London); Bundesarchiv/Filmarchiv (Berlin); Ceskoslovenska Socialisticka Republicka, Ministerstvo Vnutra (Bratislava); Brigitte J. Kueppers, Julie Graham, and Lauren Buisson, Arts Library Special Collections, Charles E. Young Research Library, University of California, Los Angeles; Anne Caiger, Department of Special Collections, Charles E. Young Research Library, University of California, Los Angeles; Cinémathèque Suisse (Lausanne); Copyright Office, Library of Congress (Washington, D.C.); Deutsches Filmmuseum (Frankfurt am Main); Eberhard Spiess and Gerd Albrecht, Deutsches Institut für Filmkunde (Wiesbaden); Jörg Wyrschowy, Deutsches Rundfunkarchiv; Embassy of the Czechoslovak Socialist Republic (Washington, D.C.); Bernd O. Rachold, The Erich Wolfgang Korngold Society; Otto G. Schindler, Fachbibliothek für Theaterwissenschaft an der Universität Wien; Emil P. Moschella, Federal Bureau of Investigation, U.S. Department of Justice (Washington, D.C.); Beth Alvarez, Ferdinand Reyher Papers, Rare Books and Literary Manuscripts Department, University of Maryland College Park Libraries; Marje Schuetze-Coburn, Feuchtwanger Memorial Library, Specialized Libraries and Archival Collections, University of Southern California, Los Angeles; Jerome Johnson and Kristine Sorensen, Filmarchivists/Filmarchivists; Filmbewertungsstelle (Wiesbaden); Francis A. Countway Library of Medicine (Boston); Fred Bauman, The Fred Allen Papers, Manuscript Division, Library of Congress; General Register Office (London); Edda Fuhrich-Leisler, Gesellschaft für Max Reinhardt-Forschung; Gary Adams, Grand Order of Water Rats (London); Handelsakademie und Handelsschulen der Wiener Kaufmannschaft; Erwin Strouhal, Hochschule für

Musik und darstellende Kunst in Wien, Archiv; Henry S. Dogin, Immigration and Naturalization Service, U.S. Department of Justice (Washington, D.C.); Institut für Theaterwissenschaft an der Universität Wien; Gustav Kropatschek and Rosina Raffeinder, Josef Stadt-Archiv, Theater in der Josefstadt (Vienna); Karl Kraus Archiv der Stadt Wien, Stadt- und Landesbibliothek; Kunsthistorisches Museum (Vienna); Herbert Koch, Magistrat der Stadt Wien; Samuel A. Gill and Kristine Krueger, Margaret Herrick Library, Academy of Motion Picture Arts and Sciences; Toni Neidlinger, Markt Garmisch-Partenkirchen; Linda Burns, Marriott Library, University of Utah; Forschungsarchiv Marta Mierendorff, Max Kade Institute for Austrian-German-Swiss Studies, University of Southern California, Los Angeles; N.Ö. Landes- Real- und Obergymnasiums (Mödling, Austria); Peter Michael Braunwarth, Österreichische Akademie der Wissenschaften (Vienna); Michael Omasta, Brigitte Mayr, and Elisabeth Streit, Österreichische Filmmuseum, SYNEMA—Gesellschaft für Film and Medien; Österreichische Nationalbibliothek (Vienna); Österreichisches Staatsarchiv-Kriegsarchiv (Vienna); Haris Balic, Österreichische Theatermuseum (Vienna); Ken Greenwald and Martin Halperin, Pacific Pioneer Broadcasters (Los Angeles); John Munro-Hall, RKO Radio Pictures Inc., Studio Collection (Los Angeles); Romania Arhivele Nationale (Bucharest); Schiller Nationalmuseum, Deutsches Literaturarchiv (Marbach am Neckar, Germany); Valerie Yaros, Guild historian, the Screen Actors Guild (Los Angeles); Janet McKee and staff, Sound Recordings Department, Library of Congress, Washington, D.C.; Staatliches Filmarchiv der DDR (East Berlin); Dagmar Bouziane, Staatsbibliothek zu Berlin; Staatsbürger-schaftsverband Mödling; Stadtarchiv Zürich; Stephen Dörschel and Sabine Wolf, Stiftung Archiv der Akademie der Künste (Berlin); Werner Sudendorf, Stiftung Deutsche Kinemathek (Berlin); The Theater Collection of the Lincoln Center for the Performing Arts (New York); Sigurd Paul Scheichl, Universität Innsbruck; Basil Stuart-Stubbs, Special Collections Section, University of British Columbia; Ned Comstock, USC Cinema-Television Library, University of Southern California, Los Angeles; Stuart Ng, Stuart Galbraith, and Haden Guest, USC Warner Bros. Archives, School of Cinema-Television, University of Southern California, Los Angeles; Paul A. DuCommun, U.S. Public Health Service; Jerry Haendiges, Vintage Radio Classics; Volksbühne Archiv / Bibliothek (Berlin); Ingeborg Weiss, Westdeutscher Rundfunk Köln; Wiener Stadtbibliothek, Handschriften-sammlung; Wiener Stadt- und Landesarchiv; Susan Dalton, Wisconsin Center for Film and Theatre Research (Madison); and Zentralbibliothek, Institut für Theaterwissenschaft, Freie Universität Berlin.

PROLOGUE

"WHO ARE YOU, REALLY?"

We live in times when there is a tremendous exaggeration
on the glamour of viciousness, of angriness, of hardness, all
the so-called basic faults. Well, kindness has become
identified almost with weakness and attractiveness. To me,
it is much more fascinating to make kindness fascinating.
—Peter Lorre

Indeed in pretending to be somebody else, he [the actor]
does not show himself; he conceals himself.
—Otto Fenichel

As a little girl bounces her ball against a *Steckbrief* (wanted
poster) pasted to a circular pillar, the shadow of Hans
Beckert falls across the sheet.
"What a pretty ball!"
The shadow bends down.
"What is your name?"
"Elsie Beckmann."
—M

Walking along Hollywood's Highland Avenue one fall evening in 1977,
twenty-five-year-old Catharine A. Lorre, sole heir to the face and fame of her
highly recognizable father, watched a police car pull up and cut her off. Out of
the vehicle stepped two undercover vice-squad officers, who flashed their badges

and demanded to see some identification. Among the papers in Catherine's purse was a photo of herself at age ten sitting on her father's lap. "Look what we've got here," one of the policemen allegedly said, handing the snapshot to the other officer. They let her go.

Two years later, former Glendale auto upholsterer Angelo Buono Jr. and his adoptive cousin Kenneth A. Bianchi confessed to the "Hillside Strangler" murders of ten women as well as an abortive attempt to abduct and murder an eleventh: Catharine Lorre. According to Bianchi, posing as police officers, they intended to order her into the car, but they changed their minds after learning that she was meeting someone nearby. Catharine told a different story, one that might have twisted her father's smile into the ironic grin so familiar to moviegoers. After abandoning the thought of ransoming her, claimed Catharine, the starstruck killers decided to spare the look-alike daughter of their screen hero who, as Hans Beckert, had won fame for his psychopathic tendencies toward young girls in Fritz Lang's *M* (1931).

Neither Catharine nor little Elsie Beckmann dreamed what was in store for them. From benign beginnings, no one, especially the intended victims, could have expected such malignant endings. With Beckert, Bianchi, and Buono's on- and offscreen admissions of guilt, persons and personas soon sorted themselves out. The "Hillside Stranglers" were confessed killers, and that was that. They would spend the remainder of their lives in prison.

For Lorre's part, he simply hung up his costume and walked away. But the paying public wasn't buying. "Look, it is not me they see," he told a friend. "It is the murderer. I am not famous. It is the murderer. . . . they think I am the murderer." After personifying the "Vampire of Düsseldorf," claimed the actor, he raced from hostile crowds, dodged stones, watched forks drop from plates, and received death threats—all signs, however exaggerated, of a mistaken identity that surely gave him pause to reconsider his statement about enjoying roles that complemented part and player. Even Fritz Lang thought better of casting him as an innocuous schoolteacher after witnessing the backlash to a performance as convincing as it was credible.

In the wake of *M*, Peter Lorre watched the "lively," "naive," "melancholy," "explosive," "carefree" personality that had found expression on stage slip from public view. The mantle of screen villainy concealed it. According to friends and co-workers, we saw only the tip of the iceberg. Beneath the surface lay unplumbed depths. Sound waves sent out saying, "Who are you, really? And what were you before? What did you do and what did you think?" came back only as vague blips. Finding the real Peter Lorre proved difficult. His "life interest" had gained the upper hand on his life long before the cinema opened up to him. He was, in a word, elusive, at times laughing at the truth, at others hiding from it. He was also modest. Opening up about himself in interviews went "against the grain," he explained to New York talk-show host Helen O'Connell in 1961. "I had a very strict father and he brought me up not talking about myself, like a decent person should. Now in an interview, all of a sudden you have nothing but talking about yourself, so you have to overcome a certain amount of inhibition." He also had not joined the throngs of actors who had penned autobiographies: "It's a racket now. I want to be the only actor who never wrote a book."

As a biographer, I soon realized I would not reconcile man and myth by treading ties. Middle ground does not accommodate who Peter Lorre was and what he became. I broadened my parameters. Spanning the wide tracks of his personality conditioned my appreciation of the extremes of his life. Along the fringes of memory, I found scattered remnants of a being long since extinct, one who had given us not what he wanted of himself, but what he thought we wanted. Between creator and creature stood a man who had lost his way.

I

FACEMAKER

Acting is a ridiculous profession
unless it is part of your very soul.

—Peter Lorre

At the beginning of the twentieth century, Arad looked to the future. Thanks to its position as an important railroad junction, the commercial center of southeastern Hungary boasted one of the largest distilleries in Europe, its own brand of flour (Arad Königsmehl, or King's Flour); a lumberyard; and wagon, machine, and barrel factories. The surrounding countryside produced grains, fruit, tobacco, honey, and cattle. Underground lay gold, silver, and copper. Above lived nearly 40,000 inhabitants. Predominantly Roman Catholic, the population also included nearly 10,000 Greek Orthodox Christians and 5,000 Jews, together with Greek Catholics, Lutherans, and Reformed Protestants. Little wonder the bustling community could afford to top its new city hall with a tower and fund a telegraph, a business school, a cathedral, a conservatory, a theater, and a horse-drawn trolley to connect the growing suburbs. Given its importance as an industrial hub, it is not surprising that the city attracted the business-minded Loewensteins.[1] Born to Savolta and Wilhelm Loewenstein, an office worker and assistant rabbi, in nearby Csene on January 27, 1877, Alajos followed in his father's footsteps. After graduating with honors from a three-year commercial academy in 1897, he established himself at the Erste Arad Fabrikshof Aktiengesellschaft, a manufacturing concern. Three years later, he stepped into the comfortable position of chief bookkeeper at Adolf Weigel and Company.

The need to supplement his income no doubt played an important part in his decision to join the *kaiserlich und königliche Armee*, the professional standing army of the Habsburgs, on September 18, 1897. More likely, his love for Emperor Franz Joseph tugged at his heart and universal military service forced his hand. Whatever his motivation, Loewenstein signed up for one year at a volunteer training school, ten years in the *Heer* (army), and two years in the *Landwehr* (national guard). The *Haupt-Grundbuchblatt* described the five-foot-four soldier as having black hair, brown eyes, a well-formed mouth, a round (dimpled) chin, and an oval face.[2] A surviving portrait of Alajos Loewenstein in his uniform shows a proud man with clear, strong features that convey a firm sense of purpose.

Loewenstein began at the bottom but advanced rapidly. After passing the volunteer's one-year examinations at the infantry regiment number 33, Kaiser Leopold II, in Arad, he was promoted to the rank of titular corporal, then field sergeant. Another exam paved the way for his rise to deputy cadet and finally lieutenant in January 1901. Believing war with Russia inevitable, the Dual Monarchy had increased its military budget in 1895. The army was slowly awakening from a period of stagnation, and active reserve officers, drawn from the ranks of the one-year volunteers, were becoming increasingly important. Alajos was among the better-paid public servants. He was soon earning six thousand kronen per year, three times what he was making behind his desk. That he was able to speak and write both German and Magyar pushed his stock higher. Besides being remunerative, the Austro-Hungarian Army—composed of "different and often hostile nationalities . . . held together by tradition and discipline"—was surprisingly liberal, becoming one of the first European forces to open its officer corps to Jews. Military historian Gunther E. Rothenberg notes that although the "well-educated and largely middle class Jewish population of the monarchy" constituted only 5 percent, it "continued to provide over 16 percent of reserve officers."

Between military exercises at nearby Grosswardein (Nagyvárad), Loewenstein found time to marry twenty-three-year-old Elvira Freischberger, a native of Zubrohlava, on September 8, 1903. The following year he accepted the position of chief bookkeeper with the Textil Industrie Aktiengesellschaft in Rószahegy, a small primarily Slovak town of 12,490 inhabitants nestled against the High Tatra Mountains on Hungary's northern border. Rising sharply out of a high plateau in the central Carpathians, they kept close company with the Transylvanian Alps. However, as the elevation dropped, wolves, bears, and wildcats gave way to spring and summer cow pastures and, lower yet, to vineyards. Closely tied to the land, Rószahegy depended on the production of textiles, wood, cotton, flax, grains, livestock, and marble.

On June 26, 1904, Elvira gave birth to their first child, László, who would become better known as Peter Lorre.[3] True to what would become an all-too-familiar pattern of enforced absenteeism, Loewenstein barely had time to greet his new son before reporting for another month of military maneuvers. Two years later, a second son, Ferenc (Francis) was born. In April 1908, shortly after giving birth to a third son, András (Andrew), Elvira died of either blood or food poisoning, depending on the brother who searched a distant and vague memory of a mother he never knew. Her death certificate cites blood poisoning (*vérmérgezés*, literally "angry blood") as the cause.

"To me, the food poisoning theory is much more plausible," said Kathy Vern-Barnett, Francis's daughter. "'Opi' [Alajos] had an absolute obsession about not saving up cooked potatoes (even when we had refrigeration). He insisted that they were poisonous."[4]

Loewenstein, who was seldom home, recognized the boys' need for a mother and married Elvira's schoolmate and best friend, Melanie Klein, who raised them (and Liesl and Hugo, her two children by Alajos) almost single-handedly. Lorre later told his first wife, actress Celia Lovksy, that when Melanie entered the house in her new capacity, he hid under his bed. His stepmother apparently neither forgot nor forgave the affront, setting the bitter tone of their relationship. Lorre admitted in 1947 that he had gotten along very poorly with Melanie, who "spoke of him only in terms of the prodigal who let them down, who wasn't there to support them when they needed it." The hand-held joy nurtured by Elvira's touch turned to closed-fisted defiance of the interloper. Young László struck off from the family. Instead of playing soccer with his brothers, he kept to his room and sketched and painted in watercolors. "At home and also in school," Francis recalled, "he kept separate from us, never joined in any play we had in mind and never helped to do the home chores, which we had to do before leaving for school, such as make the beds, clean and so on." Kathy recalled that the "extremely pragmatic" Melanie, who insisted that the boys learn to knit, sew, and cook, disapproved of László's sloppy ways and late hours, habits that were, to her mind, symptomatic of an artistic temperament. Described by Andrew and Francis as a strict but loving parent who doled out equal treatment to the boys, she won no recognition from László, who willfully resisted her efforts to mold him in the image of her successful brother-in-law, Oskar Taussig, and resented her harangues about the importance of good grades.

Lorre's childhood memories of what he called the "dark mountains" yield little else. Those who imagine a Kafka-like tragedy in his youth that will solve the mystery of Peter Lorre are disappointed. It did not exist and he knew it.

The best lies couldn't hide the truth. Nonetheless, by steering people away from his early years, he helped create the mystique of clouded beginnings.

His memory of the period ran to extremes, when it flowed at all. In 1936 he confessed that the death of his mother had "taught me what sadness can be." Lorre disingenuously credited his father with being "a very rich man, owning many castles." History again took a back seat one year later when he dug into his early memories of Christmas for interviewer J.M. Ruddy.

> To my small boy's mind, no other event could compare in grandeur and enchantment with the thrill of Christmas. For nights my dreams were filled with wonderful thoughts of a bag full of beautiful toys and luscious candies dropped down our chimney by the ever-thoughtful Kris Kringle.
>
> But always I was doomed to disappointment. My family was thrifty and exceedingly practical. My father and mother realized how much wiser it was, if not so pleasing, to supply their son with a pair of extra warm boots, or a new pair of pantaloons, than to give him something which would fill his heart with joy but not further material welfare.

Forty years later, Andrew had only one thing to say about his brother's Yuletide tales of colorfully garbed country folk, full larders, street dancing, and plaintive carols: "Unadulterated B.S." Peter, he maintained, would have remembered little about life in Hungary because by 1910 the Loewensteins had moved on to Brăila, Romania, where Alajos had been promoted to inspector at another division of the Textil Industrie Aktiengesellschaft. Brăila, with its nearly sixty thousand inhabitants, was far from rustic. The one-time military fortress was now a transportation nexus. Both hub and harbor, it lay on the Barbos-Buzau line of the Romanian state railway and trafficked grains to Constantinople by steamship down the Danube River to the Black Sea. Here, László and Francis enrolled in a private German school. Although Alajos had been transferred to nonactive status in the *Landwehr* in December 1907, the breakout of the Second Balkan War in August 1913, and the likelihood of a larger conflict, in which he most certainly would be called to play a part, induced him to move his family to Vienna (Landstrasser Hauptstrasse 123) in September.[5] There they stayed with "Uncle" Oskar Taussig, who was married to Melanie's sister, "not a real uncle," said Francis, "but he definitely was a good friend of my father and helped him on many occasions when he was in trouble, which, unfortunately, was very often."

Loewenstein's military service record, somewhat inexplicably, ends here. According to Francis and Andrew, their father was called up August 5, 1914, one day after World War I erupted. As the oldest ranking lieutenant in his regiment, he was automatically promoted to *Oberleutnant* and assigned to the Third Army's operations on the Eastern Front, where he witnessed the collision of the Austro-Hungarian and Russian forces in the Carpathians during the winter of 1914–15. Bitter fighting produced heavy casualties, while subzero temperatures and severe food shortages pushed the death toll higher. By 1916 the Austro-Hungarian Army had suffered eight hundred thousand dead and another 1 million sick or wounded. Although a German-supported counteroffensive repelled the Russians, thousands fell into enemy hands. After heart trouble forced him to retire from active duty, Alajos was put in charge of a Russian prisoner-of-war camp. "I believe the Russians praised him," said Kathy, who recalled hearing her grandfather tell stories about "cleaning up the barracks where they were living and feeding them, because by the time some of those Russian soldiers were finally caught by the Germans in that particular area, they were on the verge of starvation." During their internment the prisoners fashioned an aluminum ring with a copper inlay inscribed "M.L. 1914/16," which they presented to Melanie in appreciation of their kind treatment.

In March 1915 Loewenstein moved his family to Ludwig-Höflergasse 20 in Mödling, ten miles south of Vienna, where they lived in a townhouse built in 1913 by the Jugendstil architect Karl Lehrmann. Since the nineteenth century, this fashionably expensive bedroom community near the Wienerwald had drawn artists who wanted to retreat to the country but stay within striking distance of the city. There they could touch nature and be touched in turn by the area's famous *Heurigen* ("new wine" from the last vintage). The city also hosted a Jewish enclave of merchants, tradespeople, and civil servants. While only 100 of Mödling's 18,680 inhabitants (fewer than 1 percent) listed their religion as Israelisch, they formed a *Kulturgemeinde* (cultural community) that exerted influence beyond its number.

Here László attended *Mittelschule* (sixth to ninth grades) at the Niederöster Landes Realgymnasium from 1915 to 1917, when the family again moved, this time to Valeriestrasse 88 (today Böcklinstrasse), near the Prater, Vienna's great amusement park. As a Jew and one of only two private students, he was in the minority. While his brothers applied themselves, studying long hours in anticipation of helping their father support the family, the "clever" László seemingly breezed through school, admitted Francis, "with an ease which was always an envy from my side." He earned A's in drawing and writing and B's in religion, German, history, geology, mathematics, and physical fitness. He lagged behind only in Latin with a C.

Grades, however, tell only part of the story of László's school years. No one has painted a more damning picture of turn-of-the-century education than the Austrian novelist Stefan Zweig. Using "unfeeling and soulless" methods, unapproachable teachers taught nothing worth knowing. School became a treadmill of lifeless lessons as coldly impersonal as the dreary, barracks-like classrooms, whose whitewashed walls smelled of mold and whose hard wooden benches twisted the spine. Doctrine, dogma, and discipline suffocated the intellect and suppressed the spirit of many but engendered in others "a hatred for all authority" that awakened a passion for freedom. For these students, the "impulse to creative production became positively epidemic," fostering an "artistic monomania." Melanie's stringent standards had edged László out of the nest, but school "spread his soul out wide" for flight into the boundless worlds of art, literature, theater, and, alas, business.

Loewenstein acquired three thousand acres along the Sava River in Carinthia after mustering out of the army. Rich in mountain scenery, the Austrian crown land, with more than 1 million wooded acres, was populated by far more trees than people, who numbered only eighty-four inhabitants per square mile. Now an agriculturalist, Loewenstein filled small timber contracts for the army. In May 1917 less lucrative circumstances necessitated relocation of the Loewensteins to the inner city. After months of deprivation in Vienna, where ration cards allowed each adult only a small portion of meat that was all but inedible, when it could be found, the family depended increasingly on their country estate. Here the boys spent "the nicest time of our youth" eating, playing, and working. To earn a little pocket money, László and his brothers harvested hay, minded cows, and collected apples from more than two thousand trees and helped press them for wine. Alajos also taught his sons the fundamentals of horsemanship. A detachment of military riders furthered their equestrian education by teaching them circus trick riding. Fit and full-bellied, the boys returned to the city of shortages.

With war's end, lands changed title. Loewenstein's property became part of the new Kingdom of the Serbs, Croats, and Slovenes, called Yugoslavia after 1929. According to Andrew, because he had served in the Austro-Hungarian Army, Alajos was classified as an "enemy officer" and his land was placed under state supervision, with a commissar to oversee its production.[6] Convinced that the government supervisor was skimming off the profits, Loewenstein sold the estate to Uncle Oskar, who, since he had not served in the army, could operate the business free of restrictions, and started dabbling in the grain export business. Through Taussig, who was on the board of Steyr-Automobil-Werke, he also developed a long association with the car company. Loewenstein's promotion to director of sales for personal cars and trucks eased the family's financial worries but kept him on the road for weeks at a time. "Practically always on the move," he would not come to rest until he moved to Australia in 1949. "My father was very intelligent, oversensitive and a good organizer," observed Francis, which was "perhaps the reason [why] he was either on top and in high position or without a job for many years." A photo taken toward the end of the war frames a face world-weary in its lean knowing. Tired and subdued, Loewenstein once again felt the weight of starting over in a city whose burgeoning population (from 476,220 in 1857 to 2,031,420 in 1910) had witnessed the growth of a housing shortage into a housing crisis. Rents ate up more than one-quarter of a worker's wages.

Unlike the stabilizing Melanie, Alajos hovered just a couple inches above the ground. "Opi was an idealist," said Kathy. "He wasn't a terribly practical man." Strongly bound to his cultural roots, Loewenstein nurtured "a passionate secret love, [which] was the establishment of a Jewish homeland in Palestine and [he] was a great supporter and admirer of the Hungarian journalist Theodor Herzl." His conversion to Catholicism during the war years had been, according to the family, only a "life-saving exercise." When asked by the Gestapo how long he had been a Catholic, Loewenstein reportedly replied, "Let's just say that I have been a Free Mason for a lot longer." Until his death in 1958, he faced east every morning and faithfully read from the Hebrew prayer book.

Alajos also prided himself on his ability to "examine a pregnant woman's hand and prognosticate as to what the sex of the child would be," said his granddaughter, "and I never knew him to be wrong. I remember him very proudly telling me that he won two dollars from Bogie [Humphrey Bogart] because he forecast his son and daughter to Lauren Bacall."

In September 1918 good marks allowed László to advance to the second year of a four-year business program at the Wiener Handels-Akademie. Already striking his independent colors, he listed his religion as *konfessionslos* (without a confession of faith or creed). The designation set the pattern for nonobservance that characterized the rest of his life. Like so many of his artist friends, he fell somewhere between agnosticism and apathy. Given his fiscal irresponsibility as an adult (euphemistically dismissed as inattention to daily details), it is easy to understand why he never mentioned that he had earned high grades in merchant and travel geography, commercial history, business mathematics, bookkeeping, business law, and economic policy. László took his final exam on June 28, 1921, and graduated the following week at the top of his class, a distinction that undoubtedly would have surprised his future creditors.

Actors who talk about being bitten by a bug or infected by a desire to act might have taken their cue from Lorre, who claimed that his addiction to acting amounted to a disease transmitted by an unknown host. Although Lorre expounded by the paragraph when questioned later about the psychology of acting, he had little to say on the subject of his beginnings. He later explained, seemingly searching his own past for the seeds of his first flowering, that as a young boy he had "read a great deal ["like somebody else is eating," said Francis] and lived in fantasies wherein I acted, all unconsciously, my many parts." Francis recalled that he and László debuted as dwarfs in a grade school production of *Snow White.* "I was the smallest of these people," recalled his brother, "and Peter the biggest one. Of course, we just had to hop around on the stage and not talk." If Lorre remembered his early introduction to the stage, he never spoke of it.

László did not act again until his *Mittelschule* years. When his German professor learned that Hans Winge was casting three one-act plays for a theater evening, he recommended a student from another class. László Loewenstein accepted the role of a quarrelsome defendant and stood upon the stage of the Vienna Kammerspiele for the first time. "He had no interest in the theater," wrote Winge, "but I infected him with my enthusiasm. . . . I dragged him into the theater and into the movies and further from the business career, which he had intended to pursue."[7] Again, Lorre seemed to have forgotten his first role as a criminal.

Lorre later downplayed his acting origins and the idea of "expressing yourself. I think they are automatic. You either make faces or are born to it, or you don't like it and that's all there is to it." He commented in 1935 that becoming an actor wasn't a conscious decision: "I did not say to myself, 'I am going to be an actor,' because I did not really know what an actor was. But somewhere, in my subconscious being, the root stirred and motivated me and I went. . . . I knew then why I had left my father's house."

Not without a word of advice. As the apple of his father's eye, László bore a double burden. Loewenstein expected great things of his firstborn and looked to him to set a good example for his younger brothers. News of his son's acting aspirations fell on unappreciative ears. Acting was barely tolerable as an avocation; as an occupation, it was downright foolish. With Vienna's economy in shambles, he warned, his son would starve. Loewenstein urged him to pursue a more practical profession, a trade with a solid future. Unable to "imagine that anybody would be wasteful enough of their talents to want to go into such a thing as the theater," recalled Kathy, Melanie seconded her husband's opinion.

Thanks to his influential Uncle Oskar, a director at the Anglo-Österreichischen Bank in Vienna's Strauchgasse, László landed a job in the foreign exchange department.[8] According to his first *Meldezettel* (residence registration forms), in late October 1922 he took up lodgings in Margarethe-strasse 56. The local authority listed his occupation as "beamter" (official) and his religion as "konfessionslos." Within a few months, the clever and efficient bank employee headed his section. His superiors smiled down on him. Herr Engel, his manager, even extended his hand in friendship. Earning his own way sat well with László. The six telephones on his desk rang to the importance of his new position. Alajos beamed with pride and sighed with relief.

What his father did not know—and the local authorities soon learned—was that László divided his life into public and private sides. In early April, when he moved from Webgasse 30 to a studio apartment in Fischerstiege 9, he again filled out the required *Meldezettel*. Alongside the designation *beamter* is a handwritten note that reads, "auch Schauspieler" (also actor). The young bank employee had, in effect, come out from behind his desk.

With "some other nuts" determined to explore their acting skills, László built a stage in a barn. After quickly learning that the inexperienced actors became self-conscious and stiff delivering memorized lines, he suggested an improvisational approach. One of the players would invent a situation and create a character. The others would then define their roles, ad-libbing the dialogue and the action until they exhausted the possibilities of the situation, and then move on to another scene.

"I am amazed when I look back now," Lorre reflected from his Hollywood home some sixteen years later. "We acted out these plays we had concocted. They were bad and we were bad—but we were acting. And do you know my parents had been so strict that I had never been inside a theater; had never seen a play? I was an actor before I had ever been part of an audience."

The late nights played havoc with László's schedule. One day he didn't report to work. When Herr Engel telephoned to inquire after his absent worker, Melanie told him that her son had left that morning at the usual time. That evening, when he returned home, she confronted her undependable stepson, who declared that he wanted to be an actor, not a bank teller. "Counting people's money is a thankless business," he later said. László vowed he would not return to work, but Melanie's strong hand prevailed. Herr Engel opened a canned speech about tardiness.

"You know," interrupted László, dropping a sure hint, "you can fire me, but you can't reprimand me so severely." (To make sure that others didn't miss the point, he appended to the oft-repeated story a postscript about wiggling his ears during the lecture.)

Engel fired him.

In a revised version of the story told to New York talk-show host Helen O'Connell in 1961, Lorre confessed that he "wasn't very good" at banking: "One day the manager of the bank told me a long story in front of all the other people. To me it was very boring. I didn't listen to him, so I guess unconsciously I wiggled my ears and everybody laughed and I was fired."

Whatever the cause, "his boss got him past the promise he had given his father that he wouldn't quit," explained Peter's brother Andrew. "From that time on he just devoted his entire attention to the stage."

It was the worst of times for an actor. Postwar Vienna knew poverty, hunger, widespread unemployment, and rampant inflation. "We got our pocket money and carried it home in two suitcases, all paper," recalled László's friend Walter Reisch, who went on to become a prominent screenwriter at Universum Film AG (UFA) and eventually wound up in Hollywood.[9] "By the time you came home you couldn't buy a cigarette with it." Against this backdrop, László decided to "run away from home." There was a ring of truth to it, just enough, in fact, to feed the movie tabloids years later. More accurately, the door closed on him and he drifted away. After losing his bank job in November 1923, László lodged on a day-to-day basis, first at the Hotel Wandl for a few months and then at the Hotel Nord for a few weeks. On nights when he could not afford even a cheap room, he turned up at home. But with Alajos away, Melanie had set new rules. She told László she could not forbid him to stay there, but if he wasn't home by nine o'clock, he would be locked out for the night. Likewise, if he failed to show up for meals, he could go hungry. Francis recalled that although László never came home again, "sometimes he was so desperate he waited in the morning in front of our flat until my sister and I went to school and we gave him the sandwiches our mother had packed for us. I know that for some time this was the only food he consumed, as he had no money to buy anything. We also gave him our pocket money and sold some of our books in order to give him something to live on." At one point, the large-hearted Loewenstein also gave László what he thought would be an adequate sum to tide him over until he found work as an actor, despite his disapproval of his son's new career. The next week, however, the jobless offspring returned for another handout, prompting heated discussions between Alajos and Melanie. To keep peace in the family, he secretly deposited an allowance with his attorney. Once a week, László rolled in to collect the gratuity.

During the making of *I'll Give a Million* some fifteen years later, Lorre told actor John Carradine that he had lived in packing crates and even "robbed people out of necessity." However much romance he read—and later related—into his poverty, he did sleep on wooden benches in the nearby Prater. With the metallic grind of its giant Ferris wheel, the pinging of the shooting gallery, and the cacophony of outdoor concerts, it is no surprise that he sought out, as he later claimed, a bed of pine needles in the woods or a quiet doorway. Reduced to selling newspapers to buy his beloved goulash, he used the extras as bedding. Celia remembered Peter telling her that hunger forced him to trade his "little lilac wool jacket for a roll."

"For a long while I went hungry and friendless and cold," Lorre told an interviewer in 1935. "I knew park benches for beds and the feel of a face pressed against the window of a sweet-shop." People didn't know it to look at him. Because of his starchy diet, he stayed surprisingly pudgy, although his health was poor: "I am the only actor, I believe, who really had scurvy."

Francis recalled that his brother was determined to act: "I know that once he decided to be an actor, he stuck to it and spent all his time either going to the theater or learning."

To shelter himself from the elements as well as gain free entrance to the theater, László joined a claque, or group of clappers, at the Burgtheater. Around seven-thirty each evening a stagehand admitted László, Walter, and a few others and planted them throughout the theater, where they were expected to sigh, whistle, laugh, and applaud at just the right moments in the show. The members of the claque received no pay for their services, but they nurtured their aspirations—for as many as thirty performances of the same play—of one day finding themselves on the stage. "Peter's great obsession and ambition was the theater," recalled Reisch, "and since at that time Vienna had an enormously rich theater life, he spent practically every night there."

While the theater filled his head with dreams, the American government filled his stomach with food. Under the direction of Herbert Hoover, the American Relief Administration supplied foodstuffs to the war-torn countries of central Europe after the armistice in November 1918. After its liquidation, Hoover helped form a private charitable organization called the European Children's Fund, which provided food and clothing to needy youngsters until June 1922. Reisch credited Hoover with saving his and Lorre's lives:

The Herbert Hoover action was one of the most beautiful things God ever invented. . . . Hoover's name was more popular in Austria than Abraham Lincoln or George Washington, much more important than Woodrow Wilson. . . . It was always four o'clock in the afternoon when the kitchen opened. . . . Anybody who lined up with a pot and a little box could, free, completely free, by the grace of the United States of America, get a big pot of chocolate, which was unheard of. Hot chocolate! And a huge piece of *gugelhupf,* which was a certain pound cake. . . . And while lining up, Peter only talked about the theater.

Destitute and malnourished, László jumped the ship of blind optimism and security enjoyed by the older generation and was swept away by the liberal tide of the times. Vienna's younger generation rejected the moth-eaten morality, "petrified formality," and "disciplined conformity" of a bourgeois existence. For László, abandoning the values he had known at home made way for a new emphasis on self-expression, intellectual mobility, and bohemianism.

While the theater satisfied his ambition to become an actor, another Viennese institution met most of his other needs. In the literary coffeehouse, László discovered the "ersatz totality" that family, profession, and political party could not offer. It was a home away from home for those who could not afford even a cramped and cold apartment. There, too, he could stay busy without purpose, receiving and answering letters, making telephone calls, discussing the merits of a play, a book, or a painting, or perusing an assortment of newspapers and journals. As an "asylum for people who have to kill time so as not to be killed by it," the coffeehouse held body and soul together, soothing what writer Alfred Polgar liked to call a "cosmic uneasiness" by offering escape "into an irresponsible, sensuous, chance relationship to nothingness." Here the "organization of the disorganized" built an inner world out of anecdote at the expense of facts.

Lying "on the Viennese latitude at the meridian of loneliness," the literary coffeehouse offered "solo voices [that] cannot do without the support of the chorus" a longitude of fellowship among the cultural elite. To an assimilated Jew with artistic aspirations, the strong Semitic presence of the coffeehouse was an intellectual magnet. At the Café Central László could huddle anonymously over a cup of coffee or rub shoulders with writers of *Kleinkunst* (small forms), such as Polgar, Peter Altenberg, Egon Friedell, and Karl Kraus.[10] Or he could walk a few steps down narrow Herrengasse and further his education in psychoanalysis at the spacious and sunny Café Herrenhof, which was frequented by Alfred Adler, Siegfried Bernfeld, Otto Gross, and Adolf Josef Storfer.[11] Something of a shining figure there, "Laczy" (pronounced Lazzy) Loewenstein brilliantly advertised his cabaret gifts. Milan Dubrovic, the doyen of Austrian journalism, remembered László "as an unmasked blitz parodist notorious and famous for his mischievous sayings, puns and bawdy rhymes, which he produced on an assembly line." Most famously, after the homosexual actor Gustaf Gründgens wed actress Marianne Hoppe, he devised the popular chant

Hoppe, Hoppe Gründgens
they don't have children.
And if they do have children,
they are not by Gründgens

Reduced to begging, László made the café circuit in the hopes of cadging a cup of coffee or collecting enough spare change to buy something to eat. At one stop, he met William Moreno, whose older brother Jacob had founded the Stegreiftheater (Theater of Spontaneity) in 1922.[12] Jacob Moreno believed that traditional theater had lost its surprise. Words and gestures had grown tired in their long trip from page to stage. To restore the lost sense of immediacy, he proposed stringing together "now and then flashes" that would unchain illusion and let imagination run free. As a young medical student at the University of Vienna, he had walked through the public gardens collecting children for "impromptu play." In his interactive kindergarten, he learned how to "treat children's problems by letting them act extemporaneously." He also conducted sessions in the streets and at military camps, prisons, and hospitals. On April 1, 1921, psychodrama, a "science" that explored the therapeutic effects of spontaneous drama, was born.

Not only social misfits, malcontents, and psychological rebels (which László must certainly have appeared to be) were attracted to the experimental theater, but also natural actors untainted by experience or orthodoxy—certainly a cut at Freud's teachings—and gifted enough to improvise both gestures and dialogue. Among those who came by the Stegreiftheater to watch, listen, and learn were Alexander Moissi, Ernst Toller, Georg Kaiser, Franz Theodor Csokor, and Arthur Schnitzler.

William Moreno was intrigued by the young waif. Zerka Moreno, Jacob's widow, recalled that William listened attentively to László's stories of street life and (somewhat skeptically) to his claims that "he had been ejected from his parental home because he had impregnated a maid" and that his parents "were middle-class people who could not deal with him, and did not support him in any way."[13] He reported to Jacob that he had met a rather odd-looking young man who was in need of a job. He "might be a suitable character for the theater, he had such a curious smile and face, quite unforgettable." Would Jacob like to meet him? He would. Jacob, who was "always fond of mavericks, being one himself," tested László at the Stegreiftheater, "putting him into a situation with a surprise element, to test and evaluate his ability." He apparently showed promise and was invited to become a regular member of the acting troupe in 1922.

Years later, Lorre remembered it as an "ideal school of acting." Instead of focusing on linear time, the actors discovered a collection of moments that aroused "the subject to an adequate re-enactment of the lived out and unlived out dimensions" of their private worlds. In this way, he pointed out, they could commit "dramatic suicide," if they were so inclined, and rid themselves of psychic complexes at the same time. Always contemptuous of conventional methods, Lorre defiantly pointed out that acting cannot be taught in school: "I don't believe in studying a thing that lies definitely in the realm of imagination." Rather, he believed that "the actor must have a feeling for it. If a person acts because he has 'learned it in school,' rather than because he has a striking talent for it, he'll just be reaching a dull medium in his performances."

Also known as The Therapeutisches Theater (Therapeutic Theater), the Stegreiftheater followed two lines of development, one purely aesthetic-dramatic, the other psychiatric. Steering a course between the "ecstatic pathos of expressionism" and direct analytical therapy, Moreno stressed the need to define the individual in relation to the group, an approach that put László in the spotlight. As a talented improviser capable of using his "facial muscle acrobatics" to instantly change his normal expression—a "mask frozen in an ugly grimace"—from the saintly face of a Tibetan beggar monk to that of a demonic lust murderer, he was an ideal actor for Moreno. The so-called star of the Stegreiftheater, according to Dubrovic, could motivate patients who played with him to "spontaneous healing reactions." Zerka Moreno remembers hearing about another side of László: "He acted particularly in roles involving streaks of cruelty, pimps, murderers, gamblers, etc. One of his best roles was that of a wealthy miser who lived, however, in abject poverty and whose sole reason for living was to count his money, neatly stacking his coins and from time to time letting them run through his hands as if they were water. His delight in this was captivatingly infectious."

One day the distraught fiancé of Moreno's chief actress complained that his angelic sweetheart, Barbara, acted like a "bedeviled creature" when they were alone. Moreno smiled his "mixture of mockery and kindness" and said he would try a remedy. Because she had taken part in his extemporaneous, living-newspaper experiment, Moreno told her that "news just came in that a girl in Ottakring (a slum district in Vienna), soliciting men on the street, had been attacked and killed by a stranger." Moreno, pointing to László, identified him as the "apache" and told the actors to "get the scene ready." László

came out of an improvised cafe with Barbara and followed her. They had an encounter, which rapidly developed into a heated argument. It was about money. Suddenly Barbara changed to a manner of acting totally unexpected from her. She swore like a trooper, punching at the man, kicking him in the leg repeatedly. . . . [T]he apache got wild and began to chase Barbara. Suddenly he grabbed a knife, a prop, from his inside jacket pocket. He chased her in circles, closer and closer. She acted so well that she gave the impression of being really scared. The audience got up, roaring, "Stop it, stop it." But he did not stop until she was supposedly "murdered."

The therapy worked. Having acted out her problems on stage, Barbara joyfully embraced her fiancé, and they went home "in ecstasy."[14]

Just as Moreno's "moments" anticipated poet and playwright Bertolt Brecht's "pictures"—there the similarity ends—László's self-presentations foreshadowed what he later described as "psychological" acting. "There is little doubt," wrote Zerka, "that Moreno was one of the sources of his awareness of human psychology and its role in acting." The psychodramatist counseled his players and patients to "lift the veil" and make evident what is genuinely there but "hidden, repressed or denied." Through nonverbal acting techniques, his actors made their bodies speak explicitly and learned to put the gesture before the word, pairing it with the abstract or unspoken.

Jacob Moreno clearly recognized László's talent for "learning to be in the core of the role, swapping skins with another's feelings and being." Helping the budding actor to find himself and a style that answered his apparent needs did not, however, preclude constructive criticism. After watching him repeat his best lines and movements—he had already adopted the "peculiar grin" he later trademarked in Hollywood—Moreno cautioned him to "de-conserve" his "mimic behavior."

Moreno drew László into his circle at the Café Herrenhof, where he and the nineteen-year-old Billy Wilder sat at the "kitten table for the children." Among this group were Franz Werfel, Franz Theodor Csokor, and the highly respected Viennese character actor and director Karl Forest, who took the aspiring artist under his accomplished wing and schooled him for the stage. Forest played the provinces—Ingolstadt, Czernowitz, Reichenberg—after mounting the boards at the age of seventeen. He moved on to Munich, Hamburg, and finally, in 1898, Berlin's Deutsches Theater, where he appeared in productions of Gerhart Hauptmann, Henrik Ibsen, August Strindberg, Frank Wedekind, Carl Sternheim, and Georg Kaiser and took classical roles as well. In 1917 he returned to Vienna and the Deutsches Theater, the Burgtheater, the Raimund Theater, and the Theater in der Josefstadt. Grounded in realist drama, he gravitated toward "an exploding expression of fate." Wilhelm Kosch wrote that he was "an episodist of the fantastic, the farcical in a human being, a macabre humor. At the same time, the strong, graphic power of his drawing shows up in his delicate lines, which let the human and his fateful background suddenly blend into each other so that one had to think of Kubin."[15] Perhaps László recognized something in Forest that he saw in himself.

Moreno couldn't release this talented unknown into the world without giving him a more suitable professional name. The psychodramatist borrowed his friend Peter Altenberg's Christian name, bemusedly recalling the actor's resemblance to the character of Struwwelpeter, an unruly young man in German children's literature "whose hair and nails grew to unreasonable ungroomed lengths." For a surname, Moreno suggested Lorre, which means "parrot" in German. (Perhaps a more accurate origin of the word is the common parrot vocalization of the phonetic equivalent of "lora," a predictably popular call name.) "This name would mean he could keep the same initial as in both his given names," said Zerka. "'Parrot' seemed the right designation for him. Probably Lorre's ability at mimicry was the source of the inspiration."[16]

Lorre told German film editor Paul Falkenberg "that he met an actor friend in Vienna, who said, 'Oh, Peter, I'm going to see an agent for a job. Can you help me read the cues?' So Peter said, 'Fine, I'll come along.' And they went to see the agent and Peter read the cues and the other guy spoke his part. At the end of the performance, the agent said, 'And who are you?' pointing to Peter. 'My name is Peter Lorre,' he told him. 'I have a job for you in Breslau,' said the agent. He forgot about the professional actor and hired Peter right on the spot."

Falkenberg stated that this account "came from Peter's mouth." For public consumption, however, Lorre standardized the story that Leo Mittler, director (along with Paul Barnay) of the Lobe and Thalia Theaters in Breslau, Germany, saw him perform at the Stegreiftheater and offered him a job. "Moreno did say that [Lorre] needed to earn more money," said Zerka, "and was ambitious for a wider audience—as what actor would not be?" Lorre later admitted that after going "through a certain period of Bohemianism, . . . then you have enough of it." The working actor claimed he didn't know what his services were worth and was afraid to ask. Bit parts, he soon learned, paid one hundred marks (about twenty-four dollars at the time) per month, an apparently tidy sum to a destitute artist, especially one who was also expected to pay for his basic costume: white shirt, dark suit, hat, and shoes. Alajos gave his son an old suit, the only thing he could spare, and train fare.

No other period in Lorre's life suffered as much sheer reinvention as his first shaky professional steps. He later shrugged off his early experience, insisting that he had no idea of what constituted acting, only that "an actor was a guy not allowed to speak in his natural voice." Lorre told George Frazier of *Life* magazine that "his efforts to disguise himself as a basso profundo were so ludicrous that he inadvertently found himself regarded as a comic." Judging by his comments about his first professional stage performance, Lorre preferred to have audiences laugh with him rather than at him, putting one of his most often told anecdotes in some kind of perspective. "I was on the stage in a small city in Germany," he later said of his role as a Teutonic warrior in Heinrich von Kleist's *Die Hermannsschlacht* (*Hermann's Battle*), "and I had a small part, but everybody laughed [at] every line I said. Well, they didn't know that it wasn't intentional. I had never been to school and didn't know how to walk or speak or anything." As punishment, the actor was stuck in a line of bearded soldiers carrying spears: "It so happened that the man in front of me pointed backward and said, 'Do you see the Roman eagles?'" Lorre wiggled his ears and the audience howled. He was fired for a second time. "Don't ask me about any more firings," he appealed to O'Connell. "The next one might be coming up."

In another version closer to the event, Lorre said he "dropped my spear, flapped my arms in true eagle fashion, and tried to look as much like a bird as possible. Everyone thought this very amusing—everyone but the producer, who promptly fired me."

All kidding aside, Lorre found himself not in stock theater, as he liked to imply, but at elegant provincial theaters with distinguished traditions. Here he performed in a variety of small roles, often seven days a week, in both afternoon and evening productions, during 1924–25. At the Lobe Theater, which sounded a higher literary note, he appeared in a bit part in Gustav Freytag's comedy *Die Journalisten* (*The Journalists*), under the direction of Hans Peppler; as a donkey in the Grimm brothers' fairytale *Die Bremer Stadtmusikanten* (*The Bremen Town Musicians*); as a soldier in the historical *Die Hermannsschlacht*; and as a tousle-haired apothecary in *Romeo und Julia* (*Romeo and Juliet*). At the Thalia Theater, which struck a more comedic and often folksy chord, Lorre could be seen—if you looked closely—as a servant in Shakespeare's *Die lustigen Weiber von Windsor* (*The Merry Wives of Windsor*).[17]

German writer Hans Sahl, then a student at the University of Breslau, "did not expect Peter Lorre to become a great actor. He was a nice guy with no particular characteristics, except for his protruding eyes." They "gave him the look of a demonic, pop-eyed frog and . . . predestined him for criminal and gangster roles. He loved to parody himself and to scare others." Sahl regarded Peter as "very intelligent, well read and very ambitious. He was very eager to become somebody, but he was not a faker, he was very, very serious about it."

The writer recalled, "We often went all night long through the little streets of Breslau and spoke about future fate and about the difficulties of making something of yourself. 'I would rather stay a little actor who plays small parts big than a big actor who plays big parts small,' he once said to me. Lorre became a great episodic actor who gave small parts a new dimension."

For now, however, failing health cramped his "dreams of grandeur." "When I got my first engagement," Lorre told Federal Bureau of Narcotics Inspector Theodore J. Walker and Agent Sam Levine in February 1947, "my appendix started bothering me, as a result of the hardships which I had experienced, after which I was operated on." Interviewed by Dr. D.D. Le Grand at the U.S. Public Health Service Hospital in Ft. Worth, Texas, several weeks later, he explained that his appendix had finally ruptured, necessitating surgery. It marked the first episode in a complex and often confusing progression of health problems that eventually led to drug addiction.[18]

Lorre developed a close friendship with Hans Peppler during his time in Breslau. A giant of a man and a former navy captain, the actor and director more closely resembled a Casanova type than a celebrated character performer of the Berliner Volksbühne (People's Theater), where he later starred as Zola in *Dreyfus*. When Peppler moved on to Zurich's Schauspielhaus the following August, he took Lorre with him.

Over the next nine months, Lorre appeared in more than twenty-five productions at the Schauspielhaus and the Stadttheater, most often with Peppler and under his direction, and usually as a *Chargenspieler* (supporting actor), playing small parts big. (As a member of the ensemble, he also put his business degree to use, working behind the scenes as secretary and treasurer of the actors' union.) In his first performance, he played two parts—Sir Oliver Martext and a farm boy—in Shakespeare's *As You Like It* (*Wie es euch gefällt*). His next role, which he performed "excellently," according to the *Neue Zürcher Zeitung*, was that of Gilman, the greasy and greedy merchant in John Galsworthy's *Gesellschaft* (*Loyalties*), the story of a wealthy Jew who tries to storm the blockade of British propriety.

From there Lorre moved on to comedies and farces. He played another apothecary in Luigi Pirandello's *Der Mann, das Tier und die Tugend* (*The Man, the Animal, and Virtue*). In the Grimms' fairytale *Das tapfere Schneiderlein* (*The Brave Little Tailor*)—which the actor also adapted with director Fritz Ritter—he gave an "extremely vivid" performance in the lead role, "sometimes, however, with a little too much volume." He also stuck out as one of a dozen noisy scoundrels in Johann Nestroy's *Die schlimmen Buben in der Schule* (*The Bad Boys in the School*).

With few words and gestures, Lorre learned to establish a character quickly. By striving to squeeze the most out of his roles in these early years on the stage, he earned the reputation of a scene-stealer. Hilde Wall, before she married film director Max Ophüls, remembered him drawing the audience's attention as a servant. "His little bit," related screenwriter Ellis St. Joseph, who heard it from Wall, "was to come in and announce that Frau Schultz was here to see her. That's all he had to do, just come in, say those words and go out." Lorre came in and sat down. "'Of course, you know Frau Schultz,' he said. 'Yes, of course, I know her,'" Wall said, simply trying to follow along. Lorre pulled out a cigarette, lit it, and looked up. "'She's been here quite a few times lately, hasn't she?' 'Yes, of course, she's a friend of mine.'" Lorre drew long drafts, puffing the moment into something greater, stubbed out his cigarette, and then got up. "'Well, Frau Schultz is here to see you,'" he said, finally delivering his one and only line. On that, he exited with a hand from the audience.

For every comedy, however, the actor appeared in two dramas, often tragedies, most notably Christian Dietrich Grabbe's *Napoleon oder die hundert Tage* (*Napoleon or the Hundred Days*), in which he doubled as Ludwig XVIII and a grenadier; George Bernard Shaw's *Die heilige Johanna* (*St. Joan*), as a castle manager; Pirandello's *Heinrich IV*, as a lackey; Goethe's *Faust*, as a happy pub patron; Ibsen's *Peer Gynt*, in the double role of a bridegroom and a madhouse director; and Schiller's *Wallensteins Tod* (*Wallenstein's Death*), as an astrologer. He even played in blackface in Leon Gordon's *Weisse Fracht* (*White Cargo*).

Except for a brief hiatus in the fall of 1925, Lorre worked steadily on stage despite "numerous episodes of abdominal cramping pain, vomiting, and diarrhea." Alajos Loewenstein arranged for Dr. P. Clairmont, a Masonic brother, to perform a second surgery in Geneva to remove adhesions resulting from the first operation, which "was not done by the best doctor," and his gall bladder. Familiar with his stage work, the surgeon took special interest in Lorre, which included pumping him full of morphine to relieve his severe pain, "no doubt having the best of intentions, but that seemed to be the beginning," according to his brother Francis.

"On and off during that time," said Lorre, "I had been given great amounts of narcotics," namely morphine, Pantopon, and Dilaudid. "I want to point out here that I was not addicted during this time. This use of drugs on and off lasted for about seven years. . . . Over this period I took narcotics only in the office of the physician who was treating me at that time."

On July 1, 1926, Lorre sent a postcard picturing Vienna's Café Habsburg to Andrew, "My Dear Brother and Kinsman," saying that if he did not hear from (Max) Reinhardt, German's most influential stage director and producer, by Tuesday, he would accept a one-year contract with the Kammerspiele, for a monthly salary of five hundred schillings. The intimate theater seated between 300 and 500 patrons (it had one-half the capacity of the Reinhardt-directed Deutsches Theater in Berlin) and specialized in small plays, often with controversial themes. Through the sheer number and variety of its "chamber plays," actors broadened themselves and sidestepped the typecasting dilemma. On September 29, 1926, Lorre stepped onto the stage of the Kammerspiele in a dual role—as a doctor and as a young lad with violin in hand—in Nicolaus Lenau's *Faust.* Over the next two years he appeared in more than thirty productions, with comedies now outnumbering dramas two to one. Lorre consistently drew positive if limited critical attention commensurate with the size of his roles. In *Die fleissige Leserin* (*The Diligent Reader*), a poorly received parody directed at the lowbrow literary pulps cropping up in Germany, he appeared in nine sketches in roles as diverse as reporter, waiter, and dance maiden, but it was his solo scene as a political protester that "was the hit of the evening." Under Peppler's direction in the farcical *Die Mädchen auf dem Diwan* (*The Girls on the Couch*), he saved another boring performance: "Noteworthy is only the young comedian, Peter Lorre, [for] whom no part, not even the smallest and the silliest, is routine, but a chance for a grotesque human portrayal. This theatrical gift, perhaps the strongest and most original of the entire ensemble at the Kammerspiele, deserves the most attentive encouragement and cultivation."

Offstage, Lorre continued to wear as many hats as he did costumes onstage, most notably those for his positions as chairman and secretary of the local chapter of the Österreichischen Bühnenvereins (Austrian Theater Union). He even earned a credit as set designer on *Die fleissige Leserin.*

During the actor's run at the Kammerspiele, three long-standing patterns emerged. No matter how mediocre the material, how poor the production, or how negative the reviews, he was able to separate himself for the better from the vehicles in which he appeared. "The only one who made an exception was Peter Lorre," wrote the *Arbeiter Zeitung*'s F.R. of his performance in the coolly received cabaret piece *Alles verkehrt!* (*Everything Upside Down!*). "His couplet was a small masterpiece of the stage art by itself but not because of its text but because of the way he presented it." Lorre seasoned his comedy with a dash of the absurd, foreshadowing the delicate balance of opposites that would trademark his screen career. "Peter Lorre tried with success to play a retired president of a court of justice," wrote the not easily impressed F.R., "with his strong talent for grotesque strangeness." Again, as the dim-witted monarchist in *Bitte, wer war zuerst da?* (*Please, Who Was Here First?*), he showcased his "acid-like grotesque humor."

True to lifelong form, he relocated often, changing rooms more often than shoes. But wherever his fortunes led him—from apartment to hotel and back again—he stayed inside Vienna's ring, close to cafés and to the Burgtheater, the Rathaus, the Stephansdom, the Staatsoper, and the Hofburg.

Another trend took tighter hold of Lorre's life. After collapsing on stage, he woke up in a crowded ward of shaking alcoholics and sweating drug addicts at the Wiener Allgemeine Krankenhaus. The cattle-pen conditions made getting a private room a priority. Alajos, who had since moved into the city, soon arrived and arranged for upgraded accommodations. For several months Lorre remained at the public hospital, where he underwent the first of many treatments for drug addiction. When Alajos asked about his son's prospects for recovery, the physician told him that his efforts had been unsuccessful and suggested hypnosis, as a last resort. Francis related that although Alajos was somewhat dubious, he did not stand in the way.

"What was the result?" he asked after his son's first session.

The doctor shrugged his shoulders and replied, "I think I'll give him more morphine."

Discharged without being cured, Lorre began forging prescriptions and falsifying doctors' names to satisfy his addiction.

Franz Theodor Csokor, in whose play *Die Stunde des Absterbens* (*The Hour of Dying Off*) Lorre had appeared at Max Reinhardt's Theater in the Josefstadt in late February 1927, unselfishly lent a helping hand to young and troubled talents. He thought the actor was ready for Berlin, "the most exciting, the most alive, the most productive, and by far the most immoral city in Europe." Its artistic milieu mirrored the hectic metropolis at large. Rattling tramways, screaming car tires, and the rumbling underground gave voice to a brash dynamism. Fed by a "striking mixture of cynicism and confidence," Germany's postwar generation rebelled against the "sticky, perfumed, sultry" traditions of its parents, expressing its detachment through *Tendenzkunst,* art with a political, economic, and social purpose. A flood of isms—futurism, Dadaism, cubism, constructivism, surrealism, impressionism, postexpressionism—interpreted industry, caricatured the military machine, and indicted middle-class morality. Artists of every stripe thronged to dazzling and decadent Berlin, where, Brecht exclaimed to his friend the set designer Caspar Neher, "Everything is jam-packed with bad taste but on what a scale!"

The efflorescence of the arts in Berlin obscured an economic downside. The same city that offered "organically structured" living accommodations to the well-to-do ignored housing shortages that condemned the lower classes to crowded tenements. Severe unemployment in the wake of the Great Crash gave rise to evictions, strikes, demonstrations, and political unrest. In 1925 Berlin was home to more than twenty-eight thousand artists, a high percentage of whom needed to take on second jobs to survive. Conditioned to higher rates of unemployment than workers in other sectors of the economy, theater personnel nervously watched joblessness rise to a startling 44 percent by early 1932, 10 percent higher than the general unemployment rate. Between the 1929–30 and 1932–33 seasons, the number of theaters in operation fell from 242 to 199. Cutting the length of their season kept the doors of some theaters open. Others trimmed salaries and turned contract players into freelance actors. By the 1931–32 season, nearly 50 percent of the working members of the Bühnengenossenschaft (Society of German Theater Employees) earned less than seventy-two dollars a month.

In the winter of 1927–28, Lorre turned up at Berlin's Renaissance Theater with a word of recommendation from Csokor to director Gustav Hartung's assistant and "alter ego," Rudolph Joseph, who had the authority to hire and fire actors, make contracts, and attend to the general running of the theater. Joseph remembered that the young man was polite enough but that "he didn't look too healthy and had rather wet hands." He asked for a job. Joseph usually knew right away whether an actor would fit into the ensemble. Lorre struck him as an "odd type," whom he might not be able to place in parts very often. Certainly, nothing about the newcomer suggested he would become one of the leading actors in Berlin. Joseph wanted to think it over and talk with him again. But Lorre didn't return. Soon after arriving in Berlin, he had suffered an internal hemorrhage and been diagnosed with pulmonary tuberculosis. He was placed in the hospital for three months and given "big amounts of morphine, as a result of which I became addicted." Csokor wrote Joseph and asked him not to be angry with the young man, who had admitted himself to a sanatorium for treatment of his morphine addiction, confident that he would "come out of here very big or not at all."

Several months later, Lorre appeared, not at the Renaissance Theater, but at the Theater am Schiffbauerdamm in search of Brecht. He carried ten marks in his pocket and a letter of introduction from Csokor.

"In my forechamber sat a small comical man who followed me with his glances," wrote Ernst Josef Aufricht, an actor turned entrepreneur who had recently leased the Schiffbauerdamm Theater (now the home of the Berliner Ensemble), located just off Friedrichstrasse.

Each time the theater manager walked by him, Lorre stood and timidly bowed.

"Do you want something from me?" Aufricht finally inquired. Lorre nodded, and Aufricht asked the young man to follow him.

"I am an actor," blurted Lorre, "and I would like to play with you."

Aufricht apologized for laughing. "You look like a tadpole." He peered into Lorre's large, protruding eyes. "They are rehearsing on stage. Ask for Brecht. I'll send you to him for the part of the village idiot in *Pioniere in Ingolstadt* (*Engineers in Ingolstadt*)."

Aufricht caught the spirit of their first meeting, if not the facts. Although Lorre did not officially move from Vienna to Berlin until March 1929, giving his address as Schlüterstrasse 48, the actor had turned up the previous summer, when Brecht cast him as Peachum, king of the beggars, in *Die Dreigroschenoper* (*The Threepenny Opera*).[19] However, when Lorre became ill—one day before opening night, according to his friend Paul E. Marcus, a journalist for the *Berliner Börsen Courier* who signed his work PEM—Erich Ponto stepped into the role, but nearly walked out on the production when Brecht reduced his part.

"[Brecht] cast me in one of the plays he was directing," Lorre later recalled, "because I did not look like an actor." People who met Lorre never forgot their initial sight of him, certainly not Brecht, who could not "hold with beautiful people," recalled actress Lotte Lenya. "Anything a little offbeat appealed to him." "In those days," said Marta Feuchtwanger, wife of novelist and playwright Lion Feuchtwanger, "so many actors were good looking. Peter's physical appearance was a new thing to Brecht, who looked for the exception. He wanted characteristics, not beauty, and sought the unique, the distinctive."

If his looks caught people's attention, his personality held it. Photographer Lotte Jacobi found him fascinating: "Whatever he said, he was unique in saying it. I would have done anything he wanted me to do. I don't know if I had the idea that I was in love with him, but I really was."

Lorre aroused the curiosity of the crowd at the Romanischen Café. "Normally, you don't care about other colleagues," said actor Jürgen von Alten, who worked with him on the Berlin stage, "but somehow he interested us. Even when he did not open his mouth, he had such a fantastic personal magnetism, an aura. We liked him because he was unique and he also transferred that to the stage. He was an actor who appeared and then the air was thick. We accepted him immediately, as an actor, an artist, though not as a human being. He was very reserved, very shy. . . . Although I didn't know him well, I remember him. Lorre is a person you don't forget."

Others thought him strange, particularly his sense of humor and his "ridiculous" views. "We didn't know if he meant [them] seriously or was making fun," said Heinz Rühmann, who shared the stage with Lorre in the 1931 production of Valentine Katayev's popular comedy-farce *Die Quadratur des Kreises*

(*Squaring the Circle*). According to screenwriter Charles Bennett, Lorre loved to tell of "making a movie in Germany that employed forty extras—supposedly soldiers—thirty privates and ten officers. When it came to the lunch break the guys dressed as officers, getting just the same as the guys dressed as soldiers, insisted on eating together; snobbism rampant; being dressed as officers they couldn't eat with those lower forms of extras who were just soldiers."

"He had such funny expressions for people when he wanted to describe them," said German writer and director Hermann Kosterlitz of Lorre's oblique outlook.[20] "The famous German novelist Thomas Mann had a very long thin face and Peter Lorre once said to me, 'Don't you think that Thomas Mann looks like when you sit way in the corner in the front row at the movies?' The president of Germany was a man who had a very quadratic head. Everything was so military about him, and Peter said to me, 'Hindenburg looks to me like every inch is square.'"

On another occasion, Lorre brought a girlfriend named Dina to a reserved table shared by Koster, director Erich Engel, and choreographer Ernst Matray at the Café Vienna on Berlin's Kurfürstendamm. When she momentarily left, Lorre asked Koster what he thought of her. "Very pretty," replied Koster. "She has the smallest mouth that I've ever seen," pointed out Lorre. "She has such a small mouth, she has to eat asparagus with Vaseline."

Lorre's sense of humor also rang in Max Ophüls's ear—he later remembered hearing the actor refer to his red sports car as an "unchained bidet."[21]

Lorre found Brecht onstage. He was a tall, slender man with close-cropped black hair and brown eyes set deeply behind steel-rimmed glasses. More often than not unshaven and reeking of sweat, he nonetheless exuded an animal magnetism that made mistresses of many of his female admirers, who described him as energetic, charming, and charismatic. "He showed himself to be like his poetry," recalled historian Lotte H. Eisner, displaying "a fierce cynicism touched by a comedian's melancholy." The dialectical combination disconcerted some and fascinated others. Such men as Peter Lorre, who described Brecht as "overpowering," and playwright Arnolt Bronnen, who recognized that "in that small, insignificant man beats the heart of our times," fell just as easily under his spell.

Brecht and Lorre talked for half an hour. "It was as if we had known each other for twenty years," the actor later recalled. Brecht told Lorre that he was "going to play the lead in another play I have." For now, however, he would step into the smaller role of a young simpleton. Brecht recommended signing the actor to a three-year contract. Aufricht wanted to think it over, at least until opening night. Meanwhile, Lorre looked up Max Reinhardt.

"Why do you want to come to me?" asked the theater director. "In Berlin, it doesn't matter where you start. Berlin's critics have the best tuned ears and the most papers. You just have to have some talent. Even if you have only a marginal appearance, you will be discovered and find yourself in the headlines. This is a better start than I can offer you. In my ensemble, you would get lost among so many prominent actors." Asked if he had any other possibilities, Lorre replied that the Schiffbauerdamm would probably engage him. "I strongly advise you to take it then," said the professor, smiling. "You know, there is a superstition about that. The Theater am Schiffbauerdamm lies directly on the Spree. From there radiates an aura."

In August 1928 Aufricht had opened the fall season in a "blaze of glory" with Brecht's production of *Die Dreigroschenoper,* adapted from John Gay's *The Beggar's Opera*, an eighteenth-century satire of British society, directed by Erich Engel and set to music by Kurt Weill. Brecht revolutionized poetic language, letting "the naked human being speak, but in a language we have not heard in years." By 1926, however, the loneliness, alienation, and disillusionment of his earlier plays had given way to a new social awareness in which man held the capacity to change the world instead of being changed by it. At the Theater am Schiffbauerdamm, Lorre met a man in progress who led the way by staying one step ahead.

The Schiffbauerdamm Theater was becoming all the more fashionable because of the lively tone of its entertainment, which was irreverent, antimilitary, leftist, and for its conservative critics, smutty and perverse. After transferring *Die Dreigroschenoper* to another theater, Aufricht staged Peter Martin Lampel's antiwar play *Giftgas über Berlin (Poison Gas over Berlin)*, which exposed illegal experiments by the Reichswehr. Censorship and critical indifference closed the show after a single private performance. Aufricht asked himself how he could top his first two scandals and not disappoint his audience. To fill the gap and buy time for Brecht to deliver a new play, he settled on Marieluise Fleisser's *Pioniere in Ingolstadt,* a comedy that had premiered to positive review as *Fegefeuer in Ingolstadt (Purgatory in Ingolstadt)* in Dresden one year earlier.

Fleisser had met Brecht in 1923 and become blindly infatuated with the man she described as "the genius, the peak, the potency, the strong flowing life, a sun, the pure dynamite, the rebel, the irreverent one, the most cried at one, the almighty, the personal lord and master, the creator." After hearing her tell about a company of soldiers on a bridge-building assignment in her hometown in southern Bavaria, he persuaded her to glue together memories of the event. "You must write like a child," he told her. To guide his Galatea, Brecht, who by this time thought of the Schiffbauerdamm as his theater, recommended Jacob Geis, a director whom he could direct. At rehearsals, he intervened to promote his own ideas for a new theatrical style, loosening the scenic connections in Fleisser's simple story to create "an epic tableau with different motifs." Brecht coaxed endless rewrites from Fleisser—"change and change again, there was no satisfying him," she remembered. The handpicked cast, including Lorre, "endured it, when they didn't complain."

On Saturday, March 30, 1929, at 8:30 p.m., an expectant audience filled the nearly eight hundred seats beneath the gilt-edged canopy of gargoyles, angels, and cupids. The entertainment was less respectable than the quaint decor. "This *Lustspiel* presents the morals and customs of deeper Bavaria," advertised a prefatory note. "Using them one can study certain atavistic and prehistoric worlds of feelings." In the first "picture," a company of soldiers on a bridge-building mission marches into Ingolstadt. Like all men-at-arms, they also look for love among the local servant girls. While the sensual Alma (Lotte Lenya) satisfies her sexual appetite with the eager soldiers, the chaste Berta (Hilde Körber) nurses a broken heart when her love is not returned. Fabian (Peter Lorre), "a half-cretin of a high school student," aspires to the soldiers' lusty and callous indifference toward women, but their ridicule transforms his feelings of inadequacy into half-baked schemes of vengeance. After wreaking havoc in the ordered lives of the citizens of Ingolstadt, the soldiers exit town over the bridge they have built. Behind them they leave the used and abused servant girls, and Fabian, who satisfies his desire with a local whore.

Fleisser recalled that Brecht "was aiming for scandal because that guaranteed success." By sexually charging the performance, he pushed public tolerance for prurient entertainment past acceptable limits and nearly pulled the Theater am Schiffbauerdamm apart at the seams. Some hissed; others cried, "Silence!" At times Aufricht thought the company couldn't go on with the show. A member of the Nazi SA (Sturmabteilung or Storm Troops, a.k.a. Brown Shirts), wrote one reviewer, voiced his protest with a stink bomb. When Fleisser and the cast came on stage afterward, members of the audience booed, whistled, and applauded for fifteen minutes. Lampooning the army was in bad taste, but that a woman should do so was intolerable. Sex in a cemetery and defloration in a heaving and pitching wooden crate was too offensive for words. A police officer, who coincidentally had been a lieutenant with the soldiers at Ingolstadt, declared, "Do you believe that we allow such things?" A threatened ban on the play forced cuts, and Aufricht invited the critics to a revised performance on Easter Sunday.

"The times had their special sharpness," wrote Fleisser with understated economy worthy of Brecht. "They were already loaded up with that which came afterwards." No one, it seemed, occupied the middle ground. Rival critics Alfred Kerr and Herbert Jhering singled out Fleisser as a most gifted young writer and her piece a natural portrait of everyday life, "splendid in local stupidity." Others condemned *Pioniere in Ingolstadt*'s sexual explicitness as sordid, unwholesome, and deliberately orgiastic and faulted the play for its undeveloped story and characters, its fragmentary construction, slow tempo, and failure to surpass the depiction of the Bavarian milieu—all failings Fleisser chalked up to Brecht's domineering influence.

The loudest voice took a dimmer view. Richard Biedryznski, writing for the *Deutsche Zeitung,* pointed to the play as a precursor to anarchy: "Things are ready to explode. The more unrestrained impudence becomes, so grows our disgust, our self defense and our exaltation of the censorship of vulgarity. Mean-ness breeds anger. . . . The concert has begun. It will continue in the street. Soon the battue can start and the best actors won't be able prevent the cultural bankruptcy of the theater and its political annihilation." What sounded like bad press was praise to Brecht's ears. Besides shocking the audience to its conservative core, he had taken another developmental step toward his epic theater. Branded as an informer and a traitor, Fleisser became a social pariah. Though her father advised her not to return to Ingolstadt, she eventually did so. In 1933 the Nazis burned her books and forbade her to write.

Lorre fared much better than the play itself—establishing a pattern of rising above theatrical storms—by sticking to Fleisser's conception of a feeble-minded youth whose helplessness of expression blocks his feelings, until he discovers the colloquial language of sex. True to Fleisser's "natural art," he traversed the border between comedy and tragedy with complete facility, expressing the most complicated of feelings—pathos and passion—by the simplest means. "Peter was completely uninhibited when he was acting," said Lotte Lenya. "Just all at once, his talent came out. It came natural to him, that same kind of tragedy that moves people without their having to do anything, just be there. Just one look of Lorre's conveyed more than any other actors could do in a whole scene."

Alfred Polgar, critic for *Das Tagebuch,* pronounced Lorre an actor according to Berlin taste: "He bills himself; through each word, each gesture demandingly pressing. . . . He stretches out a second. A slow motion actor."

Kurt Pinthus described the new discovery in Berlin's *8-Uhr-Abendblatt:* "And a new face was there, a frightful face: the hysterical son of the petty bourgeoisie, whose bug-eyed, bloated head swells in a yellowish manner out of his suit; how this lad staggers between sluggishness and hysterical outbursts, as he timorously walks and grasps and sometimes greedily fumbles. Even people older than I am have never seen anything so uncanny in the theater. This person is *Peter Lorre*. If he can also portray other figures in such a comprehensive manner, then here is a first-class actor."

After the performance, Lorre stood on the stage and looked out into the cheering crowd. "I was afraid," he recalled, "that it was mock applause, that it was like the laughter which greeted me when I rehearsed my first part in Breslau. Then I realized that these people were really cheering me. It was heady wine. I thought, 'Now, I can buy a new suit.'"

Lorre told Quentin Reynolds of *Collier's* that Aufricht threw his arms around him and said, "Lorre, my boy, you were wonderful. What do you need? Money, perhaps? Ask me for anything and it is yours."

Presumably stretching a point, Lorre related that he "was still in a daze. I didn't have, literally, a mark in my pocket. I said to him, laughing, 'My friend, you might give me 30,000 marks [$7,200].' The manager reached in his pocket and peeled off thirty thousand-mark notes. I had never seen money like that— no, not even when I worked in the bank. I took it and said, 'In the morning I will buy a new suit.'"[22]

"I was the hottest thing on the Berlin stage," Lorre later told film historian Joel Greenberg. The "facemaker," as he dubbed himself, had arrived.

Aufricht placed Lorre under contract. Peter told Celia that the following Monday morning Reinhardt sent an assistant to sign him. As it turned out, Aufricht, who considered *Pioniere in Ingolstadt* the most successful production under his management of the Theater am Schiffbauerdamm, was agreeable to lending Lorre's services, but not to selling them. And Lorre preferred to stay with Brecht.[23]

Rave reviews and morphine kept Lorre on his feet. During the run of *Pioniere in Ingolstadt,* he suffered another hemorrhage. Rather than admit him to a hospital, a physician supplied the actor with enough morphine to ensure his continued appearance in the play.

In the audience on opening night sat a thirty-two-year-old actress named Celia Lovsky. Once she recovered from the shock of seeing Lorre pick flies off the window pane and pull out their wings and feet, she felt the full weight of his performance. Even by Berlin standards, his was a singular talent. When the curtain fell, she squeezed backstage to congratulate the actor, but "there were women all over him." Celia closed the door and left. She often stopped by Schwannecke's, a pub just around the corner from Peter's apartment on Eislebener Strasse. Arriving there at noon one day, she spotted him sitting alone contentedly devouring a dish of *Knödel* (dumplings). Celia walked over to his table and held out her hand: "I congratulate you on your sensational success." He invited her to sit down. After the prerequisite shop talk, he asked if he could escort her home. They chatted, but he was obviously nervous. Peter and Celia strolled past the Kaiser Wilhelm Memorial Church and took either Budapester Strasse by the zoological garden or the Kurfürstendamm to the Spree. Following along the riverbank, they crossed over the Potsdamer Bridge and down Schöneberg to Victoria Allee in the theater and culture sector. The farther they walked, the quieter he became. Suddenly, he blurted out that he loved her. "I laughed," recalled Lovsky, "and told him anybody could say that." Angry, Peter screamed "Untier" (monster) in her face. The nickname stuck.

Lovsky may well have been unaware of Lorre before March 29, but he had known of her for some time. He later told her he had seen her as Desdemona in Shakespeare's *Othello* at an open-air restaurant in Kritzendorf, ten miles northwest of Vienna. "I was only a schoolboy," said the presumably bemused Lorre, highlighting their seven-year age difference, "but night after night I visited the theatre there and—and worshipped."[24] He confessed it had been "love at first sight."

"I always wanted to play romantic roles," Lorre later admitted, "but after I had gotten some small roles, in which I had to wrap my arms around my partners on the stage, I decided that I would rather save love for my private life."

Lovsky was born February 21, 1897, in Vienna, to Bratislav Emil Lvovsky, composer and chief editor of the *Österreichische Musik und Theaterzeitung*, and cellist Walburga "Wally" Prochaska.[25] Cäcilie Josephine Lvovsky (later simplified to Celia or Cecile Lovsky) attended the Akademie für Musik und darstellende Kunst (Academy for Music and Performing Arts) from 1913 to 1916. Although she received no financial support her first year, Celia won a two-hundred-kronen scholarship "for exemplary and needy students" her second and third years. A model student, whose studies included acting, drama, German, Italian, and French languages, and dance and fencing, she received an A on her final exam and graduated June 13, 1916, just after appearing in the title role of Hofmannsthal's *Elektra*. She had also portrayed Amine in Goethe's *Die Laune des Verliebten* (*The Mood of the One in Love*) and Countess Blandine in Oskar Blumenthal's *Wenn wir altern* (*When We Grow Old*). Lovsky soon stepped onto the New Wiener Bühne, where she earned a reputation as a gifted and versatile actress whose ability to "form her parts out of her heart and her mind" ranked her alongside Maria Orska and Elisabeth Bergner. During her tenure at the Deutsche Volkstheater (1925–27), Lovsky developed a deeply devoted personal connection to playwright Arthur Schnitzler, from whom she solicited letters of recommendation, including one to Franz Herterich, director of the Burgtheater.[26] By 1928 she had moved to Berlin, "the city which consumes one totally." Performing continuously for a year without a free evening, she still found time to lobby him for a role in *Fräulein Else,* starring Elisabeth Bergner.[27]

The boyish, fun-loving Lorre and the stunning, experienced Lovsky made an unlikely pair.[28] On holiday in the Black Forest, he was warned against sledding down icy trails. "If somebody said don't do it, he did it," said Celia. "Peter sat in front on the sled and chauffeured it. My job was to work the brake. We almost collided with a horse and cart. I couldn't control the brake and yelled, 'Stop immediately, I want to get out.'" Headlong in love, the couple careened toward a more permanent living arrangement and soon moved into his apartment on Eislebener Strasse.

To mark the anniversary of *Die Dreigroschenoper,* Aufricht planned another Brecht-Weill collaboration "in the same combination." Although a little embarrassed by the "middlebrow popular success" of the stage blockbuster, which, according to the official German Communist Party paper, *Die Rote Fahne* (the *Red Flag*), "contained not a hint of modern social or political satire," Brecht couldn't turn his back on the financial possibilities. He proposed that Elisabeth Hauptmann, his "best" collaborator, piece Chicago underworld and Salvation Army elements from her short stories into a play. Under the pseudonym Dorothy Lane, Hauptmann produced the basic script for *Happy End.* Kurt Weill wrote the music and Brecht the lyrics, in addition to creating roles for Carola Neher, Helene Weigel, Kurt Gerron, Oskar Homolka, Theo Lingen, and Peter Lorre. After bullying director Erich Engel into quitting, Brecht continued to participate but dragged his feet at every stage of production.

Happy End premiered on Saturday, August 31, 1929. It got off to a good start, playing just as well with the audience as *Die Dreigroschenoper* had one year earlier. And then came the third act. Cheap rhymes, filthy language, and sacrilege taxed the public's patience. Between "a couple of nice ideas," Brecht and Weill had sandwiched too many songs, clogging an already unfocused and flighty story line. Disappointed spectators fidgeted and coughed. Aufricht waited in the wings for the ensemble to sing a finale. Suddenly, Helene Weigel walked to the front of the stage. He couldn't believe his eyes. She pulled a slip of paper from her pocket and in her piercing voice delivered an anticapitalist diatribe filled with "vulgar Marxist provocations." Brutally roused from their boredom, the audience booed and whistled for the curtain to fall.

The public probably had even better reason to shun the *Singspiel* than the near-riot atmosphere inside the theater. It quickly became apparent that Brecht, who disowned the play after having represented himself as the author (discrediting Hauptmann with a failed production that he had consciously sabotaged), had repeated himself. Stand still and "build your position" or move forward, advised Herbert Jhering: "Both positions are impossible." The avalanche of criticism, however, did not bury Brecht's acting ensemble, which performed superbly. Lorre played Dr. Nakamura (the Governor), a sinister Oriental thug, whose pidgin English, karate chops, and gun play made good practice for his role as Mr. Moto, the Japanese detective, eight years later. Lorre also turned his vocality loose on "Song of the Big Shot" ("If you want to be a big shot / Start by learning to be tough").

When *Happy End* closed after only three performances, Aufricht found himself with a cast of players on full salary, but no production. A solution came easily enough with Lorre. After learning that Aufricht looked to lend out the young actor, Franz Theodor Csokor had put Lorre in touch with stage director Karl Heinz Martin at the Volksbühne.

Berlin provided a politically correct setting for Georg Büchner's bleakly fatalistic tragedy *Dantons Tod* (*Danton's Death*), set in the aftermath of the French Revolution. It is 1794. The battle is won, but revolutionary rhetoric now strangles freedom. "Death to all who have no holes in their clothes!" shout the People. "Death to all who can read and write!" Lorre, as Saint-Just, a member of the Committee of Public Safety, allows that "humanity comes out of the cauldron of blood." Georges Danton, author of the Revolutionary Tribunal, cannot stop the People, "who smash everything to see what is inside." Although he is disillusioned, his voice is still strong enough to accuse Saint-Just, Robespierre, and their hangmen of high treason for seeking to suffocate the Republic in blood.

Berliners heartily endorsed the four-hour production, which opened on the same day (and hour) as *Happy End*. Critical approval of the "world-view drama" focused on Karl Heinz Martin's energetic and innovative direction. Draping the drama with verse from contemporary Communist marching songs did not, it seems, undermine the play's historical authenticity. The reality of the street detail and mass scenes, the thundering of the Marseillaise and Hanns Eisler's music intoxicated the audience with the spirit of revolution.

According to Lorre, Brecht enabled him to overlap appearances as Dr. Nakamura in *Happy End* and Saint-Just in *Dantons Tod* by "killing off" the Governor in the first act. A waiting taxi, in which Lorre hastily changed from gangster garb to general's uniform, sped him from the Schiffbauerdamm Theater to the Volksbühne am Bülowplatz. When Brecht learned that Lorre had time to return before the end of act 3, he resurrected the seemingly slain Nakamura: "You thought I was shot? No, I'm just a little bit injured."[29]

Lorre presented a radically different spectacle from the heavy-lidded simpleton in *Pioniere in Ingolstadt*. Outfitted in a military uniform and wearing a blond wig, he appeared older and physically commanding—all the more so, one imagines, since the actors spoke their lines directly to the audience.

Berlin critics singled out Lorre's "philosopher of terror" as the high point of the evening. "Hypocritical, mollusk-like with soft effeminate gestures of a spoiled child is Peter Lorre's St. Just," wrote drama critic Alexander von Sacher-Masoch for *Vorwärts*. "His ability peaks in his speech to the people." Far more important to Lorre's marketability as an actor was the recognition that his uniqueness did not type him. On the contrary, he displayed "many natural possibilities," keeping his "great histrionic talent" before the Berlin public in a variety of roles.

For now, however, Lorre might do as another pathetic teenager. Martin arranged to hold the actor over for a starring role in Frank Wedekind's controversial child-tragedy *Frühlings Erwachen* (*Spring's Awakening*). Inspired by the alarming rate of suicide among young people, Wedekind had earlier addressed himself to the adolescent sex drive. Society, he believed, could attain a more natural and healthier complexion if liberated from moral constraints. By keeping young people ignorant of their awakening sexual feelings, stupid, prudish adults—caricatured as grotesque brutes pitted against lyrically simple children—held them in a bondage of shame.

Fourteen-year-old Moritz Stiefel, played by Lorre, suffers from the pangs of puberty. He feels awkward about "manhood's emotion" and grapples with the shame brought on by his urges: "To be overcome by such a sweet wrong and still be blameless seems to me the fullness of earthly bliss." Melchoir Gabor (Carl Balhaus), whose liberal parents have enlightened him on the matter of sex, gives him a pamphlet that he has written and illustrated. It is entitled *Cohabitation*. The soulful Moritz, full of angelic simplicity and hounded to death by his conscience, decides to kill himself. Alone in the woods, he reflects on self-destruction until interrupted by Ilse (Lotte Lenya), a former classmate who has freed herself from the constraints of home life. A simple girl, she is also a nymphomaniac who shares the company of an entourage of male devotees in a wild, animalistic existence. After Moritz declines Ilse's offer to join her band, she leaves him and he takes his life.

Melchoir is held responsible for Moritz's suicide and sentenced to reform school, but escapes. Wandering through a cemetery, he meets Moritz, who steps from behind a headstone with his head under his arm and tells his friend that only in the afterworld will he find peace and joy. From behind another tombstone emerges a masked man who discloses Moritz as a charlatan unhappy in death and convinces Melchoir to rejoin the world of the living.

Max Reinhardt had first staged *Frühlings Erwachen* in 1909. Shocked by the play's explicit sexual situations, censors touched off a firestorm of criticism that led to a purged version of the text and court-imposed restrictions on its dialogue and content. Its power stripped, Wedekind's drama became just another romantic love poem rife with pathetic sentimentality. The play had not been performed for fifteen years when Martin decided to restore the raw power of the original drama. Updating it to the present, he scrapped the Bavarian for a Berlin dialect and substituted, with Caspar Neher's expert help, an attic for a hayloft, a canal for a river, and big-city housing blocks for a small-town milieu.

Frühlings Erwachen polarized an already divided audience. Liberal forces stood for ten curtain calls and applauded "the breath of our times" that blew over the scenes. For the more conservative element, however, modernizing the play had compromised its timelessness and redeeming value. The 1929 version of *Frühlings Erwachen* was smutty, indecent, and empty, and the "gliding togetherness of both children" was now seen as an act of rape.

Once again, Lorre escaped unscathed. He seemingly could do no wrong. As "a youth to whom hardness and heaviness make everything a problem," Lorre's Moritz Stiefel won the undivided praise of Berlin critics, who credited him with imbuing the play with a newfound spiritual dimension that penetrated the heart of eternal human feelings. "Probably no words from a hands-saved fallen-off head have ever been so full of resigned longing for the torso," wrote critic Walter Benjamin, "than those spoken by Peter Lorre." Tortured by the perplexity of his helplessness, Lorre expressed "the quiet Vulcan of a soul, which explodes—and how!" Alexander von Sacher-Masoch dissected his performance without puncturing its magic: "An extraordinarily capable technician. He builds his portrayal out of small, apparently inconsequential gestures and accentuations into powerful effect. He hardly plays, sometimes one has the sensation that he would be talking with himself. Raw guttural sounds, hasty, rushed language, sudden hesitations, awkward posture, sloppy movements. All of this creates the impression of a great naturalness and is indeed thought and weighed out in the finest detail. His originality helps him not to lose himself in technical details." It was his second role as a neurasthenic, schlemiel figure in six months, but surprisingly no one drew a comparison to the similar character in *Pioniere in Ingolstadt.* Everyone agreed only that Lorre's talent had once again confirmed itself.

No one knew this more than Celia Lovsky, who couldn't stop talking about him. Putting his career before hers, she invited Germany's leading film director, Fritz Lang, and independent producer Seymour Nebenzal, cofounder with Richard Oswald of Nero Films, to a dress rehearsal of *Frühlings Erwachen*. Lang later claimed to have already seen Lorre in *Pioniere in Ingolstadt*, but Lovsky knew better. Certainly, he had followed the actor's success. He had even seen him at the Mutzbauer restaurant, where the Viennese colony of writers, composers, artists, filmmakers, and actors (among them Elisabeth Bergner, Rudolph Forster, Robert Stultz, and Walter Reisch) gathered for Wiener schnitzel. Whenever the director entered, they politely bowed.

What Lang saw struck him as an unlikely means to a murderous end. "If he is cast properly," he told film director and historian Peter Bogdanovich, an actor "must have either the ability to play the role, or already have the characteristics of the part." Lorre had both. Already a specialist in troubled teenager roles, the fleshy, pubescent actor "looked like a negative superman," said Lang, who "wanted to get away from the typed murderer with broad shoulders and dark eyes." Celia introduced Lang and Lorre backstage and left. The actor was awestruck. He too had seen Lang at the Mutzbauer and had even exchanged social courtesies, but he had never talked with him or sat at his table. "I will do my first sound picture," said Lang, bridging the gap. "I don't know yet what it will be and I don't know when it will be.[30] I am aware that you will receive many offers from pictures. But if you don't accept any other offers, this picture will be written for you. You will be the star of it."

Lorre was skeptical. "I was really a success on the stage and I did not want to appear in pictures," he recalled in 1944. "I did not know then what it would be and I had no faith in it." He remembered telling Lang that "my puss could not be photographed," adding, "with a face like mine who could expect a career in films?" Lang held the thought, appreciating the irony in it. For now, Lorre balanced the fear of rejection against his "belief in miracles" and told Lang he would wait. "It was hard enough to turn down film offers just because of this future music," confessed Lorre in an article for *Mein Film*, in which he reviewed his meteoric rise and naively announced plans for his next German film production. He posted the piece just days after fleeing Berlin in the wake of the Reichstag Fire.

What Lorre failed to mention to Lang he also neglected to tell anyone else. Perhaps he attached no importance to it. Or maybe he had just forgotten about it. There was no reason to upset the director's plans with news that he had already worked in film, albeit in a very small way. Anyway, Lang wanted to make a sound picture, not a silent one.

Earlier in the year, Lorre had made his screen debut as a patient waiting to be seen by the dentist in *Die verschwundene Frau* (*The Missing Wife*), one of

Austria's last silent films. Despite his brief appearance, there was no mistaking his boyish looks and pained facial expressions. Produced by the Österreichisches Filmindustrie and directed by Karl Leiter, the "frightening occurrence in seven hilarious acts," according to a publicity release, was originally released in Vienna on March 22, 1929 (and in Berlin on May 3, 1929). More curious than this inauspicious beginning in the movies was the fact that he told no one about it, not his brothers, not Celia, not the scores of interviewers who scoured his screen past. For the record—his record—*M* was his first film. He said it again and again. Far more crucial to Lorre was the fact that he had crashed upon the scene in an important film and catapulted to international success. He wanted to be remembered for *M,* not *Die verschwundene Frau.* And it worked . . . until 1996. Believed lost, a nitrate Belgian release print of the film surfaced in 1984. Twelve years later, during its restoration by the European Union's Lumière Project, Lorre's appearance was rediscovered. Not only was he uncredited on the film, but his name did not appear in any published cast lists, and obviously, as an obscure bit player, he was not mentioned in any review. His tracks were easy to cover.

Although Alajos and Melanie had moved to Budapest in 1928, Lorre still had occasion to visit Vienna and see friends, drop by old haunts, and attend lectures by Alfred Adler at the Café Siller. Along with other members of the Kammerspiele, he also performed literary *Kleinkunst* for the film community at Café Kosmos. His performance in the variety show, along with a youthful photo of the actor wearing a white shirt and tie, even found its way onto the pages of *Mein Film.* There, too, Celia Lovsky drew him back to Café Central, whose "cool twilight" provided "the ideal lighting for recluses and eccentrics." Its sky-lit inner court gave the café an "oddly ecclesiastical" impression, without the incense. In deep alcoves darkened with the "thick cloud-drift of cigarette smoke," denizens cut circles of light with their intellectual vivacity.

Satirist Karl Kraus, however, seemed more interested in cutting his opponents to ribbons. An acrimonious misanthrope, implacable cynic, and intransigent polemicist, he harbored a fanatical hatred for corruption in bureaucracy, vacuity in political life, and feuilletonism in the press.[31] Kraus directed incessant attacks against Viennese newspapers from his militantly ethical periodical *Die Fackel* (the *Torch*), making mordant wit his shield and language his weapon in his war against the intellectual prostitution of the written word, whose impurity he considered a direct index of the moral decline of mankind. His outrage climaxed in the apocalyptic world-war drama *Die letzten Tage der Menschheit* (*The Last Days of Mankind*), which Lorre later cited as one of his favorite books.

Allegedly once "the great love" of Kraus's life, Lovsky, who had appeared in productions of his surrealistic fantasies *Traumstück* (*Dream Play*) and *Traumtheater* (*Dream Theater*) in 1925, drew Lorre into his circle. The actor apparently satisfied Kraus's stringent criteria for a great artist, who must act naturally and not rely on "pose and pathos," and offstage must be a genuine, unpretentious, and warm person. Being a member of Kraus's *Stammtisch* (reserved table), however, did not spare Lorre from his sarcastic wit. "My brother and I once went with Peter to the coffeehouse where Kraus used to hang out," recalled Andrew. "And Kraus looked up over his glasses—he always peered above his glasses—and said, 'Well, here is Peter with the boy scout troupe.'" At the lower end of the pecking order and owing what station he held to Lovsky, Lorre felt privileged to be at the center of the literary storm in Vienna.

On October 20, 1929, Lorre appeared in Kraus's documentary satire *Die Unüberwindlichen* (*The Unconquerable*), written between December 1927 and February 1928. The play chronicles the Békessy Affair, in which Vienna press czar Irme Békessy whitewashed a deadly crackdown on a political demonstration instigated by the city's chief of police, Johannes Schober, in 1927. Kraus used the piece to expose the corrupt partnership between the press, the financiers, and the police of Vienna. He took his case to the progressive circle of Berlin, where he officially premiered the piece at the Volksbühne am Bülowplatz. Kraus had assembled an outstanding cast: Lorre as Barkassy (Békessy), Hans Peppler as police chief Wacker (Schober), Kurt Gerron as the shady profiteer Camillioni (Castiglioni), Ernst Ginsberg as the crusading journalist Arkus (Kraus), Leonard Steckel in the role of Veilchen, a golden-tongued bureaucrat, and Celia Lovsky as a secretary. Playing the small role of a civil servant was Josef Almas, who had taken over the role of Moritz Stiefel when Lorre had dropped out of *Frühlings Erwachen* five weeks into its run. Doubling up on stage work and rehearsals may have compromised Lorre's already fragile health. It is also conceivable that having made his mark as Moritz Stiefel, he accepted the lead role in *Die Unüberwindlichen* out of respect for its author.

The production held few surprises. Kraus characterized Barkassy as a porcine figure with blond curly hair, soft manicured hands, and a nasal tone. The dogmatic publisher congratulates himself that his readers—who are spoon-fed truth and lies until they see spots before their eyes—have come around to his point of view. In a split-stage technique, the journalist presents evidence of Barkassy's criminal past—and present—to the police chief. True to life, he kicks the crook out of Vienna. Kraus, however, confuses fact and fiction by staging the newspaper magnate's phoenix-like triumph over the forces of righteousness. The real journalist actually prevailed against Békessy, who fled to

Paris and then to his native Budapest. Schober went on to become the chancellor of Austria in September 1929.

Despite expectations of a longer run, the Volksbühne canceled the play after only one Sunday matinee performance, citing low ticket sales and Lorre's health. "In reality, Lorre is well again and wants to play," reported the *Berliner Börsen Courier*. Kraus surmised that the Volksbühne was not being honest about the "technical reasons" for dropping the evening performance and threatened to sue for damages. According to Kraus scholar Harry Zohn, the Austrian Embassy requested the cancellation of further performances, undoubtedly prompting Kraus to reflect about winning the battle but losing the war against the combined forces of his enemies.

Given its topicality, *Die Unüberwindlichen* could not have sustained itself in Berlin. No one doubted Kraus's ability to shred his victims with the sharpness of his words, but the audience regarded his mordacity as nonproductive, sterile, and monotonous, no matter how just the cause. Lorre barked, bellowed, and burst from within, but could not save the bone-dry piece. He yelled too much, although Kurt Pinthus, writing for the *8-Uhr-Abendblatt*, felt that "Lorre took the part with such devoting power one hardly noticed that he sometimes over-exerted himself." The influential Herbert Jhering thought that the quick succession of roles had inhibited the maturation of Lorre's acting skills: "He becomes loud instead of strong and, unsure of such an extraordinary part which demands new sides of him, has to save himself in self-conscious shouting."

The stress and strain proved too much for Lorre's perennially poor health. When a persistent cough triggered more bleeding from his bronchi, he took the advice—and probably the proffered financial assistance—of his friend Franz Theodor Csokor and sought shelter at a sanitarium in Badenweiler. From there he wrote Csokor on January 3, 1930, conveying deep appreciation for his friendship. "At a time when the fates had me in such a way in their claws," wrote Lorre, "[there] seemed no residue of strength in me to carry further this senselessness. I thought I had finally reached an end . . . you know better about that than anyone else . . . the pain of those endless minutes in which the gray self of time took the last comfort and imposed sadness in eternity! . . . in these days it really went to an end with the old Peter with whom I have nothing any more in common, only this confounded image which you so often and flatteringly sang about."

Lorre recovered and credited his newfound health a "miracle" in which Csokor played a large "and maybe the most beautiful" part. He told Csokor:

There can be no sense in the creation that I should store up this investment of sorrow and experience and fate to be dry and barren and should like the old Rockefeller play golf.

(That's certainly meant symbolically, Herr Doctor.)

We shall sit together quite often and maybe I will tell you as the only one about it. And you will see an abyss which will make you shudder.

But I am redeemed! As if a destiny is fulfilled and has freed me to act now. (You once wrote the face is there which is waiting for a destiny.) You can imagine how happy it makes me that a friend is there who has faithfully believed and waited where there didn't seem to be any more sense and gave me a credit in his heart—far above the incidents of the profession—up to a calling!

Lorre asked Csokor if he knew "how much it means to me to have you as a friend?!" Lorre knew and never forgot Csokor's kindness. He believed that the curtain did not go up and down on a lasting friendship with him who had "seeing eyes and a knowing soul for me." Although many of his friends had "behaved inhumanely," said Lorre, it was "too small an experience to be named disappointment. Many friends behaved humanely and made it possible for me to recuperate here."

Anxious to tell Csokor everything, Lorre broke the news that he and Celia had become engaged at Christmas. "Believe me, it is good and we are good for each other. That all will be told. She comes now up to me and we shall probably stay here for fourteen days."

Obviously reluctant to jump back into the "witches cauldron," he confessed that he "missed a lot—meaning nothing. I have a kind of *Heimatgefühl* here! For a gypsy—like me!! Write right away. I am full of joy."[32]

After a brief run in Carl Sternheim's *Der Kandidat* (*The Candidate*), a political satire translated unsuccessfully from the French to the German political scene and staged at Berlin's Kammerspiele, Lorre took a breather that ate up much of the rest of the year. By fall he felt sufficiently recovered to accept the first of what would become a long and happy association with radio. On October 5, 1930, he debuted on *Funkstunde Berlin* (Berlin Radio Hour), as a counselor in Jacques Offenbach's *Die Seufzerbrücke* (*The Bridge of Sighs*), a two-act operetta set in Venice and arranged by Karl Kraus.[33] Celia Lovksy played the part of a confidant to the wife of the doge.

That same month, two years after Lorre's introduction to Rudolph Joseph, he finally played at the Renaissance Theater, supplying some of the few laughs in an otherwise riveting murder mystery by celebrated Berlin jurist Max Alsberg and newspaper editor Otto Ernst Hesse.[34] *Voruntersuchung* (*Preliminary Investigation*) underscored the mistakes of modern jurisprudence. Even the crown prince and Albert Einstein, who attended the premiere, "had a chance . . . to think about the relativity of the legal process and research of the law." Contributing to the thundering success of the production by comically shading their parts were Lorre, Julius Falkenstein, and Ludwig Stössel. Already experienced in "proving again and again [his] impressive liveliness and performing power with smallest means," Lorre squeezed every comic possibility from the supporting roles with the "amusing impudence of the cabaret performer."

Lorre returned in December to the Schiffbauerdamm Theater, where he appeared in *Die Quadratur des Kreises*, a love story set against the Russian housing shortage. Unbeknownst to each other, roommates and fellow Kosomols Wasja (Lorre), "a boy of normally serious inclinations . . . somewhat uncomfortable and self-conscious in his gaudy butterfly tie, the shiny puttees, plastered hair and well-pressed coat," and Abram (Heinz Rühmann) marry on the same day. In order to accommodate both couples, they use a chalk line to divide their quarters into two apartments. Each half assumes the personality of its mistress. Wasja's wife, Ludmilla (Hilde Körber), adorns her half with middle-class comforts, while Abram's spouse, the liberated Tonya (Lotte Lenya) favors empty-walled austerity. Dividing their lives along party lines proves impractical. Abram finds Ludmilla's home-cooked cutlet more filling than Marxist ideology, and Wasja satisfies his intellectual craving with Tonya's party literature. The four decide they are mismatched and swap partners after the prerequisite divorces and marriages.

Always the businessman, Aufricht pushed the play's comic appeal at the expense of its political overtones. Given its warm reception—"so much laughing . . . that the walls shook and so much clapping the people's hands hurt"— he comfortably projected at least a six-month run. After a few weeks, however, the turnout fell off. The worsening financial crisis ate away at Berliners' pocketbooks, putting expensive theater tickets beyond reach. Street fighting between Communist and Nazi youths also discouraged theatergoers from venturing out at night. Aufricht made tickets available at discount prices, but he could not fill the theater.

If critics faulted director Francesco von Mendelssohn for losing sight of the play's instructive quality and for overemphasizing nonessentials, they rallied to the support of the actors, crediting Lorre and Rühmann with "terrific" virtuoso performances. "Peter loved the play," observed Lotte Lenya, "because he was very funny when he did it. He loved anything which furthered his talents."

In 1946 scholar, critic, and translator Eric Bentley, who was the first to champion Bertolt Brecht's cause in the United States, told the playwright that he had "a conception of art which few understand" and encouraged him to explain himself to American audiences. Since the 1920s, when he had borrowed the term *epic* to describe his own theater, Brecht had muddied the waters of understanding, first frustrating critics who scoffed at his ideas and later perplexing scholars, who took on the thankless task of doing what he should have done in his own lifetime. Like Brecht himself, of whom set designer Wolfgang Roth said, "he was very human, but it didn't come through," his epic theater suffered in translation.

Brecht had begun railing against traditional theater, which he condemned as bankrupt, stupid, lazy, and degenerate, in the early 1920s. Always ready to take a swipe at "culture," he championed boxing, which satisfied the demands of its audience. If German theater found its own form of sport, suggested the playwright, perhaps it too might connect with the public. The rules of the game lent character to his idea of creating a useful, objective, and entertaining activity that reflected "the mentality of our time." In his 1926 stage production of Christopher Marlowe's *Edward II*, he began laying the foundation for his epic style—simple gestures; clear, cool delivery; emotional realism. While sports gave him a new perspective on theater, Brecht's studies in Marxism structured his theories with scientific method, further estranging him from the "sentimental element of a worn out bourgeoisie." To his mind, by not keeping up with the times, classic theater, where "wit sparkles like fireworks or some sad occurrence moves my heart to compassion," had become static, cramped, and superficial. The logical cycle of change demanded an adaptable form, at the same time dynamic, realistic, and functional. Brecht learned that diagnosing an illness and treating it were not one and the same. "Invent a theory, dear Brecht!" advised Kammerspiele director Rudolf Frank after witnessing the artistic chaos of his *Edward II*. "If one presents Germans with a theory, they will swallow anything." One theory, however, did not allow room for growth. For what ailed the theater, Brecht prescribed a course of treatment that borrowed eclectically from the medieval Japanese playwright Seami, Soviet director Vseolod Meyerhold, Karl Marx, Charles Chaplin, and the *Neue Sachlichkeit* (New Objectivity), among others. He built his theories from the ground up with methods that invited radical changes in form and content. While "bourgeois" theater lulled its audiences into a "magnetic sleep by warming up the numbed senses and giving the imagination a gentle rocking," what Brecht wanted to do, wrote Eric Bentley, "is something closer to waking them up." Peeling away the decorative layers of "irrelevant emotion" to uncover "not . . . a higher reality, or a deeper reality, but simply . . . reality" amounted to an intellectual adventure. Only by appealing to reason—and de-emphasizing emotion—could the-ater open the door to change.

Brecht's actors bore the burden of putting his theories into practice, but not before another blackboard lesson. In 1931 the dramatist schematized a formula that suggested "changes of emphasis" contrasting dramatic and epic methods. To limit the swept-away feeling of illusion inherent in "culinary" theater, an actor must detach himself from his character, not so much by stepping out of his role but by placing himself between it and the audience. By cooling off his performance, he could distance the spectator from feel-ings that dulled his ability to think critically about what he had just seen. Making the familiar seem unfamiliar challenged the audience to see things with fresh eyes.

During his lifetime—and well after—Brecht's theories took on a life of their own, growing from simple guidelines into oversized rules. *Verfremdung,* which accurately if clumsily translates as "defamiliarization" or "making strange," most often appears simply as "alienation" or "estrangement." The concept lost more than meaning in translation. Members of Brecht's ensemble later acknowledged that his theories did not meet his own standards for prac-ticality. In a word, they did not work. Lenya said so. Eisler told him so to his face. Even Lorre gave voice to the same thought after Brecht's death. Gerhard Bienert, who appeared in the 1932 Berlin production of *The Mother,* main-tained that actors cannot distinguish between "being" and "pretending" to play a role. Roth also believed that Brecht eventually "realized that you can't pre-vent the audience from developing a relationship with the actor."

Just how seriously Brecht took himself and his theories is as hard to say today as it was in 1929, when "you never knew what he meant," said Roth. "He said one thing and meant something else. You had to get to know him. . . . I took it literally what he said very early until I learned to listen in between. And he said, 'Don't take it so god-damned seriously. Who cares, anyhow?'"

Certainly not Gerhard Szczesny, who, in his book *The Case Against Bertolt Brecht* (1969), maintained that "what Brecht called his theories were on the whole very superficial and mechanical attempts to apply a simplistic Marxism to the dramatic structure of the pre-existing vaudeville theater of types."

Apparently, his ensemble of actors didn't care either. "I am so tired of hearing that [*Verfremdung*]," said Lotte Lenya. "At that time there was no sign of alienation. It was just good acting or bad acting. . . . And I don't think that alienation ever entered in—neither when we did *Threepenny Opera.* I don't think Brecht paid much attention to that alienation. Later maybe."

Brecht himself may not even have cared. After the war, when Lenya was rehearsing the song "Surabaya Johnny" with Brecht, she "stopped for a second and said, 'Brecht, you know your theory of epic theatre—maybe you don't want me just to sing it the way I sang it—as emotional as "Surabaya Johnny" has to be done?' . . . He said: 'Lenya, darling, whatever you do is epic enough for me.'"

Brecht's co-workers also agreed on his practice without theory. Lorre thought him a great director. While Bienert rejected his idea of standing next to his part, he found Brecht a pleasure to work with as a director who helped awaken his actors' artistic abilities by demonstrating for them the full range of emotions—"enigmatic, demonic, full of humor, crafty, to the point." Roth, too, marveled at his capacity for deriving productive use from "whatever he learned from everywhere."

What role Lorre played in the development of Brecht's ideas on stagecraft is open to discussion. As much as he liked "strange faces, strange types," Brecht had an eye for talent and knew what to do with it. "He didn't want actors at all, but people on the street," claimed Roth. "Bring those people in," joked Brecht during times of high unemployment. "We can offer them twelve marks." Actually the dramatist sought out trained actors who looked and behaved like ordinary people. Oskar Homolka had butcher written on his face. Ernst Busch looked like and had been an untrained metal worker. To breathe political conviction into *Die Mutter (The Mother),* Brecht even suggested hiring unemployed workers.

Bentley believed that Lorre had a significant influence on Brecht: "Brecht followed the performers and when he saw a performer that offered him something, he studied it very closely." He found much about Lorre's style that gave form to his developing ideas about "the right kind of acting."

"Brecht found Peter such a new kind of talent," said Marta Feuchtwanger, who attended many of the playwright's rehearsals. "He tyrannized everyone to get his will into them. Peter did not need this. He immediately knew what the part meant. There were no fights between them. Peter and Brecht understood each other without words. Where there is such understanding, no influence is necessary."

Probably Lorre's most appealing feature was his duality, which nicely fit Brecht's theories of opposites. Balanced contrasts and contradictions, after all, underlined the "other possibilities" of human behavior and argued for man's capacity for change. "Brecht was fascinated by the doubleness in Lorre's performances," said Bentley, "in the two elements, in the clashing of characteristics . . . the peculiar combinations in his personality between the naive and sophisticated or between comic and grim, or not comic." Co-workers sensed an unconscious "split" in Lorre's stage persona that was consistent with a type of acting in which the feelings don't directly come out in a flood but in some way are veiled or kept at a distance. . . . Because of the gap between the suffering in the creature, the real feelings, which are usually suffering in a person, and the expression in voice and gesture, but very noticeably in voice in his case, there's an emotional block or lack of flow of communication in himself. . . . For example, the feelings don't get expressed in the voice. If the character is a fiend, the voice will sound like a little child and innocent. . . . Lorre could have played the Hitler of Brecht, where his idea was not to present the demonic Hitler with barbaric forces from the depths and strange pathological developments, but to show him as a strange buffoon whose buffoonery has destroyed millions of people. There's something in Lorre that isn't there. It's comic, but it's not really, but on the surface, yes, it makes you laugh, but then underneath, boy. . . . This quality of being at a distance from your own emotions might come from your studying Brecht's theories, but it might just be that you were born that way. I tend to think the second is true of Peter Lorre, and it fascinated Brecht because here is someone whom nature made the way he thought an actor was supposed to be in any case, a natural Brecht actor.

"It might be that this style suited Lorre because of his own personality make-up," suggested Zerka Moreno.

We live in two dimensions; I call them objective and subjective reality. If the objective reality becomes too lacking in emotional nurture, the child will withdraw into the subjective one and there be once again all-powerful. This is the matrix for later psychotic, deeply neurotic, drug, alcohol and criminal experience. We have all sensed these parts in us. . . . [Lorre] may not have been ill, but he may have been more evidently split when he came into Moreno's arena. It is even possible that acting, or at least the training he received from Moreno, help put some of the parts together.

Whatever the source of Lorre's duality, Brecht looked only at the result, including what Feuchtwanger called Lorre's "natural gestures." One of the most important means to Brecht's "epic" ends was his concept of the "gestus." In language that tends to put people off, he defined it as "the most objective possible exposition of a contradictory internal process." Theater historian John Willett, who collected Brecht's theoretical writings under one title—*Brecht on Theatre*—brings us a step closer to understanding by explaining that it "means both gist and gesture; an attitude or a single aspect of an attitude, expressible in words or actions." In simpler terms, "showing" rather than "being" a character enables an actor to distill the essential meaning of an incident, a scene, or a role. By adopting a "socially critical" attitude—rather than an illustrative or expressive one, wrote Brecht, an actor "can show what he thinks of [the character] and invite the spectator . . . to criticize the character portrayed." In this way, he turns his performance into a discussion between actor and audience.

Already trained in putting the gesture before the word—something Lorre continued in Hollywood, where he preferred showing to telling his feelings—the actor bridged theory and practice by instinctively expressing the idea underlying his roles. This he accomplished in a style—clear, controlled, economical—consistent with Brecht's criteria for good acting as well as his own personal standards. "He used freedom with great concern for honesty and psychological truth," said Hollywood director Joseph Pevney, echoing Brecht's theoretical writings. "Peter battled pomposity, dishonesty, and had little patience with stupidity. He adored sensitivity but debunked sentimentality. As an actor he laid bare man's cupidity."

With his collaborative experience at the Theater for Spontaneity behind him, Lorre adapted well to the everyday realities of Brecht's working methods. Pacing back and forth, waving his cigar, the playwright solicited suggestions from everyone, even the cleaning lady at the Schiffbauerdamm Theater, but mostly his co-workers—Hauptmann, Neher, Lenya, Busch, and Lorre—and transferred their input to a blackboard. "When an actor said I have an idea," said Lenya, "Brecht said, don't talk about it, show me. . . . If I like, I take it." Collaborative give and take appealed to Lorre, who later "recalled how [Brecht's] actors would invent bits of business and even dialogue in their efforts to create the playwright's special brand of 'epic' theatre. It was, he said, essentially a group enterprise, with an extraordinary rapport among its participants." The actor cultivated a similar rapport with Hollywood filmmakers. As a director himself, he not surprisingly stressed the importance of a kind of teamwork—*Mannschaft*—that harked back to the "harmonious cooperation which has a creative counterpart in the 'ensemble' of the European theatre."

Fun is not one of the key words associated with Brechtian theater. Unfortunately, it saw more play in theory than in practice. According to Roth, however, the dramatist prized humor above all. "If there's not laughter in the theater," he told him, "you should not be in there." Brecht wanted to liberate audiences by provoking them to think with their heads and not with their hearts. As a result, "they might well simply see theatre—a theatre, I hope, imbued with imagination, humour and meaning." At rehearsals, remembered the set designer, they "worked hard, but it was fun, a very creative fun." Beginning with Brecht, on through Alfred Hitchcock, John Huston, and Rouben Mamoulian, Lorre did his best work for directors who shared his sense of humor. It is not surprising that Roth credited the actor's aptitude for comedy as his greatest contribution to epic theater.

However you translate it—*A Man Is a Man, Man Is Man* or *Man Equals Man*—*Mann ist Mann* got its start as early as *Galgei*, a poem about a butter vendor forced to assume the permanent identity of another man after falling "into the hands of bad men who maltreated him, took away his name and left him lying skinless." Completed and renamed *Galy Gay* or *Man=Man* in late 1925, it premiered as *Mann ist Mann* the next year in Darmstadt and opened at the Berliner Volksbühne in 1928. By the time Brecht directed a revised version at the Staatstheater in 1931, his political outlook and theories on the theater had come together, enabling him to introduce a new, and to him superior, "human type." Once its hero, Galy Gay, surrenders his personality and ceases to be "a private person," wrote Brecht in an introductory speech for a Berlin Radio broadcast in 1927, "he only becomes strong in the mass."

In her notes on his work, Elisabeth Hauptmann wrote that "Brecht declare[d] that *Man is Man* is altogether a classic comedy." Relinquishing his "precious ego" and eliminating his individuality does not harm Galy Gay, maintained Brecht. On the contrary, "It's a jolly business." If the inhumanity of human nature seemed less amusing than Brecht had anticipated—*Galgei*'s "monstrous mixture of comedy and tragedy" sat uncomfortably with him—he allowed that "possibly you will come to quite a different conclusion. To which I am the last person to object." As his Marxist studies had conditioned Brecht's subordination of the individual to the collective, so the rise of fascism cried for an updated interpretation. In keeping with the changing times, Galy Gay now became a "socially negative hero" and the play's theme "the false, bad collectivity (the 'gang') and its powers of attraction."

On the face of it, *Mann ist Mann* is a parable about the mutability of man. The place is Kilkoa, India. Galy Gay, a simple, poor Irish dock worker goes out to buy a fish but instead agrees to purchase a cucumber that he does not need. When a machine-gun unit of British Tommies—in the 1931 production, standing on stilts and wearing false noses and hands to effect, according to Brecht, the depersonalization of the actors and enforce the need for external gestures—that has lost its fourth man realizes that here "is a man who can't say no," they propose a business deal. If Galy Gay will agree to replace their missing comrade, they will sell him an elephant at a bargain price. "For about any kind of deal I am your man," says Galy Gay, who soon disavows his wife, his name, his past, altogether his sense of identity. Because "one man's as good as another," the soldiers take Galy Gay apart like a car and reassemble him bit by bit. To complete the transformation, the soldiers arrest him when he tries to sell the fake army elephant and convict and sentence him to death. "I'm not the man you're looking for," says Galy Gay, throwing himself on the ground. "I don't even know him. My name is Jip. I swear it." The soldiers smell progress. Time is up. Galy Gay walks to the place of execution "like the protagonist of a tragedy" and stands against the "Johnny-are-your-pants-dry-wall." At the shout of "three," he faints. Entreated to prepare the former Galy Gay's funeral oration—since "you knew him—better than we did, maybe"—the reconstructed Jip sings "The Song of the Both" ("What's a Man? Something and nothing.") before delivering his own eulogy. The conversion of the weak-minded, soft-hearted docker into a human fighting machine—armed with pistol, rifle, hand grenades, and a knife between his teeth—is complete.

Mann ist Mann opened on February 6, 1931. Thirty-one years later, Lorre told an interviewer for *Newsweek* magazine that "the only compliment I've ever had about my acting that meant anything to me was from Brecht. In the notes to 'Mann Ist [*sic*] Mann,' he talks about me for several pages." Negative reaction to Lorre's performance by confused critics prompted Brecht to address a clarifying letter titled "The Question of Criteria for Judging Acting," which was published in the *Berliner Börsen Courier,* March 8, 1931. Opinions fell into two categories. Some rejected his way of acting. Others judged it consistent with the playwright's "new point of view." Brecht used the controversy as a platform to defend Lorre's performance within the context of his epic style, focusing on Herbert Jhering's criticism that the actor had summoned sufficient charm for the early Galy Gay but lacked the decisive prerequisites—"clarity and the ability to make his meaning clear." In rehearsals, Lorre had turned in a traditional performance. On opening night, however, the "hallmarks of great acting faded away," wrote Brecht, "only to be replaced, in my view, by other hallmarks, of a new style of acting." To the objection that Lorre had "acted nothing but episodes," he explained how "his manner of speaking had been split up according to gests," which, for the long speeches or "summings-up" had seemed to hinder their normal meaning. Lorre shouted and mumbled, withdrawing sentences and preventing the spectator from getting "caught up" in the contradictions. Thus the theatergoer "was not led but left to make his own discoveries." If this seemed peculiar, epic theater had "profound reasons" for such a "reversal of criteria." By pacing the tempo by mental processes rather than emotional ones, Lorre had "delivered his inventory" in a "truly magnificent way." Just how well he managed "to mime the basic meaning underlying every (silent) sentence" struck Brecht when he saw Carl Koch's 16mm film of the production: "The epic actor may possibly need an even greater range than the old stars did, for he has to be able to show his character's coherence despite, or rather by means of, interruptions and jumps."

During rehearsals of *Edward II* in 1926, Brecht had quizzed his assistants on how soldiers looked before battle. They shook their heads. Asked the same question, comedian Karl Valentin said simply, "They're pale, they're scared, that's what!"—which gave Brecht the idea of instructing his actors to chalk their faces. Though Lorre hadn't formed the idea, he used it to great effect in 1931. Four masks, wrote Brecht, marked the phases of Galy Gay's development: "the packer's face, up to the trial; the 'natural' face, up to his awakening after being shot; the 'blank page,' up to his reassembly after the funeral speech; finally, the soldier's face." After long consideration, Lorre chose to whiten his face for the third mask. Said Bentley, who heard it from Brecht: "He had put his head in his hands as he turned away from the audience and his hands were covered with white paint, so he just rubbed off all the white paint on his face. When he turned back, he was as white as a sheet."[35] Rather than allow his acting to be "influenced by fear of death 'from within himself,'" Lorre chose the "fear of life . . . as the more profound."

"Brecht laughed over that," said Bentley. "He thought it was just terrific. It was the use of an external device to get the effect."

Lorre, who, according to Eric Bentley, could discourse on Brecht's theories by the hour, understood what was expected of him and filled in between the lines of his rules on epic stagecraft. "Peter's quietness, subtle humor and his ability to underplay were his strengths," observed Marta Feuchtwanger. "Brecht liked this." The actor delivered an emotionally restrained performance that contrasted favorably with what Bentley would later label "the Hitlerite actor . . . who sounds for all the world like the late Führer addressing a mass meeting." At the same time, his rational, socially minded, and credibly alienated Galy Gay gave concrete form to Marxist doctrine.

Apparently sensitive to the idea that critics perceived his theories to be not only confusing but also monotonous, Brecht called for more "fun" in the theater and appreciated Lorre's suggestions, which checked and balanced the comic-tragic nature of the drama. Like Pieter Brueghel the Elder, whom Brecht later singled out for balancing his pictorial contrasts without merging them into one another, Lorre practiced "the separation of comic and tragic; his tragedy contains a comic element and his comedy a tragic one." In later interviews about his film portrayals, Lorre said the same thing, in almost the same words. By mixing and matching comedy and villainy (or tragedy), he undercut audience expectations, though even those contradictions eventually stamped his distinctive style.

Lorre also understood what Galy Gay asked of him. "There was an accidental meeting of the minds there," said Bentley of Lorre's split style of acting. "Galy Gay was an absolutely sensational coincidence for it calls for exactly that, a man cut off from his own feelings. The other actors in the story are taking a knife and cutting off the channel of feeling so that he has none. He's totally calloused, but you can still tell from his calloused tone what he's gone through."

Soon after *Mann ist Mann* closed (after only six performances), Brecht and Lorre spun up to the door of Berlin's Staatstheater in the writer's "singing Steyr" roadster. Gazing up at the democratic motto inscribed in stone on the theater's facade, Brecht predicted, "This will be the last play around here for a very long time." While Lorre as Galy Gay sat on his coffin and delivered his own eulogy, Brownshirts laughed, chattered, and whistled, threatening to close the show. For a moment, the gnome-like Lorre stood there helplessly. On the verge of tears and gripped by an intense excitement—not a very Brechtian thing, said Bentley—he decided to pit himself against the disturbance. Softly speaking his lines, he grabbed the audience and held it, powering it into silence. "He is a neurasthenic Kaspar Hauser," wrote a Berlin theater critic, "and the laughing died in him and in us."

2

M IS FOR MORPHINE

One of the first movies Monty [Clift] and I ever saw was
M. We couldn't stop talking about this marvelous actor. We
went back three times to see it. And Monty said, "Wouldn't
it be wonderful to be like him as an actor."

—Andrea King

I was a murderer, but I was a matinee idol.

—Peter Lorre

Absolutely convinced that Peter Lorre was perfect for the lead in his new
picture, Fritz Lang saw no need to screen test the "virgin" actor. With script in
hand, he turned up at the Theater am Schiffbauerdamm. "I sometimes cursed
him secretly," Lorre looked back twenty years later, "as I must have waited fourteen months and couldn't accept any film offers." He had even turned down an
overture from director Richard Oswald, who promised a three-day guarantee
to reprise his role as Moritz Stiefel in a film production of *Spring's Awakening*.[1]
Indeed, Lorre supposed Lang had forgotten about him. "I never paid any attention to it," said the actor, later claiming he had accepted the role out of
politeness.

"Peter confessed to us that he didn't believe he really would go through
with it," recalled Walter Reisch. "If Lang realizes how small he is . . . when he
sees the dailies, he may not like it. Peter had a complex about that, but that's
exactly what Lang wanted." The director told him he would begin shooting in
six to eight weeks. Lorre then learned a closely guarded secret (one that he was

sworn to keep): he would play Hans Beckert, a compulsive child murderer, in *Mörder unter Uns* (*The Murderer among Us*), later shortened to *M*.[2]

"A director should not talk or speak about his films," Lang said in 1973. "If his films don't convey his ideas, he's a lousy director and shouldn't make any movies." To his credit, he took his own advice and spoke about his films only when asked, which, as it turned out, was often. Like most filmmakers who become legends during their lifetimes, Lang formatted his answers to questions about his work posed by journalists, students, and biographers (and somehow still left room to maneuver around his own mythmaking). Behind the glib generalizations, however, lay a trail of differing details. Tired of making what he later called "big canvasses," films of colossal construction, such as *Die Nibelungen* (1924), *Metropolis* (1926), and *Die Frau im Mond* (*Woman in the Moon,* 1929), the director opted for a simple story about a real human being and "what makes him do what he does, what makes him tick." Lang asked his wife and collaborator, screenwriter Thea von Harbou, what was the most unspeakably heinous crime to which man put his hand. Writing poison-pen letters topped the list. They began work on a synopsis. Scanning the newspaper headlines one day, Lang hit upon another idea, one more symptomatic of the times. Rape, robbery, and mass murder filled the front pages. Karl Denke, of Munsterberg, had smoked the bodies of his thirty victims. Berlin's Carl Wilhelm Grossman had cut twenty-seven women to bits. Fritz Haarman, the "Ogre of Hannover," had dismembered and potted the meat of young boys and afterward said he remembered nothing. And Peter Kürten, the highly intelligent, naturally reticent "Vampire of Düsseldorf," strangled, axed, hammered, drowned, and knifed to death forty men, women, and children. "The first idea for 'M' came to me," recalled Lang in his notes for a 1948 showing of *M* at Princeton University, "when I read a news item in the local part of the *Berliner Tageblatt* that criminals through their underground organization had offered their help to the police in their effort to catch [Kürten]."[3]

Like the police, Lang needed a motive for the murders. Recognizing that "every human mind harbors a latent compulsion to murder," he believed that guilt and innocence walk a fine line: "Yes, you, you and you, are all potential killers needing only the flick of a mental trigger to send you before a jury of your peers."

"Let's make a film about a child murderer," he said to von Harbou. "A child murderer who is forced by a power within him to commit a crime which he afterwards resents very much."

In his own way, Lang was as compulsive as Kürten. He conducted his research at the "Alex," Berlin's Police Headquarters at Alexanderplatz. Believing there are no small details, he studied its methods and procedures. Through his discussions with psychiatrists, he got into the heads of the criminally insane. He even claimed to have interviewed several mass murderers and talked with members of the Berlin underground that were looking for Kürten. Thea von Harbou, according to Lang, declined an invitation to scrutinize the criminal "types." "This is not necessary," she told him, confident in her ability to work from the inside. "I see everything before me."

Lang did not need to be asked on what particular crime or criminal he had based his story. As much as he considered *M* a factual report, he was quick to point out that the script had been completed before Kürten was apprehended. Only after the murderer had urged his wife to turn him in for the reward—a courtesy expected to subsidize her old age—did the public hear his confession. Before he was caught, however, Kürten's description (based on two thousand eyewitness accounts), case histories of the murders, profiles of his victims, and even symptoms of a growing psychosis in Düsseldorf had been graphically chronicled in a special edition of *Kriminal-Magazin*. Although Lang could afford to pick and choose from both the secret police files and the popular press, the outline of the case indulged his need "to explain Kürten, to account for him, to explain his mind. Just to label him with disapproval was not enough. I saw him not as a criminal, not as a corpse in a police mortuary slab but as a man, not as an isolate, a phenomenon, but one of many criminals of this time, as a unit in a disintegrating social system." Lang later admitted to journalist Gretchen Berg, who interviewed the director in 1964, that he and von Harbou had based their script not only on a "synthesis of facts" taken from the Denke and Haarman cases, but also on Kürten's "habit of sending notes to the police telling them where his hammer-killed bodies were to be found." Although the script was completed before the murderer confessed, filming did not begin until January 8, 1931, giving Lang and von Harbou time to further document the script.

Lang recognized that it was best to leave some details of Kürten's history out of the script. Committed to presenting "an objective account, showing neither harshness nor pity for such a sick mind," he chose to omit the psychological and sociological roots of the murderer's pathology. Gone were scenes of a drunken, abusive father and a local dogcatcher who taught Kürten how to torture animals. Lang took from Kürten only what he needed for Beckert.

A chronic criminal and sometime construction worker, Kürten cultivated a refined exterior. He dressed impeccably, read widely, and behaved properly. He was, according to friends, a most unlikely murderer. But he also had a weakness for women. By his own admission, he derived a heightened sexual gratification from shedding the blood of his female victims, sometimes breaking into song. He confessed that while committing his crimes, he lost touch with his human side. Becoming more animal, he said, felt good. Kürten rationalized taking revenge on a world he was trying to better. Afterward, he seemed strange to himself and disconnected from his deeds, reason, he believed, to deny responsibility and reject moral judgment. He was, as his wife described him—and as he characterized himself—"a two-natured human being." This concept was a theme central to Lang and von Harbou's efforts to "fill in some of the gaps" in their own treatment. But unlike their murderer, no conscience followed Kürten to bed. He felt no remorse, suffered no inner torment.

Invited to Lang's apartment on Berlin's Breitenbachplatz, Lorre, by his own account, bored the guests with his silence. "Wordless, he sat at the bar," reported *Der Spiegel.* "Wordless, he gulped down his cognac, wordless he stared with lost, deeply sad eyes at the guests." His hectic theater schedule—performances in *Squaring the Circle* overlapped rehearsals for *Mann ist Mann*—had relegated Lang's film project to a rather trifling third place. Suddenly, Lorre lashed out at Lang, denigrating his idea as *Schmarren* (tripe). Lang, who believed that "a director should be a kind of psychoanalyst [who] must be able to go under the skin of his characters . . . so that he can explain to the actor why a scene is the way it is, why a character does something—in case the actor doesn't catch on after reading the script," sketched out the story. The actor now understood. He cursed himself for his outburst, jumped from his barstool, and excitedly picked up where Lang had left off.

Lang described *M* as "simply a cops-and-robbers story." A murderer runs loose. Neighbor suspects neighbor. The public demands results. Police raids yield silverware, burglary tools, brass knuckles, guns, knives, binoculars, and even furs, but no clue to the identity of the culprit. "Keep up your investigations," the killer advises. "Everything will happen just as I have predicted. But I haven't yet FINISHED."[4]

"This is wrecking our business," laments a landlady. "If they catch that bastard, they'll wring his neck."

"Wherever you spit," cries a burglar, "nothing but cops."

Tired of "someone who is not a member of the Union" screwing up their business, a crime boss takes the moral high ground: "We are not on the same level as this man. . . . There is an abyss between him and us. . . . We're just doing our job. . . . because we have a living to make. But this monster has no right to live. . . . He must be exterminated, without pity, without scruples." With its reputation at stake, the criminal community decides to catch the murderer in their ranks.

The race is on. While the police search from house to house and hedge to hedge, mapping their methodical progress in concentric circles, the underground mobilizes its beggars' union, which monitors every corner and courtyard.

A stranger whistles. "I've heard that somewhere before," says a blind beggar who remembers selling a balloon to a "fellow [who] whistled just like that" the day Elsie Beckmann was killed. "After him," he orders, "and don't let him go." A young man chalks a letter on his palm and marks the murderer's back. When the killer sees the letter M reflected in a mirror, his eyes bulge in panic. The underworld closes in. After rooting him from the attic of an office building, the criminals put the killer on trial. He tells them there must be some mistake, that he is not responsible for his actions. The mob offers "no mercy . . . no pardon . . . kill him." At the last moment, policemen show up and arrest the murderer "in the name of the law."

Behind what one reviewer dismissively labeled a "plain thriller" lay what Lang called "higher instincts." He believed that film should educate as well as entertain. It is this counterpointing of convictions that gave *M* a sense of equilibrium. Asked if Brecht's *Die Dreigroschenoper* influenced him, Lang replied that he had been open to many outside impulses. As a "witness to the 30s," *M* mirrored the trends of the times, which checked and balanced his vision of a society precipitately poised on the edge. Realism and expressionism set parameters that embraced light and dark, sound and silence, emotion and reason, sanity and sickness, revenge and justice. Lang was at his artistic best when searching out common ground among them.

In the opening scene, Lang coldly observes a group of children playing a game. A little girl, standing inside a circle of her playmates, points a finger from one to another as she ominously chants a gruesome nursery rhyme:

Just you wait a little while,
The evil man in black will come.
With his little chopper,
He will chop you up.

Counted out, a child leaves the circle. The camera then scans the gray face of a tenement block. On the balcony hang wet clothes. A pregnant woman lugs a load of laundry up the stairs. Life's repetitions weigh pleasure and pain.

Later, the director intercuts the cool efficiency of the criminals, headed by the sleek Schränker (Gustaf Gründgens), with the crippling inefficiency of the police, led by the fat, feet-soaking Lohmann (Otto Wernicke).[5] Lang seems to be saying they are only opposite sides of the same coin, knocked off its slim edge by an outsider who has upset the balance between the separate but some-how equal worlds.

Throughout the film, stretches of silence throw sound into sharp relief, giving objective voice to subjective reality: a cuckoo clock, a stone-cold stair-way, a ball smacking the sidewalk and then noiselessly rolling to a stop, a doll-shaped balloon flailing silently in utility wires before flying off, a *Hampelmann* (jumping jack) soundlessly convulsing in a toy-store window, an electric drill boring into a floor while a knife covertly turns the screws of a lock.

Like Brecht, Lang wanted to awaken his audience, in this case to the need to "look after the little ones better," a theme close to von Harbou's heart. He also accurately predicted that his message about capital punishment would trigger heated debate about the "pros and cons" of the death penalty. Lang said it wasn't his place to take sides, though it is obvious where his sympathies lay. He sought to explain the murderer's base crimes, not to defend them. He counted on Lorre to sing the higher notes.

A shadow of a man falls across a wanted poster.

"What a pretty ball!" says an offscreen voice. "What's your name?"

Later, tunelessly whistling the "Hall of the Mountain King" theme from Edvard Grieg's *Peer Gynt Suites,* a sinister leitmotif that runs the course of the story, the man buys a balloon for little Elsie Beckmann.[6] The audience sees only his back, concealed by a long, dark overcoat.

Writing a note to the newspapers on his windowsill, Beckert remains face-less to both the audience and the handwriting expert who determines that "the very particular shape of the letters indicates a strong pathological sexual-ity." His conclusion that "some of the broken letters reveal an actor's personal-ity, which is indolent and even lazy," is voiced over the reflected image of a facemaking Beckert searching for the murderer in the mirror.[7]

"It's a man who looks like a peaceful little family man, who wouldn't hurt a fly," predicts a detective.

When buying a bag of apples, the symbolic forbidden fruit in Judeo-Christian tradition, the murderer finally steps into the light. He appears terri-fyingly normal.

Looking at a window display in a cutlery and silverware shop, Beckert is framed by the rhomboid reflection of a knife arrangement. In a diamond-shaped mirror he sees a little girl, whose image is also outlined by the geomet-ric pattern formed by the shiny blades, ornamental details sharply suggestive of an overwhelming sense of fatalism. The script very specifically directs Lorre to stand "transfixed, staring at her. He wipes his mouth with the back of his hand, eyes bulging. . . . [his] arms fall limply to his side, he gasps for breath and his eyes close as he sways forward against the shop front. Then the fit subsides and he recovers slightly." Lorre invests the scene with inner struggle, assuming a brutish, almost feral, look before bursting once more into *Peer Gynt,* the barometer of his bloodlust. When the girl's mother shows up, he ducks into a doorway and then steps onto the sidewalk and scratches his hand in frustration. Beside him, in a bookshop window, an arrow incessantly bounces up and down, stabbing space with phallic thrusts. Next to it, a cardboard circle spirals inward.

The murderer retreats to a nearby café, where he orders a brandy and peers out from behind a trellis of climbing plants. Like a cornered animal, he distorts his features, externalizing the evil force inside him. Whistling "gives wordless expression to his inner urges." He puts his hands over his ears, but cannot block out the sound. The melody floats behind him as he leaves.

Lang later said he had only one complaint about working with Lorre. "Though Peter had the script eight to ten weeks before," said the director, "and knew that the first scene called for a whistle, he didn't think it necessary to tell me that he could not whistle." Lang "told Peter to fake it," but the actor remained mute. "I am a musical moron who can't carry a tune," Lang told film historian Gene Phillips, "but I decided to dub the whistling myself. It was off key and turned out to be just right since the murderer himself is off balance mentally."

Lang credited von Harbou with writing the climactic courtroom scenes, in which the tribunal of thieves and burglars try Beckert. Like the dialogue itself, the "fear . . . horror . . . pain" directed in the script does not touch Lorre's performance, which sealed his fate as an actor. Rawly emotional and physically racking, it is as exhausting to watch as it was to give. "If I play a pathological part," Lorre later admitted, "I put myself into this character until I begin to display his symptoms." He sweats, screams, pants, pleads, and squeals. His eyes bulge, his fingers clench, and his voice pitches toward an ecstatic frenzy:

I can't help myself! I haven't any control over this evil thing that's inside me— the fire, the voices, the torment! Always . . . always, there's this evil force inside me. . . . It's there all the time, driving me out to wander through the streets . . . following me . . . silently, but I can feel it there. . . . It's me, pursuing myself. . . . I want to escape . . . to escape from myself! . . . but it's impossible. I can't. I can't escape. I have to obey it. I have to run . . . run . . . streets . . . endless streets. I want to escape. I want to get away. And I am pursued by ghosts. Ghosts of mothers. And of those children. . . . They never leave me. *Shouting desperately.*

. . . I see the posters and I read what I've done. . . . I read . . . and . . . and read. . . . Did I do that? But I can't remember anything about it. . . . But who will believe me? Who knows what it feels like to be me? How I'm forced to act. . . . *His eyes close in ecstasy.* How I must . . . Don't want to, but must . . . *He screams.* Must . . . Don't want to . . . must. And then . . . a voice screams . . . I can't bear to hear it. *He throws himself against the wooden barrier in a paroxysm covering his ears with his hands.* . . . I can't . . . I can't go on. Can't go on. . . . Can't go on. . . . Can't go on . . .

Nor could Lorre go on. Like Beckert, he had spent himself. "Lang wrung him like an old towel," recalled Paul Falkenberg, who edited *M* and spent almost every day on the set. "He was completely worn out. Tongue hanging out. He had given his all and his best." Lang knew what he wanted and how to get it. Beginning at eight in the morning, he shot the "court" scenes until one the next morning. "Peter fainted," said writer Kurt Siodmak, who stopped by to visit his cousin Seymour Nebenzal. "That was what Lang wanted and he used that shot." Siodmak was anxious to meet Lorre, but Lang had given instructions that no one talk with the actor, who, broken down and isolated, had become one with his role.[8]

The bruises soon faded, but their memory did not. By 1931 Lang had earned a reputation as the "Stalin of Film." Like the Russian dictator, he ruled with an iron fist. "Look, if you want me to make a picture for you," Lang had told Nebenzal (whom he later credited for courageously financing a social drama "in which there is no love interest and the 'hero' is a child murderer"), "I have the choice of everything—script, actors, cutting, everything. And nobody else has anything to say." He got his way. Described as brutal, abusive, exacting, driven, omnipotent, imperious, and autocratic, to name only a few of the more charitable adjectives, Lang was a perfectionist, who, according to actor Gerhard Bienert, "liked to stir up actors, to keep them off balance. He felt more creative in an atmosphere of tension."

In Berlin for an auto show, Andrew Lorre stopped by the makeshift studio at the Staaken Zeppelinhalle to see his brother. "I came upon the scene," he recalled, "when Mr. Fritz Lang was seized by one of his frequent rages and there was no way to calm him down. I mentioned to Thea von Harbou, Mr. Lang's wife, who was his assistant, that I had brought some Hungarian salami for Peter. 'Fine,' she said, 'we'll slice some up and give it to him.' Lang really calmed down immediately and polished off the salami."

"A director," said Fritz Lang, "crawls under the skin of an actor and gets out something maybe he doesn't even know exists in himself." If, as Falkenberg claimed, Lang cast a magic spell over Lorre that "unloosened" realms of possibility, the enchantment also harbored a darker side: "Lang sort of plucked him from the gutter and made him feel that he was the boss and he was the creature. He didn't do it outright, like coming and hitting him in the face right and left. No, he took the opportunity to use him for a perfectly innocuous scene that anybody could have done. There is a shot, if you look very closely, in the final scene of *M*, where he is trying to escape and these plug-uglies, these gorillas, try to push him down the stairs so he can face the trial by the criminals. There is a close-up where a nailed boot hits him against his shin. Now this shot was taken at least thirteen times and it wasn't second unit shooting. It had to be Peter, who had his whole leg bandaged and couldn't walk for three days. Lang insisted that he lend his own shin to this close-up, which was perfectly idiotic. Anybody could have done that."

Celia Lovsky also recalled watching Lang film eighteen takes of Peter being dragged down a staircase inside a bag. Although in the scene his rug-wrapped body comes to no physical harm, consensus of opinion would tend to support Lovsky's claim that Lang put Lorre through more than appears onscreen.

Lorre knew perfectly well that Lang could have used a double and shot around him, possibly explaining why he took the liberty of requesting a leave of absence from the set to appear in *Mann ist Mann* the first week of February. According to Lang, Lorre didn't want to listen to reason. "If you don't come," threatened the director, who reminded Lorre that he had three hundred extras on the payroll, "I'll have to bring an injunction against you."

Normally full of jokes, good humor, and funny stories, Lorre "muttered dire threats," said Falkenberg and "spoke about the bastard, what's he's doing to him. I don't recall that there was ever an open conflict in the sense that Peter openly revolted and walked off the set. He knew where his bread was buttered and what kind of an important part he was playing. . . . Ms. von Harbou was always trying to pour oil on the waters, trying to heal the wound and make up for Lang's transgressions in her own idiotic way. She used to say to me, 'Where there's lots of light, there's lots of shadow, so you can't avoid it.' These idiotic truisms she threw out, trying to keep things on a steady keel."

As a "genius who sometimes gets his finest effects independently of his director," Lorre claimed to have researched his role from within: "I did not see the actual murderer. I did not need to. I saw a few photographs of him, that was all. It did not matter to me what he looked like, or what his mannerisms were. It only mattered that he did what he did, and my only concern was to understand *why*. And I did understand." But not without outside help. Lorre had not studied the police files or canvassed the criminal community. However, he held a deep interest in psychology and read widely in the field. Moreover, as Lang pointed out in a 1967 interview with the BBC's Alexander Walker, the climate of experimentation on his first sound film invited a careful exchange of ideas between director and actor.

"Create your own method," Konstantin Stanislavski advised young actors. "Make up something that will work for you." Described by his daughter Catharine as "a very emotional man" who learned to "suppress a lot of his emotions," Lorre heeded the Russian stage director and developed a method that accommodated the extremes of his nature. "You can't portray a character," he echoed repeatedly. "You have to *be* that person while you're in the role." Even the *Deutsche Filmzeitung* agreed that "Lorre brings a realism to all the problems Lang avoided." That he so convincingly transformed himself into a compulsive child murderer goes far toward explaining public reaction to the actor in the streets of Berlin, where mothers with children allegedly fled from him.

Lang and Brecht wanted—and got—the same thing from Lorre, a split style of acting that left a gap between the person and his actions. The actor seamlessly stepped in and out of character, one minute exploring the "contradictions of existence" at a critical distance, the next swept away by the catharsis of confession. His performance is not so much what Brecht pejoratively labeled a "psychological operation," but is rather a dissection in which the actor becomes both doctor and patient, alternately looking at himself from within and from without. Through "interruptions and jumps," he broke the spell cast by conventional actors, shocking rather than beguiling the audience into understanding. Sympathy pulls them in and repulsion pushes them away. By distinguishing the cause of Beckert's behavior ("There's an evil force inside me") from its effect ("I read what I have done"), Lorre allowed for an outcome that was not tragically inevitable. This process made strange bedfellows of Brecht and Stanislavski, playing their means against an end that achieved what all acting methods strive for: reality.

Where a director as controlling as Lang leaves off and an actor as psychologically intuitive as Lorre begins is impossible to say. Bienert stated that Lang "never guided actors, rather pushed them to overdo it." (Lorre confided to Lovsky that he would have played the climactic courtroom scene "more simply, in his own way.") The director, however, coldly claimed that he only photographed "the feelings of a person," using his camera to show things from "the viewpoint of the protagonist; in that way my audience identifies itself with the character on the screen and thinks with him." Lorre, through what

Graham Greene called his "sympathetic grasp," suffused Lang's form with sensibility. Committed to explaining the murderer's motives, he presented Beckert not as a monster but as a divided human being whose darker side acts independently of his will. "If you could examine that film more closely," he told an interviewer in 1935, "you would perceive that it was a tragedy—as real a tragedy as ever Shakespeare conceived. One felt for the murderer—as one does for Macbeth—an overwhelming pity."

On the set of *Island of Doomed Men* some nine years after *M*, a conversation between Lorre and his director, Charles Barton, turned to his portrayal of Hans Beckert. "In *M*," recalled Barton, "Peter didn't come on as strong as I think he wanted to. He wanted to overplay it. I didn't want him to do it in this picture. . . . When you do that you become weak." Unbeknownst to Fritz Lang scholars—and likely forgotten by Lorre himself—was *M le maudit* (*M the Damned One*), the French-language version of M, shot at the same time as Lang's original and rediscovered in 2004 in the archives of the Centre Nationale de la Cinematographie, outside Paris. In this film the actor indeed went "over the top." There is no longer any record of whether Fritz Lang supervised the French *M* himself, but it seems likely that the work was not his. The final result is a mixture of dubbed scenes from the German original (notably Gründgens in the kangaroo court) and sequences reshot with French actors (the phone conversation between the Government Minister and the Chief of Police). There is one exception: Peter Lorre. He reprised his role in French, but for whatever reason—most likely his imperfect command of the language—another actor, a *French* actor, revoiced all his dialogue. Although Lorre had obviously taken the trouble to learn his role phonetically (his lip movements match perfectly), he apparently wasn't polished enough for a French audience.

But the performances stand further apart than merely the language gap. For the German version, Lang had literally beaten a performance out of Lorre in the film's finale. Lorre was clearly pushed past the limits of physical endurance. The same actor who verges on collapse in the German *M* is far fresher in the French version, obviously shot at a different time entirely. The sets and lighting are pale imitations of Lang's original, and, unfortunately, so is Lorre's performance. Freed of Lang's notorious sadism and left to his own devices, Lorre took his performance where he felt it belonged. His renewed energy feeds an agitated reenactment that fails to capture the immediacy of the original. In the less-centered French version, he stands instead of crouches, wildly flipping his head and shaking his body. He directs himself outward rather than inward in a portrayal that is more personified than personal. And all this coupled with a voice that, while technically fluent, has little of the passion, anguish, and individuality that is Peter Lorre's original German. That his performance in *M le maudit* falls short of that in *M*, there can be no doubt. But it hardly matters. It is, after all, the original that has become film history.

M intersected the latitude of life and the longitude of death. The film premiered at 6:00 p.m., Monday, May 11, 1931.[9] Moviegoers blocked the sidewalks. Automobiles jammed the street. Inside the theater, spectators clapped and whistled for and against capital punishment while Kürten sat on death row. He had asked to die, then to live. Condemned to death on April 22, he was beheaded on July 2, 1931. Classic stature came to Lang's favorite film overnight and stayed. After two hours' deliberation, the politically conservative *Filmprüfstelle* (Film Examiner's Office) announced: "Mr. Lang, this film has practically everything about which we disagree and which we cannot accept but it is done with such integrity that we don't want to make any cuts."

It was the first of many mixed notices. While the jury of critics reached an easy verdict on Lang's mastery of technical details—provocative camera angles; newsreel atmosphere; dramaturgical use of sound, tempo, and tension; expertise with mass scenes; casting; and even the writing—it hung on content. Debunking the film's documentary ambitions, Herbert Jhering pointed out that where *M* was most cinematic, it was also most inaccurate. He argued that Lang's *Threepenny* reality made "a gruesome mockery of social custom," undermining police authority and romanticizing the criminal element. Both conservative and liberal voices warned that arousing feeling for a murderous underdog would only feed the frenzy of psychotic types. Even those swept along by the sheer entertainment of the film stumbled over its anticlimactic ending. It came down to a matter of style. Pick one, advised Jhering—"cold or neutral" or "amusing or satirical"—but not both. Like a firefly, Lang flitted between morality and suspense, never alighting on a consistent point of view, provoking the criticism that he "only ever peeps into the great problems. . . . Lang has only thought of his subject; he has not felt it. *M*, like *Frankenstein*, is a fullblown tragedy that has been diminished in the creation to a mere 'sensational.'"

Critics bit into Lang without drawing blood. *M* played at film festivals, and scholars confirmed its place in cinema history. Nonetheless, the movie had struck a collective nerve. As a *Zeitstück* (period piece), it not only mirrored the time in which it was made but also documented the time that made it. Regarded today as Lang's masterpiece, *M* was, to the best of the director's knowledge, "the first film to deal with social and psychological aspects of crime." That he put this pill in a jelly sandwich didn't bother the moviegoing public. Although it lumped in the throats of some squeamish Americans, those who put European cinematic art on a pedestal considered *M* ahead of its time. With two years' hindsight, the *New Republic*'s Bruce Blevin held that "the film is one which deserves to rank with the very best things in this field which have come out of Germany, with 'Mädchen in Uniform,' 'The Last Laugh,' 'The Cabinet of Dr. Caligari,' and 'Variety.' It is a picture which I do not believe could under any circumstances have been made in Hollywood—indeed, any American director who suggested such a thing would probably find his own sanity suspected. Nevertheless, Hollywood will make better pictures after seeing this one. And so we progress."

Time has vindicated the few German critics who credited Lang with exploring both sides of a complex question "with delicacy and fine feeling." Indeed, old weaknesses have been heralded as new strengths, namely "every attempt to explain, exhaustively, the murderer's viewpoint and the question of his punishment." Although Lorre later confessed that he found the film "old-fashioned," for generations of moviegoers, *M* "remains as fresh as on the day of its release."

Lang believed that Lorre gave "one of the best performances in film history and certainly the best in his life." Most critics agreed. Reviewers coined fresh superlatives for the director's discovery, who was cast over the objections of those who thought it rash to pin the success of his first sound picture on a newcomer. "The murderer Peter Lorre," wrote *Film Kurier*, "is captured in the nuances of an extraordinary mimic art. He is an individual who is not crushed by the monumentality of the surrounding, but within the whole work penetrating to the moving touch."

Dr. Hans Wollenberg, writing for the *Lichtbildbühne*, also credited the actor with achieving "the scarcely comprehensible that gives the lust murderer's features life!—which follow one into the dreams. Unbelievable . . ."

However dazzled by Lorre's unique gifts, German critics allotted more weight than space to them in their columns. It was the *Nation*'s William Troy who identified the classic element of his performance:

> For the crystallization of these symbols in an emotion absolutely realized in the spectator and effecting in him a genuine Aristotelian catharsis, the flawless acting of Peter Lorre is perhaps finally responsible. In his rendering of the paralysis of frustrated lust in the scene on the cafe terrace, for example, he gives us an intuition of the conflict of will and desire such as we are accustomed to only in the great classic dramas when they are played by great tragic actors. And in the last scene, when he stands at bay before the assembled underworld seated in judgment, his wide-eyed, inarticulate defense is made the equivalent of those long passages of rhetoric at the close of Greek or Elizabe-

than plays in which the hero himself is forced to admit his helplessness before the forces which have undone him. The modern psychopath, through Peter Lorre's acting, attains to the dignity of the tragic hero.

The actor had the added benefit of not having worked extensively in silent films, whose visual histrionics often carried over to early sound movies. Nonetheless, what some critics pinpointed as *M*'s abrupt change in style from "nerve-tickling" suspense to moral manipulation left Lorre seesawing from a soap box, "on the whole indescribably bad, he overacts and diminishes the impression." Even Herbert Jhering believed that "physiognomically he is so terrifyingly good that he should not have felt it necessary to go through the streets with such an obvious play of the bad conscience shortly before the pursuit by the beggars." In any case, such ripples dissipated in the pool of favorable public opinion.

Lorre also had his own doubts about *M* before it was released. "To show you how much faith I had in the film at that time," he said later, "I was faithfully rehearsing Brecht's new play while I was appearing, I thought quite indifferently, in Lang's *M*." That would have been in January, just after shooting began. After stunned audiences spilled out of the UFA-Palast am Zoo on to the Ku'damm, Lorre knew his life would never be the same.

Ellis St. Joseph saw something deeply personal in the actor's portrayal of Beckert, something that sprang from another irresistible impulse—morphine. "Do you realize how important *M* is to Peter Lorre?" he asked. "When he cried out in the kangaroo trial, 'I cannot help it,' he is telling you everything about his victims and if you translate the child murderer drive into another kind of drive, you can see why there was such an explosion of genius in that performance." For those who knew Lorre well, the letter *M* on his back stood for *morphine* as well as *murderer*. That his drug addiction neither numbed nor stimulated his performance—at least directly—testified to Lorre's ability as an actor. It enabled him to keep his habit at arm's—however punctured—length.

"My trouble is that I try to cover a part entirely," Lorre said, looking back several years later. "When you do that there's the danger that the patron will leave the theatre feeling that you are so perfectly suited to the character he has just seen that he can't imagine you in any other part." Women seemed most convinced of this—and at least one little girl. To the six-year-old Inge Landgut, who played Elsie Beckmann, Lorre seemed "eerie," not least because Lang told her nothing about the story, "so that I wasn't influenced by anything." Only after the war did she see *M* for the first time. Fifty years later, Landgut remembered Lorre as "not unfriendly, not friendly either." What stuck most in her memory was holding his sweaty hands: "I wanted to run to my mother. When I remember the scene I become uncomfortable."

Friend and screenwriter Axel Eggebrecht wrote in his autobiography that *M* remained important to him because he had "never before so directly observed that fruitful and, at the same time, alarming impact a great actor can have on viewers who are no longer able to distinguish between the real person and the person portrayed." At a gala reception after the premiere, an obviously nymphomaniacal high-society lady forced her way up to Lorre and confessed that the ghostly character of his child murderer had left a deep impression on her: "He couldn't get rid of her and finally looked at her with his kind, bulging eyes and said ironically, 'Did it really please you so much, madam? Well, then send me your daughter in the morning.'"

In the coming weeks and years, women who wanted both to suffer at his hands and to mother him penned invitations to tea. "Terrible letters came to me," recalled Lorre. "Letters from strange people; people who I never believed lived in the world; depraved and disturbed minds, thinking they saw in me the perfect companion, a fellow psychopathic. A success can be too great, I tell you."

While filming *Secret Agent* (1936) at Gaumont-British film studios in London, he told a publicist about a man who claimed the actor's eyes haunted him: "Obsessed with the idea that they were watching him, he wrote weird and threatening letters to Lorre. It seems that he woke up nights and saw those eyes peering at him. The horror became unendurable and one day the maddened wretch wrote that he was going to kill the actor." An incredulous Lorre showed letters from society women—including one who begged "*M*" to whip her—to journalist and historian Heinrich Fraenkel, who recalled that "it was a giggle to him that they thought of this timid little Jew as a tough guy."

Although Lorre and Lang's working relationship during the filming of *M* had been rancorous, the actor told friend and set designer Harper Goff that the director had thought of using him in a film about "a schoolteacher, an unsung hero who was fighting the problems of education during World War I." Lorre apparently resented Lang's assumption that audiences "would imagine he was going to end up seducing the boys in the school." Whatever the reason, the picture wasn't made. Lang and Lorre saw little of one another in Berlin after *M* was released. Thrown together at émigré gatherings in Los Angeles a few years later, they socialized and, judging from the photos, even shared a laugh. Never one to hold a grudge, Lorre nonetheless sounded fairly disparaging when interviewers brought up Lang.[10] Only shortly before his death, at a

UCLA showing of *M* attended by both men, was Lorre able to laugh off Lang's callous treatment. By then, these fossils of the Weimar age apparently had come to accept their shared past.

In early March 1931, Lorre stepped on to the Schiffbauerdamm stage for the last time as Pipi the Clown in a French circus farce by Alfred Savoir. *Der Dompteur* (*The Lion Tamer*) starred Carola Neher, Fritz Kampers, and the elegant Gustaf Gründgens, who had dieted down for the role; that fact possibly accounted for his moody behavior. The slim actor kept his composure onstage, not batting an eye at the unexpected toppling of a circus tent around him. Offstage, however, he kicked holes in the scenery and demolished his dressing room with a stool, "in order," explained Aufricht, "to quiet his nerves."

Picked apart by the critics for its cheap sophistication, Savoir's love triangle between a circus rider, a lion tamer, and a decadent lord quickly collapsed, despite finding a receptive audience that appreciated the production's erotica and diverse surprises. The ensemble fared well with theatergoers and critics alike. With only the thinnest thread of interest given to his role as a melancholic clown, who sighs with his "suggestive voice," the gifted Peter Lorre was hailed in "mask and play, truest circus."

On May 25, 1931, the actor returned to *Funkstunde Berlin* as a servant in *Blaubart* (*Bluebeard*), a Jacques Offenbach operetta adapted by Karl Kraus and costarring Celia Lovsky as Princess Hermia.

Tagged as a screen menace, Lorre claimed he was offered dozens of villainous roles after *M*. "I wanted to do them," he later recalled, "but the attitude of the public made me think. Here they were trying to type me. Once you are typed your field is limited and your screen life is apt to be short." Intent on demonstrating his versatility, he turned down picture after picture until a comedy turned up. *Bomben auf Monte Carlo* (*Bombs on Monte Carlo*, 1931) afforded him both comedy and caricature, although on a small scale. In the supposedly true story of a ship captain's efforts to win his crew's back pay at a casino in Monte Carlo, Lorre played the chief engineer, relegated to the role of cook. Emerging from the galley holding a large ladle, he quizzes, with "cannibalistic innuendo," according to editor Paul Falkenberg, "Guess what I am making beef goulash out of, gentlemen? Well? Well?"

Thinking it was children, audiences laughed at what appeared to be a sardonic reference to *M*.

"Out of the beard of a billy-goat," he retorts.

In his remaining moments on the screen, he clowns, mugs, and even sings. "Now people began to forget *M*," celebrated Lorre, "and the belief that I was strictly a horror actor." Critics, however, took little notice. Hans Albers,

Germany's blue-eyed Clark Gable, carried the picture. *Bomben auf Monte Carlo* couldn't decide between reality and cheap operetta, but it hardly mattered. Albers electrified the low-voltage script, encasing the movie in a "glimmer-magic" that guaranteed box-office returns and passing marks from critic Herbert Jhering for its "lyrical frivolity, sexual patriotism and heart in the right place."

In the summer, Lorre enthusiastically tackled one of the most unusual roles of his movie career, that of a happy, healthy husband and father in *Die Koffer des Herrn O.F.* (*The Luggage of Mr. O.F.*, 1931). When the titular luggage arrives in sleepy Ostend, excitement spreads as the town readies itself for the announced arrival of millionaire Oscar Flot. The local hotel becomes "Grand Hotel Ostend." The hairdresser renames his shop "Coiffure Jean." The tailor turns into "The Old Gentleman Tailor Dorn." A movie theater, a casino, an opera, a town hall, a department store, and a cabaret all go up. The flurry of activity triggers an economic boom during times of financial crisis, making Ostend the focus of international attention. By the time editor Stix (Lorre) decides to end the hoax by reporting the stranger's death in an automobile accident, myth has eclipsed the man and no one remembers who he is. As the 78th World Economic Conference opens in Ostend, a travel agent in another city fires one of his secretaries, who sent the thirteen trunks of movie star Ola Fallon to the wrong town.

Critics complained that director Alexis Granowsky forged his actors into a team instead of giving free reign to their individual styles. He offered film audiences a Peter Lorre—earnest, exuberant, ardent—better known to theatergoers than movie fans. "It is amusing to see Peter Lorre, the terrible *M*," observed a French review, "as a bon vivant, a good boy, well-scrubbed, his face innocent, with a romantic lock of blond hair, singing joyfully of love and guile."

The Nazis didn't find Lorre and *Koffer*'s other Jewish performers and writers as endearing. In 1933, after Hitler came to power, the Reichsfilmkammer forced the removal of most of the songs in the picture and trimmed many of the performances. The censored version was released under the title *Bauen und Heiraten* (*Build and Marry*).

In October Lorre returned to the Volksbühne am Bülowplatz for the starring role of the Pawnbroker in Georg Kaiser's *Nebeneinander: Volksstück in fünf Akten* (*Side by Side: Popular Play in Five Acts*), under the direction of Karl Heinz Martin. Set against the economic and moral degradation of post–World War I Germany, it tells the stories of three isolated individuals connected only by an undelivered letter discovered in a hocked suit. Because the address has been effaced by cleaning fluid, the Pawnbroker opens and reads the message, which appeals to the owner's jilted lover not to commit suicide. The Pawnbroker's conscience and sense of duty impels him to help a fellow human being: "Nothing has any sense, if all are not ready at all times to save the life of a single person." However, he is arrested for wearing a pawned fur and loses his license. The policemen deride him for trying to help his neighbor. The Pawnbroker breaks under the realization that his brotherly love has gone to the dogs. He seals his room, turns on the gas, and dies before experience robs him of his lost illusion, "The imperceptible gain of the most wonderful feeling: to do something for a stranger! Therein lies the sense and the completion of the adventure. It douses its object—but the wave of which it tore up foams silver white. I perceived the voice of my neighbor—for which others closed themselves off—I heard it! . . . Or should one not take some part in the fate of a neighbor??—But how come this urge—erupting precipitously—is planted in our blood????"

Meanwhile, the woman who had contemplated suicide has received a second copy of the letter and marries a young engineer. The amoral, egotistical writer of the letter rises in the business world to the station of manager of a film company.

Under Berthold Viertel's successful direction, *Nebeneinander* had premiered in 1923 at the close of the expressionist era. By 1931, pointed out Norbert Falk in the *Berliner Zeitung,* the *Zeitstück* "goes down the throat as historical reminiscence." Without updating the story, Karl Heinz Martin had no hope of connecting with contemporary audiences, which found the tragedy hollow and false. Critics also faulted the production for its lack of uniform tone and continuity, imperceptible structure, and lifeless diction. Worse yet, the director was accused of tipping the delicate balance between comedy and tragedy in the altruist's favor, overburdening the play with compassion.

Critics took specific aim at Lorre, damning his performance with faint praise. Oddly enough, the same reviewers who found *Nebeneinander* "too stale, too strange" by contemporary standards charged the actor with being un-Kaiserly. In 1923 Rudolph Forster, as the seducer, had amplified the Pawnbroker's comic possibilities for appreciative audiences. Reprising the role, Ernst Busch played "without the shine and aura of a life winner," weighting the play in Lorre's favor but disadvantaging him with the critics, who accused the actor of "hopelessly drowning in the mush of empty tragic tirades." Instead of "streaking like a shot out of a gun" in Kaiserly fashion, he carefully brooded over each word, spreading on too thickly "the mask of misery and imposed sentimentality." Even the *Berliner Börsen Courier*'s Emil Faktor, who commended the actor for his "able, intensive performance" and said his excellent "facial expressions give good insight into one driven by demons," tempered his approval with the disclaimer that Lorre did not sustain his vision and lapsed into "a monotone lament." Another reviewer suggested that Lorre was simply too young for the role.[11] "Playing more out of a whim than direct tragedy," capped Norbert Falk, "one can pity him as a poor fool but not lament him as a hero of the old clothes shop."

No one lodged the same complaint about his next assignment, which followed closely on the heels of the unhappy pawnbroker. In Ödön von Horváth's *Geschichten aus dem Wiener Wald: Volksstück in Drei Teilen* (*Tales from the Vienna Woods: Folk Piece in Three Acts*), inspired by Johann Strauss's enchanting waltz, the actor starred as a flesh-and-blood villain far more frightening than anything he had played on-screen. By his own admission, Alfred (Peter Lorre) weighed in on the human scale as "a weak person," incapable of mending his lying, cheating, philandering ways.

Following what Jhering called the "sweet kitsch" of romance with the "sour kitsch" of reality, Horváth scratched Vienna's golden veneer to expose the bitter truth about a petite bourgeoisie that consumes itself in an endless search for personal happiness. The last Berlin production of Max Reinhardt, who cast the play but did not oversee it, Horváth's "slice of life" premiered at the Deutsches Theater on November 2, 1931, under the direction of Heinz Hilpert. His dark satire of human "mistakes and vices" won over critics accustomed to seeing the city's heartland idealized on stage and screen. That year Horváth received the Kleist prize for drama. Lorre drew accolades as the rascally seducer of females of all ages, "for whose immeasurably shabby soul [he] finds a surprisingly fitting cover and an expression of a smiling, slick meanness that almost borders on innocence."

On December 12 Lorre again performed on *Funkstunde Berlin* (which was also broadcast by *Radio Wien*), this time starring in *Fortunios Lied* (*Fortunio's Song*), a one-act comedy by Offenbach. Kraus, who adapted the piece, cast Celia Lovsky as Charlotte, Fortunio's scribe. Friedrich Hollaender, with whom Peter and Celia would share fate and fortune in Paris after their emigration, conducted the music.

Lorre made his final stage appearance in Berlin quite inauspiciously as a crooked teller in Louis Verneuil's bitter comedy *Die Nemo Bank,* which opened at the Komödienhaus just before Christmas. Max Pallenberg swindles his way up the ladder from bank porter to financial minister. However, the world of finance does not speak a universal language. German fraud, Alfred Kerr indignantly pointed out in the *Berliner Tageblatt*, bore its own homemade stamp of specificity. From inside Germany, *Die Nemo Bank* looked French provincial, despite the well-publicized coincidence that Pallenberg had earlier lost his fortune with the collapse of the Holland Umstelbank.[12] Audiences came to laugh at the popular actor, who held them in his hands, but ended up laughing with him, although not hard enough to leaven the flat satire.

Brecht had tentatively cast Lorre as the teacher, Nikolai Wessovschikow, in *Die Mutter* (*The Mother*), set to premiere at Theater am Schiffbauerdamm on January 17, 1932. When he failed to show up for rehearsals, Gerhard Bienert stepped into the role. Perhaps nothing more than the result of a scheduling conflict with his next picture, it likely signaled the actor's growing interest in movies and the money he could make by appearing in them, no small consideration to someone addicted to drugs and tired of just getting by on Brecht's low wages.

Lorre's busy radio schedule further complicated his calendar. On January 14 he had performed on *Funkstunde Berlin* as Bellecour, a singer in Offenbach's comic opera *Vert-Vert* (new text and dialogue direction by Kraus). The following week, he returned to the Radio Hour as a swindler in Nestroy's *Das Notwendige und das Überflüssige* (*The Necessary and the Unnecessary*), arranged and directed by Kraus.

Between film assignments, the actor also performed a double role in an abridged radio production of a play that did not reach the stage until 1959. Where theater feared to tread, radio stepped in. *Funkstunde Berlin* premiered *Die heilige Johanna der Schlachthöfe* (*St. Joan of the Stockyards*) on April 11, 1932. One of Brecht's most daring dramas, the *Lehrstücke* (learning play) not only took on classical drama, which it boldly parodied, but also indicted the corrupt partnership between Christianity and the capitalist system. Stock was as specific to Chicago as it was universal to the world exchange and the current German economic crisis in particular. In the larger of his two parts, Lorre played Sullivan Slift, a Mephistophelian character who brokers more than beef. With honey-smooth slickness, he set off the free-market magniloquence of meat magnate Pierpont Mauler (Fritz Kortner) to full effect and paved the descent of Joan Dark (Carola Neher) into the depths of poverty and degradation. As the broker Graham, the actor further flexed his vocality in the longest speech in the play, recounting the battle between the meat packers with a rolling rhythm broken by Hitlerian bombast.

In 1928 screenwriter Hermann Kosterlitz had seen Lorre in *Pioniere in Ingolstadt* and had bookmarked his comic aptitude for later use.[13] Kosterlitz and stage and film director Erich Engel returned to the page when casting a film adaptation of the popular musical comedy *Fünf von der Jazzband* (*The Jazz Band Five*, 1932). To Felix Joachimson's story of a struggling group of acrobatic musicians, the writer added a thread about a couple of look-alike car thieves played by Robert Klein-Lörk and Peter Lorre with deadpan delivery and studied insolence:

> Policeman: Do you two know the lady?
> Lorre: Maybe we know the lady. Who knows?
> Policeman: Do you know her or don't you?
> Klein-Lörk: Well, you're getting paid to find out those things.
> Lorre: We cannot do the work of other people. That's too much.
> Policeman: Get them out.

Herbert Jhering, the influential drama critic for the liberal-minded *Berliner Börsen Courier,* had treated Lorre with an even hand since 1929, singing his praises for *Pioniere in Ingolstadt* and *Frühlings Erwachen* but faulting him for *Die Unüberwindlichen.* Between his reviews, Jhering sandwiched critiques of the rising stars of stage and screen, including Ernst Busch, Leonard Steckel, and Peter Lorre. Jhering offered constructive criticism that pointed the way to perfected talent. He also pointed out the pitfalls for even the most consummate actor, making the case that how an artist's talent is used is just as important as how an artist uses his talent. For example, Jhering noted that under Reinhardt, an actor's distinctive physical appearance won contracts. With his pudgy body, round face, and protruding eyes, Lorre would have become "in a time of specialty a specialty." Producers and directors were now looking for a more typical appearance, leading them to use Lorre "for criminal types, for underworld figures." Jhering suggested in June 1932 that the former cramped Lorre's talent as much as the latter. His "areas," hammered the critic, "are the ironic, ambiguous, charming-infamous border figures. Not the obviously sick, not the obviously uncomplicated." As an agent for "the wicked harmlessness, the infernal friendliness, the cynical gentleness, the cunning naiveté, the ironic smugness . . . his 'ability' and 'being' come together. Here Lorre is first-class. Here he is a modern actor."

Lorre next appeared as a trigger-happy thug in UFA's *Schuss im Morgengrauen* (*A Shot at Dawn,* 1932), based on *The Woman and the Emerald* by Harry Jenkins, a bullet-ridden crime drama centered around a jewel heist. Convinced he could do nothing with the "underwritten" role, the actor suggested making his character a frustrated sex maniac. "He played it like that," remembered Rudolf Katscher, who coauthored the screenplay. "He followed every young female character from behind, with his hand and fingers outstretched to pinch her bottom. So when he started that gag, the audience knew what was coming and roared with laughter. In fact, he never got to 'grips' with any unsuspecting bottom!"

Mixed reviews leaned in *Schuss im Morgengrauen*'s favor. Critics didn't bother to build up or tear down the minor work "off the rack." However, they credited producer-director Alfred Zeisler and his writers, Katscher and Otto and Egon Eis, for tightening the tension with humor and singled out the "splendid acting" of the criminal types, including the "horribly grotesque" Lorre, who made the most of his small part.

Screenwriter Walter Reisch, who was under contract to UFA, had helped push fellow scenarist and friend Karl Hartl up the ladder and into a director's chair in 1930. When the studio assigned Hartl to direct German, French, and English versions of *F.P.1 antwortet nicht* (*Floating Platform 1 Doesn't Answer*, 1932), he returned the favor and persuaded Reisch to write the screenplay. Based on Kurt Siodmak's novel, it tells the story of a courageous flyer who prevents the destruction of a mid-Atlantic refueling point for transoceanic flights. Hans Albers would play the German lead, Charles Boyer the French, and Conrad Veidt (of *Caligari* fame) the English. But who would lighten what Reisch described as "a heavy science fiction drama?"

Since the hero had a sidekick, Hartl suggested, "Why don't we write the part of the little newspaper photographer so that Peter can play it?"

"We decided to have this cameraman played by the smallest actor in Berlin," recalled Reisch, "and that was Peter Lorre." And so they did, tailoring the role to better fit his talents. "Peter was very happy to get a part in which he could show his sense of humor, in which he could bring out laughs to get a different note from that monster, the child killer."

Hartl shot all three versions simultaneously on Greifswälder Oie, a small island in the Baltic, where a full-scale "floating platform" was built.[14] For three months, cast and crew, including pioneer German producer Erich Pommer, shared the only hotel on the nearby island of Rügen. There Lorre met Veidt, an actor who, like himself, was capable of switching on and off his demonic personality. Reisch recalled that Veidt "always died with laughter at whatever Peter Lorre did." While Veidt—"Connie" to his friends—found Lorre amusing, Hartl did not and threatened to have him thrown overboard for ruining takes with his jokes.

After the sun set at five-thirty, everyone returned to the hotel for dinner, where one man "provided more fun than anybody else in the whole star roster," said Reisch. "That was Peter. He could tell the most incredible stories with little nuances, hardly changing his face, just touching upon it and bringing the house down. It was inconceivable after working hours to have an evening without Peter. It would have been gloomy. He had an enormous sense of humor and was the happiest man on earth when people laughed."

After dinner, there was only one diversion—Ping-Pong. Much to everyone's amusement, the six-foot-five Veidt and the five-foot-five Lorre—who tipped the scale at the same undisclosed weight—paired up. "And these two guys, the one who played 'Caligari' and the other one who played the mass murderer in *M* became a team in Ping-Pong that was unbeatable," said Reisch. "It was not just if we win tonight, it was a matter of life and death to win the tournament. Not for the money, but there was a gala reception afterwards and a medal. And these guys played together like a team, with beautiful timing."

F.P.1 antwortet nicht delivered two star attractions, each of which guaranteed box-office success. Hans Albers, "the human dynamo with a heart of gold," stretches beyond his blue eyes as a prototype of *Casablanca*'s Rick Blaine and loves, loses, and rallies. The only attraction big enough to hold its own against the popular actor was the technical setting of the film, a utopia that lay within human reach. Critics who faulted the film for being long on applied science and short on logical development were shouting in the wind. It created a major sensation at both the Apollo Theater in Vienna, where tickets were hard to come by, and the UFA-Palast am Zoo in Berlin. Even *Variety* hailed it as "Ufa's greatest picture of this year."

Although Reisch enlarged the very small role of Johnny in the Siodmak novel, *Kinematograph* noted that "Peter Lorre easily steps, in spite of noticeably great virtuosity, into the background." Nonetheless, the actor left his mark. "The most complete and impressive acting performance is by Peter Lorre as a photo-reporter," stated Vienna's *Arbeiter Zeitung*. "The person he portrays is outside of the technical puppet world of the film. He is a human being possible in reality."

It is easy to see today how and why Lorre answered Albers's cocky attitude with comic understatement. When the hero is expansive, Johnny is laconic, even droll. It is just this chemistry that set the German version of *F.P.1* above its English counterpart, titled *F.P.1 Doesn't Answer,* which paired the mutually monotonous Conrad Veidt and London-born character actor Donald Calthrop, who was often cast as a villain, most notably in Alfred Hitchcock's *Blackmail* (1929). It is far less a matter of the length of Lorre's on-screen time (which is slightly longer) than of what he did with it. While Calthrop dispassionately distanced his character from the audience, Lorre made himself conspicuous by posture, gait, and attitude. Even his frowsy, flyaway blond hair contrasted comically with Albers's Aryan elegance.

Some 1930s audiences read the polarity in personalities quite differently. At a showing in Cairo, some Jewish viewers who felt that the photojournalist gave *F.P.1 antwortet nicht* an "anti-Semitic accent" generated a disturbance that resulted in an invitation to leave the theater from others in the audience, which included 120 attending National Socialists, Italian Fascists, and Greek Royalists. Historian Dorothea Hollstein accused Lorre of caricaturing his part, making it easier for a prejudiced viewer to misinterpret the role as a representation of the "National Socialist cliché of the Jewish journalist: he is small and a little rotund, he moves himself slowly and in an indolent manner, but gold directed; he carries out every assignment without asking; he hardly gives his own opinion, rather he always agrees with the superior one, as soon as he hopes to gain profit therefrom; he is sufficiently lacking in character to allow himself to be humbled and picked on without defending himself; if he is thrown out, he returns again through the back door."

Such a performance certainly was not intentional. Far from reinforcing anti-Semitic stereotypes, Lorre's character displays no qualities that could be considered typically Jewish. Intelligent and resourceful, Lorre's Johnny is a devoted sidekick to Albers's hero, who affectionately teases him with a string of descriptive nicknames, including *Rollmöpschen* (pickle with herring wrapped around it), *Rollfilm*, and *alter Affe* (old ape). Moreover, the only people who could have given the role an anti-Semitic spin—author Kurt Siodmak, producer Erich Pommer, screenwriter Walter Reisch (who expressed shock to hear such accusations, for the first time, some forty years later), and Lorre—were Jewish.

When Lorre's next film project, *Der Kaufmann von Hamburg* (*The Merchant of Hamburg*)—reportedly set for direction by Fritz Eckhardt after his own script about corporate greed, and costarring Gustaf Gründgens, Paul Wegener, and Fritz Kampers—failed to materialize, the actor stayed at UFA for *Der weisse Dämon*. The studio publicity department went all out to convince moviegoers that in the part of the hunchbacked drug dealer (nicely balanced against his butterfly collecting), he eclipsed his earlier performances: "Lorre creates the symbol of the narcotic. He is the evil that becomes flesh, the creepy one . . . a warning sign to all, whenever they run across a human being like him who knows nothing of luck, love and true humanity. Tell your audience that Peter Lorre creates a type, which, far from all cliché, is psychologically highly interesting and must be called a unique performance, and at the same time will not miss giving the audience a moral imprint."

Complaints that the film didn't take a stand against drug addiction sent the script through rewrites and the picture back for retakes. Not until UFA toned down the title, scrapping the inflammatory *Rauschgift* (*Dope*) and judiciously reedited the picture, did *Der weisse Dämon* pass the censors. The final version struck an acceptable balance between adventure and finger-pointing instruction.[15] What remained was the story of an honest coffee planter (Hans

Albers) who chases, swims, boxes, and jumps to the aid of his sister, rescuing her from the evil clutches of dope peddlers.

Lorre's addiction undoubtedly lent him a special understanding of the sale and distribution of narcotics. One wonders if holding a syringe gave him pause to consider how art imitated his own life. However he approached his role, he apparently convinced audiences and critics that he "haunts like a nightmare that finds a form . . . with silent seeming eeriness, leaving a trail of dreadfulness and fear; it is a typical counterpart to Albers; he makes himself the executing voice of his own horribly evil instincts. Is he still a human being or a robot pushed by invisible forces, who as well as he sells narcotics, can crush cities and worlds or trade with corpses? Great, unforgettable and his style a unique portrayal!"

Lorre often said that once you're typed, "people just demand it over and over again." Had the actor first appeared in *Was Frauen träumen* (*What Women Dream*) instead of *M,* he might just as easily have been typecast as a comic songster instead of a child murderer. For that reason—what might have been—it is one of his most important movies. As a clumsy criminologist, Lorre little resembles the childlike Beckert. His eyeglasses, smart moustache, and suit and tie give him a more mature look. He even stays miles ahead of his commissar cohort in solving the crime, although his methodology is laughably moronic. But it is not his attempts to free himself from foolproof handcuffs or his drunken efforts to put his coat on backward that single out his aptitude for comedy. It is a song. With head back, body bouncing, and hands pounding the piano keys, he exuberantly belts out:

> Yes, sir, the police, they are the cutest fellows.
> Yes, sir, the police, they're always at their best.
> The lieutenants are adept at handling women.
> And when the men kiss them, they're impressed!
> Yes, sir, the police, they fascinate every girl.
> Who can't just pass by, one two, three.
> Sure, ev'ry little town has got good looking guys.
> But the handsomest of all are the police!

Co-worker Gustav Fröhlich remembered that "in so singing the little stout Lorre turned an ironic coloring through his enthusiastic intonation." He was "completely different than usual," noted *Lichtbildbühne*, "a type you feel a little bit sorry for, mostly shoved to the side, but excellent in the refrain of his duet with Nora Gregor, spirited, funny, happily contented."

The fun was short-lived, however. Because German censors did not approve of a "picture [that] makes the police force look ridiculous," *Was Frauen träumen* premiered in Budapest instead of Berlin. The film finally opened in Germany more than two weeks later, on April 20, 1933, Adolf Hitler's forty-fourth birthday. Berlin's Atrium Theater prefaced the feature with a documentary short commemorating the death of World War I flying ace Manfred von Richthofen with scenes celebrating the development of German air technology. After this patriotic prelude, the slick, elegant comedy about a jewel thief was deemed so much *Mätzchen* (silly nonsense). By the time of its release, both Lorre and coauthor Billy Wilder, whose name had been struck from the credits, had fled Nazi Germany.

In the winter of 1932–33, with *Was Frauen träumen* in the can and Hitler in the chancellorship, Lorre and Eggebrecht, a leftist literary figure with ties to Brecht, began work on *Ein Kaspar Hauser von Heute* (*A Casper Hauser of Today*), an updated telling of the "strange tale of the foundling of Nuremberg, whose origin never was revealed and who has become the hero of many a legend, thriller, novel and thesis." Born in 1812 and raised by an illiterate day laborer, Hauser turned up in Nuremberg in 1828 with a letter of introduction to the cavalry captain of the 4th Eskadron, 6th Chevauleger. Lord Stanhope adopted the slender, reticent boy, whose aristocratic hands and feet hinted at noble origins, and placed him as a clerk in a law office. On December 14, 1833, he returned home mortally wounded by a dagger, triggering rumors about the suspicious circumstances of his death and his princely origins.

More shadow than substance, the story lent itself to reinvention. In Lorre and Eggebrecht's hands, Hauser became a child from the Tatra region of Czechoslovakia lost in World War I. Lorre not only set the story in his homeland, but planned to shoot on location in the Carpathians. The first of numerous projects conceived to break the mold, "Kasper Hauser" held Lorre's interest for the next two decades.

Walking along the Ku-damm with Rudolph Joseph one wintry evening in early 1933, Lorre spoke intensely of his upcoming picture without mentioning its name. "He wasn't telling anyone, not even me," recalled Joseph. "I looked at him and said, 'Casper Hauser.'"

"How did you know?" asked a surprised Lorre.

"It was written on your forehead," laughed Joseph.

With outline in hand, Lorre and Eggebrecht first approached actor Fritz Kortner, who had plans to begin his own film company. According to Lorre, however, it was UFA that signed him to star in and direct the film in three versions—German, French, and English—that would get under way after he completed his next picture, *Unsichtbare Gegner* (*Invisible Opponent*, 1933), an unlikely story of a South American oil swindle, set to begin shooting just after the March 5 elections.

When Lorre left for Hollywood a few years later, recalled Lotte Eisner, he took with him everything he could find on Casper Hauser and asked her to send him the poetry of Verlaine. Anticipating possible objections to the idea of casting Lorre as a teenager, she told readers of *Cinématographe,* "Why not. Lorre's face expresses all ages."

Producer Sam Spiegel had scheduled Kurt (Curtis) Bernhardt to direct *Unsichtbare Gegner.* When Bernhardt became involved in another project, he suggested Rudolf Katscher, who had just successfully turned out his first feature, *Teilnehmer antwortet nicht* (1932), to replace him. Having worked with Lorre on *Schuss im Morgengrauen,* in which he had performed a "similar half-funny, half-sinister part," Katscher thought him the obvious choice for Pless, a sidekick to the main villain, played by Oskar Homolka.

A less imaginary drama was taking shape outside the walls of Germany's "dream factories." As the Fascists hammered words into weapons, and hatred into ideologies, Hitler's Storm Troops escalated their campaign of terror against Communists, Socialists, and trade unionists. Some four hundred thousand strong, the NSDAP's private army targeted Jews. They had become all enemies in one, the single foe on whose doorstep the Nazis laid blame for Germany's defeat in World War I (the "national humiliation"), the country's economic depression, and revolution. As perennial outsiders, Jews held no claim to a sense of German national identity or community; no *völkisch* ideology embraced them. As part of his "national awakening," Hitler promised a solution to the Jewish question. Nazi-sponsored anti-Semitic legislative proposals providing for the elimination of non-Aryans from public life soon took root in decrees, boycotts, and acts of terror.

Tucked away in the studios, many actors had either shut their eyes to the dark shadow on the horizon or had quietly defied the expectation that they would celebrate the new spirit of the German people. But politics soon pervaded the stages and back lots. On the set of *M,* Fritz Lang, who followed political events with "passionate attention," had probed and prodded his politically nonconversant star to distraction. Brushing aside the burgeoning number of anti-Semitic associations and periodicals wasn't quite as easy. Or news that the Jewish actress Helene Weigel had been dragged to the police station during a performance of *Die Mutter.* An expected ban on Jews in the film industry had almost halted production by April 1933. Later that month, Joseph Goebbels, the new minister of propaganda and popular enlightenment, told party members at UFA that "German films must be made by Germans who understand the spirit of the German people." Even before the requirement became law, film companies voluntarily began to ease Jewish actors out of their films. Beginning in July, new film laws administered by Goebbels would completely exclude Jews from the film industry.

Lorre soon found himself caught in the political current. His old friend Egon Jacobson, editor-in-chief of the *Berliner Zeitung am Mittag*, had sharpened the newspaper's political and cultural edge with articles on Nazi atrocities and commentaries on censorship by noted humanist writers Erich Maria Remarque and Heinrich and Thomas Mann. When one of the thirty provincial newspapers that subscribed to his columns used his article on calendar reform as a pretext to sever relations with the publisher, Ullstein-Verlag, Jacobson read it as "a sign of the times." A few days later, he called Lorre.

"I'll pick you up Sunday morning," he said cryptically. "I need you. We will be back before night." Only after reaching the Avus River did Jacobson confide that he was driving to the Baltic Sea: "I know a deserted beach close to Ahrenshoop. There you have to help me burn records and membership lists which they entrusted to me." If a single name is revealed, he told Lorre, "the unhappy one" will be lost.

When Lorre asked who owned the car, Jacobson replied that it was the actor and director Johannes Riemann: "He's reliable."

"Then you could have gone directly to Eugen Rex," suggested Lorre, who clearly knew more about party politics than he let on.[16] "Riemann is for quite some time a member of the party."

"Riemann?" replied the stunned newspaperman.

"I could give you a list of prominent pretenders," said Lorre, "who just can't wait to appear as cleansed stars in the heaven of the German acting profession." He listed [Werner] Krauss, [Emil] Jannings, [Heinrich] George, and [Veit] Harlan. They were, said Lorre, "friends from today who have boozed with us and who would stick a knife in our back with the same charm."

When they reached the Baltic shore, the beach was deserted. Jacobson and Lorre changed into swimsuits, placed a handful of twigs in a pit, and piled on the papers. Inexperienced arsonists, they worked up a sweat trying to start a fire in the capricious sea breeze. Suddenly, a policeman showed up.

"What are you doing here?"

As he trudged back to the car for a camera, Jacobson explained that they were filming a scene for the new Peter Lorre movie, *The Fire Victim of the Baltic Sea*.

"Oh, Mr. Lorre in person. Can I be of any help?" he said, beaming.

"Yes," answered Jacobson, "we need a stronger fire. Could you please help us burn the papers?"

With the policeman's help, they finished their work in about an hour. "The eye of the law did bravely what it could," Jacobson noted sarcastically. They thanked the civil servant, who left with Lorre's autograph for his wife.

On Saturday, February 25, 1933, Sam Spiegel sat down for a shave. His barber told him he had "better not be home that night," recalled the famed raconteur in one of several versions of his flight from Berlin. "He was a member of an S.S. [*Schutzstaffel*] troop that was supposed to arrest and beat us up or kill us. We had no idea this was going to happen. I simply called Homolka and Lorre and told them to get the hell out of Berlin and join me in Vienna a few days later. I went to a little suburban station in Berlin, took a local train to Leipzig, changed to a train for Vienna without an overcoat and without bags or anything, just with my script under my arm, because we had to pretend that we were just going into the country for the weekend so as not to be molested on the train. Lorre made it. Homolka made it with me on the same train. Josef von Sternberg was on that same train by accident, and Jascha Heifetz. Several weeks later we started shooting in Vienna."

Shot at Sascha-Film studios and produced by Spiegel's Pan-Film, *Unsichtbare Gegner* featured the fourth-billed Lorre as a criminal agent overcome by magnanimity. Spiegel knew the actor was absolutely right for the part of Pless.[17] He was also very much aware that Lorre was most anxious to avoid being typecast: "We chose him [because] he had a good reputation, a good name, but it was really typecasting. In those days, I wasn't adventurous and clear enough about what movies should be about [so] the typecasting came naturally to me, as it did to everybody else in one's early stages of a career. But I do remember this kind of preoccupation whether he would like to play something unlike Peter Lorre."

Typecasting notwithstanding, Lorre seemed "very docile and easy to handle" until "moments of great tension [when he] suddenly became intractable." These he dissipated by playing pranks on Oskar Homolka. Katscher recalled that when they had an important dialogue scene, using a "stand" microphone, Lorre, as the nervous Pless, "twiddled his hat in his hands, always surreptitiously covering the microphone with his hat whenever Homolka's lines came, which drove the sound-recordist to distraction. Time and time again, he stopped the 'take,' shouting: 'I cannot hear Oscar's lines!'"

The strong cast could not save what the *Deutsche Allgemeine Zeitung* characterized as an unbelievable and unbelievably awful picture.[18] Even actors who obviously "felt no creative joy during work" outshone the flawed script and lumpy direction. Katscher was very good with actors, said Spiegel, but he was "not an extremely astute director." Knowing that Lorre had accepted the assignment somewhat reluctantly, Spiegel turned him loose on Pless, out of which, said the producer, he "created an extremely interesting character." Critics, however, thought Lorre's presentation represented the lackluster performance of the film. While *Die Filmwoche* said he "was frozen and without interest again," the *Lichtbildbühne,* less charitably, echoed Herbert Jhering's warning that cramping his ability will result in his giving "only a double of his earlier films."

Celia had arrived in Vienna several weeks earlier for rehearsals of Ferdinand Bruckner's *Die Marquise von O* (based on Heinrich von Kleist's novel) at Max Reinhardt's Theater in der Josefstadt. She had been reluctant to leave Peter in Berlin, believing that his friendship with Brecht put him at risk. On February 25, two days before the burning of the Reichstag paved the way for the suspension of basic civil liberties, Lorre joined her at the Hotel Imperial on Kaerntnerring 2–25, just a few hundred meters east of the Staatsoper (Royal Opera). To Celia, more than the times must have seemed unsettled. The critics judged her performance as the mother in Bruckner's play either "completely colorless" or "beautiful in her sympathetic, quiet, subdued way, very noblesse especially in such seconds of fate in abyss-deepest silence." About the production, which was directed by Otto Preminger, they agreed: it was long and laborious.

In mid-April, Lorre found work as Judas in Professor V.O. Ludwig's *Golgotha.* Presented for the first time in Vienna, the Passion play was sponsored by Cardinal Dr. T. Innitzer and performed at the newly remodeled Zirkus-Renz with a cast of three hundred—including Hans Schweikart as Jesus and Ebba Johannsen as Mary.

Believing that his dream of a Greater Germany was divinely inspired, Hitler justified any measure that would "lead back his homeland into the Reich." The Austrian-born chancellor concentrated his efforts on politically destabilizing his native land in anticipation of *Anschluss* (union). On May 29, 1933, he imposed a fee of one thousand deutsche marks on German visas for travel to Austria. Although it wrought havoc with the tourist trade, the levy did not trigger the contemplated collapse of the Austrian economy. That summer, Hitler rocked Austrian independence with a terrorist campaign of bomb attacks, sabotage, and cross-border skirmishes conducted by the Austrian Legion, a Nazi paramilitary group that operated from the German side of the frontier. Clashes between Nazis and Socialists turned the streets of Vienna into a bloody battleground. In the face of a general strike that threatened to cripple his Christian Socialist government, Chancellor Engelbert Dollfuss dissolved Parliament and proclaimed, in effect, the end of democracy, bringing Austria to the verge of civil war. Vienna was under martial law.

Lorre shared lodgings with his friends and fellow actors at the Hotel Kranz-Ambassador. "We were under an eight o'clock curfew," said Walter Reisch. "There was absolutely nothing you could do. You couldn't go to the theater, you couldn't go to a coffee house. Everything was closed. . . . At the hotel there was a subterranean Bohemian wine place called Majolica Hall. When the curfew started, we had to go down there and get our food. There was no radio. There was no light. Outside we could hear pop-pop-pop and police cars racing around. After dinner there was not great fun demanded. It would have been out of place because while we were sitting there everybody knew the houses in the district of the workmen were being shot at. People were dying. It was the kind of climate in which you would rather talk about anything else but the shooting outside. There was a moment when everybody was rather gloomy and Robert Stoltz, the composer of 'Two Hearts in Three-Quarter Time' started to talk to Lorre and said, 'You know, it is funny that they always give you parts in which you play either a monster or a second violin, just a Greek chorus, Dr. Watson, that sort of thing. What would be wrong if you played once an important classic part?'"

"You are thinking of *Hamlet*," Lorre replied. "I know the whole play from beginning to end, all the parts."

Rosa Stradner, who later married director-screenwriter Joseph L. Mankiewicz, urged him to recite some of the play: "We have no audience here. We are all friends. Come on, shoot." "And the others felt a little funny about that," recalled Reisch. "After all, he with his shoulders hanging down and the fat face. He was very, very overweight at the time. He looked much older than he really was. Everybody said, 'Come on, don't be silly.'"

"Yes," agreed Lorre. "I want to do it, really. It has been deep in my heart ever since I was twelve. Ever since I ran away from home. Ever since I saw *Hamlet* with all the great stars of Europe, it has been the great dream of my life. If you will really keep quiet, I will give you a bit."

"Everybody really tried very hard to be serious," continued Reisch, "although we knew that it could be nothing but a disaster. After all, everybody knew *Hamlet*. It was part of our education."

Lorre called the waiter over. "No serving for the next quarter of an hour."

"He didn't start with 'To be or not to be.' He started reciting the first gravedigger from beginning to end."

After finishing, Lorre scolded his audience, "You sons-of-bitches, you thought I was going to play Hamlet and make a fool of myself. My part is the gravedigger and if I had ever played it on the stage I would have stolen that play. There would have been no Hamlet and no Claudius, no Polonius, no Laertes and no Ophelia. It would have been me."

"And I tell you something," concluded Reisch. "It was terrific. After the first lines he got up and took a knife, as if it were the gravedigger's spade, and he started to dig into the earth. You forgot the shooting outside, you forgot the Majolica Hall, you forgot everything. You forgot Hitler. You forgot Hamlet. You saw Peter Lorre as the gravedigger and that showed to me this guy knew his limitations, and at the same time made the best of his shortcomings, his figure, his funny face, his reputation as a monster."

In Berlin, Lorre had relied on the acumen of politically minded friends such as Brecht and Lang (who undoubtedly winced with incredulity at his salute "to the readers of *Mein Film* [that] all is good"). Lacking these connections, he grew anxious in Vienna, where the anti-Semitic clamor had grown more audible. With his narrow escape still fresh in mind, Peter and Celia retreated to Vranov, Czechoslovakia, a town of just over nine thousand inhabitants that sat peacefully on the River Thaya. There they visited her mother in early summer.

Mulling over their few options did not take long.[19] Rumors of work in Paris—Lorre boasted a fluent use of French—and the fear that Nazi troops would any day march into Czechoslovakia, brought them to the gray, high, narrow Hotel Ansonia on the Rue de Saigon, where, according to fellow exile Friedrich Hollaender, the rooms "are small, but dirty. Dirty, but cheap. What do you want, the Ritz?" For as long as three months, a refugee might pass himself off as a tourist, but then he was required to obtain a Carte d'Identité. Although it was much easier to secure than a labor permit, and allowed a refugee to work, importuning the officials too eagerly could result in a trip to the border. Lorre did not play the despairing exile. *M* still played in theaters, and on the streets people followed after him and called out, "*Le maudit!* [The Damned One]," a reference to the French title of the picture. Instead, he viewed his stopover as a respite in a grand design, with Hollywood the final destination. "It is necessary to wait for one's luck to change," he said. "If I did not have the courage to wait, all that I suffered until now would have been in vain. In that case it would have had more value if I had not become an actor." That fall, Lorre optimistically told an interviewer for *Cinémonde* that if he didn't enjoy Paris, he wouldn't be there, and boldly stated that he intended to make the city his headquarters. Not only was he set to make some French language films, but he would soon get *Caspar Hauser* back on track.

A mood of humor and expectancy welded the Ansonia group together. In addition to Lorre and Hollaender, the vertically arranged nest of exiles included Billy Wilder, Franz Wachsmann (who later changed his name to Waxman), Hans G. "Jan" Lustig, Hanna Luke, Max Kolpe (who later became Colpet), and Rudolph Joseph. "Emigrant four on the second floor," mused Hollaender in his autobiography, "listened to emigrant nine coughing on the fifth floor. Knows that he also cannot sleep." Lorre's brother Andrew had lent him and Celia money to travel to Paris. Beyond that and the help received from fellow émigrés such as Wilder, who worked illegally writing under other people's names, they scrimped and scrounged, bound by their meager purses. "There's an old proverb," explained Andrew, who visited his brother in Paris, "that in all Hungary, there are only one hundred pengös, but every night they belong to someone else."

"Do you remember," Lorre asked German refugee Manfred George, who interviewed the actor in 1951, "what a three-cornered life we led, among the nearest delicatessen store, the subway and the psychoanalyst?" By day, they ate hard-boiled eggs at Café du Dome or sat at the small sidewalk tables of the Café Colisée and looked back to their life in Berlin. Lorre loved to tell of the time Joseph Goebbels toured UFA just after he had fled Berlin. He related that the minister of propaganda had one day asked a studio executive, "Tell me, where is that little man who did so many marvelous pictures? The Führer wants to meet him."

"There is a slight difficulty," the executive nervously stuttered.

"There can be no difficulty," Goebbels impatiently replied. "Send him to me." Informed that the actor in question was Peter Lorre, who was Jewish, he snapped, "I never want to hear that name again."

It made a nice story. Actually, after seeing *M* on May 21, 1931, Goebbels wildly praised the film in his diary and predicted that Lang would be "our director one day," but did not even mention Lorre. Furthermore, one year later, on May 31, 1932, *Der Angriff*, a National Socialist paper edited by Goebbels, caricatured Lorre as a prototype killer, who had "lost nothing of his gruesome repulsiveness to this day."

Lorre said that shortly after arriving in Vienna, he received a telegram from Goebbels asking him to come back. The "darling actor of Hitler" reportedly replied, "For two murderers like Hitler and me, there's not enough room in Germany." Unable to improve on this story, Lorre repeated it until 1963, when he appeared on the *Hy Gardner Show* with Boris Karloff. He offered a revised account in what turned out to be close to a deathbed confession. His sudden departure, he said, had left the *Caspar Hauser* project in limbo and

UFA somewhat nervous about film rights. The studio asked Lorre to sign over the German rights to the project; in exchange, he could keep "all the outside versions."

"One night I just happened to be in a mood," admitted Lorre. "I don't know whether I had a drink or not. Most probably I did. I addressed a telegram, not to Hitler, but to the general manager of UFA, and I said, 'There is no room in Germany for two murderers like we are, Hitler and I. Signed, Peter Lorre.'"

The restive energies of the captive audience demanded an outlet, a cooperative walking of wits. Together they assembled around the table in scenarist Max Kolpe's first-floor room to hatch an idea for a film. Usually their efforts dead-ended on page two, or with the seconded motion to adjourn to Korniloff's, a nearby Russian restaurant, or to an American movie at the Cinéma Madeleine. When Kolpe attracted a sponsor from the executive ranks of the Pantheon Lightbulb Factory, who agreed to back their venture on condition that his wife star in it, they forged ahead, "each one toying, gagging, and advising, anticipating a share of the kill," with a suspiciously familiar story line: Lorre would play a "lust murderer" who strangles his female costar. The actor found the idea lacking and stood up. "In an expressionist hand movement," wrote Hollaender,

> he part[ed] the waves: A moment please. With the distance which apparently is removing you and which only an actor can possess, I have just recognized the club foot in the manuscript. It came to me like an enlightenment. The character of our lust murderer is still lacking the essentials: warmth of heart, amiability, nicety, with a word, he is lacking our sympathy. After all, if *I* am supposed to play this role, something of scope has to stick to this character, something popular. I would like to say something which appeals to the simple man in his child's soul, unless it doesn't matter to you if I play him or not. Then naturally, I don't have to!

Lorre then sat down and looked at a spot on the ceiling while Wilder unraveled a second plot and Waxman and Hollaender worked out a musical theme.[20]

"Don't get so excited," piped up Lustig. "The picture will never be made. This Galliard woman is a cow. The whole thing will collapse. She can never play that part. Besides both would hardly agree that she will be suffocated after the first 150 meters of film."

"Just the opposite," laughed Wilder. "Galliard would be delighted to see her strangled."

"Children, stay on the carpet," interrupted Lorre. "I'm prepared to rewrite the role myself for a pair of grubby per cents of the entire profit. Now, isn't that an offer?"

The group had decided to remove to Korniloff's when Hanna Luke broke in with the news that Max Alsberg, the famous Berlin defense attorney, had shot himself in the head.

"I just crossed out Korniloff's," said a dampened Lorre. "I'm not hungry anymore."

Alsberg's suicide in September of 1933 marked the first of two setbacks for Lorre. Soon after arriving in Paris, his addiction had again gained the upper hand. "Because of my physical condition, and the depressed condition mentally and physically which I had been under," he told narcotics authorities in 1947, "I went to various doctors and got prescriptions for morphine, and kept using morphine for longer than I had a medical need for the drug." Contradicting his own statement that he had become addicted five years earlier in Berlin, he asserted that "this was the first time I considered that I was really addicted to the use of narcotic drugs."

In late summer, Lorre approached Paul Falkenberg, who had arrived in Paris a year earlier, and told him that he was a morphine addict: "I have to have a cure. Can you help me? Can you give me the money?" Falkenberg's generosity placed Lorre in a sanatorium on the outskirts of Paris. When film director G.W. Pabst learned of the actor's need of a job, he and his wife paid their ailing friend a visit. "Lorre was at a terrible stage," remembered Rudolph Joseph, who had since emigrated to Paris. "He was in the middle of treatment." Pabst not only picked up the balance for Lorre's cure, but created a small part for him in his current French production, *Du haut en bas* (*From Top to Bottom*, 1933). The gesture would appear to have been an afterthought, given the extraneousness of the role and its awkward placement in the story. In the picture, Lorre plays an unsuccessful beggar whose luck turns a corner once it has been pointed out to him that he doesn't look shabby enough to elicit sympathy. After he rips his pants leg, his door-to-door business picks up—until a kind seamstress too poor to give him any food decides that the least she can do is sew up the tear. At his benefactress's instruction, the beggar retreats behind a screen to take off his pants for mending. She turns her back on him as she bends to her task. The camera closes on a pair of shears hanging on the wall. When the beggar's hand stealthily creeps out to grab the potential weapon, the audience is sure that the unsuspecting seamstress is about to pay dearly for her generosity. But then comes the punch line: the beggar has cut his coat to ribbons in order to compensate for the newly mended trousers. It had been three years and several striking departure roles since the release of *M*. Nonetheless,

Lorre still could not step out of the shadow of Hans Beckert and the expectation that behind his sad innocence lay something more sinister than subtle impudence.

By October 11, only days after completing *Du haut en bas,* he was once again under treatment for morphine addiction. Of the many roles Celia played in Peter's life, none was more important than financial manager. Early on, she developed, out of necessity, a proficiency for keeping creditors at bay. A loan of three thousand schillings from Karl Kraus had enabled them to get this far. Lorre had promised to pay it off in several weeks and even put up his life insurance policy of ten thousand deutsche marks as security. On October 15 the full sum, plus interest, came due. Celia wrote Dr. Oskar Samek, Kraus's attorney, that they were unable to repay even one schilling at this time because a "life-important" cure had placed Peter back in a clinic until the twenty-sixth. Not only had poor health forced him to decline other film offers, but his earnings for four days of filming also went for the cure.[21] "The moment Lorre makes money," she assured him, "it won't be hard to honor his debt." Clearly embarrassed by their "awful situation," Celia asked his forgiveness. It was a closing she would have reason to repeat in the future.

Job prospects looked no better for the other refugees. Newborn ideas that "hummed about like flies" died just as quickly, wrote fellow Ansonian Paul E. Marcus. "It was one large market of illusions." Waiting for something to turn up caused "a mixture of depression and revulsion against the times, with an added hazardous tension," conditions symptomatic of a prevailing epidemic called "stay-in-bed disease." It developed, said Hollaender, "when the monotony of the days and their lack of events became stronger than the increasingly thinner humor with which one tried to meet them."

Lorre suffered a full-blown case of this "form of paralysis, this proneness to hibernation" that stole "from us the concept of time. Sun and night sky, day and darkness were not any longer kept apart." He and Celia lay in their twin beds, eyes open, without speaking. Sleep was impossible with the thunderous speeches of Hitler coming over the radio from the floor above and the angry, indignant rejoinders of their fellow Germans: "False! False! . . . Lies."

In *Those Torn from Earth,* Hollaender's fictionalized account of the emigration, Lorre brooded over his success in Berlin and his frustration in Paris: "There, one had played outstanding parts, acquired an enviable screen-name. His pictures had inspired all the servant maids with horror, made them shudder, and now? Barely able to get a 'bit' for three days; 'atmosphere' in tails. Dammit, it wasn't that one *had* to be an actor, a clown! Smearing grease paint on one's face was disgusting enough. Sooner or later he would have chucked this so-called vocation, and turned to some honest labor."

Like most refugees, Lorre vacillated between believing in the transience of his own fate and vegetating into decline. Offers of work fell through with discouraging regularity. "Sometimes things look more hopeful, sometimes gloomier," wrote Marcus. "Every day is the same. Everything is so unending. You get blunted. There was a time when you were a useful member of human society; now you are an outsider . . . without, indeed, a regularized right to exist."

3

ESCAPE TO LIFE

Ever since I came to this country I've been trying to live
down my past. That picture "M" has haunted me
everywhere I've gone.

—Peter Lorre

A benign fate—as he liked to believe—intervened to end Lorre's *Hungerjahr*
in Paris. At Lime Grove Studios in Shepherd's Bush, more commonly known
as "the Bush" to film habitués, Alfred Hitchcock and Ivor Montagu, his associate producer, readied production of *The Man Who Knew Too Much* (1934) for
Gaumont-British film studios. From his German comrade Otto Katz, who held
a position on the Soviet-backed Comintern press, Montagu learned that Lorre
had left Germany "for conscientious reasons" and was living "professionally at
liberty" in Paris.[1] He reminded Hitchcock of the actor's forceful performance
in *M*. "We wanted him at once," said Montagu. "There was never any question
about his coming over to be inspected or tested—even his English was not in
question, for a German accent was no obstacle in the part. He came over, not
to be approved, but to be engaged."

Katz knew where Lorre was staying and offered to get in touch with him.
With the ready consent of Michael Balcon, director of production at Gaumont-
British, they cabled the actor to come over. Balcon also agreed to cover Lorre's
expenses and secure a period immigration permit to allow him to work in
England. Before leaving, Peter contacted his brother Andrew, who was in town
for the Paris International Motor Show, an annual event scheduled the first
Thursday in October. He shared his good fortune (he had a job in England)

and his bad fortune (he was, as usual, short of money). Tapping the filial rock once more, the improvident brother drew French francs and was off to London.

Despite his German triumph in *M*, Lorre was little known to English-speaking audiences. That, along with his presumably poor English, had relegated him to consideration for only a small role in the picture, said Montagu: "Hitch and I both considered that Peter would be excellent as the 'Hit Man' of the gang in the situation Hitch had envisaged." They "admired him and jumped at the chance to get him and to do him a good turn at the same time, but the production company needed a certain amount of persuading."

Sidney Bernstein—impresario, showman, exhibitor, theater owner, builder of supercinemas, and founding member of the National Film Society—undoubtedly put in a good word. Along with Ivor Montagu and Otto Katz, he belonged to the Committee for the Victims of German Fascism, which had initiated the "Reichstag Fire Trial of 1933." Bernstein also played an equally active role on a private level, supporting a public boycott of German goods, coauthoring a pamphlet titled *The Persecution of the Jews in Germany*, boosting membership of the Committee for Co-ordinating Anti-Fascist Activity, and extending a helping hand to needy refugees.

An acquaintance from the Berlin days, Bernstein invited Lorre to stay first at his flat on Albermarle Street, where the actor bumped into intellectual luminaries and film celebrities—including Charles Laughton—and then at Long Barn, a Tudor house in Sevenoaks Weald, featuring low ceilings, sloping dark oak floors, exposed beams, and leaded windows, which he had leased from Vita Sackville-West.

"Peter told me that he was deeply embarrassed," recalled Paul Falkenberg, "because he had never been in England before. He was lying in this beautiful bed and he had only one pair of underwear and in comes the butler and opens the curtains and says, 'Good morning, sir, would you like your tea,' and so on. It was a totally new world that opened to him."

German refugee Paul E. Marcus (PEM), who now published a newsletter in London recording the activities of fellow exiles, also remembered hearing Lorre dress up the story of his arrival in London

> with a single suit on his body and dress coat in his suitcase. . . . Every morning the proper butler asked him which suit he should put on, where there was no choice. One evening his host invited Lorre to go out with him. "Put out the dinner jacket," said Lorre proudly to the butler. While getting dressed, Lorre noticed that the dress coat had a built-in hump from his last movie role, which

he could not get rid of. Hence, there was nothing for him to do, except to explain the thing to Mr. Bernstein. He only laughed and they both went out together. Wherever they went on this evening, girls fought their way to Lorre to touch his hump because it would bring good luck.[2]

Bernstein introduced Lorre to Hitchcock and Montagu at London's Hotel Mayfair in Berkeley Square. Lorre listened while Hitchcock sounded out his plans and took in first impressions. "Now all I knew in English was yes and no," recalled the actor, "and I couldn't say no because I would have had to explain it, so I had to say yes to everything, which doesn't quite befit me. Sidney put me wise to the fact that Hitchy likes to tell stories, so I used to watch him like a hawk and whenever I thought the end of a story was coming and that was the point, I used to roar with laughter and somehow he got the impression that I spoke English and I got the part."

"As soon as Hitch saw him," said Montagu, "he agreed, so did Peter, and we developed his part in the picture." Not that of Levine, the hired gunman, as originally intended, but of Abbott, the diabolical mastermind of the gang. From all appearances, the actor answered his search for new and different faces. The director later remarked, "Your big problem in casting is to avoid familiar faces. . . . I've always believed in having unfamiliar supporting players even if your stars are known." Actually, in *The Man Who Knew Too Much*, Hitchcock's supporting actors were familiar to British audiences. It was the scarred visage of the second-billed Lorre, his cigarette smoke wafting menacingly out of frame, which appeared in poster artwork for the picture. Alongside ran the byline, "Public Enemy No. 1 of All the World."

Despite his desperate need for work, Lorre was cautious in accepting the role of an international archcriminal. Abbott's kidnapping of a young girl and his almost Oedipal deference to the androgynous nurse Agnes recalled Hans Beckert's perverse sexual presence in *M*. The part was a purely menacing one, however, calling for malefic amiability rather than tortured pathos. In the end, a first-rate script and Hitchcock's reputation dispelled Lorre's fears. The actor recalled that he was

almost in despair when I was given the script of *The Man Who Knew Too Much* to read, with a view to my taking the part of the spy. This, although of course it did not allow me to get away from my "horrid" screen nature, was a really intelligent and constructive film, and the part called for subtle characterisation. . . . There was no obvious terrorism in it. I had to be a villain without making it apparent until the film had half developed. I had to be a villain enough for a child, with the clear perception of childhood, to dislike me; and yet for grown-ups to see nothing out of the ordinary in me at all. This gave the role a background of reality and I was very glad to play it.

When all was settled, Peter wired Celia in Paris with big news. At a press party, he told her, Rufus LeMaire had walked up to him and put the question: "How tall are you?" After that, the casting director kept his ear to the ground. If Hitchcock liked this newcomer, perhaps Hollywood had room for him. LeMaire cabled Harry Cohn, chief of Columbia Pictures, and received a clearance decision to sign the diminutive Hungarian actor. On May 15 Lorre reportedly inked a five-year contract, renewable in six-month options, that carried a weekly salary of five hundred dollars. Celia hurriedly packed up, said good-bye to their fellow exiles in Paris, and sailed for London, where she and Peter moved into Carlton Court in Pall Mall Place. There Celia once again devoted herself to looking after Peter's happy-go-lucky ways, keeping meticulous accounts, and staying one step ahead of his creditors.

How quickly Lorre learned English is difficult to say. "I wasn't the man who knew too much English when I started the picture," he later explained. "At that time Peter's English wasn't exactly great," confirmed screenwriter Charles Bennett. "Hitch had recently employed a young female Oxford graduate named Joan Harrison . . . with high honors in French. With language difficulties existing, and since Peter was known to be a French linguist, Hitch asked Joan to discuss the next scene or such with Peter in French. Peter listened bewilderedly for a while, then said in his halting if hopeful grasp of the English tongue, 'Please—please, speak English.'"

Lorre claimed that he learned English in two to three months with the aid of a tutor. At night he sat up with a cup of black coffee and mentally translated his dialogue into German in order to firmly fix its meaning and inflection. After getting a handle on his characterization, he returned to his English lines, rehearsing and memorizing them word by word. However he managed it, by the time filming began on May 29, Lorre had more than a working knowledge of English. His acting is far too subtle and well-shaded to be dismissed as mere parroting.

Whoever conceived the idea—Hitchcock claimed collaborative credit— *The Man Who Knew Too Much* got its start as "Bulldog Drummond's Baby." At the suggestion of Walter Mycroft, story editor at British International Pictures, which owned the rights to Herman C. "Sapper" McNeile's Bulldog Drummond character, Bennett wrote an original scenario for Alfred Hitchcock to direct. John Maxwell, head of B.I.P., allowed that it was "a brilliant scenario, a tour de force," but told Hitchcock he would rather keep his ten thousand pounds, a modest budget even by the studio's parsimonious standards.

Hitchcock decided to move on. After a brief stint with Alexander Korda, he signed with independent producer Tom Arnold to direct *Waltzes from Vienna* (1933), "a musical without music, made very cheaply," which was being filmed at the newly organized Gaumont-British at Lime Grove Studios, Shepherd's Bush. One day Michael Balcon stopped by the set. Asked what he was doing after this picture, Hitchcock told him about a story he had "worked up" with Charles Bennett and Edwin Greenwood toward the end of his unhappy tenure at B.I.P. Balcon invited Hitchcock, Bennett, and Bulldog Drummond to join him at Gaumont-British. When he learned that Maxwell held the rights to Bulldog Drummond, Balcon commissioned Hitchcock to buy them, which he did for 250 pounds. Hitchcock reworked the story with Bennett and Montagu, introducing sights and situations he had mentally jotted down during his honeymoon in St. Moritz. In the end, they scrapped the names of the characters, including Sapper's hero, settled on a gentleman agent less articulate in crime detection and the niceties of international intrigue, and retitled the scenario *The Man Who Knew Too Much.*

In the film, a terrorist gang plots to assassinate a visiting foreign diplomat at Albert Hall. At the last moment, however, a woman's scream foils Abbott's well-orchestrated plan to synchronize the sound of a bullet with the climax of William Walton's "Storm Cloud Cantata." In an enhanced reconstruction of the famous Sidney Street Siege of 1911, in which Metro police and Scots Guards received automatic pistol fire from Russian anarchists holed up in a house in Stepney, bobbies storm Abbott's hideout. Behind a door, the chiming of a pocket watch invites a burst of gunfire; the door closes, and Abbott unceremoniously slumps to the floor.[3]

The shooting script did not end so predictably: "The door is turned back. Behind it can be heard the last notes of the chiming watch. In the foreground creep one or two of the police with [Inspector] Binstead, their guns outstretched. Binstead advances and swings the door suddenly back—only a waistcoat hangs on the peg—a watch chain dangling from the pocket." More closely resembling the final version was an alternate ending in which Abbott shoots himself behind the door. No matter how much he preferred the more typical "cupboard empty" ending, Hitchcock didn't dare invoke the wrath of the censors, who demanded that miscreants be punished, or Gaumont-British, for incurring reshooting expenses.

Like Brecht and Lang, Hitchcock understood that the cleft—real or imagined—in Lorre's personality expressed itself in his understated acting style.

Knowing his own strengths, the actor reasoned that "little men are ineffectual only in direct relation to their noisiness and boastfulness in trying to delude others into believing they are 'walking dynamite.'" Fortunately for Lorre, Hitchcock believed in "getting good actors who know how to express a mood or intention with the slightest gesture or change of expression, like Peter Lorre. This is the way to make your characters stand out effectively." The director wanted "an actor to play a part for which his personal experience in life has raised him. In this way he does not have to resort to cheap mannerisms and unnatural movements. The best actors are those who can be effective even when they are not doing anything. Understatement is priceless." Most directors engaged Lorre for an express purpose and gave him a character so narrowly defined that he could do little with it. Hitchcock likewise retained the actor for what he could bring to his role, but he allowed him—a rare confession—an unusual degree of creative freedom.

Film critic and historian Andrew Sarris aptly pointed out, "Lorre . . . embodies much of the charming irony of a European sensibility in conflict with the stolid British passion for decorum." In *The Man Who Knew Too Much,* a chilling malignancy masks his benign humor. No matter how discordant the fit, he accommodated it to his personal acting style. "Peter had the amazing ability," observed Ellis St. Joseph, "which we see again in Marlon Brando, of the delayed reaction, the surprising delivery, a softness which has the effect of a bullet when it is delivered."

A script note describes Abbott as merely "a round-faced person about 45. He is an invalid . . . helped by a rather straight-faced woman who is apparently [his] nurse." Hitchcock went one better, introducing the character as a gregarious tourist ripe for a good laugh. Asked if he is all right after a ski jumper flattens him, the murderer cracks, "Better ask my nurse. My English is not good enough for me to know." Abbott discomposes his victims with spasms of laughter, then menaces them with well-mannered restraint. "Mr. Lorre, as the anarchist leader," wrote Andre Sennwald in the *New York Times,* "is able to crowd his role with dark and terrifying emotions without disturbing his placid moon face." It is just this kind of ambiguity that unsettled audiences, heightened dramatic tension, and fascinated Hitchcock. While Beckert baited his victims with candy, Abbott entreats a young girl's silence with a shiny pocket watch. "I'm not a baby," she indignantly remarks as she thrusts the watch back into his hand. After kidnapping the child, he figuratively twists the knife with sardonic duplicity: "One of the sweetest children I ever met. You know, to a man with a heart as soft as mine, there's nothing sweeter than a touching scene . . . such as a father saying good-bye to his child, good-bye for the last time." In a deleted scene, the "unctuous but deadly" Abbott—so called in the script—winds the same sort of duality around her father's neck with the polite warning, "I am pained by your headache, Mr. Lawrence, and I should be quiet if I were you, in case of a very much more painful ache in the head—yes?" He controls his gang—"my children" in the script—with a malicious grin rather than an iron fist and seems to care only for the severe Nurse Agnes, who dies in the gun battle. In a moment of awkward emotion—not in the script—Abbott tenderly embraces his fallen comrade. With this simple gesture, Lorre underscores the humanity of evil.

Modestly budgeted at forty thousand pounds, *The Man Who Knew Too Much* drew plaudits from audiences as a fine thriller and from critics as a technical masterpiece. Likewise, those within and outside the film world singled out Lorre's performance as a masterwork of staccato violence. "One of the striking things about the picture is the way grimness and terror are heightened by pitching the acting in a low key," wrote James Shelley Hamilton for Britain's National Board of Review. "Nothing is done violently or loudly—a careful style of understatement achieves in the sum total a remarkably gripping force. All of the actors are casual and unassertive, and particularly effective is this method as used by Peter Lorre; always low-voiced, with sometimes a slow, deprecating smile moving over his melancholy face, often completely motionless and devoid of expression, he creates one of the few really sinister characters of the screen."

Andre Sennwald, an ocean away, continued the thought in a piece for the *New York Times:* "Even Charles Laughton, who comes the closest to resembling him in physical appearance and in talent, seems by comparison to be an impish and rosy-cheeked gentleman striving to play the bad boy."

Lorre was, in Montagu's words, "a brilliant actor who would concentrate attention by his timing and explosion and take direction easily, filling into Hitch's conception." In the process, he catapulted himself to stardom in the English-speaking world.

As cogs in intricate mechanisms, or more derisively, pawns in methodical chess games, Hitchcock's players often found themselves the object of his caustic wit. When Johnny Carson pointed out on *The Tonight Show,* April 21, 1976, that he was quoted as saying, "All actors are cattle," Hitchcock dryly corrected, "What I probably said is actors should be treated like cattle."

"He told some they were kittle-cattle," said Montagu, "and that his film was finished when the script was written, and so got on terms of humor with them. If they were dunces, he did not waste time on them unnecessarily. If they were intelligent of course he would be grateful for and encourage and readily snap up any suggestions. This is doubtless the relationship Peter and he had."

Hitchcock and Lorre found common ground in their unconventional senses of humor and fondness for elaborate practical jokes. Excusing the director's well-documented sadistic streak, Montagu commented, "Hitch loved and frequently played practical jokes, BUT ONLY on people who liked them equally and enjoyed them and were in a position to (and usually did) reciprocate." Several years later, a newspaper story credited Lorre, dubbed "the walking overcoat" for his floor-length mantles, with sending fifty singing canaries to Hitchcock at his Cromwell Road flat. As the versions of the story multiplied, so did the number of birds—to three hundred in some accounts. In retaliation, Hitchcock reportedly bombarded a shipboard Lorre with hourly wires giving him news of the birds.

In his biography of Hitchcock, *The Dark Side of Genius,* Donald Spoto charged the director with sending a dray horse to Lorre's flat. Montagu debunked the story, declaring, "I regard this as totally absurd. Hitch indeed had a horse delivered to the theatre dressing room of an English actor [Sir Gerald du Maurier]—it was one of the most well-known jokes of the West End for a long time. How could Hitch possibly have repeated such a joke? He would only have invited contempt for plagiarizing himself and shown his imagination grown dull. Besides, as far as I remember, Peter's flat was on what we call the first or Americans call the second floor." While not completely factual, such stories well serve the spirit if not the letter of their shared fun.

Peter decided that he and Celia should legalize their five-year romance before sailing to America. "We were married in Austria," she told a reporter, "but it was a marriage by consent—not valid here in England or in the United States." Red tape, Celia later explained, had frustrated all their earlier efforts to tie the knot. In England, however, only passports and certificates of good behavior were required. Celia preferred to wait, but Peter insisted. Just before noon on June 22, 1934, she appeared at the General Register Office in Westminster and quietly waited for Peter to arrive from Lime Grove Studios, where Hitchcock had kept him overtime shooting *The Man Who Knew Too Much.* They had twenty-five minutes to obtain the license and be married. (Hitchcock later claimed to have allowed Lorre two hours off in the middle of a scene.) In costume and full makeup—purple smoking jacket, frosted hair, and a three-inch scar created by an astringent that puckered the skin—Lorre rushed off the set and hailed a taxi. Combing his hair over the scar apparently failed to soften his sinister image. "It petrified the official who married us," recalled the actor. "He didn't look at us, at first. He just read out of a book.

Then he looked up, and nearly dropped the book." The brief ceremony ran its official course, but not without a hitch. Celia spoke no English and had to carefully repeat the vows of matrimony. When the groom realized he had forgotten the wedding ring, a friend slipped his own band to Celia. Afterward, the newlyweds hurried back to the set, where Hitchcock greeted them in mock outrage: "THIS IS A SCANDAL! THEY'VE BEEN LIVING TOGETHER FOR FIVE YEARS! LIVING IN SIN!" It was all in fun and Hitchcock soon dared to call Celia "Untier" or "Untie" for short.

Before leaving for America, Lorre invited his father to London. "You will be surprised to learn," said Francis, "he even sent him a ticket." Alajos spent "a beautiful fortnight" there, but Peter had to cable Francis for money to send his father home. "That was my brother, Peter," said Francis. "But then, of course, he was already world famous and we could easily follow his career in the newspapers. I am sure that this invitation to London was not only out of love for his father, but to impress him."

During the 1920s, the Hollywood movie moguls, men of business who traded in the written word, the moving image, and the human soul, began dispatching their emissaries far and wide in search of European film talent. They wanted not only box-office returns but also critical recognition. They wanted "art" and with it respectability. In Europe they could buy both. Agents canvassed the Continent for art and culture, ferreting out those who could be bought. Trophy hunting, the studio sport, netted a bagful of "highbrow" properties, among them Swedish actress Greta Garbo, German actor Emil Jannings, and directors Ernst Lubitsch, F.W. Murnau, Paul Leni, Michael Curtiz, William Dieterle, and E.A. Dupont. Hollywood quickly weeded out those who would not accommodate art and commerce, or failed to make the transition to sound. Some fell afoul of the studio star system and quit America to seek greater artistic freedom elsewhere, while others stayed on in diminished capacities.

Although Harry Cohn had no assignment for Lorre, he urged him to report for duty as soon as possible.[4] The mogul's hunting instinct was unmistakably American—to shoot first and ask questions later. Certainly, he knew little about his prey. *M* (1931), *Schuss im Morgengrauen* (1932), and *Was Frauen träumen* (1933) had received only limited exposure in the United States. At New York's Mayfair theater, in April 1933, *M* grossed $15,000 its first week, $11,300 in a second, and $8,000 in a third—a nice showing, but not good enough to hold it over a fourth week.[5] In Los Angeles it played to a negligible take at The President, a second-run house offering its first first-run film, and bowed out after a two-week run. Audiences, claimed the press, found the grisly nature of its subject material shocking and offensive. "Why so much fervor and intelligent work was concentrated on such a revolting idea is surprising," wrote *New York Times* film reviewer Mordaunt Hall. Columbia looked past the actor's screen image—first that of a compulsive killer, then that of a smiling villain—and focused on his international stature. *M* was art and Peter Lorre a classic actor.

On Wednesday, July 18, 1934, one week after obtaining visitors' visas at the American Consular Service in London—and just one day after wrapping up production at Gaumont-British—Peter and Celia boarded the Cunard White Star Liner *Majestic* in Southampton and sailed "First Cabin" for New York. In preparing his "Manifest of Alien Passengers for the United States Immigration Officer at Port of Arrival," the ship's officer grilled the Lorres with a long list of perfunctory but provocative questions. Asked the name of the "nearest relative or friend in country whence alien came," Lorre unhesitatingly answered Sidney Bernstein. He described himself as being five foot, eight inches—chalking up three inches to creative license—having a fair complexion, fair hair, and brown eyes. He also responded that Columbia had paid his passage, that he possessed at least fifty dollars, that he planned to spend six months in the United States, that he had never been in prison or an insane asylum, that his mental and physical health were good, that he had not been supported by charity, and that he was neither a polygamist nor an anarchist. Asked if he planned to return to England "after engaging temporarily in labor pursuits" in the United States, Lorre answered yes. Moreover, he and Celia stated that they did not intend to become American citizens and—incorrectly it would seem—that they had not come "by reason of any offer, solicitation, promise, agreement, expressed or implied to labor in the U.S." Although Lorre had high hopes for Hollywood, in the past year, he had, like Brecht changed "countries oftener than our shoes." He now exercised a caution that told him to forge ahead without burning his bridges behind him.

Six days later Peter and Celia stepped off the gangplank at the West Fourteenth Street dock. Camera bulbs popped. Lorre was not the "repellant spectacle" the press had expected. "The pathological murderer in 'M,'" described a reporter for the *New York Times,* "is a round-faced, smiling young man of 30 years." And questions flew. Lorre reflected on his work with Hitchcock and his future in the American cinema. "If it were not for *M,*" he said regretfully, "I would have started on my trip to Hollywood long ago." On the matter of reconciling marriage and career, Celia said she would give up acting, at least for now. "Both of us feel this will make for matrimonial happiness," echoed Peter, showing his true European colors. "It is not a case of possible jealousy. But a man does like to see his wife when he comes home at night."

On Thursday, July 26, Peter and Celia stepped aboard the *Twentieth Century Ltd.* When the train pulled into Chicago the next morning, switchmen uncoupled the sleeping cars and tacked them onto the rear of the *Santa Fe Chief*, which rolled out the red carpet for the Hollywood celebrities who routinely crossed the country by rail. Deluxe accommodations featured plush drawing rooms trimmed in wood paneling, private bathrooms, spacious observation decks, and gourmet dining. While rolling plains built to rocky mountains and then fell to desert expanse, the passengers observed the scenic wonders, talked shop, and partied into the early morning hours. The lull of the track seductively beckoned them to the end of the line, where, as actor Clive Brooks observed, "The links of our chains are forged not of cruelties, but of our luxuries."

News of Lorre's arrival in Los Angeles had preceded him by over a month. "In all of the newspapers here, we read of his coming," Elisabeth Hauptmann wrote Walter Benjamin in Paris. "One has to congratulate the man who engaged the 'genius actor.'" Hollywood extended a warm welcome to the Lorres. Invitations summoned Peter and Celia to lavish Viennese and Tyrolean dinner parties, where they mixed with old friends such as Fritz Lang, G.W. Pabst, Billy Wilder, and Franz Waxman and met new ones, among them Jean Negulesco, Delmer Daves, Paul Muni, and Olivia de Havilland. The Friedrich Hollaenders also enrolled Lorre—along with Ernst Lubitsch, Conrad Veidt, and Josef von Sternberg—for their Sunday afternoon Ping-Pong tournaments.

Soon after his arrival, Lorre found himself at the Brown Derby, a popular watering hole for film celebrities. Several tables away sat Charlie Chaplin, flourishing his menu in an effort to catch the actor's eye. Chaplin confessed that he had seen *M* three times and later said of Lorre: "There is much of the born poet in Peter Lorre. His is a fresh and original talent. He is endowed with such intuitive, emotional and imaginative powers that he impresses me as one of the greatest character actors. I look forward to seeing him make a genuine contribution to the art of acting on the screen." Compliments came in no greater size. Lorre told one interviewer he kept a clipping from the *Los Angeles Times* in which Chaplin had called him Europe's greatest actor. He even returned the favor, citing the silent clown as his favorite film star.

Lorre again met the celebrated pantomimist at a dinner given for Chaplin and Paulette Goddard by King Vidor. They instantly hit it off and entertained each other with some facemaking; Lorre recreated tense moments from *M*, nearly frightening his audience of one to death, and Chaplin improvised a skit about a blind man. The two men also traded ideas for pet projects. Feeling that Chaplin, who had played a hapless private in *Shoulder Arms*, would share his enthusiasm for Jaroslav Hasek's *The Good Soldier Švejk (Osudy Dobrého Vojáka Švejka za)*, Lorre told him he held an option on the novel and one day hoped to portray the soft-headed batman in a film version of the World War I comedy.[6]

Just as there was much of Hasek in Švejk, there was also some of Švejk—both real and imagined—in Lorre. Hasek described "the good soldier" as a short stocky figure who is quiet, unassuming, and shabbily dressed, with the "kindliest of smiles" and the gaze of a "guileless lamb." However, Hasek makes it clear that Švejk "is no mere idiot and that his innocence is only simulated." Pretending to be "a half-wit for the sole purpose of concealing his rascality under the mask of imbecility" is his modus operandi. "The little man is indestructible," wrote Czech literary critic F.X. Šalda of Hasek's anonymous hero. "Švejk's . . . idiotic cunning protects him more and is of more use to him than the greatest imaginable acumen and ingenuity."

Lorre identified with people, especially writers, who actively represented views that he inactively subscribed to. Who better than Hasek, who also out of necessity had clerked in a bank before pursuing avocations—as anarchist, atheist, rogue, mischief-maker, hoaxer (before losing his job as editor of a magazine called the *Animal World,* he had advertised "thoroughbred werewolves" for sale), vagabond, satirical caricaturist, writer of sketches and feuilletons, and above all, "idiot of genius." No one was immune to his "epic phlegm." He ridiculed do-gooders, the nobility, the church, the police, marriage, school teachers, children, censors, professors, experts, and so on.

The Austrian Army called Hasek to arms in 1915. After being taken prisoner on the Eastern Front and spending several years in a Russian POW camp, he enlisted in the Czech Army. Hasek encapsulated his army experiences in his Švejk stories, which first appeared in *Karikatury* (*Caricatures*) in 1911. Six years later, Slav Publishing House in Kiev brought out a second series of stories titled *The Good Soldier Švejk in Captivity (Dobrý voják Švejk v zajetí)*. Between 1921 and 1923, Hasek completed three of four projected volumes of *The Good Soldier Švejk* before dying at age forty. Lorre undoubtedly latched onto the German-language version, which was published in 1926.

At close view, *Švejk* is pure propaganda aimed at winning support for the Czech national struggle and at pillorying the Austrian military machine, whose gross mismanagement of the war took little account of human suffering. However, the novel's enduring importance lies in its pacifist message. Described as a deeply unhappy man, Hasek treated serious subjects humorously. "By seeming to make fun of its horrors," wrote Cecil Parrott, author of *Jaroslav Hasek: A Study of Švejk and the Short Stories,* "he draws attention to the ghastly waste of human life in a way that no one can fault." Saying one thing and meaning another, Hasek, like Švejk, "shows up the world war in all its infamy, idiocy and inhumanity so vividly . . . He stood above it from the very beginning. He just laughed at it."

"It is a book about a dumb soldier, a half comic, half pathetic character," Lorre explained. "It is a psychological study of this soldier. I want to play that soldier very much. Everyone reads the book and laughs. 'That is not screen material,' they tell me. I say, 'All right, forget it,' but you know some day I will play the part. Some day someone will make the Good Soldier Schweik." Chaplin suggested that he would like to direct an American version of the Švejk story with Lorre in the leading role. Although their plans never materialized, the actor took Švejk to the movies in many of his best screen portrayals.[7]

Lorre had caught the first flight of European artists from Hitler. In 1934, 4,392 immigrant aliens (at least one-third of them Jewish) listed Germany as "Country of Last Permanent Residence." Those who followed the refugee trail to America in 1933–35 included a cross section of the German intelligentsia— scientists, scholars, writers, and artists, among them mathematician Richard Courant, physicist Albert Einstein, composer Erich Korngold, philosopher Herbert Marcuse, actress-singer Lotte Lenya, and theologian Paul Tillich.[8]

America extended a cold shoulder to the "huddled masses" of refugees from Nazi Germany, who ran headlong into the Quota Act of 1921 and the Immigration Act of 1924, restrictive barriers symptomatic of an isolationism rooted in the nineteenth century. In the wake of World War I, a wave of national spirit fed the strong distrust of foreigners. The State Department suspected an invasion of criminals and subversives, while labor unions feared a deluge of cheap workers. Rigid legislation reflected the national mood to stem the "alien flood." In 1929 the United States had adopted an annual quota ceiling of 153,774. The great crash in October of that year, widespread unemployment, and the influx of refugees had prompted President Hoover to resurrect the "public charge" clause of the Immigration Act of 1917. On September 8, 1930, he issued a White House statement instructing consular officials to judge whether an applicant was "likely to become a public charge" at any time, even long after arriving. In an avowed effort to prevent immigrant aliens from becoming burdens to their communities, Hoover reminded them that they must possess sufficient resources to support themselves for an indefinite period without employment or be able to enlist the support of friends or relatives. At one time, an immigrant with $100 could gain entry to the United States. Now, as Vice-Consul Burke, an immigration official in Hamburg since 1924, pointed out, he doubted that a man possessing $10,000 "should be regarded as unlikely to become a public charge."

Under section 7 of the act of 1924, American consular officials also required applicants to provide police certificates of good character (on October 18, 1934, the chief of police of Berlin had certified that Peter Lorre had no criminal record), passports, birth and marriage certificates, and other available public records. Émigrés encountered yet another hurdle in a "contract labor" provision, which denied admission to those under employment contracts. Along with this, the Immigration Act of 1917 demanded the "exclusion of persons whose ticket or passage is paid for by any corporation, association or society, municipality or foreign government either directly or indirectly."

"They were expected to be self-sufficient though penniless," wrote Arthur D. Morse in *While Six Million Died: A Chronicle of American Apathy*, "capable of supporting themselves though unemployed, and prepared to pay their passage without accepting help from friends." The consular officers had the final word, sealing fates with a rubber stamp. Charged with stringently applying the acts and provisions, they arbitrarily exercised their prerogatives, screening out undesirables, political radicals, and immigrant aliens who, upon their discretionary judgment, should be turned away. Diligent enforcement of the quota restrictions sharply curtailed the arrival of newcomers. The number of immigrants admitted to the United States fell from 241,700 in 1930 to 97,139 in 1931 and to 35,576 in 1932. Only 6,514 of 63,000 Jews who fled Germany in 1933–34 entered the United States.[9] America's "closed door" policy ideally suited Hitler, who used the United States' racially discriminatory immigration policies to justify his own anti-Semitism. "Through its immigration law," he stated, "America has inhibited the unwelcome influx of such races as it has been unable to tolerate within its midst. Nor is America now ready to open its doors to Jews 'fleeing from Germany.'"

Despite the barriers, 1935–36 saw an increase in the number of Jewish immigrants from Germany admitted to the United States. Presumably years of preparation finally had paid off. Also, worsening conditions in Europe enforced the necessity of hurdling obstacles erected by the American government. In 1937, when President Roosevelt relaxed the restrictions of the "Hoover Directive" of 1930, the trickle of German and Austrian refugees swelled to a flood.

Sociologists quickly began to study them, to record their impressions of America—and America's impression of them—and to chart the progress or failure of their integration into American society. Their field notes, interviews, and graphs shaped the refugee profile: middle- or upper-class; primarily business-oriented, professional, and white collar; well-educated; city-dwelling; cosmopolitan; generally older; learned English rapidly; aspired to a high standard of living; tended to join American organizations; migrated in family units; and naturalized rapidly and in high proportion.

The reality of exile lived harder than it read. Most refugees arrived with limited funds and became dependent upon the generosity of friends and relatives. Jews leaving Germany after Hitler came to power were allowed to take out up to $10,000, but this ceiling soon fell to $6,000, then $4,000, and finally $800. In October 1934 the Nazis further restricted the currency outflow to ten reichsmarks (about $4) per emigrant. Finding work was imperative, but refugees often encountered a "closed shop" policy, only one aspect of an intangible animosity toward foreigners. In the throes of an economic depression, America offered few jobs, at least on a level commensurate with the experience and aptitude of the refugees, who were ineligible for work relief; judges became clerks and dishwashers, and university professors worked as night watchmen. Unfounded fears that cheap labor would flood the marketplace and displace American workers unleashed a wave of anti-Semitism. Immigrants (predominantly Christian) of an earlier period, who were of lower economic and educational backgrounds, did not readily extend a helping hand to the apparently better-off latter-day arrivals—roughly 80 percent of whom were Jewish—who sought to continue their European style of living. Strongly nationalistic Germans viewed with suspicion the refugees of fascism, whose abandonment of the Fatherland invited their contempt. Those sympathetic to National Socialism (an estimated fifty thousand were ardently anti-Semitic) even defamed emigration with anti-refugee propaganda.[10]

A microcosm of isolationist America, "Hollywood was still a closed society," observed writer-producer-director John Houseman in 1939, "whose social, financial and professional structure, though subject to constant shifts, remained basically rigid and unchanged." Big names took refuge in the studio star system, while those whose reputations did not precede them bumped their heads against a brick wall of indifference. Hollywood, it seemed, took more interest in the loss of foreign revenue and in the closure of American-owned cinemas brought on by the war than in the plight of the refugee artists from Hitler's Germany.

Hollywood's reception fractured the émigré community into cliques along geopolitical, literary, professional, artistic, and philosophical lines; in short, the makeup of their lives before emigration. Pre-exile Germans clustered around Emil Jannings, the Viennese sought out Max Reinhardt, and the Hungarian enclave identified with George Marton. What you did and who you worked for also defined social spheres. Former stage actors banded together. Likewise, studio employees formed their own clans. Only the larger salons crosscut the colony. German director William Dieterle and his wife Charlotte's circle attracted politicians, preachers, film people, artists, and writers, including Bertolt Brecht, Lion Feuchtwanger and Thomas Mann. At the Mabery Road cottage of Salka Viertel, an MGM screenwriter and active member of Hollywood's "Popular Front," exiled intellectuals mingled with European and American artistic and literary figures such as W.H. Auden, Aldous Huxley, Christopher Isherwood, Charlie Chaplin, Greta Garbo, Charles Laughton, John Houseman, Oscar Levant, Otto Klemperer, and many others.

Ideologically, the émigré colony fell into two camps, those who burned their bridges and forged ahead, and those who resisted the urge to assimilate. Many refugees viewed America as a temporary residence and their stay as a brief stopover. For them, going to America was in itself an admission of defeat that was only partly mitigated by efforts to preserve a "culture in exile." These émigrés suffered an especially severe case of displacement. They behaved as outsiders, belonging nowhere. Some made a fetish of their exile condition, ready at a moment's notice to discard their uncomfortable hotels and provisional furnishings for flight. Lingering between arrival and departure, they developed a taste for transience.

"The experience of defeat, of emigration, of the breakdown of hope," wrote German Jewish academic Henry Pachter, characterized exile literature. Klaus Mann found the American landscape hostile and alien, and glamorously unreal. The stars in the sky, he noted ironically, were perhaps only "a subdued reflection of the electric stars below." This Lotus Land harbored a deceptive beauty where beneath the illusion of splendor the common run bargained away their souls for fame and money.

Émigrés with diverse backgrounds expressed their lostness in common metaphors. Thomas Mann wrote disparagingly of the "soulless soil" that knew nothing of him and to which he owed nothing. "Neither the things that grow nor the people seemed to have any real roots," continued English actor Sir Cedric Hardwicke, as if finishing the thought.

That America fell short of their preconceptions was partly their own doing. The German art movement of the 1920s, with its romanticized images of a modern, urban, vibrant land of the future, took root in the consciousness of the so-called educated bourgeoisie. What the émigrés saw—and deprecated as emotionally immature and politically ignorant—was a "pop" culture choked with mindless melodramas and soap operas. Nothing prepared them for the culture shock they experienced and, in many cases, continued to feel. Although

New York lived up to its reputation as a cosmopolitan hub, Los Angeles failed to meet expectations. There, most of all, émigrés complained of geographical and cultural isolation.

More defensive than discourteous, cultural elitism echoed a loneliness of the transient heart that, in exiled writer Karl Zuckmayer's words, had made "a journey of no return." As outsiders who looked in on a strange and hostile environment, they turned their feelings of despair inward.

Such exiles clung to one another out of the need for sympathetic contact with fellow sufferers. They maintained their separate identity by reading German newspapers, listening to radio broadcasts in their native language, and singing familiar folk songs. As Americans were wont to forget, refugees from Hitler's Germany were not immigrants but emigrants who looked to the day when they would return to reestablish democracy in Germany. Meanwhile, these unhappy guests idealized the past and dreamed of Strauss waltzes, Tyrolean mountains, and Unter den Linden. "The poor refugees had a hard time settling down," wrote exiled Austrian actor S.Z. Sakall. "They roamed the streets like masterless dogs. The only joy in their tragic situation was the same innocent little lie. They told the Americans and each other that in the old country they had been prosperous and had held jobs of authority and importance."

Peter Lorre was one of a special and select group, whose transition from Europe to America was made easier by his stopover in London. There he had learned enough English to convincingly convey a studied malevolence in *The Man Who Knew Too Much* and had acclimated to filmmaking techniques and production methods that were only one step removed from those in Hollywood. Moreover, it had earned him a movie contract and a ticket to America, where Columbia Pictures—although it boasted little more than poverty-row status—had parted the waves of red tape. While others, such as novelists Leonhard Frank and Franz Werfel, won their freedom after close encounters with death, Lorre had effortlessly flung open the golden door to opportunity, arriving in America as an international film star whose singular looks made him one of the most recognizable actors of his day. He took passage first to a state of mind, Hollywood, and second to a geographical reality, California. "As long as Hollywood wants me, I want Hollywood," he celebrated. "I am convinced that my future, from an artistic point of view, definitely rests here. I have no desire to return to Europe for some time."

For Lorre, America was the end of flight and the takeoff for new beginnings. He believed that Berlin's "consequential position" in world cinema was a thing of the past: "Germany's artistic resources have been scattered to the four winds, leaving her poor indeed in this respect." The actor had broken with the past and, he hoped, with the legacy of his German screen image. In launching a new film career in America, he strove to put away the old and place before him the new, not obtrusively, but quietly. America, he felt, owed him nothing but a chance to start over. Like noted émigré Max Berges, he believed that "we have only a future now, a future which demands of us only one thing of which we can be proud: To be Americans, and nothing but Americans!"

Lorre neither romanticized the past nor identified with American-bashing Germans who judged Los Angeles provincial and its local customs quaintly inferior; they were now his customs. Unlike many refugees, he was better off in Hollywood, where there was a ready market for his talents—or screen identity, as it turned out—and where he now enjoyed a higher standard of living than he had known in Europe. In an economy where actors, musicians, and writers—many of whom, bitter and disillusioned, returned to Germany after the war—faced occupational adjustment problems because of the importance of speaking and writing English, he had comfortably nestled under the studio wing, easing his introduction to the American lifestyle. Hollaender recalled that Lorre, "who but a short time ago . . . had shuddered to crawl into his only suit not completely in rags," found himself "in a peaceful villa close to the ocean, sauntering through the hall, in flannels, or trimming roses in the garden."

Lorre had fallen for the California lifestyle and exulted that "we have a home at [326 Adelaide Drive] Santa Monica, near the sea, because I love the water and sunshine and fresh air and flowers. I am delighted to be here, because I can have a home. I am now busily engaged in putting in a badminton court and planting flowers, many flowers." He had known change, daily and epochal, and transience. He had witnessed a culture spiraling toward dissolution and had retreated to seedy hotels and lived at the expense of friends. The glazed red-tile detail and glistening white stucco walls of his Spanish colonial house, which overlooked the ocean, washed away the gray memory of exile. He padded along the beach, sat in the sun, played tennis and badminton, and counted his blessings.

Celia wanted to live near the studio, so her husband wouldn't spend all of his time commuting. However, Peter preferred to stay as far away as possible. He isolated himself in the tropical setting, far from the grim political realities of Europe. "I love everything about it," declared Lorre. "The people, they are charming. The climate, it is perfect. The life, it is ideal. We live on the beach and never dress up, and we adore the lazy, lounging clothes of Hollywood." He felt renewed and ready to plan his future in the New World. In the sudden shift of fortune, Lorre was on the inside looking out:

László and Elvira,
ca. 1907.

László Loewenstein,
ca. 1908.

Left to right: Liesl, András (Andrew), Ferenc (Francis), and László (Peter), ca. 1911.

Peter Lorre's father,
Lieutenant Alajos
Loewenstein, 1903.

Alajos Loewenstein during the war, ca. 1916.

Die fleissige Leserin (*The Diligent Reader*), Kammerspiele, Vienna, 1926. Peter Lorre is second from right.

As a merry deserter in *Marlborough zieht in den Krieg* (*Marlborough Goes to War*), Kammerspiele, Vienna, 1926.

Grete Witzmann
and Peter Lorre
kneel in prayer in
Die Stunde des Absterbens
(*The Hour of Dying Off*),
Theater in the Josefstadt,
Vienna, 1927.

"Die Ohrfeige" ("Box on the Ear") in *Ein Abend der Überraschungen* (*An Evening of Surprises*), Theater in the Josefstadt, Vienna, 1927. *Left to right:* Egon Friedell, Karl Ehmann, Fritz Strehlen, Hans Ziegler, Peter Lorre, and Rudolf Beer; *in front,* Gisela Werbezirk.

An early publicity postcard addressed to "Bundy," Peter's brother Andrew, 1927.

Celia Lovsky, ca. 1924.

Lotte Lenya and Peter Lorre in Marieluise Fleisser's *Pioniere in Ingolstadt* (*Engineers in Ingolstadt*), Theater am Schiffbauerdamm, Berlin, 1929. Photo by Lotte Jacobi.

As Moritz Stiefel in Wedekind's *Frühlings Erwachen* (*Spring's Awakening*), Volksbühne, Theater am Bülowplatz, Berlin, 1929. Photo by Lotte Jacobi.

Playing a dental patient in his only silent film, *Die verschwundene Frau* (*The Missing Wife*), 1929.

M le maudit (*The Damned One*), French film poster, 1932.

Peter Lorre and Fritz Lang study the script on the set of *M*, 1931.

"In the name of the law," Peter Lorre's final scene in *M*, 1931.

As editor Stix in *Die Koffer des Herrn O.F.* (*The Luggage of Mr. O.F.*), 1931.

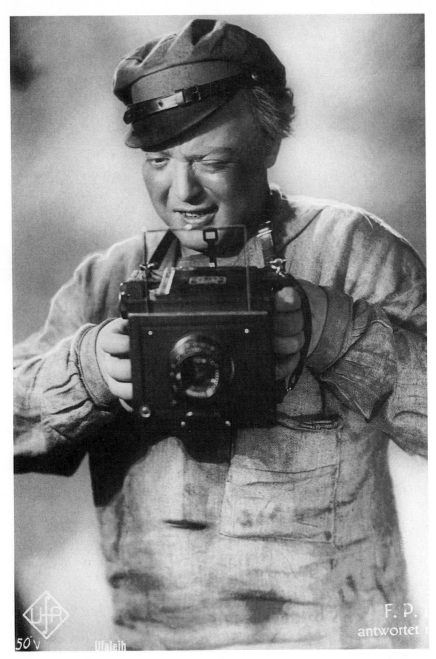

As "Foto Johnnny" in *F.P.1 antwortet nicht* (*Floating Platform 1 Doesn't Answer*), 1932.

I confess that I have looked forward throughout my professional career to this visit. . . . No question exists in my mind that the American motion picture is the finest product of its kind in the world.

Hollywood definitely is the place where picture making is natural, like champagne is natural to France. The huge smooth-running production organization you have here—and there is nothing to equal it anywhere—has developed step by step over a period of years. It has a tradition behind it by now. Regardless of competition, it will be the main factor in the world market for a long time to come.

Even the matriarchal nature of American society, often singled out for comment by European émigrés, suited his and Celia's living arrangement, in which she functioned as wife, mother, friend, and accountant—though not actress.

When he returned from the studio, Lorre closed his door on publicity. Whereas most actors thrived on getting their names into the industry trade papers, he tried to keep his out. "I am the worst actor in private life," he explained. "I can't make nice faces, pay nice diplomatic compliments. When I am not acting I can't pretend. A man like me needs solitude. In Hollywood I have often gone out of my way to please people, lest I be taken for a snob." With telegraphic punch, the *Hollywood Reporter*'s "Rambling Reporter" crammed its columns with tantalizing news bits, party lists, and the names of notables lunching at the Vendome, a posh restaurant-nightclub hot spot belonging to Billy Wilkerson, who also owned the *Hollywood Reporter*. The celebrity roll call very seldom mustered Lorre into its ranks. "One of the most amusing paradoxes," he confessed, "is that most of my screen activities should be concerned with the sinister things of life, for by nature I am almost too shy." He admitted that "the constant excitement and activity of the big cities makes me fidgety" and added that "meeting people, talking, exchanging ideas draw too much vitality from an actor. I find it is better to conserve my energy for work." Even at home, said Celia, "he still is strange and remote in some mysterious way. We have never quarreled nor had disagreements. He just retains some remoteness inside which I cannot penetrate. He is wise, quiet, and happy, like a Buddha."

Although he enjoyed a healthy isolation from Hollywood's cliques, communities, and salons, Lorre occasionally turned up at Salka Viertel's home for exchanges that delicately accorded past and present. He did not wish to parade his good fortune, or what the German colony—divided between "haves" and "have-nots," or between those who sold out and those who, in spite of their protestations otherwise, waited to be bought out—begrudgingly viewed as commercially stepping up and artistically stepping down. Lorre lent his presence to these occasions, but seldom his participation. By casting himself in the role of a party clown who unsurely played off his monstrous screen image, he sidestepped the partisan wrangling that routinely marked the discussions.[11] Among his fellow exiles, he no longer knew where he stood; to his old-world compatriots he was an insider whose subsequent film work was of little consequence, and to moviemakers, he was an outsider banished to permanent exile on-screen. At a gathering of German and Austrian émigrés, William Dieterle told the members of his table, including Klaus and Erika Mann, Luise Rainer, and Lorre, that he could barely remember an actor that he liked better to work with than Paul Muni. Klaus and Erika Mann recorded the reaction to his comment:

"And where do I come in?" asks Peter Lorre, turning his bearded face to the producer, his round eyes full of surprise and disappointment.

"You keep quiet, Mr. Moto," says Dieterle. "You're silly and you haven't even shaved!"

Lorre registers indignation. "It's for your sake," he complains, "that I am growing a beard. Only for you, for your good. It's you that will profit by it when you see my incomparable presentation of a tramp. You've got no gratitude—no, not even you, Ma," he wails, stealing a bit of roast beef from Luise Rainer's plate. "You are cold and perfidious!"

"Assimilation," wrote Donald Kent Peterson in *The Refugee Intellectual*, "is a process of absorption. It is a process by which one body ingests a foreign body and so incorporates it that its original identity is lost and it becomes an indistinguishable part of the absorbing body." Lorre met American society, with its expectation that refugees wanted to assimilate as quickly as possible, more than halfway. Like the child émigrés, who most easily absorbed new ways, he was boyishly optimistic about his New World adventure. He didn't feel obligated to demonstrate his good intentions by participating in community projects, joining civic organizations, or attending classes in American history, customs, and politics sponsored by the refugee aid groups. The need to belong came naturally.

The process of "de-nationalizing" and "renationalizing" was too political to describe Lorre's easy adjustment. He jumped in with both feet. "We were into Americana," said fellow émigré Billy Wilder, who never regarded America as a foreign country, but as a place where he belonged. On Wednesday nights Lorre and Wilder motored to the Olympic Theater to watch professional wrestling. The actor later boasted to interviewer Mike Wallace that soon after he arrived in America, some Hollywood friends threw a party so that he could meet another European sensation, Greta Garbo. "I was very pleased by the prospect," he proudly recalled, "but on the night of the party, I forgot all about it and went instead to see Man Mountain Dean wrestle." An enterprising Fox publicist later parleyed Lorre's wrestling mania into a fitting press release: "Lorre hasn't missed a wrestling match here in more than a year, and whenever Dean wrestles is on hand in Dean's corner as an unofficial second." It was the only profession, he said, where you can overact without being punished for it.

People were sure to see the actor even if they didn't recognize him. Like a prisoner freed from long confinement, he cast off musty old-world formality for the latest and loudest fashions. He sported polo shirts, informal combinations of colorful shirts and loose ties, a yellow greatcoat, and even a gray buckskin jacket bristling with metal zippers. "He looks like a Jack Pepper stooge," slammed one onlooker. "Maybe a Ted Healy stooge." Personal freedom also gave free rein to his appetite, which he satisfied with hot dogs and Coca-Cola mixed with raspberry vinegar.

For many émigrés, surmounting the language barrier presented a daunting challenge. "If I had known the tremendous ordeal ahead of me in learning English adequately," moaned a Czech actor, "I believe I would rather have stayed in Europe and faced Hitler." Slang, colloquialisms, and conversational language isolated the refugees, who clung together out of the need to hear their own language. Lorre, in contrast, immersed himself in the "racy" vernacular, with its colorful jargon and idioms. One of the original "hipsters"—so called by a close friend—he strained the latest smart talk through a Continental accent.

The hospitable corporality of America all but submerged Lorre's European identity. As much as a "rococo cherub gone slightly astray" could, he melted into the Hollywood landscape. Some German émigrés, intent on preserving old customs and habits, which they felt were superior, disparaged America for a perceived lack of seriousness, especially on political and cultural issues. Americans, in turn, attacked the "European stiffness of behavior." No one accused Lorre of anything less than irresistible enthusiasm. He took refuge in the openness and natural informality of his adopted countrymen. If being an exile was a state of mind, as Henry Pachter observed, and not a matter of needing a passport, then Lorre had found a permanent home in America.

At first, his sinister screen persona had amused him. But in true Hollywood fashion, it had grown larger than life. Lorre was weary of being reminded of *M*. Unless he expunged his identity as a "horror hero" from public consciousness, he could not hope to reorient his image or his career. After *M*, Lorre told the press, Hollywood had deluged him with offers to play homicidal maniacs. "I am a young man," he said, justifying his refusal. "If I should play nothing but horror pictures, when the craze for murder pictures is through—which will certainly be in a year or two—I would be through. I have no wish to be through. I want to act forever."

Lorre took Harry Cohn at his word that signing on the dotted line guaranteed him a fresh start in Hollywood. Their verbal understanding assured the actor a variety of roles in mutually acceptable screen vehicles. "I am having less trouble about being typed," explained the hopeful actor, "because Mr. Cohn feels the same way—that my work requires a change. That's why I signed with Columbia." Undoubtedly, he recalled for Cohn his varied experience on the European stage and screen, of his roles in farces, comedy revues, and historical and political dramas. "What I would like to do is to play many characters," he said, "and be known as a general character actor as at home." He pointed out, somewhat inaccurately, that until he made *M* he had "never played a bogey man. . . . I was an out-an-out [*sic*] comedian, of the broadest sort. When I was on the stage in Berlin and Vienna, no producer ever thought of me as anything except a funny character." Intent on demonstrating his versatility, the actor asked to play the kind of half-comic, half-tragic characterizations that had earned Charles Laughton his popularity. "I am, of course, physically limited to a certain extent," conceded Lorre. "I could not, for instance, play the sort of part that calls for Clark Gable. I could not play a tall Viking with a crest of gold on my head. But those are minor limitations. It does not mean that I cannot play the lover, the adolescent, the dreamer, the murderer, the Falstaff—since all of the emotions, love and hate and fear and sorrow and joy are *in the mind*."

Cohn assured Lorre that his production staff was searching for a suitable vehicle, one to garner critical success and box-office returns. Not content to leave it at that, Lorre broached the idea of filming Jakob Wassermann's *Caspar Hauser* (1928) and suggested fellow Ansonia expatriate Hans Lustig, a Berlin theater and film critic turned scenarist, to adapt it for the screen. In September 1934 *Variety* reported that Columbia had set Lorre to play the name part in "Kasper Hauser" as his first picture, but nothing materialized of the actor's earliest attempt to chart his own course.[12] "It is the same in Germany," Lorre sadly commented. "There, too, they remember what you have done last. If it is good, then you must do it again, in another play or in another picture. It doesn't matter what it is. They give you no chance at doing anything else. So I would rather do nothing than be typed like that."

Weeks of leisure turned into months of waiting. Lorre studied the works of Carl Jung, greedily devoured the macabre tales of Edgar Allan Poe, tended the garden, and played with his Airedale terrier. Meanwhile, Celia stalled Dr. Samek. Since she and Peter had arrived in Hollywood, the attorney had kept up pressure with monthly reminders of his overdue debt to Karl Kraus. Just as often, she asked for short extensions, which she met with payments that fell far short of the promised sum. In January Columbia extended his option for another six months, but still had nothing for him to do. With Lorre on full salary, Cohn asked himself what he could do with his trophy, this actor for whom casting presented such a vexing problem. Perhaps, he felt, he had another Charles Laughton on his hands, a specialty, an oddity nearly impossible to classify. Laughton's recent appearance as a maniacal doctor in *Island of Lost Souls* (1932) came easily to mind. Even the press lumped them together as unconventional evildoers, though exaggerating their physical similarities as pop-eyed, spongy-faced ogres. Laughton had effectively sidestepped the type-casting dilemma with his Oscar-winning performance in *The Private Life of Henry VIII* (1932). Cohn doubted Lorre would as summarily escape the same fate.

Whether or not Cohn was aware of it, Lorre walked in Hans Beckert's shadow. Both, it seemed, searched for an identity. The *Lustmörder* found no home among the gunmen and molls of the popular cycle of gangster movies of the 1930s. For many, the outlaw served as a depression-era Robin Hood, who, through his criminal acts, defied a corrupt system and reaffirmed the myth of individual success. After all, John Dillinger robbed banks, not people, and even flirted with older women bystanders. American criminals were adventurous pirates, not sexual psychopaths. Beckert was no more welcome in the ranks of movie-made monsters, fiends, and madmen. In an industry where filmmakers thrived by satisfying public expectations rather than contradicting them, Columbia was at a loss to explain Lorre as anything but what he appeared to be, an outsider who hinted at things better left unknown.

In their "color biographies," studio publicists sold the real Lorre as a boyish, affable, would-be comedian who had taken his hard knocks on the Continental stage, playing everything from broad comedy to tragedy. Only on screen, they emphasized, was he typed as a "monster man." To prove it, Columbia sent a photographer to peer in on his private life. His camera recorded—and reinvented—enough sides of Lorre's character to warrant a diagnosis of multiple personality. There was the dutiful Lorre swathed in domestic bliss with Celia, the landed gentry Lorre surveying his—rented—estate, the pensive Lorre in high-waisted white slacks leaning against a baby grand piano, the debonair Lorre in double-breasted suit and slicked hair, the gardener Lorre, the quiet intellectual Lorre, the dog-lover Lorre, and the smiling, good-natured, secretive, and mysterious Lorre, along with the bogeyman Lorre just to top off the photographic essay on a familiar note. Sympathetic with their motives, although not with their methods, Lorre played along with whatever gags and gimmicks studio publicists cooked up. To prove he was not a murderer, but an animal lover, a press agent even shoved a dog into his hands, snapped a shot, and released the story to newspapers: "Lorre Saves Dog . . ."

Truth is often stranger than fiction, and sometimes the press gave better than it got. *Los Angeles Times* columnist Philip K. Scheuer proved there was more to Lorre than met the public eye with a story titled BERLIN BURIAL:

> Peter Lorre, expatriate, has just buried a dachshund in Germany. Eight years ago . . . he played a farm boy [*Pioniere in Ingolstadt*], and in one scene came on stage carrying a small bewildered dog. In time Lorre grew to regard the dachshund as a mascot. One night a flat fell on the dog behind the scenes, breaking its shoulder and a foreleg. The actor placed it in the care of a stage hand, with the promise to send a monthly check for its maintenance, come what may. . . . From Hollywood he continued to mail money orders to Berlin. This week the stage hand wrote that the old trouper, age 10, was dead. "I gave the dachshund a beautiful funeral," went the letter, "and I had a headstone made by a monument maker for his grave. It cost me the equivalent of two months' care." A money order, the last, is on its way home.

While Columbia covered all angles, making the highs higher and the lows lower, Lorre decided the best way to unseat his screen image was simply to be himself. To get his point across, he freely gave his time to interviewers, some of whom pegged him—quite accurately—as a bibliophile who could enlarge upon his appreciation of Schiller, Goethe, and Sardon. Yet another journalist characterized him—quite rightly—as being "as quiet and dignified as he is voluble and gay. . . . In Hollywood, where it is better to be gay, Peter's the gayest of them all!—the life of every party." One woman even described him—quite sympathetically—"as a sweet little fellow with the sad look of a wounded raccoon." Lorre just wanted people to know he was quite normal:

> I am afraid that I must disappoint you. I know what you expected of me, what you hoped of me. . . . You would like me to tell you that I sleep in a darkened room, inhabited, perhaps, by bats and evil spirits, lit with a red lamp, the evil eye. You would like me to say that I am familiar with visitations from another world, that I spend my days and nights reading ancient tomes of old devils,

that I am drenched in the lives of murderers and mental criminals. No. I am sorry. I am afraid that I am a very normal, happy, wholesome individual, with no complexes.

Other émigré artists who had been brought over on the strength of their reputations discovered that admiration and accolades didn't always translate into steady work. After codirecting only one picture, the disastrous *A Midsummer Night's Dream* (1935), the legendary stage director Max Reinhardt opened an acting school and theater workshop. Stage and film actor and director Fritz Kortner traded the classics for small character roles, appearing in eight films in almost as many years before returning to Germany. Max Ophüls sat idle for six years before directing *Letter from an Unknown Woman* (1948). Fritz Lang, signed by David O. Selznick in 1934, passed more than a year without directing a feature film. His poor English, smart "Prussian" bearing, and monocle too easily recalled the arrogant and autocratic Erich von Stroheim, an independent producer and director who had been similarly chafed by the lack of creative control in Hollywood. During his idleness, he traveled extensively, even living with the Navajo Indians; devoured newspapers and comic strips, a common denominator of American life; and mingled with the man on the street, gauging the national character by taxi drivers, bartenders, and grease monkeys.

Lorre may well have wondered if the same fate awaited him. The hiatus generated deep concern about Columbia's intentions. Already Cohn had invited the actor to accept a featured part in one of the studio's Jack Holt melodramas. By his own telling, Lorre had said no in several languages. Frustrated with the studio's seemingly endless search for a suitable role, Lorre took matters in hand. His literary tastes inclined toward the Russian masters. Fyodor Dostoyevsky especially suited his aptitude for psychological investigation, for crawling inside a character and unmasking its motives. More than once he voiced interest in bringing *Crime and Punishment* and *Notes from the Underground* to the screen. MGM had built its reputation on prestige pictures such as *Mutiny on the Bounty* (1935), *Romeo and Juliet* (1936), and *The Good Earth* (1937). Lorre found this willingness to branch out, to experiment with the classics, a hopeful sign: "The boy, the girl, the villain—with a dash of this and a sprinkle of that—this old formula for the sure box office hit no longer is so sure. In fact several of the recent pictures made on the old pattern have been failures. This is why there are producers now who are seeking desperately for new formulae, and this is why they are willing to experiment with opera, with Shakespeare, with such stories as 'Crime and Punishment.'"

At the same time Lorre praised MGM, he took Hollywood to task for the censorship of ideas: "There's too great insistence, not only on films that won't corrupt the child-like mind, but also on films that won't strain it." He also berated "West Coast acting," which he found, in many cases, wasn't acting at all, but "a trick of personality, a histrionic gag."

Realizing that Harry Cohn would not be strong-armed into reading the Russian novel, he presented him with a two-page summary of the book that had been prepared by a secretary and slyly added, "You can have the rights for nothing." Lorre, who never missed a chance to mock the mogul, loved to tell the story of how he put over *Crime and Punishment* on Cohn, who supposedly exclaimed, "Has this story got a publisher yet? This would make a great suspense story." With time, the story got better, until it outgrew its own credibility: "As a matter of fact, Tolstoi was credited in most of the credit sheets. The publicity writers, who didn't know how to spell Dostoievski's name, just said, 'Oh, yes—it's by that Russian guy,' wrote 'Tolstoi' and let it go at that."

Lorre had the last laugh, but Cohn had the last word. Crediting the actor with "a rather Napoleonic understanding of tactics," the *New York Times* reported that Lorre knew how to "concede a minor position in order to execute a devastating flank attack." In order to recoup the studio's investment in the actor, who had been on the payroll for nearly a year, Cohn considered lending Lorre to MGM to star in *Mad Love* (1935), the story of a crazed surgeon who grafts a guillotined knife-murderer's hands onto the mutilated stumps of a concert pianist, based on Maurice Renard's *Les mains d'Orlac* (1920) and converted to celluloid in 1924 for Austria's Pan-Film by Robert Wiene, best-known for the expressionist classic *Das Kabinett des Dr. Caligari* (*The Cabinet of Dr. Caligari,* 1920). "I'll do the Metro picture," offered Lorre, "if you promise to make 'Crime and Punishment' and give me (Josef) von Sternberg as director." It was a masterful move. As the *New York Times* put it, "The Hungarian Napoleon had outsmarted the Hollywood Wellingtons."[13]

But he had not outflanked his Austrian creditor, Dr. Samek, who was becoming impatient with his habitual excuses, solicitations, and broken promises. When the attorney threatened to take legal action, the cracks began to show. "I can't give you a time when I can send money," pleaded Celia, "because I just don't know in or out." She explained that the studio spread Peter's twenty-week pay period over one-half year. Instead of earning $500 per week, he was actually making only $380. Worse yet, he brought home only $160 per week. The rest went for agents, insurance, and support of family and friends in Europe. Celia hoped they could send $100 per month and repay most of the loan by October, but she couldn't promise. She could only assure him that they would do everything in their power to square accounts. "It is hugely depressing," confided Celia, "that we have nothing for ourselves. We can't even put away a dollar for times of need or sickness." She hung all her hopes on his first American film: "It's a very big work on which everything depends."

The big work was, of course, *Mad Love*. Budgeted at $217,176.53 and scheduled for twenty-four shooting days, the picture began principal photography on May 6, 1935, under the direction of famed German cinematographer Karl Freund, who had compiled a list of impressive credits behind the camera during the 1920s, including *Der Golem* (1920), *Der letzte Mann* (*The Last Laugh*, 1924), and *Metropolis* (1926). His innovative moving-camera technique had opened the door to the dramatic possibilities of the new medium. In 1929 Freund immigrated to the United States, bringing his genius to Universal Pictures, where he further distinguished himself on Tod Browning's *Dracula* (1931) and Robert Florey's *Murders in the Rue Morgue* (1932), besides directing seven pictures—most notably *The Mummy* (1932)—for that studio between 1933 and 1935. In early 1935 the "great master" moved to MGM, which gave him license to "specialize in unusual themes." *Mad Love* marked the end of his directorial career and the renewal of his original vocation as cinematographer.[14]

For atmosphere, Freund looked to a past that he had helped to make, steeping *Mad Love* in German tradition rich in dark, brooding imagery. Before the picture even begins, the ominous shadow of Dr. Gogol (Peter Lorre) passes over the opening titles. Suddenly a fist draws back and knocks out the glass on which the credits are printed, setting the stage for what is to follow—a miscellany of sinister shadows, oblique angles, staircases, and reflections. After gently pulling his audience into a fantastically macabre Théâtre des Horreurs, past hideous masks, a hanging dummy, and a headless hat checker, Freund shows Dr. Gogol sitting alone in his box seat. A shadow vertically splits his moon face and gleaming bald head, masking one side of his divided psyche. Later, Gogol returns to his operating room, whose walls Freund had painted black and brown to heighten the fantastic shadowy effect. Attired in a surgical cap and mask, which letterbox Lorre's bulging eyes, the doctor tensely brushes his hand across his dripping forehead. Unable to continue, he pulls away the medical disguise and peers in the washroom mirror, which reflects the personification of his evil impulses.

Veteran horror scenarist John L. Balderston (*Dracula, Frankenstein, The Mummy*)—who shared screen credit with Guy Endore and P.J. Wolfson—took another page from the same book. Arriving late in the process, he continued writing three weeks into filming, polishing dialogue and tailoring the starring role to Lorre. Described as "a mixture of saint and devil, fiend and child," Gogol harks back—very loudly—to *M*. One moment the doctor comforts a lame girl whom he will make walk. The next, he witnesses a guillotining with sadistic satisfaction. Later in the script, the screenwriters, capping the point, instructed Freund and Lorre: "As he says these last two lines, and actually starts his strangling, his 'M' look, the ecstasy of the moment of murder, is on his face; his eyes protrude."

Lorre balanced the constraints of the script against the independence allowed him by Freund, who, according to costar Frances Drake, "couldn't leave the camera alone, which suited Peter very well."[15] Untethered from the director's control, he sought to inject elements that set Gogol apart from any character he or anyone else had ever played.

"I believe the low-spoken villain," explained the actor,

> who is absolutely blasé about what he does, who works out a murder like a mathematical problem, for instance, is a much more terrifying fellow than the human fellow who commits a murder in a fit of anger. That type of villain is really not a villain at all—only the fellow whose temper got the better of him, and more to be pitied than anything else. . . . But at the same time this fellow is kind and tender to little Cora Sue Collins. He only is dangerous to a person when there is a reason for it. He does not hate mankind. But he is willing to ruin anyone to gain his ends. If being dangerous to a person doesn't pay, he can be perfectly kind.

"Peter had definite ideas as to his character portrayal," confirmed co-worker Keye Luke. "He was careful that his character had a sense of reality and vitality." Where a gesture or look more economically expressed emotion, the actor scrapped dialogue. Likewise, when grease paint got in the way, he uncovered himself. "Make-up's an excuse for an inability to act," stated Lorre. "You can cheat people with a lot of make-up. An actor should find his expressions in his naked face. I would rather depend on facial expressions and the right shading of light to get the effect I desire, instead of resorting to the actual methods of disguise." He even took credit for shaving his head, explaining, "It gives the idea that this character thinks of his science only and not of personal appearance." These techniques, he allowed, didn't apply so well to actresses. "They must be their beautiful selves," said Lorre, "and lights and shadows do not beautify. But for the character player it is a perfect method."

Although Freund and Lorre reportedly spent a day observing surgery at the Lutheran Hospital, the actor researched his role from within. "I never look at a person with a view of using his characteristics in a role. I don't believe in imitation," he explained. "My trick is to imagine. I imagine I'm the character, figure out what it would do, and thus live the role in a way. It may sound foolish—it is a certain strain. Other actors may work differently but I find that in my case it's the best way to get what I want. I like to feel that I have really given the picture something, and don't feel that way unless I am completely absorbed in the character."[16]

Lorre credited his imagination with introducing a new kind of villainy to the cinema. However, he balanced that menace against a soft vulnerability that was more real than imagined. "Peter was a very complex man," said Drake, "who had a pathetic, sad quality about him. He wanted to meet me before his head was shaved so as not to scare me. My impression was that he was a very sensitive person, easily hurt."

Like so many of his female friends and co-workers, handwriting analyst Shirley Spencer also diagnosed this aspect of his personality in his penmanship, which offered "an explanation of his ability to assume characters so utterly different from his own." His signature reflected "his finesse, his subtle mind, his cleverness, and intriguing, unconventional imagination. . . . There is so much sympathy revealed in Mr. Lorre's writing that I wonder he can hide it at all. He is warm-hearted, ardent, quickly responsive, and has a great desire to help others."

Mad Love (subsequently retitled *The Hands of Orlac,* but previewed under its original title) opened at New York's Roxy Theatre on August 2. As a satirical homage to the horror film, it bit a little too hard, falling "right in the middle between Art and Box Office." Even by the horror-hyped standards of the day, the sexually frustrated Gogol, like Hans Beckert before him, struck a perverse chord. Public rejection of the "sick" picture, more horrible than horrific, registered at the box office, where it earned a domestic gross of only $170,000. Even with the better foreign earnings—it took in $194,000 abroad—MGM still lost $39,000. All the more reason for the studio to put *Mad Love* behind it.

Billed as the "Screen's Strangest Sensation," Lorre could not as easily forget his "first American production" in which he "triumphs superbly in a characterization that is sheer horror. That is the important thing. Unfortunately, the picture is neither important nor particularly compelling, but it should serve to build a new star for American pictures. . . . His face is his fortune . . . his subtle changes of expression make it a fortune to be conjured with in no mean terms."

The actor's sharp-edged delineation of aberrant behavior was a tour de force that critics could not ignore, regardless of their opinions of the film. "With any of our conventional maniacs in the role of the deranged surgeon, the photoplay would frequently be dancing on the edge of burlesque," wrote

Andre Sennwald in the *New York Times*. "But Mr. Lorre, with his gift for supplementing a remarkable physical appearance with his acute perception of the mechanics of insanity, cuts deeply into the darkness of the morbid brain. It is an affirmation of his talent that he always holds his audience to a strict and terrible belief in his madness. He is one of the few actors in the world, for example, who can scream: 'I have conquered science; why can't I conquer love?'—and not seem just a trifle silly."

It was to the actor's range that writer Graham Greene so eloquently spoke in an article titled "The Genius of Peter Lorre," which appeared in *World Film News,* July 1936:

> To Lorre alone we owed the goodness, the tenderness of the vicious man. Those marble pupils in the pasty spherical head are like the eye-pieces of a microscope through which you can watch the tangled mind laid flat on the slide: love and lust, nobility and perversity, hatred of itself and despair jumping out at you from the jelly. His very features are metaphysical. . . . He is an actor of great profundity in a superficial art. It will always be his fate to be cramped, not only by the shortcomings of directors, not only by the financiers with their commercial demands, but by the Board of Film Censors [which threatened to ban *Mad Love* in Britain]. The financiers are not interested in psychological truth, and the Board do [*sic*] not recognize morality.

Beyond crediting *Mad Love*'s "very good" photography and direction, Lorre failed to muster any kind of endorsement for the film. On the contrary, he told one interviewer he didn't think it a good picture and added that he did it only because he was tired of being idle. Asked if he enjoyed making it, the actor dissembled, "Well, that's a tough question. I enjoy being myself more than I was permitted to in that film. I made it while we were preparing the script for 'Crime and Punishment'—so my mind wasn't entirely free for it." Such reservations ran a distant second to the need for exposure. All he asked of his American debut was audience recognition. Unfortunately, the actor made too big a splash—and in the wrong pool. Overnight, he became one of the "horror boys" . . . "a one-man chamber of horrors" . . . "a pint-sized Boris Karloff." Metro's lurid ad campaign added insult to injury:

> A WOMAN'S LOVE WAS WHAT HE CRAVED . . . and could not have! To win her, he would stop at nothing this side of Hell! Not since Lon Chaney, has the screen seen a performance to top this for soul-shattering thrills! Brilliant Star of "M" and "THE MAN WHO KNEW TOO MUCH." Now . . . THE SENSATION that TOPS THEM ALL!

Phantom of the Opera, Hunchback of Notre Dame, Dracula, Frankenstein. To the great character creations of screen history . . . add the most amazing of them all! Peter Lorre, as the mysterious Dr. Gogol . . . feared by men . . . fascinating to women . . . achieves the acting triumph of years!

Silver Screen's Whitney Williams predicted that "this offering of terror will climax all horror films." Horror!—there was that word again. Lorre hated the sound of it. He took a strong stand, the first of many, and challenged Hollywood's definition. "The way I feel about it," he said, "is that the situation, not the acting, is what arouses the excitement and terror in a horror story. You can get the effect by means of inanimate objects just as well: a shadow on the wall, for example, or the sound of footsteps on a dark street. You could take my barber and put him in a horror story and, if the events were frightening enough, he would frighten the audience."[17]

Lorre disliked horror films and thought that the recent spate of pictures in that genre appealed to base instincts:

I hold no brief for the purely horrific film. I agree, with its critics, that its appeal is essentially evil. The average horror film from Hollywood is either absolutely obvious and silly, or else it appeals to the sadistic emotions of the audience by showing scenes of torture, whippings, etc. It is not only the horror film which does this. Certain films purporting to be historically accurate make it their business to stress licentiousness and cruelty. Something should be done to prevent film producers from deliberately setting out to appeal to base instincts by glorifying depravity. . . . There is all the difference in the world between a film which is uncanny and fascinating because the psychology of evil has been carefully studied; and the entirely worthless effort intended merely to bring shekels to the box-office. Although I condemn the latter, I do think that, just as there is room in literature for imaginative horror, so there is room for it in films.

But Lorre's war of semantics fell on deaf ears. As late as 1963, he still protested his association with horror movies: "How this image always remains I don't know, but it does remain. I have never played a single horror picture, as far as I can remember. I somehow got into that category, but it's actually psychological terror I used to play, or do play."[18]

Lorre likewise labeled himself a psychological actor who, paraphrased *Variety* interviewer Cecilia Ager, "gets his effects from within, intuitively—like an artist—not from scientific observation." His portrayals, he pointed out, were realistic, not fantastic; intellectual, not physical. Nor did he resort to cosmetics to simulate disfigurements, and held that actors coated in latex were no more than impressionists. Makeup, he reminded, should characterize, not scare.

In the realm of psychological terror, Lorre's tastes inclined toward Poe. "It is a shame that people know so little about Edgar Allan Poe," he lamented. "They all recognize his name, of course, but how many people today have read much of Poe? His achievements as a critic were great, and his sarcasm and wit are qualities of which few are aware." On the Producers Studio set, the actor halted production of *The Raven* for one minute of silence on October 7, 1962, in honor of Poe's death exactly 113 years earlier. "I cannot find any expression for my respect for the poor wretched life of that man," he said, "and what [we have] to thank him for." Lorre was especially grateful for "The Tell-Tale Heart," which crosscut his interest in psychoanalysis: "Poe never heard of psychoanalysis, or modern psychology, but he knew about it, just the same. The double symbolism of the 'eye' and the 'heart' in 'The Tell-Tale Heart' anticipated Freud by many years. You can find a 'scientific' explanation of that tale in Freud, but Poe was nearer the truth, because he knew that psychoanalysis is not, as Freud said, a 'nature study,' but an expression of the deepest secrets of the heart and mind."

Lorre talked of bringing the tale to the screen. He noted that Poe had portrayed a murderer who was "perfectly harmless and inoffensive" under normal circumstances. Said Lorre: "But he was not responsible for his highly strung personality, which snapped under the strain. It was because this young man was perfectly ordinary that the story became terrible. This is the sort of horror we should aim to show in the cinema. The only way I can describe it is to say it is psychological horror."[19]

Above all, Lorre wanted people to know that he did not want to become typed, as anything: "I am less complicated than anyone I know. My interests and instincts, I am afraid, are strictly normal, but I have always had, even as a child, a fanatical absorption into getting into people's character—in trying to unmask them and their motives. This, I suppose, is what has interested me so much in playing pathological roles, but has not, I want to say emphatically, circumscribed my ambitions, for I want to play all kinds of parts. I don't care whether it is tragedy or comedy if it is an authentic portrayal of life."

His words were swept away by the landslide of public opinion. "Lorre hopes that he will not become typed for horror roles," wrote Kate Cameron in the New York *Sunday News,* "but since he seems to possess an uncanny power for projecting horror, I'm afraid Hollywood will have little else for him to do." Lorre's plans to make his mark in a literary classic had backfired. The shrewd strategist had outsmarted himself. Hollywood was ready for him, but only on its terms; if it could not sell the actor, then it would market the image.

Mad Love had finished production on June 14. Lorre barely had time to grow out his hair before beginning work on *Crime and Punishment.* Already he had been sitting in with S.K. Lauren, who was working on the screenplay. Now, in the last week of June, he went into a script huddle with his director, Josef von Sternberg.

At that time, von Sternberg enjoyed the reputation of a temperamental artist-poet who painted his pictorial canvasses with broad strokes of light and shadow. "The screen was his medium," wrote Aeneas MacKenzie, "not the camera." Von Sternberg looked high and low for abstract human emotion; in gutters and palaces he found the spiritual power for his visual ideology. Many felt that von Sternberg had surrendered to self-indulgence in his Hollywood pictures with Marlene Dietrich and charged the "Leonardo of the Lenses" with wallowing in feminine mystique, drawing exotic—and erotic—fantasies from his own private dream world.

Von Sternberg also had earned a reputation as a vicious autocrat. In his mean-spirited and self-serving autobiography, *Fun in a Chinese Laundry,* he fed his image as a martinet—and a neglected genius. He possessed "an irresistible need to create and to carry alone the weight of his creation," wrote Jean de Baroncelli in *Le Monde.* When von Sternberg exercised creative control, he accepted full responsibility for the outcome. Similarly, he disowned anything he felt didn't carry his signature. He utterly repudiated *Crime and Punishment:*

> In this decelerating interval two films were made in the cart-before-the-horse system. . . . A novel by Dostoevski is to be transferred to the screen. This, to begin with, is a redoubtable assignment. At best it can be no more than a film about a detective and a criminal, no more related to the true text of the novel than the corner of Sunset Boulevard and Gower is related to the Russian environment. As mixed a collection of human beings as can be imagined is before me, members of a cast of players herded together by a Hollywood studio. Some are literate, some are not. Among those present are trained performers and those who have made the jump to the screen from the trampoline of a mattress. A few have been chosen for their skill in characterization; still others are there because they are under contract to the studio. . . . [None] have read the novel to be filmed, with the sole exception of Peter Lorre, who, though unsuitable for the part of Raskolnikov, has been contracted for it. . . . All values in a film must be predetermined, and when a director is called upon to

direct a story and players over which he has had no choice, his contribution can be only a routine one.

Von Sternberg introduced *Crime and Punishment* with a prologue, or, as some felt, a disclaimer:

> The time of our story is any time, the
> place anyplace where human hearts respond
> to love and hate, pity and terror.

The film opens on a college commencement. Two lines of students stand at attention, hands clenched behind their backs. One alone upsets the symmetry of the design. In shadowy silhouette stands Roderick Raskolnikov (the "celebrated European film star" Peter Lorre)—head bowed deferentially, arms at his side, his white hands piercing the somber lighting. Crude sets molder into gray translucent backgrounds, a touch of German gothic. The players sport no greatcoats, no pointed beards. This is not nineteenth-century St. Petersburg, but 1930s anywhere.

Film historians later asked themselves whether von Sternberg had answered an impersonal assignment with indifference or had merely attempted to live down his reputation as a mad genius and put his best professional foot forward. Had his genius gone dry, his personal vision blurred? His co-workers, and especially Lorre, didn't think so. Columbia had given von Sternberg free rein with the filming. No one interrupted him on the set. The subject interested him, he was reportedly delighted with the script, and he evinced profound respect for the abilities of Lorre and Edward Arnold, who played Inspector Porfiry. One interviewer watched him enthusiastically bob about the set acting as head gaffer and sitting on the camera dolly and watching every move as it was seen by the lens—while the cameraman stood beside him. Robert Allen, who played Raskolnikov's friend Dmitri, even recalled seeing von Sternberg touching up a crack in a stone wall with his paint brush. Contrary to his image as an insufferable megalomaniac, he impressed Allen as a gentle, low-key director who quietly monitored every detail of the filming: "We were called in several days before they started to shoot the picture, and we all sat around a big table and we read through the script for two days. And if you threw in an extra 'but' or an 'and,' or a handle to get you into the dialogue, von Sternberg went, 'No, that is not in the script. We're sticking to it. We're not changing a word.'"

Filming began in fall of 1935. Von Sternberg stayed ahead of schedule, despite taking time to get it right. "Oh, yes, he rehearsed more and he shot more film," said Marian Marsh, who played Sonya. "We'd do the same thing over and over again. It was nothing to do it twenty times. . . . He changed the lights and the lighting. He changed all kinds of things, had you come in a different way and by a different entrance. He tried many, many things."

Von Sternberg found his biggest supporter in Lorre, who praised the director for his fluid and straightforward storytelling, free of heavy Russian despair: "For the first time in a long while he had a script to work with, a story good enough and important enough to interest him, to keep his attention focused upon the core of the screen instead of letting it get preoccupied with the composition and decoration of its outer edges." Lorre added that "he takes more pains with players than any man I have ever worked with, and he takes the camera over completely. If the picture is a success, he will deserve nine-tenths of the credit."

Nine years later, Lorre picked up where he had left off in a column titled, "The Role I Liked Best . . ." for the *Saturday Evening Post*: "It was a stark, honest part and, happily, most of its honesty was preserved in the film. Not a single extra was used in the picture because director Josef von Sternberg wanted to eliminate everything that might possibly distract the audience from the story itself. For the same reason, no exotic settings or costumes were used. Unfortunately, this very interesting film technique was so smoothly successful that it was practically unnoticed."

Lorre felt lucky to be playing Raskolnikov. He knew he fell far short of the physical requirements of the role. After all, Dostoyevsky had described his protagonist as "exceptionally handsome, above the average in height, slim, well-built, with beautiful dark eyes and dark brown hair." Marsh, who met the actor in von Sternberg's office on the Columbia lot, took exception to Lorre's image of himself:

He was attractive. His eyes were so expressive. And he was so well-mannered. He had that European politeness, in which he greeted you with a little bit of a bow and looked you right in the eye. It was not just a casual, "Oh, hello, glad to meet you" sort of thing. It was a little ceremony. . . . And he turned to von Sternberg and said, "I really have told you before I don't think I'm handsome enough for the part. Why should she love me that much?" I was amused by that and said, "I find you most attractive, Mr. Lorre." And so we were good friends right away.

On the face of it, Lorre and von Sternberg were also good friends. "Everybody warned me about him before we started the picture," the actor told an interviewer shortly after completing production, "but I found him helpful and sincere." Soon after arriving in Hollywood, the actor had suffered another internal hemorrhage and had been put on Dilaudid. Tests performed by Dr. Joel Pressman revealed that he was not suffering from pulmonary tuberculosis, earlier thought to explain his coughing blood, but from bronchiectasis, a disorder of the large bronchi, often caused by a severe respiratory infection in childhood. Working back to back in *Mad Love, Crime and Punishment,* and *Secret Agent,* Lorre explained, had put him under great strain. He fatigued easily. In order to keep going, he resorted to drugs.[20] Von Sternberg answered Lorre's need for rest with either close-up work or an invitation for the actor to retire to his dressing room.

Behind the scenes, however, the actor walked on eggshells. In his autobiography, *Lorenzo Goes to Hollywood,* Edward Arnold recalled arriving on set after working on retakes at another studio; he now began to grow drowsy. "Joe looked like a thunder-cloud all through the scene," recalled Arnold. Afterward, he asked a script girl what was wrong. "'You yawned in his face,'" she replied. "I laughed, and said, 'Oh, tell him to go to——.' So I was on the warpath once more. Peter Lorre, who was playing the criminal I was tracking down, met me a few minutes afterwards, and inquired rather naively, it seemed to me, 'Did you tell von Sternberg you were sorry?' 'No,' I replied, 'why should I? It was nothing personal. I am dead tired. I worked all last night at the Universal Studio.' 'Well, if you don't do something about it,' insisted Lorre, 'he'll take it out on the rest of us.'"

Described by Arnold as a "RAPER OF EGOS . . . [who] crushes the individuality of those he directs in pictures," von Sternberg contended that "an actor is chosen for his fitness to externalize an idea of mine, not an idea of his." Marsh remembered that

> Peter tried to do it the way von Sternberg wanted it done, but somehow his own way would creep into it. Von Sternberg wanted you to do it his way, but he wanted it to be you at the same time. He didn't want you to be just a puppet. He wanted your own feelings. . . . When Peter would do a scene and do it so well, he never thought it was good enough. He really wanted to be exactly right, to do it von Sternberg's way. But I know that von Sternberg liked what he did. He'd say, "Don't worry, it's different."

For twenty-eight days of filming—a record time for von Sternberg—Lorre lived the role, on-set only, as he was quick to point out. "You see," he told a reporter, "to be an actor is to understand quite thoroughly what the individual you portray is like—how he thinks, what his daily habits are, and why he does the things he does." Looking back, he noted, "When I am studying a part and working out its shades and nuances, I become so absorbed that I'm in a fever pitch." This was true behind the camera as well, according to Celia, who told a reporter that when Peter is working, "he is overwrought. He doesn't sleep well. He dreams constantly of his role. He is not like himself, but seems moody and has little conversation with me or any one else. These roles seem to take a great deal out of him. We make no social engagements whatever while he is working." A visitor to the set confirmed that the actor appeared tense and nervous.[21] Co-workers likewise found him introverted and very quiet. According to Catharine Lorre, her father "more readily identified with strongly emotional characters. He would reach a boiling point, which was as close as possible to an actual physical breakdown." Marsh recalled that "Peter was really very into it, really being that person, the illusion of the character. We'd get into a scene and read through and get the words right before walking through it. Then something would come over both of us. A few times I remember him looking at me and saying, 'Do you feel it? Do you feel something?' And I'd say, 'Yes, I feel it.' We just had an understanding. It was comfortable. . . . I don't think Peter ever really planned what he was going to do until he got into it, but there was a lot of thinking in back of it."

Lorre drew greater attention for his effort than for his achievement: "Lorre plays . . . with dazzling force and finish"; "Lorre bares the soul of the tormented homicide with brilliant flashes of histrionics"; "Lorre keeps it on a high level"; "Mr. Lorre provides a performance . . . [that] can be placed among Hollywood's greatest thespic efforts." Audiences and reviewers alike, who took their literature with a little levity, also applauded the actor's sardonic sense of humor, if anything so heavy-handed as pounding Lushin's hat flat with his fist falls under that heading. "It was a cheap little piece of comic relief," wrote Graham Greene, "but Lorre got from it every possible laugh."

Nonetheless, the weight of critical opinion fell heavily against him. Critics faulted his portrayal as hectic, hysterical, disconnected, unmotivated, roughhewn, erratic, and unconvincing. "He has no more psychological continuity than a marionette dancing on a stick," wrote Andre Sennwald. "His behavior is a series of unrelated and meaningless moods which tell us nothing of what is going on inside of him. The drama, in brief, has been completely externalized so as to make a pattern for a detective story."

Joseph Alsop Jr., writing in the *New York Herald-Tribune,* noted "frequent gleams of the old Lorre in his performance" and pointed out that "occasionally he takes the bit between his teeth and starts to gallop along in his old form." However, he concluded that "Mr. Lorre has offered his customers the same old stuff, and plenty of it. His performance is an unearthly blend of 'M,' and his work in 'The Man Who Knew Too Much' . . . Mr. Lorre's trouble may be that Hollywood has just a trace of the Upas tree about it. The place has a savage habit of killing actors, and then making them into profitable zombies."

Others accused him of making Raskolnikov just another blood-stained psychopath. Edwin Blum, a scenario editor for producer Lester Cowan, "thought Lorre was miscast as Raskolnikov—and in fact threw the whole picture out of whack. The reason? Raskolnikov was a classic intellectual murderer and not in the least psychotic—whereas Lorre was the very archetype of the psychotic murderer. . . . So in this sense, Dostoievksi, who was studying the Nietzschean rationality in Raskolnikov, was betrayed not only by von Sternberg (who was too dense to grasp anything), but by Peter Lorre, who in his nature and performance set forth the responsive psychotic state to the Hitlerian aggressive psychotic state. One could, in fact, conceive of Lorre—as a rather demented lesser underling, a clerk, perhaps—turning and stabbing Hitler in the heart as he passed by—and saying he didn't do anything."

Even his old friend Franz Theodor Csokor, who found Lorre a quiet, sad man of "Dostoievskian dimension," hoped that "nobody stamps him to a type that doesn't reach above a mask."

An article titled "Lorre in New Horror Role" stung the actor. Clearly on the defensive, he told the press that *Crime and Punishment* "is by no means a 'horror' film, but great tragedy." Raskolnikov is "a comparatively normal person," he emphasized. "He does not kill because of an inner compunction [*sic*], like 'M,' but from force of circumstance. What happened to him might happen to anyone. He is a subject for psychologists, but not for pathologists."

Lorre had struggled to squeeze some meaning between his lines, seesawing between the possibilities of intuition and intellect. He enacted the cool, arrogant Raskolnikov at a Brechtian distance with simple direct gestures and studied and stylized yells, scowls, and poses. At the same time, he submerged himself in the sensitive and suffering student. In a scene charged with psychological agonizing, Raskolnikov retreats to his shabby apartment, slams the door, and throws a temperamental fit. Anger and confusion struggle for the upper hand. "MONEY! MONEY! MONEY!" he screams as he sweeps the books from his table and then collapses. Lorre also delved inside himself for the final scene, finding, as one reviewer wrote, a "childlike martyr, radiant in redemption." But Lorre was spinning his wheels. No transitions bridge the duality of Raskolnikov's personality, prompting one contemporary reviewer to complain that the actor was "baleful and spineless by turns." Spanning the psychological rifts in the story was impossible. Blocked by the script, Lorre's performance is lost and labored, searching for a center where there is none. Little wonder that on the bill with *Crime and Punishment* was the Columbia comedy short subject, *Oh My Nerves.*

Unwilling to swim upstream against the edifying current of classic literature, most reviewers shuffled about for some suitable—and superficial—stock phrases to voice their approval of the new trend toward fiction into film: "Classic Crime Film," "Absorbing Mental Study," "Powerful Drama," "Enthralling Picture of Dostoievsky Classic." The few who had read the book understood just how far *Crime and Punishment* fell short of the original work. Stripped of substance—Raskolnikov's careful preparation of the crime, his subsequent feelings of loneliness and estrangement, his "extraordinary man" theories, the recurring motif of confession—it became "just a good detective story," as von Sternberg himself had predicted during filming.

In response to a letter accusing film producers of "butchering" famous novels, Britain's *Film Weekly,* in the interest of a frank and open discussion of the question, invited contributions from screenwriters. Joseph Anthony and S.K. Lauren, who coscripted the film, answered "the increasingly common complaint" in an essay titled "Novel into Film." In their own defense, they stated their good intentions of rendering "as accurately and as consistently as possible the creations of Dostoievsky's mind," yet admitted that "small deviations from the book" may be brought up against them. Getting the psychology of the character absolutely right, retaining the dramatic value of the soliloquies, and scrupulously selecting dialogue from the novel, argued the screenwriters, weighed heavily in their favor. After all, reducing some two hundred thousand words to ninety minutes of film was a daunting task. The greatest difficulty, however, lay in adapting the well-known personalities of the principal players to the characters in the book. "As scenario writers," wrote Lauren and Anthony, "we could not allow ourselves to submerge completely the valuable and well-known personalities of Lorre, Arnold and Marsh." Recycling some of the "same old stuff" had been part of the plan to effect a "character compromise."

Coming some four months after the November 26 release, however, their exposition sounded warmed-over, a case of too little, too late. The verdict was in and it was not good. "Peter Lorre is beaten before he begins," wrote Andre Sennwald in the *New York Times,* "and can offer nothing, except in individual scenes. . . . Having a vast regard for Mr. Lorre's talents, I refuse to charge him with failure to create a full-length portrait of a character who is psychologically meaningless in the very writing of the American script." Another reviewer praised von Sternberg for allowing Lorre to tell the story through facial expressions instead of dialogue. Nonetheless, by reducing the psychological drama to visuals, he left the actor holding an empty bag.

Moderating the extremes of critical opinion, Sennwald granted that "within the limits permitted him by an indecisive script, Mr. Lorre gives a fascinating performance, revealing once again his faculty for blending repulsion and sympathy in the figure he projects to his audience." In his scrapbook, the actor kept a German review that set his performance apart from the film: "Now Lorre has reached the climax of ability. He has a touching human power, something demonic; one can feel it in his humor and he is equipped with the rare ability to say the unspeakable with the sparest means of expression."

Crime and Punishment suffered by comparison with *Crime et châtiment,* a vastly superior French film version of the novel that opened in New York one week ahead of the American production. "The difference between the French and the American screen versions of 'Crime and Punishment,'" wrote Sennwald, "is the difference between Dostoevsky and a competent wood pulp fictioneer." Against the dark, grimly realistic *Crime et châtiment, Crime and Punishment* appeared vulgar and hollowly optimistic. Critics praised the gaunt and hypersensitive Pierre Blanchar's beautifully fluid and mannered movements. Even Lorre confessed to friends that *Crime et châtiment* was altogether a better film. Despite the disagreements in film circles, no one denied that the two pictures canceled each other at the box office.

Lorre felt there must be some higher motive for moviemaking than box-office receipts: "There are many actors who consider pictures merely as an easy way to make big money. Acting, if money is its only object, is a childish, undignified work." The actor believed that life's struggle had qualified him to play Raskolnikov. Like Dostoyevsky's character, he had kept company with a guilty conscience. And like Dostoyevsky, he had kept faith with the idea that through suffering came understanding. Chemical dependency had sent him on an odyssey in search of himself. Lorre tried to come to grips with his drug problem through psychoanalysis, "though he never had any formal knowledge on the subject," said noted psychoanalyst Dr. Ralph Greenson, whose thirty-year friendship with Lorre fed a profound understanding of his dreams and demons.[22]

> Peter was uneducated, yet he was an intellectual who had a marvelous intuitive grasp. Intuition—this is how Peter felt—empathy, psycho-mindedness, and rigorous intelligence. He analyzed himself because one, he wanted to help himself. He didn't want to be put in the position of a patient. And two, he didn't believe that enough was known to help him. He believed that no one

could help him. He never could abide anything orthodox and made fun of all psychoanalysts. Peter was hostile to Freud early in his life. Freud seemed to have the answers and Peter couldn't abide anybody that knew the answers.

Lorre's quest for self-understanding put him in touch with himself and the characters he played on screen. The actor felt that by helping himself, he was helping others. "There is great satisfaction," he said, "in the thought that you may be helping people to understand their fellow men, even if these be monsters such as I played in 'M.' And people did understand that poor creature—at least thousands and thousands who wrote to me said they felt a certain amount of pity for the man who suffered himself as he became the victim of his pathological abnormalities."

With Brecht six thousand miles away and his chemical addiction as close as his own shadow, little wonder that psychology informed his acting style. "An actor, to be good, *must* be a psychologist," declared Lorre. "He must outstrip the professional psychologists, who concern themselves only with a few phases of a subject's mind. An actor must be a *hundred percent psychologist*— for he takes his character apart and reconstructs ALL his emotions. Then he takes those emotions into himself, becomes that character, be the character mad or not." Sounding more like a disciple of Stanislavski—though he scorned "method" acting—than a student of Brecht, Lorre stated that the "actor must be the character, utterly." Lorre repeatedly compared acting to an addiction: "Acting is like a drug and I'm an incurable addict." He admitted that it was "the only thing I am really serious about. I'd get sick if I didn't act. I need it for my nerves, just as others need stimulants."

Through the lyrics of facial expression, Lorre invited his audience to enter into the lives of the characters he portrayed on screen. To Lorre, the face "was an entrance way to some human being," said Greenson. "It was the face that let you into the soul." Corinne Calvet, a co-worker on *Rope of Sand* (1949), observed that "Peter Lorre's mind was like a puppeteer, controlling the strings that pulled each of his facial muscles individually, setting the perfect expression for his role." Lorre's eyes told most of the story. Wide-eyed glances, minatory gazes, and baleful looks gave him, in one writer's words, "the appearance of a Buddha contemplating the mysteries and miseries of the human soul." Writers described them as bulging, protruding, globular, and poached.[23] Writer and producer Hal Kanter said they were "very far apart, like a hammerhead shark." One day, explained Kanter, he and Lorre dropped by the Key Club across the street from NBC on Sunset and Vine for a loosening libation after rehearsals for *The George Gobel Show*. While sitting at its horseshoe bar, they looked in the mirror and noticed a man glance up and down.

"There's a guy to my right," said Peter, "who wants to engage me in a stare-down and make me blink. Wherever I go, people try to do that to me, like a gunfighter who goes into a small town. You watch this guy. I'm going to turn and look at him and I guarantee you he's going to blink first." Suddenly he turned and engaged this guy's eyes and stared at him. It took about twenty seconds and the guy got up and left. Peter said the secret is that no one can stare him down because his eyes are so far apart.

"I defy you to look into both of my eyes at once. You can't do it. Now when I worked with actors that I liked—Bogie was a prime example—I taught him how to act with me: 'Just pick one eye and look at it. The camera will never know the difference.'"

If Lorre looked like a tadpole, he behaved like a chameleon, able to adjust himself to any director's style, whether expressionist, epic, or method. While speaking a gestic language in *Mann ist Mann* for Brecht, he had crawled under the skin of a child murderer in Fritz Lang's *M*. He was, in a word, adaptable. In America, his "psycho-minded" acting methods, which showed not only the influence of Jacob Moreno, but also the stimulus of his inner demons, had crystallized almost overnight. Fortunately for the actor, he made his first two appearances in literary properties—*Les mains d'Orlac*, a French novel, and *Crime and Punishment*, a Russian classic—that had a built-in tolerance for traditional acting styles. Lorre seemed at times stiff and mannered in his early American outings, but as the past receded and he became more comfortable with his new home, his outlook relaxed and his acting became more spontaneous.

Others were not so lucky. Many émigré actors carried their European backgrounds in their voices and gestures, like so much cultural baggage. "Closely obliged to their spiritual origins," they felt the need to preserve the past. Breaking with tradition became one of the most difficult steps in the integration process. What they failed to understand was that in America, acting was as much an attitude as an art. Lorre's theatrical training and experience had been more avant-garde than classical, allowing him a flexibility denied others. He had never developed the histrionic flair and overprojection of silent film actors. A perceived staginess stigmatized European actors and, rightly or wrongly, relegated prominent actors—Fritz Kortner, Alexander Granach, Curt Bois—to minor roles. Having "an inborn gift for the naturalistic style, an inexhaustible imagination for the details of modern life," American actors behaved informally, independently, and freely, all qualities that encouraged Lorre to steer his own course.[24]

By the time Lorre had the opportunity to assess critical reaction to his performance in *Crime and Punishment,* he was no longer in the country, having left for London three weeks prior to the film's release. In April Michael Balcon had signed him for the role of the "Hairless Mexican" in Alfred Hitchcock's *Secret Agent* (1936). Even before von Sternberg had finished his rough cut and shot retakes, Balcon was cabling and telephoning Harry Cohn daily for a clearance decision on the actor. Unless Lorre arrived at Gaumont-British within the week, threatened Balcon, he would recast Conrad Veidt in the role of the tittering assassin.

The Lorres, along with Billy Wilder, who planned to visit his mother in Vienna, climbed aboard the *Santa Fe Chief* on October 21. Wilder looked forward to an evening repast, a pleasant reunion. "That was the plan," he recalled. But the next morning a sharp rap on his compartment door woke him.

> It was Celia Lovsky, and she seemed very agitated.
>
> "What is it?" I asked.
>
> "Peter is in trouble. He's taking a medicine and we need help right away because he is in very bad shape." Whatever the medicine was in—she didn't describe it to me—had broken.
>
> "Well, have you got the prescription?"
>
> She gave it to me and I went to the conductor and I told him to radio to the next stop. And I told him there was a very sick man and he needs this medicine. Then I went back to the compartment and Celia was trying to calm Peter down, hold him down. He was in excruciating pain and absolutely suicidal. If he would have been able to open the window, he would have thrown himself out of the train, so we pacified him. Now the train is slowing down and I go out and it stops and there is a man. I instantly recognize by the little satchel in his hand and his straw hat that this must be the doctor. So I identify myself.
>
> "Let's go," I said, "because we only are stopping here for five minutes. Did you bring the medicine?"
>
> "I did not bring the medicine," said the doctor, "and I cannot help this man because the prescription is for morphine."
>
> I begged and pleaded, but he said that he absolutely could not do it. The train started again, and again we had to calm down Peter and it was not an easy task. He was just like a mad man. Then Cilly and I decided to send a wire to the next stop, which was Albuquerque, to have an ambulance ready for

him. There indeed was an ambulance. And there were two nurses and a doctor. It was a Catholic Hospital [St. Joseph's] and we got him off the train with Cilly and their luggage. And I went on because I knew this man needed hospital attention.

"Well," I said, "I've lost my chums and I've got to go alone."

Now we dissolve and I'm on the boat, and lo and behold there's Celia and Peter.

"How is this?"

"I'm absolutely marvelous," said Peter, "just fine. Those were wonderful people there in that hospital. In fact, I think I've got enough medicine to get me to Europe."

Peter had been provisioned by the nuns at the hospital. Naturally, he charmed them all. He gave me the long story about his operation and why he needed the morphine. . . . So, we were on the *Berengaria* and he was in high spirits, winging it, innocently.[25]

By the time Lorre arrived in Southampton on November 1, *Secret Agent* was well under way at Shepherd's Bush. Montagu had met the actor when the ship made an interim stop at Cherbourg, France, and briefed him on the story and his role in it. He and Hitchcock had been assigned by Gaumont-British to make a film from Somerset Maugham's Ashenden stories, based on the author's own experiences as an agent of the British Intelligence Division of the army in World War I.[26] They chose to develop "The Hairless Mexican" and considered Lorre ideal for the name part. Maugham's "hairless Mexican" is just that, hairless and Mexican. However, in the film he is called that "chiefly because he's got a lot of curly hair and isn't a Mexican." Lorre was glad he would not have to make the supreme tonsorial sacrifice twice in six months. "In any case," he said, "the hairless Mexican is the name of a dog in America—a nasty, naked looking little animal." The makeup man joined the train at Southampton and curled the actor's hair.

Deeply grateful to Balcon, Montagu, and Hitchcock for launching his career in the English-speaking world, Lorre was anxious to show his appreciation. He especially enjoyed the sense of continuity at Gaumont-British, where he would work with the same unit that had made *The Man Who Knew Too Much*, from the director to the electricians.

In *Secret Agent*, Richard Ashenden (John Gielgud) is charged with the mission of preventing a German agent from reaching the Middle East and enlisting Arab support in World War I. Finding no glory in sanctioned murder, he is fraught with moral doubt about killing in cold blood. Elsa (Madeleine

Carroll) has been assigned by British Intelligence to pose as Ashenden's wife, a role she plays with stereotypical vacuity. They are assisted by the General (Lorre), a professional assassin to whom murder is child's play. Sporting oiled locks, gold earring, wing collar, king-size carnation, and capacious checked overcoat, he splits the difference between pantaloon and pander, with heavily accented pidgin English to round out the paradox. Both cherub and imp, he impulsively plots assassination one moment and scuttles after his companions like a lost waif the next.

"When we wanted for 'Secret Agent' a potential murderer," said associate producer Ivor Montagu, "engaged by a British spy to kill a suspected German spy (and finally killing the wrong man by mistake) in Switzerland during the First World War, a very difficult part, we all (Hitch and I especially, Balcon too) wanted Peter. Because we had got on with him so well and knew what he could do." Hitchcock put Lorre's "extremely deceptive" screen personality to use. Knowing that humor made his menace more powerful—and ambiguous—the director and his screenwriter Charles Bennett wittingly built on the legacy of sexual pathology in M and The Man Who Knew Too Much.

Hitchcock introduces the General as a notorious womanizer pursuing a young girl from a cellar during an air raid. "I'd rather be upstairs with the bombs than downstairs with some people," she squeals.

"A lady killer, huh?" queries Ashenden.

"Not just ladies," answers R (Charles Carson), his boss.

The General is beguiled by Elsa, "beautiful woman—lady—girl!" Infuriated that Ashenden and not he has been assigned a wife as part of his cover, the General rampages through the bathroom. Only after he has pawed wildly at a roll of toilet paper, mussed his hair, wrenched his tie, and swept the shelves of bottles does his tantrum subside. He is a whimpering child once again. Later, the realization that Elsa is not married to Ashenden renews his hope that "maybe affections of beautiful lady are free for me? Completely free?"

Ashenden and the General discover that their Swiss contact has been strangled in a church. The corpse's hands rest on the organ keyboard, producing an eerie drone. Initially impressed by the job, the artful assassin offers a professional critique with an innocent smile: "Nice work! Very neat!" However, after finding a button from the murderer's coat in the victim's hand, he recants: "Not so neat after all. . . . Me better, much better." Throughout the scene, he plays with his knife as if it were a toy, like a youngster who has no conception of good or evil.

They locate their target. Delighted, the General mimes the cutting of a throat. When Ashenden declines to participate, he eagerly takes over. Later

Ashenden and Elsa sit soberly at a village celebration, while the General teases a buxom native girl, tossing a chocolate croquette down her décolletage. (In the script, she "waves a comically deprecating finger at him . . . he offers to get it out for her, but she shakes her head as she inserts her fingers to retrieve the chocolate.") News that the agents have assassinated the wrong man numbs Ashenden and Elsa, but for the cackling General, the mistake is a great joke. In a later scene, a sharply focused Ashenden grapples with clear moral issues. Behind him looms the murky image of the General, who is unburdened by his conscience.

Bound for Constantinople on the Orient Express, Ashenden, Elsa, the General, and Marvin (Robert Young), the enemy agent, confront each other only minutes before the troop-filled train on which they are traveling is derailed in a bomb attack. Trapped beneath the wreckage, the mortally wounded German agent pleads for a drink of water. Incautiously, the General puts down his pistol, reaches into his coat pocket to retrieve a flask, and is shot in the back by the dying spy.

The shooting script of *Secret Agent* contained alternative endings. In the first, the General responds to Marvin's cry for water with a flask of brandy and then with a grin shoots the entrapped spy in cold blood. Grabbing the flask off the floor before it runs out, he wipes the mouthpiece and offers it to Ashenden and Elsa, adding, "This job take much long time, my friends, maybe perhaps I am getting old." They both turn away "shudderingly," and the General, "with a show of nonchalance, proceeds to drink the brandy himself." The picture fades out. In the second, the General aims his pistol at Marvin, but the spy dies before he can shoot him. On this note Ashenden cries, "He's beaten you—thank Christ, he's beaten you!" as Elsa breaks down, sobbing, into his arms.

According to the press, the British Board of Film Censors refused to allow the General to murder Marvin in cold blood.[27] But Balcon, Montagu, and Hitchcock did not recall any problems with the scene. Montagu maintained that "Mich [Michael Balcon] would never have liked to be so rough as the first ending (which shows Peter grab the falling flask after the shot Young has dropped it, and drink from it himself). We probably shot both and however much we may have preferred it realized it wouldn't do for GB. . . . I do not think the censor ever saw the first 'rougher' alternative."

During shooting, it also occurred to Montagu to make the train crash more realistic. He asked Len Lye to hand-paint the trade-show copy of the film, so that

> at the moment of the crash, chaos resulted on the screen, sprocket holes flashed
> about and then tongues of red and yellow (hand-painted fire), then darkness

a moment, before the scene resumed with various characters dead or alive amidst the wreckage. Hitch was a bit reluctant at first, but in the end, when we got it ready and viewed our handiwork in the projection theatre we had an instant triumph—too much of a triumph, because the projectionist instantly stopped projecting and when he'd examined the film and found out what we'd done he came down out of his box into the theatre and threatened to break both our heads. There was a bit of a barney afterwards. I wanted to keep it in and at least see how it went at the trade show. Mich hesitated. Eventually at the eleventh hour, Mui Diche, in charge of negative cutting and lab work etc. prevailed on Mich to order it taken out. Neither trade show nor censor, nor anyone else ever saw it, except ourselves.

Although "this part [the General] was much more important and unusual," said Montagu, "Peter interpreted it excellently. No acting problems or disappointments—Hitch, I and he understood each other easily and there were no directing or acting problems between us."

Memory failed the associate producer: there was one problem—Lorre's drug addiction. "That Lorre needed his shots, there was no doubt," recalled studio manager John Croydon, who had the unenviable job of keeping a lid on the actor's addiction. Negative publicity would have tarnished the studio's image. Hugh Finlay, publicity chief at "the Bush," was assigned the task of handling car transport at the end of the day's shooting, when he smuggled Lorre to and from a Harley Street specialist for injections of morphine. Croydon believed that the production high flyers never caught on, although the unit knew of the frequent trips.

Lorre was up to mischief behind the scenes as well. Each day the makeup man sat him down, tinted his skin with grease, and curled his hair into tight ringlets. Getting the actor to sit still for the primping was often a lost cause. Lorre just disappeared and wound his way through the sets or ran off to hide in the studio attics. Just as suddenly he reappeared, late but ready to take up the business at hand.

Hitchcock, who thought John Gielgud a bit of a "Shakespearean highbrow," took a vicarious pleasure in Lorre's misdeeds behind the camera. In rehearsals the actor was very nice to Gielgud, saying he reminded him of Gustaf Gründgens, who had played Schränker, head of the underworld, in *M*.[28] He spoke his lines as written and kept to his marks on the floor. Then the camera rolled. Lorre put in odd lines and positioned himself so that the camera would favor him, stealing the scene. Gielgud had seen this done on stage, but new to filmmaking, he did not know it could be done on a movie set. He stood helplessly by, fascinated but a little chafed, since his own role had been cut down by Hitchcock to divide interest between Lorre's and Young's roles. Lorre's pranks lengthened the already long shooting days. Close to five o'clock every afternoon, Gielgud grew anxious about getting away in time to the New Theatre, where he was directing *Romeo and Juliet* and alternating the roles of Romeo and Mercutio with Laurence Olivier. Hitchcock often urged him to stay for just one more shot. A good sport, Gielgud chalked up the minor irritations to experience, leaving a memorably pleasant recollection of his work with Hitchcock and Lorre.

Eventually, however, Lorre's antics wore thin. One day the actor came onto the set wearing an intricately woven waistcoat of many colors, of which he was obviously proud. "He displayed it to Hitch," recalled Croydon, "who was standing with a cup of coffee in hand and made no bones about his opinion—just uptilted the coffee over the waistcoat. Lorre's reaction was curious. He was taken aback, for a moment did not react and then merely adopted that furrowed forehead and pained expression in the eyes, turned on his heel and left the set!"

In his article for *Film Weekly* titled "My Spies," Hitchcock discussed every major and minor player in *Secret Agent*—except Lorre, whom he conspicuously did not mention.[29] Years later, Montagu shot down reports in the Hollywood trades of a third picture: "Sheer rubbish. . . . Hitch would not at that time dream of engaging him again. Beyond saying cryptically that the circumstances were less for Peter's fault than ours I shall say no more."[30]

Critics reacted less enthusiastically to *Secret Agent* than to either Hitchcock's *Thirty-Nine Steps* or *The Man Who Knew Too Much*, charging excessive dialogue, a faulty sense of continuity, and a heavy-handed treatment of the romance. Even Hitchcock felt that the picture was static, the natural by-product of a story whose hero had a negative purpose.

Mexican audiences took special exception to the "hairless Mexican." *Secret Agent* was passed with deletions by the original Mexican censor and ran two weeks at the Teatro Rex in Mexico City. However, when protesters almost burned down a second-run house, the Department of the Interior censor withdrew the film from exhibition.[31]

To the actors went the accolades. Once again, in an important and unusual role, Lorre fared better than the film itself. Hitchcock gave him much to say, and he said it in spoken and unspoken ways. The comic aspect of his characterization, wrote Hitchcock, had in it "something of Lorre's humorous personality as his friends know it," both heightening tension to a nerve-wracking pitch and underlining the political implications of placing loaded guns—and knives—in the hands of mischievous children to whom right and wrong is an expedient rather than a moral choice.

As "rather a jolly little fellow with a sense of humour and a deep appreciation of murder as a fine art," Lorre struck Britain's *Film Weekly* as "Sinister— But with a Difference." *New York Times* film critic B.R. Crisler did not fail to note that Lorre "plays one of the most amusing and somehow one of the most wistfully appealing trigger men since Victor Moore; a homicidal virtuoso, a student of the theory as well as the practice of garroting and throat-slitting, repulsively curly and Oriental in make-up."

No reviewer sang his praises louder or more eloquently than the *New Republic*'s Otis Ferguson:

> He is one of the true characters of the theatre, having mastered loose oddities and disfigurements until the total is a style, childlike, beautiful, unfathomably wicked, always hinting at things it would not be good to know.
>
> His style is most happily luminous in the intense focus and supple motion of movie cameras, for the keynote of any scene can be made visual through him. In close-ups, it is through the subtle shifts of eyes, scalp, mouth lines, the intricate relations of head to shoulders and shoulders to body. In medium-shots of groups, it is through his entire motion as a sort of supreme punctuation mark and underlineation. A harmless statement is thrown off in a low voice, and it is felt like the cut of a razor in Lorre, immediately in motion— the eyes in the head and the head on his shoulders and that breathless caged walk raising a period to double exclamation points. Or the wrong question is asked, and the whole figure freezes, dead stop, and then the eventual flowering of false warmth, the ice within it.

In the endpaper of Celia's diary, Lorre had written, "Dear Untier, for 1936, the memorable year in which the fairylike rise of the owl begins," and signed it with a sketch of an owl. Peter and Celia now called Santa Monica home. They needed only to formalize their two-year romance with America. On January 10, 1936, the Lorres declared their intention of residing permanently in the United States and applied for "Quota" immigration visas at the American Consular Service in London.[32]

By the end of the month, however, Lorre found himself in a Wellbeck nursing home, once again pursuing a fast cure for his addiction. Gaumont-British generously stood the cost of his treatment and Celia's hotel bill at the Mayfair. The weekly checks of sixty pounds, along with his monthly earnings from Columbia, dutifully recorded in her diary, even allowed them to repay some of the money borrowed from Paul Falkenberg during their Paris sojourn. They also loaned two pounds (approximately 140 dollars in today's currency) each to Marcus and Leo Mittler, whom Lorre credited with discovering him at the Stegreiftheater and putting him on the Breslau stage eleven years earlier. Though Peter was "very sick" and "without a chance to make money," she wrote Dr. Samek on February 5, "we tell everyone that we are very well and that [he] went back into a sanitarium for a rest, because if people knew the truth, it would hurt him very badly in this business." (As far as the public knew—at least those who read the trade papers—a case of the flu had delayed the actor's return to Columbia for three weeks.) What she penned to Samek was the confidential truth. The studio payments were not enough to cover expenses. In a nutshell, they didn't have a "Heller." Taking legal action against them, she said, would do no one any good, especially Peter, whose condition couldn't withstand such agitation. In four weeks, Celia assured the attorney, he would be healthy and ready to accept "some great offer here as well as in America." Once he was again under contract, "we will pay."[33]

Lorre was apparently well enough to attend the British premiere of *Crime and Punishment* at the Plaza on March 13. With some time to spare before their scheduled sailing from Southampton on April 22, the Lorres railed to Vienna, where the actor "showed his original face" to the public at the opening of his "Raskolnikov film." While there, Peter and Celia also saw Franz Theodor Csokor and Karl Kraus, for the last time, as it turned out.[34] They also stopped off in Budapest to visit Melanie and Alajos, still employed with Steyr-Werke, before returning to England and boarding the SS *Washington*, which docked at West Fourteenth Street in New York on April 30.

On May 7 Lorre gave his first American radio performance on Rudy Vallee's *Fleischmann Yeast Hour*, broadcast from the NBC Studio in Washington, D.C. "Doctor Mallaire," wrote *Variety*, "gives both Jean Hersholt and Peter Lorre equal opportunity to shine in the sort of roles to which they are best suited." Kindly playwright Hersholt creates a medico (Lorre) so ghastly that he takes his own life in order to rid himself of his creation. Overnight, the course of his movie career had found its correlate in radio. With a voice as recognizable as his face, Lorre was a natural radio talent. The actor later joked to Bob Hope on *The Pepsodent Show* that he was born in a library and that's why he talked in a low, quiet voice. Indeed, several years later, a movie pressbook featured a promotional piece titled "Bogey Lorre on Radio Kiddie Hour" that claimed the actor's voice had been chosen from a recent survey of recorded deliveries as "best suited for child audiences" because it combined "soothing and calming qualities most likely to instill confidence and quiet at the approaching bedtime hour." Whispering menace, childlike mewling, frantic inflections of an unhinged mind—all and much more comprised his vocal repertoire.

Even Lorre took a hand in overlapping the mediums. Shortly before guest starring on the *MGM Radio Movie Club* on November 20, he telegrammed Fritz Lang ("Dear Mole") and asked permission to perform the monologue from *M* over the airwaves. Lang shot back his okay.[35]

Back in Hollywood, the actor was long on plans but short on work. On May 12 the *Hollywood Reporter* announced that Paramount Pictures—after having failed to interest John Barrymore or Paul Muni—had signed Lorre to star in *The Monster,* the next Ben Hecht–Charles MacArthur film, adapted from Frederick J. Thwaites's novel *Mad Doctor,* about a mentally twisted physician who murders his wives. Three days later, the trade paper reported that casting difficulties had put the skids to the planned production. When Michael Balcon denied rumors that Paramount would make the movie for Gaumont-British at its studios in Astoria, New York, *The Monster* was, to quote the trades, all washed up.[36]

The *Pariser Tageblatt* even rumored that Lorre and Paul Graetz would costar in a Hollywood production of Max Gorki's *Nachtasyl (Night Refuge).*[37]

Lorre also figured in casting discussions for Cecil B. DeMille's *Dimitri,* the story of an ambitious Cossack captain who passes himself off as Dimitri, the son of Ivan the Terrible and rightful heir to the throne, and becomes the czar of Russia.[38] DeMille had worked the idea into a play as a teenager and later, with historian Harold Lamb, had set to work on a book.

By 1936 the director felt the time was ripe for the Russian Pancho Villa. "Dimitri is a character that American audiences will understand," he told a conference of Paramount executives headed by studio head Adolph Zukor on August 23. "He is a Russian cowboy and will do all the things that our cowboys do." DeMille said he wanted to forgo spectacle and bring the film in on a modest budget, without a star. Eliminating elaborate—and expensive—battle scenes, he argued, would allow him to concentrate on the intimate story of Dimitri, caught between two women's love. "It is from rags to riches and back to rags, with a happy ending," enthused the director. But Zukor pressed for a big cast. Without star backing, he cautioned, selling "a piece of Russian history that nobody knows about" would prove difficult. For the role of the dashing and courageous Dimitri, they talked Gary Cooper, Errol Flynn, and Frederick March; and for the female lead, Claudette Colbert and Marlene Dietrich. Lionel Barrymore came first to mind for the part of the hated Boris Godonov, who murdered the real Dimitri. Zukor reminded them that Barrymore had been ill, looked bad, and would not do. Anyway, he was too old. They settled on

Peter Lorre for the role, but like so many story ideas, this one died on the conference table.

The trades also rumored that Paramount had engaged Lorre for *A Gun for Hire,* an English murder mystery in the impressionistic style of *The Cabinet of Dr. Caligari,* which would be directed by Robert Florey.

According to the *Hollywood Reporter,* September 19, 1936, a fan poll encouraged Universal to go ahead with plans to remake *The Hunchback of Notre Dame,* with Lorre as the probable star, nudging out Frederick March, Paul Muni, Ronald Colman, and Lionel Barrymore. This project, too, failed to materialize.[39]

Realizing full well that Columbia's commitment to his film career had flagged, Lorre turned to the stage and a special project dear to his heart. Napoleon Bonaparte conquered the performing arts in the 1930s—it seemed that most actors secretly yearned to strut. Claude Rains, who had portrayed the "Little Corporal" on stage in *The Man of Destiny,* reprised his role in the Warner Bros.' *Hearts Divided* (1936). The next year Metro released *Conquest,* with Charles Boyer playing Napoleon to Greta Garbo's Countess Walewska. After acquiring the screen rights to Emil Ludwig's *Napoleon,* Warner Bros. also announced—prematurely—that it had set Edward G. Robinson to star in a film version of the popular novel. Even John Barrymore, Charlie Chaplin, and Dick Barthelmess, reported the *Los Angeles Times,* had set their sights on the coveted role.[40]

Because of his striking physical resemblance to Napoleon—in height, weight, and beam—Lorre claimed that at least thirty theatrical producers had urged him to play the Corsican general. "I have wanted to play or rather to be Napoleon for many years," he told a reporter for the *Indianapolis Times.*

In the spring of 1936, he finally threw his bicorn hat into the ring. While in Vienna in early spring, Lorre had renewed his acquaintance with Ferdinand Bruckner, a poet and playwright and founder of the Renaissance Theater, and learned he was working on a play about the French general. To play Napoleon on stage or screen, he maintained, would satisfy one of his three great ambitions, the others being to play "the good soldier Švejk" and to assume the title role in *The Hunchback of Notre Dame.* Moreover, the actor was bent on alternating stage and screen and claimed that "for full artistic development, as well as for fun, the actor should work in both." He and Bruckner talked it over. "Ironically I was the one man who shied away from the part," explained Lorre, "because the figure of Napoleon has been so standardized, even unto his gestures and every small characteristic. All the existing plays held no surprises." Lorre thought that any production about Napoleon would need a "new angle." That angle, as Lorre put it, was the man behind the myth. "Most Napoleon plays tell the story of his rise to power," said Bruckner. "Mine starts as Napoleon reigns and tells about the man—unfortunate in love and private life—the man who suffered—the man who died, disillusioned. I have tried to do that without taking away from his greatness—for he was a great man." Lorre predicted that the role would take him "a long way from the torture man I am becoming on the screen."

On April 30, after arriving in New York at midnight, Lorre telephoned playwright Sidney Kingsley and discussed the play until four in the morning.[41] At noon the next day, Kingsley sailed for Europe to see Bruckner. He called on the playwright in Paris and paid him an advance to complete *Napoleon the First*, which he would adapt, produce, and direct for the fall season in New York.

Well before Bruckner had put the finishing touches on his play, the trades speculated about the when and where of a probable film version. Several studios, they announced, were negotiating with Kingsley for screen rights. Paramount, which had put Bruckner under contract, even contemplated assigning Ernst Lubitsch to direct a film version at its Astoria studios. Louella Parsons also noted that Warner Bros., which had abandoned its Napoleon picture, was negotiating the sale of the Emil Ludwig script to Columbia, where Josef von Sternberg had just finished shooting tests of Lorre as Napoleon.

While Kingsley managed the logistics, Lorre gave thought and voice to his approach to the role: "If I were going to do Napoleon, I would look at his portraits and read about him—especially his letters—to get the feel. I would do my hair as his was done and wear his clothes, but otherwise I would merely put myself inside him."

In the midst of preparations for the play, Lorre won release from his Columbia contract. Clearly, Harry Cohn did not know what to do with him. To the studio chief, Lorre was little more than an overspecialized actor for whom casting presented a persistent problem. In a year and a half, he had loaned him to Metro for *Mad Love* and agreed to *Crime and Punishment*, Lorre's own idea. The actor longed for lighter roles to balance the darker side of his screen persona. But he was no match for the moguls. In November Darryl F. Zanuck, vice president in charge of production at 20th Century–Fox, lured him into another long-term contract, again with the promise to showcase his versatility in a variety of screen roles. Lorre believed him. Even before the studio had time to retail the actor, it marketed his image as one of the "horror boys" in *One in a Million* (1936), a musical comedy introducing Norwegian Olympic skating champion Sonja Henie and featuring the Ritz Brothers as Karloff, Laughton, and Lorre ("I tell you! It's not me! It's the parts they give me!").

4

SOFTLY, SOFTLY, CATCHEE MONKEY

In a company of fools a mental giant
always sounds ridiculous.

—Peter Lorre in *Crack-Up*

I made the "Moto" series purposely. I wanted to get the
flavor of *M* out of the cinema palate of the American fan.

—Peter Lorre

Lorre wanted to play comedy. 20th Century–Fox, which had accepted him—and he it—on a trial basis, met the actor halfway with a dual role in an action-melodrama. Director Malcolm St. Clair had reportedly read the screenplay for *Crack-Up* (1937) and then sketched his ideas of what the characters might look like. Following his drawings, the casting department came up with Lorre for the role of Colonel Gimpy, the apparently feeble-minded, bugle-blowing mascot of an airship factory.[1] "Colonel Gimpy was a character worth any actor's while," explained Lorre. "He's just this side of sinister, but real, with a sense of humor and a fanatical fidelity to his code. I studied the role very carefully before accepting it, as I wanted to be sure that it was not the type to horrify audiences."

Gimpy toots his horn, makes day and night owl faces—a bit of business added by Lorre—and roams the hangar spouting his own quirky version of

"The Walrus and the Carpenter." Hidden in the verbiage is a poetic wit that is discrepant with Gimpy's reputation as a nitwit: "Madness . . . is a very common malady. Can it be that they are mad themselves who call me mad? If you only knew what was going on in this head of mind. If you only knew . . ."

Behind closed doors, however, Gimpy trades giddy for grave when he assumes his true identity as master spy Baron Rudolf Maximilian Taggart, a cold-blooded operative who bribes world-famous pilot Ace Martin (Brian Donlevy) into stealing the blueprints for a newfangled airplane propeller.

In the final scenes aboard a cracked-up airship, blown off course in a raging storm over the Atlantic, Gimpy and John P. Fleming (Ralph Morgan), whose company built the plane, race paper sailboats—again, Lorre's own idea—in the flooded cockpit. With water rising, the self-exposed spy, the disillusioned-in-love airplane manufacturer, and the double-crossing pilot—each a failure in his own way—chum up for a last smoke, three on a match.

Crack-Up was, by all accounts, a weak entry in the single-feature circuit. Critics complained that the director had put Lorre on too short a lead, tugging him back into conventional stereotyping. More freedom, they argued, would have earned its own reward in a greater show of versatility. Hollywood had "not got within a mile yet of Mr. Lorre's special quality," reproved film critic C.A. Lejeune in the London *Observer*. "For that matter, as long as they go on taking carbon copies of '*M*' indefinitely, each fainter and more derivative than the last one, I can't see that they ever will."

If Fox had not handed Lorre a blank check, it at least had asked something new of him—comedy. Discharging a debt to his screen past and at the same time unleashing his comic instincts, Lorre's dual role bore the stamp of his best performances. First as Gimpy, then as the Baron, he demonstrated his range, disjoining good and evil and ultimately absorbing them into a human whole in death.

The studio pushed production of *Crack-Up*—compressing its schedule to eighteen days—enabling Lorre to check out early. On October 26 he hopped the "*Chief*" and headed to New York to begin rehearsals for *Napoleon the First*. Before leaving, however, he took time to file a "Certificate of Alien Claiming Residence in United States," the next bureaucratic step toward becoming a citizen. Darryl F. Zanuck urged the actor to postpone his appearance on Broadway until he had made several pictures under the new agreement.[2] No longer the babe in the woods who trustingly swallowed the sugarcoated promises of studio chiefs, Lorre said no and insisted on a clause that would allow him to remain with the play to its finish and to accept the title role in a possible film version, even if it were acquired by a rival studio. Unless Fox bought the rights to *Napoleon,* his contract gave him the option of indefinitely postponing his return to the West Coast.

Ferdinand Bruckner had been collaborating with Lorre and Sidney Kingsley on the Napoleon script between film assignments: an original story for Sylvia Sidney, *Lucretia Borgia* for Marlene Dietrich, and a screenplay from *Hotel Imperial* for Ernst Lubitsch. Actually, Lorre had not followed the development of the play since their early discussions. Bruckner had worked on the play alone, devoting only his spare time to it. In an interview for the *Los Angeles Times,* the actor had optimistically stated that the play was "marvelously written," though it is doubtful he had read a complete draft. Closer scrutiny told a different story. "We had anticipated a fine play," lamented Kingsley, "but it was slipshod. We were very disappointed in the play and with Bruckner," whom Lorre had earlier cited as his favorite author.

One need only read the surviving manuscript to understand their letdown. *Napoleon the First* is an ungainly and contorted jumble of scenes that falls woefully short of its goal of presenting a psychological study of the dictator projected through the medium of his private life. Far from preserving his greatness, Bruckner's pitiably clay-footed hero staggers between the bedroom and the council room like a lovesick schoolboy.

When he arrived in New York, Lorre learned firsthand that further complications threatened to hand this Napoleon his Waterloo. Kingsley had been unable to cast the role of Josephine. Tallulah Bankhead, Judith Anderson, Fay Bainter, and Ruth Chatterton were all under consideration, but each was busy elsewhere. Gladys George, his last hope, had also turned down the part. With ten thousand dollars invested in costumes, set design, and advance payments to Lorre and Bruckner, Kingsley postponed the production in late November. Although his option on the play had another three months to go, *Napoleon the First* definitely was not for the 1936 season.

With the cancellation of the play, Zanuck ordered Lorre to return for a supporting role in *Nancy Steele Is Missing* (1937), a prison melodrama starring Victor McLaglen, already in production. At Fox awaited the role of an erudite extortionist by the name of "Professor Sturm," who admits going to the funeral of his last victim, not out of sentiment, but curiosity: "I was curious to see what they could do about that hole in his head." On November 29, the latest of several projected opening dates of the play, the disappointed actor boarded a plane for Los Angeles. "A number of times in Europe I was scheduled to portray 'Napoleon,' and something always came up which necessitated canceling the production," Lorre told a reporter in late December. "I'm not a superstitious man, but I am beginning to think insofar as Napoleon is concerned, I'm a jinxed man." With production of the play tentatively scheduled for the next year, he still looked to fulfill the chief ambition of his life, to play Napoleon. "Will I ever get to do it?" he reflected. "I don't know."

On December 14 Fox set Lorre for a featured role in *Slave Ship* (1937), an action-drama starring Wallace Beery and Mickey Rooney that was scheduled to begin shooting the following week. At the last minute, however, health problems forced the actor to drop out. During production on *Nancy Steele Is Missing*, Lorre had taken a fast cure for drug addiction in Culver City. Barely able to complete the picture, he collapsed at the end of filming. In February he retired to Palm Springs for what the *Hollywood Reporter* euphemistically termed a ten-day rest, ruling out any immediate film appearances.[3]

In 1925 playwright and novelist Earl Derr Biggers introduced the Chinese sleuth Charlie Chan in a serialized version of his novel *The House without a Key*, published in the *Saturday Evening Post*. Hollywood wasted no time in converting the popular stories to celluloid. Pathé Studios released a ten-chapter serial of *The House without a Key* under the same title in 1926. Two years later, Universal produced the second Charlie Chan film, *The Chinese Parrot*, directed by Paul Leni. The popularity of the Chinese detective soon caught the attention of Fox Film Corporation (which merged with 20th Century Pictures in 1935 to form 20th Century–Fox Film Corporation). Between 1929 and 1942, the studio produced twenty-nine Chan films, cornering the market on Oriental detective pictures for more than a decade. Only after Chan's tired legacy moved to Monogram Pictures in 1944 did his appeal begin to fade.

Biggers's death in 1933 sharpened the public appetite for Oriental fiction. Not to be outdone by *Collier's*, which was serializing Sax Rohmer's "Fu Manchu" stories, the *Post* sent John P. Marquand, a well-established contributor to popular periodicals, to Peking in search of, in the author's words, "a new Chinese character and a Chinese background," with the idea that he translate his junket into a series of short stories for publication. "With the ignorance of a complete stranger, where every sight is strange," Marquand recorded in his notebook, he traveled extensively throughout China, Korea, and Japan.

In the summer of 1934, one month after returning from the Orient, Marquand completed *Ming Yellow* (1935), a mystery novel rooted in firsthand impressions and secondhand anecdotes of bandit adventures. The next year he blended memory and imagination into *No Hero*, which introduced a counterespionage agent named Mr. Moto.[4] Like Biggers's celebrated Honolulu policeman, Marquand's "Japanese G Man"—supposedly based on an ingratiating detective caught shadowing the author in Japan—captured the public's imagination. What the author had planned as a single spy story quickly developed into a series of detective thrillers. From 1936 to 1942, the *Post* and Little, Brown, and Company, which brought out trade editions of Marquand's novels, inundated its readers with Moto tales.

To say that Marquand attached little importance to his Moto stories is something of an understatement. Like his critics, he denied them the title of literature and dismissed them merely as "carpentry work." Although their obvious deficiencies—contrived plots, stock characters, and happy endings—argue against their artistic merit, Marquand's biographer rightly singled out their redeeming strengths: the stories are well written, evoke a strong sense of place and history, and ring with the sights and sounds of the Orient.

Mr. Moto's growing popularity also demanded a wider audience. In October 1935 Warner Bros. picked up the screen rights to *No Hero* for contract player Pat O'Brien. *Variety* also reported—incorrectly, as it turned out—that Metro had purchased *Think Fast, Mr. Moto* in July 1936.[5]

On January 11, 1937, Marquand signed a contract with Fox that committed him to submit "two stories . . . which we have the option to purchase for $5000 each" and provisioned an "additional $2500 for each story so purchased if the same is published in THE SATURDAY EVENING POST prior to the general release date of our motion picture based upon the same." Marquand also gave Fox the right to create its own staff originals, for which the studio agreed to pay him three thousand dollars. To keep their agreement alive, the studio had either to purchase one of Marquand's original story outlines or exercise the right to "make one picture based upon an original story utilizing the character created by our staff writers."

The first year Fox purchased two of Marquand's stories, *That Girl and Mr. Moto,* which became *Think Fast, Mr. Moto,* and *Thank You, Mr. Moto,* and created one staff original, *Look Out, Mr. Moto.* To get Mr. Moto off on the right foot, Zanuck promised to pump up production on *Think Fast, Mr. Moto.* Kenneth Macgowan, an associate producer with a string of A productions to his credit, was the man for the job. But kicking off what had the earmarks—and trappings—of a budget serial meant a step down the studio ladder. When Macgowan spurned the assignment, Mr. Moto became grist for executive producer Sol M. Wurtzel's "sausage factory" B unit. Norman Foster, an actor turned writer-director who had been relegated to low-budget features, fell heir to the project. Thirty years later the benevolent director, who was loath to harm a fellow writer or to malign a dead one, admitted that the first draft screenplay for *Think Fast, Mr. Moto* horrified him. He set to work rewriting it, retaining only the story's main figure, the names of several characters, and in the broadest sense, the setting. If the revised scenario bore little resemblance to the original screenplay, he thought it a good thing.

Foster was troubled by more than a second-rate script. To fill the starring role of Mr. Moto—described by Marquand as a "small man, delicate, almost fragile"—Wurtzel cast Peter Lorre, whose penchant for understated and subtle characterization seemed consistent with the Oriental ideal of philosophic calm. Foster felt that Lorre was utterly unsuitable for the part. "Peter was so unlike the Japanese," he complained. "Everything was wrong with him, except the eyes." Something else was wrong with him. When Foster asked to meet Lorre, he learned that the actor was undergoing treatment for drug addiction at West Hill Sanitarium in New York's Riverdale-on-the-Hudson. A trip east confirmed his worst fears that Lorre was physically no match for a leading role in an action-adventure picture.

Foster counted on makeup and a stuntman to transform, albeit superficially, an ailing actor with a European accent into an athletic Japanese detective. With hair blacking, eyeliner, a blending of grease paints, and steel-rimmed glasses (the teeth were his own), the makeup department attuned cosmetic detail to current stereotypes. Except in scenes where Moto appears in disguise, Lorre resisted paint and putty, preferring to create his character from within. "Acting comes from the inside. As you think, so you look and so you appear," he told a studio publicist. "Mr. Moto is a Japanese, a clever, swift-thinking, rather suave person. Well, then, I become that person and what I do is right. I do not need to study a real Japanese man to know what to do. That is wrong. There is a typed idea of each nationality and actors think they must imitate that idea, as if Japanese or Chinese men were not as varied as we are ourselves! All Chinese do not clasp their hands and run about with a jumpy step. Each man moves according to what he is. When you have imagined what he is, you must move as he does."

Think Fast, Mr. Moto (1937) went over big with its preview audience. Wurtzel had wisely instructed Foster to build up the jujitsu and action sequences, elements lacking in the more methodical *Chans*. Harvey Parry was engaged to lend the character a vitality Lorre could not summon. Regarded by his peers as the "Dean of the Hollywood Stuntmen," Parry (1901–85) was a living legend whose career spanned the Keystone Cops to *Airplane II: The Sequel* (1983). In over sixty years—and some six hundred-plus film and television credits—he worked for every major studio in Hollywood. During that time he stunted for such screen notables as Harold Lloyd, Tom Mix, Jimmy Cagney, Humphrey Bogart, John Wayne, and Clint Eastwood, to name only a few. *Think Fast, Mr. Moto* gave the stuntman plenty to do: he leapt over a counter, mixed it up hand-to-hand, and hurled bodies through the air. Lorre's attachment to the wiry, self-effacing stuntman and the popularity of Mr. Moto's gymnastics assured Parry's future as the actor's on-screen alter ego. Parry not only stunted for the actor at Fox, but also, on Lorre's request, later at Warner Bros. and American International Pictures.

"At first it wasn't supposed to be a series," said Foster, who aspired to bigger and better productions. "The whole thing was done tongue-in-cheek. The producer didn't know we were kidding." Whether naive or simply resistant to the Moto hysteria gripping Fox, Foster definitely was ill-informed. Even before *Think Fast, Mr. Moto* went public on July 27, 1937, *Variety* served notice that the studio planned to plot Moto through Chan's successful footsteps, facetiously predicting a cavalcade of *Moto* movies: "'On Your Toes, Mr. Moto,' 'Be Lively, Mr. Moto,' 'Come Quickly, Mr. Moto,' and ad infinitum until [the] inevitable climax of 'Charlie Chan at Mr. Moto's.'" *Variety* even carried news of Wurtzel's upcoming trip to the Far East to draw out reaction of the Japanese government to the characterization of their fictional countryman by the "Continental horror specialist."

Think Fast, Mr. Moto secured a foothold in the public imagination, multiplying itself by eight. Between July 1937 and July 1939, Lorre appeared in *Think Fast, Mr. Moto; Thank You, Mr. Moto; Mr. Moto's Gamble* (which began as *Charlie Chan at the Ringside*—a.k.a. *Charlie Chan at the Fights*—but was redesigned as a *Moto* after Warner Oland, suffering from poor health, withdrew from production and died soon after); *Mr. Moto Takes a Chance* (from the staff original titled *Look Out, Mr. Moto*); *Mysterious Mr. Moto* (originally titled *Mysterious Mr. Moto of Devil's Island*); *Mr. Moto's Last Warning* (originally titled *Winter Garden,* then *Mr. Moto in Egypt*); *Danger Island,* based on John W. Vandercook's novel *Murder in Trinidad* (originally adapted as a *Chan* and then converted to a *Moto* and retitled *Mr. Moto in Trinidad,* subsequently renamed *Mr. Moto in Puerto Rico,* then *Mr. Moto in Terror Island*); and *Mr. Moto Takes a Vacation.* For the two years the films were in production, Mr. Moto's public rivaled that of Charlie Chan, no mean achievement.[6]

As Marquand's formula became more familiar, Fox decided it could give better than it got. In 1938 it accepted his *Mr. Moto in the Persian Oil Fields* (which it never made) but rejected his *Mr. Moto Takes Them On* and *Mr. Moto Is So Sorry.* The studio also created five staff originals.[7] At least a dozen writers helped fashion the inexorable succession of Moto movies. Norman Foster exercised quality control over the six screenplays for the films he also directed. "The first Moto script that was given to me was terrible," he recalled, "and so were the rest." Before they reached the actors, Foster felt compelled to rework them. The late-night revisions exhausted him. Nonetheless, he sharpened the narrative in the unwrought screenplays and created a more authentic background, one drawn from his own experience as a young vagabond traveling about the Far East on tramp steamers.

Marquand's reading public may well have asked themselves what Hollywood had done with his Orient, which was supremely merciless and abounding in secrets incomprehensible to the westerner. It wasn't there. Working around tight shooting schedules—usually three to four weeks—Norman Foster barely managed to preserve even a semblance of eastern flavor. To help what he described as a "ridiculous situation," he spiced the pictures with documentary footage from Fox's "Magic Carpet of Movietone" travelogues. In *Think Fast, Mr. Moto* he matched shots from a Chinese New Year's celebration with the narrative action filmed on the studio's Sound Stage 7. In this way, and by planting period details, such as a Cambodian temple in *Mr. Moto Takes a Chance*, Foster worked to heighten the Oriental atmosphere. Because Marquand set his tales in exotic locales, Foster likewise varied the settings, using as his background San Francisco's Chinatown; Peiping, China; Angkor, Cambodia; Devil's Island; London's Limehouse District; Port Said, Egypt; and Puerto Rico's Great Salinas Swamp.

Abandoned, too, was Marquand's political forecast. His apprehensions about Japan's surging military might and global designs of expansion carry a portentous weight in retrospect. The only film to take an anti-Axis stand was *Mr. Moto's Last Warning* (1939), which vaguely suggested that Fascist powers were up to no good in the Mediterranean. Inasmuch as Fox relegated Mr. Moto to a shoestring budget, discarding Marquand's monitions caused no ripple in the writers' pool. In the end, Fox salvaged little more than Mr. Moto himself, translating him from a supporting role in the novels to a leading character on the screen.

Marquand characterized I.A. Moto—an agent in the service of Japan—as suave, polite, self-controlled, resourceful, and inscrutably furtive. "Adventurer, explorer, soldier of fortune," says actor Thomas Beck in *Thank You, Mr. Moto*. "One of the Orient's mysteries. No one knows very much about him, except that whenever he shows up, something usually happens." In *Mr. Moto's Last Warning* (1939), his dossier describes him: "Nationality, Japanese. Age 35–40. Short. Ju-jitsu expert. Uses various disguises. Adept at magic. Usually works alone. Has been known to use doubles." The on-screen Moto is scholarly, dutifully ingratiating, improbably indestructible, stoically imperturbable, and fond of cats and milk. To compete with Charlie Chan, Foster and his cowriters also sharpened his sleuthing skills, which are almost nonexistent in the stories.

In his film debut, "Kentaro" Moto is also supremely sinister, a skilled hunter who kills without compunction. When a ship's steward pulls a knife, he hurls him overboard with studied cold-bloodedness. Foster believed that the actor's "unusual sinister quality" tallied nicely with Moto's shadowy image. Lorre explained this threatening edge to a studio publicist:

> Menace in nature always is silent. Sometimes it is beautiful. A copperhead snake has little or no facial expression, yet it needs only to raise its head to strike terror into the heart. The famous Gila monster, native American lizard, resembles a beautiful beaded bag. Yet its bite is more deadly than most of the poisons known to mankind. Therefore, Mr. Moto, as I see him, is the character who never quite lets anyone know what he is going to do next. He completely fools the rest of the cast as well as the audience in the theatre—they don't know whether he is on the side of crime or is an ally of justice.

Moto's prowess as a killer is unnerving. In *Thank You, Mr. Moto* (1937), the second installment in the series, the Japanese detective is attacked one night in the Gobi Desert. He stabs an assailant three times and buries the body in the earthen floor of his tent. "If I was casting a horror picture," added a remarkably straight-faced Chick Chandler, speaking of Lorre as Mr. Moto in *Mr. Moto Takes a Chance* (1938), "I'd have him play the murderer."

In the first Moto film, Foster kept audiences guessing. Only after he is suspected of narcotics smuggling does Mr. Moto reveal that he is the managing director of the Dai Nippon Trading Company and a detective by hobby. In the second, however, he emerges as a confidential investigator for the International Association of Importers and an international policeman. Finally, his own popularity and the Chan legacy curbed Moto, bringing his shadowy form into clear focus. Foster and coauthor Philip MacDonald firmly tied Moto to the International Police, as Agent No. 673, in *Mysterious Mr. Moto* (1938). With wholesome respectability, the body count fell off, although not his glibness in the face of murder and the cold intensity of his violence. Shelving the clutter of Lorre's menacing screen persona, the Moto-makers forged a Hollywood hero that was human and likable, if a more conventional protagonist. The publicity department, for reasons of its own, resisted the whitewashed Moto. Even after the character had metamorphosed into something more salutary, it clung to the mercurial Moto. A trailer for *Mr. Moto's Last Warning* proclaimed, "KILL TO LIVE BECAME MOTO'S MOTTO!"

"Instead of wrecking the series with poor production, as was done in the 'Jeeves' series with Arthur Treacher," wrote Douglas W. Churchill, Hollywood reporter for the *New York Times*, "Fox has promised to embellish the J.P. Marquand yarns to make them first string entertainment, and in between give Lorre vehicles worthy of his talent." Four months later, he observed that

> shooting is characterized by a happy indifference impossible in the more imposing epics. . . . Mr. Moto's personal jungle is located just outside the stage where a political rally in "In Old Chicago" was taking place, and just as the players were in the mood of the eons of jungle silence, "The Blue Danube" from a healthy brass band would crash upon them. But if they have their limitations, they also have a latitude not possible in films made for more discriminating customers. Action had taken place beneath a tree in one scene and the next was a wider shot showing the tree and a man emerging from the temple. The camera man looked through his finder and said, "You'll have to move either the tree or the rajah." So they moved the tree.[8]

Although Foster fiercely denied modeling one series after the other, the *Chans*—three of which he also directed—set the pace for production. "In those days, those were 'B' pictures," pointed out Leon Ames, a co-worker on *Mysterious Mr. Moto* and *Danger Island.*

> It was sort of plotted for you from the head office and you just kept your schedule and finished the picture. . . . There was no great depth of characterization you had to do. You did your day's work and went home at the end of the day and came back the next morning and did the next day's work. There was no great creative requirement in the *Motos*. It was all spelled out and you did your job the best you could. You didn't get any great histrionic things from anybody. They hired very proficient actors and you got them done on schedule and that's it.

Sensitive to the criticism that he fell headlong into the clichés of the *Chans,* Foster claimed he worked hard to set Moto apart from his Chinese cousin. Each *Chan* plot, he pointed out, contained a raft of red herrings, a series of clues and coincidences, a stoic Chinese conversant in Confucianism, and often an impetuous offspring. The Chinese gumshoe systemically plodded his way to the resolution of a mystery, whereas Moto watched, waited, and sprang. Often working undercover and assuming an assortment of imaginative disguises—peddler, Mongolian camel driver, ancient guru, curio dealer, archaeologist—he most often played a lone hand. Moto collaborated only twice and both times in pictures without Foster at the helm. In *Mr. Moto's Gamble,* a re-adapted *Chan* directed by James Tingling, Moto teamed up with Lieutenant Riggs (Harold Huber) to solve a boxer's murder. Even Charlie Chan's son, Lee Chan (Keye Luke), and "Knock-out" Wellington (Maxie Rosenbloom), students in Moto's criminology class, manage to stumble onto a few clues, as well as a few laughs. Again, in *Danger Island,* directed by Herbert Leeds, the dimwitted "Twister" McGurk (Warren Hymer) tags along with the graciously chagrined Moto.

Feeling that the same Fox contract players turned up again and again in the *Chans,* Foster went out of his way to people the *Moto* movies with new faces, such as Virginia Field, Dick Baldwin, Chick Chandler, and Amanda Duff—and established character actors, such as John Carradine, Sig Rumann, Joseph Schildkraut, Douglass Dumbrille, and Leon Ames, just to name a few. Foster prided himself on presenting as fresh a format as possible.[9]

In 1938 a magazine fan writers poll tagged Lorre as "poor copy." Whether or not Fox believed it, the studio went to work on his screen image. In his autobiography, *The Name above the Title,* director Frank Capra wrote that "95 percent of Hollywood's 'news' originates in studio publicity departments." Publicity director Harry Brand blitzed readers with stories of the actor's immersion into Japanese culture, all in preparation for his role as Mr. Moto. "A stickler for realism," he claimed, Lorre frequented Japanese restaurants, interviewed Japanese laborers in the fields, and read Japanese novels and poetry and the religious writings of Buddhism and Shintoism.

Brand also endowed the actor with a mastery of martial arts. Overnight, Lorre became a jujitsu expert under the tutelage of Professor Haiku Watsutu: "The first guy he tossed about was Foster himself . . . [who] landed on his back, right in the middle of the set, without having the remotest idea how he got there." Lorre and actor Warren Hymer reportedly "attended the professional heavyweight matches to get ideas for their own clash before the cameras" in *Danger Island.* The actor even "invaded the gymnasiums in the Oriental section of Los Angeles and matched his skill against one of the Judo students." Because he "performed all the accepted movie stunts himself" in the *Moto* movies—including wrestling 220-pound Sig Rumann and having bullets pumped at his steel vest in *Think Fast, Mr. Moto*—the Stuntman's Association, whose members had purportedly coached Lorre in jujitsu, boxing, wrestling, and acrobatics, accorded him active membership in their select organization.

None of it was true, of course, but the invented bruises, falls, broken fingers, torn ligaments, and nervous breakdowns, all incurred on behalf of the physically demanding role, nicely explained his retreats to area sanitariums, where, in reality, he wrestled with his chronic drug addiction.[10] Years later, in a statement to the Federal Bureau of Narcotics in New York, Lorre maintained that after two and a half to three months in the West Hill Sanitarium, he "came out of it completely cured" and that he did not again resort to narcotic drugs until November 1946. His memory had failed him. He had not, as he claimed, stayed completely free of addiction during his years at Fox. In 1936–37, Lorre reeled between the "on and off" prescription of Dilaudid and what he termed "fast cures" at various sanitariums. Before undergoing treatment in New York, a doctor had "furnished me with narcotics by means of injections in his office and by issuing prescriptions to me . . . always in my own name, Peter Lorre."

One day Harvey Parry walked into the actor's dressing room as a doctor stuck a needle into his arm. Lorre looked up, but said nothing. Parry turned away and left. Later, Lorre invited the stuntman to lunch at Fox's Café de Paris.

"Were you surprised today?" asked Lorre.

"What's that?" replied Parry.

"When you walked in and saw me doing that thing."

"I never noticed."

"You're a liar."

"Well, Peter, it's none of my business."

"I've got to do something to relax. I've made a couple of these things and they're a little more than I imagined. The physical end of it bothers me, the running, the jumping, even driving a car—I'm a lousy driver. I've just got to get some relaxation and the doctor told me that this would help me."

Parry suspected someone at the studio of playing a little game to quietly discourage Lorre's use of morphine. The Narcotics Bureau would receive an anonymous tip the actor had some "stuff" on the lot. Investigating officers would be promptly dispatched, but by the time they arrived, any trace of the drug had disappeared. Always, claimed Parry, someone on the inside had warned Lorre.

During the making of the Warner Bros. film *All Through the Night* a few years later, Lorre balked at repeating a take that, to his mind, hardly merited another try. Vincent Sherman, the director, said to him, jokingly, "Don't give me that, Peter. Don't tell me that you're so particular. How the hell did you make all those Mr. Motos over at 20th Century–Fox?"

"I took dope," Lorre solemnly answered.

"Everybody laughed like hell at that," said Sherman, who later learned it was true.

Foster felt that Lorre's addiction got in the way of his characterization of Mr. Moto.[11] "Though Peter didn't make Moto as believable as Oland made Chan," he said in his defense, "he did his best to be like the Japanese. 'Oh, so's' might not have made it, but it was a step in the right direction." Where the actor fell short, Foster stepped in as writer and director. "Peter was very sick during the making of these films," said Foster. "Only when I could con him into doing it did he do any judo or stunts. He was hardly able to run up the stairs. So we took many takes and wrote and rewrote." In *Mysterious Mr. Moto*, Moto was scripted to perform a coin trick. "Peter couldn't do this either," added Foster. "I finally gave up stunts requiring manual dexterity because it was just too expensive."

Lorre's chemical dependency put him on an emotional rollercoaster. On good days, he buttonholed cast and crew members into rounds of cribbage and gin rummy. Or made time for a little monkey business. Ames recalled that "Peter was not an attractive physical specimen to women, but he had a great sense of humor. He would say, 'Do you think you could get used to my body?' But I didn't know whether he meant it or was kidding. He was a he-man as far as I knew in every respect because he was on the make for every broad in the picture, but he did it in kind of a funny, charming way."

On the downside, however, it darkened his disposition. During those times, the actor became anxious and depressed. "In the mornings on the set," Robert Anthony Foster remembered his father telling him, "he would turn up his sad eyes like an abandoned waif: 'Oh, Norman. Too early to be making faces.'" Between scenes, he retreated to his portable dressing room, where he listened— entranced, incredulous, dispirited—to Hitler assailing the Jews over the air-waves. Foster once interrupted him, saying, "I'm sorry, Peter, but we need you."

"The whole world is falling apart," screamed Lorre, nose running, saliva dripping from his mouth, "and you want me to make a picture!"

"Sickness?" said Parry. "Yes, you could tell Peter was sick for the simple reason he was sulky. He would go in a hole. He'd say, 'I'm going to my dressing room.' And he'd be there lying down on the couch and have a book, eyes wide open, and not be reading. His home life got bad and he didn't call the people he used to."

Before the camera, however, Lorre left it all behind him. "He was a good actor," said Leon Ames.

> He was a dependable actor and every scene we did was fun. He was very punc-tilious and he did everything by the book. He was very precise. All of his busi-ness and everything that he did in front of the camera was very studied. He was sharp. That man never missed a word or a line in his performance, ever. He was like a computer. That's what threw me about him. If you had a scene that you'd rehearsed in a long shot, a medium shot, and a close-up, if he had a

cigarette that was half smoked or if he had to do this or that, he never varied in matching the shots. He was an expert at it. . . . It was part of him. I saw no evidence of him ever being influenced by anything other than his job. He was a technical actor and you had to be good to cope with him.

Harvey Parry agreed and thought that Lorre enjoyed the characterization: "I would hear him sit down with various people, whether it be Foster or the fellow he was doing the scene with, and he always referred to, 'This is how I think he lives. This is what I think he'd do. I don't think this man would do this.' So he was studying the character. He was serious. It wasn't a case of trying to duck something, then let the writer put it in."

Lorre, perhaps naively, credited the sustained popularity of the *Moto* series to "brain above brawn." More realistically, it was plenty of action that spelled success at the box office. Although he performed few of his own stunts, the actor played along with anyone gullible enough to believe he did. Lorre and Parry were discussing the previous day's shooting when they were joined by a writer who didn't recognize the stuntman without his makeup.

"Harvey," said the actor, "you tell this gentleman what Peter Lorre did yesterday."

Parry related Mr. Moto's adventures, which included a car chase, a foot race, an underwater fight, and fisticuffs on a pier.

"Jesus, Peter, weren't you tired?" marveled the writer.

"I'll never do it again," quipped Lorre.[12]

Lorre actually saw more action than audiences supposed. In *Mysterious Mr. Moto*, the Japanese detective, disguised as a convict, and Paul Brissac (Leon Ames) escape from Devil's Island. Ames recalled the scene, which Foster shot on the Fox back lot:

This particular night we were escaping in the jungle and the swamp. The guards were shooting at us and we were in this boat and all of a sudden we saw little splinters of wood and some things happening in the water that were too close for comfort. We stopped the scene and said, "Just a damn minute here. What the hell's going on?!"

"Don't worry," said Norman, "we've got expert marksmen."

They were getting pretty damn close and those were live bullets.

In addition to using real ammunition, the prop department dug deep holes in the set floor. "All of a sudden," said Ames, "you would step in this hole and you'd go underwater. Tricky little people they were in those days."

In *Mr. Moto Takes a Vacation,* Parry jumped from a second story window, inadvertently turned in the air, and dislocated his shoulder when he landed. The accident-prone Lorre fared little better in the scene. For one of the film's close shots, Foster directed him to step from a table, over another stuntman's head, and fall to the floor. Lorre planted his foot squarely in the stuntman's stomach, tripped, and twisted his shoulder, separating the joint.

Like the original stories on which they were based, the *Moto* pictures shared obvious strengths and weaknesses: they were exciting, fast-paced, and suspenseful, yet wildly melodramatic and farfetched. Since the pictures didn't take themselves too seriously, neither did the critics. "In the long run Mr. Moto's adventures . . . are of the kind that breeds soft tolerance in a reviewer," wrote the *New York Times* critic B.R. Crisler.

> What is to be gained, after all, from swimming against a trend apparently as well established as the Gulf Stream? Therefore we herewith formally and for all time accept the phenomenon of Mr. Moto, together with his invariably able supporting cast, and the fact that Providence, or its equivalent in Shinto or the Shogunate, has enabled him to be (1) everywhere at once (2) aided by almost supernaturally mysterious allies in all parts of the world (3) unsusceptible to ambush, espionage, riot, hail, tornado or falling aircraft and (4) invincible, when the issue descends to anything so vulgar as physical assault.

Even the roster of civic and censor-minded women's groups, which found the pictures overdosed with "horror, brutality, and murder," endorsed them for "mature" audiences.

Variety speculated that "Peter Lorre was presumably cast in 'Think Fast, Mr. Moto' as a trial balloon to determine whether his screen work as an Oriental would click with audiences." It did. Audiences liked Lorre in the role of Moto and welcomed—as he did—his departure from villainous roles. "As Mr. Moto I have been given the opportunity of gaining popularity which otherwise would have taken years longer," he was quoted as saying. "The following which would have come to any actor selected to star in the Moto adventures will enable me, I hope, to play parts to which I have looked forward for many years."

Nevertheless, Lorre soon wearied of the hackneyed plots and characterizations. In interviews he pressed the point that repeated casting bored audiences and demeaned actors. He feared, and rightly so, entrapment in another persona. People everywhere greeted him as Mr. Moto. No one, it seemed, missed an opportunity to lend credence to his identity as the Japanese sleuth. According to his brother Andrew, one day someone at the studio removed the actor's identification from his wallet and substituted phony documents, including a card that read, "Mr. Moto—Japanese spy." Stopped for speeding, Lorre unwittingly produced the false I.D. Fortunately, the officer recognized the actor and realized he was the victim of a practical joke.

Parry knew Lorre had reached the breaking point when he said he was not going to do Mr. Moto anymore. "I'm tired of Mr. Moto," he told Parry. "He gives me a pain in the ass." Toward the end of the series, Lorre bumped into Lotte Lenya in New York. They had not met since Berlin. When Lenya asked what he did in Hollywood, Lorre replied, "Nothing, I make faces."

"Mr. Moto was fine for a while," he said later. "But the role is really childish. I'd rather play any kind of part in a picture with a good dramatic story." Over the years, his bemused intolerance turned to outright hostility. When someone brought up the subject during a rehearsal for Spike Jones's *Spotlight Revue* in 1948, Lorre exploded. "He hated the *Motos,*" said head writer Eddie Brandt. "Thank God I didn't say to him it was my favorite thing he did." The actor told a reporter for Omaha's *Evening World Herald* in 1963 that he had "found the Mr. Moto arrangement was much harder to get out of than into." Referring obliquely to his treatments for addiction, he added, "It was so hard that I had to become ill for at least six months around contract time and I had to utilize the services of many good doctor friends while I was 'sick.'"

"We're like a couple who have been married too long," Lorre wearily remarked to Foster one day.

"Want a divorce?" replied the director.

In early December 1938, just before starting production on *Danger Island,* the final *Moto* picture, Lorre had "inked a new ticket," trade talk for renewing his contract. Given his obvious—and vocal—discontent, it was a surprising move. The studio had promoted him from thirteenth ranking in its "featured" player category in 1937 to number nine in its "star" list in late 1938. As his stock rose, however, his salary had stayed put. In *Crack-Up,* the actor had earned $2,500 per week, with a four-week guarantee. Nearly three years—and a hit series—later, Fox still held him to $10,000 a picture, making him one of the most underpaid actors at the studio. Warner Oland pulled down $40,000 per picture as Charlie Chan. If he read the trades, Lorre learned what he probably already suspected, that according to a 1938 exhibitor's poll, his dollar value as a supporting player ranked second only to Walter Brennan's.[13] Despite starring in nine Fox titles, he reverted, quite inexplicably, to "featured" status in 1939.

Whether star or featured player, Lorre knew he wasn't making ends meet. Chronically short of money and long on bad luck, the Lorres had good reason to fret about finances. Legal threats and promises of payments still passed between Dr. Samek and Celia. Finally, in 1937, Lorre turned the matter over to his business manager, Eli Leslie, who bought more time with a request for a full accounting, which, with interest, had climbed to 3,609.28 schillings (approximately $866). Demands for full payment by July 1 fell on deaf ears. The best Lorre could do, explained Leslie, was regular payments of $45. This was unacceptable to Samek, who "was very sorry that Peter Lorre doesn't know in what unheard of ways he misused my good will." After emigrating to America, Samek eventually received the full amount, but Lorre's delinquency in discharging the debt irreparably damaged the friendship.

One and a half years after returning from England, Peter and Celia also grappled with outstanding obligations to Ivor Montagu and Dr. D. Hunter, London Hospital, Whitechapel, stemming from drug treatments. Leslie regretted the delay but felt certain "that we can now start sending you sums at regular intervals and alternate each time with Dr. Hunter." In a personal letter to Montagu on Fox stationary, Lorre asked forgiveness

> for not having sent my money yet—but things were very, very tough—and still are!
>
> (Untier was very ill, had operation but is better now—etc.)
>
> Here are my first 50- Dollars and I will keep sending more in regular short intervals. . . .
>
> Ivor dear, I only write very shortly to day [sic]. (I have a little bronchitis.)

By April 1939 things had only gotten worse. Celia wrote Mrs. Montagu:

> You must know Peter is away since 2 months, and I am opening all his letters to see whether there is something important among them.
>
> Please forgive if I am not able to send you the money now, although I know that you are in need of it. Peter has a contract, but he is in ill-health and had to take a leave of absence. Since the beginning of January he is without salary because of illness. You never heard from us because the last years have been very hard for us owing to illnesses and great excitement about the happenings in Europe where our people lived. Six months ago we had a terrible car-accident and I had broken in a very complicated way the wrist of my right hand.[14]
>
> I was ill for 4 months, and Peter, who was under the car at the time of the accident, had a terrible schock [sic], and hat [sic] to work at the same time.

Please keep it only to you and Ivor, but I am very much worried about Peter's health, and the Motos are really hard work. P. is expected to be back at the end of May and to start work at the beginning of June. I promise you to do everything in my power that you should get a payment every week. It will be, however, impossible to send all the money at once, as taxes and everything had to be postponed to 1st of June when P. will start to work. Please write me a line that I might know you are forgiving us.

Lorre would not have needed to run over to Metro's *David Copperfield* and consult Mr. Micawber to know that "annual income twenty pounds, annual expenditure nineteen six, result happiness. Annual income twenty pounds, annual expenditure twenty pounds ought and six, result misery." Working so hard for so little heightened his awareness that the studio had fallen short of meeting his financial needs.

The actor's salary problem was symptomatic of other, larger issues. He believed Fox had, in the words of friend and later publicist Irving Yergin, "sold him up the river" in more ways than one. The Front Office realized that "there was something fermenting," said Leon Ames, and weighed the possibility that his ripening disenchantment with the *Moto* series might prompt him to do something rash—namely check off the set. Anticipating a walk-out on *Danger Island,* the last film entry in the series, Fox headed Lorre off. "We were signed and put on salary immediately for some legal, technical reason, to force Lorre to go to work," said Ames. "They locked the cast in. He didn't refuse. He was just bored."

History played into Lorre's hands, accomplishing what he was unable to do. Rising anti-Japanese sentiment in the late 1930s dealt Mr. Moto his final blow, at least until after the war. Under the "Here and Now" column in the Anti-Nazi League's *Hollywood Now* (formerly *Anti-Nazi News*) for February 19, 1938, appeared the entry "THINGS WE WOULD LIKE TO SEE: That Japanese boycott button in Peter Lorre's buttonhole. Especially when he's all dressed up for his part in 'Mr. Moto'—as a Japanese." Actually, the *Hollywood Reporter*'s "Rambling Reporter" had caught the "Moto-ing" Lorre wearing a "Don't Buy Jap Goods" button several weeks earlier. Charlie Chan "continued solving high society murders" during the war years, wrote Number One Son Frank Chin. "His effectiveness as an anti-Japanese tool depended not on his exploits but his being visibly and actively not Japanese with all his heart and soul." With the series pictures petering out, Fox disclosed in January 1939 that it was abandoning four of its seven series, retaining only *The Jones Family, Charley* [sic] *Chan,* and *Mr. Moto,* the success of which the studio attributed to attractive characters and good stories.[15] By June, however, Moto was "Outo," according to *Variety*, which carried news that Fox had shelved three Moto pictures slated for production over the next two years.[16] On December 4, 1939, Wurtzel wrote to E.C. Delavigne that "we would like to pass up the entire Marquand contract as we will not make any more MOTO's in the future."

Hollywood had not heard the last of the ubiquitous detective. Earlier in the year, Warner Bros. had satirized Mr. Moto in *Porky's Movie Mystery*, starring, of course, Porky Pig as the Japanese gumshoe "Mr. Motto." On August 10 Lorre reprised the role for radio opposite vaudeville comedian Lou Holtz on *The Royal Gelatin Hour*. The following week, after turning in a detective sketch on *George Jessel's Celebrity Program*, Lorre coolly announced, "To everyone who was good enough to see the Mr. Moto pictures, I would like to say this: that tonight you have heard me play Mr. Moto for the last time. . . . As far as I'm concerned, there's no more Mr. Moto." But shedding his movie-made persona wasn't as easy as he supposed. Lorre again stepped into the role in October, this time working alongside other great detectives on *The Texaco Star Theater*. In August 1942, 20th Century–Fox announced plans to bring together Charlie Chan (Sidney Toler), Michael Shayne (Lloyd Nolan), Philo Vance (Warren William), and Peter Lorre as Mr. Moto in *The Four Star Murder Case*, but the collaboration of the celebrated sleuths did not materialize. In a comic turn, Lorre—as Moto—and comedian Fred Allen—as One Long Pan—competed for the title of World's Greatest Oriental Detective in "The Missing Shot" on *The Texaco Star Theater*, January 3, 1943. The following June, the actor uttered his final "Oh, so" when Mr. Moto and One Long Pan again faced off in "More Murder on the Fred Allen Program."[17]

In the midst of *Moto*-mania, the studio seemingly lost sight of its commitment to supply Lorre with a variety of screen roles. Jimmie Fidler expressed what was on the actor's mind in his column "Movie Medley" for the *Chicago Sunday Times*:

> Peter, apparently, has been doomed to an endless and disheartening succession of 'Mr. Moto' pictures. . . . He didn't want to play such pawkish roles, but, ordered to do so, he put his shoulder to the wheel like a real trooper and did the best he could with the material at hand. . . . Peter ought to be given an opportunity if for no other reason than it's a crime to waste his talent. And if that argument needs reinforcement, I submit that since he has worked like a trojan in a thankless task and made money for the studio—it is no more than sporting that his willingness should be rewarded with a role into which he can sink his teeth.

In another column, which Lorre kept in his scrapbook, the Hollywood columnist again went to bat for the actor, stating that

> the way he's been kicked about from pillar to post, overlooked whenever a great role suiting his particular type was to be awarded, and finally shunted aside into a nonsensical series of 'Mr. Moto' quickies, is puzzling.
>
> In simple fairness, the powers that be ought to give Peter Lorre a decent break. He was signed with the assurance that he would be tendered fine acting roles, would be an important star.
>
> He didn't want to play those Mr. Moto parts, which he could have been excused for considering an insult to his ability. He played them simply because he's such a non-temperamental, obliging person that he refused to fight.
>
> He's done his part. How about giving him a deserved reward?

An ad in the *Hollywood Reporter* belatedly boasted that "Peter Lorre, as the famous Saturday Evening Post sleuth, has steadily become a more firmly established boxoffice asset" and promised that "added impetus will be given his popularity by the stronger material afforded him in 1939–40." However, the studio's guilty conscience was a case of too little, its good faith a case of too late.

In April 1937, shortly after *Think Fast, Mr. Moto* finished shooting, Zanuck had set Lorre to star in *Life of a Lancer Spy* (released as *Lancer Spy*), a World War I spy melodrama, scheduled for immediate production under the direction of Gregory Ratoff. Philip Dunne wrote the screenplay from the novel by Marthe McKenna: "I had him [Lorre] play a civilian. I was in effect trying to say here was a pre-Nazi Nazi, that there were already Nazis in Germany and this was the type, sort of a Goebbels. He was the principal villain.... There was already talk of putting Peter in the part. He still carried the aura of *M* around with him. That may have colored a bit of what I did with it thereafter."

One day before the scheduled shooting date, Zanuck yanked the film so that the story could be extensively rewritten—unbeknownst to Dunne—ostensibly to get a steeper budget after revision. Meanwhile, Lorre went to work on *Mr. Moto Takes a Chance. Lancer Spy* got under way several weeks later. "When I saw the film," recalled Dunne, "and I never saw all of it, I walked out. Peter turned out in a uniform and it spoiled the whole character for me; it made him just one more German in uniform." Lorre's featured role had been cut to little more than a cameo—as a staff underling in the Kaiser's Imperial Army—that any bit player might have filled.[18]

Wedged quietly among the *Moto* films was *I'll Give a Million* (1938), originally budgeted at one million dollars, with John Ford directing. Walter Lang ultimately stepped in, settling for much less. In this parable of wealth and poverty, Lorre played Louie the Dope. Described in a press release as "somewhat mentally disordered, the 'philosophical knight of the road'" jumps to a drowning death, only to be rescued by a disillusioned millionaire who exchanges identities with him. Louie bumbles through the story with lamblike innocence, dumbfounding local journalists who seek the real identity of the millionaire and confounding restaurateurs, from whom he orders "lobsters with thermidor." Although Lorre delighted audiences as another "little man" in the Švejk mold, *I'll Give a Million* made far too imperceptible a splash to rank him as a comedian.

Other projects fell by the wayside, among them *Love under Fire* (1937), a romance-adventure set against the Spanish Civil War, with Lorre as "Captain Delmar." When he became ill, John Carradine stepped into the role. Frank Capra had also considered Lorre for a role in *Lost Horizon* (1937). That year Darryl Zanuck refused to allow Lorre to play opposite Miriam Hopkins in *Wine of Choice*, a Theater Guild production set for Broadway in December 1937. Lorre was too busy as Mr. Moto, it seemed, to parade around as anyone else. His name also came up in casting discussions for *International Settlement* (1938), a smuggling yarn starring George Sanders and Dolores Del Rio.

Lorre's appearance is credited in a cast list for 20th Century–Fox's *Four Men and a Prayer*, directed by John Ford. It was not so, although the actor had figured in the picture at one point, as script revisions testify. Today, *Four Men and a Prayer* looks as if two directors, working independently from different scripts, had crudely interspliced their work. With the sophisticated charm of *The Thin Man* in mind, Zanuck had wanted to treat the story "with a delightful sense of humor instead of as a melodramatic thriller" and wrote Lorre's "monk-like, odious character" out of the script. John Ford, however, held out for the dramatic ending to David Garth's novel, which was restored, along with Lorre's role. Two weeks into filming, Zanuck suddenly rewrote the script, substituting his own ending and cutting the supporting role to a bit part, played by Paul McVey.

Why Zanuck recast the role is difficult to say. Always eager to plug his contract players into as many holes as time and tide permitted, he would have thought nothing of relegating Lorre to a mere cameo. Nor does a scheduling conflict appear to have ruled him out. After temporarily canceling production of *Charlie Chan at the Ringside* on January 17, 1938, the studio had decided to rework the stalled project into *Mr. Moto's Gamble*, starring, of course, Peter Lorre. However, the picture was completed well before Ford began shooting the secretary role for *Four Men and a Prayer*.

Ironically, the actor's best offers of substantive roles came not from Fox, but from MGM. In August 1937 Lorre and Oskar Homolka tested for the role of Louis XVI—originally set for Charles Laughton—in *Marie Antoinette*, opposite Norma Shearer. They lost out to Robert Morley.

Soon after, gossip columnist Louella Parsons reported that Lorre had satisfactorily tested for the role of Quasimodo in *The Hunchback of Notre Dame* (1939) at Metro.[19] This part, wrote Fox publicist Harry Brand, satisfied one of the actor's two great ambitions, the other being to play Napoleon. Lorre claimed he had earlier turned down the role because Lon Chaney's portrayal was too fresh in the public mind.[20] Apparently, he had thought better of it. "Chaney's results were gained through painstaking experimentation with make-up," a Fox publicist quoted Lorre as saying. "My method is to study the character psychologically. I try to bring my characterization from within and for that reason I feel that my portrayal of the part would be different." In the end, Charles Laughton captured the coveted role.

One of the most interesting unproduced projects was *War Is Declared*, an original story by Waclaw Panski, in which news that war has been declared—a hoax perpetrated by a neurotic wireless operator—divides passengers aboard a luxury liner into hostile camps symbolizing democracy versus fascism.[21]

In September 1934 Paramount had submitted for approval an early draft of the script for *S.O.S.* (the film's original title) to the Hays Office. Four months earlier, the Motion Picture Producers and Distributors of America (MPPDA), under the leadership of former postmaster general Will Hays, had created a self-regulatory code of ethics governing the film industry. The "Hays Code," which took effect July 1, 1934, with Joseph I. Breen as director of the Production Code Administration (PCA), set standards of good taste, regulating sex, violence, and language in the movies.

With the exception of two minor changes, Breen found nothing "reasonably censorable" and approved the script. There the matter sat until February 1937, when producer B.P. Schulberg, apparently convinced the timing was right, wrote Breen, "I think at the moment the world is clamoring for a picture with pacifistic doctrine." Breen reported back the next day: "There is a thought in our minds that a number of European countries are not likely to allow the exhibition of any picture, which graphically suggests the outbreak of another European war. . . . The British board has a more or less standard policy of refusing to approve pictures, in which characters are shown to be demented or crazed for any reason." Although Lords Max Beaverbrook and Valentine Castlerosse offered to publicly sponsor the highly timely picture and even get it past the film censors, Paramount decided to abandon the project for "international political reasons."

Late in 1938 Universal sought to borrow Lorre from 20th Century–Fox to costar, as Baron Wolf von Frankenstein, with Boris Karloff and Bela Lugosi in Rowland S. Lee's grimly expressionistic *Son of Frankenstein* (1939). However, Lorre turned down the role because, explained the *Hollywood Reporter* "he has left the menace field since he became the popular, sleuthing Mr. Moto and doesn't want to take a chance on another meanie." Universal recast Basil Rathbone in the part.

In January *Variety* reported that Lorre would "go comic" in *The Gorilla*, an "old house" thriller, starring the Ritz Brothers. To sidestep the popular movie subgenre in which murder walks the halls of a gloomy, rain-swept mansion, the actor produced nothing short of a note from his doctor—he supposedly had been ordered by his physician to take another month to recuperate from "pneumonia"—forcing 20th Century–Fox to hire Bela Lugosi for the role of the mysterious butler. By summer he was well enough to collaborate with Hans Rameau on a scenario titled *Jack the Ripper*. The project apparently progressed no further.

After six idle months, Lorre was given an okay on his bid for release from 20th Century–Fox. In mid-July, the *Hollywood Reporter* announced that the actor wanted out of his contract "because of too few parts since dropping of the 'Mr. Moto' series." Lorre hoped that freelancing might steer him around the typecasting rut. Over the next four years, he found himself in constant motion between the back lots of MGM, 20th Century–Fox, Columbia, Republic, Warner Bros., Universal, and RKO. Hollywood now arranged his career in installments—one, two, or three films at a time. He lived an existence as marginal as that of his screen persona. Pushed out of starring player status at Fox, he increasingly landed in featured and supporting character work. His next twelve assignments followed no pattern, unless it was that his services as a specialist in menace and mayhem were routinely recycled in low-budget pictures. He stood in the shadow of his screen past, relegated to the edge of the film frame, where his malevolent presence is more felt than seen.

Offscreen, Lorre had assumed another persona. A member of the Screen Actors Guild (SAG) since May 1936, he was elected to a three-year term on the board of directors in September 1938. The actor faithfully attended the first few bimonthly meetings, then disappeared from the minutes until July 1939, when racketeers made an abortive attempt to "kidnap" the actors' unions. Among the stars who made a pledge, cast a vote, and signed a petition that defended the right of representative unions to govern themselves democratically was Peter Lorre.

During his tenure on the board, he also brought the plight of Adolph Eisler, former head of the Austrian Actors Union, to the attention of Associated Actors and Artistes of America. Being "very anxious to see if something can be done to get him out of the country," Lorre suggested that Eisler might be valuable to one of the guilds here. Despite his efforts, the actor remained in Europe and was last heard of appearing in a German documentary in 1988.

In October 1939 Lorre returned to MGM to put his stamp on yet another villainous role. *Strange Cargo* (1940), a "Devil's Island" tale with a religious twist based on the novel *Not Too Narrow . . . Not Too Deep* by Richard Sale, presented Lorre as the loathsome stool pigeon M'sieu Pig, who informs on Clark Gable and lusts after Joan Crawford.[22]

On the recommendation of director Gregory Ratoff, who believed Lorre quite capable of turning in an exceptional comic performance, 20th Century–Fox recalled the actor in December to appear in *I Was an Adventuress* (1940), a comedy-melodrama about a motley trio of jewel thieves played by Erich von Stroheim, Peter Lorre, and Vera Zorina. After finishing work on *Strange Cargo* at noon on December 19, Lorre immediately reported to work at Fox, where he put in fourteen-hour days, returning to Metro nights and Sundays for retakes and added scenes. The actor played a charmingly dim-witted pickpocket. "I guess I'm just a pathological case," says Polo, confessing to a kleptomaniacal bent. Accused of endangering their operations with his small-time thieveries, the pop-eyed idiotic lout ingenuously purrs, "I am a weak character. So is my whole family."

"I hope the movie fans will laugh at me," said a hopeful Lorre. "If they do, maybe Hollywood will give me another chance to be funny. This horror business, you know, gets rather tiresome, and no fellow ever particularly enjoys seeing himself constantly as a heel on the screen. He'd rather be a clown once in a while."

Indeed, Lorre had some of his finest comic moments in *I Was an Adventuress*. While posing as Nicholas, the cousin of Tanya (Zorina), he is asked: "Are you a White Russian?"

"No, I cannot say that I am white."

"Oh, then you must be Red."

"No, no, no—I cannot say that I am red."

"Well then, what are you?!"

"Pink! I am pink, yes? A pale, pale pink! In other words, a conservative."

The London *Times* noted that "Mr. Peter Lorre has a part in this film, and the pity is that it is not a more substantial one. . . . Polo has the air of a change-ling, a faintly malicious sprite, not quite of the world in which he makes so lucrative a living by indulging in his own peculiar talent. It is a subtle and unusual piece of acting." Critical praise notwithstanding, *I Was an Adventuress* has been all but forgotten and in Lorre's case overshadowed by a darker and much larger body of work.

When Columbia executive Irving Briskin, who headed the studio's B-picture unit, got wind of Lorre's availability, he assigned producer Wallace MacDonald to develop a starring vehicle for the actor. On March 20, 1940, Lorre went into production on *Island of Doomed Men* (1940), in which he played a "fastidious connoisseur of human suffering," who, advertised the trailer, "cannot bear the sight or sound of physical torture." He recruits paroled con-victs to labor on Dead Man's Isle—the film's original title—where he pays them off with a pine box. Working undercover, a government agent instigates a breakout that climaxes in the stabbing death of the "gentle fiend" by his ser-vant and the emancipation of his long-suffering wife.

If the use to which Columbia put Lorre smacks of budget banality, the use to which the actor put himself prevailed in an unoriginal situation. *Island of Doomed Men* reveals the ready crystallization of the actor's psychological canon. He is never a garden-variety sadist; his villainy is never matter-of-fact. Playing amiable ends against a maleficent middle was, to his mind, as predictable as human nature.

After shooting a government agent, he takes his place in a crowd of spec-tators.

"What happened, sir?" he innocently asks a bystander.

"Oh, but that's shocking, isn't it?" Lorre purrs, underlying his expression of moral outrage with an obliquely sinister rhythm.

He supervises the flogging of enslaved men with cold courtesy, then lets the melancholy nocturnes of Chopin calm him. Only the sight of his servant's pet monkey breaks his icy control. After shooting it, however, his rage gives way to remorse. Throughout the film, Lorre's movements, in their choreo-graphed stiffness, suggest a form of Brechtian enactment.

To be at the same time cruel but gentle, diabolical yet genial, loathsome and pathetic took tightrope balance. However infinite the weighed possibili-ties of doing two or more things at once, Lorre's trademarked duality invited one contemporary reviewer's sweeping indictment that since *M* "Hollywood has used his tricks but not his talent."

When director Charles Barton learned he would be working with Lorre, he told MacDonald, "I think we should give him a little freedom to let him say the same thing, only in the words he wants to use." Barton maintained that Lorre was "a very good screenwriter. He could write lines for himself that the writer couldn't write. He would take a line in the script or a whole scene and he'd work it out pretty well his way, not that he was domineering or anything, but he just thought it was for the best, and he did very well." Barton and Lorre listened to each other, lending an easy understanding to the assembly-line pace of production. "If I didn't lay it out right, or bring it up to what he thought," recalled Barton, "he would very nicely, very gently, but not loud in front of everybody, say, 'Charlie, I'd like to do this with it.'"

Of course, it worked both ways. Barton felt that if "Peter wasn't natural, if he was trying to ham it up, he was no good at all. He agreed with me on that, because you take sixty minutes of pounding, pounding, pounding and you won't get anyplace. A couple of times he'd go overboard, and then when we'd finish, I'd say, 'Cut—well, alright now, Peter, now we'll do it my way.' And he just looked at me and laughed like hell."

According to Barton, Lorre understood that his role in *Island of Doomed Men* would strengthen his screen identity as an arch villain. He also knew that these "thrown-together quickies," as he pejoratively put it, kept the Front Office happy and paid the bills.

Columbia had no second thoughts. Parading Lorre before the public as a deranged sadist in an overcharged ad campaign made box-office sense:

Beauty and the Beast
Men die under the lash . . . of his TORTURING WHIP . . .
Women SHUDDER at the touch . . . of his CRUEL CARESS!
There's no escape . . . from his FIEND'S PARADISE of torture!
ISLAND OF DOOMED MEN
Paroled prisoners ENSLAVED . . . in a tropical TORTURE TRAP!
A beautiful woman . . . THE VICTIM . . . of this connoisseur of CRUELTY!

Charles Barton did not see Lorre again for many years. Standing under an arch on Fifth Avenue in New York during a blizzard, he felt a hand touch him on the shoulder: "'Meet me in the Casbah.' I almost died," exclaimed Barton. "It was Peter. He quickly walked away and I had to run after him."

After completing *Island of Doomed Men*, Lorre signed a nonexclusive contract with Columbia, commencing August 1, that guaranteed him $3,500 per week (with a three-week guarantee) for two more pictures.

In August 1939 J.J. Nolan, vice president in charge of studio operations at

RKO, had sent two stories, "The Eyes of Max Carridos" and "International Spy," to Frank Orsatti, who, along with the William Morris Agency, owned Lorre "fifty-fifty." Busy trying to line up properties for his client, Orsatti agreed they would be "great" for him. A cautious Lorre wanted story approval, however, leading executive producer Lee Marcus to size up the actor as a prima donna. "After all," he wrote Nolan, "he is not a Cary Grant or a Carole Lombard, and if he has not sufficient confidence in us and enough knowledge to realize that if we invest our money in the story, we're going to try to do it well, I anticipate difficulties with this young man." On top of this, Lorre was asking for the same salary he had received at Columbia.

Marcus looked for another property, keeping in mind that if the idea grew too expensive, RKO would drop the project. By the following May, he had settled on Frank Partos's unpublished scenario *Stranger on the Third Floor*.[23] Lorre liked it but still held out for his normal fee. RKO and Lorre's agents struck a deal. On May 29, 1940, the actor agreed to appear in two pictures at a weekly salary of $3,500 for a guaranteed total of six weeks.[24] Perennially short of money, Lorre arranged personal advances totaling $4,000 between June 13 and July 26. The William Morris Agency negotiated top billing in the first picture (*Stranger on the Third Floor*) and first feature billing in the second (*You'll Find Out*). Contractually bound to complete both pictures within six months, or between June 15 and December 20, RKO set production to begin on or about June 20 and asked the actor to report to the Stills Department on June 1.[25] Filming began June 3 and ended July 1. RKO's timetable frustrated Universal's plans to put Lorre in the top spot in *The Mummy's Hand*, which was scheduled to go into production the last week of May. The role—presumably that of Professor Andeheb—was ultimately played by George Zucco.

Stranger on the Third Floor is set in an "urban nightworld" of restless, sweat-soaked dreams that blur the border between reality and illusion. When newspaper reporter Michael Ward (John McGuire) becomes a key witness in a murder case, he earns a raise and a byline. However, misgivings gnaw away at his confidence in the testimony on which a man's life hangs. Haunted by guilt that the condemned man (played by Elisha Cook Jr.) may be innocent, Ward dreams that a web of circumstantial evidence incriminates him for the murder of Meng, his prying "third-floor" neighbor.

Ward's repressed fears take shape in a paranoid dreamscape of "light-and-shadow effects and unique angle treatments said never before to have been seen on the screen." A distorted skyline hovers over Jane (Margaret Tallichet), his girlfriend; two-foot-high newspaper headlines scream "MURDER!"; a forest of oblique lines silhouette Michael's cell wall; the figure of blindfolded Justice hangs over the courtroom; an electric chair casts its giant shadow against a wall barred by diagonals.

When Ward awakens, he discovers that the petulant tenant has indeed been murdered, his jugular vein cut. He claims to have seen a stranger (Lorre) with an "evil face" hanging around the building on the night of the killing. Convinced that the stranger committed both murders, Ward points out to the police the similarities between the two killings, but he overlooks the most obvious coincidence: he discovered both crimes. One by one, the events in his nightmare come to life, from implication to arrest.

Jane roams the streets in search of the stranger, described by Ward as a thick-lipped, bulging-eyed figure in a shabby overcoat and a long, dirty-white scarf. Weary and discouraged, she stops at a diner for a cup of coffee. When a stranger asks for two uncooked hamburgers, the proprietor jokes, "Kinda like the taste of blood, huh?" Jane follows him outside and watches him feed the meat to a stray dog, which he compassionately warns, "Don't eat so fast, you'll get a tummy ache." Together Jane and the stranger stroll lonely streets lined with seedy tenements. She learns that he is an escaped lunatic who fears being taken back and locked up. "They send you," he reasons, "because they know I would trust a woman." Before he can harm her, he is run down by a truck. Death only seconds away, he confesses to the murders and then murmurs, "But I am not going back."

In one scene, Jane describes the person for whom she is searching to a postman, who tells her that people are just names to him. Sometimes, he says, he thinks about what the names might look like as people, "but I never thought of anybody that would look like that!" And no one did, except Peter Lorre, whose pubescent fleshiness had given way to ghostly leanness. He moves in and out of the shadows, one moment skimming down stairways in furtive silence, the next rolling through the city streets like a phantom tumbleweed, at the same time sprung from the noir milieu and detached from it.

Stranger on the Third Floor owed a debt to the past that Lorre probably did not want to pay. Subtle differences notwithstanding, his urban stranger is an updated version of the murderer in *M*. "I remember that he referred to his work as an actor as 'making faces,'" recalled co-worker Margaret Tallichet, "and I'm sure there was a bit of boredom and bitterness that he did always get the same type roles." Frank Partos, who adapted the screenplay from his own story, tempered the repulsive elements of Lorre's character with just enough sympathy to allow some understanding of the nameless stranger. Feeding stray animals and killing people evokes the ugly memory of the childlike Beckert, who kindheartedly offered his young female victims candy before murdering them.

Even his menacing sexual presence harks back to *M*, although in a twist on the past, the only kindness he has known is from a woman.

Lorre worked five days with three days idle, punching in at the RKO Ranch in the San Fernando Valley on June 20 and checking out on June 28. On night shoots, he took a special lunch with him. "This snack," said Tallichet, "invariably consisted of wine and the most smelly cheese one could find. So in the scene where Peter is trying to strangle me and I am shrieking—the agony came easier because the smell of mingled wine, garlic and smelly cheese coming from Peter was agony in itself."

Critics found *Stranger on the Third Floor* confusing and pretentious, in a word, "arty." (RKO, possibly sensing something of the sort, advertised it as a horror-thriller.) B movies ordinarily satisfied the public appetite for a plain genre repast, palatable and instantly gratifying. Director Boris Ingster had served up something far more imaginative and important. The darkly original partnership of Partos's grimly cynical story and script, Ingster's Germanic direction, cinematographer Nicholas Musuraca's "visual italics," and special-effects artist Vernon L. Walker's spiraling miniature sets went almost unnoticed at the time. Today, however, film scholars consider *Stranger on the Third Floor* the "first true *film noir*," demonstrating "the most overt influence yet of German expressionism on American crime films to that time."

In August and September, Lorre fulfilled his second commitment at RKO, putting in forty-four days (twenty-seven working and seventeen idle) on *You'll Find Out* (1940), a modestly budgeted musical-comedy-mystery about three confidence men intent on divesting a wealthy widow of her fortune. Director David Butler had suggested that RKO assemble, in his words, "three notable heavies" for box-office value. Together with Kay Kyser—for whom the picture was originally titled *The Professor*—and his band, he paraded out Peter Lorre, Boris Karloff, and Bela Lugosi in their horror guise, assuring the commercial success of an otherwise doltish effort. The *New York Times*'s Bosley Crowther supposed that "the script writers were scared out of their wits by their own ideas, for the dialogue and plot developments indicate that little was devoted to them." Word that sneak-preview reaction persuaded RKO to sign Karloff, Lugosi, and Lorre as a comedy trio for the next Kay Kyser picture, with Butler producing and directing, was apparently premature.

During filming of *You'll Find Out,* Lorre turned in his only performance as a leading man, not for the movies, but on a baseball diamond. The annual charity game benefiting Mt. Sinai Hospital and free medical clinic matched the Comedians (including Jack Benny, Fred Allen, Andy Devine, Buster Keaton, the Ritz Brothers, Edgar Kennedy, and Leo Carrillo) against the Leading Men (including Gary Cooper, Tyrone Power, Errol Flynn, Fred Astaire, Randolph Scott, John Wayne, Roy Rogers, Peter Lorre, and others) before a capacity crowd of 37,700 at Wrigley Field on August 8. Paulette Goddard captained the comics and Marlene Dietrich the principals. Milton Berle announced and Kay Kyser, James Gleason, Chico Marx, and Thurston Hall umpired. Lorre apparently lost himself in the "charity fracas," which advertised the Jack Benny–Fred Allen rivalry (Allen: "Did you warm up?" Benny: "Yes." Allen: "I thought I smelled ham burning.") turned "first-class riot," which was broken up by the Keystone Cops. Although Boris Karloff (dressed as Frankenstein, but not listed in the lineup for either team) scored a home run, the Comedians beat the Leading Men 5 to 3.

You'll Find Out reached American audiences on November 22, 1940. Seven days later, Lorre made an unbilled appearance in what German film historian David Stewart Hull calls "the most hideous three-quarters-of-an-hour in film history." *Der Ewige Jude: Ein Dokumentarfilm über das Weltjudentum* (*The Eternal Jew: A Documentary about World Jewry,* 1940) is one of three anti-Semitic movies that looked to prepare the German populace for the "Final Solution to the Jewish Problem."[26] This anti-Semitic pseudodocumentary is a "black masterpiece" of racial hatred. Compiled primarily of newsreel footage from the Warsaw ghettos, it profiled the poorest segment of Jewish society in its "natural state" of squalor. Maps and supporting footage of rapacious rats chart what is described as a plaguelike spread of Jews across the face of Europe. Driven out by civilized nations that will not tolerate the "pestiferous" people, says the commentator, they learned to assimilate themselves camouflaged as Aryans. But the most effective disguise cannot hide the "inner being" of the "vilest of parasites," which design to rule the world of commerce and degrade the hardworking Aryan with their degenerate art. Contrasting the ordered lives of the German people, underscored the *Illustrierter Film-Kurier,* "leaves the visitor grateful to belong to a people whose Führer has fundamentally solved the problem of the Jews."

Dr. Franz Hippler, who headed the film division of Joseph Goebbels's Propaganda Ministry, scripted the film. Based on "an idea by Dr. Eberhard Taubert," *The Eternal Jew* indicted every segment and strata of Jewish society, including theater and film folk, for being "instinctively interested in everything that is abnormal and depraved." Singled out for censure were "stage dictator" Max Reinhardt and actors Curt Bois, shown performing in drag in *Der Fürst von Pappenheim* (*The Prince of Pappenheim,* 1927); Fritz Kortner (introduced by his original name, Kohn), pictured committing a brutal murder of an old man and the rape of a young woman in *Der Mörder Dimitri Karamasoff* (*The Mur-*

derer Dimitri Karamasoff, 1931); and "the Jew Lorre in the role of a child murderer with the notion that not the murderer but the victim is guilty. Normal judgment is twisted by a sympathetic portrayal of the criminal to gloss over and excuse the crime." Ripping out Lorre's final confession from *M,* a film that had been banned in its entirety by the National Socialists, served a doubly diabolical purpose. Besides accusing Jews of being incapable of checking their compulsive desires and hence posing a danger to "moral society," *The Eternal Jew* appealed to a paranoid perception that, for Jewish actors, person and persona were one and the same.

In November Lorre returned to Columbia to appear in the first of two pictures signed away earlier in the year. Promoted—again somewhat erroneously—as a horror film, *The Face behind the Mask* (1941), based on the radio play by Thomas Edward O'Connell, promised to be a routine programmer. According to the trailer:

> Men see and *shudder!*
> Women look and *scream!*
> You'll see it . . . and GASP!
> THE FACE BEHIND THE MASK
>
> Why must the underworld's most hated man of mystery
> always wear this mask?
>
> Is it fear of his enemies?
> Is it to hide a strange secret?
>
> What *fiendish fury* lurks behind this mask?
> What WEIRD VENGEANCE is brewing?
>
> Peter Lorre . . . man turned monster.
> The underworld's PHANTOM TERROR.

The preface to the film sent a more prosaic message:

> Just a few years ago—
> when a voyage to America
> meant adventure and
> not flight . . .
> When a quota was a number—

and not a lottery prize to be captured by
a lucky few.

As the film opens, a young Hungarian immigrant (Lorre) practices his English: "Excuse me, please. Could I trouble you for a light? Thank you, I do not smoke." Opportunity knocks when a dishwashing position opens up at a New York hotel. Asked if he can wash them without smashing them, he bursts with boyish enthusiasm, "In America, I can do anything!" His dreams go up in smoke when a fire horribly disfigures his face. No one will hire him. His hands outstretched, he cries pitifully, "I know, but my face makes no difference how I can work with my hands." Driven to the brink of suicide, he turns to crime. A plastic surgeon creates a rubber mask for him. As the new face covers the old, so coldness conceals the warmth beneath. But his mask is like a palimpsest on which the old imprint can be written over but not completely erased. He collides with a woman on a city sidewalk and he reproaches her for her clumsiness, then realizes she is blind and tenders an apology. Coming face-to-face with his sinister mien is a disturbing revelation.

"If you could see my face, you would feel sorry for me!" he bitterly confesses to her. "People who look at me, they see a mask, artificial, but the face behind the mask, it's mutilated, a horrible nightmare out of which I can never awake!" She does not perceive the masked criminal, but senses the gentle person within. They decide to marry and begin a new life. When his old gang suspects treachery, they plant a bomb in his car, killing his wife by mistake. He hijacks their airplane and takes them to a remote desert spot. "Keep thinking, thinking your little brains out," he declaims in cool resignation, "turning round and round in circles, looking for a way out, but you will not have the courage to take the way out yourself. Foolishly and vainly you will hope, hope that somehow you will be saved, and slowly you will surely die. For my sins, I have earned my punishment. I shall die too."

Lorre had only to give and withhold of his seemingly limitless reservoir of bodily and facial gestures. As an immigrant, he expresses the wide-eyed innocence of new beginnings. After turning to crime, his body language becomes taut, or as Brecht would have preferred, cooled down, and his face freezes into icy detachment. "I put on dead white make-up," explained the actor, "used two strips of adhesive tape to immobilize the sides of my face, and for the rest of it I used my own facial expression to give the illusion of a mask."

The real face behind the mask had undergone a remarkable improvement since *You'll Find Out.* In 1936 Fox had insisted on a "special provision" in the actor's contract stating, "Artist agrees, at his own expense, to have such dental work done as may be necessary in the opinion of producer." The studio even had reserved the right to cancel the agreement for noncompliance. Lorre had finally replaced his rotten, protruding, splayed teeth with dentures. "He had terrible pyorrhea when we played together," recalled Leon Ames, recalling their work on the *Moto* films. "His teeth were shot and he hadn't gotten them fixed yet, and it was just awful to even have him breathe in the same room with you." Makeup departments hardly could have furnished him with a set of teeth more becoming his screen roles as repulsive, hideous monsters. Dentures incalculably improved his looks and softened his screen image. In *The Face behind the Mask*, they warmed his boyish smile. He was now less macabre, more suavely villainous; less mad, more smoothly menacing.

In writing their screenplay, Allen Vincent and Paul Jarrico worked from the persona and not the person of Peter Lorre, whom they never met. "The role *was* 'tailored,' as I recall," said Jarrico, "in the sense that Lorre had already been cast." Yet their script is curiously biographical. As Lorre's "typecast" restricted him to villainous roles, so the immigrant's grotesque physical appearance bars honest work. Turning their "maskedness" to commercial advantage spelled a kind of suicide for both. More broadly read as an "eloquent statement on the failure of the American dream," *The Face behind the Mask* portended for Lorre a sort of grim, apocalyptic vision of his future in Hollywood.

Given his performance, it is disappointing to learn that, after all, it was just another job. "I don't think Peter was very much impressed with *The Face behind the Mask*," said actor Don Beddoe, who played Officer O'Hara. "His other successes, such as *M*, made him pretty blasé about this particular venture." On a day of location shooting at the Oxnard sand dunes, the actor left his house on Havenhurst Drive in Hollywood in the early morning, only to arrive before the plane needed in the first scene. While waiting for filming to begin, he drank his breakfast, a glass of Pernod, then another mixed with a split of Moet. Disquieted, director Robert Florey sat and listened to Lorre joke about needing liquid refreshment to forget the silly dialogue and grimaces called for in the role. The actor promised to behave, said Florey, but "didn't keep his word and he didn't hold his liquor well. I could handle him till lunch time without much difficulty, but as the afternoon progressed Peter foundered into a world of his own, becoming gloomy or playful, melancholy or senseless, not taking direction but never hostile. . . . I tried to get all his important scenes photographed during the morning hours, which was not always possible."

Budgeting time to direct his players was a luxury Florey could not afford with his twelve-day schedule. He concentrated on the narrative, which he told with masterful economy, and on the subtle handling of "masked" themes and images. By costuming Lorre in a long black overcoat with a turned-up collar and a dark scarf that concealed his neck, the director, in essence, severed the actor's head from his body, symbolically cutting the character off from his own feelings. Ten years later, Lorre employed a similar technique in his own film, *Der Verlorene*. Pernod notwithstanding, Lorre delivered a deeply empathetic performance that earned him critical praise, especially from Florey, who credited the actor with "one of his best creations since the unforgettable *M*." With a host of strong supporting performances, *The Face behind the Mask* was a cut above the usual assembly-line picture. It played well enough at the box office to merit re-release two years later, something unusual for a B picture. It also earned Lorre the number one rating—ahead of second-place Boris Karloff—on Columbia's "Featured" player list in 1941.

Lorre closed this fragmented and frenzied time of filmmaking with two cameo performances. Hoping to capitalize on the popularity of the long-running radio program *Mr. District Attorney,* which had first broadcast over NBC in 1939, Republic Pictures acquired the motion picture rights and projected a continuation of the series on film. In February 1941 the actor lent his name and his screen presence as the sinister "Mr. Hyde" (who is shot by his wife) to the studio's *Mr. District Attorney* (1941).

In May he briefly stepped before the camera in Metro's *They Met in Bombay* (1941) as Captain Chang, a mercenary freight skipper who double-crosses jewel thieves played by Clark Gable and Rosalind Russell.

Lorre wanted out, but he had nowhere to go. He feared betraying himself and his future by acquiescing to public expectations and studio obligations, but he gave nothing less than his creative best—sometimes in spite of himself. By taking his assignments one at a time, he kept his perspective and his sense of humor, which "was wicked, frequently obscene, but always in good taste," said Beddoe. "His was a wonderfully wry humorous touch, well salted with the comical scatological rejoinders. He had a rare bawdy approach to life that was never offensive that swept you along with his realistic appreciation of the 'lovelies' who were never outraged by the tongue-in-cheek forthrightness of his glistening-eye approach." Above the moment, Lorre kept the spirit alive.

5

BEING SLAPPED
AND LIKING IT

When you're slapped, you'll take it and like it.

—Humphrey Bogart to Peter Lorre,
in *The Maltese Falcon* (1941)

I've played mostly badmen—killers—but the audience
loves me. You know, I can get away with murder.

—Peter Lorre

Fed up with losing control over his work, John Huston, who had coauthored his way into high standing at Warner Bros. in the late 1930s, asked his agent to write a provision into his contract that said if the studio took up his option, he would be allowed to direct a film. After scripting *High Sierra* (1941), Huston told Henry Blanke, his producer on *Jezebel* (1938) and *Juarez* (1939), that the time had come. He wanted to direct.

Asked what he had in mind, Huston replied, "*The Maltese Falcon.*" After all, the studio owned the rights to the best seller, which it had acquired from Dashiell Hammett and Knopf Inc. for $8,500 in June of 1930, and it could be shot on a limited budget, perhaps for $300,000 or less. Blanke warned Huston that he would have little luck in putting it over. Warner Bros. had filmed the book twice before, with little success.

In May 1931 the studio had released *The Maltese Falcon,* directed by Roy

Del Ruth and starring Ricardo Cortez as Sam Spade, Bebe Daniels as Ruth Wonderly, Dudley Diggs as Gutman, and Otto Matieson as Joel Cairo.[1] Huston's attitude toward this version—from simple disapproval to downright virulence—is hard to understand, given its straightforward if somewhat stagnant retelling of the story. *The Maltese Falcon,* however, lost its way in the deluge of crime and detective films that inundated moviegoers in the early part of the decade. Five years later, Warner Bros. disguised the original story by substituting an eighth-century hunting horn for the jewel-encrusted statuette of a falcon. William Dieterle's eccentric and heavy-handed *Satan Met a Lady*— produced, coincidentally, by Henry Blanke—bordered on burlesque, with Warren William refashioning Spade into a flamboyant rake and Bette Davis, who later referred to the movie as one of the worst turkeys she had ever made, anxiously looking for an exit from the set.

Huston told author Gerald Pratley that Warner Bros. indulged him: "They liked my work as a writer and they wanted to keep me on. If I wanted to direct, why, they'd give me a shot at it and, if it didn't come off all that well, they wouldn't be too disappointed as it was to be a very small picture. They acted out of friendship towards me, out of good will. This was Jack Warner [vice-president and head of production], but largely Hal Wallis and Henry Blanke."

Believing that the earlier film versions hadn't kept faith with the story, Huston told Blanke, "We'll do the book as it is."

According to office-mate Allen Rivkin,

One day [Huston] came in, tossed a book on my desk, took a stance, pointed a finger at the book and said, "Kid, Warner said if I can get a good screenplay out of this Dash Hammett thing, he'll let me direct it." . . .

. . . "Let's go," I said, eager for another assignment. "Fine, kid, fine. But first, before we do that—let's get it broken down. You know, have the secretary recopy the book, only setting it up in shots, scenes and dialogue. Then we'll know where we are." . . .

About a week later, John ambled into my office, looking very puzzled. "Goddamnedest thing happened, kid," he said, giving each word a close-up. My eyes asked what. "Something maybe you didn't know," he said. "Everything these secretaries do, a copy's got to go to the department. This *Maltese* thing our secretary was doing, that went there, too."

Jack Warner read the breakdown and told Huston to start shooting within the week.[2]

Huston's casting coups nicely served the spirit if not the letter of Hammett.

When George Raft refused to work with a first-time director in an unimportant picture, Huston fell heir to Humphrey Bogart for the role of the "blond Satan," Sam Spade. A veteran of countless gangster roles, Bogart was well prepared to play a hard-boiled detective whose wry grin walked hand in hand with his gritty integrity. Casting submitted the names of seventeen actresses (including Olivia de Havilland, Loretta Young, Rita Hayworth, and Paulette Goddard) for the role of Brigid O'Shaughnessy. When Geraldine Fitzgerald, Huston's first choice, was unavailable, he went with Mary Astor, who breathed credibility into her congenital liar by hyperventilating before going into her scenes. Blanke and Huston found their "Fat Man" appearing in Robert Sherwood's *There Shall Be No Night* at the Biltmore Theater in Los Angeles. Sydney Greenstreet, a veteran of the British and American stages, made his first screen appearance in *The Maltese Falcon* at age sixty-one. Jowly, gregarious, phlegmatic, there is more of Pickwick than of rogue in his portrayal of Kasper Gutman. On May 19, 1941, Warner Bros. casting director Steve Trilling submitted the names of twenty-four actors for the role of Joel Cairo. Among them were Peter Lorre, Sam Jaffe, Curt Bois, Gene Lockhart, Oskar Homolka, Conrad Veidt, J. Carroll Naish, and George Tobias. Lorre also ranked fifth on the list for the part of Wilmer Cook, right under Elisha Cook Jr.

Much as Alfred Hitchcock had rescued Lorre in Paris, transforming imminent anonymity into international fame, John Huston now saved the actor from fading into the world of B movies and beyond—including overtures from Monogram Pictures for the role of a zombie-master in *King of the Zombies* (1941)—by casting him in *The Maltese Falcon*. Warner Bros. tacitly expressed little interest in Lorre as a versatile character actor. To the studio, he was a curiosity, a freak whose scope and ability had been circumscribed by repeated casting. John Huston disagreed. The actor's performance in *M* had left a strong impression on him, and although he had not seen *Crime and Punishment*, he had heard about it. "The flight of his talent was just unlimited," said Huston. "Peter could do anything. He had himself such a rich and varied personality that he could incorporate anything into it." Huston saw no one but Lorre in the role of the malefic milksop Joel Cairo, whose real-life counterpart had been picked up by Hammett (then working as an operative for the Pinkerton National Detective Agency) on a forgery charge in Pasco, Washington, in 1920. "Peter just seemed to me to be ideal for the part," recalled Huston. "He had that international air about him. You never knew quite where he was from, although one did of course." Like other directors before him, Huston also caught on to the possibilities of the natural duality of his screen personality: "He had that clear combination of braininess and real innocence, and sophistication.[3]

You see that on screen always. He's always doing two things at the same time, thinking one thing and saying something else. And that's when he's at his best."

On May 29, 1941, Lorre signed a "Screen Actors Guild Minimum Contract for Free Lance Players" at a salary of $2,000 per week, with a minimum five-week guarantee and featured billing. Trilling snidely noted to Jack Warner that the actor was short of cash "for some reason, which appears prevalent" and had requested a partial advance of "500.00—or more if we would so grant it to him—against his first salary. Will that be o.k. with you?"

Production began on Monday, June 9, 1941. Huston stuck to the story. In *The Maltese Falcon,* he said, "I attempted . . . to transpose Dashiell Hammett's highly individual prose style into camera terms: i.e. sharp photography, geographically exact camera movements; striking, if not shocking, set-ups. . . . As the book is told entirely from the standpoint of Sam Spade so also is the picture." He asked his cast to study Hammett's novel and thoroughly familiarize themselves with the characters. Huston posted sketches of camera setups, entrances, and exits on a large board: "About half the time they would themselves fall into the set-ups that I'd designed, and about a quarter of the time I'd have to bring them into those set-ups. The remaining quarter of the time, what they showed me was better than what I had drawn." He also commandeered a closed set for rehearsals—unheard of. Run-throughs meant few takes and an express schedule. Shooting pretty much in sequence, he invested the gathering momentum of the filming into the narrative action, trailing Hammett as closely as the censors permitted.

Spade's quick paging through Cairo's passport tells moviegoers he was born May 5, 1903, in Lepanto, Greece, and is a professional "Traveler" who now resides in San Francisco. Apparently indifferent to the political consequences attendant upon King Alexander Koryzis's consent to the landing of British forces in Greece, Huston did not heed the suggestion of Carl Schaefer, head of foreign publicity, "that the 'heavy' character . . . not be identified as Greek and therefore that no insert or close up be made of his passport."

Joseph Breen, watchdog of the nation's morality, read the temporary script for *The Maltese Falcon* in May and found the basic story acceptable. However, he warned, "certain objectionable details" must be eliminated before the picture could be approved. Since drinking apparently offended audiences, he recommended it be kept to an absolute minimum necessary to the development of the plot.

Expletives—Spade's "damn" and Gutman's "by Gad"—were also objectionable. Intimation of illicit sex between Spade and Iva, and also between Spade and Brigid, had to go.

Cairo's homosexuality posed one of the biggest obstacles to securing overall approval of the picture. Hammett didn't mince words in the novel. "This guy is queer," says Sam Spade's secretary as she hands him an engraved card bearing his name—Mr. Joel Cairo. He speaks in a "high-pitched thin voice," carries "gaily colored silk handkerchiefs fragrant of *chypre*," and walks in "mincing bobbing steps." Introduced as a "gorgeous young customer" to an unwitting Spade in the pre-Code 1931 version of the film, Otto Matieson's "Dr. Cairo" comes across merely as a starched sophisticate. Arthur Treacher, a tall, lanky English actor who specialized in impeccable butlers, including Jeeves to David Niven's Bertie Wooster in *Thank You, Jeeves* (1936), played Cairo for a wacky Wodehouse-type humor in the post-Code *Satan Met a Lady.* Hal Wallis realized that American audiences—not to mention the Hays Office—were not ready for a candid look at homosexuality, which traditionally drew laughs and jeers out front.

"We cannot approve the characterization of Cairo as a pansy as indicated by the lavender perfume, high pitched voice, and other accouterments," Breen wrote Jack Warner. "In line with this, we refer you to Page 148, where Cairo tries to put his arm around the boy's shoulder and is struck by the boy for so doing. This action, in light of Cairo's characterization, is definitely unacceptable." After reading the final script a few days later, Breen also noted his objection to Cairo's effeminate behavior in scenes 21 and 155, where he rubs the boy's temple.

After seeing Lorre's first day's work, Wallis dashed off a memo to Huston: "Don't try to get a nancy quality into him, because if you do we will have trouble with the picture." Huston bent to Breen's will. In the film, secretary Effie Perine (Lee Patrick) presents Cairo's calling card to a bemused Spade, who holds it to his nose.

"Gardenia," says Effie.

"Quick, darling, in with him," replies Spade.

The rest Huston left to Lorre's subtlety and the viewer's imagination.

Wallis kept a close watch on production with a mind to polishing the rough edges. He found need for improvement all the way around. Lorre, he said, needed to enunciate, to round out his words. Greenstreet likewise. Wallis felt the film's tempo was too leisurely and singled out Bogart, with his "suave form of delivery," for dragging out the scenes: "All of the action seems a little too slow and deliberate, a little labored and we must quicken the tempo and the manner of speaking the lines."

The svelte 137-pound Lorre who stepped before the camera on June 18 seemed younger, fitter, swifter. More was asked of him and he asked more of himself. It was partly a change in attitude. Lorre's stuntman, Harvey Parry, drew this analogy: "I would say it would be like you're going to be a clerk at Woolworth's 5 & 10 cent store, and suddenly you get moved to Saks Fifth Avenue. So now you put on a tie and you're a little cleaner and your diction is a little better. You say, 'Good morning, may I help you?' where before you said, 'What do you want?'"

The role of Joel Cairo was the best of its kind to come his way in years, and Lorre knew it. He kept it that way by deftly cross-graining layers of subtle characterization. Fastidiously arrayed in a black three-piece suit, wing collar, and bow tie, the actor articulates with delicate exactness as he mindfully fondles his umbrella, suggestively brushing the phallic handle across his lips. Each nuance finds its own pose and posture; meticulously gaited movements pause his body language; his forehead furrows, rustling his greasy curls; groomed fingers ceremoniously smooth a white glove over the brim of his upturned hat; the lines of his mouth bend to a shy intimacy, then twist to a silkily menacing grin. But his malevolence, veiled behind guileless eyes, is benign. After telling Spade he intends to search his office for the falcon, Cairo orders him at gunpoint to clasp his hands together at the back of his neck. Spade easily disarms him, punches him in the face with his own right hand (not once, but twice), then jabs him onto a couch. Minutes later, Cairo comes to and steps to the mirror to assess the damage to his appearance. "Look what you did to my shirt," he pitifully whines.

When Gutman chips the enamel coating on the falcon and uncovers the lead beneath, Cairo squeals in rage: "You! It's you who bungled it! You and your stupid attempt to buy it! . . . You—you imbecile! You bloated idiot! You stupid fat-head, you!" Sobbing, he collapses into an armchair, his tantrum spent. With hearty truculence, Gutman announces that the quest will take them to Istanbul. Cairo's mewling tapers off and his face brightens. "Are you going?" he whimpers. Roused by the Fat Man's resolve, he meekly proposes to go with him.

"I'd often shoot a scene with Peter and find it quite satisfactory, nothing more," recalled Huston.

> But then I would see it on the screen in rushes and discover it to be far better than what I had perceived on the set. Some subtlety of expression was seen by the camera and recorded by the microphone that the naked eye and ear did not get. He'd be doing little things that the camera close on him would pick up that standing a few feet away you wouldn't see. It was underplaying; it was a play that you would see if you were close to him, as a close-up, as a camera is

close. Things would flicker there and burn up slightly, like a lamp, and then dim down, and come on again. You're watching something as if it were in motion.

Behind the scenes, Huston nurtured a family feeling. "You felt you were working in an atmosphere of love," recalled Patrick. "You were with a director who loved every one of you and wanted everyone to be good in his own way. He made everything very intimate to you. What he had to say to you was very quiet, in your ear. He could illuminate just what he wanted with a few words. He made you feel somehow that you were so important to the picture. And it only led to good performances."

Members of the crew likewise felt this warm embrace. Script supervisor Meta Wilde, William Faulkner's mistress, recalled in her autobiography that when Lorre learned she spoke a smattering of German, he delighted in engaging her in conversation on the set.

Huston set up an open table by the pool at the Lakeside Country Club across from the studio. He kept attendance voluntary and the spirit festive. Ahead of schedule, the company took long lunches, leaving shop talk behind. After shooting, the bitter-enders—Huston, Bogart, Lorre, Astor, and Ward Bond—reassembled for a few drinks and stayed on until midnight.

The camaraderie nurtured by Huston fed a repertory spirit among the cast and crew. In 1962 Lorre reminisced that filming was "one of my happiest memories and [a] very nostalgic one, because for a few years we used to have a sort of stock company, an ensemble.... It was a ball team.... Each one of those people, whether it was Claude Rains or Sydney Greenstreet or Bogart, or so on, there is one quality about them in common that is quite hard to come by. You can't teach it and that is to switch an audience from laughter to seriousness. We can do it at will, most people can't."

As the cast grew more comfortable with each other, the line between work and play faded, setting the stage for an elaborate practical joke called "Shock the Tourists." "We didn't want people around watching us," wrote Astor in her autobiography, *A Life on Film*. "We had an odd childlike territorial imperative about our set. It was hard work, and we didn't want anyone looking over our shoulder, so to speak. Also, we had a sneaky feeling that we were doing something different and exciting, and we didn't want to show it to anyone until it was finished."

Each player had a move. The arrival of starstruck onlookers prompted Huston to call out "Number Five." Bogart would suddenly launch into a prepared harangue, calling Greenstreet a "fat old fool" and viciously berating the actor for upstaging him. In a mock attempt to check Bogart's temper and quell the racket, Huston would intervene. Lorre, too, had his charade. "Whenever VIPs would come on the set to witness the shooting," said Huston, "Peter would slip into Mary Astor's dressing room and come out buttoning up his fly as people were passing. This was a regular procedure. Peter loved to shock people."[4]

Their "goddam gags," so called by the long-suffering publicity man, put an end to gaping visitors. Huston got his closed set.

"The combination of Huston, Bogart and Lorre was very fast company in the wit department," wrote Astor.

> There was a kind of abrasive, high-powered kidding-on-the-level thing that went on, and you joined in at your own risk. . . . I did the best I could for a while, but it was more than I could handle. I got sort of backed into a corner: "Then you *admit* you don't like pointillism, that the Fauves were a bunch of jerks?" "I didn't say that, I just said——" My eyes started to smart and I whimpered, "I just can't keep up with this!" Bogie laughed his head off, along with the rest and then got up and came around the table to my place. He wiped my tears with elaborate care. "You're O.K., baby," he said. "So you're not very smart—but you know it and what the hell's the matter with that!" Although it was still on a kidding level, Bogie really meant what he had said. "Be yourself. Be yourself and you're in."

Huston wrapped production at 2:00 a.m., Saturday, July 19, two days ahead of schedule and at a cost of $327,182—$54,000 under budget and only $50,000 above the production costs on the 1931 Del Ruth version. Undergoing several title changes—preproduction as *Knight of Malta* and postproduction as *The Gent from Frisco*—*The Maltese Falcon* was released October 1, 1941.

"It was not the effort," Lorre said of the film, which he cited as his best, "but the form which was unforgettable." Huston is foremost a storyteller respectful of his source material. Beyond a simple fitting and trimming, he took few liberties with the novel. His sharply stylized images, oblique compositions, and comic-strip economy charges Hammett's world with energy and visual wit without intruding on it. His hand as director was only heavy enough to keep Hammett and Hollywood apart, upholding the fidelity of the living language in the author's crisp dialogue and the hard-edged realism of his noir mood. Holding down the clutter of gloss, gimmicks, and generic trappings, he stepped behind the scenes and into Sam Spade's shoes. His eyes rove, seeking to uncase and react, to know all the angles and report all the facts. He adjusts the tension through the camera's lens, seeing all, one moment downright equivocal, the next pressing his specimens behind glass, defined in captive space. His is a subjective and often cynical view, commenting and caricaturing, seeing in and through, all told drawing a curtain on a dark underworld of greed and treachery.

Nominated for three Academy Awards—Best Picture, Sydney Greenstreet in Supporting Actor category, and John Huston for his screenplay—*The Maltese Falcon* lost on all counts. Spurred by public favor, Warner Bros. projected *The Further Adventures of The Maltese Falcon,* with Huston writing and directing and Bogart, Astor, Greenstreet, and Lorre reprising their roles. Plans for a sequel, however, never materialized.

Lorre also figured in casting discussions for a stage dramatization of *The Maltese Falcon,* set for fall of 1949. Dashiell Hammett wrote his sister in Pleasantville, New York, that the play would proceed "*if* we can get a good script and *if* we can get a good cast." Both Howard Duff, who had starred in *The Adventures of Sam Spade, Detective* on radio, and Fred MacMurray were favorites for the gumshoe. Instead of reprising the role of Joel Cairo, Lorre was under consideration for the part of Kasper Gutman. "I think we'll ignore the written-in-fatness," wrote Hammett. "He should do a pretty good job on it, used to be a fine actor." The play was not produced, with or without Lorre.

Lorre had shuffled from one studio to another for years, displaced and unanchored, always for hire. Separated from Celia, he now lived alone. The vacuum drew him to an extended family that embraced him as one of its own. Physically, Warner Bros. was on the small side, more intimate and cozy than Metro or Fox. From the moment a player passed through the gate, where he was met with a warm greeting from the guard, to the time he entered makeup and gulped his hot coffee and donuts, the sense of familial surroundings was reinforced. Overnight, Lorre became a fixture at the studio. In the Green Room, the noncafeteria part of the commissary reserved for actors, directors, and executives, sports fans crowded around Pat O'Brien for the latest scores, while those with a psychological bent attended Lorre's discussions on extrasensory perception, congenital memory, and déjà vu. "He was a font of knowledge," recalled set designer Harper Goff, "or at least knew about things in that vein. People who leaned toward that huddled around Peter."

Lorre labeled his Warner Bros. cohorts "journeymen" actors. It was an exclusive club of peers built on mutual respect and shored up by fierce loyalty. They lost patience with no-talents and slackers. No matter how bad the hangover—or the picture—they showed up on time.

"Peter was a director's dream," confirmed actor Bob Cummings, a coworker on *The Chase* (1946). "He arrived prepared and ready to shoot, and was very facile at converting the director's ideas quickly and efficiently into usable film with seemingly no effort. He knew his trade and was skillful in his 'under' playing of the part. If asked to 'give' more to heighten the tension of the film moment he was capable of supplying the extra projection. . . . There was nothing pretentious or up-stage about him."

"Peter was glad to be working," recalled producer-screenwriter Milton Sperling. "He was an actor with grease paint on his collar and that was the way to be. . . . We were just a bunch of working stiffs who were going from picture to picture and there was no sense of history involved, or giant contributions to cinema being made."

Working with Humphrey Bogart represented the best of times for Lorre. They became good friends during filming of *The Maltese Falcon*. Bogart barely survived his stormy marriage to the irascible Mayo "Sluggy" Methot, an actress of little stature with a fiery temper and a fancy for Scotch. After their bouts, he found a neutral corner at Lorre's house.

"One night Mayo walked out on Bogey from my house and Bogey stayed with me," Lorre told columnist and critic Ezra Goodman over martinis at a San Fernando Valley hash house in the early 1960s.

Finally, I got fed up with Bogey and threw him out. He disappeared into the night. He was making the rounds.

At 6 a.m. I got a phone call. It was Bogey's voice or the remains of it. "Pick me up and take me to the studio," he said and gave me a certain telephone number. I didn't know the address. I finally phoned and got the address. The place was two blocks from me in the Hollywood hills.

It was a private house. After all the joints had closed, Bogey kept wandering in the hills. We were then doing "Passage to Marseilles" [*sic*]. He was unshaven and dirty for the part. It's ugly enough, his face, without it. As he was wandering around in the hills, he smelled coffee from a house. He puts his face against the lit up kitchen window, his horrible face. "Could I get a cup of coffee?" he said. The woman inside let out a horrible shriek. But then she recognized him. She had just arrived in Hollywood and was a movie fan. "Mr. Bogart, come in," she said. So there he was, when I got there, sitting with four kids around him, drinking brandy and coffee, talking to the kids, a big story conference.[5]

It was the pixie in Lorre, the elfin charm, that struck a chord with Bogart. Bogart, said Lorre, had a heart as soft as goose liver, and just as big. Whatever they saw in each other—scamp or Samaritan—Bogart and Lorre didn't trade in images. "I like Bogie because he is one hundred per cent what he is and that is very rich if you know him," said Lorre. "So you take all the disadvantages with the advantages." "Bogie called a spade a spade," said Dan Seymour, who played greasy villains in numerous Bogart and Lorre films. "Peter did this, too."

While their methods sometimes differed, their goals remained the same. Bogart was confrontational, always willing to take a suspension to press his point, while Lorre took a page from *Švejk,* mocking his victims—usually the patriarchal echelon—in the very act of subordination.

During the making of *The Cross of Lorraine* (1943) at Metro, L.B. Mayer one day crashed the set with a company of Washington brass. "Colonels were just errand boys in that group," said director Tay Garnett.

> Mayer was playing every instant the big boss over all this big thing. And he was showing off pretty well and Peter walked by him and he had on, of course, the Nazi uniform, the black shirt.
>
> "Oh, Peter, come over here," called Mayer.
>
> So Peter turned around and said, "Yes, Mr. Mayer," and walked over to him.
>
> "It seems strange to see you in a Gestapo uniform. How do you keep yourself in character?"
>
> And Peter looked him right in the face and said, "I eat a Jew every morning for breakfast." Well, it got a hell of a laugh from the brass, because they all knew Mayer was Jewish and a lot of them didn't know that Peter was.

More often, Lorre and Bogart set their sights on the Warner brothers. They labeled Jack a "kreep."

"How dare you call me that?" demanded the studio head. "The dictionary says that a creep is a loathsome, crawling thing."

"But we spell it 'Kreep,' not 'Creep,'" explained Bogart.

Lorre shared the "honor" for introducing the descriptor into the Hollywood vernacular with *New York Journal-American* critic John McClain, writer John O'Hara, and actor Gilbert Roland: "They used to use the word 'jerk' for everybody and we got sick and tired of it, so we made up our minds to invent a new word and so we invented 'kreep.' Now 'kreep' is spelled with a 'k' and it doesn't come from creeping. It's just a word." One of the most recurrent epithets in Lorre's vocabulary, it described anybody and everything, depending on the given inflection. "Those kreeps that steal the show," he explained, are the big stars. "That kreep!" with an exclamation point, is synonymous for "That jerk!"

"In any case," said Lorre, "the word today is more misused than 'jerk,' so let's drop both of them." Jack Warner, who held that "every actor is a shit," didn't buy it and returned the favor in his autobiography, *My First Hundred Years in Hollywood* (1965), in which he called Lorre "a plump little fellow with a deceptive baby face [who] deliberately upstaged other actors because there was no other way he could compensate for his lack of height and good looks."

One afternoon Harry Warner conducted a decked-out delegation from the Iranian air force around the studio.

"Listen, you creeps," said Lorre, feigning almost uncontrollable indignation, "get those uniforms the hell back to wardrobe in a hurry."

In an interview with *Life* magazine entertainment editor George Frazier, Lorre told how he had found himself in the midst of a group of studio syco-phants during a break on *The Mask of Dimitrios*. He began to pace nervously up and down and pretend to pull out his hair. "God damn that Jack Warner!" he shouted. "I sent the creep out for a beer for me ten minutes ago and he isn't back yet." "Lorre says that it was wonderful to watch everyone suddenly drift away from him," wrote Frazier in his Hollywood memoir, "as if mere proxim-ity to a heretic would indict their own willingness to die for dear old Warners."

At Finlandia Baths, a steam room on Sunset Boulevard where Hollywood's glamour boys relaxed after a tough day before the cameras, Lorre took a high colonic.

"Jesus, it stinks in here," Bogart greeted him.

"It's a lot of those Warner Bros. scripts I'm getting rid of," Lorre returned with stinging quickness.

"When he pulled these dirty cracks," said director Tay Garnett, "he'd have that innocent expression on his pan, which made his menace infinitely more powerful, but he was anything but innocent. Some of these shafts had barbs on them and some of the barbs had venom on them, because he could be vindictive when he disliked anything, but his delivery was always the same."

Like Bogart, Lorre crusaded against pomposity, toppling the highbrows and cutting through the posh and pretension. "Peter claimed that people never listened to what you say in a social context," recalled Hal Kanter. To prove it, Lorre took him to a party. The hostess greeted them and asked, "How are you?"

"I've been terrible," said Peter, smiling. "I caught your husband fucking my maid."

"Oh, how nice," replied the inattentive hostess.

Prefacing his forecasts with a favorite expression—"I can feel it in my urine"—Lorre scorched ears and raised eyebrows.

No one bored them for long. Together, Bogart and Lorre choked off hard cases by puffing smoke in their faces. They called it their "smoking gag."

Director Michael Curtiz was another of their victims. Lorre told Goodman,

> When he was directing "Passage to Marseilles" [sic], in our drunken stupor we decided to blackmail Curtiz into a sense of humor. Curtiz has no sense of humor when shooting. He eats pictures and excretes pictures. Bogey and I are one-take people. In addition to that, we were not supposed to waste any film during the war.
>
> We came in from a horrible night. Bogey apologized to Warner. Then we went on the deck of a big boat set. Bogey was in the first shot. Mike says to Bogey: "You do this," and Bogey says: "I heard the most wonderful story" and tells some stupid, square joke, endless. Bogey gets through and Mike says, "Now we shoot." He made nineteen takes and didn't get it. He almost went out of his mind. Then I started to tell a long story. It took him about two days to find out whenever he laughed he got the scene in one take and whenever he didn't laugh he didn't get a take. Two mornings later, Bogey and I, two staggering little figures, arrived on the big set. Mike saw us a block away on the set and he started laughing like crazy in advance.

Jack Warner wasn't laughing. "I noticed today that there was a tremendous amount of takes of one scene on your picture," he wrote in a letter to Lorre. "Upon investigation, I find that you did not know your dialogue, after the director had told you on Saturday you were going to have an important scene today. . . . There is a war going on, and we are trying to save film. This one scene used up many unnecessary hundreds of feet of film."

Passage to Marseille notwithstanding, "the bum true-blue," Truman Capote paraphrased Bogart in his own language, "was any fellow who shirked his job, was not, in meticulous style, a 'pro' in his work. . . . Never mind that he might play poker until dawn and swallow a brandy for breakfast: he was always on time on the set, in make-up and letter-perfect in his part."

At Shepperton Studio, where Bogart and Lorre were completing *Beat the Devil* in spring of 1953, the two actors told an interviewer, "Acting's our racket, so we do our best." Doing their best, however, meant not taking themselves too seriously, either.

"You're supposed to be a tough guy?" someone once belligerently queried.

"Yes, but only for the money," Lorre softly answered.

"As long as we have to do this meaningless shit," he told a co-worker, "let's have fun while we're at it." He loved to stir up trouble, to charge situations with humor and excitement. "Whenever they were setting up for a shot," recalled Frank Capra of Lorre's antics on *Arsenic and Old Lace,* "the assistant director would always measure the distance from the camera to the subject so that they would have the proper focus. He would hold the tape in his right hand and back away from the camera to the subject holding out his hand with the end of his tape behind him. The assistant was a rather elderly man and every time he approached Peter, whom he couldn't see, he would snarl, giving the old guy seizures."

"Peter was always ready for a laugh," said Lorre's friend and East Coast attorney Jonas Silverstone. "He was always ready to provide one. He could see humor where the average run-of-the-mill Joe may not have seen it. He'd laugh very well, very heartily. As a matter of fact, he laughed so heartily his face became red. He would guffaw, really. He would explode with laughter if something struck him as being funny. He loved a good story. He loved primarily good situations from which he could draw fun."

If the situations didn't exist, Lorre happily created them. He often carried a makeup bag. Broderick Crawford related that when Lorre heard the call, "We'll be ready in five minutes," he would cry out, "I've got to check my makeup and fix my hair." He would then retreat to his portable dressing room, where he closed the door, unzipped the bag, and retrieved his schnapps. After a relaxed drink and a cigarette, he appeared, looking exactly as before. Among his cohorts, his familiar greeting, "Want to check your makeup?" meant a welcome break from filming.

"Peter told me," said Frankie Avalon, who starred in *Muscle Beach Party,* one of Lorre's last pictures, "that he and Bogie were once doing some publicity work for a picture. When the public found out that the two were at '21,' a crowd began to wait for Bogie to come out and sign autographs. Bogie didn't want to and asked the maitre d' for a large napkin. Peter tied it around Bogie's writing arm and explained to everyone that he could not sign autographs because he had broken his arm."

"Another night Bogey and I were bored at Chasen's," Lorre told Goodman and countless others. "With two other guys, we dragged out the safe from Chasen's office and onto Beverly Boulevard, several blocks away from the restaurant. We were loaded at the time. It took twelve people to drag it back."

Together they even lifted a rubber hand from the property department and draped it over the side of an open casket at the Utter McKinley Mortuary showroom on Wilshire Boulevard.

At a party stocked with studio executives and contract players, Erich Wolfgang Korngold, the Academy Award–winning composer of musical scores for many Warner Bros. pictures, was, as usual, asked to play the piano. "As he was playing," related his son Ernst W. Korngold, "my mother faced him with her back to the other guests. She suddenly felt a sharp nip in the nether regions of her anatomy. She whirled around to discover Henry Blanke, the producer and a close friend, directly behind her. Assuming he had pinched her, she slapped Blanke's face at the same time—sort of—apologizing by telling him, 'I'm sorry, but I don't like that.' Blanke protested his innocence but did not elaborate until the next day when he sent her flowers and a note in which he affirmed that he had not pinched her, that, in fact, nobody had pinched her, but that Peter Lorre, who was setting next to him, had bitten her. So much for the Golden Age of the cinema."[6]

"Everything was looked at with a great sense of humor and skepticism," Paul Henreid warmly remembered. It was an attitude, a hearty response, but more than that a well-rounded life of hard work and stress-dissipating, bonding fun. At Warner Bros., it was the Dead End Kids grown up.

In his autobiography, Jack Warner told of receiving news in late summer of 1936 that Nazi thugs in Berlin had trapped Joe Kauffman, "our Warner Brothers man in Germany," in an alley and "hit him with fists and clubs, and kicked the life out of him with their boots, and left him lying there." Joe Kauffman was presumably Phil Kauffman, the studio's general manager in Germany, who had fled the country in 1933, was transferred to London, where he continued in the same capacity, and died later that year of natural causes in Stockholm. Warner didn't need to concoct a story about the brutal slaying of a loyal employee to justify the studio's stand against fascism. The Warner brothers— Harry, Albert, Sam, and Jack—were no strangers to oppression. Anti-Semitic pogroms in their native Poland had forced the family to flee in 1883. A lack of formal education "was the seed that made me strive to make movies the way I did," recalled Harry, the eldest son. "I didn't want to just entertain, I felt the need to educate." When it came to "combining good citizenship with good picture making," the Warner brothers put their money where their mouths were long before they could afford to do so. In 1917 they went far out on a financial limb to make a motion picture of Ambassador James W. Gerard's *My Four Years in Germany*, which carried a "stirring warning about the menace of the German military threat."

Anti-European sentiment ran high in postwar America. Senate Republicans, in the ascendancy following the 1918 congressional elections, opposed ratification of the Treaty of Versailles, which included membership in the League of Nations. The unsettled political climate abroad during the 1930s drove

American heads deeper into isolationist sands. A majority wanted no part of "a foreign war for whatever idealistic purposes." Abiding the letter of America's neutrality policy, Warner Bros. courageously violated its spirit in a series of successful historical dress biographies—*The Story of Louis Pasteur* (1936), *The Life of Emil Zola* (1937), and *Juarez* (1939)—that drew veiled parallels to recent developments in Europe.

Warner Bros. looked no further than national headlines for their next foreign policy statement. After uncovering a German spy ring in America in 1938, G-Man Leon Turrou sold his story, "Confessions of a Nazi Spy," to the *New York Post*. On June 23, the same day the first installment was scheduled to appear in print, the studio purchased the film rights to his forthcoming book, *Nazi Spies in America,* and immediately began to transform the news story into a topical exposé of Nazism.[7] With *Confessions of a Nazi Spy* (1939), the most overtly anti-Nazi film made in Hollywood before America declared war on Hitler, Warner Bros. heralded the threat to world peace: "The Nazis are Coming!"

Those already here called the Warner brothers alarmists. Because the German-American Bund, from whose ranks spies had been recruited, protested the making of a movie that advertised the Nazi threat to the internal security of the United States, the studio skirted litigation by fictionalizing the principal characters. Dr. Georg Gyssling, consul for Germany in Los Angeles, not only voiced his government's objections with Joseph Breen, but met with Hal Wallis and asked that he cancel the film. The producer stood firm. When *Confessions of a Nazi Spy* opened on April 28, 1939, Hans Thomsen, the German chargé d'affaires, in a message to Secretary of State Cordell Hull, denounced the picture as an example of "pernicious propaganda poisoning German-American relations." Gyssling even warned the film industry that Germany would ban any motion picture featuring an actor who had appeared in *Confessions of a Nazi Spy.* Back in Germany, Joseph Goebbels threatened the State Department with retaliatory documentary films about American unemployment, gangsterism, and judicial corruption. Calling his bluff, Harry Warner fired back with a series of fourteen Technicolor patriotic shorts "driving home to Americans the manifold advantages they enjoy under a flag Warners has been proud to wave." Although Warner Bros. reportedly lost more than $1,250,000 on the production, promotion, and booking of the series, Warner vowed to turn out one film every three months because the studio had "a tremendous investment in the future of America and . . . the technical losses are justified in helping to secure that future."

In a speech at a St. Patrick's Day dinner in 1939, Harry Warner pledged to disregard "threats and pleas intended to dissuade us from our purpose. We have defied, and we will continue to defy, any elements that may try to turn us from our loyal and sincere purpose of serving America."

Out of deference to President Roosevelt, Jack Warner announced there would be "no propaganda pictures from Warner Brothers." No prowar pictures, however, did not mean the studio could not slip in the back door with anti-Nazi and pro-Allies films. As America's involvement in hostilities looked increasingly inevitable, the "Roosevelt Studio" prepared moviegoers for action with such titles as *The Fighting 69th* (1940), *Dive Bomber* (1941), *International Squadron* (1941), and *Sergeant York* (1941).

Credited with being "among the country's first industrialists to recognize the menace of the Fifth Column," Warner Bros. also packaged a wake-up call in *All Through the Night* (1942), which pitted tough and territorial gangsters against a group of Nazis muscling in on the American way of life. "I've been a registered Democrat ever since I could vote," says racketeer Gloves Donahue (Humphrey Bogart), protesting his patriotism. "I may not be citizen number one, but I pay my taxes, wait for traffic lights and buy twenty-four tickets regular to the policeman's ball." When a woman declares, "It's about time someone knocked the Axis back on its heels," Donahue retorts, "It's about time somebody knocked those heels back on their axis!" American audiences took pride in homegrown hoodlums defeating Nazi spies at their own game. As in *M*, where the criminal underworld rallies to expunge the evil in its midst, American gangsters—"Damon Runyan types," director Vincent Sherman called them—oust Nazi fifth columnists—The Fivers—an element far more rancorous in the minds of domestic audiences.[8]

Once again, Lorre figures as a foreigner, this time as Pepi, a Nazi agent pursued by the underworld. However, he is no longer pitiful, but a savage and sadistic assassin, aptly characterized by Donahue as a "goggle-eyed little rat." As in *M*, he prefaces murder with music, this time by humming "Frohe Botshaft" ("The Joyful Message"). By adding a touch of humor to villainous parts and shading his comic roles with sinister overtones, Lorre liked to keep audiences guessing.

In his opening scene, the script called for the actor to squeeze some information vital to the Nazi sabotage operation from Papa Miller, a reluctant informant played by refugee actor Ludwig Stössel. "He was always inventing business," said Sherman.

> He would never try to hurt another actor. But he had a way of doing a scene so that your eyes would be on him. He would do something offbeat with it that

would attract attention. He was very inventive about props. I remember one incident where he came into a shop. "Brother Vince," he said, "do you think you could have a popcorn machine on the outside so I could come in with a bag of popcorn, be eating popcorn while I play the scene with this man [Stössel]?" He was playing a scene in which he was very menacing and he thought it would be more effective if he casually ate popcorn, which is an interesting way for an actor to do things. I said, "That's a very good idea, Peter," and sure enough I had a popcorn machine outside and he came walking into the store. It was a bakery shop, and before I knew it he was running his hand over the icing on the cake. And he did two or three different things, and he was doing so damn many things, I said, "Peter, would you like a feather duster?"

He said, "A feather duster, what for?"

I said, "You can stick it up your ass and dust the furniture while you're at it."

He laughed.

Production on *All Through the Night* began on August 4 and lasted nine weeks. Sherman understood that the studio only wanted to put the picture behind it. Anti-Nazi films were finding only a lukewarm reception at the box office.[9] "We had a great laugh kidding the thing," recalled the director. Nonetheless, Lorre's patience could wear thin.

One day there was a scene in which Peter was running down a hallway with a revolver, followed by Judith Anderson. And she was saying, "Was ist los? Was ist los," or some damn German thing, and he shot into the lock of a door and kicked the door open. They did the scene once, and I said, "O.K., cut." And I wasn't quite sure whether I wanted to do it again or not, and I hesitated for a moment before I said, "Print that one." And Peter said, "That's all, brother Vince. It's six o'clock. I can only do this kind of crap once."

In the legal sense of the word—and only that—Peter and Celia had separated in 1940. Friends supposed Bogart, booze, and broads broke up their marriage. That's all it was, supposition drawn on distant memory. Lorre had barely met Bogey, rarely drank to excess, and hadn't gotten up to speed on the carnal highway. In Celia's silence, it is easy to read self-sacrificing indulgence of almost every possible peccadillo. Letting him off lead hardly mattered. However far he strayed, she knew he would always come back. Their relationship never really broke apart; it simply changed shape. Nothing—failure, setback, disappointment—tarnished his image as an unappreciated genius in Celia's eyes. Years after their divorce, his name still figured frequently in her diaries. As companion, mother, and agent, she kept her situation. She remained a constant in his life, unchanging, dependable, and above all, loyal. Except for several brief intermissions, Celia took care of Peter to the end of his life. After his death, she venerated his memory from her basement apartment—a veritable archive of his life and career—in their one-time home on Crescent Heights. It is Celia who is likely to be remembered as Mrs. Peter Lorre.

Cast opposite Humphrey Bogart and Conrad Veidt as a nightclub singer and Nazi pawn in *All Through the Night* was the "violet-eyed, blonde and vivacious"—so described in a Warner Bros. press release—Kaaren Verne.[10] Born in Berlin on April 6, 1918, and christened Ingeborg Greta Katerina Marie-Rose Klinckerfuss, Karen inherited a musical background from both sides of her family. "They lived music," said Barbara Sykes, Karen's younger sister, "though none were really musicians, except my [paternal] grandmother, Johanna Schultz Klinckerfuss, [who] was a pianist and the last pupil Franz Liszt took." On her mother's side were the Bechsteins, an internationally famous family of piano manufacturers. Although Ella, Karen's mother, gave private vent to her operatic singing skills, her station in society prevented her from going public with her considerable talent. "They were immensely rich," said Barbara, "and she wasn't even allowed to go by herself to the mailbox around the corner of the house in Berlin."

Apollo Klinckerfuss, Karen's paternal grandfather, had rented and repaired pianos and even dabbled in design. At the turn of the century, Erich Klinckerfuss, Karen's father, came to America for a business education. When Erich wed Ella in 1904, he married into the firm as a franchise manager for the United Kingdom. The advent of war in August 1914 caught them on holiday in Germany, cut off—permanently as it turned out—from their household possessions in London. Commissioned to an artillery unit, Erich survived the war to eventually become general director of the Bechstein piano company.

At age six, Karen attended the Lehwess-Schule, a private school in the Nikolassee district of Berlin. Students who expected to continue their education through the thirteenth grade and take the *Abitur,* a rigorous three-day written and oral exam, began the study of languages in the fifth grade. First came English, then French, and finally Latin in the eleventh grade. Under protest, Karen and Barbara also took piano lessons. "We hated it," said Barbara, who remembered Aunt Margarethe Klinckerfuss sitting beside them with a ruler. If they did not hold their fingers in the correct position, "we got it on our knuckles but really hard." Harsh discipline, along with a minimum of one hour of practice each day, backfired with both sisters. After six years, Karen admitted being "never too good at it."

"She was a very bad student," said Barbara. "She was artistic and she could sing—not like our mother—but otherwise she was hopeless." An inventive child who "could put everyone around her finger," she openly nurtured the dream of becoming an actress. She was and remained starstruck. Matching famous names and faces came easily with her collection of movie stills and autographs. Soon after enrolling in the Lyzeum und Deutsche Oberschule Zehlendorf, Karen won an acting scholarship to Berlin's Staatstheater. The youngest student in her class, she began her lessons on April 6, 1934, her sixteenth birthday. Her decision to become an actress won family acceptance. She clearly had talent. Moreover, tuition was free, no small consideration to the Klinckerfusses, whose fortune had collapsed in the wake of the 1929 crash.

Contrary to reports generated by studio biographers that she had won awards for her acting, Karen passed through almost unnoticed, playing small roles in yet smaller productions. Graduation hinged on a political examination, which she failed. Asked what office Joseph Goebbels held, she correctly answered, "Minister of Popular Enlightenment and Propaganda," but could not remember the name of Theater Chamber president Rainer Schlösser, who had succeeded Otto Laubinger in September 1935. Goebbels's Reichskulturkammer (State Chamber of Culture) also directed that members of the State Theater sign a loyalty oath to Hitler. Karen refused. According to Barbara, the new requirement didn't accord with her political conscience, which went "against anything where you had to do something she didn't like."

Soon after, she met and fell in love with pianist Arthur Young, who was appearing in Berlin with the Jack Hylton Orchestra. When Erich died of tuberculosis in 1934, his brother Walter assumed guardianship of the girls—until they turned twenty-one. Karen, then eighteen, and Young laid plans to elope outside Germany. Tipped off to the scheme and assuming they would travel to England, her Uncle Walter alerted the police, who monitored the western border crossings. But Karen and Arthur headed north to Taarbeck, Denmark, where they married on August 30, 1936. After completing a concert tour of Norway, Young and his pregnant bride returned to Berlin, where Karen gave birth to a son, Alastair, on April 8, 1937. By 1939 the couple had separated. Arthur reluctantly agreed to a divorce on one condition: that he keep Alastair. Without setting legal machinery in motion, both parents went their own way, leaving the boy in the care of a nanny.

A British subject by marriage, Karen decided to pursue an acting career in England, where she worked as a model. Her perfect teeth, featured in toothpaste advertisements, gave her the exposure she needed. It is at this point that Karen is usually "discovered" by film producer Irving Asher. The storybook beginning leaves out a few things. In September 1938 she failed to win a role in Gaumont-British's *The Outsider* about an osteopath who makes a crippled girl walk. By mid-January 1939, 20th Century–Fox had signed and then released the young actress over a contract dispute about an allowance, which was needed, Karen wrote, "not so that I could support myself and the child, but so that I could be deasently [sic] turned out and a credit to the company." Her screen test brought Karen to the attention of Asher, who gave her a list of names, told her to pick one, and cast her opposite Rex Harrison in the London Films production of *Ten Days in Paris* (1939).[11]

On the strength of the producer's recommendation, MGM offered Karen a contract and brought her to Hollywood in the spring of 1940. Five days after arriving in California, she suffered an acute case of appendicitis and underwent surgery. Traveling "under convoy!" through Nazi-infested waters had also exacerbated a skin condition "brought on by nervousness." Karen wrote Rosalind Martin, Alastair's babysitter, that she "couldn't even think of starting a picture or making a general test for Metro-Goldwyn-Mayer." After convalescing under the care of the Ashers, she began a daily routine designed to eliminate her German accent: "I am beginning to get how seriously they take it making pictures here and what a lot of training they give you, before you start on a picture." The *Hollywood Reporter* announced that the actress was "slated for a top role in *Witch of the Wilderness,* her first Hollywood picture." Metro also considered her for a supporting part in Jeanette MacDonald and Nelson Eddy's *Bitter Sweet* (1940), a musical remake of Noel Coward's 1929 operetta. "I have made one test that's been quite a success," she told Rozzie, "so it looks as if I'll get a start soon." What she got was *Sky Murder* (1940), a Nick Carter mystery. Frank Orsatti, Karen's agent (also Lorre's) had assured her "that once I had done a picture, they would get me an entirely new deal at the studio." Despite her lackluster beginning in a budget whodunit, Karen believed that "they liked me in this last picture I did and also realize that this illness [anemia followed by a tonsillectomy] wasn't my fault." After "talks" with Louis B. Mayer, she was told that her option would be taken up. It wasn't.

"A beautiful German girl . . . was brought to my office by an agent," recalled director Vincent Sherman in his autobiography *Studio Affairs: My Life as a Film Director.* "She spoke English with only a slight hint of an accent and seemed to be a good actress." He immediately cast her as Sylvia Helmuth, the female lead in *Underground* (1941), an anti-Nazi melodrama about a German family split along party lines. In February 1941 Karen had signed a freelance contract with Warner Bros. Because her extended work permit was due to expire in October, she was only too glad to grant the studio an option for a long-term contract in August. Steve Trilling even promised her that Warner Bros. "would give her whatever aid we could" in obtaining a quota number.

Visiting the set of *The Maltese Falcon*, Karen heard "that voice" on the other side of a partition.[12] She had to meet him. The starstruck newcomer told Peter that she was his biggest fan, despite the fact that "in Germany my folks would not let me see any Lorre pictures because they were too gruesome." During the making of *All Through the Night*, Peter and Karen became inseparable. She sat on his lap for studio photographers. They strolled around the back lot, hand in hand, and turned their lunch break into a picnic retreat. By the end of the picture, everyone recognized that their friendship had grown into something more serious.

To Peter, Karen was beauty, elegance, excitement. To Karen, Peter was celebrity, intellect, and old-world charm. On the set of *Kings Row* (1942), whose production schedule overlapped shooting of *All Through the Night*, she spoke very lovingly of Peter and admitted to co-worker Bob Cummings that she found him surprisingly gentle and romantic. "Karen admired him a great deal," said Naomi Yergin, Irving's wife. "Peter was a very charming man. He was an 'I kiss your hand, madam' type of man. European men have a way of making a woman feel important and Peter had that down."

Vincent Sherman first suspected the romance when Lorre asked if they would be working on an upcoming Saturday. "He was like a different person when he was with Karen," said the director. "He was a romantic young man then. I'll never forget that when he came on the set, he was wearing a little slip-over sweater and his hair was neatly combed and he was very well dressed. I think it was in late spring or early summer and I thought, my God, how attractive he looks, very dapper. He was obviously very happy."

Lorre had Gilbert Roland to thank for the brush-up. The athletic Latin lover had encouraged him to lose weight and get in shape. Lorre heeded his advice and dieted on steak and spinach. On August 8, 1941, the five-foot-five American citizen weighed in at a svelte 130 pounds. Lorre felt like a new man in more ways than one. That same day, by order of the U.S. District Court, "Ladislav Lowenstein [*sic*]" officially became Peter Lorre.

Lorre's exuberance showed, on and off screen. On weekends Peter and Karen headed to the beach, where he confidently braved the waves for the first time. Roland also shoved a racket into his hand and pushed him onto the tennis court. Three times a week he battled the likes of Billy Wilder, Paul Lukas, and tennis pro Bill Tilden at the Beverly Hills Tennis Club. Lorre was "an active physical type," recalled friend Burl Ives, with "arms of steel." Keen to work his mischief on his tennis mates, Lorre cut Paul Lukas from the flock, targeting him as a lamb ripe for slaughter. Stomping onto the tennis court, he raged, "You thief! Kleptomaniac! You stole my shirt! Don't deny it! Look here, the initials P.L!" Lukas knew the routine all too well. Denial was futile. He wilted under fire while Lorre ripped the shirt off his back.

Less than two months after *All Through the Night* was completed, the Japanese attacked Pearl Harbor. Wrenched from its isolation, America geared up for war. Mobilization bred conviction, commitment lashed rhetoric into patriotic fervor, and Hollywood joined the armed forces in earnest. Director Frank Capra expected to enlist in the Army Signal Corps and make training films.[13] "Anytime they wanted to call me," he said, "I was ready." Before leaving for duty, however, he needed to crank out "a cheap film for a fast buck to keep [his] family going." Capra had earlier seen Howard Lindsay and Russel Crouse's sellout stage hit *Arsenic and Old Lace* and had fallen in love with it. It was just the show he needed. Back in New York, he caught Lindsay backstage between acts; "Howard, I've got a yen to film your great show. Any hopes?" Lindsay told him they had already sold the rights to Warner Bros.[14] Anyway, a film version could not be distributed for theatrical release until the play closed on Broadway, in three to four years.

"Jack Warner was sort of a mercurial man," said Capra. "He'd go for things that maybe other people wouldn't go for, if he had the right incentive." The director counted on that and did his homework. After all, Warner would be a fool to invest money in a film and then lock it in a vault for three years, maybe longer. Capra learned that Josephine Hull, Jean Adair, and John Alexander had four weeks' vacation coming. He negotiated their salaries beforehand, conditionally, of course, and arranged to bring them to Hollywood. He next set Cary Grant, a sure box-office success, to star as Mortimer Brewster, and asked the production staff at Warner Bros. to secretly draw up budget estimates for a four-week schedule. Capra handed the set designers interior and exterior sketches for a single set, a spooky old house next to a cemetery in Brooklyn. With production costs calculated to the last dollar, he went to see Jack Warner and made his pitch.

"Don't throw me out the window until you hear me."

"What the hell you got?"

"I want to make *Arsenic and Old Lace*."

"What window do you want to be thrown out of?"

"No, no, I got it all set. I got the cast, the star, the sets, the budget, everything's all set."

"You know I can't make the picture."

"You got me to make the picture. Now that's an asset. And I've got it all set up and I'll make you a hell of a picture and that's an asset."

"Why, you son-of-a-bitch, you got everything ready, you could go tomorrow, couldn't you?"

"Yes, I can."

And he did.

Lorre was Capra's first choice for the role of the diffident plastic surgeon, Dr. Einstein. The director was a great fan of Lorre's, "as an actor, as a personality, and as a man who could do almost anything he wanted to do." There had been talk of the two working together in 1935, while they were both under contract to Columbia. In 1939 Capra had turned independent, forming his own production company, Frank Capra Productions. Jack Warner had been his first customer. From a one-picture commitment had come *Meet John Doe* (1941). Now Capra asked for Lorre, who was ready and willing to cross over to comedy. He was also available, since he was not scheduled to begin work on *The Constant Nymph,* his next assignment, until early spring.

Lorre built Einstein into a fawning and frantically squeamish adolescent, the victim of his own waywardness. "You could give him a little bit of a part and he'd just milk it and add to it and be that character," said Capra. "I think he had more to do with his own characterizations than anybody else, because he knew himself better than anybody else."

In his autobiography, *The Name above the Title,* Frank Capra wrote that he "let the scene stealers run wild; for the actors it was a mugger's ball." There was no reason to stick to the script "word for word with actors [who] were so much better than the script." He often kept the cameras rolling, just to see what would happen. "There's one scene especially where Peter was telling Raymond Massey what a beautiful face he was going to give him if he could find a place to do it, and that's what they were going to do upstairs. . . . I just let them go—Peter telling him how beautiful he was going to make him look, how different he was going to make him look, a face that nobody would recognize. . . . 'I'll do it by cutting here and there.' That one scene went about three or four minutes beyond the scene and it's all in the picture."

Capra let Lorre and Grant ad-lib "because they were both very good at it." In one scene the two come down the stairway as Einstein tugs on Mortimer's arm and tries to warn him about his brother (Raymond Massey) "and Cary says, 'Don't touch me. What are you doing, doctor? What kind of a doctor are you?' And then the frustration of not being able to make this guy understand that he is in danger. All this was happening while they were coming down a stairway in the Brewster manor." Lorre stayed in character, but Grant sandwiched a friendly jibe between the rapid lines of dialogue: "Speak up, sonny, I can't hear you. . . . Will you stop underplaying, I can't hear you."

When Lorre had an idea, he didn't tell Capra, "I think I've got a great idea for you." He respectfully offered, "How would you like this?" Before filming a scene in the cellar where Dr. Einstein tries to dissuade Jonathan from using the gruesome, bloody "Melbourne" method to kill his brother, Lorre suggested, "Would it be good if we would just play part of it in the shadow? I don't see anything, just the shadow doing some terrible things and I can react to it." Capra thought this "very professional" and also "a very wise thing to do because he had himself a scene." So Lorre sat on a cellar step and played opposite Massey's hideous profile in shadow, creating a macabre scene to match the grisly dialogue of murder.

Capra considered Lorre

fully one-third of the show. He was a remarkable innovator, also a remarkable maker of his part, a man who built his part—he, himself, built his part with little tricks that were almost indiscernible, with his eyes, with his face, with his body, and with a little look at the right time, a little shrug of the shoulder. Each of these built a character and built up a love in the director for that person who's thinking of things that he should be thinking of. You're so grateful to him that his part just grows because he is making it into a real character. That is acting before your eyes!

Capra shot *Arsenic and Old Lace* between October 20 and December 16, 1941, bringing the picture in one day over schedule and $99,825 under the $1,220,000 budget. Previewed by servicemen around the world in 1943, *Arsenic and Old Lace* did not receive its theatrical release until September 1, 1944.

Testing Lorre's versatility in a small way, Warner Bros. next cast him as a romantic playboy in *The Constant Nymph* (1943), based on Margaret Kennedy's best-selling novel. In the book, the stage play, and two earlier film versions, the character of Jacob Birnbaum, played by Lorre, smacked of anti-Semitism. For the Warner feature, however, writer Kathryn Scola reworked (and renamed) the part, eliminating any hint of ethnic overtones. Certainly Kennedy's description of the "fat little Jew" did not draw casting to Lorre, who looked boyishly handsome and elegantly at ease in the role. Unfortunately, the editors trimmed his already small part to little more than a cameo. Even though the studio had dared to cast against type, it did not catch on to the possibilities of the actor's potential.

Not bound by contract, Lorre was free to come and go, and in May 1942 he punched in at Universal, where he was set to play Baron Ikito, a diabolical agent in *Invisible Agent* (1942). The face looked familiar; it was Mr. Moto behind the round glasses, but without the ingratiating smile. Toying with a paper cutter, he casts an eye on its utility for torture and purrs with sardonic mirth: "This is really a very useful machine. You know, if a person weren't careful, it could cut off his fingers, or his whole hand. Very *handy* machine, huh? *Handy,* isn't it?" Out of character for Ikito, it fit Lorre perfectly.

Cast opposite Lorre is Jon Hall as Frank Raymond, the grandson of the Invisible Man, who uses his grandfather's formula to spy on the enemy. Geared for wartime audiences, *Invisible Agent* trades in racial stereotypes, depicting the Japanese as inhuman fiends and the Nazis as brutes and buffoons.

"Your kind doesn't just kill men," denounces Hall. "You murder their spirits. You strangle their last breath of hope and freedom, so that you, the chosen few, can rule your slaves in ease and luxury. . . . You're drowning in the ocean of blood around this little barren island you call the new order. . . . killing your own, dog eating dog, until only the biggest and hungriest are left."

Americans swallowed it, in a big way. Produced at a modest $322,291, the picture grossed $1,041,500 in 116 weeks, making it one of the most successful pictures featuring the "invisible" special photographic effects by John P. Fulton.

When his uncle died and left him ten thousand dollars, Murray Burnett realized his "romantic dream" of sailing to Europe on an ocean liner. "I was married to a girl whose parents lived in Antwerp," said the New York teacher and playwright, "and I always wanted to go there. We were going to spend the summer (of 1938) with my wife's relatives—and we were going to have a marvelous two weeks vacation in the south of France. But by the time we reached Belgium, Hitler had invaded Austria and *Anschluss* had taken place." His wife's stepfather offered to underwrite their trip to France if they would pass through Vienna and help other relatives smuggle money and valuables out of Austria. "I was a kid and said, 'Well, great, wonderful,' and off I went to the American Consul, who said to me, and I quote, 'Mr. Burnett, we don't advise this trip. If you get into trouble, there's nothing we can do to help you.'" By that time the "City of Dreams" had become a nightmare. Only the Hotel de France took Jews, which was more than could be said of the taxi drivers. In the Opernplatz a monstrous sign pictured a hook-nosed Jew above the caption "Murderer, Thief." Real-life tragedy played on crying faces.

"I was excited about it and very angry about it," he later recalled. "I felt at that time and I still feel that no one can remain neutral in a world like that.

You had to take sides, no matter how cynical you might have been, no matter how much you wanted to be uninvolved. You had to side with the refugees. You had to."

At Cap Ferrat, a resort town on the southwestern coast of France, Burnett and his wife took in a nightclub whose black pianist knocked out the blues and jazz tunes of the day for enthusiastic tourists.

"'What a setting for a play!' That's all I said to my wife," Burnett mused some forty years later.

> The nightclub was a great contrast to the tragedy and tears. It was a gay, happy atmosphere. . . . Here was Hitler and there was no question they were on the brink of terror, not only anti-Semitic terror, but terror and war, and no one gave a damn. . . . By the time I had come back to New York, I had solidified all the experiences with the refugees and then it was a fairly simple matter to write the play [*Everybody Comes to Rick's*]. . . . Everybody in Casablanca came to Rick's, but everybody must come to a decision. Now that's pretty abstruse, but that's why I titled it, "Everybody Comes to Rick's." It was a double meaning.

Burnett and his writing partner, Joan Alison, wrote the stage play in six weeks. Their agent, Anne Watkins, sold it in one. Theater producers Martin Gabel and Carly Wharton optioned *Everybody Comes to Rick's* for Broadway, but artistic differences of opinion—Wharton could not accept the idea that Lois would sleep with Rick to get the Letters of Transit—spelled trouble. Burnett and Alison said no to a rewrite. The option was dropped. Watkins finally suggested they sell it to Hollywood. Contrary to reports that every studio in Hollywood turned it down, Burnett claims that within three weeks of its availability, Warner Bros.—which paid $20,000 for the screen rights—outbid Paramount for *Everybody Comes to Rick's* and retitled the play *Casablanca*.

Nazis had become an "obsession" for European émigrés, noted writer Henry Pachter. "It is no exaggeration to say that at that time we needed the Nazis as our *raison d'être*." For actors with Continental accents, Nazis also meant a reason to work. *Casablanca*'s credits read like a European refugee list. Executive producer Hal Wallis, who went to elaborate and costly lengths to assemble an ideal cast, conscripted nearly seventy-five émigré actors, not only for the rank and file parts, but for three of the principal roles as well. They formed a motley troupe whose mingled accents and cosmopolitan flair gave *Casablanca* a sense of shared past.

Austrian actor Paul Henreid had refused to sign with UFA after learning that an additional agreement would bind him to join the National Socialist Actor's Guild and uphold Nazi ideology. He originally turned down the rather flat supporting role of Victor Laszlo, *Casablanca*'s Resistance leader, in what promised to be a "flagboiler," but reportedly changed his mind in the aftermath of Pearl Harbor. Conrad Veidt, a native German, freely advertised his hatred of the Nazis, but never more so than as the sardonically malignant Major Strasser. S.Z. "Cuddles" Sakall, who played Carl, the head waiter at Rick's Café Américain, had fled Europe after building up a screen reputation for comedy in Germany and his native Austria.

Lorre came late to the cast of *Casablanca* and was nearly passed over because of his prior commitment to Universal for *Invisible Agent.* After coaxing Ingrid Bergman from David Selznick, freeing Lorre from Universal—which had lent his services to Warner Bros. for $2,500 per week—seemed almost too easy. Now Lorre was back at Warner Bros. and earning $1,750 per week for what turned out to be one and one-third weeks' work, a total of $2,333. For sheer publicity, Lorre was invaluable. In his telling, he had rebuffed Hitler, scoring a high spot on the Nazi hit list. His reinvented past even placed him at a Nazi rally, where he made sport of a monograph on poison gas written by a party member. These and other apocryphal odds and ends trickled down into the studio biographies and press releases.

Success has a thousand fathers. Murray Burnett conceived *Casablanca* and embellished it with "As Time Goes By," a bittersweet ballad written by Herman Hupfelt for a 1931 Broadway show called *Everybody's Welcome,* which flopped. Irene Lee, head of the story department at Warner Bros., persuaded Hal Wallis to buy the play and assigned Julius and Philip Epstein to write the screenplay. The Epstein twins adapted the play for the screen, rough-drafting the master script, simplifying the plot, tightening the structure, and working in character types; they brought Rick more in line with Bogart's screen image and saturated the film with memorable dialogue. Howard Koch revised and polished the screenplay, developing the Paris flashback and sharpening the political focus, then anxiously delivered scenes to the set on the morning they were to be shot; Casey Robinson shaped the love story. Wallis perfectly cast the picture and rode shotgun every mile of its rough ride; Michael Curtiz stamped it with the Warner Bros. style.

The cast also left its mark. In its "character analysis," the story department described Ugarte, a dealer in black market visas, as "mean, sneaky, is generally despised." It supposed he might be from Hungary or the Balkans. Concerned about the fragile foreign market, Jack Warner and Hal Wallis wanted to know for sure. Carl Schaefer assured the Front Office that Ugarte "could be Italian rather than Spanish so as to avoid the possibility of offending Latin America." Still not convinced, Wallis wrote Curtiz on May 25, the first day of shooting, that "'Senior Ugarte' should also be Italian, and if the name 'Ugarte' is definitely Spanish, then we will want to change his name."

The thumbnail sketch only hinted at the enhancement worked by the Epsteins and Koch on *Everybody Comes to Rick's*. More catalyst than character, Guillermo Ugarte crystallizes out of "an impalpable air of sophistication and intrigue" only to fade back into the hum of voices and the soft serenade of "Stardust" after initiating the action.

The finished screenplay describes Ugarte as "a small thin man with a nervous air. If he were an American, he would look like a tout." Beneath the veneer of respectability, he is deferential and deadly, a human jackal in dress clothing. "With his round baby face and wide, bulging eyes," wrote Koch, "Peter could mask his deviousness under a self-mocking innocence. Like his partner in crime, Ferrari, played by Sidney [*sic*] Greenstreet, he is a natural to be involved in black-market operations."

Rick Blaine and Ugarte's stage dialogue crawls at an expository pace. The Epsteins rewrote most of it. In a low-key verbal duel, Rick's wry candor and Ugarte's predacious conceit face off in a cross fire that crackles with tension:

> Ugarte: You are a very cynical person, Rick, if you'll forgive me for saying so.
> Rick: I forgive you.
> Ugarte: Er, thank you. . . . You despise me, don't you?
> Rick: Well, if I gave you any thought, I probably would.

Lorre had his own way with Ugarte. "Directors didn't direct him much," said Koch, "because they wanted what Peter himself could do with the role." Like a blanched weasel, he whisks into view, fawning and fulsome, oozing greasy charm and puffing on a cigarette, turning even the simple act of smoking into a menacing art. His long delays are highly charged and followed by a softness of speech that explodes as if another man had yelled. In putting the finishing touches on Ugarte, Koch admitted letting Lorre's screen past guide his brown Eagle Number One pencils. Four days of shooting (May 28–29 and June 1–2) translated into only about four minutes of screen time, but thanks to Michael Curtiz, who seemingly enjoyed letting character actors get the better of leading men, Lorre dominated his scenes. Bogart's self-containment is no match for Lorre's nervous animation. With well-integrated bits of business—corrugating his forehead, expressively gesturing with his hands and body, lighting a fresh cigarette from an old one, and milking his dialogue—Lorre captured the camera and gleaned a virtuoso performance from leftovers.

"One of the troubles was that we had to get rid of him so early in the picture," recalled Koch. "I liked his acting so much I would have liked him throughout."

In early November 1942 Allied forces landed on the North African coast and captured Casablanca. Capitalizing on the headlines, Warner Bros. launched its own offensive to put *Casablanca* into theaters as soon as possible. The picture opened in New York on Thanksgiving Day, 1942. On January 23, 1943, one day before Franklin Roosevelt and Winston Churchill wrapped up their "Casablanca Conference," it went into general release. *Casablanca* garnered eight Academy Award nominations that March, taking home Oscars for Best Picture, Best Directing, and Best Written Screenplay.

For all the hoopla and backslapping in the Front Office, no one was more surprised by *Casablanca*'s success than those who made it. "Peter told me that nobody wanted to make it," recalled television director Buzz Kulik. "Neither Bogart, nor Bergman, nor anybody. They thought it was a horror, an awful thing. But they made it, almost sloughed it off. He was telling me that the greatest thing that he and Bogart looked forward to was to slip out and go get a couple of boozes as quickly as they could. Apparently, nobody really knew what they had, even when they had finished making it. From his point of view, they were just going through the motions, and were absolutely stunned by the reception."

Lorre best remembered *Casablanca* for what went on between takes. In *Casablanca*, the spinning of the roulette wheel in Rick's Café Américain symbolized a refugee's chances of securing exit visas. For the cast members, it meant recreation. The actor claimed that his gambling winnings totaled more than his paycheck.

Some thirty-one years later, Howard Koch conceded that "none of us involved in its production could have foretold that *Casablanca* was to have an illustrious future—or, in fact, any future at all. Conceived in sin and born in travail, it survived its precarious origin by some fortuitous combination of circumstances to become the hardiest of Hollywood perennials, as tough and durable as its anti-hero, Humphrey Bogart." For whatever reason—its timeliness, its topicality, its idealistic self-portrait, its immutable values, its flight into nostalgia, its perfect cast, its repertory spirit—or perhaps the magical combination of all of them, it was, as film critic Andrew Sarris put it, "the happiest of happy accidents."

On March 5, 1941, *Variety* had announced that Boris Karloff would take a hiatus in June from the smash Broadway play *Arsenic and Old Lace* to return to Columbia to costar with Peter Lorre in *The Boogie Man Will Get You* (1942), a "comedy-horror yarn" by Robert Andrews. With the stage hit breaking box-office records and the film version contractually locked up until the play completed its Broadway run, what better way to capitalize on the *Bodies in Our Cellar* angle than to offer a cheap imitation? Reluctant to release their star attraction with the production in full swing—Karloff eventually gave more than fourteen hundred performances as Jonathan Brewster between 1941 and 1944—Russel Crouse and Howard Lindsay won a rain check from the studio, which agreed to postpone filming until the following March. Meanwhile, the producers promised to recompense Lorre for the delay.

In a mere four weeks, Edwin Blum, better known for his Alice Fay and Tyrone Power vehicles, turned out a screenplay about a mad scientist who lures lonely traveling salesmen to his basement. Irving Briskin's B unit took it from there. Decked out in cowboy hat and six-shooter, Lorre played a hit-and-run entrepreneur—his first of only several roles as an American—with his finger in every paying pie in town. He wheels and deals as local sheriff, justice of the peace, physician, coroner, and loan shark.

"The secret of Lorre's indelible and unforgettable power lay, of course, in absolute innocence," said Blum. "The sweeter he smiled, the softer he spoke, the more dangerous he became. Karloff had this quality in his lisp and sweet gentleness, but Lorre faced the great master off in *Boogie*."

According to Blum, the studio had envisioned *The Boogie Man Will Get You* as a "goose pimple" picture. At the premiere, however, audiences laughed rather than trembled. Briskin blasted Blum, who responded with a four-letter rejoinder. He was canned on the spot. "*Boogie* turned out to be a film of some minor historic meaning," claimed the screenwriter.

> You see, nobody realized it was "camp," because no camp existed in those days. Lorre didn't know it was camp, nor did Karloff. They played it absolutely straight, which is the only way camp can come off—that is, if the camp is in the writing. The reason the camp was in the writing was that I was and still am incapable of writing a straight horror film. Without knowing it, I tend to secretly kid it. There was not a single person in that company who thought they were doing anything other than another horror story. . . . this special brand of film has culminated now in Mel Brooks' "Young Frankenstein."

The whole idea is incomprehensible. *The Boogie Man Will Get You* reeks of plot contraptions, tired gags, and giddy dialogue; it's as humorless as it is horrorless. Karloff and Lorre kidded the story themselves, salvaging an uncertain situation with mock malevolence.

Horror-comedy didn't rattle the publicity department for an instant. Advertising a "Double Dose of Chills," it followed through on the original premise, even coming up with the gimmick of asking critics to select the ten best screen menaces. When they elected three Disney characters—the witch in *Snow White*, the wolf in *Three Little Pigs*, and the cat in *Pinocchio*—for the top slots, the scheme quickly withered.

In September 1942 *Variety* carried notice that Jack Barry's New York–based Minoco Productions would make *Captain America*, its first full-length feature film, based on the popular comic-book hero. Frank Wisbar was scheduled to direct from an original story by himself and Marilyn Barry, the producer's wife. Minoco had planned to star Lorre, presumably in a villainous role. However, commitments on the West Coast apparently blocked his involvement in the independent production.[15]

At the end of the month, Lorre returned to the front in Eric Ambler's wartime spy novel *Background to Danger* (1943). Directed with a cops-and-robbers edge by Raoul Walsh, the picture starred George Raft, Brenda Marshall, Sydney Greenstreet, and Lorre as Zaleshoff, a vodka-slurping Russian agent, high-strung and full of benign petulance.

Ambler had known Lorre fleetingly in Hollywood and last saw him in London in the early '50s. "We spent an evening in his suite at the Savoy Hotel," remembered the writer. "He wanted me to write a picture for him that he would produce. I wanted only to get away. The only drug I understand is alcohol and am no good writer [when] under the influence of any other, heavier kind." However brief their acquaintance, Lorre's screen image seemed to have taken root in the writer's imagination. He might well have had the actor in mind when he created Zaleshoff, a character who "gave the impression of being almost childishly naive [and] . . . possessed a subtle sense of the value of histrionics. Violent displays of emotion, if well timed, distract the shrewdest observer and hamper his judgment. Zaleshoff's timing was invariably perfect." In the film, his time was shortened and reduced in importance to accommodate George Raft, whom Ambler called a "putty-faced dummy."

One of Warner Bros.' more turbid spy melodramas, *Background to Danger* is probably better remembered for the fireworks behind the scenes. According to Mack Grey, Raft's personal assistant, in one scene Raft sat tied up in a chair while Lorre blew smoke in his face. Cautioned to "knock it off," Lorre instead laughed and persisted, earning him a belated clobbering in his dressing room. Harvey Parry, Lorre's stuntman, offered another version:

Peter was a little character and he knew exactly what he was doing when he was in a scene. And he was on this little bench, tailor style, with a cigarette and talking at the same time. George and Brenda Marshall were also in the scene and George asked Peter what the hell he was doing.

Peter says, "What do you mean?"

"With that cigarette."

He says, "I'm stealing the scene."

"You're stealing the scene from whom?"

"From you and Brenda."

"How can you do that?"

"They're like you, they all watch me."

George says, "You son of a bitch."

So the scene was over and they had a little confrontation.

"Don't put that cigarette in your mouth again."

He says, "Georgie, I do what I want, you do what you want. I wish you good luck." He bombed him. He hit poor Peter. He knocked him right off the little couch he was on.

Walsh grabbed him and said, "Now come on, George. He's just a little helpless guy."

Jack Dales, executive secretary of the Screen Actors Guild, told Warner Bros. general counsel Roy J. Obringer, that he would take no action on the George Raft–Peter Lorre matter unless a formal complaint was filed. In such a case, he added, the guild would have full jurisdiction to make a binding decision. But things never got that far. After Lorre agreed to return to work, Obringer assured Jack Warner that he found both actors "are working this morning."

From 1936, when he debuted in "The Creation of Dr. Mallaire," until 1942, Lorre enjoyed a fleeting acquaintance with radio, performing in variety shows (*The Lifebuoy Program, The Royal Gelatin Hour*) and dramas (*The Lux Radio Theater, The Philip Morris Playhouse*). On *Hollywood Hotel* he also performed— in full makeup—in sketches with movie tie-ins, either anticipating or coinciding with the release of pictures in which he was currently starring, such as *Nancy Steele Is Missing* and *Lancer Spy*.

At 9:30 p.m., Tuesday, December 15, 1942, church bells rang over the CBS airwaves, and *Suspense* host Joseph Kerns, the "Man in Black," introduced "one of the screen's past masters of the art of suspense" to listeners of the weekly radio broadcast. In an episode titled "Till Death Do Us Part," Lorre played an insanely jealous mathematics professor who carefully plots to kills his wife but inadvertently poisons himself instead. Produced and directed by William Spier, who built a reputation as "the Hitchcock of the airlanes," *Suspense* presented tales that kept its listeners guessing until the last possible moment. During the 1940s Lorre returned often to the popular series, performing in stories rife with morbid ironies woven around his screen image.

In the next five weeks, he gave as many radio performances. On December 17, Lorre, Grace Moore, and Jane Cowl gathered around the microphone on the stage of New York's CBS Radio Theater to benefit the Stage Door Canteen, which offered live entertainment for servicemen. After appearing on the *Al Jolson Colgate Show, The Texaco Star Theater,* and *The Kate Smith Show,* on which he performed in Edgar Allan Poe's "The Cask of Amontillado," the actor returned to *Suspense* as a Hungarian count who harbors a dark family secret in "The Devil's Saint" on January 19.

In February 1943 *Variety* reported that the Music Corporation of America had signed a flock of film clients—including Shirley Temple, Maureen O'Hara, John Garfield, Jean Arthur, Paulette Goddard, Marlene Dietrich, and Peter Lorre—for radio bookings.[16]

Later that month, Lorre appeared in "All Star Convoy," a benefit for the A.W.V.S. (American Women's Voluntary Services) Motor Transport Service at New York's Alvin Theater. In addition to performing at charity events, the actor also donated his services to wartime radio shows such as *Stage Door Canteen* (even as a singer), *Treasury Star Parade,* and *Stars for Humanity,* most often in roles to which producers felt he was best suited. For the Hollywood Victory Committee, he performed on *Mystery Playhouse* and *G.I. Journal,* which were broadcast over the Armed Forces Radio Service (AFRS) to servicemen overseas. Besides freely providing their programs to the AFRS, the network studios felt a patriotic duty to boost morale at home. The second installment of NBC's five-part series *The Day of Reckoning* on March 6, 1943, put Benito Mussolini on trial for his crimes against the Italian people, with Mephisto, played by Lorre, acting as his counselor.

Long before Hollywood extended his options with caricature roles, Lorre lampooned his menacing screen image over the airwaves. On *Duffy's Tavern,* he described plans to write a children's hour: "The first story is about a little boy and girl. And they are late for dinner because on their way home from school they have fallen in a concrete mixer. Their parents would have been there, but they were strolling down a country lane and got their heads cut off by a windmill." His appearance on the June 4, 1944, broadcast of *Texaco Star Theater* came complete with a disclaimer: "Ladies and gentlemen, any knives, daggers, stilettos, dirks or other cutlery found sticking in people's backs after Mr. Lorre leaves tonight must be wiped off and returned to the Keen-Kut Kutlery

Company at once. These utensils have merely been loaned to Mr. Lorre. Remember, just because it's in you, it doesn't mean it's yours."

Fast-paced, broad-based, and easily digestible, radio anticipated television by several decades by pushing programming to popular extremes, from Nazi-bashing to hee-haw humor, from variety acts to virtuoso performances. Accommodating all tastes, high, low, and in between, radio likewise stretched Lorre in opposite directions. On *Texaco Star Theater*, Fred Allen said to Portland Hoffa, his wife and sidekick, "Peter Lorre isn't anything like we expected, is he? . . . You sure are a let-down, Peter. . . . I thought you'd come creeping in here on all fours, drooling arsenic with a buzzard on a leash. You're supposed to be a brutal killer. You couldn't take a kumquat away from a Chinese baby."

Accused of being a "slab [*sic*] happy . . . odious little runt" by Allen, Lorre puns, "Fred, why do people think I'm such a monster? I'm just a loveable little guy trying to get ahead. . . . If people knew the story of my life, they'd see that I'm not a mad, twisted creature. They'd feel sorry for me. . . . When I was two years old, I was an orphan, no father, no mother."

"You poor kid. What happened to your father and mother?"

"Oh, I strangled them with a yo-yo string."[17]

When director Tay Garnett learned that MGM had purchased the screen rights to German émigré Hans Habe's *A Thousand Shall Fall*, a novel about the French Resistance Movement, he picked up a copy of the book and read in it the potential for "a whale of a picture." In *The Cross of Lorraine* (1943), as it was retitled by the New York sales office, Nazis promise French soldiers that, under the armistice, they will be demobilized and returned to their homes and families to begin rebuilding France. Instead, their captors throw them into a military prison, where, through a program of torture and starvation, they crush body and spirit. Although rumors of Nazi death camps had reached America as early as the summer of 1941, most Americans did not believe them. Ring Lardner Jr., who coscripted *The Cross of Lorraine*, was an exception, judging by the line: "The Germans don't bury you; they make soap out of you."

From a list of actors given him by the casting director, Garnett set contract players for most of the roles. One part, however small, called for someone who was not on the studio payroll. For the brutally vicious and bloodthirsty Sergeant Berger, Garnett thought of only one actor: Peter Lorre. "I knew his capacity," recalled the director. "I thought he was magnificent, because for a small man he was so much more menacing than anyone we have today." Lorre put extra menace into his role. With fiendish delight he tosses a loaf of bread on the ground and watches the starving prisoners scramble for it. Shooting a praying priest puts a cruel smirk on his face. In a befittingly gory end, the ruthless Nazi is stabbed in the neck and tossed from a moving truck, blood draining away the little life in his veins.

Despite the heavy subject matter, cast and crew gave production the atmosphere of a social club. Lorre and Cedric Hardwicke affectionately needled each other about most everything. "Anytime Peter would say anything," remarked Garnett, "Hardwicke would try to find something wrong with what he had said. And Peter would do Hardwicke's English accent right back at him with a slight German tinge."[18]

At best, war pictures were risky business. Box-office success often hinged on split-second timing. *Variety* credited Warner Bros. with "a lot of luck picking its spots to coincide with front page news." More often, "happy coincidences" depended upon delaying or rushing a film into production and distribution. Not all efforts ended so successfully. The question still remained: to whose timetable must Hollywood set its watch. America had urged the invasion of France in 1943, but prolonged fighting in North Africa made such a plan impossible. Winston Churchill, however, preferred a Mediterranean offensive, to strike "at the soft underbelly of the Axis." Not until the early hours of June 6, 1944, did the great armada, as Churchill liked to call it, finally cross the Channel.

Release-date tactics backfired with *The Cross of Lorraine,* which, reported *Variety,* had been thrown back into production for "a new ending in case of an early invasion of the continent." Thomas M. Pryor, for the *New York Times,* complained that the picture "should have been on the screen a year ago, when the future of French resistance was not as apparent as it is now." History alone, however, was not enough to temper the studio's projections that the "stark, heavy and unrelieved drama" would have to be double-booked with a supporting feature. At a time when audiences preferred lighter fare, *The Cross of Lorraine*'s harsh realism, including Lorre's "expected masterpiece of cruelty as a Nazi jailer," left no room for comedy or romance.

On June 2, 1943, Lorre signed a standard five-year contract with renewable options "to act, pose, sing, speak or otherwise appear and perform for and as requested by the Producer," with Warner Bros. Pictures Inc. It had not happened overnight but had taken five films and two years to soften the skeptics in the Front Office. Hal Wallis realized early on that "Peter was a unique and fine performer and added considerably to any picture he was in." Acknowledgment from Jack Warner arrived only after Lorre had prominently figured in two studio blockbusters—*The Maltese Falcon* and *Casablanca.*

Inscribing his name above the word "Artist" committed the actor to appear in no fewer than two films per year for "the sum of Seventeen Hundred

Fifty Dollars ($1750) per week for a period of not less than six (6) consecutive weeks with respect to each of the aforesaid motion pictures." Provided the studio picked up his option, Lorre stood to earn the same pay the second year, $2,500 the third year, $3,000 the fourth, and finally $3,500 the fifth and last year of his contract. The arrangement tied him to the past in more ways than one, limiting his compensation for the first two films to the "highest wage or salary paid Artist between January 1, 1942, and September 15, 1942," during which time he had appeared in *All Through the Night, The Constant Nymph,* and *Casablanca.* Warner Bros. retained the right to "lend, rent, or transfer" his services to "any other so-called 'major' producer of motion pictures."[19]

The agreement grudgingly honored Lorre's prior commitment to direct and star—as himself in the role of a sadistic actor—in *I Play the Devil,* a stage play written by his friend Ernest Pascal, proposed for the upcoming Broadway season. Under the conditions of the contract, Lorre agreed to advise the studio on or by August 15, 1943, if he wished to appear in the play. Warner Bros. granted him a "single engagement . . . during the theatrical season commencing October 1, 1943, and ending June 1, 1944, and for no other period of time" if it did not interfere with completion of work in progress. Possibly because of all the strings attached, the project never materialized.

With his seemingly permanent move to Warner Bros., Lorre's affair with radio blossomed. The studio parted the airwaves, granting Lorre the right to absent himself once a week to perform on radio, providing it did not interfere with "studio services." Lorre's radio and movie work proved mutually reinforcing. In the next three years, the actor gave over forty radio performances, most typically in roles with a sinister aspect.[20] *Inner Sanctum Mysteries'* "Death Is a Joker" cast him as an ugly, clumsy comedian who finds black humor—and tragic irony—in becoming "a criminal all because he thought he had committed a crime and had to think like a criminal." In an episode for *Suspense* titled "Nobody Loves Me," he played a murderer who gets something like love when he kills, because "there won't be anyone else in the world for you, but me. No one else will matter." In June 1944 the actor was offered a package thriller, *Journey into Fear,* written and directed by Norman Winters, as a half-hour evening show. Apparently, his agent's asking price—$2,000 for the first thirteen weeks, $4,000 for the next thirty-nine, $4,500 for the next fifty-two, and $5,000 thereafter—put it beyond reach.

Although his contract did not stipulate it, the studio also asked that Lorre obtain the necessary releases, submit scripts to the publicity department forty-eight hours in advance, and plug his current Warner Bros. feature. Lorre's official reply to this request came from Ann Rosenthal, an attorney for the William

Morris Agency, which represented the actor, in a letter to Roy Obringer: "In a spirit of cooperation, Mr. Lorre will agree to use his best efforts and endeavors to have the producers of said radio program comply with your request."[21]

It was not the kind of body and soul agreement the studio originally had in mind. Steve Trilling, promoted from casting director to Jack Warner's personal assistant, subsequently sought to sign Lorre to an exclusive seven-year contract limited to six pictures annually and feature billing.[22] "PETER LORRE has been up at [Lake] Arrowhead," he wrote the production chief on July 24, 1943.

> [He] is not returning for at least another four or five days, and telephone conversations are very unsatisfactory. LORRE is trying to avoid an exclusive deal, would rather not be tied down, hoping eventually to become a director. We therefore suggested, as bait, to make ours a two-way contract and if sometime later on in his career he showed proclivities as a director, we might be interested. . . . However, with LORRE's attitude, not wanting to be exclusively committed, I do not know what we will arrive at until I can get him in my office and talk to him personally.

But Lorre didn't change his mind. In fact, a supplemental agreement to his multiple-picture deal, dated September 9, 1943, indicates that he stood his ground and then some. His nonexclusive contract allowed the actor to work outside the studio in two A pictures annually. By committing himself to three pictures (instead of the original two), Lorre also won permission to direct one outside feature per year. "In such event," casting director Phil Friedman wrote Roy Obringer, "the contract will be suspended and extended for a period equal to that consumed in connection with such directorial work." However, Warner Bros. held the right to preempt outside work by serving twenty-one days' notice on the starting date of his next picture. By invoking paragraph 26 of Lorre's contract and rushing him into a new assignment, it kept a tight rein on his services. The arrangement forced Lorre to turn down offers to appear in Universal's *Her Primitive Man* in October 1943, William Cagney Productions' *Blood on the Sun* (1945) the following August, and Paramount's *The Private Eye* in April 1946.[23] Burgess Meredith also remembered thinking of Lorre for *Diary of a Chambermaid* (1946), which he coproduced, coauthored, and starred in. The director, Jean Renoir, was fond of him, said Meredith. "I know there was talk about seeing if we couldn't use Lorre in *Diary* . . . but at any rate they didn't want to get too many accents."

Warner Bros. was so disinclined to allow Lorre to work for other producers that when Roma Wines proposed filming his August 30, 1945, radio broadcast of *Suspense* as part of an exploitation campaign, the studio jumped at the opportunity to further limit their employee's outside activities. On August 17 Obringer disingenuously wrote the actor's agent inquiring whether "Lorre plans to use this as one of his two 'allowable' outside pictures." If so, continued the general counsel, the studio would not stand in his way by exercising its pre-emptive rights. The resulting 16mm filmed radio performance runs thirty minutes. While providing rare footage of Lorre behind the mike, it hardly qualifies as an A feature.

Warner Bros. even held a patent on Lorre's "physical likeness," caricaturing the actor in animated cartoons that depicted a baby-faced villain with bulging eyes and nasal whine. He had presumably signed away his screen image as early as 1941 when, on May 24, during preproduction on *The Maltese Falcon,* Warner Bros. released "Hollywood Steps Out," which featured a gallery of stars, including Peter Lorre. Eying a naked woman clothed only by a bubble, he diffidently whines, "I haven't seen such a beautiful bubble since I was a child." In Dr. Seuss's "Horton Hatches the Egg" (April 11, 1942), an incredulous "Peter Lorre Fish" spots the elephant atop a bird's nest, pulls out a pistol, and shoots itself in the head, a scene later deleted by several television networks for its violent content. Other animated appearances included "Hair Raising Hare" (June 8, 1946) with Bugs Bunny, "The Birth of a Notion" (April 12, 1947) with Daffy Duck, and "Racketeer Rabbit"(September 14, 1946), in which he again shared the screen with Bugs Bunny—and an ersatz Edward G. Robinson.

Probably the most original appropriation of Lorre's screen image appeared in a thirteen-week episode of a *Batman and Robin* newspaper strip entitled "The Two-Bit Dictator of Twin Mills," which ran from October 30, 1944, to January 26, 1945. Drawing on the William M. "Boss" Tweed and the Tammany Hall scandals that rocked New York City in the 1860s, Al Schwartz (who went on to become a regular writer for the *Superman* strip) "wrote the strip like a film scenario, even describing how the characters should look." The Lorre character, "Jojo the Flinker," was "a good example of the way I would develop a personality," explained the writer, by "having him use words in his own peculiar way and exaggerating certain personal mannerisms and idiosyncrasies." Batman creator Bob Kane (who used W.C. Fields for his inspiration to pencil Tweek Wickham) gave his Lorre look-alike an old face and a new voice. The parted hair (on either side, depending on the frame), dangling cigarette, and sloe-eyed imperturbability were familiar to moviegoers. However, the voice was pure New York mobster, with "boid" for bird and "poifect" for perfect. Schwartz used another of what he described as "speech markers" to delineate Jojo: "flink." The trigger man flinks birds from the hip and guys between the eyes. He practices his flink, makes a perfect flink, saves a flink for a double-crosser. Both noun and verb, it meant sudden death by pistol shot.

Sheltering as it did an ensemble of character actors, Warner Bros. held a strong attraction to the rootless Lorre. It was a studio built of specialists of every size, shape, and nationality. A haven for this human mélange, it was also a prison for the creative artist. The Front Office took few chances, seldom risking a backlash at the box office by casting against type. Pigeonholing was good business, but too often prototype gave way to self-impersonation. Repetition begat perfunctory portrayals and mechanical predictability. "They were always trying to latch on to aspects of a personality and use them just for commercial purposes," said contract player Geraldine Fitzgerald, "use the person as a kind of product and not really give them a chance to develop, which in the long run would have made them much more interesting a product. They would try to cash in on us in an instant way."

Celia said that Peter had been "happily unhappy" at Warner Bros. The simple contradiction nicely accommodated the extremes of his experience there. Character work assured a certain present, but threatened an uncertain future. Weighing prescribed stardom against creative confinement spawned nagging doubts in Lorre's mind, although not about his appearance in cheap exploitation pictures. Before the ink had dried on his contract, and with Metro's *The Cross of Lorraine* still in production, Universal announced plans for *Chamber of Horrors*. According to *Variety,* June 9, 1943, George Waggner, who was then directing *Cobra Woman* (1944), cooked up the idea of rounding up Boris Karloff, Bela Lugosi, Lon Chaney Jr., George Zucco (all under contract to Universal), Peter Lorre, and other "goosepimplers" in a "ghostly rodeo with Frankenstein, Dracula, the Wolf Man, the Mad Ghoul, the Invisible Man and kindred spirits prowling into one cinematic nightmare." The "Chiller-diller to end all chiller-dillers" progressed no further.[24] RKO also failed to deliver Lorre, Karloff, and Lugosi in *Star Strangled Rhythm*—a play on Paramount's 1942 *Star-Spangled Rhythm*—in which Boris and Bela's movie-made horror personas take possession of their bodies.[25]

Having worked the anti-Nazi sentiment of the *Casablanca* cast into a successful advertising campaign, Warner Bros. went to the well again with *Passage to Marseille* (1944), based on Charles Nordhoff and James Norman Hall's *Men without a Country.* The studio paid a whopping seventy-five thousand dollars for the novelette and set the "*Casablanca* kids" on French Guiana, now as convicts desperate to exchange their penal servitude for a crack at the Nazis.

"As you may already have discovered, mon capitaine," Lorre, as the convict Marius, confesses, "I'm a very clever man and sensitive, sensitive down to my fingertips. In fact, these fingers made me the best safecracker in Paris and a virtuoso among the pickpockets." Although Nordhoff and Hall fashioned Marius as "the worst rogue of the lot," screenwriters Casey Robinson and Jack Moffitt softened the role, giving Lorre a sympathetic bent. Hardly the knave in the story, Marius advertises his droll humor and dies for the cause behind a machine gun poised at the attacking Luftwaffe.

Warner Bros. pressed production on *Passage to Marseille,* intent on scheduling its release to coincide with the expected Allied invasion of France. But invasion talk, heavy in the air since 1942, proved a poor barometer of progress on the war front. When the offensive did not materialize, the studio delayed release until February of 1944, anticipating, though somewhat prematurely, the Allied landing in Marseille six months later.

Passage to Marseille was the fourth outing for Bogart and Lorre. Once again they teamed up with Michael Curtiz, whom they goaded to distraction with their practical jokes. For Lorre, however, the mood turned sour when the smoky battle scenes triggered his "house dust" allergy. The actor complained that he would not work under such conditions, prompting an assistant to report to the Front Office: "I am very much afraid that we are creating a 'FRANKENSTEIN' by using doubles for PETER LORRE because you must not lose sight of the fact that there are other members of the cast in the same smoke, such as CLAUDE RAINS, SYDNEY GREENSTREET, etc., who, when they find out we are using doubles for PETER LORRE and HUMPHREY BOGART, will also demand doubles, and where in the hell will we be then—might as well shoot the whole picture with doubles."

In late 1943 Warner Bros. decided that the hugely popular *Amazing Dr. Clitterhouse* (1938) might enjoy a repeat success. The studio assigned producer Wolfgang Reinhardt and writers Alvah Bessie and German émigré Leonhard Frank to update the story of a doctor whose research into the physiological reactions of criminals leads him into a life of crime. By giving it a new title, renaming the characters, and changing the setting—to nineteenth-century London—but keeping the story essentially the same, the Front Office hoped to pass the picture off as something new. It was clearly a matter of out-and-out theft, without being too obvious.

The availability of Peter Lorre and Sydney Greenstreet gave the writers an idea for an "interesting (and pathetic)" twist. As Clitterhouse, Greenstreet would be in love with a young girl who treats him "like a dog," but feigns affection in exchange for expensive gifts. "We added some new characters and cast Peter Lorre in the role of a feebleminded gangster called Willie the Weeper," wrote Bessie in his autobiography, *Inquisition into Eden,* "who was constantly trying to snitch Greenstreet's whisky, so that Greenstreet would whack him on the back of the hand with a ruler and roar, 'Whisky's not for children!'—and Willie would weep."

Five or six weeks later, they showed their treatment to Reinhardt, who gave it an enthusiastic nod. Audiences would never remember where they had seen it all before. At a story conference, however, Steve Trilling threw the manuscript on the desk. "Greenstreet *in love* with a young *girl?*" he raged. "That's *disgusting!*" Bessie explained they were going for the pathos in the situation, but Trilling said audiences would laugh it off the screen. "Now look! We're going to remake *The Amazing Dr. Clitterhouse,*" he exploded. "It was a very successful picture. It made a lot of money. . . . *I want exactly the same picture— word for word!*"

Bessie and Frank went back to work, writing a treatment that differed only slightly from the original screenplay. Trilling was livid. If he had wanted the same picture, he screamed, he would have re-released the original picture. "*I don't want to make a picture about a crazy man!*" he finally bellowed. "*Forget it!*" He assigned the project to two other writers, who resurrected Bessie and Frank's original treatment, only to have it shelved for good.

When John Huston made *The Maltese Falcon,* he had unknowingly pulled the project out from under Jean Negulesco. He later apologized and told Negulesco that the studio owned a book every bit as good if not better than *The Maltese Falcon* in Eric Ambler's popular novel of international intrigue and espionage, *A Coffin for Dimitrios.* "Take it to Henry Blanke," advised Huston. "Just do the book page by page."

Negulesco broached the idea of filming the story in a memo to Jack Warner, who was bent on cultivating a crop of young directors capable of operating on small budgets. Frank Orsatti, Negulesco's agent—also Lorre's—did the rest.

Negulesco and Blanke, the film's producer, took a copy of the book and cut and pasted up the individual pages, improvising a script as they went. Because, in his words, he "respected character actors more than stars," Negulesco wanted only featured players in the picture. For the darkly sinister Dimitrios, he got newcomer Zachary Scott, whose screen debut earned accolades from Lorre. Negulesco credited himself with the idea of costarring Lorre and Greenstreet in their own movie. Blanke approved the casting and arranged for the actors to test for the leads.[26]

"Let's do a scene," said Negulesco. Lorre and Greenstreet rehearsed their lines. The director heard giggling. "Go to it, boys," he instructed. The actors clowned their way through most of the test. Negulesco said nothing, just letting them go. Anything to be different. "I saw the rushes," Blanke scolded the next morning. "They are terrible. I want to tell you something, Jean. This is your first chance to make a picture. But if the first day's rushes are as bad as the test I've just seen, you won't be doing the film."

"It was a great gamble," said Negulesco. "They were fooling around, improvising from their characters. It was a test of what they should not do. Fortunately, next day I had quite a good scene. They liked the rushes of that and the picture proceeded smoothly."

In *The Mask of Dimitrios,* Lorre uncomfortably wears his departure role as a diffident Dutch mystery writer swept up in a real-life mystery. "It's hard to break old habits," the actor joked about his performance, which is uncharacteristically wooden. "I can't control my leers. My glowers get out of hand. I snarl when I should be wincing with fear. That'll last only for a few days, at least I hope so, and then we'll be making better time."

Negulesco, however, credits him with saving the picture. "Lorre was the most talented man I have ever seen in my life," said the director. "If you watch *The Mask of Dimitrios,* you'll find that the whole picture, its entire mood, is held together by him. Without him, you're a little bored by it. I think his chief asset lay in the element of surprise. When you expected him to be quiet he was loud. When a scene in *The Mask of Dimitrios* threatened to run down, for example, this little man would shout for no reason at all; and as you were slowly recovering from the shock he'd say mock-innocently: 'Did I scare you?'"

Indeed, the director thought him so perfectly cast that when Orson Welles considered remaking *The Mask of Dimitrios* and playing Greenstreet's role, Negulesco could suggest no one to play Lorre's part.

What *The Mask of Dimitrios* lacked in budget, it made up for in production value. Negulesco put his talent as a painter to good use, sketching scenes beforehand, crowding his canvas with Balkan backgrounds. Art directors Ted Smith and Harper Goff "had to make it look like Constantinople, Sophia, or wherever by using stock backings. But if the door swung the wrong way, so that it got in the way of the camera or the entrance, we literally could not rehang it. We took the set as was, moved in and went to another set." The potted palms, louvered doors, circular fans ("to give a sense of heat"), and a cosmopolitan cast—including Steven Geray, Kurt Katch, and Victor Francen—gave *The Mask of Dimitrios* a strong international flavor.

Negulesco directed his first full-length feature with deliberate care, integrating the numerous flashbacks without cost to the narrative action. The picture drew generally favorable reviews as "a strange, absorbing drama of crime, intrigue and vengeance" and has since earned a footnote in the noir canon—primarily for its somber, low-key visual style. Ambler thought "it wasn't that bad; and bits of it, those in which Sidney [*sic*] Greenstreet could compel an audience to overlook the miscasting of Peter Lorre, were almost good." *Los Angeles Examiner*'s Sara Hamilton thought it much better, including Lorre, "who is so much more an actor than a mere personality . . . he can play anything."

Peter Lorre and Sydney Greenstreet are inseparably linked in the public mind as the Laurel and Hardy of the crime set. "There seemed to have been what the Italians call *simpatico* between him and me," said Lorre. "That was self-evident from the outset." For Don Siegel, who directed them in *The Verdict* (1946), the secret of their appeal "was that they were like a marriage of a beautiful girl and an ugly man. They appeared to be diametrically opposite—and opposites attract."

Greenstreet savors crime, making a hearty repast of its sinister flavors. He is father to the boy, master to the pupil, affectionately paternal, benevolently corrupting. Lurking in a dark corner, peering out with bulging eyes, Lorre whines and feeds on the scraps. Whereas Sydney is openly civil, belching cordiality, Peter is secretive, reckoning his masks in layers. He is infernally friendly, warily effusive, always the droll and deadly schoolboy. Somewhere in the musty film vaults must lie a lost scene of the two actors walking away from the camera side by side, Greenstreet waddling with jaunty grace and Lorre mincing in youthful tread, the one jovially guffawing, the other tittering in 2/4 time. The contrast of the pixie and the behemoth has taken on a dimension that is larger than life and one their films cannot fully document. Paired or pitted against each other, they formed a celebrated complement.

Behind the camera, they gave shape to another contrast, one of working styles. Greenstreet, claimed Siegel, was deadly serious about rehearsing. Steeped in formal training, the disciplined actor knew every period, comma, and dotted *i* in the script and expected exact cues. And then Lorre arrived on the set, apparently unfamiliar with his lines, the scene, the film, even the studio, and as giddy as his partner was grave. "So this is the script," Lorre casually mused, holding it upside down. Gay, voluble, spontaneous, unflappable, uninhibited, and not temperamental, he was everything Greenstreet wasn't—except professional.

"He used to tell me how he drove Sydney Greenstreet up the wall," remarked Richard Matheson, who scripted a series of horror-comedies for Vincent Price and Peter Lorre at American International Pictures in the early 1960s. "Greenstreet was this theater trained perfectionist and he would deliver a line and Lorre would just throw something back at him that seemed to have no relationship to the picture." When the cameras rolled, however, Lorre was letter-perfect. Greenstreet marveled at Lorre's sangfroid and heaved a sigh of exasperated relief. "It was all a game to Peter," said Siegel, who felt a happy set was a relaxed set. "He knew the script and had studied it."

In their game of cat-and-mouse, Lorre did the stalking. When Greenstreet warned him he would cut off both his hands if he did not stop projecting himself into his scene, Lorre amiably checked, "Fine, then I'll play the scene with stumps and steal the whole show." Irving Yergin said that Lorre loved to tell of being on the set of *The Conspirators* (1944) with Sydney Greenstreet and Hedy Lamarr, who was wearing a low-cut dress. "Hey, Sydney," he joked, "you're the only person on the set with a pair of tits." According to Lorre, production was held up for two hours while Greenstreet and Lamarr chased him around the set, no doubt fitting one reviewer's description of the actors as a "Pekingese and a great dane out for a romp." Lorre wrapped his take on one of his favorite stories with Jack Warner fining him ten thousand dollars for the delay.

John Huston reassembled most of the principal cast from *The Maltese Falcon* for *Across the Pacific* (1942). The company and crew enjoyed being together again but missed Lorre, who secretly arranged with Huston to visit the set. "One afternoon," wrote Mary Astor, "he donned a white coat and walked through a scene in which Sydney, Bogie and I were being served breakfast on the ship. We didn't know John had made the switch with the actor who was playing the waiter. He was behind us, so we couldn't see him, and Peter served us, making tiny mistakes—holding a platter a bit too far away, just touching Sydney's arm as he lifted a cup of coffee. Finally he leaned down and kissed me on the back of the neck and we all broke up."

To Lorre, Greenstreet was "the old man." Greenstreet called Lorre "Puck." They competed for the camera's eye, yet they relished each other's company, although away from the studio they rarely socialized. They shared much in common: a sense of humor that lightened the atmosphere of filmmaking, a feeling of ease and comfort on the set, an erudition that cross-fertilized their very literate minds, and a respect that reached well beyond their admiration for one another's craftsmanship. "Sydney Greenstreet was not only one of the nicest men and gentlemen I've ever known," said Lorre, "I think he was one of the truly great, great actors of our time." Joan Lorring, who worked with the actors in *Three Strangers* (1946) and *The Verdict* (1946), saw Lorre as the stronger magnetic force, "which sought out other minds like it." She added that "neither were impressed by being a recognized human to other humans. They were both on the same wave-length." Nevertheless, Lorre always had the last word. "It's fun to work with Sydney," he once told an interviewer. "The only problem is staying out of his shadow."

Five weeks after wrapping production on *The Mask of Dimitrios,* Lorre once again suited up, metaphorically speaking, for the war effort, as one of *The Conspirators* (1944). Hal Wallis had hoped to reunite much of the *Casablanca* cast but only reassembled Paul Henreid, Lorre, and Greenstreet, loosely teamed, but all on the side of the Resistance.[27]

Freely adapted from Frederic Prokosch's novel of the same title and uncertainly directed by Jean Negulesco, *The Conspirators* is substandard wartime fare about anti-Nazi undergrounders in Lisbon. "I have just been to see my first film after a year and a half abroad," wrote Prokosch to the *New Republic*. "All I felt when I rose to go was weariness, intense boredom and certain amazement. . . . amazement at the mentality which can concoct such nonsense with a straight face." The film editor, Rudi Fehr, joked, "It was a mishmash of leftovers from *Casablanca* and *Passage to Marseille*, so we re-titled it *The Constipators*, starring Headache Lamarr and Paul Hemorrhoid. But Hal Wallis liked it; that was enough."

The Hollywood Canteen, a serviceman's club cofounded by Bette Davis and John Garfield, opened its doors to visiting soldiers on October 3, 1942. At no cost, they could dance, mingle, and be waited on by movie stars, including Lorre, who donned an apron, greeted the boys, and even joined in the sing-alongs. Inspired by the activities of the Canteen, writer-director Delmer Daves fashioned a scenario to showcase Hollywood's war effort. With barely a thread of a story—a veteran of the South Pacific visits the Canteen and is overwhelmed by the number of celebrities he meets there—*Hollywood Canteen* (1944) is no less than a benefit show boasting sixty-two marquee names, including Bette Davis, John Garfield, Paul Henreid, Jack Benny, Tommy Dorsey, the Andrews Sisters, Roy Rogers and Trigger, Sydney Greenstreet, Peter Lorre, and many more.

Daves, who also directed the picture, put it to Lorre and Greenstreet: "What would you be comfortable doing?" They got back to him with their ideas for a sketch, which he used to develop a one-and-a-half-minute exchange in which the two, supposedly playing themselves, help Patty Andrews escape from a determined but hopeless dance partner:

G.I.: Honey, I'm going to dance your hips right out of your sockets.
Miss Andrews: Oh, please!
Greenstreet: I beg your pardon, young man, but exactly what did you say you were going to do with Miss Andrews' sockets?
G.I.: Dance her out of them, Mr. Greenstreet.
Lorre: Say, Sydney, doesn't that constitute mayhem?
Greenstreet: Definitely, Peter.

Lorre: And besides, it would be very gruesome.

Greenstreet: Horrible sight.

G.I.: Uh, now look, gentlemen, it's only a figure of speech. You know, like you'll say you'll tear a guy limb from limb. You wouldn't really tear a guy limb from limb. (*Laughs*)

Lorre: Huh?!

Greenstreet: Wouldn't we?

Lorre: Uh, pardon me, sir. Would you mind stepping outside with me for a moment?

G.I.: Uh, now, now, excuse me, gentlemen. I've got to join my outfit.

Lorre: All I wanted to ask him is to join me in a cigarette.

Greenstreet: He didn't trust us, Peter.

Lorre: No. And we are such gentle people.

Greenstreet: Are we?

Lorre: Hey, Sydney . . . (*shaking his head suspiciously*)

Clearly, Lorre and Greenstreet yielded to audience expectations. The compressed characterizations lampooned their familiar images as screen menaces. Lorre meekly whines, always the menacing milksop. Greenstreet is imperious but gracious, brimming over with malevolent affability. Only a very small part of the picture, the sketch is a delightful interlude in two hours of musical acts.

Production on *Hollywood Canteen* had begun in December 1943, but a dispute with the Screen Actors Guild over the salaries for cameos by freelance actors forced Warner Bros. to shelve the picture until a settlement was reached. The studio felt that the performers should accept nominal remuneration for their brief appearances as a patriotic gesture. This violated Guild Rule 33, which stated, "It shall be conduct unbecoming a Guild member to perform in any motion picture without compensation or for compensation substantially lower than the normal payment of the performer." More than the issue of money troubled the guild, which feared that studios would pressure actors to appear in *Canteen*-type movies and expose them as unpatriotic if they turned down the roles—even if their reasons for refusal were artistic rather than political.

After a five-month hiatus, Warner Bros. and the union finally got together, settling on a minimum of one week's usual salary for freelance actors, but also granting them the right to freely bargain above such an amount. Contract players, however, were compensated on a pro rata basis. For their one-day shoot, Lorre earned $291.67 and Greenstreet $416.17. In *The Maltese Falcon*, their first film together, Warner Bros. had billed Lorre over Greenstreet and paid him $2,000 a week. Greenstreet had reaped exactly one-half that amount in a larger role. Lorre was never again billed over Greenstreet or earned as much, no matter how their roles compared in size. Even in *Casablanca,* Greenstreet received a whopping $3,750 per week to Lorre's $1,750. Although it never caused any hard feelings between the actors, Lorre felt that Warner Bros. selfishly profited by the inequity, which reflected his depreciated stature at the studio.[28]

Lorre didn't press the point, at least directly. The day actress Andrea King signed with Warner Bros., she went to the business building, opened the door, and looked down the hall to Jack Warner's office. There she saw "this very pathetic, ragged, scrubby little man with a tin cup and some pencils in it, and his head was bowed. I thought, what is that crouched in the corner next to Jack Warner's door? I said to myself I'd better look and see if I can help. I quietly went down the hall about three hundred yards and here was this creature. All of a sudden, these enormous eyes looked up and I about fainted. I knew right then and there it was Mr. M himself—Mr. Peter Lorre. He wriggled his tin can with these pencils and said, 'This is my way of asking Jack Warner for more money.'"

For a time, it looked as if Columbia would sign his next check. After paying almost $350,000 for émigré Franz Werfel's play *Jacobowksy and the Colonel,* a "Comedy of a Tragedy" about a Polish-Jewish refugee and an anti-Semitic Polish military officer who flee Nazi-occupied France together, the studio decided against using the Broadway cast and opted for Lorre in the lead role. By the time it reached the screen—as *Me and the Colonel*—in 1958, Danny Kaye and Curt Jurgens had filled the starring roles.

With production on his next assignment scheduled for fall, the William Morris Agency set Lorre, billed as "The Man of Intrigue, Mystery and Melodrama," for a three-week—later extended to nine weeks—house tour, beginning with the Earle in Philadelphia on August 18, 1944, and finishing up at the National in Louisville, in late October.[29]

Vaudeville-houses-turned-movie-theaters combined new and old by prefacing their feature presentation with a stage show. For an actor between assignments or willing to promote his new release, treading the boards was a common enough pastime. At the least, it meant making a personal appearance to plug a picture. In Philadelphia Lorre headlined a bill that included singer Ray Kinney, whose Hawaiian orchestra backed him on "Hawaiian War Chant" and "Sweet Leilani"; the dancing Aloha Maids; the Oxford Boys, whose impersonations ranged from popular radio figures to President Roosevelt; and comedic acrobats Jean, Jack, and Judy. Breaking the ice, Lorre whispered into the stage microphone, "It's so-o-o-o nice to see live people again, only they don't stay alive very long, I'm afraid, when I'm around." On walked the statuesque blonde singer Marcella Hendricks, who, as a breathless, starstruck reporter—and foil—from "The Woman's Home Companion," posed questions about his toughness and penchant for monstrosity, which he fielded with ghoulish rapture. His "favorite hobby," he tells her, "is digging, his favorite flower the lily and his favorite color, black."

As the laughter died down, a new tone crept into Lorre's voice. "What I would like to do is very different," he told the audience. "With this I will need your serious attention and your talents. I've chosen a story written by Frank Wilson. It's a very powerful study of a psychopathic killer. It is as exciting and breathtaking as any story ever conceived by the imagination of a great writer. The title—*The Man with the Head of Glass.*"

Lorre had earlier engaged veteran radio writer Frank Wilson to work up a story that sounded a familiar note with audiences.[30] Wilson gave him just what he wanted, a spasmodic monologue he could further tailor; each performance bore small changes and elaborations. In fitful, frenzied jump cuts, Lorre reprised the spirit of his screen past:

But you said you were my friend. You said you were doctors and that you understood me and what I have done. And now you've come in here and you look into my head and you watch and you laugh at what I am thinking.... You said you would give me back my hat. I won't let these people look into me . . . all right, I will tell. . . . I will tell you and then you will give back my hat. The first time? The first time I think it was in a streetcar. Yes, a woman, she stared at me and she got up in a terrible rage and she called the conductor and he put me off the car. And then I knew my head is glass and she could see through me. And she knew what I was thinking—how wonderful it would be to put my hands around her fat ugly throat and press and press. And then I know what I have to do. I get myself a large heavy black hat that comes way down over my eyes and I'll be safe. Now I can think and think and no one can catch me while I am thinking. . . . And then out of nowhere came a little girl and she laughed with me. She was so sweet. She took me by the arm and she pulled me along. Oh, I'm so tired and I slipped and she mocked me and she pulled my hat over my eyes. And the hat fell off. No. No. She must not get away. . . . I am shoving through the crowd and people laugh at me. . . . Why do they laugh? There's no air. I can stand it no more. And I rise. They can see. They close in on me, striking and biting and tearing and kicking. . . . They are going to kill me now. What are you pushing me for? What do you want? You want me to sit down on this chair? . . . What are you doing to my hands? What are you doing to my feet? You're strapping me in, but you said you would give me back my hat. . . . You're putting my hat back on for me. (*laughs*) Thank you, my friends. This is very nice. But gentlemen, this is not my hat, this is only the band of a hat. . . . Hey you, what are you doing over there at the switch? Get away from that light. . . . I CAN'T STAND TO BE IN THE DARK!

Variety applauded Lorre for spending "some time figuring out just what he was going to do on a personal tour, and taking care to do it well." During his performance in Hartford, "the audience sat enthralled and absolutely still." Afterward, applause thundered throughout the State Theater and "demanded Mr. Lorre's continuous curtain calls." At the National, reported the *Louisville Courier-Journal,* Lorre left the stage "with great dignity and with the exhausted appearance of a great tragedian of the time of Mansfield, Mantell, John Barrymore or E.H. Southern."

Reporters in nine cities buttonholed Peter—and Karen—for interviews in which they covered familiar ground: the future of pictures, his bogeyman image, her movie career, and his tours of army hospitals. Lorre also mentioned their three-year marriage, although he and Karen would not wed for another seven months. (Reporters who knew the falsity of his statement were polite enough not to challenge it, possibly in light of the standard "morals" clause in studio contracts.)[31] Along with the thumbnail reprise of his life before and behind the camera, Lorre threw out a rare reference to his contractual arrangements with Warner Bros., which apparently was still dangling the proverbial carrot, stating that after his return he "hopes to direct a couple of movies, free to do whatever he wants." Meanwhile, *Hotel Berlin* and *The Fountainhead* awaited him in Hollywood.

In 1944 Warner Bros. paid fifty thousand dollars for *Hotel Berlin '43,* Vicki Baum's timely updating of her best-selling novel *Grand Hotel,* set during the crumbling of the Third Reich. *Collier's* serialized the story in late 1943. Doubleday brought out a trade edition in 1944. Warner Bros. put it on the screen in 1945. *Hotel Berlin* (1945) crowds a swanky Berlin hotel with a disaffected Prussian general, a duplicitous Nazi actress, a vicious Gestapo chief, a smoldering blonde floozy, and a handsome underground leader. It was, wrote Harrison Carroll in the *Los Angeles Evening Herald-Express,* "like seeing the whole high German kit and caboodle dropped like rats in a barrel with a terrier on their necks." Added to this collection was the drunken and disillusioned Professor Johannes Koenig (Peter Lorre), who acts as the film's conscience. Beaten into submission at Dachau, he nonetheless scoffs at the idea of Germany's rebirth: "There are not ten good Germans left. . . . We shall be wiped off the face of the earth. Serves us right, absolutely right."

Aiming "to hit the jackpot again, as it did with *Casablanca,*" Warner Bros. raced to get *Hotel Berlin* into the theaters before the Russians felled the German capitol. On January 31, 1945, *Variety* trumpeted, "WB Hypos 'Hotel Berlin' on Strength of News. . . . Two-way drive in Germany has developed a third campaign in Burbank." Jack Warner pressed all departments to get the picture out within the next thirty days. Double crews of cutters edited 50,000 feet of film to 9,000 in five days, while mixers and dubbers worked around the clock and three orchestras readied Franz Waxman's musical score.

Warner Bros. released *Hotel Berlin* on March 17, beating the Russian army to the German capitol by over a month. What the picture gained in time, however, it lost in continuity. For Lorre, scooping history had a downside. On the cutting room floor lay remnants of a larger role, now inexplicably disconnected. (His appearance in underground headquarters at the end of the film is not only unexpected, but also unexplained.)

As if audiences needed to be reminded of Warner Bros.' patriotic commitment, studio publicists advertised *Hotel Berlin*'s "Violently Anti-Nazi" cast, singling out those who had "brushed up against the Nazis" in Europe, including Peter Pohlenz and Trudy Berliner, who had seen the inside of a concentration camp.

During his brief tenure as a screenwriter at Gaumont-British in the mid-1930s, John Huston had conceived the story of three strangers who meet at midnight on Chinese New Year and cosign a sweepstakes ticket in the hope that Kwan Yin, the goddess of fortune and destiny, of life and death, will grant their wish. The ticket is drawn in the lottery but becomes a clue linking one of the strangers to murder. Thereafter, she deserts her suitors, tainting their lives with tragic denouement. Huston had told his story to Alfred Hitchcock, who liked it, but apparently Michael Balcon did not, and that was the last he heard of it. In 1937 he sold "Three Men and a Girl" to Warner Bros. for five thousand dollars, with the provision that he write the screenplay.

Lorre learned of the story, presumably from Huston, and saw an opportunity for a romantic leading role. He asked Howard Koch, with whom he had become friends during *Casablanca,* to read Huston's treatment. "He always began when he would see me with some deprecatory remark about the heads of the studio, whom he cordially disliked," said Koch. "'These damn Warner brothers,' complained Peter, 'all they can think of is that I fit into a category.'"

Because the story was what Koch described as "Hustonesque, somewhat reminiscent of *The Maltese Falcon,*" with its "bizarre twists and turns," he told Lorre that he really ought to take it up with Huston. "It wasn't my kind of picture," said Koch. "I had been more concerned with pictures that had some social theme. But, for once, Peter was not kidding. He wanted to make *Three Strangers* outstanding." Lorre kept after Koch to read the story. Touched by his conviction and convinced of his dilemma—and because he liked him—Koch lent a sympathetic ear. "Finally, I said, yes, alright, I'll do it. And the studio wanted me to do it."

Huston and Howard Koch completed the script for *Three Strangers* in 1942, just before Huston accepted a commission in the Signal Corps. Koch said that his "contribution was mostly in writing the scenes that [Huston] had indicated in his treatment—although I probably stressed the romantic elements more than he had intended." Huston planned to shoot it with Humphrey Bogart, Mary Astor, and Sydney Greenstreet in the leads. Before war's end, however, the project fell into Jean Negulesco's hands.[32] When Jack Warner learned that Negulesco wanted Lorre in lieu of Bogart, not slyly sinister, but warmly romantic, he laughed and told him he was crazy. But knowing he had little to lose on the modestly budgeted picture, the cost-conscious studio chief agreed not to stand in his way. Opposite Greenstreet's rudely dignified solicitor, Lorre's philosophic drunk showed just how far his Hollywood experience had separated him from his European sensibilities. As his body became leaner, so did his performances. By 1940s standards, Lorre's earlier work seemed as stiff and self-conscious as the old-world milieu that shaped it. His acting had moved away from the psychological introspection of *Mad Love* and *Crime and Punishment* toward a bold immediacy that was, at the same time, casual and comfortable, off-center and ironic. Where he was, philosophically speaking, offscreen had come of age on-screen.

Given freedom to improvise on *Three Strangers* (1945), Lorre brought to his portrayal, in Negulesco's words, "his own melancholy whimsy, the calm of a poet." The actor openly stood apart from his movie-made persona and looked at his surroundings with a sense of floating detachment: "I was looking at all the lights in all these houses. . . . Well, you see, each light cuts a tiny little circle out of the darkness, and each circle is the center of somebody's life. People swing around these lights like planets swing around the stars."

Lorre worked for the first time with Joan Lorring in *Three Strangers*. Although she had earned accolades in *The Corn Is Green* (1945), she described herself then as a naive and diffident youngster: "I was a retard at the time, nineteen going on eleven." Working with veteran actors fed her feelings of insecurity and self-consciousness. Lorre sensed his costar's discomfort. Recalled Lorring:

> The first time I met him, I was coming out of the make-up building, and he was coming in. Somebody introduced us. I have to preface this by saying I

was so painfully shy and so absolutely certain that I was ugly enough to stop a clock and had legs that should never been seen. . . . Well, I had never met Peter Lorre before. . . . As we were introduced, he said, "How do you do?"

"I just wanted to tell you something. Do you know how many years I have been in this country?"

"No," I said.

Then he said, "Do you know how long I have waited to play a romantic part?"

"No," I said.

He said, "It's been a number of years. All of my dreams of playing with the most glamorous women, and here is my first romantic part, and look what I get to play with!"

This comment crushed me, but I laughed. This was Peter's therapy for me. After that I didn't feel like such a freak. I don't think I could have done the role with anybody else. He changed the way I felt.

One day, when Lorre plopped his tired body next to Lorring on a bed on the set, she mistook his meaning and slapped him. "I felt very embarrassed about it afterwards," she admitted. "But he didn't even look angry. He understood more than I did."

In a scene beneath the clammy Battersea Bridge, art imitated life when Icy (Lorring) tells Johnny (Lorre), "You make me feel as if I was . . . somebody. At first I thought you were makin' fun of me. But you're not. That's just the way you are."

Lorre drew Lorring to him, first offscreen, then on, reinvesting their rapport into what the actress felt "was the best work I have ever done." Koch recalled that "Peter had a very good kidding relationship with the other members of the *Three Strangers* cast and never tried to upstage them. He didn't seem to have that kind of competitiveness that he wanted to bring anyone else down, except the people who were running the studio."

Production on *Three Strangers* began on January 10, 1945. The common cold, inclement weather, and differences of opinion between Negulesco, producer Wolfgang Reinhardt, and Lorre on the interpretation of a scene encumbered the usual assembly-line pace at Warner Bros. The director completed production on February 22, eight days behind schedule and nearly $50,000 over the $440,000 budget.

Reviewers were less critical than curious about *Three Strangers*, finding it novel, esoteric, even arty, a melodrama cast in the noir mold. Adolph Deutsch, who had scored *The Maltese Falcon* and *The Mask of Dimitrios*, composed the music for *Three Strangers*. And cinematographer Arthur Edeson's sure hand was present, smudging the characters in shadow tones of gray and black, saying more with the camera than the writers did with their lines of dialogue. Huston said he didn't think much of the film, which he felt had been "rather sentimentalised." Critics grudgingly acknowledged Negulesco's skillful weaving of three stories, saving their accolades for the leads. *Life* praised Greenstreet as "a polished, patrician villain, whose cold, sinister machinations lurk beneath the apparent dignity and wisdom of old age." Lorre fared no less well with *Variety*, which complimented him for handling the part, "one that is difficult in its transitions, with telling skill." Cast against type, he drew only a peripheral glance for his "under-acting." The Front Office caught on in a small way, plugging him into a similar role in *The Verdict* (1946). After all, amiable drunks were as readily recyclable as psychotic killers.

For Lorre, the new beginning had already dead-ended, except in his own imagination, where he role-played better parts. Co-worker Andrea King remembered that "he would go to wardrobe and put on these incredible costumes, such as the *Mutiny on the Bounty* Charles Laughton costume, and right in the middle of a take on Errol Flynn's set, as Errol would be speaking, he would let out, 'Here we go! Mutiny!' And Errol would say, 'Oh God, it's Lorre again. Will you get him off the stage?!' And I had a feeling that he felt one day he would give anything to be able to be some kind of a leading man in one part or another."[33]

Little more than a week after wrapping *Three Strangers*, Lorre found himself on a plane to New York to attend the premiere of *Hotel Berlin* at the Strand on March 2. Besides plugging his new release, the actor revived his house act for three weeks, restaging his bloodthirsty gags with Marcella Hendricks and reciting "The Man with the Head of Glass." Seven days into his run, the *New York Times* bylined Lorre as a "Sensation!" then upgraded him to "Chilling on Screen—Super Thrilling on the Stage!"

Lorre made for "the exception to the usual dullness when a Hollywood star makes a personal." He mesmerized audiences. People couldn't get enough of him. Perhaps it was because he was so recognizable. Or possibly that they wished to see firsthand how he stacked up to his movie image. They wanted to touch him, to talk with him, to connect with that part of him that was larger than life. After a show at the Roxy, Peter, Karen, John Garfield, and Irving Yergin headed for Greenberg's delicatessen on New York's Lower East Side. When an unruly crowd of admirers gathered outside the restaurant, Greenberg called in four squad cars, but it was an undaunted cabby who warded off fans with a tire iron.

Confusing person and persona only enhanced the attraction. Women especially fell under his spell. A fan magazine in the 1940s had mused that its readers would "probably wind up trying to mother him." Co-worker Hazel Court found that the middle-aged Lorre "actually had tremendous sex appeal. When he talked to you, you felt you were the only woman in the world. And the eyes were hypnotic. . . . They were most expressive—not beautiful—but they were incredible. They used to look at you, as much to say, I'm going right into your soul." June Vincent, Lorre's costar on Universal's *Black Angel* (1946), recalled finding the actor sitting alone at the postproduction party. He was covered with lipstick, evidence of kisses bestowed by a bevy of young actresses who had worked on the picture. "You know," she said smiling, "you must be terribly popular. Have you looked at your face?" Lorre sat there with an impish grin. "I like to make people happy." Jonas Silverstone saw another side of this chemistry: "When you blend a star with menace and his obvious potency, he became attractive to some women and I saw this happen."

When Lorre played at New York's Roxy Theater in 1947, he received a constant stream of fan mail and personal notes at the Sherry Netherland Hotel. Returning early one morning, he found "Shorty the Nurse," a beautiful young woman swathed in fur, sitting on his living room couch. According to Irving Yergin, she had paid the maid ten dollars to get in. When Lorre learned she was naked beneath her coat, he told Irving he would see him later. Afterward, she kept sending him cards and even several paintings.

Not surprisingly, the criminal element closely identified with him. At the Earle in Philadelphia, nitery owner Benny-the-Bum Fogelman clenched his fists in anxious anticipation of Lorre's execution in "The Man with the Head of Glass." He couldn't take it. With tears streaming down his face, the mobster sobbed, "Ain't he the sweetest little son-of-a-bitch you ever seen!" Yergin recalled that "Benny became quite attached to Peter. He offered Peter his car and bodyguard. He even recommended to the manager of the Earle that Peter should have a better dressing room." He backed up his suggestion by threatening to burn down the theater.

To be on a first-name basis with a movie villain delighted gangster fans. It was their payoff. According to Yergin, a small-time hoodlum in Cincinnati sent up a refrigerator stocked with beer and cheese. When Lorre learned that Amadeo "Mimi" Capone planned to visit him in Chicago, he sent Karen out to shop. "If there is anything you need," offered Capone, "just let me know." The flattered if incredulous Lorre thanked him for his concern and assured him that if his services were required, he would get in touch.

Actress Betsy-Jones Moreland, who worked with Lorre, Boris Karloff, and

Lon Chaney Jr. on "Lizard's Leg and Owlet's Wing," a *Route 66* episode aired in 1962, recalled that

> Peter Lorre and other actors of that sort, Humphrey Bogart and so on, were always loved by "the darker side," if you know what I mean. The Mafia. The hoods of this country. Those actors were always treated with great respect and love and devotion. We went one night, Peter Lorre and I, and I forget who else, a whole bunch of us—we were taken by "gentlemen" from that world to a nightclub, to dinner, and we were treated like royalty. Absolutely like royalty! Peter Lorre wasn't allowed to pay for anything, there was no way that anybody like Lorre could ever pay for anything when the *other* kind of people were around. And everything was done first class. It was very interesting. You sort of had a feeling there was an undercurrent *all-l-l-l* the time, that other things were going on that you didn't know about and didn't *want* to know about, but you'd read about them in the paper tomorrow. There'd be little exchanges at the other end of the table, somebody would step out from the shadows and whisper in somebody else's ear, and you thought, "Oh, God, somebody was just macheted somewhere!"

Asked by film historian Tom Weaver if "she got the feeling that Lorre knew more than you did about what was going on," Jones-Moreland said, "I don't think so, I don't think he was part of it. I think he was like a mascot. He was a pet, but *not* a pet who knew anything!"

Silverstone said that "Peter was very well liked in Las Vegas, where the syndicate operated. Whenever he would enter one of the places, the doors would open wide. They couldn't do enough for him." His gangster fans adopted him as one of their own, extending their protection against threats, real or imagined. "I remember once some people got close to Peter," continued Silverstone. "Some of the guys in one of the casinos thought they were a little too close and presumptuous. They moved in and blocked these people off, just got rid of them. They were too close. They were threatening their idol." How did Lorre feel about this endorsement? "That was his reward," said Catharine Lorre. "He was honored because he had touched that closely."

"I guess there was originally a sexual attraction," said Paul Falkenberg, who had known Peter and Celia since 1931, "but I think it was more of a mother-son relationship in the end. She kept a protective hand over him and saw to it that everything went as smoothly as possible, saw to it that he got married again when they got divorced." They had lived together—by bureaucratic default—for six years before marrying. Karen and Peter had gone half that distance by 1944 and Celia felt it was high time they legalized their living arrangement. Karen was not oblivious to the legal kinks in her and Peter's situation. In November she filed for divorce from Arthur Young, now a bandleader with the British armed forces, on grounds that he had failed to support her, and asked for custody of Alastair, who was still in England. Having repeatedly failed to contact Young, Karen filed notice in the *Los Angeles Legal Journal.* That was not good enough, ruled Superior Judge Robert H. Scott, who "continued the case for three months during which time proper service on the husband must be made."

Meanwhile, Celia took steps to clear the way for Peter and Karen. Toward the end of January 1945, she escorted Karen to Las Vegas to satisfy the six-week residency requirement necessary to obtain a divorce in Clark County, Nevada: she from Peter and Karen from Arthur Young. On March 13 Celia filed a complaint alleging that she and Peter had lived "separate and apart from one another without cohabitation for more than three (3) consecutive years." Lorre didn't appear before the Eighth Judicial Court. Because his attorney "failed to introduce any evidence in support of the answer," District Judge George E. Marshall awarded Celia a decree of divorce and $200 weekly in alimony until she remarried or died.

Karen refiled her own complaint for divorce on the same day, stating that she and Young had not cohabited for more than three years and charging "extreme cruelty without cause therefor, causing plaintiff great and grievous mental suffering and resulting in impairment of plaintiff's health." According to Karen, she had begged her husband to let Alastair come over after she had settled in. Cable after cable asking him to send the child in July 1940 went unanswered. Finally came Arthur's reply: "Alastair must stay here, letter of explanation following." The letter never arrived. And the boy remained in the custody of the nanny who took him for an afternoon and ended up raising him as her own after both mother and father abandoned him. Payment for his support dribbled in, when it came at all. However she felt about Alastair, in her complaint Karen relinquished her son to the defendant, "who is a fit and proper person to be awarded the care, custody and control of this child," simply to expedite the divorce.

On May 16, which also marked the studio's extension of his one-year option, Peter and Karen announced plans to marry. Taking a page from Bogart's book, Lorre, who was forty-one, tied the knot with twenty-seven-year-old Verne in a private ceremony on May 25 that was officiated by Judge Marshall. Only minutes before, he had granted Karen's divorce from Arthur Young, who had failed to answer or make a defense to the plaintiff's complaint, served on April 23 in London. Friends Paul Mentz and actress Patricia Shay witnessed the wedding. Afterward, Peter and Karen flew back to Hollywood to celebrate with newlyweds Bogart and Bacall. Lorre had become one of Bacall's biggest supporters. Bogart had told him that he loved Bacall, but confessed that the twenty-five-year difference in their ages bothered him. Lorre had dispelled his doubts: "What's the difference? It's better to have five good years than none at all."

Lorre put their honeymoon on hold, pending completion of a tour of army camps in northern California. Then in July Peter, Karen, and Celia drove to Big Bear Lake. After all, Celia had brought them to the altar. If not for the first Mrs. Peter Lorre, Karen would very possibly not have become the second Mrs. Peter Lorre. Karen apparently didn't think the arrangement strange. "Celia didn't have anyplace to go," she honestly explained to inquisitive acquaintances. "We had to take care of her." Celia later returned the favor. For a short time, Peter and Karen lived with his first wife before moving into a rental property on Queen's Road in the Hollywood Hills.

The newlyweds spent much of their honeymoon in the saddle. Celia was no equestrian, but she was not ignored. Before trotting off on moonlit rides, Peter and Karen arranged for a car to drive her to the planned destination. Peter had earned a reputation as an expert riding instructor. On earlier visits to Palm Spring's B-Bar-H Ranch, he had crawled out of bed before the birds, told a sleepy Karen he was going for a walk, and reported to the stable. After brushing up his own equine skills, he taught her to sit erect and keep her heels down.

As a wedding present, Lorre rented a three-acre ranch in Mandeville Canyon, which he and Karen furnished in early American style and populated with a menagerie of goats, cats, a St. Bernard called Bum, a Boston terrier named Happy, a seagull identified as Cornelius S. Gull, and horses. "Peter and Karen had so much fun there," recalled Naomi Yergin. "They really blossomed into country gentry with the riding." Galloping off together into the Hollywood Hills became a daily routine.

On May 24 Lorre starred in the radio broadcast of "An Exercise in Horror: A Peculiar Comedy" for *Arch Oboler's Plays*.[34] In the opening minutes, he asks Oboler to write him a nice horror story, like the one about the guy who wears his girlfriend's ear on his key chain. "I'm really very sorry, Mr. Lorre," replies Oboler. "I'm not going to write a horror play for this series." Lorre prods him but gets nowhere. "I can't write any horror plays," says Oboler, "because some people in recent years have been writing far more potent ones than I can ever do. . . . Here, Mr. Lorre . . . is horror such as I could never invent."

The first story tells of a benign German family that turns a blind eye to the existence of a nearby concentration camp whose victims' ashes are canned for use as garden fertilizer. Touring the camp after the war, the father laments to his son that the most terrible thing of all was "that it was not hidden. . . . It is the duty of Germans to do things to perfection."

Lorre narrates the second story, building to a fevered, guttural pitch:

> Fill the Yankee Stadium in New York with one hundred thousand people. If there isn't room for that many, no matter, jam them in and shut the gate. Let them wait there. Go to Chicago. Take Chicago Field. Jam another one hundred thousand into it. Lock the gates. . . . Go to the Sugar Bowl . . . to Cleveland, San Francisco, New York, six hundred thousand people, some relatives, neighbors, friends, most of them strangers, but people drawing breath as you do. . . . Give a signal. All at once turn machine guns on these people (*sound of gunfire*). Kill them. Kill the people. Spray the bullets around the stadium, into the faces of the girls. . . . Listen to the screams, but don't stop . . . never stop until they are all dead, until not a groan is heard, until the mass of flesh is silent and the only sound you hear is the rush of their blood as it pours down the cascades of the seats and gurgles into the gutters right to where you stand.

"That is my last horror story," concludes Oboler, "but I haven't written even that. It happened already. Yes . . . the place, the ghetto of Warsaw."

It happened also in Budapest in 1944, after a Nazi coup put the Fascists in power and the lives of one-half million Hungarian Jews, including Lorre's own family, at risk. Recalled Francis Lorant,

> During the war, as you can imagine, we were not in a very good situation being right in the middle of Budapest after the Nazis took over. One fine day my grandfather and aunt were dragged off in front of the Gestapo. My father was in a forced labor camp somewhere at this stage and my poor mother was landed with the responsibility of trying to manage the family to the best of her ability. Anyway, the story goes that Peter was making some anti-Nazi speeches on the American short wave, which of course we didn't hear because we didn't have any of those privileges, but obviously the Nazis did. My aunt was dragged off to Auschwitz, but got sick on the long march towards the Austrian border and fell by the wayside and was too ill to continue. So that probably saved her life, for the time being, anyway. And my grandmother, who was very, very upset by the whole thing, tried to commit suicide, unsuc-

cessfully, but at least having landed in the hospital at that stage we prevented her from being dragged in front of the Gestapo.

On June 5 Lorre reported for his last tour of duty in the Warner Bros. armed services. He began his third year under contract with an adaptation of *Confidential Agent,* Graham Greene's story about an antifascist Spanish Republican agent on assignment in England. The studio had originally set Humphrey Bogart and Eleanor Parker to costar but recast Charles Boyer and Lauren Bacall in the leads. By May, late in the preproduction stage, Lorre also had joined the cast.

Topical then, dated now, *Confidential Agent* (1945) was, by the standard of the times, an excellent spy melodrama. The *Motion Picture Herald* singled out Lorre, who "tops almost all his previous portrayals in one high-tension fit of hysteria." When the confidential agent (Boyer) corners Contreras (Lorre) and accuses him of murdering a young girl, the actor unleashes his extraordinary vocality in a jagged crescendo of anxious flutters, torrential gasps, and raspy whimpers as his hand anxiously spreads across a face convulsed with frenzy: "I swear to you I wasn't there when it happened. It was Maria. It's her you want. She did it. . . . DON'T—DON'T FRIGHTEN ME! I have a bad heart. The doctor has only given me six months to live. . . . WAIT! LISTEN TO ME! If you only had six months to live and no hope at all, wouldn't you choose a little comfort and respect? . . . WAIT! HEAR ME OUT!"

His breakdown dead-ends in a heart attack on the bathroom floor, "which he executed beautifully," said director Herman Shumlin, after "I described to him the way I saw the scene and the way I wanted it to happen. I think he felt that I should have taken it for granted that he would know how to do it effectively. When I described how I wanted him to fall and how I wanted him to lie as he died, he looked at me expressionlessly and said, 'Show me.' It was a deliberate challenge, so I showed him, falling and lying on the dirty floor."

Co-worker Dan Seymour recalled that Lorre also tested cinematographer James Wong Howe. "He used to drive Jimmy nuts," said the corpulent character actor, "because he was always smoking cigarettes and when he looked through the camera, he'd always hold his cigarette in back of him. Peter used to have a little eyedropper with water in it, and he'd put a drop of water on the end of the cigarette. Jimmy would blow his top. He couldn't figure out why the cigarette would go out and why it tasted so bad."

In 1944 Warner Bros. paid $13,500 to RKO for the motion picture rights to Israel Zangwill's *The Big Bow Mystery,* first published in 1892 in England and three years later in the United States. Originally brought to the silent screen as *The Perfect Crime* by Film Booking Office of America (FBO) in 1928 and again as *The Crime Doctor* by RKO in 1934, the Victorian whodunit underwent another refashioning by Warner Bros. scenarists Peter Milne and Barre Lyndon, resurfacing as "The Open Verdict."

After making the Academy Award–winning *Star in the Night* (Best Two-Reel Short of 1945) and *Hitler Lives* (Best Two-Reel Documentary of 1945), second unit director Don Siegel—who had done montage work for *Casablanca* and the mutiny and escape-from-Cayenne scenes in *Passage to Marseille*—held out for a feature assignment. Jack Warner gave him *The Verdict*, a mystery built around the pitfalls of circumstantial evidence, with Joan Lorring as a music hall entertainer; Sydney Greenstreet as George Grodman, superintendent of Scotland Yard; and Lorre as Victor Emmric, an artist who is partial to young women and old bottles.

Finding a ghoulish little man with a macabre interest in painting cadavers—"I can do corpses exquisitely"—was easy, claimed a Warner Bros. publicist. Peter Lorre, the "pocket sized menace man" and Greenstreet's foil, was the obvious choice. "Come on, Victor, I have a delightful stabbing for you to illustrate," invites Grodman, who is writing a book about his famous cases.

"Oh, no, I've done three stabbings in a row," whines Victor. "How about a nice strangling for a change?"

Emmric knows more than he cares to tell. With sardonic mirth, he plants false clues and casts sinister gazes, throwing audiences off the scent. "No one could be as guilty as he is made to seem," wrote Jack Grant in the *Hollywood Reporter*. Just as often as Lorre secretes himself in a dark closet or lurks in the shadows, he trots out his affable lush. It is a good trick, playing on public expectations, then turning around and casting himself against type, all smoothly done in the same film.

Peter and Joan Lorring picked up just where they had left off in *Three Strangers*. Lorring was self-conscious about wearing tights in a song-and-dance number. Always the psychologist, Lorre sensed her fears and soberly remarked, "Oh, you should never show those [her legs]. . . . You don't even have them screwed in right. You've got the left one on the right and the right on the left." Lorring laughed and felt better: "By the end of that movie, I had such a crush on him. I couldn't stand it. I have to tell you that my skirt got shortened [and] I didn't wear jeans . . . or slacks as much. I got other dresses and they were shortened. Now, how this looked, I can't tell you."

Lorre kept Greenstreet on the hot seat, too. At one point in the film, the bulky actor rises from a chair and says, referring to the angling George Coulouris, "He's already made one [mistake]; he's misjudged the size of my britches!" Then his massive backside moves to black out the frame. Indeed, it was Greenstreet who persuaded Siegel to shoot him from behind at a low angle. When the director voiced doubts about using the scene, Lorre, with a devilish grin, piped up, "If I had been asked to do that shot, it would have been much more difficult." After all, he pointed out, the "old man" had managed his bulk so well.

In the final moments of *The Verdict*, Grodman laments that "things over which we have no control have come between us." He was more right than he knew. Playing with Greenstreet was "one of the most satisfying times in my life," said Lorre, but "we didn't want to end up like Abbott and Costello." *The Verdict* rang down the curtain on "the little man and the fat man."

On December 4, 1945, Siegel brought in *The Verdict* eighteen days behind schedule. No one blamed him. In October the studio's union employees had struck over low wages and poor working conditions. Riots broke out between opposing guilds. Pickets marched and rocks flew. Armed guards reconnoitered from rooftops. Hired goons wielded clubs and leather straps. Siegel remembered being the only director working during what became known as the Battle of Burbank. He fought his way into the studio without knowing from day to day who would be his cameraman or which members of the cast might show up.

Lorre put his personal safety and the stigma of being called a scab ahead of Steve Trilling's instructions to report to work. "He said he was afraid he would have to refuse," reported Trilling on October 19, "[and] would not cross the picket line no matter how few the number." Trilling reminded Lorre that "he had been passing picket lines for the past six or seven months; that he had come through the picket line last night at 5 p.m. with no threats or any intimidation." The set was ready. The director, cameraman, and crew were waiting. The stand-ins were standing by. Even a call from Siegel—with William Jacobs in attendance—did not budge Lorre, whom Trilling characterized as one of the "timid guys." The guild had told its members to be careful: "If there is mass picketing, if there is any threat of violence, don't go through."

Siding with the union against Warner Bros. ran true to Lorre's liberal form and at the same time twisted a knife in the sides of the patriarchal echelon. Moreover, his guild-sanctioned absence nicely covered an upswing in his drug problem. The mists, hazes, and banks of fog required by the story—and needed to cover the sets that did not fit the period—were produced by dry ice fumes, burning cans of charcoal, and vaporizing mineral oil. Lorre blamed the artificial fog, earlier a problem on *Passage to Marseille,* for triggering "what I think is now called 'house dust' allergy, which affects the sinus." For his "very great pain and misery," he sought out an allergy doctor, whose treatment did not include the use of narcotic drugs. "That was the time I found out I could not stand the suffering anymore," Lorre told federal narcotics inspector Theodore J. Walker and agent Samuel Levine. "I didn't think I could even finish the picture." In November, complaining of "headaches, hay fever, severe attacks of pain in the region of his liver, and a marked depression," Lorre visited Dr. Louis I. Sokol, who had treated him for addiction in 1939. His physical examination confirmed fever, migraine, biliary dyskinesia, and depressive psychosis. Among other things, said Lorre, Sokol "gave me at first Dapirin with Codeine; then when that did not work any more he slowly and reluctantly gave me Dilaudid, knowing full well that I was in danger of becoming addicted. He gave me approximately 6 to 10 prescriptions in my own name which I had filled at Turners, on Sunset Boulevard." Lorre took his first injection of Dilaudid with the understanding that he would travel to New York after the finish of the picture and take a cure.

Lorre's health threatened to close down production, but Greenstreet's actually did—for two weeks without pay. With the second lead down with pneumonia, Lorre and Siegel took off for sunny Palm Springs, where they vacationed at the B-Bar-H Ranch. When Siegel admitted that he didn't know how to ride, Lorre offered to teach him.

"You're too effete to ride," replied Siegel.

"All Hungarians ride horses and women," Lorre proudly returned.

Siegel recalled that Lorre taught him standard corrective technique: "'If the horse wants to go left, make him go right. If he wants to stop, make him move forwards. If he wants to go forwards, make him stop. It's that simple.' Believe it or not, it worked. In half an hour, I was in control of the horse. Peter rode superbly. I never saw him with a woman." Back at the studio a tanned Lorre teased a pallid Greenstreet that he "must have lost at least a pound." Greenstreet, recalled Siegel, just patted his protruding belly and chuckled.

Siegel and producer William Jacobs ran the picture for Jack Warner, who registered genuine surprise—and consternation—at the last-minute revelation that Greenstreet was the murderer.

"You can't make Sydney Greenstreet the killer," objected Warner.

"You know the story," countered Siegel. "We just followed the book." Siegel and Jacobs were delighted that they had fooled Warner, but they were up against a brick wall. Warner had fingered Lorre for the killer and felt that audiences would do the same. To avoid confusion, he instructed Siegel to insert several clues pointing to Greenstreet's guilt.

Overwritten, overplayed, and overdirected, *The Verdict* was, in the minds of contemporary critics, overconstructed with well-worn materials. *Variety* complained that the picture's "heavy-handed" treatment offered no relief from its "sombre monotone," completely overlooking the comic touches gently prodding the story. Greenstreet lightened his sinister machinations with levity, even making sport of his own girth. When he is not satisfying audience expectations, Lorre cuts a dapper figure who is tenderly charming and immensely likable for all his faults. Returning from a night out with Lottie (Lorring), Emmric savors the moment with a satisfied smile and an impromptu bump-and-grind. It is Peter Lorre as few audiences saw him and as he wanted to be. According to Lorring, he was "thrilled" to be playing a leading man. Lorre swept up Siegel with his energy, input, and versatility. With the director's blessing, he struck off in a new direction, if only momentarily.

In December 1942 Warner Bros. had purchased the screen rights to W.F. Harvey's short story "The Beast with Five Fingers" from the author's widow for two hundred pounds. The property kicked around the studio for several years, with more than one writer failing to come to grips with it. Finally, screenwriter Curt Siodmak solved the problem of the Harvey story, which was, in his words, "not big enough or interesting enough for a motion picture," by creating a screenplay about a murderer whose guilt is manifested in hallucinations about the severed hand of his first victim.[35]

Siodmak said that he was thinking of Paul Henreid, who was starring in *Casablanca* at the time, when he wrote the screenplay. "Paul didn't go for it," said Siodmak. "He told me that he wouldn't play opposite a bloody hand. My idea was to make the murderer inconspicuous—one would never suspect a leading man like Paul to kill the pianist. . . . Paul was wrong, and that is still my opinion."

The Front Office, however, decided on Lorre for the role of the demented bibliophile Hilary Cummins. Before the actor had time to groan and roll his eyes, studio publicists had announced, "Peter Lorre continues to be the busiest little 'horror man' in pictures, with new assignments piling up before he can finish up the old!"

Director Robert Florey expected better of Warner Bros. than *The Beast with Five Fingers* (1946) after bringing in *The Desert Song* (1944) and *God Is My Co-Pilot* (1945), both box-office successes. Adamant in his dissatisfaction with Siodmak's screenplay as well as the shooting schedule, he took a three-month suspension. But when he returned to Burbank, Jack Warner stuck him with the same assignment.

"I read it," Lorre greeted Florey in his office. "Don't worry. Since you are in trouble I'll keep two Pernod bottles in my dressing room."

Florey decided that the only way he could possibly make something out of the story was to "shoot it as seen through the eyes of Hilary Cummins." He designed and photographed the sets in an expressionistic style and edited the film accordingly, "as I conceived my adaptation of 'Frankenstein,' and wrote and directed 'Murders in the Rue Morgue' at Universal in 1931." Florey discussed the idea with Lorre. Interested in his conception, he accompanied Florey to the producer's office. William Jacobs dismissed the project as "commercially unthinkable."

"A glimpse of what *The Beast with Five Fingers* might have been," said the director,

> remains in the sequence in which Hilary, alone in the library, sees, then struggles with, the cut-off hand. He is terrified as the hand comes at him again and again until it becomes apparent that there is a bizarre connection between the hand and the crazed astrologer who nails the hand to his desk—it escapes and Hilary chases it. This sequence and a series of quick flashes cutting to inserts of objects and shadows in the room and flashing back to distorted angles of Hilary's face and close shots of the severed hand crawling—weird sound effects and strange music being recorded later—strident sound when a string is snapped from a mandolin hanging on the wall—each motion of the hand synchronized with a jarring shrill sound—the picture would have been a success if entirely directed as I visualized.

The finished screenplay was not what Siodmak had envisioned, either. "When a writer has finished his screenplay, everybody gets into the act and improves on it. I told Peter that I was the worst writer in the world, everybody can do it better. . . . Peter fooled around with that screenplay after he got the part. It lost, in my opinion, its brittleness and menace. A threatening Paul Henreid would have been something new and with much more impact than bug-eyed Peter, whom everybody suspects anyhow to be the monster."

Filming got under way at the Warner ranch in Woodland Hills in November. Lorre swung between emotional extremes that were undoubtedly symptomatic of his growing frustration at Warner Bros. Humor mediated his highs and lows. On the second day of shooting, co-worker Andrea King went to put on her bathrobe: "I always had to be careful when I went to my dressing room. THAT HAND could and would be somewhere in my drawer or pocket of my dressing gown, I never knew. But I did know it was Peter." It "was really an ugly, hideous thing and he fell in love with it. Well, the first time that I'd had this happen was [when] I went to put on my bathrobe while the hairdresser was fixing my hair. I put my hands in my pocket and of course here was this hideous hand. I threw it across the room, with catsup falling everywhere. And then you'd find it in your dressing room drawer [or] squished in your shoe."

On another occasion, the cast was assembled for a dining room scene. The camera rolled, and the players began their lines. King said that when she turned to talk to Lorre, he "would have a piece of celery or a carrot in his ear or up his nose. Well, we got the giggles." During another take, he told those gathered around the table he didn't feel well. Suddenly, he pitched forward and made a retching noise, prompting King to scream and cover her face.

Not everyone found his shenanigans amusing. When Lorre had acted up on *Hotel Berlin,* the dignified Raymond Massey had chastised, "After all, Peter, you're supposed to be an actor. You *are* an actor, unfortunately. But God didn't give you any talent for this sort of behavior, so stop it, please." If he had stopped then, he did not now.[36]

Victor Francen, who played the part of the pianist, was suffering from a bronchial condition. When he had had enough of Lorre's pranks, he simply got up and left. "This is just impossible," grumbled Florey, who also walked off the set and canceled production for the rest of the day.

Lorre was also up to old tricks. Some called it "bits of business." John Carradine, who remembered Lorre mugging for the camera when they worked together on *I'll Give a Million,* called it scene-stealing: "The director [Walter Lang] would tell him to save it for the close-up. Of course, there would be no close-up." Whatever you called it, green actors had to stay on their toes. "I think it is common knowledge that he was a tremendous scene-stealer," said actor Robert Alda, who costarred in *The Beast with Five Fingers,*

and that you had to be prepared for this all the time. You were able to study some of the pictures that he had done before and see some of the little tricks that he did. A lot of times, you might be doing a scene with an actor and he turns his back on you and you think, well, he is out of the scene. Not Peter. He would turn his back on you and his hands would be going behind his back, and he would have things to do with his back pocket, or that famous trick of his of unleashing his collar from the front, or those hands were giving themselves a self-manicure, or anything to keep the camera's eye on him.

Lorre had made it especially interesting for friend and co-worker Broderick Crawford, whom he had met through Bogie. "One night in Chasens we started making faces at each other for the fun of it," said Crawford, "because he was known as 'the little monster'—because of the picture *M*—and he called me 'the big monster'—because I did 'Of Mice and Men' in New York. So every time we'd see each other we'd make the worst faces we possibly could at each other and it became kind of a gag around town that we were trying to scare each other." Crawford regarded the actor as "one of the greatest scene-stealers in the business. He'd light a cigarette in rehearsal and then you'd wait for him to light a cigarette when you got into the take, [but] he wouldn't light the cigarette, which threw your timing off. These are little tricks that actors have and do to each other. The actor doesn't resent it, and when he says, 'You bastard, don't do that to me again,' he's laughing, because Peter trapped him. And the next time you make sure Peter doesn't trap you, that's all."

During the fourth and final week of shooting, Lorre took more interest in his work, greatly facilitating Florey's job. "I think he started out tongue-in-cheek," said King, "and then he became involved and thought it was a colorful role. . . . I don't know whether his sense of humor gave further energy for what he did, but he would just be hilarious, then he would all of a sudden—boing—go into a dramatic scene and play it to the hilt! . . . His whole being was in it. He didn't use tricks. It just came from inside him."

Florey gave *The Beast with Five Fingers* as much expressionist style as he dared with lighting and photography, but Lorre, under no such restraint, remained true to the director's original idea. Any number of his screen performances, most notably in *M, Crime and Punishment,* and *Der Verlorene,* bear moments of expressionist acting. As Cummins, the crazed librarian who seeks to "rediscover the key to the future known only to the ancient astrologists," he exteriorizes the emotional "inner rhythm" of his character, nearly sending his repertoire of familiar mannerisms over the edge. He furrows his brow and bulges his globular eyes. His broad hands knead his face, distorting its features. No longer able to distinguish between imagination and reality, Cummins moves in a "sleepy delirium, like a somnambulist." Lorre avoided the jerky, robotlike movements of early German expressionist actors and smoothly synthesized his role, reducing thought and action into a single word or gesture.

Florey dressed Lorre in dark clothing, contrasting his white face, front-lit from below, with his black body, as he had done in *The Face behind the Mask.* Eerily luminescent, Lorre's face hangs in space, severed from rational sensibility. Visually italicizing Cummins's mental deterioration, Florey, like Karl Freund in *Mad Love* (1935), vertically divided the actor's face with light and shadow, symbolizing his split psyche. Caressing the hand arouses conflicting passions of pleasure and revulsion, each read on his mobile visage. One moment it is tender, the next terrible. With insanity grown to homicidal mania, Lorre pumps panic into full-blown hysteria. He purrs and pants, rants and raves, reaching a crescendo of guttural cries when the hand crawls to his neck, strangles him, and vanishes.

Between its completion in January 1946 and its premiere in December, *The Beast with Five Fingers* underwent extensive editing, including the elimination of visual effects that would have drawn the audience into Lorre's sense of reality. In the original ending, for example, Bruce Conrad (Alda) and Julie Holden (King) discover the charred remains of the hand in the fireplace, indicating that Cummins had imagined the attack. The scene was deleted from the final cut. Critics were divided as to whether Lorre had turned in a forcefully introspective portrayal of grotesque proportions or merely overplayed his hand. "Without any explanation of the switches from straight narration to scenes registered by Lorre's deranged mind," observed *Variety,* his madness lacked a constant point of reference, a sense of perspective.[37]

The utter believability of the hand remains one of the film's strongest assets. In his short story, Harvey described the living hand as "moving quickly in the manner of a geometer caterpillar, the fingers humped up one moment, flattened out the next; the thumb appeared to give a crablike motion to the whole." The studio's special-effects department did justice to Harvey's macabre conception. For long shots, a mechanical hand, mounted on two small wheels, wound its way across the set like a toy train. Its fingers humped up and flattened out, scuttling along a tier of books, wriggling in agony. In close-ups at the piano, the hand was that of pianist Erwin Nyiregyhazi, who was otherwise covered in black velvet. In another scene, the hand belonged to Florey, who pushed open the cover of a box on a desk and moved his fingers threateningly. Still another hand was made out of wax and wood.

Florey all but disowned the release cut of *The Beast with Five Fingers,* which the studio advertised as "THE MOST *TERRIFYING ADVENTURE* EVER HURLED FROM THE SCREEN." Indeed, the director left Warner Bros. after the project was completed. He advised friends not to see it, and in their own way, critics said the same thing. They called the picture "grisly," "repulsive," "tasteless," "bloodcurdling," "for strong stomachs only," "gruesome and horrible," "for the ghoulish trade, a must," and a "cinematic nightmare." *Time* concluded that "Director Robert Florey, plainly untroubled by considerations of taste, concentrated on peddling gooseflesh to cinemagoers who dote on being frightened." Ironically, *The Beast with Five Fingers* did better business than expected, perhaps because it had no competition in the horror market. Although the picture turned out to be the requiem for the horror genre, which had been supplanted by another Hollywood perennial, the science fiction movie, it is regarded as a "classic," wrote Florey biographer Brian Taves, "innovative and influential in its day and still effective and successful with modern audiences."

Lorre's screen persona had also become obsolete. In May 1946 his contract came up for renewal. Although it had two more years to run, Lorre sensed the studio would not exercise his option. He had proved himself readily recyclable in film noir after ending his time at Warner Bros. on loan to Nero Films for *The Chase* (1946) and Universal for *Black Angel* (1946), both based on Cornell Woolrich novels. Nonetheless, with the end of the war films and the eclipse of the Lorre-Greenstreet team, he felt his stature shrinking.[38]

"There has not been a script written bad enough to cause me to take a suspension," Lorre told a friend. "As long as they pay me, and well, I'll be anything they want me to be, a Martian, a cannibal, a monster, a king, even Bugs Bunny. I don't give a damn."

Jack Warner had called his bluff.

Sinister currents at Warner Bros. indicated that something stronger than suspension was in the air, something equally shadowy but far more pernicious. Lorre believed the political insinuations attendant upon his friendship with Bertolt Brecht had further alienated him from the Front Office. Those who knew the dangers inherent in associating with a supposed Communist never doubted Lorre's suspicions that Jack Warner—a friendly witness who, in May 1947 would name names in a preliminary hearing of the House Committee on Un-American Activities investigating alleged subversive influence in motion pictures—had graylisted him, in effect putting a safe distance between the actor and Warner Bros. By "mutual agreement," Lorre and Warner Bros. agreed to "release and discharge each other" on May 13.[39]

The actor later joked that he had spent several years of hard labor at the studio. Metaphors of prison life, of a sort of chain-gang existence, haunt the memories of those who worked at Warner Bros. "We were all rather unhappy there," recalled contract player Geraldine Fitzgerald. "The way the studio was run was very confining. For example, writers couldn't come on set unless they had permission from the Front Office. The whole atmosphere was restrictive and prison-like. We all felt this since we were under really iron-clad contracts. Warner Bros. had a lot of talented people there. We clung together to make our lives interesting. The camaraderie on the Warner Bros. lot was remarkably strong, but the reason for it was not such a good reason."

Sentenced—as he liked to believe—to a maximum term of character work, Lorre squeezed through the prison bars, under cover—ironically—of the movie camera. He milked his parts, feeding audiences fragments of self-expression. For all the artful dodges, however, Lorre sensed his was a sealed fate. "For the rest of his career he would remain a character actor," said Florey, "a fact he deplored more than once. He told me that if he had been a foot taller he might have become a leading man, but with his globulous eyes, his short legs, his soft hands and his gnomic appearance, he had to be satisfied in sharing his lot with 'Old Man' Greenstreet. Realizing the hopelessness of his 'leading man dream,' he had become a philosopher hiding his melancholy behind a disabused grin."

What lingered in Lorre's nostalgia-softened, anecdotal memory of his years at Warner Bros. were the pranks, camaraderie, and home-away-from-home life. Among the selected high points was not, but perhaps should have been, a time of steady, lucrative work. For an artist of Lorre's stature, if not of his ability, Warner Bros. presented a workable compromise. He most often went his own way—within obvious limitations—rising above the constraints of his typecast and giving more. "Any director who was striving to get him to do anything else than be just what he was," said Harper Goff, "was wasting his time." That Lorre played the game on both the studio's terms and his own was as much a testimonial of his ability to serve two masters as of his inability to commit to celebrity or to himself. Only being kicked out of the nest enforced some kind of decision.

6

INSIDER AS OUTSIDER

I'm here, free as the wind, fountain of extraordinary knowledge,
splendidly corrupt, and eager to be of profitable service.

—Peter Lorre

An actor is the meanest, most contemptible sort of creature alive.
So debased that he throws away his own self, his own
individuality, and takes on the personality someone else wants
him to be—for what?—for money, or maybe for fame.

—Peter Lorre

By all appearances, Lorre had gone Hollywood at Warner Bros. With pal
Humphrey Bogart, he frequented popular watering holes—Chasen's,
Romanoff's, the Villanova—and steamed the alcohol out of his pores at
Finlandia Baths. He pulled pranks and practical jokes and cracked wise. He
spent more than he made, even tapping Bogart for loans both knew he would
never pay back, and romanced a woman fourteen years his junior. He made
fifteen films in six years, playing sinister villains, insidious foreign agents, a
disenchanted scientist, an obsequious writer of detective yarns, a volatile plastic surgeon, a contemplative barfly, an artist about town, a homicidal librarian, and on several occasions, a true-blue patriot. He had made the team.

In the shadow of the movie marquee, however, stood another Peter Lorre,
one whose Hollywood lifestyle gave no hint of a secret existence as hard to
believe as some of his screen roles. Behind the scenes, the stage was set for a
collaboration that would have turned his career inside out. Even as he had

trundled between RKO and Columbia, he looked to more substantial roles. In late 1940 screenwriter Jo Swelling (*Pennies from Heaven, Made for Each Other, The Westerner*) had broached the idea of adapting émigré novelist Lion Feuchtwanger's novel *Der falsche Nero* (*The False Nero*, 1936) "as a play and at the same time as a vehicle for me."[1] Lorre had his sights on the role of a corpulent red-headed potter named Terrence, whose resemblance to the slain Nero sets the bloody stage for his impersonation of the late emperor. Anxious to move forward, he dashed off a short letter to Feuchtwanger in January 1941, asking when he would return to Los Angeles. If not in the "foreseeable future," perhaps they could correspond. Failing that, he proposed coming to New York between film assignments. Despite Lorre's enthusiasm, his efforts progressed no further. What he most wanted to make public—his aptitude for artistically worthy roles—seemed destined to remain private.

On July 21, 1941, two days after Lorre completed work on *The Maltese Falcon*, Bertolt Brecht sailed into San Pedro, California, with his wife, the actress Helene Weigel; their two children, Stefan and Barbara; and his collaborator-mistress-agent Ruth Berlau. Having fled Berlin one day after the Reichstag Fire in 1933, he had hugged the German border with a mind to making a quick return when the Nazi regime collapsed: "Don't go too far away. In five years we shall be back." Hitler's advance, however, forced Brecht's retreat through Prague, Vienna, Zurich, and Paris. In December 1933 he took shelter in Denmark. As the Reich grew and free Europe—"this moribund continent"—shrank, Brecht began to fear for his safety. Clearly, he could not remain "perched on one of these little islands at a time when the slaughter seems to be on the point of breaking loose." Stripped of his German citizenship and facing possible deportation, he applied for American quota immigration visas for himself and his family in March 1939. In April Brecht moved to Sweden. While he was there, he received an invitation to join the faculty of the New School for Social Research in New York, putting him a giant step closer to securing an entry permit to the United States. On April 9, 1940, German forces invaded Denmark and Norway. Denmark resisted for two hours, Norway for two months. Brecht sailed for Finland. Painted into a tiny corner of the globe, he waited until May 3, 1941, for an immigrant quota visa number, then traveled across Russia on the trans-Siberian railroad and boarded a Swedish ship bound for America from Vladivostok on June 14.

Even given his limited access to the grapevine of émigré news, Lorre likely knew of Brecht's flight and his pressing need for money, sponsors, and an affidavit of support.[2] Just how helpful he was is difficult to say, although Elisabeth Hauptmann, Brecht's friend and collaborator, had no doubts. "Lorre has made it big in Hollywood and in the press," she had confided to Walter Benjamin in fall of 1934, adding that her "faith that anyone would make the slightest move to help is totally gone. I don't even muster the courage to write to him, although he owes me money."

Martha Feuchtwanger and refugee actor Alexander Granach met Brecht's party at the pier. Lorre's absence underscored the privacy in which he held their relationship. For reasons more personal than political—or financial—he divided past and present, keeping silent on what would become the darker half of a double existence during Brecht's exile in America. Of all the dichotomies, or as Brecht would have it, dialectics, that encapsulated their friendship, the most striking was that his arrival as an unknown with no audience for his plays coincided with Lorre's greatest commercial success.

The next day Brecht visited his old friend and collaborator Lion Feuchtwanger, who advised him to stay in California "where it is cheaper than in NY, and where there are more opportunities for earning." Touted as "the New Weimar," Los Angeles housed not only a community of literary émigrés in whose company Brecht might feel contentiously comfortable, but also theater and film people like Lorre, Fritz Lang, William Dieterle, Fritz Kortner, Alexander Granach, and Salka and Berthold Viertel, all close friends who had cultivated ties with the film industry.

The Brechts (minus Ruth Berlau, who took up lodgings nearby) moved into a small furnished apartment on Argyle Avenue in Hollywood near Columbia and Paramount Pictures, just minutes by car from Lorre's home on Poinsettia Place. One month later they relocated to a modest two-story frame house in Santa Monica. There the family lived in near poverty on an income of $120 per month provided by the European Film Fund, to which refugee film workers—including Peter and Celia—pledged 1 percent of their income. To make ends meet, Weigel shopped for clothes and furniture at the Salvation Army and Goodwill stores. Brecht quickly converted his cramped bedroom into a study equipped with only a few books, a typewriter, and a map charting Hitler's advance in "lobster-red."

In Hollywood terms, Brecht had an image problem. From the first moment, he cast himself as an outsider who had been sentenced to "involuntary exile." He was a man on the run, and America was only a stopover. Not surprisingly, he made an ungracious guest who deprecated popularity by being unpopular. From his haircut, which "looked like a treatment for lice or an attempt to humiliate him," to the tips of his smelly toes, which suffered from a chronic foot condition, Brecht advertised his nonconformity. His crumpled shirts, whiskered face (he made it a point not to shave in expectation of meeting prominent movie people), old weather-beaten jacket, and visor cap—true proletariat apparel—singled him out as one of the worker class. The stench of his cheap cigars told people he had arrived, even before he did.[3] "He hadn't many teeth," remembered actress Elsa Lanchester, whose husband Charles Laughton became one of Brecht's closest friends and collaborators, "and his mouth opened in a complete circle, so you'd see one or two little tombstones sticking out of this black hole. A very unpleasant sight." He once turned up at a party in his honor, only to be turned away by an unknowing porter.

In the 1920s Brecht had imagined America as a never-never land—vibrant, dynamic, exotic—far removed from the constipated mediocrity of the German intelligentsia. But his studies in Marxism, followed by the Great Depression, tempered his romantic notions about "The New Atlantis." Nothing, it seemed, measured up to his expectations. He abhorred fast food ("One doesn't eat such things in Augsburg") and pronounced the bread tasteless and spongy, the fruit tasteless and odorless, and the air just plain tasteless. Although he had "no feeling for nature," according to Ruth Berlau, Brecht liked greenery. All the more reason to hate the desert heat and the artificial landscape, which, like a mirage, would fade away if the water bills went unpaid. Scenic seascape vistas bored him. He preferred instead the waterfront slums and storehouses of Los Angeles harbor. The same Brecht who later packaged urgent requests to find him a car—preferably another Steyr—in love notes to Ruth Berlau disparaged America's automobile-oriented society, in which "houses are extensions of garages." Americans, he judged, lived a synthetic, transient existence "from nowhere and are nowhere bound." In a setting so repulsive, yet so seductive, where "a universally depraving, cheap prettiness prevents people from living in a halfway cultivated fashion, ie [sic] living with dignity," Brecht quickly came down with a severe case of culture shock.

"Almost nowhere has my life ever been harder," he wrote, "than here in this mausoleum of easy going." From his letters and work journal emerge a portrait of a man suffering a sense of intellectual isolation. Contact with refugee artists and intellectuals at dinner, garden, and house parties only served to feed his sense of separation. Instead of filling his plate with content, they heaped it with contention. "Enmities thrive here like oranges," Brecht wrote a friend shortly after arriving in America, "and are just as seedless. The Jews accuse one another of anti-Semitism, the Aryan Germans accuse one another of Germanophilia." In his journal, he named names, describing how Bruno Frank jumped to his feet and shouted, "I will not permit the president to be criticised here." Oskar Homolka threw him out. Kortner caught Fritz Lang making an anti-Semitic remark, then split the émigré community along unemployment lines by accusing those who earn well of "talking with their pay-checks in their mouths." In a postscript to the proceedings, Brecht briefly noted, "[Rolf] Nürnberg hates Lorre etc."

Lorre's friends painted a picture of a lost soul turning up on the actor's doorstep with armfuls of books and manuscripts, searching for emotional equilibrium. "They would talk for hours," observed Irving Yergin, "not about the industry or pictures, but about Nazi Germany, actors that had stayed, world conditions, Brecht's own writings, etc." Their conversation often stretched into the early morning hours. Some even thought Brecht lived with Peter and Karen from time to time. More likely, he just slept over rather than violate the 8:00 p.m. curfew on "enemy aliens."

During his first few months in America, Brecht produced little other than vitriolic comments about Los Angeles, a kind of hell, which "stink[s] of greed and poverty." Ruth Berlau confirms that "he was able during the whole of 1941 to write hardly anything of serious concern to him." All the more reason to make some quick money with an English-language production of *Der aufhaltsame Aufstieg des Arturo Ui (The Resistible Rise of Arturo Ui)*, a dark comedy written in 1939 that cast Hitler as a Bronx-born gangster. Thinking it could be staged swiftly, Brecht approached Lorre, Oskar Homolka, and other actors he had worked with in Germany. "That, unfortunately, was wrong," wrote Berlau. "Nobody in America was interested in the play, and it was neither staged nor filmed."

However intellectually "out of the world" he felt in Los Angeles, Brecht was not socially insulated. Between Sunday evening *Kindergarten* at the Brechts and Salka Viertel's soirees, he networked, in a contemporary sense, with an important cross section of Hollywood's literati. In addition to renewing old acquaintances, he made professional contacts in the film world, names like Ben Hecht, Clifford Odets, Arch Oboler, Jean Renoir, Orson Welles, Lewis Milestone, John Huston, Groucho Marx, and Charles Chaplin. By fall, Brecht had shaken his lassitude and gotten down to the business of earning a living. His "first priority," wrote Berlau, was to collect some dollars, something he thought he could do writing for films; if fifty-nine other refugee German screenwriters could do it, so could he. At the same time, the medium would provide "a platform for his political as well as for his artistic views."

During his American exile, Brecht wrote stories, sketches, outlines, and notes for more than fifty films, most of which, says James Lyon, author of *Bertolt Brecht in America,* he tried to peddle in Hollywood. From an article about a model Ohio farm family put on display in a living diorama of daily life, Brecht developed a film treatment that included a household dispute, shattered furniture, and divorce papers—in short, the breakup of "all-American domestic bliss." In October 1941 he told Hollywood screenwriter Ferdinand Reyher of his plans for *The Bread King*, about the "production, distribution and enjoyment of bread." From this idea, they developed a fifteen-page story outline in a couple of hours.[4] Four days later, Brecht related the story to MGM assistant producer Gottfried Reinhardt, the son of theatrical producer-director Max Reinhardt. In his December 17 journal entry, he also indicated progress on other film stories: *Days of Fire* for Charles Boyer with Fritz Kortner, a film farce called *Bermuda Troubles* with Metro screenwriter Robert Thoeren, *The Snowman* with Ruth Berlau. After listening to the plot of his *Caesar's Last Days* in spring of 1942, director William Dieterle, under contract to MGM, encouraged Brecht to write an outline, although there was no chance of bringing it to the screen. "The industry isn't making costume films," Dieterle told Brecht. According to a June 1, 1942, entry in his journal, Metro even expressed interest in filming *The Threepenny Opera*. Later that week, at a luncheon hosted by Fritz Lang and attended by Clifford Odets and Hanns Eisler, Brecht also discussed a film version of *The Private Life of the Master Race*, the American title of *Furcht und Elend des Dritten Reiches* (*Fear and Misery of the Third Reich*).

Brecht had taken his "place among the sellers" and found it a dirty, degrading business. With one exception, he sold no stories and wrote no screenplays. The struggling scriptwriter must have felt that he had buttonholed nearly every influential person in Hollywood into listening to his story lines. One can imagine them politely lending an ear and between yawns rolling their eyes in wonderment at his blindness to commercial reality. For all his success, or lack of it, he might just as well have sold vacuum cleaners door-to-door.[5]

While in Denmark, Brecht had applied unsuccessfully for an American immigration quota visa. From 1938 he had tried a new tack, putting out overtures to screen and stage celebrities in the hope that getting an American production of one of his works would open, if not the golden door to opportunity, then at least a back entrance to asylum. Ferdinand Reyher, who in 1939 had lobbied intensely, but without success, for an American production of *The Private Life of the Master Race* "on the main hope for the play, the hope that we can make it the reason to get you in America ahead of your quota number," wrote Brecht that "with few exceptions it doesn't do much good to work through actors in this country" and recommended he "tackle" producers instead.

When that door closed on him, Brecht thought better of taking an actor's celebrity to the bank. As featured or supporting player, Peter Lorre was a star whom "almost every American knows." While Brecht had crossed countless borders, Lorre had paid his dues as a freelance actor, climbing steadily toward his commercial pinnacle at Warner Bros. If the writer could not interest producers in his scenarios, perhaps he might secure a foothold in the movie business through the aid of a friend like Lorre, who had made a name for himself.

Brecht believed that Lorre needed a suitable vehicle as much as he needed a well-placed contact to champion his cause. Sometime during his first year in America, he and Berlau collaborated on *The Grass Must Not Grow over It,* the first of eight known film stories written for Lorre—and one of almost a dozen for which no manuscript copy exists.

In *Rich Man's Friend,* which he had developed in fall 1941, Brecht stylized Lorre's story of how he had first come to London and enjoyed the hospitality of Freddy (Sidney Bernstein). Although L. (Lorre) at one time owned ten suits made by Berlin's best tailors, he now has only two, one aged beyond repair, the other a dress coat with a hump sewn in it, the legacy of his role as a "devilish hunchback."

Before he gained lodging in Berkeley Square, L. lived in Green Cottage with Maisie (Celia Lovsky), who "treated him from the very beginning as a great actor, which he indeed is." L. tries to make the boarders understand how poor he is and shows them a pair of shoes, but "they only clap like those possessed: wonderful how he simply puts something like that forth and pretends." At a wrestling match, L. hatches the idea of working up a theater act based on the choreographed infliction of pain—a dig at Stanislavski?—by the combatants. But it comes to nothing.

Freddy arranges to introduce the actor to a Hollywood producer at a great dinner. When he misses his ride, L. decides to go by foot. It begins to rain. Arriving at the Savoy, he is not well dressed enough to enter; "He turns around and there it happens."

L. sees a ghostly procession of sandwich men coming toward him in the fog. Their boards advertise *M.* On long poles swing giant heads: it is L's. The rain increases. When the sandwich men rest their poles against the wall of an underground station, he captures one and runs away with it. Carrying his own head, the small man in rags runs into the great producer, who is on his way to the train. "In this way," finishes Brecht, "L. became engaged in Hollywood."

The war years caught Brecht in a didactic mood. *Rich Man's Friend* is a *Lehrstück* with a personal touch. Ostensibly for public consumption, it taught Lorre a private lesson in *Verfremdung* (distanciation), of looking at his own past in a new light and seeing himself in the present, forever crossing the shadowy line between illusion and reality, guilty still of marketing his screen fame to the highest bidder. Weaving Lorre's reminiscences into a comical film story probably sounded like a good idea at the time. Besides planting the incentive, even the obligation, for the actor to get behind the project, it brought him into the creative fold. Between lip and leaf, however, it lost something, or so Brecht apparently thought, judging by his disclaimer that Lorre "doesn't tell a story in a very stringent manner, rather he strays and loses himself in details, episodes." Whether Lorre garbled the tale in the telling or Brecht in the recounting hardly mattered. The surreal jumble so departed the Hollywood norm that Lorre most likely showed it to no one. For whatever reason—and there are many—it didn't sell.

What Lorre could have done to help Brecht is unclear. He had no friends at the Front Office—declining to sign an exclusive contract had alienated Jack Warner, who returned the actor's antipathy—and enjoyed only a casual acquaintance with several writers at the studio.

Rejection of his work, indeed his mission to "effect change," invited Brecht's open contempt of Hollywood. When it fired on him, he answered back with all his senses. In his journal, letters, and poems, he excoriated the "dream factories of Hollywood," which "are filled with the oily smell of films." Here buyers and sellers operate a "market where lies are bought." "The very centre of world drug-trafficking" intoxicated audiences, reproached Brecht, dulling their senses and clouding their thinking with suspense, shocks, and surprises, sentimental devices he deprecated as "laxatives of the soul." Into this "cesspool" he cast the screenwriters, whose "spiritual mutilation," he said, "makes me ill. It is scarcely possible to stand being in the same room with these spiritual cripples and moral invalids." Even the actors belonged to "a cult of types which has almost nothing to do with art."

"Life in the most advanced capitalist country of the world," wrote Lyon, "contained enough new experiences to transform culture shock into mordant social criticism." *Cold, sharp, contentious, intransigent, refractory, dogmatic,* and *irreverent* are just a few of the words used to describe Bertolt Brecht in America. No doubt he would have enjoyed the obdurate impression these words and images forged of his steel-hard resolution to divorce emotion from intellect. Cutting himself off from his own feelings, he cast a rational eye on human relationships, subordinating the individual to the idea; he judged people good and evil, issues black and white.

In her politically partisan reminiscences, *Living for Brecht,* skillfully woven into an autobiographical narrative by Hans Bunge, Ruth Berlau furnished "Brecht's Everyday Vocabulary: A Small Dictionary," tabulating his likes and dislikes. One learns that he praised people who were normal, kind, useful, helpful, gifted, amusing, and genuine. In the theater he asked for contradiction. Why? why? and again and again: why? He enjoyed new potatoes, carp, dumplings, horseradish, and cheese, and on the beverage side lemon juice ("never, on any account, water"). He liked old clocks and fine pipes and needed tables, typing paper, pupils, gifted actors, discussions, detective stories, and to be left in peace. Though Lorre scored well in the "Words of Praise" and "What he Needed" categories, he fell short in "Words of Condemnation": America had *corrupted* him; he had *sold* out to Hollywood and his weaker instincts; he had *exploited* his own acting tricks instead of putting his talent to use; his performances were *nondialectical;* he was *non-Marxist.*

Happily for Lorre, there was more to Brecht than Berlau's inventory of likes and dislikes. His "tough-guy" image accounts for only one-half of the "contradiction between conflicting forces and ideas [which] taken together in their 'synthesis,' comprehend the essence of what is true." His lesser-known— at least to most—tender side provided the other half of the dialectical equation. Like Lorre, Brecht wasn't who he pretended to be, but rather, in Martin Esslin's words, "a person basically tender, driven to suppress his emotion, to appear hard and rational."

The dialectical gears in Brecht's mythmaking machine afforded him "the luxury of contradicting himself and everyone else within a consistent framework." After all, his rigid standards were just that, something to go by, not necessarily to live by. On the wide inviting avenue of logistical loopholes— and not a few potholes—Lorre walked back into Brecht's life.

Most of the writer's friends met certain qualifications: "political compatibility . . . usefulness in making a name or getting a production, availability to collaborate, and willingness to be a disciple." All except Lorre. Where he fell short, Brecht either looked the other way or propped him up. "If he saw people as being artistically useful in any number of ways," observed Rhoda Riker, a philosophy major at UCLA drawn into the Brecht circle by classmate and boyfriend Stefan Brecht, "Brecht could excuse a lot of other things about them." Lorre had a lot to answer for. To Brecht's mind—and Lorre wouldn't have disputed him—he was weak. Dr. Ralph Greenson agreed with both of them that "Peter was undisciplined and didn't always apply himself." While Brecht wore exile like a badge, Lorre submerged his foreignness—except on screen— sacrificing his true identity, including his accent, to the integration process.

One day Lorre and screenwriter Walter Reisch, whom the actor had known in Vienna, sat next to each other on barber chairs at a fashion shop on Rodeo Drive in Beverly Hills. Reisch invited Lorre to come to his new house, which, he said, had "a certain European flavor." Lorre accepted the invitation and thanked him. After leaving, Reisch found him waiting for him outside, his face pale.

Peter said, "I meant to tell you something, which I didn't want to say in front of the others. I don't want to come to your parties." I said, "Why not?" And now he said something which is absolutely the one and only time that I ever heard of such a thing:

"I am doing my darndest right now to improve my accent and to play not only parts as a foreigner, but parts in which the accent doesn't appear, or isn't noticed. And if I come to your parties, all of these guys will be there, like Lubitsch and Negulesco and Milestone and Billy Wilder and Garbo and Ingrid Bergman. And you, Walter, you speak with a terrible accent. I am working nightly six hours to get that foreign nuance out of my vernacular, out of my language. And when I am there at your parties everybody will speak with an accent or in the old language. I cannot afford it."

And you know what, he never came to a party of mine, in my house. And I never invited him again. It didn't hurt really, I understood what he meant, but I thought it was ridiculous, because I don't think that with his face and the parts he played the accent mattered. To the very contrary, the accent was part of his chemistry. It was part of his mystery. But, in all honesty, I must say that he absolutely cut me down. It was like ack, ack, ack, shrapnel, and I was shot down by him and in a way it was the last time that we really had contact with each other.

The surface signs of Lorre's Americanization must have also puzzled Brecht. At his ranch home in Mandeville Canyon, Lorre lived out a kind of frontier fantasy. He rode Western, not English, and outfitted himself in tooled belts, silver buckles, piped pockets, and stitched boots. He especially liked cowboy hats—each distinctively creased by its owner, he pointed out—which he collected from local wranglers. At least Brecht, who used and abused the colorful slang and idioms of colloquial English, could more easily identify with his friend's love of the vernacular. Lorre spoke hip talk fluently. At Las Vegas, where audiences often matched wits with comedians, heckling a young comic called Milton Berle was good sport. One night Lorre sat quietly with Burl Ives, ready to enjoy the show. However, when he spotted Groucho Marx sneaking in the back, he loudly exhorted, "Cream him, daddio!"

"Peter immersed himself in things American, or rather western," said actor Tony Martin, "especially slang. His jargon was right up to date, right in with everybody, always right today, like 'Hello, pop,' or 'What are we doing after work? Let's have a couple of boozes and maybe we'll get a couple of girlies.' He was opposite of what he was on screen. Real hip."

Like most émigrés, Brecht was impoverished, unrecognized, and, according to Ruth Berlau, very lonely. Lorre was none of these. Unlike Fritz Kortner, whom Brecht praised for his "ability to resist assimilation," Lorre worked hard to be an insider and to enjoy the fruits of his labor. In Brecht's stringent view, his friend had sunk into the "glamorous swamp" of Hollywood up to his neck. Writing to Ferdinand Reyher, he observed that "Just like [Charles] Laughton, Lorre is living in shamefaced poverty with four horses and several Japanese gardeners in a $50,000 villa." Far from enduring a slavery forged of golden chains, however, the actor actually lived less extravagantly than most film notables of his stature. Perhaps it was just that Brecht found it harder to understand excess in one who should have known better. Lorre rented, never owned, and in that way was more transient than Brecht. Until he moved into his ranch house in Mandeville Canyon around 1945, he lived rather modestly indeed. Even then he employed no servants.

When Brecht looked out his window, he witnessed poverty and inequality. Lorre saw only Joshua trees. His political résumé was painfully thin. Andrew Lorre described his brother as a "salon socialist." Like most actors, he readily fell in behind Roosevelt and remained a Democrat thereafter, although he might change sides at a moment's notice just to stir the political pot. "Peter was not a Communist," said director John Huston. "He would have been a Communist if he found himself in the presence of Orange County Republicans. He would have been a Communist at the dinner table with [President Richard] Nixon. He would have chosen to be. On the other hand, he would have been a die-hard Republican among black militants. Peter loved to shock people for fun." A sign, Brecht believed, of a healthy intellect.

Eric Bentley reported that

the circle who would gather at the Brecht home at Santa Monica on Sunday evenings was, of course, very German. Brecht didn't make a lot of contact with real American Americans. It was also very left wing, very much in a Communist clique of German refugees or people sympathetic to that. I remember I didn't know whether Lorre had anything to do with that kind of politics and in fact I never really found out in any direct way, but I recall that once there was some vigorous political discussion in German going on there with the German word for communism occurring a lot. And Lorre came in as this was happening, into this flood of dialogue. I remember him standing in the doorway and there's this little stop for him to come in and he was saying, "Ah, der Kommunismus, Kommunismus," communism. He picked up this word and grinned about it. I couldn't tell just from what point of view the grin was, whether it was from someone antagonistic or someone friendly, or what, but in some humorous way he teased them for being on that topic. In the further discussions he tended not to tangle.

Although Brecht never joined the Communist party, one knew where his sympathies lay. In émigré circles, he enjoyed the reputation of an "ardent fellow traveler" who "was unfriendly to anyone who wasn't friendly to the Communist party." Unable to separate art and politics, he had no time for nonpolitical actors or what was to his mind politically incorrect behavior. In 1939 Alexander Granach had appeared—as a Russian comrade—in the Ernst Lubitsch comedy *Ninotchka*, which satirized the foibles of Communism. "From that time on," wrote Berlau in her autobiographical reminisce, "Brecht ceased to mention Granach's name. Previously, when he was writing a film script, Brecht would express the opinion that Granach might play one role or another. But after his political blunder, as far as we were concerned, he was as good as dead." If "Red" Ruth held the party line, Brecht wavered as it suited his needs. Granach, one of his favorite actors, turned up as a member of the Gestapo in *Hangmen Also Die*.

Given the increasing brittleness of Brecht's political intolerance in the 1950s, one wonders how he would have reacted to Lorre's reprisal of the role in *Silk Stockings* (1957), a musical remake of *Ninotchka*. There is no way of knowing whether their friendship would have weathered the crisis; Brecht died in 1956.

If Brecht extended a particularly cold shoulder to those who abandoned Marxism, it was probably a good thing Lorre had never embraced it. "He didn't talk like a Communist," said Bentley. "He talked more like an independent radical of some sort. I'm not sure he felt any political commitment." Knowing Lorre as "an angry nonconformist, a dissenter with limited courage," Brecht never expected too much of him, or got it. Lorre was not among the fifty-six signatories—including Lucille Ball, James Cagney, Joan Crawford, Bette Davis, John Ford, Henry Fonda, Edward G. Robinson, Jack L. Warner, and others—of Hollywood's "Declaration of Democratic Independence" endorsed on December 21, 1938, which, according to *Hollywood Now*, petitioned the president and Congress to sever all economic connections between the peoples of the United States and Germany "until such time as Germany is willing to re-enter the family of nations in accordance with humane principles of international law and universal freedom." Nor had he signed the appeal of the Motion Picture Arts Committee to protest the "inhuman bombing of defenseless women and children in the cities of Loyalist Spain." Two ambulances purchased by the Motion Picture Arts Committee for the Spanish government bore numerous signatures of Hollywood personalities, but not Lorre's.

For Brecht, the Peter Lorre with whom he held so many apparent philo-sophical and ideological differences was only an adulterated version of his old comrade. As *M* fixed Brecht's pejorative attitude toward Lorre's Hollywood career, so their early association conditioned his view of Lorre's integrity as an actor. They had much to build on. They referenced the present by keeping faith with a past that had witnessed poverty, malnutrition, and the early struggle to establish a new theater; each knew where the other had been and where they might have gone together had Hitler not intervened. Both believed that America had stifled the free expression of their talent; and each knew he was among the few who truly appreciated the other's gifts.

Eric Bentley asked Lorre to write something for the jacket of his second Brecht book, *Parables for the Theater* (1948). After he did, Bentley could

> imagine, reading from Lorre's original note, that Frau (Elisabeth) Hauptmann sat him down at the desk or table and said, "Now you," and he tried a few phrases with her, as I see he was first going to write, "Brecht is a great writer . . . I think Brecht is the great writer . . ." He crossed that out and put, "Even an actor has a right to an opinion. Brecht is the poet—he chose that word—of our generation and to my mind its greatest writer."[6]
>
> Now at that date nobody was saying that, I can assure you. The only per-son from the theater or movie world that gave us a thing like this was Peter Lorre. There was one American or English figure out there that was coming around to an opinion like this. That was Charles Laughton, though he dropped it. He no sooner arrived with opinions of this kind than he dropped them under influences from political sources.
>
> When I got it I was not only pleased, I was surprised how far he went, because although I had been arriving at the same opinion, I had not found people in the German colony to agree. Most of the older generation people didn't.

Lorre publicly advertised Brecht as the greatest writer—and director—of his generation. "I knew that he would be one of the great poets of all time, which slowly turns [out] to be the case," he told interviewer Hy Gardner in 1963. "You don't really need much foresight to know that twenty years from now it will probably be Joyce and Brecht."

"He worshiped Brecht," said screenwriter Ellis St. Joseph. "When every-body in the world put Brecht down, when Brecht wasn't wanted, nobody could see any talent whatsoever in Brecht, except for one or two people like Lorre." Celia Lovsky characterized their relationship in much the same way Ruth Berlau described Brecht's friendship with Walter Benjamin, as a "comfortable intimacy" where each understood the other without the need of speech. In later years, Lorre's first wife cast a transcendent glow over their instinctive rapport, remembering, as did Lorre, that Brecht represented the best, unrealized, part of himself. Long before it meant something to have been one of his original ensemble and long after their collaborative ventures had been forgotten, Lorre still considered himself "Bertolt Brecht's actor" and Brecht "the only great friend he ever had." By his own admission, he "[did] not love many people or things but love[d] the few intensely."

Brecht did not conceive of human relationships in such terms, but in his own way he regarded Lorre just as highly. If he hadn't been forced to flee Germany and become just another cog in the dream factory, claimed Brecht—always ready to take a poke at Hollywood—Lorre would have realized his unlimited potential. Nonetheless, remembered friend and collaborator Hans Viertel, "Brecht thought Lorre the greatest German actor." When his name came up at home, he fell on it with an anger born of frustration. Lorre's typecasting as a heavy infuriated Brecht, who "thought of him primarily," added Hans Viertel, "as this sort of deft, light, extremely adaptable kind of actor he liked."

"In our wonderful days of washing dishes," recalled Rhoda Riker, "Brecht would stand there and say he's better than what they give him. He's a great actor and they are giving him shit."[7] In much the same way that Helene (Weigel) assumed the role of earth mother, taking under her strong wing presumably wayward souls, so Brecht was "a bit possessive about people . . . and Peter Lorre was one whom he regarded as properly his, but in this period seduced by American capitalism and possibly to be won back."

"Brecht was very opinionated and very determined about people that he thought had tremendous talent," said Riker. "He would just get these damned ideas and would decide about each of us, this is what we ought to do. Sometimes he'd just get damned pushy about it. When he thought he was right, he was pushy."

While others—Kurt Weill for his "culinary" opera and Christopher Isherwood for being "bought"—got "chewed down to nothing in a very short time" or "thrown out like old shoes," Lorre fell into a different category. "Brecht treated him with great gentleness," said Riker. "He never spoke of him with contempt, and let me tell you I heard a lot of people spoken about with contempt. Lorre wasn't one of them. . . . Brecht was always deferential and polite to him. He never put him down in front of other people."

The tough Brecht could be brutal, derisive, and insensitive, but his softer side did not exploit other people's weaknesses, noticeably Lorre's "sad and inevitable seduction." He "regarded Hollywood as deadening to a career like Lorre's," said Morton Wurtele, a graduate student in physics at UCLA who lived with the Brechts in 1945–46. "Yes, he (Lorre) was corrupted, but . . . there wasn't a significant alternative. Brecht could always write what he wanted to write, but an actor can't do that. There isn't any alternative for an actor except to go with the tide." He even allowed that Lorre "was doing very well in Hollywood and therefore should be treated in a certain regard."

"For Brecht, criticism was effective and useful," realized Berlau, "only when it was made in a spirit of real love." Brecht expressed his feelings for Lorre by tailoring film stories to the actor's capabilities—as he saw them—with only a gambler's chance that his efforts would pay off. His actions spoke louder than his words, shoring up Lorre's sagging self-confidence and rehabilitating his bruised self-image as an actor. For all his care and concern, however, Brecht never forgot that "the aim of criticism should be to aid production." Intent on weaning Lorre from his own celebrity, Brecht teased him about hanging out with his old cronies. Breezing in with news of the latest card game at Bogie's only invited ridicule. "Brecht was very tough," said Riker, and felt "obligated to behave that way and wouldn't let Peter get by with one single sentence which sounded as though he was being Hollywood. . . . He cut the turf out from beneath him."

Though Riker identified Lorre with the Hollywood crowd rather than the political-intellectual or émigré circles, most often he turned up alone, oftentimes sporting a red flannel shirt. One wonders whether he wore it in order to fit in or to pique the party-liners. From their conversations, Brecht distilled that Lorre, like himself, lived as an outcast. It showed up in his attitude, offscreen in a cynical distrust of the studio star system and on-screen in a kind of whimsical detachment. Acting, it seemed, had become a joke.

Early one morning, the bleary-eyed actor stumbled into the makeup department and moaned to actress Lee Patrick, who played Effie Perine in *The Maltese Falcon*, "For a grown man to come in at this hour just to make faces for a few minutes is ridiculous. It's really very humiliating."

"Me act?" Lorre told a reporter, "I just make faces! Really, that's all I do. I make lots of faces and they pay me for it. The director says: 'You're mad. Make like you're mad.' So I make like I'm mad. Then pretty soon someone calls out 'one hour for lunch!' I follow the others to the commissary and later return to the set. 'Make like you did before lunch, Peter,' says the director. 'Make like you're mad.' So I make like I'm mad again and before long someone says 'wrap 'em up. That's all for today.' So I go home, have dinner, go to bed, get up, report for work again and the director says: 'Make like you're mad again, Peter. Make like you did yesterday.'"

"His whole attitude toward the picture business, toward acting, was very funny," said director Tay Garnett.

> The other actors used to look at him in wonderment because he always referred to acting as making faces. He'd say, "Well, I'm going down to make some money today. I have to go and make some faces." He always said that. Had the desire for self-expression been there, Peter would have been the last one to let anyone know it. He would have been very, very careful to hide it. Peter didn't want anyone to think he took anything seriously. But actually he was a very thoughtful actor [who] gave a great deal of thought to his part, to what his character meant to the overall construction of the story.

The other side of the sword says that behind the banter hid the hurt of not being taken seriously as an actor. Lorre no longer talked about acting, but kept his thoughts to himself, preferring instead to let people know that, like Brecht, he shrugged off moviemaking as a "business, like any other racket. Either you know your business or you don't. What is there to get excited over? A good musician doesn't set up a wail or clamor when confronted with a new scherzo or gavotte. He knuckles down and learns the thing."

"I get a kick out of actors who say they can't do a part because they don't 'feel' it," said a surprisingly apostatic Lorre. "If I had to 'feel' every role I've done, I'd have been a stumble-bum years ago."

"I felt a kind of cynicism about his career and about life in general," recalled director Vincent Sherman. "I think he found that instead of being regarded as a very serious actor in this country he was regarded as kind of a freak."

Either way, Lorre deprecated not his talent, but the waste of it. In the beginning, wrote Paul E. Marcus, Lorre "jokingly referred to himself as a 'facemaker' because he never thought of himself as a serious actor in full-length, feature films. That also must have been the secret of his friendship with Bert Brecht."

Now he sold gestures to the studio middlemen, who bought them and packaged them into salable commodities. Undoubtedly, Lorre's Hollywood experience informed Brecht's harangues about the "commercialisation of art," where "custom here requires that you try to 'sell' everything, from a shrug of the shoulders to an idea . . . so you are constantly either a buyer or a seller, you sell your piss, as it were, to the urinal."

What began as a joke, however, ended with Lorre "play[ing] both a role and its own commentary." Whether Brecht, who believed that an actor "derives his morality exclusively from his attitude [toward] what he produces as an actor," heard only what he wanted to hear, or only what Lorre wanted him to know, this kind of talk was music to his ears.

"Brecht was very much preoccupied," explained collaborator Hans Viertel, the son of Salka and Berthold Viertel, "with making all the people he knew productive who he thought could make valuable contributions. He thought Lorre something valuable, a national treasure, so to speak, that had to be recovered." Bentley wondered if he could persuade Lorre to launch English translations of Brecht's plays in America. "When you heard Lorre's conversation," he recalled, "you kept thinking he would come back into serious theater. . . . His conversation would suggest that would be one of the things he would most like to do."

Brecht was determined to wean Lorre from Hollywood. Clearly, the actor was no good to anyone until he was good to himself. What better way to make him productive and useful than to bring him into the creative fold. Many of the writer's collaborators were bilingual exiles, such as Fritz Kortner and Robert Thoeren, who had established themselves in the film industry. For Brecht, the act of creation was a collective enterprise. He needed an audience to stimulate, entertain, and listen to him. While Helene Weigel prepared hot *Gugelhupf* and coffee downstairs, Brecht roamed his spacious studio collecting opinions from his guests. Through discussion he clarified his own thoughts. He invited criticism and often gave better than he got. Every word, idea, and impression was grist for his mill. "When he liked it, then he used it, adopted it, and formed it," said Marta Feuchtwanger, "and then all of a sudden it was his."

Lorre had the advantage of being a willing and intelligent disciple, "bright enough to offer ideas but too weak to give him resistance." His rigorous intelligence impressed Brecht, like everyone else. Eric Bentley remembered meeting Peter and Karen at the premiere of *Galileo*, which starred Charles Laughton, at the Coronet Theater in Los Angeles on July 30, 1947:

> Lorre was talking very vigorously and somewhat in monologue as he did when he had a favorite subject and was somewhat correcting everything about this American event from the point of the German, who knew much better what Brecht was all about. . . . He gave the impression of one who with a different spin of fate might have been an intellectual, might have chosen to be an intellectual. I wouldn't say he was pretentious, it was just that he was rather widely read. And very intelligent. He would speak to the point and he would speak

with real eloquence even in a language that wasn't his own. . . . I recall being very captivated by his persuasiveness, the cogency of his personality. I was very surprised at how bright he was. I was going around telling everybody he's really so bright. One doesn't usually expect that, at least from members of the acting profession. Since I only knew him as a moviegoer and knew the kind of parts he played in Hollywood, I was terribly impressed to find how much he tried to stay in contact intellectually with various things that were going on and how much grasp he had.[8]

In his journal, Brecht, who judged people by their thoughts and actions rather than by their feelings, noted, "Talked to LORRE in the evening about v[erfremdung]-effects. He finds that in my productions (he mentions the production of THE MOTHER in Berlin) the manner of the actors' technique was neglected, except when they could manage it anyway, and he advises me at least to mention the need for technical maturity."

Brecht tolerated intelligent dissent from one capable of making a contribution. However willing he was to subordinate himself to genius, Lorre was no yes-man. Andrew Doe, a theater professor at the University of Southern California who tried to interest the actor in staging a student production of *Mann ist Mann* in the early 1960s, remembers that Lorre "was not enthusiastic about Brecht as a theorist, rather as a great director." As much as Brecht valued him as a sounding board, Lorre probably played a more important role as an informant. Who better to give him a behind-the-scenes look at the off-set Hollywood. Too ingrained in the system and too addicted to the lifestyle in which it supported him, Lorre gave private vent to what Brecht said publicly in his poems and plays.

"I think Brecht to Peter was a form of friendship," said mutual friend Dr. Ralph Greenson, "in which Brecht represented some of Lorre's idealistic views which he, Peter, was unable to carry out."

Their "oppositional stance" stood them on common ground. In one of the most often quoted testimonials to his perennial dissidence, actress Elsa Lanchester remembered: "[Brecht] was anti-everything; so that the moment he became part of a country he was anti-that country. . . . He wasn't a bitter man. He was always funny about institutions and authority. He didn't want to be in power himself. But he was anti-any power, really; I think he was a professional anti-." Deprecatory of authority, especially the studio bosses, Lorre likewise rattled his cup on the prison bars. Whether or not he mocked the mogul or remembered his own brief and ineffective campaign to reorient Hollywood's thinking about literary classics, the spirit of his struggle lodged in Brecht's imagination. As a fellow victim of movie capitalism, Lorre could help him build his case against Hollywood. Mining the vein of collected injustices gave them a firm footing for a new beginning and a common denominator from which to wave the flags of mutual discontent.

Distancing the actor from Hollywood was the first regimen in a therapeutic course that included nurturing talents unrecognized by the movie capitalists. Brecht encouraged Lorre to recultivate the art of poetry reading and gave him a copy of his *Svendborg Poems* (1938). Unconfirmed reports even suggest that they collaborated on several poems. Lorre returned the confidence placed in him at a reading of Brecht's works in New York City on March 6, 1943. Sponsored by *Die Tribüne für Freie Deutsche Literatur und Kunst in Amerika* in the Studio Theater of the New School for Social Research, the program featured commentary by Wieland Herzfelde, songs by Lotte Lenya, and poetry readings by Lorre and Elisabeth Bergner.[9] Like Brecht, who read his own poetry "with dead-pan face, in the totally flat, antirhetorical manner he had intended it," Lorre stood there "like a piece of wood" and spoke his lines "better than anyone could speak," very simply and with complete understanding. He undertook the "thankless task of reciting Brecht's loose, thought-encumbered poems," wrote Henry Marx in the *New Yorker Staats-Zeitung und Herold*. "One of his oldest co-workers, he interpreted them well, thanks to his excellent sense for the humor and the deeper meaning of the poems, and by avoiding, above all, pathos." Brecht apparently agreed, judging by his comment that both Lorre and Bergner "have forgotten nothing, their techniques have remained completely fresh." After an afternoon reading, he told Morton Wurtele he regarded Lorre "as the finest reader of German poetry alive."

Serving two masters was nothing new for Lorre. In 1931 he had worked by day for Fritz Lang in *M* and by night for Bertolt Brecht in *Mann ist Mann*. Twelve years later he rendered purrs and guttural bursts over the radio and delivered ironic understatement to Brecht. Little wonder he believed he could bridge the extremes of his acting career.

The press didn't pick up on Lorre's cutaway to New York, or its symbolic import, which was just as well, given the prudence of low-profiling his association with leftist literary figures. Nonetheless, 1943 represented a high-water mark in the American chapter of Brecht and Lorre's relationship; common need, it seemed, had bred mutual commitment. Brecht wrote one play and two film stories expressly for Lorre within this twelve-month period.

In 1942 Brecht had dusted off plans for a stage version of Jaroslav Hasek's *The Good Soldier Švejk,* which he accorded a prominent place in twentieth-century world literature. No one, argued Brecht scholar Herbert Knust, influenced the dramatist's writing as much as that indestructible little man; "in many of his great figures one finds Schweykish attitude, Schweykish dialectics and Schweykish tone." Brecht had kept company with Schweyk since 1927, when he had worked—along with left-wing stage director Erwin Piscator, writer Felix Gasbarra, and artist George Grosz—on the script for a stage version performed at the Theater am Nollendorfplatz in Berlin. Though unfaithful to the spirit of the book, the enormously successful production catapulted German comedian Max Pallenberg, who played Schweyk as "a sly batman and, in some scenes, an idiot," into an independent tour of the provinces.

The prospect of collaborating with Piscator on both stage and film versions kept Schweyk simmering on Brecht's back burner during the 1930s. En route to England in November 1935, Lorre had stopped off in New York long enough to confer with Piscator and writer Albert Bein about a spring production of "Schweyk," which did not materialize. However, random references in his work journal in 1940 and 1942 document Brecht's continued interest in the project. In early 1943, conversations with Piscator turned on the possibility of reviving the successful 1928 adaptation for the Theatre Guild. Piscator went ahead with preparations on the assumption that Brecht would collaborate on the stage play and even introduced him to actors Zero Mostel and Sam Jaffe as possible Schweyks. Gathering momentum toward something definite finally crystallized during Brecht's stay in New York in the spring of 1943. On April 3 he attended an antifascist rally at Hunter College entitled "We Fight Back," where two Czech comedians performed a comedy act called "Schweik's Spirit Lives On."

In his journal, dated unhelpfully March–April–May 1943, Brecht noted: "Weill has a big Broadway hit . . . Aufricht arranges for us to meet. . . . we plan a Schweyk," which he also wanted Piscator to direct. Hoping to duplicate the spectacular success of *Die Dreigroschenoper,* Aufricht, Weill, and Brecht also had their eyes on a fall production on Broadway.

By mid-May Brecht had completed a story outline for *Schweyk im zweiten Weltkrieg (Schweyk in the Second World War)*, and Weill had written some of the songs. With two planned productions in mind, the dramatist returned to Los Angeles on May 26. Three days later, he related the plotline to Lorre, whom he thought of as the prototypical Schweyk, the archetypal—and literal—little man, subversively wise, full of ironies and contradictions, master of small opportunities. Brecht saw no one else in the role. For Lorre, it was the coveted opportunity of a lifetime.

Lorre "really went for it," reported Brecht, but objected to "the scene where Schweyk slaughters a stolen dog and brings it to the landlady at the Chalice so that his friend Baloun can have a decent goulash." Brecht understood that the actor had "a grisly past in horror films to live down, so the moment he appeared with a parcel everybody would see the dog's skinned carcass, the skeleton in the brown paper bag as he calls it." Lorre also may have reminded Brecht that the audience had laughed at the "goulash" scene in *Bomben auf Monte Carlo* (1931). "But the errors that arise from that kind of thing are productive," rationalized Brecht, who nonetheless split hairs over Lorre's enthusiasm "about Schweyk's being a dog-lover. Which Schweyk of course isn't, being a dog-dealer."

Brecht balked at the first draft of the contract drawn up by Weill's attorneys, which branded him as "a pure librettist, without any author's rights." Already apprehensive about plans to turn the production into a musical comedy, he wanted it clearly stated that *Schweyk* was their joint property, with Brecht supplying the play and Weill the music. In a less restrained letter to Berlau, Brecht vented, "I must have a reasonably 'influential position,' I'm not just the bottle washer. . . . Moreover, political problems are involved in this play, I must have a say."

Brecht completed the first draft in German the last week of June. With *Schweyk* "largely finished," he acted on his hope to "make some money soon" on two film treatments written for Lorre with the understanding he would attempt to sell them to his friend and screenwriter Ernest Pascal, who Brecht mistakenly believed was also a producer.[10] Brecht told Berlau that the prospect of a solid contact meant that "something permanent *could* develop out of it, one or two films each year with United Artists."

Over the Fourth of July weekend, Lorre brought Brecht and Pascal together at Lake Arrowhead, where, according to Brecht, the actor "rides, swims, drives a speedboat, shoots clay pipes and is generally nice, somewhere between my patron and my student." Brecht didn't find the posh surroundings conducive to selling film stories and confessed to Berlau that he didn't know if anything would come of Pascal's plans to do a film. Two days later, again in a letter to his mistress, he voiced his frustration with the "playground of the rich . . . It's as quiet as living in a forest between two sawmills, because speedboats are always thundering across the lake. Lorre is living with a millionairess, the daughter of a Chicago meat king, the children bite mummy's pearls to see if they're real or prove to the guests that they are."

Brecht knew better. Well aware that neither Lorre's seeming affluence— nor Karen's apparent inherited wealth—had any basis in fact, he nonetheless did not miss this opportunity to stylize the difference between the rich and the poor.[11] "We discuss the story in the morning," he wrote Berlau, "that's a con-

Peter and Celia, Berlin, 1932.

Peter and Celia on holiday in the Black Forest before fleeing Hitler, 1932.

As Judas Iscariot in *Golgotha*, Zirkus-Renz, Vienna, 1933. Courtesy of the Österreichisches Theatermuseum, Vienna.

Peter and Celia, just married at the General Register Office in Westminster, June 22, 1934. Lorre arrived at the ceremony in full makeup for his role in Alfred Hitchcock's *The Man Who Knew Too Much* (1934), which was being filmed at Lime Grove Studios.

Fritz Lang takes anthropometric measurements of the plaster cast of Lorre's head from *Mad Love*, 1935. Courtesy of Tom Kelley Studio.

Émigré dinner at the Schildkrauts. *Left to right, seated:* Joseph Schildkraut, Peter Lorre (*almost hidden*), Mrs. Erich von Stroheim, G.W. Pabst, Marie Schildkraut, Fritz Lang, Mrs. G.W. Pabst, Erich von Stroheim, and Celia Lovsky. *Standing:* Alice Waxman, Franz Waxman, and Mr. Rappaport. Hollywood, 1935.

Peter and Celia, ca. 1935.

Peter Lorre caricature by Paolo Garretto, 1935.

On the set of *Crime and Punishment*, 1935. *Left to right:* Douglass Dumbrille, Tala Birell, Marian Marsh, Peter Lorre, and director Josef von Sternberg.

Character study, ca. 1935. Courtesy of Motion Picture & TV Research Service, Los Angeles.

A Columbia photographer shapes Lorre's star image, Santa Monica, 1935.

Reveling in his new American lifestyle, Santa Monica, 1935.

Peter Lorre as Hairless Mexican in *Secret Agent.* Caricature by Gitano, 1936.

John Gielgud, Alfred Hitchcock, and Peter Lorre on the set of *Secret Agent*, 1936. Courtesy of National Film Archives / Stills Library, London.

Alfred Hitchcock (*on left*), Peter Lorre (*second from right*), and extras on the set of *Secret Agent*, 1936.

Publicity shots in anticipation
of the stage production of
Napoleon the First, 1935.

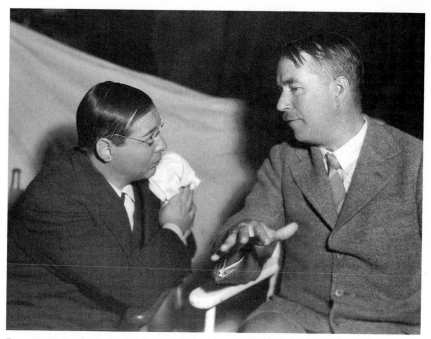

Peter Lorre in character as Mr. Moto on the set with John P. Marquand, author of the Mr. Moto stories, 1938.

Peter and Celia, ca. 1939.

Film program featuring a collage of images from Fritz Hippler's *Der Ewige Jude* (*The Eternal Jew*) 1940, including a scene from *M*.

Publicity shot of Lorre in *The Face behind the Mask*, 1941.

Karen Verne, ca. 1940.

Humphrey Bogart, Karen Verne, and Peter Lorre relaxing during production of *All Through the Night*, 1941.

Candid with cactus, ca. 1945. Photo by Robert Mack.

cession to me; otherwise it's not normal to work if one goes out to work. I don't feel a single cubic metre of ground under my feet, merely Lorre's bank balance, in this polluted continent in a lost century."

Brecht came away with, if not a firm commitment, at least sufficient interest in a story idea he called *The Crouching Venus* to engage Hans Viertel as translator. Viertel recalled that "Brecht had a full-length photo of Toulouse-Lautrec, if one can call it that, which he had cut out of some magazine. And he said to me this is Tottin, a museum curator and Lorre is going to play him. That was how he introduced the character."[12]

In his forty-page treatment, Brecht prefaced his film story with an eye for the movie frame: "Marseilles. Autumn 1942. A few days after the German occupation of the city." Professor Aristide Tottin, director of the National Museum, hides the gallery's more valuable pieces and displays its comparatively worthless ones. When members of the German Art Commission accidentally discover the prized Venus de Fontainbleau, a sixteenth-century wooden statue, concealed in the basement, Tottin fends off further inquiry by convincing them it is a copy. Chief inspector Heinz Kippenheyer, an art expert intent on exporting France's art treasures to Germany, is not so easily fooled. With the help of the influential Madame Coupeau, owner of the Pot des Fleurs, a cabaret in the waterfront district, a plan to steal the statue and smuggle it out of the country—in a coffin—takes shape. Kippenheyer charmingly insinuates himself into the cabaret scene, hoping to get behind the scenes. He invites Yvonne, one of the entertainers, and Tottin to an improvised supper in the singer's dressing room, where he discovers the statue dressed as a dummy. Asked if he still believes it is a copy, the tipsy Tottin answers no and even nods stoically to Kippenheyer's accusation that he arranged its theft. Suddenly, however, his apparent apathy takes a bitter tone. Tottin rages at the thieving hyena and sinks back into his chair, but the chief inspector recommends that he save his strength for his talk with the Gestapo. Weakly, Tottin asks for his cane. When he pulls on the ivory handle, the Florentine stick comes apart, leaving Kippenheyer with the sheath and Tottin with a sword, which he plunges into the German. While General Todleben, the German commander of the Marseilles District, rattles the windowpanes with his shouts to close all the dives on the waterfront, the Venus de Fontainbleau sails safely to Lisbon.

In describing Tottin as "a middle-aged gentleman, very distinguished and elegant in an old-fashioned way" and making the character a connoisseur who speaks with lyrical eloquence on subjects he feels passionately, Brecht flattered his friend. Likewise, casting him as a professor appealed to Lorre's own self-image as an intellectual and indulged patriotic fantasies about which Brecht was doubtless unaware. Tottin's naïveté, however, better served the actor's movie-made image than the man, clouding the issue of how tightly Brecht fit the role to Lorre.

Whether or not they consciously patterned *The Crouching Venus* (subsequently retitled *The Fugitive Venus* for marketing considerations) after *Casablanca*, which had gone into national release earlier that year, the story was far more original than many of the anti-Nazi resistance spin-offs. Unfortunately, the Paul Kohner Agency was unable to place the property. Unlike others of his film stories, which were considered too Brechtian for Hollywood, it seemed geared to box-office return. Brecht actually followed the Hollywood formula, placing plot before political platform and skillfully interweaving mystery, intrigue, and politics. One can easily imagine Lorre and Conrad Veidt in the principal roles, with Faye Emerson and Florence Bates in the supporting parts.

Brecht also went ahead with the second film treatment for Lorre mentioned in his June 4 letter to Berlau. From his antiwar poem "Children's Crusade," about a group of hungry Polish children who attempt to "flee the slaughter" to a "country without war," Brecht adapted a nine-page treatment in German for a film version. He set his story in a rural New England school, where a snowstorm interrupts a "War Stamp Campaign." Explaining that snow can mean something besides fun, the schoolteacher tells his students about a troop of children who set out in search of a "land of peace" and perish in the drifting snow.

Brecht's letters and journal are silent on the matter of placing *Children's Crusade*, which was as hopelessly unconventional as *The Fugitive Venus* was potentially commercial. American filmmakers waged World War II in black and white, reducing global conflict to heroes and villains, right and wrong. Starving, snowbound children fell into that grey area in between and outside the sanction of acceptable propaganda.

Believing the time was right for *Schweyk* to go to war, Brecht planned for the possibility of a fall Broadway production, even without Lorre, who he doubted would be available, because "I wouldn't want to wait for him, as I'm against wasting time."

While at Lake Arrowhead, Brecht urged Berlau to engage the poet and politically correct Alfred Kreymborg to translate *Schweyk* into English.[13] In August Brecht sent Kreymborg a copy of his manuscript and a one-hundred-dollar advance borrowed from Lorre.

Lorre helped out financially on other occasions too. Morton Wurtele remembered one time when "he was ashamed to bring just the money. That was too coarse, too crude, so he brought a bottle of brandy. 'Well, here, I brought a bottle of brandy. We're going to drink and talk and celebrate. And, incidentally here's the money.' It was only the money that they were concerned with, of course."

In June 1944 Lorre covered the pregnant Ruth Berlau's airfare from New York to Los Angeles, where she planned to give birth to Brecht's baby. When he learned that she had lost her job with the Office of War Information, "he drew a key from his pocket and gave it" to her. "Go to Santa Monica," said Lorre. "You can stay with us." He even paid Berlau's medical bill at Cedars of Lebanon Hospital, where tumor surgery resulted in the premature birth of Michel Brecht, who lived only a few days.[14]

Lorre later put Elisabeth Hauptmann on his payroll as his private secretary, whose household duties ranged from letter-writing and cooking to general economizing. Naomi Yergin, Irving's wife, who visited Peter and Karen at Mandeville Canyon almost daily, remembered her as a "hanger on who just took up room. I was chopping up some scallions and I didn't use too much of the green part. You should have heard the two German women bitching. You'd think it was a million dollars I was throwing away."

After receiving a copy of *Schweyk in the Second World War*, Alfred Kreymborg wrote Piscator, for whom he was expected to adapt Brecht's 1928 script for the Theatre Guild production, that he had crossed over to the Brecht-Weill-Aufricht camp. Stunned by his translator's defection, Piscator fired off an angry letter to Brecht, branding his theft a "swinish Brechtian trick." However, no sooner had Kreymborg begun work than Kurt Weill informed Brecht that "some American writers had told him the play was too un-American for Broadway, etc. etc."[15] Moreover, Aufricht "doesn't seem to believe in the play" and later returned eighty-five thousand dollars to the play's backers.

Having instructed Berlau to secure exclusive rights to *The Good Soldier Švejk* from the Czech government in exile, Brecht returned to his collaboration with Hans Viertel on *The Crouching Venus* on August 14. That night, he attended a birthday party for the refugee writer Alfred Döblin at the El Pablo Rey Playhouse in Santa Monica. Among the 180 guests were a list of émigré luminaries, including actors Alexander Granach, Fritz Kortner, and Peter Lorre, who read from Döblin's works.

In September Brecht received Kreymborg's translation, which "has as many mistakes in it as a dog has fleas," but whose tone, he congratulated the writer, "seems perfect, simple and powerful." However, Brecht's son Stefan, Hans Viertel, and Ruth Berlau gave him pause to temper his guarded optimism. "In despair about the Schweyk translation," Brecht predicted that "we'll never get a production on the strength of it. Lorre and the Americans he's shown it to are greatly disappointed." With Weill now out of the picture and Lorre getting cold feet, Brecht scrambled for a backup plan. Hanns Eisler agreed to do the music. Having lured Kreymborg away from Piscator, Brecht now wanted Zero Mostel for the role of Schweyk:

> [He] would solve many problems. An American (and especially a comedian) would have a much surer judgment about what the public here would and would not understand. He'd be more productive. Less timid. Has he read the play? . . . The position on Lorre is this: He advanced me the money for the translation. . . . So my only possibility was to say to him: I have such and such an opportunity, can you too offer a production? He knows I need the money badly. The more practically and realistically you can work out a production with Mostel, the more easily I can sell it to Lorre—or drive him to make a counterproposal.

It was nothing short of blackmail. Indulging Brecht's obvious genius, regardless of cost, flattered Lorre, who felt privileged to be used in such a way. Nonetheless, Brecht typically overestimated Lorre's influence and earning power. Perennially short of cash and very likely counseled against investing in such a speculative theatrical venture, he didn't budge, prompting Berlau to write: "Peter Lorre supported us on many occasions, but Brecht never obtained from him what he really wanted. They often talked about a production of *Schweyk* in America, but Lorre never played Schweyk. I have letters from Brecht in which he declared that his only reason for writing his *Schweyk in the Second World War* was because in America he had Peter Lorre for the main part. But Lorre let him down, as did Kurt Weill, who was to have written the music."

Realizing the unlikelihood of getting *Schweyk* produced without Weill, in November Brecht asked the composer to reconsider. In a letter of December 5, Weill outlined his conditions for collaboration; more music, revision by a prominent American author capable of capturing the humor of the story, and the untangling of legal rights to the property.

Refusing to give up, Brecht asked Ferdinand Reyher to translate one scene, hoping to convince Weill a good adaptation was still possible. When he declined, Brecht thought to align at least one star in his favor. The following April, he wrote Berlau to say Charles Laughton had read the play and "seems, so far at least, to be sincerely enthusiastic. Perhaps something will come of it." But nothing did, and *Schweyk* did not step onto an American stage until 1977.

Certainly, Brecht's blame came back to Lorre in feelings of guilt that he carried to his death. At the time, however, the actor doubtlessly asked himself whose *Schweyk* he was playing. "The good soldier" had cut his political teeth early in life. Liberals, conservatives, Marxists, and non-Marxists kicked him back and forth like some sort of ideological football. For the radical left, he became the flag-bearer for revolutionary change. Conservatives, however, condemned his defeatism and moral cowardice. He was, in a word, an antihero whose slackness tainted the best tradition of soldierly self-sacrifice. Pressing the "little man" into the German Army and casting him as the Nazi nemesis also served Brecht's own end. In the last scene of the play, Schweyk has lost his way in a blinding snowstorm fifty kilometers from Stalingrad. From behind a bush emerges a starving mongrel, for which he paints a picture of his dog-dealing duties in the coming peace. Trudging through the deepening snowdrifts, Schweyk and his newfound canine friend run into Hitler, who cannot go back: "to the north there is the snow; to the south, mountains of corpses; to the east the Reds; and home?" While the Führer turns from one direction to another, the "little man" and his mongrel dog press on. In his journal Brecht wrote on May 27, 1943: "Under no circumstances must Schweyk become a cunning, underhand saboteur. He is just an opportunist specialising in exploiting the little opportunities that remain open to him. . . . His wisdom is devastating. His indestructibility makes him the inexhaustible object of maltreatment and at the same time fertile ground for liberation." For Hasek authority Cecil Parrott, Brecht updated history but outdated the character, shelving the passively resistant Schweyk for one "who is boastfully conscious of his demoralising influence."

Lorre clearly had another play in mind, one based on the book. Like Schweyk, who "recognizes that political considerations are beyond him and left them to others to sort out," the actor had no agenda. On the tangled question of "the good soldier's" simplicity or shrewdness, he no doubt would have tipped the equation toward the triumph of innocence. Lorre's Schweyk, one supposes, would have haplessly waged his struggle for bare existence with only the "help of comedy, humour and parody," just as Hasek had intended.

In writing his Schweyk play, Brecht looked past Broadway to Europe. Although his exile experience as "a non-heroic individual with no power over the course of events, who struggles only to survive," reinforced his identification with the indestructible "little man," whom some believe he reinvented in his own image, the updated play kept its peculiarly European flavor. Neither comic nor tragic, Schweyk did not even qualify as an antihero, only a half-baked saboteur with a genius for surviving (and, in Brecht's telling, resisting) the Fascist regime. With "Operation Pastorius" capturing newspaper headlines, Americans probably would not have found sabotage, real or imagined, comically appealing. This, along with the play's loose structure and central European language—Schweyk and his fellow Czechs talk in a southern German dialect, whereas the Nazis speak proper high German—left it in literary limbo.

As early as 1941, Ferdinand Reyher had introduced Brecht to Edgar Lee Masters's *Spoon River Anthology,* a collection of poetic monologues in which the dead of Spoon River narrate their own biographies from the cemetery where they lie buried.[16] In free verse, they speak to the disparity between the pious epitaphs on their tombstones and the personal frustrations and disappointments exhumed by Masters. Several years later, Brecht asked Reyher, who knew Masters, to locate him and broach the idea of a film version of *Spoon River Anthology.* Reyher set up a meeting in New York City to discuss the project, but miscommunications and financial difficulties thwarted their plans.

Lorre also expressed interest in bringing *Spoon River Anthology* to the screen. Who first read in the "lives-in-death" the possibility of a film is hard to say. Reyher's familiarity with American literature weighs heavily in his favor for planting the seed in Brecht's mind. Nonetheless, in an interview published June 23, 1944, Lorre referred to Masters as a "national debt" that needed to be paid. He reportedly wanted to assist the destitute author, who was suffering from pneumonia and malnutrition, by purchasing the movie rights to *Spoon River Anthology.* But, he cautioned, assistance should not be given in a "shameful charity way." Lorre apparently planned to interest either Warner Bros. or Sidney Buchman at Columbia in filming the American classic. However, with Lorre's efforts contingent upon the successful meeting of minds in New York, when one plan failed, so did the other.

Infecting his impressionable friend with stringent views that found a public forum must have given Brecht vicarious pleasure. If Lorre actually shared the ideas he spouted, so much the better. In his work journal, August 10, 1944, Brecht criticized "KORTNER and HOMOLKA, and to a much lesser extent LORRE, [who] judge this country by its theatre, in which conventional evening entertainment is sold by speculators." Six weeks later, Lorre gave voice to Brecht's sentiments in an interview for the *Hartford Times:* "Commercialism has a chance of ruining the theater in the United States. Though we are a country of many parts and many thoughts, our whole theatrical thinking is concentrated between 44th and 52nd Sts. in New York. Between eight city blocks our concepts of what is good and bad in acting and play-wrighting is determined. This monopoly is disastrous. It has come to be, that a Broadway success is more damaging than rewarding to an actor of any integrity."

Lorre's apparent willingness to take a stand held the promise that perhaps he was coming over to Brecht's side. During a visit to New York City in spring of 1943, Brecht and a handful of German exiles had formed the Council for a Democratic Germany, provisionally chaired by theologian Paul Tillich. Despite disclaimers about playing such a role, it functioned as a quasi-German government-in-exile whose purpose "will be to help promote establishment of a democratic order in Germany and facilitate constructive relations between a renovated German Reich and the world." New beginnings demanded that "all who shared in the responsibility for the rise of nazism [sic] should be excluded" from reconstructing a democratic Germany. While the council sought to purge all educational institutions and media—including movies and theater—of Nazi and racist teachings, it opposed the economic and political dismembering of Germany, which "would create fertile soil for new Pan-Germanist movements." On May 3, 1944, the New York Times published a manifesto of the council, subscribed to by sixty-five sponsors (in addition to the original committee), including Hollywood actors Oskar Homolka and Peter Lorre. The FBI claimed that New York council members had canvassed the West Coast émigré communities and told "every outstanding personality of the German political emigration, sometimes in sweet, sometimes in less sweet tones . . . to hurry up and jump on the bandwagon before it was too late." It specifically accused Lion Feuchtwanger, Marxist composer Hanns Eisler, and Brecht of mobilizing support among "Hollywood Communist literati, artists and theatrical folk."

By early 1945 the gathering momentum of evidence, however spurious, collected by field agents confirmed J. Edgar Hoover's suspicions that "Brecht has been closely associated with German Communist leaders in the Los Angeles area and is allegedly a Soviet agent."

For Lorre, it was not a case of what he knew, but whom he knew.[17] The FBI judged him guilty by association. An early entry in his dossier cites the name of Comintern veteran Otto Katz, who had brought Lorre's availability to Alfred Hitchcock's attention in 1933. Little more than an acquaintance, Katz was forced at his "trial" to "confess my guilt . . . as an active spy against the Volksdemocratic Czechoslovakia . . . working for France, England and America" and was hanged in Prague in 1952.

Brecht's friendship with Comintern functionary Gerhart Eisler, who headed the Free German Movement in Mexico, spelled something more sinister for Lorre. This secondhand acquaintance meant to the authorities that Lorre had firsthand knowledge of "confidential information" about the commissar's alleged activities as an agent engaged in Soviet espionage in America.

Sailing into San Pedro, Brecht had dumped overboard the writings of Marx, saying, "I don't want any trouble with U.S. authorities." Good to his word, he maintained a low profile in America. Still, the FBI, which dubbed him "a revolutionary writer and minion of Marxian [sic] thought," had kept a watchful eye on his activities. Closer examination of his writings and statements by unidentified sources condemning Brecht as "a radical and an associate of persons with Communistic tendencies" had by 1944 cued the FBI to reclassify him—from the benign "enemy alien" status applied to all German émigrés during the war years—to the more malignant "internal security" category reserved for cases of suspected espionage.

Between 1936, when he took out first papers, and August 1941, when he became a naturalized citizen (a scant three weeks before Brecht's arrival), Lorre had kept his political convictions to himself.[18] What induced him to throw political caution to the wind is difficult to say. Perhaps a latent desire to burn bridges in Hollywood and throw in with Brecht. Or, just as likely, a combination of guilt and naïveté. Fully aware that the Federal Bureau of Narcotics had been monitoring his activities since the late 1930s, he seemed oblivious to the fact that the FBI considered him a security risk and had placed him on the National Censorship Watch List for ninety days in January 1943. Three months was apparently more than enough time for authorities to reach the conclusion that he willingly played a small but not unimportant role in the Comintern apparatus. His appearance at the Brecht Evening on March 6 received much coverage and commentary, first by Alfred Kantorowicz, who authored a monthly column—"New York Letter"—for *Freies Deutschland*, mouthpiece for the Free German Movement, and subsequently by the FBI, for whom the mere appearance of the announcement in a left-wing periodical was incriminating. By default, *Die Tribüne für Freie Deutsche Literatur und Kunst in Amerika*, innocuously described as originating in New York City on May 18, 1942, with the "express purpose of publishing the works of German authors through their own cooperative publishing house," was (in FBI eyes) a Communist front organization.

The FBI also maintained surveillance on the Council for a Democratic Germany ("reportedly formed for purpose of consolidating work of all left-wing German organizations active in Free German Movement in this country") and its members, including Brecht and Eisler, who had played key roles in its organization, and signatory Lorre. Eisler's contact with Brecht, however infrequent, and Brecht's with Lorre completed the circle of suspicion. The FBI had Lorre down in its book as a suspected Communist sympathizer or "fellow-traveler."[19]

Lorre's portrayal of a mystery writer in *The Mask of Dimitrios* gave studio publicists an easy promotional angle. After all, he did say he liked "to spend his evenings on scenarios with other writers and actors." Offscreen, they claimed, the actor had written three detective stories while shooting the picture. Better yet, he housed "desks and trunks full of manuscripts of his own concoction." Not desks and trunks full, but one, a thirty-page film story by Bertolt Brecht, Peter Lorre, and Ferdinand Reyher.

When Reyher visited Los Angeles in September 1945, Brecht broke off work on *Galileo* to make "a COPY OF MACBETH for a film with Lorre and Reyher." He wrote Berlau that they were working hard on a treatment for the actor: "Maybe I can sell it." Irving Yergin remembered that Lorre played an active role in developing the property. Brecht very likely involved him but limited his actual contribution to his experience and expertise, such as they were, as a sounding board for salability. Moreover, the writing style bears Reyher's signature, just as the conceptual framework shows Brecht's hand. Their collaboration left little room for Lorre's influence beyond the obvious need to sell the story on the strength of his name. Back-to-back appearances—with two overlapping weeks—in *Confidential Agent* and *The Verdict* most certainly ruled out his active participation. Conceived in Los Angeles, *All Our Yesterdays* came of age in New York, where most of the actual writing was done by Brecht and Reyher the following February. Lorre's name—listed third—was crossed off the title page of the first treatment, renamed *Lady Macbeth of the Yards*. On the second draft, again *All Our Yesterdays*, but subtitled *Macbeth 1946*, his name was not only restored, but elevated to second place. The final version, *Lady Macbeth of the Yards*, included a foreword signed with the initials of the three authors, who explain that they "have chosen to adapt Shakespeare's play of Macbeth into a modern equivalent" because it is "a good crime story . . . a good acting story . . . a good love story [and] a good story not of far away and long ago but recurring again and again in common life without losing its profound appeal."

Speaking in a "dry police-report style," they cynically predict that "the famous supernatural elements . . . will be accepted by a land of hunch-players which supports tens of thousands of spook-merchants; stuffs its amusement parks with Princess Silver Stars, Clarices, yogis, mechanical palm readers; buys two million dream books a year; takes numerology seriously, and can't even put a penny in a slot machine to find out its weight unless it gets its future with it."

Lady Macbeth of the Yards updates *Macbeth* to the Chicago stockyards. Guided by the fortune slip in a Chinese cookie advising him to "*Be bold in your undertakings and fortune is yours,*" steer cutter John Machacek rescues a wealthy cattle dealer named Duncan from being trampled by a herd of cattle. Asked what he wants most in the world, Machacek reveals that he and his new wife have daydreamed about owning a little market specializing in choice meats.

"You now got a market!" shouts Duncan. When he fails to deliver on his promise, however, Mrs. Machacek darkly suggests, "If he makes fools of us again, maybe we'll fool him." At his wife's urging, Machacek kills Duncan with a cleaver. Later, the Machaceks receive word that Duncan had ordered his attorney to find them a market the day after the steer cutter saved his life.

Because Machacek can't stand the sight of blood, he hires a butcher for his meat counter. But recurring nightmares of oncoming steers disturb his sleep. Mrs. Machacek commits a second murder to cover the first. The burden of guilt weighs on both their minds. When Machacek finally breaks, his wife confesses: "I made him do it."

Lady Macbeth of the Yards has all the makings of a classic film noir. Beneath a dark fatalism that you could cut with a cleaver toiled and troubled a surrealistic patchwork: a distorting mirror maze, a singing witch, hallucinations, and dreams of "a distant rumble growing into thunder, and a cloud of dust . . . kicked up by the hooves of an oncoming herd of steers."[20] Altogether, the balance of ideas to action provided a rare piece of common ground for Brecht and Hollywood.

Lorre broached the subject to Steve Trilling and subsequently submitted the twenty-eight-page treatment—retitled *Blood Will Have Blood*—"by Bertolt Brecht, Peter Lorre, Ferdinand Reyher" to producer Jerry Wald, who recommended it to Jack Warner's assistant in November, saying it was "quite good." Story analyst Judith Meyers received the manuscript on December 3 and quickly reduced it to a one-page synopsis. She "RECOMMENDED" the film story, calling it "a grim and bloody modernization of Macbeth—packed with horror and suspense and practically certain to go over with those people who have strong stomachs. The story impressed me as being real, satisfactorily motivated, and quite different from anything we have done before. I was particularly impressed by the lack of trimming and furbelows. The original is written with utmost economy and disdain for mere words—everything that's in it is basic and screenable."

Blood Will Have Blood quickly climbed the story department ladder. Assistant editor Tom Chapman wrote editor Ellingwood Kay that he was "pleased with this story. It's out of the ordinary and screenable. It has lots of overtones. It certainly would be something Lorre could play brilliantly. . . . I think we should send it around and give it a little push."

"It's grim and unusual, and obviously something that Lorre could play to perfection," Kay relayed to Trilling. But the ball stopped there. Trilling, who thought the story too gory, asked Kay to phone Lorre and tell him "we weren't interested for now and to go ahead and sell it elsewhere if he could." The studio officially rejected it February 4, 1946.

Brecht also had Lorre in mind for a less likely, at least to most, Shakespeare role. According to Eric Bentley,

> The kind of actor he was was very, very important to Brecht in thinking out, not only how to do his own plays and how to act them, but secondly a fresh but not perverse rendering of the classics. And he said more than once that the modern Hamlet would be Peter Lorre. That was a favorite idea of Brecht's and he had a reply ready when a person would say, but for one thing, he's too fat—namely, the text says that Hamlet is fat and it's never played that way. The line exists in *Hamlet* about Hamlet—"He is fat and scant of breath"—and some editors try to explain away the fat as meaning something else, but it was Brecht's notion that it means exactly as it says, that this image of the slender young prince is not Elizabethan, it is romantic and nineteenth-century and that the real Hamlet Shakespeare would like to come back and see of our time would be an actor who never played it—Peter Lorre.

Separating reason from instinct is a delicate business. As symbionts in a mutually beneficial relationship, Brecht and Lorre made good friends, who gave more than they took. But hidden in the give and take of their friendship lay seeds of conflict. In one of Brecht's stories, the character Keuner tells a questioner that when he loves someone, he makes a sketch of that person, "and ensure[s] it is a good likeness," with the expectation that the subject will conform to his drawing. Brecht pictured two Peter Lorres and sent mixed messages to both. "You have the natural ability to do with the left hand what should be done with the left hand," he reportedly assured the actor, "and to keep the right hand free for when it is needed." Brecht expected the insider Lorre to pass him through the studio gates under the cloak of his own screen fame so that he might storm Hollywood with his artistic and political platform. At the same time, he held the outsider Lorre in "mental reserve [to] play a great part" in the rebuilding of his theater in Germany. Making the actor a means to antagonistic ends further amplified a struggle whose roots ran deeper than Brecht knew. What he failed to understand was that Lorre would not give up celebrity for intellectual respectability. He would have both, becoming all things to all people, a crony to Bogart, a colleague to Brecht. The actor and the playwright were more alike and different than they knew. Nonetheless, they both stood for something and would not be silenced. A "dissenter by disposition," Bogart prided himself in being an "againster." He could just as easily have been describing Brecht, who, in turn, would have admired Bogart's colloquial candor. Both men advertised strong personalities that represented sides of Lorre that never found expression.

Between the lines of closeted regrets during the Warner Bros. years, one reads larger issues and greater conflicts than that of a frog who wanted to be a prince. Lorre regretted the choices that were made for him and sidestepped the ones he needed to make himself—between the emblematic personalities of Brecht and Bogart. Addicted to a celebrity lifestyle, with its limelight and luxury, he at the same time condemned—in private conversations with Brecht—the crass commercialism of an industry he held responsible for suffocating his career. Vacillation, or what Brecht flatly considered weakness, kept Lorre straddling a fence of his own making, falling neither into a confident choice nor the recognition of mutually exclusive goals.

7

THE SWAMP

I must say, when Peter Lorre looks upon you with his face
filled with contempt you know you have been loathed.

—Bill Slocum

I am not a self-centered man and I think I am quite simple
myself, but you wouldn't call me the all-American boy.

—Peter Lorre

When Mickey Rooney passed through Pittsburgh on a promotional tour
in 1943, he met "a beefy guy with a raspy voice." Sam Stiefel made his pitch
over dinner. The theater operator wanted to sell out his interests on the East
Coast and manage the actor. His self-confidence swept Rooney off his feet.
They shook hands. With easy handouts, Stiefel took up the slack in the actor's
MGM salary, which was proving unequal to his increasingly luxurious lifestyle.
Before long, Rooney decided it was time for his new manager to "put the wheels
of my independence in motion." In March 1944 the actor signed incorpora-
tion papers for Rooney-Stiefel and Samick Corp. Rooney served as president,
Stiefel as secretary-treasurer, and producer Mort Briskin filled in as legal counsel. Once Stiefel took charge of Rooney Inc., however, he mostly managed the
actor's money, commandeering "whatever cash there was."

Two years later. Same pitch. Different actor. Stiefel's timing was perfect,
his message simple. He promised the moon. Lorre hired Stiefel to give shape

to his plans to wrest control of his film career. Stiefel in turn persuaded Briskin, who had strong reservations about working with a "narcotic," to "take a gamble on Lorre." On June 24, less than three weeks after he had left Warner Bros., Lorre signed a three-way ticket with "Rooney Inc." to act, direct, and produce under his own trade name. Stiefel formed Lorre Inc. to handle the actor—and his money—personally. The new company embraced the several associates of the Rooney firm, which functioned as the parent firm and actually owned the offshoot concern.

For an actor with no head for business, the move was out of character. "Peter had no concept of the value of the dollar, absolutely none," said Jonas Silverstone. "He was lavish with money when he had it. He was even lavish when he didn't have it. It's a strange thing to say, but Peter was that kind of man." In short, Lorre loved to spend money. He squandered it, frittered it, and gave it away. He was liberal with his own money and generous with that of others. He insisted on picking up the tab, even if he had to borrow to do it. He disbursed a small fortune in tips. "He always had a wad of money with an elastic band around it that would choke a cow," recalled Burl Ives. "He'd peel off bills to doormen and chefs. He liked to do it, but it wasn't done in a show-offy way." However, his prodigality never kept him from helping those down on their luck. "Peter was greatly interested in the welfare of the fellow about him who was subjugated, who was without," continued Silverstone. "He wanted to give. He wanted to give of what he had of his corporeal acquisitions. He would have shared with anybody who he thought needed it, and he would have gone out of his way to help anybody, and he did when he was never expected to. Peter gave more than he took."

After checking into a hotel with his friend and agent Lester Salkow, Lorre asked about a bellboy whom he had met earlier. The desk clerk reluctantly confided that money problems hounded the poor fellow to distraction. His wife, it seemed, was hospitalized and needed surgery. Lorre tracked down the bellboy, who was astonished to learn that the star remembered him by name. "There was little conversation between them," said Salkow. "Peter reached in his pocket and pulled out a bunch of one-hundred-dollar bills and gave them to the bellboy." Lorre's generosity and helping hand won him many friends, but his lack of attention to personal finances spelled trouble for the years ahead.

Before striking off on his own, Lorre fulfilled an old commitment to (Bob) Hope Enterprises Inc. In *My Favorite Brunette* (1947), a parody of the detective film genre, he played a foreign mobster. Nicknamed "Cuddles" by Hope, the sharp and sober Kismet (Lorre) takes pride in his lethal work: "Such a neat job! Such an artistic job!" When he wards off police inquiries with his ingenuousness, cop Ray Teal observes patronizingly, "You're not a bad guy, for a foreigner."

"Oh, but I am going to be a citizen," Lorre purrs in return. "I am studying for my examination. By the way, could you gentlemen tell me who was the eighth president of the United States?" He later reviews his civics lesson while practicing his knife-throwing on a ham. *My Favorite Brunette* marked only the third time Lorre's menace had been translated into a comic setting. Although not a full-blown caricature role, it was a portent of self-parody, and of things to come.

Lorre needed money. The regular checks from Warner Bros. had ceased, and he had saved nothing. He could not say no to Brecht, to whom he continued to slip cash contributions and for whom he kept Elisabeth Hauptmann on his payroll. Nor could he say no to his St. Bernard, which, he complained, ate seven pounds of meat daily; or to his horses, whose upkeep placed inordinate demands on his budget. Maintaining his gentrified lifestyle, with its incumbent dinner parties and open bar, pushed him into the red.

To finance Lorre's promised return to New York to take another cure, Stiefel booked him into the Roxy Theater for a three-week engagement that would begin in February. Lorre arrived on the East Coast in late December and placed himself in the care of his old friend Dr. Max Gruenthal for insulin shock therapy, a treatment that lacked clear evidence of patient benefit and risked forceful contractions resulting in pulled muscles, broken bones, seizures, and even death. An ear, nose, and throat specialist also started him on histamine desensitization. Still unable to get off drugs, "apparently . . . because he was under the strain of his professional activities," Lorre impatiently insisted that Dr. Kalinowsky, of the New York State Psychiatric Institute and Hospital, perform electric shock therapy, even after he was warned about memory loss following treatment.[1] After six sessions, Lorre stopped by *The Kate Smith Show* on February 9 for a guest spot in "The Painting" and gave a difficult, but drug-free performance.

The actor opened at the Roxy on Tuesday, February 11, along with jitterbugging harmonica player Gil Lamb, songstress Evelyn Knight, unicyclist-juggler Boy Foy, vocalist Pat Terry, the Roxyettes, and the Paul Ash Orchestra. Given his long-standing interest in Edgar Allan Poe, it is not surprising that Lorre chose "The Tell-Tale Heart" (adapted by Frank Wilson) to entertain and enlighten his audience.[2]

"When I told people I was going to do this, for the first time in a Chicago theater," he told the press, "they said I would be hooted off the stage. They said the bobby-soxers wouldn't go for it, and that it would be over the heads of the audience. I am happy to report that the opposite was the case. Poe knew a thing or two about bobby-soxers and audiences in general, and my trust in him was not misplaced."

A mob of rowdy youngsters made up the matinee audience. "You're crazy to go out there," warned the stage manager. Credited with "pulling in a goodly share of the trade," Lorre brushed his concern aside. "What makes a great actor?" he later reflected. "It's hard to say. Maybe it's the man who wants to interpret something important. But then we would all like to play great parts in literature. Maybe it's the guy who walks on stage and something magic happens and the house is hushed while he's on." Lorre mastered his audience, just as he had done on the opening night of *Mann ist Mann* at Berlin's Staatstheater sixteen years earlier when he stilled a contingent of unruly Nazis. "He knew what to do before an audience," observed Frank Capra. "He knew how to entertain them. He knew everything about the stage that you could possibly know." Even Caspar Neher's stark sets seemed lavish by comparison to Lorre's lack of adjuncts. Engulfed in darkness, the gnomic figure stood alone on stage, his face suspended by a soft green spotlight. With rhythmic whispers and maniacal screams, he incised Poe's morbid workings into the impressionable minds of the young audience. After Lorre completed his recitation, they sat there, paralyzed. He turned and walked off. "As his audience applauded," related Hal Kanter, who heard it from the actor, "the empty stage sank slowly into the pit, with the spot following it down." Scheduled to appear four times daily, he squeezed in a fifth performance at the behest of the management and the bidding of the audience.

"Those kids! For some extraordinary reason they have started going for me," marveled the actor. "It makes me shiver. And I'll be damned if I know what it is. . . . I can see the bobby-soxers getting agitated over Sinatra, but this is a case for Freud. I've even had my stage door exit changed every day. I should try to fight my way through those kids five times a day?" Swimming against the tide of popular opinion with the observation that Lorre's "heavy declamation" seemed "out of place with the generally light tenor of the show," *Variety* acknowledged that "the crowd shows respect for his ability and he's away to a hearty salvo."

Few cared that at some of the shows Lorre read from the script or simply held the folio. No one, in fact, realized that he had come close to collapsing. "I was unable to remember my lines," said Lorre "or to proceed with the show; only then did Dr. [Gruenthal] realize that the cure was not successful." Fearing that his professional career was at stake, and suffering from laryngitis, sinus problems, and depression, he convinced the psychiatrist to place him on

Dilaudid. Yet another doctor attended the actor in his dressing room at the theater and furnished him with injections of other morphine substitutes.

These developments clearly alarmed Dr. Gruenthal, who had good reason to fear that narcotics agents might arrive on his doorstep to question him for continuing prescriptions beyond necessary use.[3] The wrong answers could cost him his tax stamp and the right to prescribe narcotic drugs. When the psychiatrist voiced his growing concerns, Lorre asked him to inform the authorities of his condition and request permission to continue the use of drugs until the completion of his engagement at the Roxy Theater on March 4. On February 27 Colonel Garland H. Williams, district supervisor of the Federal Bureau of Narcotics, asked Lorre to come in. Narcotic inspectors Theodore J. Walker and agent Samuel Levine took Lorre's statement in the office of the Federal Bureau of Narcotics. The next day a physician examined him and certified that he was an addict, both physically and psychologically dependent on narcotic drugs. Williams, who had crushed whiskey smugglers during Prohibition before combating traffic in narcotics, demanded that Lorre surrender his syringe; he willingly did so, since he kept another. Knowing what the press would do with the story—the New York Journal-American had already called the district supervisor to ask whether the actor had been arrested—Irving Yergin scrambled to head off damaging publicity. That afternoon, he called and asked to see Williams, who declined on grounds that Lorre was currently under investigation. However, on February 28 the publicist showed up unannounced at the Church Street office. Yergin appealed for both secrecy and permission for the actor to "stay on drugs though there was no medical reason to justify same" through his run. A wary Williams wanted to swear out a warrant for Lorre's arrest. However, Commissioner Harry J. Anslinger found "a reason to help an addict who has no criminal record and who is sincere in trying to kick his habit."[4] He made Lorre an offer the actor was not in a position to refuse. Because private institutions had failed to successfully treat his narcotic addiction, Anslinger agreed to allow Lorre to complete the New York play date (including a March 1 appearance at the Kabarett der Komiker's Nacht der Prominenten [Night of Prominent People] in a sketch titled "Der letzte Österreicher" ["The Last Austrian"] by Kurt Robitschek) and to hold charges in abeyance if he would voluntarily admit himself—which he did on March 3—to the U.S. Public Health Service Hospital in Fort Worth, Texas.[5] Lorre accepted the commissioner's terms on condition that the implicated physicians would not be prosecuted. Believing the arrangement an excellent opportunity for the government to show its "humane" side by giving the addict "every break," Anslinger accepted Lorre's stipulation, but cautioned, "The rest is up to him."

On March 5 Peter, Karen, and Irving flew to Texas. "Everyone was crying," Yergin sadly recalled, "but we realized it had to be." Lorre entered the hospital under his real name, which was recorded as Lazlo Lowenstein, for an estimated three-to-six-month stay at the cost of one dollar per day for his subsistence, care, and treatment.[6] He listed his occupation as "movies," his religion as "Protestant," and his reason for leaving home as "work." In the event of serious illness or death, he directed that his "FRIEND, Irving YERGIN . . . be notified, and in case of death, that all my personal effects, including any money remaining to my credit in the Inmate's Trust Fund . . . be transmitted to him." After turning over his property—1 tweed overcoat, 1 gray coat, 1 pair white trousers, 1 gray tweed shirt, 1 pair red socks, 1 bow tie, 1 money clip with the initials P.L., 1 yellow metal key ring with 6 keys, and 1 ring with purple stone— he underwent a second, more complete physical examination, which found no sinus pathology but confirmed bilateral bronchiectasis. "The patient," summarized Dr. D.D. Le Grand, the examining physician, "gives a history of depressive and anxiety symptoms precipitated by physical disease and by exhaustive work. These symptoms have apparently been important reason for previous addictions." In a "pleasant, friendly and cooperative" mood and showing no abnormal mental symptoms, a "correctly oriented" patient embarked on what he hoped would be a final and lasting cure for his addiction. Between March 5 and 17, Lorre underwent a slow withdrawal from Dilaudid and Demoral. He generally ate and slept well, but still lost four pounds. He kept to his room, his ear to the radio. His mood ran the emotional gamut from cheerful and talkative to reclusive, tense, depressed, and anxious. Found crying in his room, he "said that his condition was due to his worry over his situation." However, a more controlled moment found him "rather disgusted with himself because of depression." Several weeks later, however, a homesick Lorre telegrammed Yergin that he "CANNOT UNDERSTAND WHY I HAVE NOT HEARD FROM HOME AND YOU FOR ONE WEEK LOVE LASLO."

For the most part, Lorre got along well during his treatment. According to Dr. William F. Ossenfort, medical director in charge, he developed friendships with several members of the hospital staff, although he reportedly also generated what the physician euphemistically described as "negative transference" toward narcotics enforcement officers. His remarkable progress even earned him consideration for a sixty-day furlough to continue his convalescent care at home. Commissioner Anslinger, however, strongly recommended against Lorre's release and threatened that if he left the hospital "under any other circumstances than with the diagnosis of being cured," the Bureau would proceed with an indictment of his New York physicians for violating the narcotics laws and would name him and Irving Yergin as co-conspirators. Just so there was no misunderstanding, continued the commissioner, representatives of the Narcotics Enforcement Bureau would be waiting for him outside the hospital, pictures would be taken, and "no limit" of publicity would go forward. Le Grand explained that the staff at the hospital had no choice but to put the furlough on indefinite hold. "These circumstances are considered unfortunate," he concluded, "but they are, nevertheless, real."

In an undated handwritten testimonial to the hospital's good work and his own best intentions, Lorre stated, "I am satisfied with the treatment here and have confidence in the medical officer in charge and his staff. My primary interest is to get well and I intend to follow the advice of Dr. Ossenfort in all respects. I am not ashamed of anything in my life and I know that neither I nor my doctor have done anything wrong. I have avoided publicity due to the adverse effect it would have on my job, but if it appears to be unavoidable I will of course face it and defend my rights."

By April 15 Lorre had been off drugs for one month. His severe headaches, which Le Grand believed were psychosomatic, "as they have been precipitated during periods when the patient was under some tension," were relieved with only small amounts of aspirin and Nembutal. He therefore determined that, at the present time, "the patient has received maximum benefit from hospitalization and it is recommended that he be discharged as 'cured.'" Dr. Ossenfort concurred. "Never in his medical experience," he told Yergin, "had he witnessed such courage and willpower in dealing with such a problem."

The medical director concluded that Lorre had previously "been treated well but not too wisely. By this, I mean he was given narcotics when other substances might have done just as well. He strikes me as being a brilliant individual who has made a success of his chosen vocation under circumstances which in many instances were most trying. He has attained a better than average insight into his problem. . . . The prognosis for remaining off drugs, provided he keeps himself under the care of an entirely reputable physician who understands him, would appear to be very good."

Lorre was discharged on April 16. Asked what he had in mind after his release, he said he planned to "remain off work" and return to the U.S. Public Health Service Hospital in the next month or two. As he got off the plane in Los Angeles, he broke down. Seeing Karen and the animals brought more tears. Four days after his return, Karen wrote friends at the hospital in Texas that Peter "is feeling fine. Of course I am terribly happy to have him back home and so were the dogs, horses, cats and even the ducks and chickens. We have been riding quite a bit already and Peter looks as fit and healthy as when I first met him 7 years ago."

Narcotics authorities kept Lorre on a short lead during the next few months. Skeptical about the efficacy of his unexpectedly quick cure, Anslinger "was very unhappy about the discharge," Yergin wrote Dr. Ossenfort on April 23. "Fortunately [he] is precluded by law from doing anything about it, so therefore I am not particularly concerned about his feelings in this matter. I know that your judgment in this matter will be more than justified."

On May 8 agents interviewed Lorre for the first time since his release. The actor cordially talked of his plans for canceling all film commitments and of keeping his name before the public through "as much radio work as possible."[7] According to the agents' field notes, he was worried about the papers picking up the story. Apparently, several others—likely his business partners—besides Yergin and Karen knew about his hospitalization. But the story never broke. Yergin later claimed to have persuaded William Randolph Hearst, an old friend from his newspaper days on the *Chicago Times* and *Tribune,* to hush up the matter. Lorre's request for permission to call a doctor to treat his flu symptoms, including discharge from the ears, very possibly explains why the agents returned five days later to take yet another interview, in which he revealed his plans to spend a week in Arrowhead Hot Springs. In late May Anslinger ordered the district supervisor of the Federal Bureau of Narcotics in Los Angeles to keep an eye on Lorre, whose activities he would closely monitor until June 1949, when the actor left for England.

"Alcohol and narcotics," noted Bertolt Brecht in a letter to Dr. Gruenthal in January 1947, had taken a heavy toll on a generation of gifted actors. Only the bad ones "can keep themselves sober in an industry that produces mental addiction." Being one of the good ones, Lorre had more easily fallen into the hands of a "racket." Brecht liked the word. Distinctly American, it threw a large net around Hollywood and the drug trade and at the same time let Lorre off lightly as a victim, however willing, of a corrupt system. Brecht wasn't sure whether Lorre agreed with him "that his situation is degrading," but he "admired the practical common sense with which he looks at his sickness." The actor, it seemed, clashed opposites even in the role of a drug addict.

At these crossroads of personal and professional crises in Lorre's life, Brecht expressed his concern—and frustration—in a poem general enough to convey a universal meaning, yet discreetly personal. When Naomi Replansky, who translated "Der Sumpf" ("The Swamp") into English, asked Brecht if he had written the poem about Lorre, he shrugged and answered, "It might be." Karen Verne also told James Powers that Brecht had confided to her that Lorre was indeed the "friend" sunk in the swamp.[8] In 1977 Ernest Pascal's widow gave Brecht scholar James Lyon permission to poke through her late husband's papers in their garage in Topanga Canyon. There he found a drawer full of odds and ends once belonging to Peter Lorre, including the German original of "The Swamp," believed lost, presumably given to him by Brecht. Clearly, the poem's epitaphic verse bears witness to Brecht's deep feelings for an old and dear friend:

I saw many friends
And the friend I loved most
Among them helplessly sunk
Into the swamp.
I pass by daily.
And a drowning was not over in a single morning.
This made it more terrible.
And the memory of our long talks about the swamp
Which already held so many powerless.
Now I watched him leaning back
Covered with leeches in the shimmering,
softly moving slime
Upon the sinking face
The ghastly blissful smile.

"For nearly a decade and a half," Brecht told Gruenthal, Lorre "couldn't find the work he wanted in his profession." Dr. Greenson took the analysis one step further, pointing out that "the addiction itself was an indication of how Peter failed to find in his work the kind of satisfaction that Brecht seemed to have achieved." Brecht had a plan to change all that. "Once again many thanks for your quick help in the Lorre business," he wrote Ferdinand Reyher in March, 1947. "It's not only that I like him, I also need him badly in Germany, if I'm going to get my theatre together again. Writing plays has become a complicated, many-sided profession; now I'm trying to disentangle Lorre's muddled affairs."

Brecht had received an offer for a theater in Berlin for the 1947–48 season. "I need Lorre, unconditionally," he confided to Gruenthal, no doubt with the idea that the physician would prescribe what Brecht conceived as a lifesaving cure for his friend. "Without him I can hardly imagine the whole thing. He has to play my parts and the great classical parts, too. We have a very definite style prepared and conversations and recitations by Lorre showed me that he has grown and that he has his best time as an actor (and director) before him." Brecht had it all worked out. While he got things in order, paid debts, and put some money in the bank, Lorre would continue his film work. During their first season, the actor would make only guest appearances at the theater and get a feel for his new situation. The next year he would reverse the process, staying in Berlin to help organize the theater and only returning to Hollywood and London for the occasional film roles, in effect borrowing from the screen to pay the stage. Keeping his foot in both worlds, Brecht felt, "would make him happy." Lorre would not only "again become a great German actor," but would be able to keep his beautiful house in America. As long as he realized that he could "only buy the possibility for the use and perfection of his great talents by not fully trading on his admirable friendliness to humans and animals," all would be well. With one foot planted on each continent, how easily Brecht forgot that Lorre stood firmly on American soil.

"Lorre may straighten out," replied Reyher, brushing aside the actor's drug problem before getting down to business. "Incidentally, do you know anything of Columbia offering a pretty fair sum for the *Lady Macbeth*, which was turned down by Lorre's agent because of additional stipulations which made it too expensive?" Brecht apparently had not kept up with developments regarding the film story, but said he would look into it: "Naturally, we would sell, if at all possible, that's what we agreed upon. Lewis Milestone showed interest, met with resistance at the box-office. He's still interested, but cutting at any moment his last film in New York." The authors then placed *Lady Macbeth* with Paul Kohner, who, in July 1952, wrote Lorre that he "just came across some copies of an old story property called *All Our Yesterdays* which are of no further use to us. I thought you might like to have them and am sending them herewith to you." Always the bridesmaid, never the bride, *Lady Macbeth* came closest of the Brecht-Lorre film stories to the Hollywood altar.

True to his word, shortly after appearing on the Armed Forces Radio Service's *Mail Call* on June 25, Lorre embarked on his first radio series. For their summer slot, NBC traditionally set a show with a crime or detective theme. *Mystery in the Air*—originally titled *Horror Stories*—replaced *The Bud Abbott and Lou Costello Show* from July 3 to September 25, 1947. On thirteen Thursday nights, Paul Baron's nerve-tingling musical score crept out of NBC's Studio A in Hollywood at 6:00 p.m. and into American homes, pausing just long enough for Harry Morgan, The Voice of Mystery, to announce gravely: "*Mystery in the Air*, starring Peter Lorre, presented by Camel (pause) Cigarettes. Each week at this time, Peter Lorre brings us the excitement of the great stories of the strange and unusual, of dark and compelling masterpieces culled from the four corners of world literature."

For the first half-hour show, Lorre once more recited Frank Wilson's adaptation of "The Tell-Tale Heart." No stranger to Poe, he drew plaudits from the trade press. The *Hollywood Reporter* credited his "finely-shaded and almost delicate portrayal" as being "the finest interpretation of 'The Tell-Tale Heart' that has ever come over the airwaves. . . . As the first in a series of 13 Camel-sponsored half-hour mysteries, it was an auspicious first and radio thriller—fans must be looking forward to the next 12 with more than modest anticipation."

"For grisliness and gruesomeness . . . POE AND LORRE'S 'TELLTALE HEART'. . . was a gem raw and red," hailed *Daily Variety*, "and a classic triumph for Lorre—a masterpiece of character etching and a cameo of narration. . . . Production-wise, the eerie mood was sustained with pin-point timing, precisioned sound effects and the isolation of music and mike-frightening by curtaining off the moaning instruments and compounding Lorre and his fellow workers in an enclosure."

Subsequent stories based on works by Edgar Allan Poe, Guy de Maupassant, Mrs. Belloc-Lowndes, Fyodor Dostoyevsky, and Ben Hecht assured the series literary respectability as well a measure of quality control. Lorre likewise stamped the series with a personal touch, blending player and part in "The Horla." In a fevered pitch, he closes, "LET ME GO! YES, I KNOW I'M PETER LORRE. I KNOW. I KNOW IT'S A STORY. I KNOW IT'S THURSDAY NIGHT AND WE ARE ON THE AIR. I KNOW IT'S BY DE MAUPASSANT. BUT, IT'S THE HORLA. (*seemingly awakening from a spell*) Oh, I beg your pardon. I'm sorry. I got so excited, but I warned you at the beginning. It's a very uncomfortable story."

Regardless how large or small the studio audience, Lorre gave performances worthy of the camera. Harry Morgan said:

I have never seen in front of a microphone anybody throw himself into a performance in every which way, including physically, which was to me so astounding, as Peter. I mean, if you're playing to a mike, you're playing to a mike. He wasn't playing to the audience. The things that he went through, contortions of the face and his whole body—everybody remarked on that. And he'd be dripping with sweat after the half-hour was over because he'd not only done a great vocal performance, he'd been through a lot physically. He used to perform with almost clenched teeth and his body so tense that the legs would quiver and his whole body would shake as he acted into the microphone. . . . At one point the intensity and the push and the drive that he had made his false teeth shoot right out about three feet and he caught them in his hand, just a reflex, and put them back in his mouth and went on without missing a beat. I've never seen anything like it in my life.

In interviews given at the U.S. Public Health Service Hospital in Texas, Lorre had told the medical staff that he was only a social drinker, and in fact, his friends and co-workers bear out the truth of his statement. However, during the broadcasts, he mixed business and pleasure, requesting that a tumbler of scotch be placed alongside his microphone. During each show, he emptied it. Yet, said Morgan, "whether it was nervousness or tension . . . it didn't affect him one way or another."

Mystery in the Air ended on September 25. Lorre subsequently gave only three or four radio performances each year, and most often in guest spots for popular variety shows, such as *Philco Radio Time,* on which "the continental Mickey Rooney" played a psychoanalyst ("I won't have to make faces anymore") and Spike Jones's *Spotlight Revue,* which offered something never seen on the big screen—a seminar on the art of impersonation by none other than Paul Frees and Peter Lorre himself. In June 1947 Jones and head writer Eddie Brandt, who opened one of Hollywood's legendary movie memorabilia shops in 1969, put Lorre-like lyrics to the song hit "My Old Flame" and hired popular voice actor Paul Frees to record the revised tune at RCA Victor in Hollywood. The next year, Jones scheduled Lorre and Frees to appear together on the Coca-Cola-sponsored *Spotlight Revue* for Chicago's WBBM Radio. Following a popularly resonant rendition of "My Old Flame" by Dick Baldwin (accompanied by the City Slickers), Frees masterfully magnified the actor's vocal mannerisms, catching rhyme and rhythm, rant and rave, to perfection in his own rendition of the song: "My old flame. I can't even think of her name—I'll have to look through my collection of human heads. . . . She would always treat me mean, so I poured a can of gasoline . . . and struck a match to my old flame."

"I think that imitation of me was just wonderful," complimented Lorre during the broadcast. And, as he learned at a rehearsal attended by several hundred spectators, quite intimidating. "The impressionists had made Lorre ten times stronger than he really had been," recalled Brandt. "They exaggerated it so much, Lorre didn't sound like Lorre anymore. His voice was so soft and quiet. And Paul Frees built it up like imitators do. When Lorre stepped in, he was a mouse against a mountain lion." Later, Brandt went by Lorre's dressing room to see how he was doing on the script and caught him "practicing Peter Lorre in the mirror and making faces at himself!"

Asked to hear "My Old Flame" done by the real Peter Lorre, the actor told "Spook-Jones . . . Spooky-boy . . . Spooky-man" that he has his own version. "My old flame," began Lorre, imitating himself for comic effect, "I can't even think of her name, no . . . I . . . Oh, yes, she had no name. My old flame was a hotfoot."

Lorre seemed a new man altogether, Elisabeth Hauptmann noted in a letter to Ivor Montagu on August 19, 1947. "Peter is in very good shape," she wrote, "and anxious to do something worthwhile." His partnership in Lorre Inc. renewed his expectations—and Brecht's—that he could make things happen.

Riding one of his cyclic waves of inspiration, Lorre had earlier told the press that "you can get anything you really want. The trouble is people don't want it badly enough or work long and hard enough for it. . . . But you must keep trying or you'll hate yourself." One had only to look at the Mandeville Canyon mailbox, where the names Mr. and Mrs. Peter Lorre and Elisabeth Hauptmann appeared, for a clue to his renewed conviction. Like all of Brecht's female collaborators who supplied "sex and text," Hauptmann turned the wheels in the Mandeville Canyon Brecht factory, churning out translations of his works with Eric Bentley and letters bearing the signature of the same Peter Lorre who had rarely put pen to paper in his life. Hauptmann gave Lorre the "kick in the ass" that he had recommended for the indecisive and insecure Charles Laughton, who seemed reluctant to commit to Brecht's *Galileo* in "the remotest part of the world just to have it put on the stage." Initially, Lorre told Montagu, "there was a terrific interest in it, the Theater Guild and others fighting for it like mad." Only after producer Mike Todd and other potential backers politely backed away from the project did the Brecht team suspect—and claim they were later able to verify—that "our old friend, his Excellency and Eminence, Mr. Pacelli [Pope Pius XII], and his outfit just don't seem to like the idea of GALILEO at all. At this moment, I don't have to inform you, they are fairly powerful."

"My interest, of course, is Brecht and the play," maintained Lorre, who had developed his role as adviser into that of middleman. Believing "it is one of the best plays written in the last twenty years, a very commercial play which is unusual for Brecht, and in any case a very important play," he asked Montagu about the possibilities for a stage production and film in London. "Being the dreamer and the ham he [Laughton] is," wrote Lorre, "he needs a push or a kick or a something at certain points in his worldly career." Perhaps "an unsolicited letter from you and possibly one or two others whose judgement he trusts," Lorre added, "might get him going very quick in the right direction instead of wasting his time here wrestling with the windmills." One of the others, as it turned out, was actor Herbert Marshall, "who is extremely enthusiastic about it and feels that it should be possible to get a serious proposition for putting the play on here if something a little more definite could be secured about the degree of Laughton's willingness to play it in England." In December *Galileo* played for four weeks in New York to unfavorable reviews. Plans for a London performance never materialized.[9]

In what for the Lorre household must have seemed like a flurry of outgoing correspondence, there also appears repeated mention of Gogol's "Coat." Brecht noted in his journal, March 24, 1947, that he had completed a film outline for Lorre of Nikolai Gogol's novella *Der Mantel* (*The Overcoat*), about a poor civil servant who procures a winter coat only to have it stolen from him. While cold overcomes his body, the lack of compassion shown by apathetic authorities crushes his spirit. Only after he reaches out from beyond the grave to secure a fur coat from the "Person of Consequence" does he rest in peace and warmth.[10]

Brecht seemed to be acutely aware of the kinds of roles that both suited and appealed to Lorre. Gogol's protagonist is a vulnerable and pathetic figure and his story one of tragic irony. Even the author's sense of the macabre lent itself to Hollywood mythmaking so foreign to Brecht but familiar to Lorre. The actor's business partners apparently showed as little interest in Gogol as they had in Brecht. Neither, it seemed to them, had any business sense. "No prospects for it in Hollywood," noted Brecht, "am thinking of Switzerland." With no hope of its production on this end, Hauptmann sent a rough translation of their script to Montagu in August: "It was meant for Peter. We did not submit the story here for reasons I do not have to explain to you." In his reply, Montagu thanked Peter and Karen for their welcome parcel and for the scenario of *The Overcoat*, whose British future looked doubtful. "It would be grand to see you over here once again," he wrote on September 22, "and to do another job together, but I feel a bit pessimistic about this subject. In the present state of affairs here a classic of non-English literature is hardly likely to make a big appeal to the companies." Brecht dropped the project, thinking, as always, of picking it up again at a later date.

Though Brecht began laying plans for his return to Germany in early 1947, he apparently had not given up on creating a screen vehicle for Lorre. In May 1948 director Joseph Losey wrote Brecht that Seymour Nebenzal, who had produced *M* in 1931, wished to remake the German classic in France or Italy, but that "Lorre is no longer acceptable for it because the producers maintain that he now is regarded by the American movie public as a clown."[11] Instead, for the role of the infamous child murderer, he envisioned Charles Laughton, who "is trying to think of other new stories that would serve as well as 'M' which he finds 'dated' and distasteful." In the end, he set *M* (1951) in Los Angeles and starred David Wayne as the serial killer, with Losey directing. Again, Lorre was out of the picture, not only for his accent, but because Nebenzal felt his acting too European by American standards. The producer's sad but telling observation, which denigrated the actor as a serious artist, likely gave Brecht the idea for *Der grosse Clown Emaël* (*The Great Clown Emaël*). In a prefatory note, he set out his twofold purpose. On the surface, the playful story shows the "touching affection of the great clown for his romantic wife, whom he loves because of, rather than in spite of, her stupidity." Secondarily, but more importantly, he intends to show how, in his opinion, Shakespeare should be performed, packaging, as it were, his epic theater principles in pink tissue paper.

Between international tours, the great clown Emaël pores over his beloved quartos of Shakespeare at his manor in Switzerland. When his foolish wife, Emile, becomes involved with a young actor in the local summer theater, he indulgently accepts that "such things spice up vacations." The ensemble embraces Emile until it learns that her husband will not attend their production of *Othello*. She applauds their mockery of Emaël but later confesses to him that "it was as if they murdered you in front of my eyes." Being laughed at washes off Emaël's back; he has made his fortune this way. However, Emile's revelation that her lover keeps a young mistress angers him. To teach the troupe a lesson for not showing his wife proper respect, he closes the brewery where they perform. Emaël ponders what to do with the hungry young rascals, who, he points out, don't even know how to study their text. When Emile says she forgives them, he tells her, "That would be too easy." Emaël decides to give a benefit performance for those he has thrown out of work and sends a letter to the actor's young mistress containing a curious note: "*Richard III, Act I, Scene 2. Instruction for an intelligent murder*"—which sets the stage, quite literally, for Brecht's lesson in Shakespeare. After murdering her husband, Gloucester wins Lady Ann's forgiveness by impudently revealing that he committed the crime to win her favor. As art imitates life, so Emaël plays with "loud provocative clown speech" as well as clumsy gestures, drawing obvious parallels to the calculating character actor who preyed upon his wife's vanity.

Gloucester's murder of Lady Ann's husband in the famous seduction scene echoes an autobiographical incident with dark undertones contained in the endnotes. Out of an unconquerable wish to possess Emile, Emaël had earlier stolen the identity of her husband, the blessed Edwardo, who played a crippled clown. Emaël simulated the lame walk of his rival, making it appear that the grinning Edwardo mocked him because of his infirmity. After enraged passersby beat his weak-hearted adversary to death, Emaël confessed his trick to Emile, on whose conceited mercy he threw himself. As Lady Ann forgave Gloucester, so Emile calmed Emaël's pangs of conscience and bought him a little castle with the proceeds from the sale of Edwardo's circus.

When Emaël learns that Emile plans to run away with the actor, he selects the proper music for their flight and watches the romantic abduction from his window, then gives chase in his Packard. Playing the scene of the betrayed lover in great style, he throws the proceeds of the benefit performance at the feet of the actor, then reclaims Emile: "She is completely happy."

Whether Brecht wished to expose the private side of Lorre's double existence to an unappreciative public or simply send him another wake-up call, he left open to interpretation. *Emaël* walks a rather crooked line, painting Lorre's life in broad Chaplinesque strokes. Brecht's infatuation with the silent picture clown harked back to his love affair with America, where he later met his idol and made overtures to work with him. Chaplin's demonstrational acting had, according to James Lyon, "exerted a profound impact on his dramatic theories and techniques of epic theater." Because they both spoke the same "gestic" language, Chaplin and Lorre appealed to Brecht for many of the same reasons. Even Lotte Lenya thought Lorre "very Chaplinesque." In *Emaël* it is impossible to know where Chaplin leaves off and Lorre begins. For biographical details, Brecht loosely worked from the pantomimist's early life. Emaël quits his career on stage for the more lucrative world of the Variété, where his personal ideas and inspirations become classic. However, "even as he grazed in the circus of the lower regions for the entertainment of the people," he quietly studied Shakespeare, putting his knowledge of drama to a practical purpose.

While Chaplin's early struggles provided the medium, Lorre's later years supplied the message. His "facemaking" for the Hollywood merchandisers must certainly have informed Emaël's selling out higher art forms for lower. Erich Engel believed that only Chaplin could have played the role. Not without limited stage experience as a clown, Lorre felt comfortable with comedy, though he believed being typed as a comedian was irreversible. Brecht needed an actor capable of doing two things at once. Lorre often boasted, not without merit, that he could charm an audience with kindness, then chill them to the marrow. He was just what the screwball comedy with a dark twist called for, a clown who stood in the shadows. Brecht intended that the film be produced in both English and German, with Eric Engel directing, Hanns Eisler or Paul Dessau composing, and Lorre, Käthe Gold, Lucie Mannheim, Therese Giehse, Will Quadflieg, and Karen Verne, as the mistress, filling the main roles. By the time Brecht finished *The Great Clown Emaël* the following year in Switzerland, time had put enough distance between him and Lorre to cool off any follow-up.

In September 1947 Lorre punched in at Marston Pictures for his first screen assignment under the aegis of Lorre Inc. *Casbah* (1948), the third incarnation of Detective Ashelbe's novel *Pepe Le Moko,* starred singer Tony Martin, who succeeded Jean Gabin and Charles Boyer in the title role of the thief who leaves the sanctuary of the Casbah for the love of a woman. Following in the footsteps of Joseph Calleia and Lucas Gridoux, Lorre played Slimane, the fez-topped police inspector who smilingly bides his time.

Believing Lorre a "dyed-in-the-wool good actor," Tony Martin, who independently produced *Casbah* with Nat C. Goldstone, gave the actor room to rework his dialogue: "The night before, when he would get the script, he'd say, 'I'd like to make this or that change.' And he'd do it." Director John Berry likewise, in Martin's words, "let Lorre have the strength" to carry out his own ideas. The actor welcomed the freedom as well as the opportunity to assume a more contemporary role. "I like the role I'm playing now," he told Martin, "because all I'm doing is being a pursuer." Martin added that the role was also a challenge: "He loved it, being the great actor that he was. It gave him a new dimension to expand his own acting career and to get out of that Sydney Greenstreet thing he was in. . . . It caught him with a sense of humor and a tenderness."

Singing his way through a string of minor musical-comedies had not prepared Martin for a dramatic debut. He knew he needed help. Lorre cast a spell over the actor and then snapped his fingers: "In those days, the black and white pictures, the close-ups, he could hypnotize you, and he could lull you into a deep inner peace. We'd do a take and I'd be rotten. He'd say, 'You know, you're the worst fucking actor I've ever seen.' I'd say, 'Really?' He'd say, 'Yes, nobody worse.' And we'd start to laugh and the director would say, 'Alright, let's go,' and I'd do a good scene. He had a way of putting me down. He had a psychological way. And we had dinner every night."

Martin was not alone. As teacher, coach, adviser, and psychologist, Lorre extended a helping hand to neophyte actors. If a co-worker felt he had not done his best, Lorre got another take. "He'd wait after work and sit in the dark while they did a close-up of me and read his lines," an appreciative Martin recalled. "And then we'd go to a bar and have a few drinks."

Reading the mixed reviews for *Casbah* begs the question: did critics see the same movie? Arguably, *Casbah*'s strongest asset—others would say its saving grace—was Lorre. The actor took "Top honors . . . as the ubiquitous Slimane. His police inspector is smooth, natural, underplayed and a worthy successor to the previous Slimanes."

Striking while the iron was hot, Stiefel, who had loaned Lorre's services for a whopping thirty-five-thousand-dollar flat rate—plus a percentage—for six weeks' work, ran an ad in *Variety* picturing Lorre as Slimane above Ruth Waterbury's review in the *Los Angeles Examiner:* "Lorre as the Inspector who knows he is going to get his man Pepe is utterly wonderful. He's lazy. He's catlike. And smart out of this world. Lorre is so consistently good in every picture that they will probably forget his work in 'Casbah' when next year's Academy nominations for 'best supporting performance' come around. But I hope they don't. This smooth job belongs right up among the best."

Waterbury was right on both counts. Neither this nor any other of Lorre's screen performances won nomination. Nineteen forty-eight was the year of the Hustons. Their work on *The Treasure of the Sierra Madre* earned John Academy Awards for Best Director and Best Screenplay and garnered his father Walter an Oscar for Best Supporting Actor.

In 1947 FBI agents knocked on Lorre's door and produced a list of names and asked if he knew the people. "If you want to know who I know," he responded, "you had better have more names." Like a "bland cherub who couldn't possibly tell a lie," as a friend once noted of his comic delivery, Lorre deferentially began rattling off the names of everyone he had ever known in Hollywood. (One supposes the list was particularly heavy with studio executives.) According to Yergin, the agents flipped their notebooks shut, hopped in their car, and sped off.

Short on political talk and shorter yet on action, Lorre, perhaps naively, never anticipated trouble. He felt safe in minding his own business and abiding by an unwritten studio policy of keeping his political opinions to himself. His credits as a civil libertarian tended toward antiheroics that never caught the public eye but accorded well with his liberal conscience. When Lena Horne's family moved into their new house on Horn Avenue above Sunset Strip, "local bigots" circulated a petition to have them removed from the neighborhood. Across the street lived Humphrey Bogart, who greeted their visit with threats to get off his property or "risk being shot at." Peter Lorre, another neighbor, likewise told them to "buzz off." At the New York Colony Club, Lorre once noticed waiting customers clustered behind a cordon while tables stood empty. He called over the manager, who scornfully explained, "They're only tourists. We prefer to seat more important guests, such as yourself, Mr. Lorre." The "celebrity" unceremoniously removed the barrier and seated them himself. On his way out, he reproached the manager, "I know what it's like to be kept out." In the White Mountains of New Hampshire, he pulled into a hotel whose manager welcomed the actor and assured him that his lodgings did not accommodate Jews. It was a common mistake. Lorre's central European accent and Continental bearing lent him a cosmopolitan mystique. "Once Peter learned that Jews were barred from the hotel," remembered Yergin, "he innocently spilled the inkwell on the desk and left." Later, he sent the hotel a three-year subscription to the *Jewish Daily Forward.*

At the same time Lorre gave muted voice to his feelings for the victims of oppression, he stanched the bleeding hearts of noisy liberals with a little shock treatment. Lorre told George Frazier that minutes after meeting Danny Kaye for the first time, the comedian loudly denounced Nazi war criminals. Lorre apparently listened intently and then shook his head: "That poor Ernst Kaltenbrunner. They want to hang the fellow. He killed a few Jews, so what?"

Such is the stuff of anecdote, but not the kind of thing that caused ripples in Washington. Heedless of warnings "not to affiliate himself with Communist Party activities because it would ruin him for more important work," Lorre went his own way, secure in the knowledge that he had not ventured too far out on a political limb. Piecing together an incriminating profile from a poetry reading and the signing of a document to which "the most important German anti-Fascist figures from the 'Catholic Center' to the 'far left,'" had also affixed their names, seemed improbable. However, what Lorre didn't know—and doubtless would have been surprised to learn—and what the FBI apparently never discovered, could have hurt him. Certainly, the actor could not have anticipated that Hanns and Gerhart Eisler's sister, Ruth Fischer, an apostate Stalinist, would finger him as a Communist. And little did he know that Jack Warner blamed Communist agitators for the 1945 labor union strike. Because he did not show up for work, it appeared to the Front Office that the actor had taken sides. A note in the January 5, 1945, issue of *California Jewish Voice* (Los Angeles) under "Our Film Folk," reporting that Lorre had been invited to Germany after the war by the Free German Movement in Moscow, also found its way into his FBI file.

What the authorities failed to note was Elisabeth Hauptmann's live-in presence at Mandeville Canyon. In her privileged position on the Brecht team, "she was Americanizing some of the things, some of the phrasing of Marxist ideology," said Bentley, who considered her "a very conspiratorial lady from the ordinary point of view, as any Communist party worker would seem." The FBI, which later shared its files with the House Committee on Un-American Activities (HUAC), monitored movements of "enemy aliens" with suspected leftist leanings, jotting down times, places, and license plate numbers. Fortunately for Lorre, Hauptmann did not own a car.

After leaving Warner Bros., Lorre more freely associated with Brecht. They socialized at each other's homes and, as best he could, given his limited access to the writer's pool, Lorre pushed Brecht's stories in film circles. Just how mindful Lorre was of the political repercussions to his career depended on his frame of mind at any given moment. Neither advertising nor hiding his friendship with Brecht, he mostly followed his conscience at the expense of his common sense. If he heard the wake-up calls—in 1940, John Leech, an alleged former "chief functionary" for the local Communist Party, had testified before a Los Angeles County grand jury about Communist influence in motion pictures, accusing eighteen actors of being "Reds," including Humphrey Bogart—he did not listen to them. Lorre balanced the threat of gray-listing, which he blamed for the slowdown of his career, against his debt to Brecht.

In 1938 Congress had established a temporary Special Committee to investigate un-American propaganda activities. Mindful of the possibility "that in any legislative attempt to prevent un-American activities, we might jeopardize fundamental rights far more important than the objective we seek," Congressman Martin Dies, who had introduced the resolution, upheld the need to protect "the undisputed right of every citizen in the United States to express his honest convictions and enjoy freedom of speech." After an initial burst of active investigation, the number of public hearings declined each year until 1941, when they virtually ceased. However, in 1945 John Rankin railroaded through Congress an amendment to create a permanent Un-American Activities Committee. On the heels of its announced intention to initiate an investigation into "Communist Infiltration into the Motion-Picture Industry," chairman J. Parnell Thomas began closed-door hearings of "friendly" witnesses—including actors Robert Taylor and Adolphe Menjou—in Los Angeles in May 1947. That September HUAC subpoenaed forty-one producers, directors, writers, and actors to testify in Washington the following month.

Affronted by the committee's infringements on constitutional freedoms—being a Communist was not illegal, after all—directors William Wyler and John Huston and writer Philip Dunne quickly recruited the Committee for the First Amendment, "not as a permanent organization, but as an immediate ad hoc protest against the abuses going on in Washington." The CFA's star-studded cast jam-packed meetings at lyricist Ira Gershwin's home. There, according to FBI sources, Lorre turned up on Sunday, October 26. As a witness to the rise of fascism in Germany, he told stories that drew damning parallels between the methods of HUAC chairman J. Parnell Thomas and Adolf Hitler. While Sam Jaffe, Bogart's agent, cautioned the actor that his political activities might ruin his career, Yergin and Lorre mutually supported each other's defense of freedom of thought and expression. From October 21 to 28, the CFA struck back with full-page ads in the trade press and several Los Angeles newspapers listing one hundred and forty names, including Lorre's, and stating that

American citizens who believe in constitutional democratic government, are disgusted and outraged by the continuing attempt of the House Committee on Un-American Activities to smear the Motion Picture Industry.

We hold that these hearings are morally wrong because: Any investigation into the political beliefs of the individual is contrary to the basic principles of our democracy;

Any attempt to curb freedom of expression and to set arbitrary standards of Americanism is in itself disloyal to both the spirit and the letter of our Constitution.

The CFA chartered a plane to fly fifty prominent members to Washington—including spokesmen John Huston and Philip Dunne, the Bogarts, Paul Henreid, Evelyn Keyes, Ira Gershwin, Gene Kelly, Jane Wyatt, Marsha Hunt, Geraldine Page, Richard Conte, and Danny Kaye—to attend the hearings and petition the committee for redress of grievances. According to Yergin, Lorre helped plan the trip and intended to accompany Bogart and Huston. But, said James Powers, who asserted that Lorre was "not a fighter," he missed the plane.

However, Lorre managed a statement for *Hollywood Fights Back*, a CFA-sponsored civil liberties broadcast that aired over ABC on October 26, at virtually the same time the nonpartisan Hollywood delegation was in flight to Washington. In the thirty-minute show, more than forty entertainment and political figures read statements prepared by CBS writer-producer Norman Corwin and members of the Hollywood Independent Citizens Committee of the Arts, Sciences, and Professions (HICCASP) defending the film industry and questioning the role and goals of the Committee.[12] Following Judy Garland, who castigated Thomas for "kicking the living daylights out of the Bill of Rights," Gene Kelly, Lauren Bacall, and Joseph Cotton, Lorre spoke his piece: "This is Peter Lorre. I hope you know what this amounts to. It amounts to this: If you like any of the pictures made by any of these accused artists, then you are not supposed to know what is un-American and what is not. So that's like saying you're stupid. Well, we don't think you are."

With about a 50 percent turnover of celebrity personnel, they did it again the following Sunday. Speakers punched specific points in their review of the week's proceedings. "In the midst of a rising tide of protest, the hearings are suddenly called off," declaimed actor Hurd Hatfield.

Chairman Thomas announces the first phase of the investigation is over. But it is not over. . . . You can't dump a bucket of red paint over a city and its citizens and run off like a bunch of Halloween pranksters. There are still a lot of questions that demand answers. Here are some:

This is Peter Lorre. Why, if these hearings were so important to the security of America, were they attended only by a fraction of the Committee's total membership? And why was John Rankin, co-chairman of this Committee—and you know who he is!—absent from all the hearings? Why?

The CFA supported rights, emphasized Dunne, not causes. The flight to Washington was made "solely in the interests of freedom of speech, freedom of the screen and protection of the Bill of Rights," reiterated Bogart in a *Photoplay* article titled "I'm No Communist." Members of the CFA had not flown east to demonstrate support for the ten "unfriendly" witnesses (out of nineteen) who were subsequently known as "The Hollywood Ten," but nonetheless they soon "found themselves lined up with a group of writers who had come across as shifty, ill-mannered, fanatical, and—well, frankly, un-American." In any case, the CFA celebrated the sudden suspension of the "de facto trials" soon after the testimony of the tenth "unfriendly" witness. The victory was short-lived. Overnight, public opinion turned against the CFA, branded as "one of the most diabolical Red Front organizations ever conceived" and its Washington delegation a "caravan of glamor Reds." Bogart's public recantation—"the trip was ill-advised, even foolish . . . they beat our brains out"—cost him some friends, but not stalwarts Lorre and Huston, who quickly put it behind them.

Lorre apparently came closer than he imagined to being summoned to testify before HUAC. In May, Thomas had asked the FBI to supply him with information concerning certain individuals in the Hollywood area, including Bertolt Brecht and Peter Lorre. Judging by the depth of its research, which depended on information about Lorre "as one of the actors trained by Bertolt Eugen [*sic*] Friedrich Brecht" drawn from *20th Century Authors* (1942), hard evidence of his suspected Communist affiliations did not exist in either the FBI field reports or at the lending library.

In the summer of 1947, Brecht had begun preparing to return to Europe. On September 19, a U.S. marshal showed up on his doorstep with a subpoena to appear before HUAC. Classified as an "unfriendly" witness, a well-rehearsed Brecht took the stand in the Caucus Room of the Old House Office Building on October 30. To counsel Robert Stripling's question, "Are you now or have you ever been a member of the Communist Party of any country?" he answered, in a word, "no," tacitly acknowledging the committee's disputed right to ask the question before leading it on a crooked chase over the German literary landscape in search of clues to his political identity. Afterward, according to screenwriter Dalton Trumbo, one of the "Hollywood Ten" fined and sentenced to a one-year prison term for refusing to answer questions about his political affiliation, Brecht apologized for breaking ranks with the other eighteen "unfriendly" witnesses. Lorre later credited himself with advising Brecht to "get out." It did not take a fortune-teller to read the writing on the wall. Or the recommendation of his well-meaning friend. "When they accused me of wanting to steal the Empire State Building," Brecht later joked, "I thought it was high time to leave." Which he did, the next day.

The "Red Menace" continued to fuel what John Huston called a "miasma of fear, hysteria and guilt." J. Edgar Hoover believed that HUAC had exposed only the tip of the iceberg—although it had failed to document even one instance of Communist propaganda in the movies. A little-known theater and film producer on the West Coast agreed that "a fine tooth combing of Hollywood is vital." Myron C. Fagan credited his 1945 stage production of *Red Rainbow* with exposing Communism in America. Three years later, at the premiere of *Thieves Paradise*, which unmasked Communism behind the Iron Curtain, he named one hundred "Red Celebrities of Hollywood" who had done "far more to siphon that poisonous ideology into our national blood stream than any other single group of Red termites in America!" The 1947 HUAC hearings "confirmed [his] charges that Hollywood was a captive of the Reds and Moscow's most dangerous propaganda machine in America!" In August 1949 Fagan came out with *Red Treason in Hollywood,* which identified "TWO hundred of Hollywood's great names as supporters of Marxism." As one of "Stalin's Stars" whom he sought to knock off their pedestals, Lorre kept company with Humphrey Bogart, Eddie Cantor, Charles Chaplin, Bette Davis, Olivia de Havilland, Kirk Douglas, Katharine Hepburn, Vincent Price, Frank Sinatra, and Orson Welles.

In response "to a tremendous PUBLIC DEMAND," Fagan followed *Red Treason* with *Documentation of the Red Stars in Hollywood* (1950), which "categorically establish[ed] the actual status of each and every individual I named in 'Red Treason in Hollywood,'" including Peter Lorre. His membership in the CFA, "organized at the behest of the Communist Party . . . *to finally bring about an open and bloody revolution against our form of Government,*" and the Actor's Laboratory Theatre, "an extension of the notoriously Communistic GROUP THEATRE of the early 30s in New York," earned him a place on Fagan's distinguished list of "Hollywood Stalinites," whom the "Red-Baiter" promised to restore to good grace "as soon as we are convinced they have *sincerely* repented." Surprisingly, he overlooked Lorre's co-vice-chairmanship (along with Fritz Kortner and Hedy

Lamarr) of an organized relief effort for anti-Nazi Austrian theater people that grew out of a meeting of actors, writers, producers, and authors at the Actor's Lab. With funds raised from the production of "suitable" plays and other performances, the group planned to "assist in the development of a democratic, cultural, internationally-minded Austrian theatre." Fagan also encouraged his readers to register their protests with sponsors who employed actors with "pink" reputations. By then, Lorre had taken his own advice and left for Europe, escaping the darkest years of the blacklist.

Always on the lookout for a good story idea to push himself up the studio ladder, Walter Doniger, a young screenwriter under contract to Paramount, paged through a travel magazine after the war. A piece about the diamond-bearing area of South Africa jumped out at him. "I was attempting to write a script that would be a character melodrama in the tradition of *Casablanca*," said Doniger. To represent the various nationalities one might find there, he reassembled on paper the cast of *Casablanca*—namely Humphrey Bogart, Ingrid Bergman, Paul Henreid, Claude Rains, and Peter Lorre—but in different roles, ones conditioned by postwar attitudes. Doniger sold his finished script to Hal Wallis, who had left Warner Bros. in 1944 to form his own production company, which released its pictures through Paramount. Although the producer could have starred Bogart and Bergman, "since they were evidently both agreeable," he had Burt Lancaster under contract "and also had tested and signed the French girl [Corinne Calvet] and felt sure she would be a star." Wallis collected only three members of the original cast. No longer a French patriot, Henreid plays a brutal commandant and Rains a menacing mine manager. Lorre, as Toady, still scavenges the fringes of society, this time keeping a vulture's eye view on the illegal diamond trade.

Like *Casablanca*, *Rope of Sand* (1949) begins with a voice-over narration and a mood-setting montage: "This part of the desert of South Africa, where only a parched camel thorn tree relieves the endless parallels of time, space and sky, surrounds like a rope of sand the richest diamond-bearing area in the world. An uneasy land, where men inflamed by monotony and the heat sometimes forget the rules of civilization." Like *Casablanca*'s Rick Blaine, *Rope of Sand*'s Mike Davis (Burt Lancaster) is, by Doniger's design, "related in a way to the essence of the philosophy of a Dashiell Hammett or Hemingway hero in that he had his own code which he must live by rather than any societal strictures."

It is Toady's code of survival, however, that puts a philosophical edge on the story: "Consider this place for a minute if you will. It often reminds me of the interior of a whale's belly. It's only an intellectual association, of course.

But it is just from the whale's sordid interior that we scavenge the base for the most exciting perfumes and that in turn we confuse with desirability, with virtue, with great passion."

Doniger developed the character of Toady with Lorre in mind, at the same time grasping on an unconscious level for a "reflection of the actor's life, a victim in and of the film world." Because of his "situation as an émigré," claimed the writer, Lorre was able to "reach this character, who belongs nowhere and who recognized that morality is a fraud perpetrated on the society in which the only morality is survival."

After the preview, Hal Wallis was ecstatic: he had a hit. Doniger was less than enthusiastic. He believed Lancaster and Calvet were miscast and that director William Dieterle, though a fine technician, did not understand the story or have any concept of how to handle actors: "They all acted out of control. I was furious because, part truth, part writer frustration over director's lack of understanding of underlying elements, I felt Dieterle had missed the sociological and character point of the film."

Nevertheless, conceded Doniger, Wallis was right, "because it was an enormous hit and made more money for his company than any picture up to that time." Largely forgotten now, *Rope of Sand* won critical recognition in its day. In his several brief scenes, Lorre once again held the screen beyond his time, "stand[ing] out . . . as a philosopher who is not beneath a bit of deceit if it fattens his wallet."

When nothing came of a deal to star in a trio of pictures produced and directed by Mickey Rooney, Lorre once again took Edgar Allan Poe on the road.[13] Between November 1948 and June 1949, Lorre spent more time on stage—approximately eight weeks—than before the camera. His monologue had not lost its luster. "By his voice, by his facial expressions, and by the motion of his hands and feet," reported the *Columbus (Ohio) Citizen*, "Mr. Lorre treats the audience to a memorable characterization. That the real-life Peter Lorre must be far different from the actor Peter Lorre is evinced in the charm he displayed before he went into 'The Telltale Heart.'" After the requisite "gags," the actor kept his audiences "breathless and spellbound" with a dramatization that sharply contrasted with the movie fare following the show, namely *Siren of Atlantis* at the Earle in Philadelphia and *Streets of Laredo* at the Paramount in New York City, and the usual variety of comedians, singers, acrobats, tapsters and even The Three Stooges. The *Philadelphia Inquirer* noted that "Lorre finishes each performance to the most thunderous applause heard in a Philadelphia house since John Barrymore played 'Hamlet.'"

As Hollywood closed down, New York opened up to Lorre. In March 1949, between spots in Baltimore and Philadelphia, Lorre moved from the big to the small screen with appearances on *The Texaco Star Theater*, on which he recited "The Man with the Head of Glass," and *The Arrow Show*, on which he played babysitter to Jack Gilford and Joey Faye. In the next fifteen years, the actor would make more than eighty television appearances, to which he then and thereafter attached surprisingly little or no importance.

In April 1949 the actor put in his final screen appearance for Lorre Inc. Mickey Rooney also tried to make it his last. According to the *Hollywood Reporter*, February 3, 1949, Rooney had sought to pull out of *Quicksand* (1950), the firm's first independent production, and to sever all ties with his manager. However, Stiefel insisted that Rooney fulfill his seven-year contract. By February 22, the partners had apparently patched up their differences and negotiations were under way to borrow Ava Gardner from MGM to costar in the picture. Fritz Lang was also under consideration for director. In the end, however, the Rooney team settled for Jeanne Cagney in the female role and Irving Pichel at the helm.[14]

In *Quicksand* the income of auto mechanic Mickey Rooney can't keep up with the expensive tastes of his mink-minded girlfriend, Jeanne Cagney. He goes from misdemeanor to grand theft, realizes that crime doesn't pay, and finally surrenders himself to the police. Although it barely filled the large screen, *Quicksand* boasted a tight story line, suspenseful direction, and honest, hard-edged performances.

Lorre stepped into the role of a blackmailing penny arcade owner with renewed relish. "I just felt that whatever he tackled," voiced Cagney,

> he did with all his might. Even though the picture was not a top drawer film, he still approached it as if it were the "A" picture of all "A" pictures. The thing that really tickled me about Peter was the marvelous sense of humor and really dingy gaiety. I did not expect it. I didn't know anybody who knew him before I worked with him, and I'd only seen his work on screen. He was so menacing that you felt as though that must have been part of the initial personality. It was like finding gold. In the first place, the slow-moving quality was all gone. His reactions were so much faster, and his feet were so much faster that I was startled. The first reaction was just pure delight in finding an elfin quality. He seemed very much younger when you met him, very much jollier, and quick on the uptake. He and Rooney were just a marvelous team as far as springing off each other with the jokes.

On the face of it, Peter and Karen's romance looked like the real thing, and it had been in the beginning. He called her "Momma." She had given up her career to become a housewife, occasionally appearing in movies to make some "mad money" for Christmas shopping. They talked about children. In photos, he in black turtleneck and khaki slacks and she in a German dirndl dress, they appeared comfortably secure in each other's affections. But as with all the Lorre marriages, by the time husband and wife said their vows, the blossom of romance had withered.

Karen often turned up alone at the Brechts'. "Be nice to her," Helene Weigel entreated Rhoda Riker. Beneath the cover girl confidence, she said, Karen is "a poor, forlorn, lost soul. Everybody thinks she's sitting on the top of the heap in Hollywood, but she isn't. She's absolutely miserable. Take her with you and let her go someplace where the pressure isn't on her." As a result, said Riker, "Karen used to be with us fairly often."

Their age difference separated Peter and Karen in more ways than just years. He held old-world expectations of marriage. In Karen he found "a clean, sweet, innocent girl . . . with no nasty habits of any kind." By relegating her to the role of hostess and hausfrau, he planned to keep her that way. According to friends and relatives, he opposed her acting career. Riker, who lent Karen a sympathetic ear during the early years of the marriage, claimed he actively destroyed it: "He resented her directors—and anybody who looked at her—and would suggest that they were trying to get her into bed. Everything they did was wrong. He killed her whole Hollywood career out of pure and simple jealousy. Oh, he was vile about it." He not only kept Karen away from the movies; he kept the movies away from Karen. He forbade shop talk at home and refused to allow her to see his films.

Karen wanted a modern marriage. She took her career seriously and expected to continue acting. "If you are a Bechstein," she told Riker, "and nothing has happened in your life except that damn piano, you want something else to come along to make your name important." Karen got Hollywood, or at least that part of the star system, like Bogart and Bacall, who found their ranch home a welcome haven. However, she felt boring and unglamorous by Hollywood standards. By those of the émigré community, she knew she was nothing more than a pretty piece of fluff.

Karen's self-esteem fared no better out of the public eye. Peter put her in charge of Bum, their St. Bernard. "The dog gave her a terrible feeling of inferiority," said Riker. "She used to come in and say, 'I can't believe this. This goddam dog is dropping two pounds wherever it happens to be. What am I going to do?'"

While bragging about his gorgeous home out of one side of his mouth, Peter chastised Karen out of the other for not performing her household duties suitably. "Cleaning shit is not something I can handle very well," she heatedly replied.

According to Riker, "Peter tried to build her up, but he didn't know how deep her feelings of inadequacy were. 'Peter, you're a beast,'" she remembered hearing Helene Weigel scold him. "'You don't understand what's happening to this girl.' 'But I'm trying,' said Peter. 'I do care about her.'"

If she could not have a career, Karen wanted a normal home life. Pushing a pram better suited her conventional upbringing than dragging around a St. Bernard. "I was hanging from the chandelier in order to have a baby, and it didn't work," Karen told her sister Barbara. "They wanted to have a baby very badly," said Barbara, "but obviously they were not able to. Karen said she tried every gynecologist in the United States and nothing helped." Unable to conceive, Peter and Karen sought to gain custody of Alastair. When Arthur Young blocked their efforts, the Lorres at least wanted to contribute financially. "As soon as Peter starts his next picture [Casbah]," Karen wrote a friend in June 1947, "(which should be in a month or so) we will have a certain amount sent every week or month . . . for Alastair's support."[15]

She added that she did not want to put him up for adoption "unless I could be convinced that it would be essential and important enough for his well being. If I make up financially for his education etc. I think it would only be right to let him decide, when he is old enough to do so, what he wants to do, where he wants to live, if he wants to be with me at all."

Isolated from Lorre and his contemporaries—German as well as American—by a generation gap, Karen spent long hours alone while Peter played poker at Bogart or Negulesco's house. If she dared turn up to retrieve him, he became snappish and demanded to know why she was there—for good reason. According to Negulesco, Lorre used these occasions to repair to the upper rooms of his house with female guests. Tales of his physical prowess soon got around. If Karen, who friends claim never made an issue of Peter's philandering because she had not kept faith with him, turned a blind eye to his infidelity, J. Edgar Hoover did not. An FBI letter of July 29, 1946, lists Lorre, along with orchestra leader Freddy Martin, actor John Garfield, and as many as seven others whose names are blacked out, as "customers" of "former part-time movie actresses . . . considered high class prostitutes." In New York, publicist Gary Stevens had arranged liaisons for the visiting actor, who complained of needing the companionship to get to sleep.

Karen blamed herself for the cracks in the surface of their seemingly perfect marriage. "She always felt she was responsible," said Riker. "She felt strongly that she wasn't adequate to the whole situation." By now, Karen's pattern of self-reproach stretched back to childhood. "Her biggest guilt about her past," claimed Riker, "was that she was a Bechstein-Klinckerfuss." She had spilled the ashes of a deceased relative years earlier in Germany. Later, she had given up Alastair, whom she would never see again. Now, she labored under the additional burden of a failed marriage.

Karen envied Peter's friendship with Celia, especially their ability to communicate, and regretted that "she couldn't be the same to him as someone who had shared all those experiences. No matter who came and went in his life, that was the primary relationship." What Peter and Karen would not get from each other, they sought elsewhere. Away from Peter and among her nonindustry friends, Karen breathed easier. At home, she dulled the distance that had crept into their marriage with alcohol, amplifying the highs and lows of a life gone to extremes. "With my sister," said Barbara, "it was always being wonderful, way up high. Nothing could go wrong. Everything was beautiful, then the next day right down way below in the dumps."

She didn't blame her father, who had suffered from alcoholism, for genetically predisposing her to the disease. Instead, Karen faulted Peter, who returned the favor. "I think both were very bitter about the other person," said her sister, "because they felt the other party was the one who drove them to their afflictions. They never saw themselves as the guilty person." A history of depression, feelings of guilt for having abandoned Alastair in England, and her failure to give Peter a son weighed heavily toward lasting escape. Late in the marriage, Karen made the first of several unsuccessful suicide attempts.[16]

After stopping over in Zurich, Brecht returned to East Berlin, where he began rebuilding his theater ensemble in late 1948. "Brecht was saying, 'we must get Lorre, he'd be perfect,'" recalled Eric Bentley. "They put it to him that while they couldn't offer money in the American sense, it would be a life because he would have the roles and be part of something. I wasn't clear to what extent he thought the political part of that proposition would appeal to Lorre. 'Part of something' to Brecht meant they were building socialism in East Germany and he might like to help. I don't know if Peter Lorre wanted that or would agree with that."

Repeated overtures from Brecht to return to Germany confirmed the actor's place of importance in the "new order." In addition to *Der Mantel, The Great Clown Emaël,* and the perennial *Schweyk,* Brecht's plans for Lorre included new productions of *Dreigroschenoper, Mann ist Mann,* and even a four-hour stage version of *Faust* for the "Goethe Year" in 1949. According to a journal entry of April 12, 1948, he also had the actor in mind for the part of the simple companion—to either Hans Albers or Ernst Busch—in *Eulenspiel,* a film story for Deutsche Film Aktiengesellschaft (DEFA) that updated the medieval rogue to a socially minded Robin Hood who mobilizes oppressed peasants. "Brecht would have very much wanted him to play Azdak in *The Caucasian Chalk Circle,*" added Bentley. "That's a Lorre role, he would say." He even thought of him as Galileo: "Peter Lorre was much interested in that play and that role and talked as one who might easily have been playing it. I think that as far as Brecht was concerned he'd be very welcome to it."

In addition to his own projects, Brecht talked with Wolfgang Langhoff about adding a studio theater to Deutsches Theater and getting "first class actors out of the emigration in short guest appearances," including Therese Giehse, Leonard Steckel, Peter Lorre, Curt Bois, and Käthe Gold.

To Brecht, the choice between something in Germany and nothing in Hollywood was an easy one. For Lorre, it was not that simple. His debt to Brecht and the guilt of having failed him, and thereby himself, had set up a collision between the private and public Peter Lorres, the one anxious to be won back, the other weak and indecisive. Brecht had banked on turning Lorre's struggle as an insider who wanted out—and as an outsider who wanted in—into a hard lesson about the need to submerge the actor's movie-made persona and restore his personal identity. Others of Lorre's friends knew that Brecht drew on a closed account. Speculating on Lorre's attachment to the status quo, Dr. Ralph Greenson observed, "I think it was not the capitalism that attracted Peter or Hollywood glamour, but that capitalism made it easier for him to gratify his periodic addictive needs."

When Paul E. Marcus dropped by Brecht's office at the Berliner Ensemble in the early 1950s, the playwright encouraged him to persuade Lorre to come to East Berlin: "As middle man between Lorre and Brecht, I appeared rather peculiar to myself, because I knew Lorre wouldn't give up his Hollywood chance.... Would he have acted differently had he known that his best times were over?"

In December 1948 Eddie Brandt heard an agent from Music Corporation of America (MCA), which block-booked its own clients onto Spike Jones's *Spotlight Revue,* tell the bandleader that he could "get Lorre cheap" because the actor desperately needed money. "Lorre was so broke," said Brandt, "he got him for $350, plus hotel and transportation."

Lorre had once told Burl Ives that "when it comes time to move under a bridge, we'll do that. But until then, we're going first class." That time came sooner than he imagined. In 1949 it all came crashing down—his management partnership, his shaky financial situation, and his dream of professional independence. Lorre was bankrupt.

During the making of *Voyage to the Bottom of the Sea* (1961), Lorre gave co-worker Barbara Eden some good business advice that was based on his own experience: "Whatever you do . . . don't let anyone else sign your checks." He told her that, in a word, Sam Stiefel had robbed him. Recognizing his own profligacy, Lorre had given Stiefel power of attorney and arranged to receive a living allowance, with his remaining earnings kept out of reach. "He wanted to be treated like a child in other words," Morton Wurtele heard Brecht tell it, "and restricted from having all this money, which he would have squandered." At the time, "Peter considered him his best friend, the one person on earth with whom he would trust his wife, his child, his life," said Eden. Later, "he blamed himself for being lazy. He said he just didn't want to pay attention to that type of business. He wanted to act and consequently was deeply disappointed and left with nothing, absolutely not a penny."

The William Morris Agency recommended a young attorney named Robert Shutan, who became one of the actor's closest friends, to handle his legal affairs. Besides owing more than $16,000 in back state and federal income taxes for 1945–47 and 1949, Lorre had left a string of unpaid bills from coast to coast. In October of 1947, the Division of Labor Law Enforcement had ordered him to appear before the Labor Commission to answer a complaint filed by Elisabeth Hauptmann, who claimed he owed her $1,202.28 in back pay. In early May 1949, Lovsky won a judgment against Lorre for $9,675 for delinquent support and maintenance, although she kindly dropped the matter of an additional $4,962 that had been orally agreed upon. In addition, she agreed to reduce her alimony from $200 per week to a flat $450 per month, beginning May 15, 1949.

To exempt his earnings from seizure, Lorre took Jonas Silverstone's advice to declare bankruptcy before kicking off a ten-week tour of Stoll Theatres in England. Lorre and Shutan sat down over a card table and listed his assets and liabilities. On May 20, the actor filed a voluntary bankruptcy petition in federal court. Informed that Lorre required an additional ten days to prepare A and B schedules, the U.S. District Court gave him until May 31 to file; the deadline was extended to June 10 and again to June 20. Auditors valued his household goods, including clothes, at $5,000, his filly and two geldings at $600. Peter and Karen's bank account held only $10.21. To more than 120 creditors, he owed $56,561.08 for services (doctors, hospitals, hotels, laundry, steam room, beauty salon, restaurants, airlines), merchandise (dog food, clothes, books), and dues (Beverly Hills Tennis Club, Screen Actors Guild,

American Federation of Radio Artists).[17] On June 15 the District Court gave notice that the first meeting of creditors, who had six months to file their claims, was scheduled for June 27 at the Federal Building in Los Angeles. On August 18 the District Court discharged Lorre from all debts. By then, Peter and Karen had left for London.

8

SMOKE GETS IN YOUR EYES

The fiftieth year means a turning point; disturbed, one looks
back to see how much of the way has already been covered
and silently asks oneself whether it leads further upward.

—Stefan Zweig

I attempted it once as a comedian and then as a clown,
but in vain; I was typecast as a villain.

—Peter Lorre

Peter Lorre's approach was always soft and silent. He left the United States, and his life in Hollywood, just as quietly. Dissembling about his sudden departure, he said, "I removed myself from the limelight to give picturegoers a rest. They deserve it. I must be a terrifying experience on occasions!" Braced by the lapse of time, he later glossed over the hiatus as a deliberate decision to say no to money and popularity and to take the gamble afresh. The grim present lived harder than the reconstructed past. Tired of "making faces," he cut himself adrift and floated into another kind of exile.

On June 29, 1949, Peter and Karen flew to England, where audiences from the Grand in Derby to the Empire in Shepherd's Bush hailed his arrival with "rapturous acclamation." "The Brits were dying to see him," confirmed comic actor Johnny Lockwood, who was the first to introduce Lorre to a live English audience. "I gave him an enormous build up and he came onto the stage to a big ovation." Lorre opened with what Lockwood called familiar patter about corpses and body counts, then moved into stand-up suitable to the occasion: "Like all tourists, I stopped off in Chicago and visited the abattoirs. All that machinery wasted on humans." The next moment a girl rushed on stage shouting, "Peter! Peter!" Lorre took a revolver from his pocket and shot her. Two stagehands then placed her body on a stretcher and took her off. "Poor girl," lamented Lorre. "She just got carried away." More patter followed, then Lorre performed Poe, alternating "The Tell-Tale Heart" and "The Bells." Lockwood recalled that he "used to tell people that he went better as he came on to my introduction than he did at the end of his act. I don't think he realised how funny he was."

Between appearances in Hackney and Bristol, Lorre reprised the role of "The Man with the Head of Glass" for the British Broadcasting Corporation on August 27—but not before the station warned television viewers that "Mr. Lorre will be seen contorting his face in close-up and we fear that children watching the performance in a darkened room would find it too alarming. We are purposely putting him on at the end so that children may see the remainder of the show before they go to bed."

The Grand Order of Water Rats issued no such caveat when it inducted Lorre into the oldest theatrical fraternity in the world the following day. Having developed a close friendship with the actor, and feeling that he would fit the requirements (two years' experience as a professional entertainer; no objections from any other Rat; fund-raising activities for charity), Lockwood proposed Lorre for membership in the elite charitable organization. Former King Rat and comedian George Jackley seconded the motion. During his initiation, a ritual filled with solemnity, tears streamed down Lorre's face. He recovered in time to deliver an acceptance speech in which he jokingly asked that no one spread word of his reaction because it would "ruin his image."

Soon after, Rat Number 501 joined a pack of his Brothers on a river outing down the Thames. Anyone who wished to do so was encouraged to give a little impromptu performance. Using his cigarette lighter as a gun, Lorre stood down the gangway so that only his head and shoulders were visible and surrendered to audience expectations. His popularity among his Brother Rats earned him a place in the Grand Order's photo gallery, alongside pictures of other famous film stars, including Charlie Chaplin, Stan Laurel and Oliver Hardy, Danny Kaye, Maurice Chevalier, Adolphe Menjou, Ben Lyon, and Vic Oliver.

During the first week of September, with the theater tour near its end, Karen flew to Germany to attend her ailing mother in Eggelkofen, putting off plans—indefinitely, as it turned out—to travel to Devonshire to see Alastair, who had been removed to the country during the London air raids. She had not seen her son since 1940, when she had entrusted him to the care of a nanny. From southern Bavaria, she continued on to the resort town of Garmisch-Partenkirchen to visit her sister Barbara and to make arrangements for Peter to rest and relax at "a clinically let sanitarium for inner and nerve sickness and those who need to recuperate, with special departments for stomach, intestinal and metabolic diseases." Founded in 1905 by Dr. Florenz Wigger, the health resort functioned as a popular retreat for overworked celebrities. Although the medical staff declined to treat mental illness and contagious diseases, especially tuberculosis, it catered to every other whim, real and hypochondriacal. For a price, it coordinated causes and cures (including morphine and cocaine addiction, "under certain conditions"), monitored meals, and designed exercise regimens to fatten the fleshless and slenderize the stout. Scenically nestled in the Bavarian Alps, with a view of the Wetterstein's *Zugspitze* (Train Peak), Wigger's Kurheim boasted both shelter and sunny exposure. Air and sun baths in the therapeutic climate, it advertised, increased the appetite, toned the muscles, circulated the blood, strengthened the nerves, and improved the outlook. The facility offered the most up-to-date diagnostic equipment and treatment, from radium to hydro-mechanical therapy. Although it made available no-frills single rooms at negotiable rates, accommodations tended toward the deluxe. Ballrooms, billiards, health bars, south-facing verandas, heated walkways, and shady parks indulged a high-paying clientele. Only two hours by train from Munich, Wigger's delivered an elevated but accessible escape from the city.

"She was very excited at that time," said Karen's sister Barbara, "that possibly the marriage would not go down the drain completely, if he could stay off morphine." Lorre's track record also put the Federal Bureau of Narcotics in a subjunctive frame of mind. Six weeks after his discharge in 1947, the district supervisor in Los Angeles had charged authorities on the East Coast to closely monitor the actor's activities when he was in New York. Good to their word, narcotics agents showed up at Manhattan's Warwick Hotel four days before Lorre was scheduled to leave the country. He told them he hadn't taken any drugs since his treatment. However, after learning that he planned to travel abroad, they returned two days later and collected a urine specimen for analysis at the U.S. Public Health Service Hospital in Lexington, Kentucky. At the meeting, Lorre asked whether he was allowed to take anything for his sinus condition, which still bothered him. The agents gave him permission to use Emperin with codeine.

When Karen picked up Peter in Munich on September 20, she knew that he had relapsed. What she intended as a respite became yet another cure. In an interview for *Der Spiegel,* September 27, 1950, Lorre said he had checked in under the name of Conrad for treatment of an acute sinus infection, a condition that presumably fed rumors in the German press that he had come to Garmisch for a head operation. (Nonetheless, pointed out the anonymous interviewer, he smoked one cigarette after another and drank his fill of strong coffee.) *Der Neue Film* also circulated news that Lorre had picked up jaundice while visiting American military hospitals in Germany.[1] Both reports contained elements of truth. During the nearly one year Lorre spent at Wigger's, he underwent both old and new treatments for addiction. Starting off conservatively, doctors first tried to wean him off morphine and then resorted to substitutes, including candy, which only served to add a few extra pounds to his slim frame. He was also treated with *Dämmerschlaf,* a drug-induced, hypnotic half-sleep intended to reduce the urge for narcotic drugs. The therapy, reported Barbara, rendered him helpless, unable to shave or even walk. He also suffered through a round of near-fatal electric shock treatments. During one of the sessions, his heart stopped. "We were sitting in the lounge," recalled Barbara, "and they said Karen should come immediately upstairs because Peter was on the edge of going." Nothing seemed to work, and Lorre later told Mort Briskin that during treatment the doctors wouldn't allow him out of the sanitarium without two attendants.[2]

Before leaving London, the actor had arranged to return to England in mid-October to appear in Associated British-Pathé's *Double Confession* (1950), a rambling mystery starring Derek Farr and directed by Ken Annakin. Producer Harry Reynolds needed a menace for his picture as well as a name to bolster the screen credits. With Lorre, he got both. Paynter (Lorre) begs to kill almost everyone in the cast, insinuates that the hero is not nice, and curses the rest as "kreeps." Occasionally, as a bit of intentional absurdity, he feigns innocence: "Look, sir, in this part of the world, we don't go around murdering people. Sometimes I wish I could." At one point, Paynter awakens from a drunken stupor, only to lapse into lethargy after a sharp guttural eruption, followed by an unprovoked rage fraught with facial contortions and vicious snarls.

The assignment asked nothing new of the actor. Engaged to lend the film what some by now coined "the Peter Lorre stamp," he savagely turned on his screen notoriety. Annakin got more than he had bargained for from the frustrated actor, who went over the top, crowding everyone else off the screen:

Peter Lorre taught me a big heap of lessons as a young director. . . . He was a great screen actor with that inborn gift of making himself stick out on screen—and instinctively and through lots of experience he did everything else to make sure his performance would stick out. . . . I was fascinated by his personality and what one could create on the screen if one allowed him to improvise, but in *Double Confession* he was playing the part of a "henchman" to a British heavy called Billy Hartnell, [who] was a very capable good tough actor but completely old time mechanical. He couldn't understand what I was doing with Peter; was afraid of him; and finished up getting quite hysterical and shouting, "If that bastard so much as touches me again, I'll kill him!!" He was afraid of Lorre (as a scene stealer) and he had every right to be, because that is exactly what he did . . . what I allowed him to do . . . with the result that he ruined my picture! It was all out of balance with the second in command bossing the boss and making nonsense of the story. And all because I admired Lorre so much and was captivated by him.

The studio's publicity department concocted a 150-word Star Story for newspapers desperate for film filler. In a piece titled "Lorre Is So Loathsome," Hartnell is quoted as saying: "Gives me the creeps, he does. Rolls his eyes and purrs like a Cheshire cat at a chap, slips a knife into him, then goes home to cry his eyes out. . . . He's a monster, not a man. . . . Take him away! I can't stand him."

"Oh yes, he wears his bow ties, and his nice smart suits—but he's crude," Lorre reportedly replied in "Hartnell Is Too Harsh." "Now he says these awful things. . . . Me—always so gentle, so understanding, so friendly. . . . Perhaps we can find a quiet corner where I can talk to him, reason with him. . . . It all makes me feel so weary, and so sad, so sad."

A publicist stirred the pot—"Sounds like trouble brewing between Elstree and Hollywood's favourite screen menaces"—and then assured viewers that "in real life Peter Lorre and William Hartnell are quite good friends, and mutual admirers."

Lorre was back in Wigger's Kurheim by mid-December. He now slipped in and out as it suited him. "It was the type of sanatorium where all the patients were not closely guarded," said Barbara. "Karen, for example, used it more like a convenient hotel." Lorre likely stayed on, not because he could afford to do so, but because he could not face the final reckoning. Karen confided to Barbara that the sanitarium never received "a penny" from the impoverished couple. "I know she borrowed from a good friend of mine in Munich," said Barbara, "and never paid it back. I felt so bad about it, but she was so charming and could talk anybody into loaning her money."

By now, Peter and Karen's marriage was as empty as their pocketbook. Barbara characterized it as "a cool, correct relationship. I couldn't see any love between them or anything." Unbeknownst to Peter, Karen, who kept a single, cheaper room on an upper floor for nearly nine months, briefly carried on an affair with a young physician there.

The marriage over, Karen left Wigger's to look up the Bechstein clan in Brauback. Soon after she checked out, Peter telephoned Barbara and asked her to stop by. "He just wanted to let me know that if he would be walking over a bridge following Karen," related Barbara, "and that if she would jump off that bridge, he wouldn't even bother trying to keep her from committing suicide. That was all he wanted and then he excused himself. He was an odd man, but very interesting, very highly intelligent."

In an undated letter meant "for your eyes only" (which he asked her to tear up), Lorre reluctantly told Elisabeth Hauptmann of their breakup: "The parting itself should have been done a long time ago and it's o.k. with me." He added that "this kind of separation makes me vomit," and admitted that an earlier attempt to end the marriage had failed. "The cast in this dusty Strindberg drama is so nauseating, as though I were to play a waiter." Peter blamed Karen's bulldozer mentality for risking his already precarious health. Although she had stopped drinking, said Lorre, she had lost herself in illusion, becoming increasingly vulgar and impulsive.

More pressing than news of the split-up itself, however, was word of Karen's planned visit to East Berlin to look for work before returning to America on his "last dollars." Lorre opposed the plan, which he dismissed as a lame excuse to tell her side of the story to the Brecht circle. He apologized for bothering Hauptmann with his personal life, but he would not suffer Karen damaging his friendship with Brecht. Writing such a letter, Lorre confessed, cost him "an enormous effort."

During his stay at Wigger's, Lorre toured Displaced Person (DP) camps, tent city centers for the homeless, service installations, and American military hospitals. He even took Karen and Barbara shopping and joined Jeanette McDonald and her entourage at the Spanish-style Casa Carioca, a nightclub built in 1945 by General George S. Patton's Third Army engineers for the troops visiting the Third Army Rest Center. Asked by reporters if he missed his California ranch lifestyle, Lorre confessed that he pined for his horses and dogs but did not miss the people. The slap in Hollywood's face did not go unnoticed, even in Germany, where he actually touched as many American lives as he had at home.

The actor had begun visiting veterans' facilities during the war. In October 1948 the *Hollywood Reporter* credited Lorre, just back from a tour of hospitals in northern California and the Pacific Northwest, with having been the first actor to enlist in the Hollywood Coordinating Committee's current program of celebrity visits to veterans' hospitals.[3] He also had made a point of visiting military medical centers wherever he performed on "house" circuits. "During the war it was horrible," Lorre told an interviewer in 1949, "horrible because you felt a face-maker from Hollywood was so useless. Now it is different. Now you want to let them know they are not forgotten. I visit all the hospitals, all the wards, mental, tubercular, even the locked-in wards. Perhaps it does some good. I don't know. I just know how good it makes me feel when I can get a sick man to smile. This is important." The press seldom got wind of his stop-offs. He preferred it that way. Believing that "we who are in the public eye through the medium of film can spread some cheer among these unfortunates," he continued to tour military hospitals overseas. The patients he visited certainly did not imagine anyone as notorious as the movies made believe. ("They tell me good villains are hard to find," kidded Lorre. "I just hope that all the people who saw how nice I was on my personal appearances believe I can be the rat the script demands.") Neither did they expect an actor utterly divorced from his own celebrity: "I would find it very distasteful to have a face-maker from Hollywood shaking hands with me." Lorre arrived not to put on an act ("I don't sing or dance, you know"), but to interact one-on-one. "In the United States," he told *Der Spiegel*, "there are 150 of the most modern, military hospitals for the war wounded, with all the amenities. But without the essential, what the human being needs, contact with the outside world. This is supposed to be done by actors. . . . Can you imagine how much that helps! And that's why I'm also in Germany." Lorre sat at bedsides and stood by wheelchairs. He shook and held hands, asked about Mama, and heard about wounds. He smiled a smile never seen on-screen. "Such visits," he said, "are very heart-rending, but also very soul-satisfying. Here you see courage and faith as nowhere else, and one comes from these visits a very humble man."

"Lorre has returned to us as an almost totally forgotten one," commented the *Münchner Merkur* on the actor's anonymity in postwar Germany. Losing himself served a greater end. He was not here to make a film, he told the press, but to visit old friends and to perform the "psychological task" of treating the victims of a war that had reduced Germany to "a land of ruins peopled by ghosts, without government, order or purpose, without industry, communications or the proper means of existence." More than 20 million Germans were homeless or without adequate shelter. By November 1948 the number of German expellees from surrounding countries residing in the Western zones had risen to 12 million, while the International Refugee Organization still worked to resettle 1.5 million Jews, Poles, Hungarians, Bulgarians, Rumanians, and Balts.

The efflorescence of Weimar—George Grosz's inflammatory cartoons, *The Threepenny Opera*, the New Objectivity—seemed tragically surreal against the "great wilderness of debris" that had been Berlin. It now presented a radically different but nonetheless "sordid caricature of humanity." Gray and yellow faces drifted through their daily existence in a kind of demoralized delirium. More than fifty thousand orphaned children lived "like wild animals in holes in the ground, some of them one-eyed or one-legged veterans of seven or so." Defeat exacted its "godless destruction" on young and old alike in the form of shortages. Two years after the war, the daily food ration had not risen much above one thousand calories, what the House of Commons Select Committee on Estimates characterized as "slow starvation." Eating meant standing in long queues for hours and even days for a loaf of bread, an onion, or a potato. Only with *Lebensmittelkarte* (food rationing cards)—also known as "Death Cards"—could one obtain a basic weekly ration of meat (50 grams), fat (10 grams), and milk (one-half liter). Raw sewage contaminated culinary water, spreading typhoid fever, diphtheria, and dysentery. As the health of the German populace collapsed, public morality sank to new depths. Want bred despair, bitterness, and cynicism. Prostitution flourished, and with it gonorrhea and syphilis. Nicotine became the drug of choice and cigarettes the basic unit of exchange on a booming black market. Berlin experienced a crime wave of murders, rapes, and robberies. The cohesive, almost benign underworld in *M* had turned willfully malignant. Fed by a "nightmare of uncertainty" about the future, bewildered youths felt a "nihilistic contempt" for government, order, and human values.

Beneath Lorre's desire to touch the lives of the war-wounded lay the unconscious need to connect with the past, to draw from it what Hollywood had denied him—a pivotal role in an artistic film. In March 1949 the *Baltimore Sun*'s Don Kirkley had posed a hypothetical question:

> What would you say if we were a producer who wanted to do a picture, regardless of box-office value, and regardless of the current taboos and censorship rules, and if we gave you a free choice of subject and character? What story and role would you choose?
>
> Mr. Lorre named a novel by a celebrated European writer, the name of which he asked us not to divulge, because he is actually negotiating for the screen rights. The role he chose was that of a "lust murderer."

This, he believes, would be box-office, according to current fancies of the audience, and at the same time, a work of art.

At Wigger's, Lorre met screenwriter Benno Vigny, who, according to publicist Hellmut Schlien, suggested "a psychological study" based on a motif by Guy de Maupassant; "this man revenges himself of the betrayal by his fiancée and later is reminded of this experience by all the women he meets." It's hard to say what de Maupassant theme informed *Das Untier* (*The Monster*). The author's hallmarks—obsession, cuckoldry, madness, isolation, loneliness, insanity, guilt, degeneration—all found their way into its text. According to a note in the earliest extant version of the screenplay, it was "The Horla," which Lorre had performed on radio, that gave psychological—and literary—shape to Vigny's short story. Like Hans Beckert, de Maupassant's victim of an "unknown force" that "pursued, possessed, governed" led "without knowing it, that double, mysterious life which makes us doubt whether there are not two beings in us." From 1931 on, Lorre too had signed his name on two lines, forever dividing into doubles that committed acts "outside himself." "The original idea of the film was the problem of a human being discovering within himself that he takes pleasure in killing," remembered editor and assistant Carl Otto Bartning, "and through this has a monstrous compulsion to kill."

Before *Das Untier* had taken its first awkward steps, Lorre's old friend Egon Jacobson—who had changed his name to Jameson after emigrating to England in 1934—turned up at Wigger's. He carried a clipping from the "News of the Day" section of a daily paper, which read: "In refugee camp E.-D. forty-three-year-old Doctor Carl N. threw himself in front of a train. His medical assistant, the former chemist Hannes N. from Kattowitz, was found fatally wounded in the stomach. According to the police, both lived with forged documents in the camp." No motive was suggested for the deaths, and the case remained unsolved after passing through German, British, and American hands.

When the newspaper published the report, it drew no comment. In the "still burning and bleeding Europe," no one cared "that one of the tortured humans lost his nerve and put a cruel end to his existence out of seeming hopelessness." Such things happened every day. The obscure notice concerned Jameson, who thought it "pointed to a danger for our future lives." Working then for Deutsche allgemeine Nachrichtenagentur, the journalist sought answers to the mystery shrouded in forged documents and dark existences. At the refugee camp Elbe-Düwenstedt, Jameson turned up a newspaper photograph of the doctor during his involvement as an expert witness in a poison murder case. The journalist circulated the picture, to no avail. He finally broke the case on assignment in Stockholm, where he uncovered a source that identified the man in the picture. Carl N. was actually Dr. Carl Rothe of Hamburg. Lorre listened intently to the tragic story. Suddenly, he interrupted the quiet that had crept into the conversation: "This will be my new film."

Actually, Lorre already had a film, but this new angle served other needs. The press reported that he had returned to Germany to, in effect, remake *M* and reclaim his international stature. Lorre denied it. "Movies that are classics or prove themselves to be hits of the time," he later pointed out, "one should under no circumstances allow to come about again." Any broad similarities between the actual tragedies were coincidental and incidental to his grand design of interfusing documentary sobriety and artistic symbolism. "I had promised myself never again to produce a film like *M* or a sex murder," explained Lorre, "and until this time I have been able to be true to this course. Just recently I changed my mind because of this remarkable eyewitness report from Egon about a figure that touched me so strongly that I wanted to make this film." Besides diffusing criticism for repeating himself, Egon's story idea furthered the greater purpose of helping Germany overcome its recent past. "If my film helps to lighten the conscience of only a single man," stated Lorre, "then it will not be made for nothing."

Having turned his room at Wigger's into an office where he held consultations and took telephone calls, Lorre got down to the business of making his dream a reality. He first called on an old friend. Born in Pozsony, Hungary (Slovak: Bratislava), in 1885, Arnold Pressburger had abandoned a singing and acting career in Vienna and cofounded Verleihfirma Philipp und Pressburger, a film distribution company, in 1909. Four years later, he moved into production, specializing in multilingual versions, an expertise central to Lorre's plans for bilingual translations of his new movie. In 1932 he established Cine-Allianz under the corporate umbrella of UFA. With the rise of Hitler, Pressburger left Germany for England to work with Alexander Korda and then emigrated to New York in 1939 and finally to Hollywood, where he produced Fritz Lang's *Hangmen Also Die* (1943). In Hollywood Pressburger founded Arnold Productions, from which Lorre had received an offer in April 1945 to star in a film tentatively titled *Vidocq*. Based on the memoirs of François Eugène Vidocq, *A Scandal in Paris* (1945), as it was subsequently called, traces the life of a crook who becomes the head of the French Sûretè. Warner Bros. exercised its contractual rights and rushed Lorre into *The Verdict* (1946), aborting what promised to be an interesting role, ultimately played by George Sanders. It would appear that Pressburger cast Lorre over the objections of the director, Douglas Sirk, who later commented that "Lorre was a good actor. He could have been a very good Richard III on the stage. But he couldn't do just anything. For example, he couldn't have done the Vidocq part." The "risk-happy" producer did not give up on the idea of putting Lorre in one of his films and even recruiting him as a director.

Pressburger, now an American citizen, returned to Germany in January 1950 to explore new film possibilities abroad. Though he failed to get his foot in the door, the producer did win reimbursement from the German government for the confiscation of Cine-Allianz by the Nazis. "Desperate to make a film," said Arnold's son, Fred, "Peter wanted my father to arrange it. It was purely a kindness on his part, because he esteemed Peter as an actor."

What Lorre wanted was another *M*, a classic film that would put him back at the top of his profession. Eager to trade grease paint for a director's chair, he imagined making a film, free of conditions and restraints, from beginning to end. The actor-director held on to an old dream of creating "a production team that sticks together and can go anywhere and do anything to make a film or a play" without "the responsibility to a company and the weight of departmental overheads." *Der Spiegel* reported that "in making frequent trips to Munich and Hamburg, he keeps his finger on the German film pulse." Lorre thought it "weak" and recommended fewer and better films. He believed that only such a team could bring about "a truly good and remarkable film." Looking ahead, he envisioned German- and English-language versions and projected a new spirit of German-American filmmaking cooperation, which, he explained, had the obvious advantages of artistic freedom, economic savings, and an expanded market. Fast developing a producer's sensibilities, he also emphasized the need to export movies.

Pressburger cobbled together a shaky financial partnership with Hamburg connections. Sugar magnate Julius de Crignis's Hamburger Filmfinanzierungs-GmbH (Fifi) supplied the bulk of the backing, with producer Friedrich Mainz and Pressburger picking up the balance.[4] Director of the Tobis Film Company from 1929 to 1937, Mainz had established himself as an independent in 1946, producing more than two hundred films by 1950. That same year he established his Hamburg-based FAMA (Friedrich A. Mainz-Film GmbH), which provided the organizational infrastructure of a parent company. For studio facilities, Pressburger turned to Junge Film Union in Bendesdorf. The newly formed National Film GmbH, also under the de Crignis banner, would distribute the film.

In July Lorre updated the press on his progress, noting his collaboration with Benno Vigny on an untitled script. If the coauthors were at a loss for words, the distributor was not. Anxious to begin publicizing the picture, National needed a name and slapped *Bestie Mensch* (*The Human Beast*) on the planned production. Lorre too had gotten well ahead of himself with expectations that shooting would begin in September. Not until August 15 did Pressburger actually sign Vigny for thirty thousand deutsche marks to write a screenplay based on his original short story. For another three thousand, he agreed to give up rights to novelization, but he was allowed to use his original story with the title "Das Untier" without reference to the Lorre film.

What National had temporarily titled *Bestie Mensch* was now *Das Untier*. Lorre was at it again, implied the *Hamburger Echo,* which claimed he "is going to kill three women this time." Although "Lorre wanted to escape his American fate," remembered friend and screenwriter Axel Eggebrecht, "he consciously connected with *M;* that cannot be disputed." C.O. Bartning agreed that "it was completely clear that he had taken up with *M*. Consciously, I don't know. He probably would have denied it."

In an interview given several days after the premiere of the picture, Lorre said "it was just common sense to take the line I have become known for in the United States. As you can see, 'The Lost One' [*Der Verlorene,* the film's final title] is a man who glides into murder. But I certainly did not want to repeat myself. So we set the story of my psychopathic hero against the background of Hitler Germany."

Continuing his thought for the Italian periodical *Cinema* the following week, he explained that the "Germany of the 1930s and that of Hitler during World War II is the same Germany. You can change without a break from one to the other. Without the murderer of Düsseldorf, the murderer of Hamburg would be unthinkable. Both represent in different form one and the same evil. The fifteen-twenty years in between are unimportant. One might have expected more explanation from Mr. Lang and his ex-wife (Thea von Harbou) about the meaning of *M*."

Catharine Lorre believed that her father "was afraid of breaking away from something in which he had been secured for so long, had made his living through and was known for." Lorre, however, balked at the suggestion he was suffering an identity crisis. "I do not object to being typed, as the saying is," he had generalized a year earlier, "so long as the role permits a certain amount of creative effort."

Invited to appear at Hamburg's newly established Amerika-Haus, the first of seven Department of State–sponsored cultural and information centers charged with explaining America to the German people, Lorre arrived in town on August 9.[5] The next evening, Egon Jameson introduced the actor to a packed house. Accompanied by Dr. Gerth at the piano, he recited "The Tell-Tale Heart" to a receptive German and American audience. According to a local reporter, those who met him for the first time found Lorre "radiantly fascinating." Nonetheless, his unadvertised appearance drew only a postscript in the *Hamburger Abendblatt*, which took more interest in Orson Welles, whose traveling show, *An Evening with Orson Welles*, played Frankfurt, Munich, and Hamburg—overlapping Lorre's appearance—before moving on to Cologne, Düsseldorf, Bad Oeynhausen, and Berlin.

Meanwhile, preparations to begin shooting ground forward. In mid-September, Mainz signed an agreement with Rolf Meyer of Junge Film Union spelling out the terms for the use of its studio. The Lorre production team guaranteed thirty days of work, at a daily rate of eighteen hundred deutsche marks. Meyer would be paid in four installments.

Several weeks later, Brecht, Ruth Berlau, director Jacob Geis, and writer Emil Burri dropped in on Lorre, whom they had expected to possibly show up in March. Although jaundiced, he was "as fresh as ever," said Brecht in a letter to Elisabeth Hauptmann, and very much impressed Burri and Geis. In January, apparently unaware that Lorre had returned to Germany, Brecht had couched an appeal in the form of a poem, "An den Schauspieler P.L. im Exil" ("To the Actor P.L. in Exile"):

> Listen, we are calling you back. Driven out
> You must now return. The country
> Out of which you were driven flowed once
> With milk and honey. You are being called back
> To a country that has been destroyed.
> And we have nothing more
> To offer you than the fact that you are needed.
>
> Poor or rich
> Sick or healthy
> Forget everything
> And come.

Already, Lorre's poor health had disappointed Brecht's hopes of starring him in a performance of *Herr Puntila und sein Knecht Matti* (*Herr Puntila and His Servant Matti*) at the opening of the Berliner Ensemble the previous November. Reluctant to give up on the actor, he now held out a very attractive carrot, the role of Hamlet. Moreover, Brecht told Lorre that he and Burri planned to move forward with *Der Mantel*. He remained silent on a third project in which he wanted to involve Lorre: a two-part morality play titled *Salzburger Totentanz* (*The Salzburg Dance of Death*). Brecht cast Lorre as Death, not a macabre or horrific apparition after Hollywood fashion, but as a dead-again wheeler-dealer. He apparently never told the actor of his plans, possibly because he had produced only five tiny fragments of the play by 1950–51.

Brecht's overtures did not bring Lorre to East Berlin. The actor had not returned to Germany—poor and sick—to work with his old friend, but to take his first, awkward steps toward independence. Brecht did not react in either letter or work journal. Whether Lorre was chasing windmills or honestly struggling to rise from the Hollywood morass hardly mattered. The invitations stopped. By failing to choose, he had chosen.

On October 27, 1950, Benno Vigny delivered a screenplay, "that he has worked on with Peter Lorre," to Pressburger. His inability to continue work because of health reasons marked the first chapter in the troubled history of a script that never reached completion. Unhappy with the screenplay and intent on integrating the story of Dr. Carl Rothe, Lorre enlisted the help of director-screenwriter Helmut Käutner. During a two-week workshop in Munich, Lorre, Käutner, and assistant director Hans Grimm produced what a cued press enthusiastically described as a second script. The revised screenplay weighed the enormity of the mass crimes sponsored by the state against the fate of a single human being, a murderer who becomes a victim of murderous times.

To shoot the picture, Lorre enlisted the soft-spoken, self-possessed Vaclav Vich, a Czechoslovakian with a strong postwar background in Italian neorealism. Bumping into many available actors in Hamburg afforded Lorre the luxury of selectively choosing his cast. He filled the male roles with experienced actors from stage and screen. Helmut Rudolph, looking more like a bank president than a Nazi officer, played the *Abwehr* colonel who cannot stand the sight of blood. Karl John, a featured character actor from Berlin's Deutsches Theater, assumed the more important role of the Gestapo agent.[6] For the role of his elderly landlady and mother of his fiancée, Lorre cast Johanna Hofer, the wife of actor Fritz Kortner.

One can't help believing, given their reports, that Lorre gave more attention to filling the other four female parts. After all, as murder victims, they defined the darker side of his character. Renate Mannhardt, who played his fiancée and the first murder victim, had worked with Käutner on *Auf wiedersehen Franziska* (1941), *Zirkus Renz* (1943), and *Via Mala* (1948). Gisela Trowe, who portrayed the prostitute, was recommended by Brecht. Eva-Ingeborg Scholz came up from Berlin's Renaissance Theater. Lotte Rausch, who had gotten her start as a comedienne under Carl Froelich in *Wenn wir alle*

Engel wären (*If We Were All Angels*, 1936), stepped into the unlikely role of a war widow whose overtures of availability end in death.

The audition process was anything but typical. Gisela Trowe met Lorre and Vich at the Hotel Atlantic in Hamburg. He asked her to sit down, while "he walked up and down in the room, then stood in front of me and had a little leather riding crop which he whipped against his thigh." After telling her that he was making a film, Lorre suddenly, "without transition," asked her to walk to the door.

> "That was quite nice. Would you please take off your shoes?" Then he asked me to wiggle my bum, which I did.
> "Now come back relaxed and a little bit provocatively."
> I have to say this appeared very strange to me. I had never had to do this before in my life.

When Trowe asked what the film was about, Lorre sidestepped the question, telling her he didn't really know yet. He then proceeded to "ask holes in her stomach" about Berlin, the theater, Gründgens, and so on. "He was enormously patient when one was talking," recalled Trowe. "I always had the feeling, how can he judge if one is an actor or not. But then he said, 'You can leave that to me. I know what I want.'" If the interview had only been strange, she later admitted, she might have run away. But Lorre's "strong sensual radiation" held her there: "He filled the room . . . though he was very thin and fragile. I had never met a man with this radiation, this aura."

Lotte Rausch arrived thinking she would be asked to supply comic relief between the darker moments. Instead of discussing the role, Lorre just sat there.

"Yes, make it good, Lotte," he finally said. As he continued to stare, wordless, into her eyes, she became frightened.

"Why are you staring at me?"

"Just be calm, yes. Nothing will happen to you," he answered with his "mocking attitude and always tortured, effective laugh."

The next day, the same thing. She wanted to run away, but he pushed her gently back into her chair.

"Fear? That's good. And—I mean by that, what happens between us in the film must also be fear. But yet still more: Hunger for life. And that strangles fear."

Nerves shot, she nonetheless returned a third time.

"Something in Lorre the demon bound her," related his publicist. "And then everything else fell away."

"Now I know what I have to play and how I have to play it," said Rausch, expressing her "moment of sudden enlightenment."

"Everyone felt at first that there was a forcing of a foreign will upon themselves," explained the pressbook, "and fought against it until they sensed that Lorre was not trying to destroy the self-assurance of the actors with his methods, but rather was pressing to the core, and wanted to dissolve layer by layer that which other directors had put into the actor or the actress."

Renate Mannhardt waited for Lorre in his dressing room. In stepped an unshaven and tired-looking little man. When she looked into his eyes, however, her initial impression melted away. "I knew in the same moment," she said, "that I would be able to trust myself to this director unreservedly, because in his expression lay goodness and knowledge about all human suffering and overcoming it."

In the smaller but nonetheless important position of personal assistant, Lorre cast Annemarie Hanna Brenning. Born in Cuxhaven in 1922, the attractive brunette graduated from the Staatlichen Schauspielschule in Hamburg in 1940. Stage work soon brought her to Berlin as one of the bright lights in UFA's new generation of artists, but the war arrested her development as a screen actress. After serving in the army, Brenning appeared at the Jungen Theater and Kabarett Bonbonniere in Hamburg before accepting work as a script assistant. A leg injury, sustained while running an errand for National Film, put her in Wigger's Kurheim. There she met Lorre, who hired her to help him with his new screenplay. Annemarie's contribution appears to have been more personal than professional. Although she served no clearly defined function and received only a nominal salary, she never left Lorre's side. "She wasn't really taken seriously by anyone," recalled Pressburger. "She was sort of a floating girl [who] appeared to be absolutely devoted to Peter."

He held an unusual track record that way. How he consistently attracted such handsome women always baffled him. After being shown a photograph of Annemarie several years later, writer Herb Meadow asked him, "How is it possible for anybody as ugly as you to be married to anybody as nice as that?"

"My dear," answered Lorre, "the good fortune of men who look like you and me is that there's no accounting for women's tastes." Still, as Mrs. Jonas Silverstone pointed out, "Peter loved women. He loved the adulation that women gave him. He wanted them at his beck and call."

Lorre cast himself as director and rather reluctantly as actor. "I'd be a better director than an actor," he had told a Paramount studio biographer several years earlier, "but I can't live without acting." In his "Peter Lorre Picture," he did both and collaborated as producer and screenwriter as well.[7]

Lorre set his story in Hamburg, which afforded both financing and film production facilities, equally hard to come by in postwar Germany. Through its long history of independence, the second largest city in Germany kept its feet on the ground and its nose to the grindstone. Temperamentally, the Hamburger was restrained and resolute, much like the Englishman with whom he had preserved trade links for centuries. As a city of merchants, Hamburg maintained stronger commercial ties to London than to Berlin. Politically, it also kept its own political conscience, giving Hitler 40 percent of its vote, 5 percent below the national average. In 1943 the R.A.F. had rained down 8,344 tons of bombs on the Hamburg area—with the stated directive of devastating "the morale of the enemy civilian population"—reducing the once cosmopolitan city to rubble and killing more than 45,000 people and destroying 253,400 dwelling units. Ironically, claimed the inhabitants, the anti-Nazi areas of the city suffered most while the pro-Nazi districts were spared.

The "Peter Lorre Film of an Arnold Pressburger Production" began shooting in what Bartning called, with telling prescience, "a dark period in November." Every stifled and creative idea and impulse of Lorre's past experience welled up, anxious to be recognized and expressed in his new film. From the "New Objectivity," a realist movement of the Weimar years, he drew a "palpable actuality" in which "artistic creation and 'true' reality flow imperceptibly together." This "unmade-up portrait of reality, a picture without retouching," so the pressbook advertised, realized a new "Lorrealismus," which looked past jack-boots, swastikas, and "accent" players shouting "Sieg Heil!" at a raw, gray world of little people in the midst of their daily lives, coping with food rationing, air raids, and street rubble. "It shall be a Reportage-Spielfilm, with artistic solidification," Lorre told Hamburg's *Die Welt*. "We will attempt to create a new realism."

Hofer remembered that Lorre wanted no "film beauties" in the picture. "The cameraman told me he would like to photograph me from my best side," she said, "but he wasn't allowed to. Lorre was naturally correct." By keeping the photography stark, simple, and gimmick-free, he felt he could better concentrate on the story. He also believed black and white was more useful in artistic construction and provided a more intense effect than color, "comprehending the human and his world in fine and clear detail."

Der Verlorene also owed a debt to American film noir, itself rooted in German expressionist cinema. During his Hollywood tenure, Lorre had appeared in no fewer than eleven pictures that wear this style. *Stranger on the Third Floor, The Maltese Falcon, The Mask of Dimitrios, Three Strangers,* and *The Chase* are all open textbooks for anyone willing to learn. The lessons are all there:

voice-over narration, tilted camera and tightly framed close-ups, intertwined destinies, characters bound to the past by flashbacks, and nightmarish atmosphere. Clearly, Lorre had kept an open mind, letting the noir mood and tone, as well as its visual techniques, percolate into his aesthetic consciousness.

As a writer, he had less to draw on. "Everyone was more or less convinced that the script was worthless," said Bartning. "Lorre was also convinced of this." His co-workers felt he knew where he wanted to go, but he didn't know how to get there. Eggebrecht, who was now working for the Norddeutscher Rundfunk in Hamburg, came on board last but stayed to the end. He called Lorre "a fantastic constructor," who "was always testing new starts." During filming, a coterie of advisers, including screenwriter Walter Ulbricht, who coauthored the screenplay for *Unter den Brücken* (*Under the Bridges*, 1945) with director Helmut Käutner, offered suggestions that fed the uninterrupted production of new scripts. Lorre quickly converted this process to a filmmaking philosophy that disallowed need for the written word. To facilitate the intuitive development of the dialogue, the actors "talked about the story, thought about it and we used their own words," said Lorre of his experimental team approach. In this way he attuned parts to players, maximizing the psychological nearness and naturalness of their acting. It also enabled his writing staff to stay one jump ahead of the camera. "A formulation in this film," advertised the pressbook, "has not been forced upon any actor which does not fit him; the details of his text have been developed from case to case out of his own personal nature, in order to achieve the highest degree of authenticity." When Karl John asked Lorre if he would be murdered in the film, he replied, "I won't tell you, because if you knew that you maybe wouldn't act as freely; that is not possible that someone knows: 'I'll be murdered.'" No less a perfectionist than Brecht, Lorre often threw out the six or more versions of the script, preferring to mold dialogue to his actors in a kind of spontaneous fit. Whatever conditioned "the kind of freedom which musicians exercise in a jam session"—immediacy, expediency, or both—it bought time to implement yet more changes. In his first—and as it turned out only—directorial outing, he aimed for visual and verbal perfection, tirelessly kneading the three columns of words, neatly divided into camera, set, and dialogue, on broad sheets he had cut for himself. "This was different from all scripts that I have ever seen," said Eggebrecht. When he found a better way to say a word or express an idea, he reshot the scene, believing, like Lang, that there are no small details. A sign on a train, the opening of a door, a shadow, all had to be right.

In the midst of cinematic chaos, Lorre needed a "well-kept corner." His love of office materials, which bordered on obsession, amused his co-workers. If he saw a file folder, he had to have it. In his flat, he kept what Bartning described as a large board supported by two sawhorses on which he piled supplies precisely arranged at right angles. On it also lay "dozens of pencils very strictly ordered parallel to each other." If someone dared to sharpen a pencil with a knife, he would yank it away and hone it with his "main pride," a pencil sharpener. "One could read out of this," said Bartning, "all sorts of things."

In the opening frames of the film, a preface superimposed on a brick wall reads, "This film is not freely invented. The factual reports from recent years underlie the events." Willy Schmidt-Gentner's demonic musical score swells and crashes over the credits, overlapping realist and expressionist styles that, for some, underlined the picture's inability to decide what it wanted to be, a newsreel or a psychological drama.[8] Just as quickly, the pounding melody, which plays less than ten decisive minutes in the film, trails off into the early morning hum of the postwar German refugee camp Elbe-Düwenstedt (the film was actually shot at a concentration camp for Ukrainians and Russians at Heidenau, ten miles southwest of Hamburg in the Lüneburger Heide). Out of the stark architecture of lines formed by a raised railroad crossing gate and towering telephone poles, Dr. Karl Rothe (Lorre) enters the fenced enclosure, which, like the brick wall, solidly stands between past and present, amnesia and acknowledgment. There, under the assumed name "Neumeister" (new master), the taciturn scientist practices medicine. It is Peter Lorre as audiences had never seen him—cool, distant, and seemingly as displaced as his patients. He wears his expressionless face as a mask. His dark overcoat cloaks him from the outside world. Inside the camp he loses himself in his work. When the prefect suggests that he hire an assistant, Rothe objects: "Leave me in peace. I am happy when I am alone." But a chemist from Kattowitz soon arrives with a shipment of patients. Administering vaccinations, Rothe hears a familiar voice: "Keep your nerve, doctor. I'm Novak." It is Hoesch (Karl John), once a member of the Gestapo and now operating under a false name. Rothe's face drains. The past has caught up with him. He rises and leaves the clinic. Outside the refugee camp, he walks along a railway embankment, his hands in his pockets. Shot from a low angle, he appears silhouetted against the gray sky, detached from earthly reality. He watches an approaching train, as hulking and unstoppable as his own personal destiny. After it passes, he follows the tracks, swept along the same course.

Back at camp, Hoesch asks Rothe for a "permanent and dependable settlement" to the past and confesses that *angst* (fear) is a habit he has developed in the last years. Now that he and Rothe are in the same boat and cannot climb out, reasons Hoesch, they can be friends. He discounts their wartime experiences as only accidental (*zufällig*). Rothe mockingly repeats the word.

The brandy gone, they retreat to the canteen. In his soft, singing Viennese rhythm, Rothe tells Hoesch, "The door is locked, the windows are closed, everything has stopped. All remains outside, also the fear. We are at the end. We are there." The doctor admits liking him much better now that he too has known the feeling of fear. "I tell you," he says, "fear kills all other feelings. All. Yes, one also kills out of fear of others." Suddenly, Rothe produces Hoesch's pistol, which he has carried since the war. The assistant only laughs. He tells Rothe that he wants something from him; "I'm on the run, but I don't have papers. After all, I helped you once."

"Well, debts must be paid," replies Rothe with mock irony. "It must be tremendous, my debt! Tremendous! In any case, you helped me once and today I have to help you—It is simple. . . . I have to see that you find peace—on your flight. I must after all begin to pay back my debts. . . . It weighs me down, since December 8, 1943—with interest and interest's interest."

Rothe paces back and forth, transported to the past in the first of ten flashbacks. It is 1943. Hamburg. Bombs fall. As the director of a bacteriological research department at the Tropical Institute, he lives only for his work. (In the "Arbeits" [work] version of the script, Rothe, like Lorre, expresses an equal interest in literature, particularly Dostoyevsky, who "can tell us more about the human being than ten books about deep psychology.")[9] Hoesch assists him in his experiments. One day Colonel Winkler (Helmut Rudolph), of the *Spionageabwehr* (Military Intelligence), visits Rothe in his laboratory, where he nervously watches the doctor draw blood from a rabbit: "From a person, fine, but not from such a harmless animal." Winkler informs Rothe that his research has recently turned up in London and identifies the leak as Fraulein Inge Hermann (Renate Mannhardt), the doctor's secretary and fiancée. Out of suspicion, the agent followed her. When she made sexual overtures, he seduced her and in confidence learned of her espionage. Hoesch tells Rothe not to let it give him gray hairs: "End it. Simply end it."

Rothe descends the stairs into the laboratory basement. Tormented by Inge's betrayal, he loses himself in thought. His fingers aimlessly ambulate into some rabbit's blood. (In the "Arbeits" version of the script, he absentmindedly finger paints on a bloody lab table.) Rothe's hand tensely passes over his face, smearing it with blood.[10] The music score wells up and over. In a scene suggestive of Beckert's examination of his reflection in *M*, Rothe peers into the mirror and confronts his darkest thoughts. The image startles him. He red-handedly looks right and left, wipes his face, and leaves. In the first of several visually innovative transitions that erase the border between past and present, Rothe walks down the basement corridor and turns right, his shadow trailing up the steps and out of frame. He next appears ascending the inside stairs of Frau Hermann (Johanna Hofer) and Inge's apartment building, where his coldly murderous form, accompanied by a dementedly beating score, methodically advances toward the camera until it fills the frame. Once inside, he is pensive and distracted. Through a glass door, Rothe and Inge watch each other's shadowy form pace back and forth. Romantic and sinister musical strains struggle for the upper hand. When Inge attempts to light his cigarette, Rothe only looks at her with heavy-lidded hatred. She drops the match.

Back in the present, Rothe steps on a burning match, extinguishing the life symbol. He tells Hoesch that Inge confessed and begged for forgiveness. At that moment, the telephone rang: "All at once it was as if you stood before me in the room." Rothe stares threateningly at Inge. His hands, seemingly under a life of their own, run restlessly over the furniture. Leaning against a mirror, Inge reflects a double image. She kneels before the transfixed Rothe and brings his hand to her face. As he softly strokes her cheek, she closes her eyes. He fondles her pearl necklace. The score works overtime. Staggering between pain and pleasure, Rothe closes his eyes and wraps his hands around her neck; his rising form blackens out the screen. According to Bartning, Lorre "played around with this scene terribly." For the strangulation, he asked everyone but essential cast and crew to leave the studio, then squeezed a doll out of frame to find the proper facial expression.[11]

Rothe's face and hands press against a window in the canteen. "What had happened could no longer be undone," he tells Hoesch. "I still don't know. In any case, I knew absolutely nothing, believe me. . . . I felt something between my hands. I played with it without knowing what it was." Another flashback finds Rothe back at Inge's apartment after the murder. He fingers her pearl necklace and studies his hands, which seem to have acted independently of his will. Hoesch and Winkler arrive at the scene and collaborate on a cover-up, but Rothe wants to confess his crime. "Your entire fanaticism for justice, what kind of reality is that?" ridicules Winkler. "Nothing more than sentimentality. . . . Our good Hoesch did you a favor. . . . Come to grips with the fact that you're going to live." Because his research is more important to the state than the life of a confessed traitor, Inge's death is pronounced a suicide. Rothe "resigns himself to [his] fate," a theme which plays a recurring role in the "Arbeits" script.

"Don't you understand?" he tells Hoesch in a passage that might well have remained in the finished film. "I couldn't live on. I was not supposed to live on.

. . . Do you have the slightest inkling what you did when you let me live?" Not allowed to atone for his sin, Rothe will kill until fate demands a reckoning.

Later, at the laboratory, he asks Hoesch to peer into the microscope: "Notice the three single ones [bacteria] there. Then give a name to the first one. . . . We will call it Oberst Winkler, the second we will name Hoesch and the third, Rothe. But if you take any one of these and put it into the blood of a healthy person, he will not remain healthy." In the same breath, he pulls out a pistol he found in Hoesch's desk. The doctor gives it back, adding that he admires it.

Rothe returns to Frau Hermann's apartment. Since Inge's death, he has played the surrogate offspring for the doting mother. There he meets Ursula Weber (Eva-Ingeborg Scholz), a new boarder (whose height forced the crew to build a platform to elevate the shorter Lorre). Baffled by her fountain pen, she turns to Rothe for help. They chat, he serves coffee, and she unwittingly brings up Inge's suicide. As she goes to fetch some gingerbread, he sees her shadow through the glass door, which once again unleashes his pathological impulse to kill. He pulls Inge's pearl necklace out of his pocket and begins to fondle it, deriving a sensual, almost erotic pleasure. However, at the last moment, he withstands the urge to kill and leaves. "Something had happened to me," says Rothe in the "Arbeits" script, "something for which I had no clear name . . . because I still was not able to look in the face of truth—a truth which as a doctor I should have realized . . ."

At a bar, he buys a prostitute (Gisela Trowe) a drink. They leave together and walk to her apartment. The light in the stairway goes out as she fumbles with her keys. "Lorre said to me very exactly," recalled Trowe, "that he would lightly nudge me when I should put the key into the lock of my apartment. And then I should only look at him and then something will come into my mind— and his mind too—and that I should only react to him." She asks Rothe to turn on the light, then tells him, "You're rather strange." He hesitates. "And then he looked at me and here it happened," continued Trowe, "and then I felt really weak." The prostitute looks into the face of a gentle madman, whose mixed expression of tenderness and evil appears free-floating against a black background. "So you're that kind," she screams. "Totmacher! (death maker). Totmacher!"

Trowe was not certain who coined the word Totmacher. "I don't know if it was written in the script, if Lorre mentioned it at the preliminary discussion, or if I said it out of anxiety," recalled the actress. "That was the only thing he said to me: 'Because she is a prostitute she notices it sooner . . . that [Rothe] doesn't only want to sleep with her, there is something else.' Afterwards it was said 'Totmacher' is a new word. Lorre said, 'This we have invented.' He said it again and again."[12]

Lorre asked her to quickly descend a dark winding staircase reminiscent of German expressionist cinema. When Trowe voiced her concern about running down the steep steps in a tight skirt and high heels, he replied, "It doesn't matter how you come down the stairs. Just look that you don't fall."

Her shrieking awakens a disgruntled neighbor, more curious than concerned about the racket: "You've never seen anything like it! I tell you that is one, a murderer!" Scanning the staircase above, another tenant sees only a hand slither backward over the banister and out of sight. Accustomed to such goings-on, what has become a group of onlookers dismisses the incident as simply another episode in the prostitute's nightlife. Rothe slowly descends the stairs. Confident no one has taken her screams seriously, he calmly explains that the woman had nothing to eat and too much to drink. Back on the street, he throws Inge's pearl necklace into a garbage can. "Now I knew it," he says in a voice-over. "What I had refused to admit to myself. She screamed it right in my face. *Totmacher*. I was saved in the very last moment."

The improvised scene, which they did in one take, put Lorre in a good mood. "He laughed a lot," said Trowe, "and constantly fed the cats, which already had eaten a lot of herring." The tenants at the apartment house in the St. Pauli district, where Lorre shot the scene, "said yes, such a nice man and he is not so mysterious after all."

Rothe decides to catch the last train home, where he meets his second victim. Helene (Lotte Rausch), a lusty, gregarious woman, laments the difficulty of the times with two small boys and a husband at the front. His annual eight days' leave is inadequate, she complains, and adds invitingly, "I'm just too spirited!"[13] Rothe plays with a *Hampelmann*—an homage to *M* or blatant borrowing?—pulling the strings just as forces beyond his control manipulate him. Suddenly, an air raid siren sounds. Passengers take shelter in the station and the train moves into the open. Rothe stays behind with Helene, who rationalizes that everyone's time will come. She alluringly rearranges her blouse and strokes her stole. As Rothe lights his cigarette, he stares at her, the burning match illuminating his face. The deadly intensity of his expression terrifies her. He drops the match. His rising form blackens out the frame, and Helene screams. Another passenger discovers her body in an overhead luggage rack: "To flee was of no use. . . . I didn't want to do it, and yet I did do it. And now I was walking through the night, blind, deaf and *verloren* (lost)." In the "Arbeits" script, he also confesses to feeling "like an animal, an animal that wants to hide in distress in its cave."

Returning to his apartment, Rothe sees a light in Inge's old room. He whispers her name, then bursts in on Ursula, who bolts upright. He checks his urges and exits, restraint masking his face. Here, Bartning remembered "pinching something from [Fritz] Lang, from *M*, a little trick. Lang had a technique in *M*, at a certain place toward the end, to produce more tension. He shows an empty room and a man goes through the room and the room again becomes empty. Always empty to empty. I remembered seeing this twenty years earlier. So I said to Lorre, we have to do that also. I don't know if this was in the final print. In any case, one sees the empty street in the camp and he comes walking through it and the street is empty again."

The Lorre team made effective use of this technique at several points, most dramatically after the second murder. When Rothe passes out of frame, the camera coldly stares down a dark, deserted street. Similarly, after Rothe leaves Frau Hermann, the viewer sees an empty room and watches the door slam. Like a specter, Rothe has passed through unseen.

"Even though I find suicide objectionable, cowardly and inexcusable," Rothe voice-overs from the present, "there was no other way out."

He returns to the institute and burns his research notes. But for one cigarette, Rothe tells a groggy Hoesch, who, he warns, will soon be able to sleep as long as he wants, he would not be alive today. Ransacking his assistant's desk for a cigarette, the doctor discovers "these strange letters from Inge." He also pockets the revolver: "You had to come along. One single time in my life, I wanted to kill—kill with a purpose." When Hoesch learns that Rothe is looking for him, he sets out in search of the doctor, who stumbles onto a political conspiracy at Winkler's villa. With the Gestapo outside and the resistance fighters inside, Rothe finds himself in "a detective novel." A chase down Hamburg's Seewartenstrasse ends at the Bismarck Monument; one conspirator is shot. Rothe and Winkler watch "the grown-up Indian game" from a bridge tower. The Colonel returns Hoesch's gun, which he had earlier taken from Rothe. "For Hoesch," says Winkler; he disappears. In soulful solitude, Rothe stands holding Hoesch's pistol.

Back at the canteen, a matching shot shows Rothe clutching the gun. "Yes, unbelievable," he says, looking back. "The bombing night was over. Thousands were dead. Thousands who wanted to live. Only I. I was still alive. Unbelievable." In another flashback, Rothe returns to Frau Hermann's apartment in the Magdalenenstrasse (just one of the streets on which Lorre lived during filming), only to discover the building has been destroyed and its inhabitants are dead.[14] Rothe decides to bury his past with the others and adds his name to the blackboard outside, marking a cross next to it. "So Dr. Rothe was dead without having died," narrates Rothe.

"I perhaps could have believed the past was buried in the rubble of the

Magdalenenstrasse," he tells Hoesch, "until you showed up this afternoon. . . . Then I knew there was no forgetting. That's not possible."

Hoesch accuses Rothe of being an amateur, who, unlike himself, never cultivated the most important survival skill—the ability to "spring to the side."

"Now, you spring to the side," says Rothe, pointing the pistol at Hoesch and shooting.

"That's yours," he adds, and tosses the gun on the floor.

He then removes the cigarette pack from Hoesch's hand, takes one, and throws the container on his chest. It falls to the floor.

"Belongs to you."

Bartning recalled that they tested this scene many times. "Then during the filming," he said, "I know that because my heart stood still—Lorre improvised that. He didn't disclose that before, that he throws the cigarette pack down and adds, 'Belongs to you.' In any case, that wasn't in the script. It wasn't ever planned. But it was a crazy moment. Yes, a crazy moment."

Rothe puts on his coat and walks to the gate, accompanied by a dog. As he leaves the fenced enclosure, the pet, his last worldly attachment, turns back, leaving him to complete the circle alone. Trudging through the forest of oblique lines that opens the film, he walks onto the railroad tracks. His back to an oncoming train, Rothe puts a hand over his eyes.[15]

Lorre later told American International Pictures (AIP) set designer Daniel Haller that the crew asked itself how they were going to make this scene look genuine. Lorre had an idea. "There were several tracks," he said. "As we laid out the scene, I walked above an over cross and along the railroad tracks. I was on the mark, with my back to the train, which was to switch tracks before reaching me. The camera was locked off. I could feel the train coming. It really put a believability in it." It also instilled a real sense of fear in both the engineer and the actor, who afterward expressed their mutual discomfort.

Lorre's experience as an actor gave his directing a personal style that, said Lotte Rausch, "was very rare and has died out today. He did not place us under the dictation of technique, but rather arranged the technical into the artistic exercise." Nothing, it seemed, ran true to form. "The way he worked was very, very different from the usual hectic ways of the studios," recalled the actress. "He started mostly around 12:00 noon! For those of us who were used to being at the studio at 7:00 a.m., it was a novelty, which, by the way, we appreciated." Sensitive to noises, Lorre held frequent script conferences in a soundproof cabin in the studio, where he also invited his actors to discuss their roles, raise questions, and offer suggestions. "This happened to me," continued Rausch, "when he warned me about the scene [cut from the film] in which he strangles me, that he would probably really hurt me and apologized for this ahead of time. Naturally, I was afraid of this at the time of the filming and was able to bring this very well into expression."

As a director, Lorre kept his input low-key. "I never heard a loud word out of him, not on any occasion," said Bartning. "He had a very strong personal radiance about him and there were people who talked with him the very first time, they loved him at once." Lorre turned any discussion into a conversation between friends. "Because he knew how to direct actors masterfully and how to explain his intentions to his cameraman," said Rausch, "in my opinion, a great career as a director stood before him. He never commanded; he convinced. He listened to other opinions and discussed quietly, almost excusing himself when he was of another opinion. He won them as friends."

Lorre forged a "unity of spirit" that embraced the members of his company, especially his female leads, whom he gently aligned into a kind of planetary rotation around his own charismatic core. "He loved his players," said Rausch. "He was very worried about them and this worrying naturally came back to him in the form of an echo." This mesmeric warmth, said Trowe, "loosened self-consciousness. . . . You have the feeling that he listens extremely well and then you begin to open yourself, but you don't feel rejected or naked or, in a mean sense, observed. This was the most important part of his work, to me at least . . . where you had the feeling that it originated, in the moment, at the most honest and truthful situation." Taking a page from Brecht, Lorre encouraged his players to show what they felt. This maximum of closeness to the material, he believed, precluded the possibility of cheating. "If you listened to him," concluded Trowe, "you weren't able to lie."

The pressbook featured a story ostensibly authored by Renate Mannhardt titled "Peter Lorre war mein Regisseur!" ("Peter Lorre Was My Director"). In it, she noted that

> working under Peter Lorre was hard, but wonderful. That was a new apprentice time, so to say. There was no false accent which he did not feel and which he didn't know through suggestive guidance to place weight on. Each sound had to be true to the human who was supposed to be portrayed. With a patience which I have never yet experienced, he tested further and further, until one gave oneself up almost unconsciously in order to be the human that one had to portray. And this remarkable engulfing aura of the great actor-director encompassed everyone already during the morning walk into the studio.

> It happened to me here for the first time that a director was capable of breaking through the thin hardened layer with which you surround yourself

for protection against the injuries of an outer world that has become hopeless, and which has bared a new human being, one previously undiscovered in oneself.

I stood in the studio and did not possess any more the least feeling of myself, but was simply my role, "Inge," as Peter Lorre wanted her to be—and have been probably never more than in this time "I."

When my work on this film ended, the daily life was not able to weaken the strength of the impressions I felt. Whosoever has worked together once with Peter Lorre will always be captured by the power and accomplishment of his artistic intentions and will always remember again and again the suggestion of his direction and acting as his partner.

Other co-workers, however, remembered different intentions. "Everything that could go wrong went wrong with that film," reflected Fred Pressburger, who took over production of the picture after his father died, "including Peter's resorting to drugs." Of all the crises and contingencies that plagued the production of the picture, Lorre's drug use topped the list. Contemporary medical texts describe the typical addict as "a worried, troubled, and harried individual" who suffers from "a poor self-image, and feelings of ineptness and being unappreciated, disapproved of, and disrespected." Did Lorre feel life's share of tragedy, frustration, and failure more keenly than others? Were his rationalizations a real or imagined smoke screen to hide human weakness? Correlating episodes of drug use and freedom from addiction with the ups and downs of his personal and professional lives is hopelessly contradictory. During his first productive years in England and America, he relied heavily on morphine, Dilaudid, and Pantopon to cope with the stress and strain of filmmaking. Yet a healthy, athletic, drug-free lifestyle characterized his successful tenure at Warner Bros. during the early and mid-1940s. Only after 1946 does his case history begin to conform to the textbook profile. Morphine put the depressed and exhausted actor in "a state of mind which is characterized by freedom from pain and worry and by a quickened flow of ideas." When the drug wore off, however, his eyes began to close and his voice slur. "He would suddenly, totally disintegrate," said Fred, "and then he would say, excuse me a moment, and he would go to the toilet and he would come back absolutely full of energy."

Fred had discouraged his father from getting involved with a "dope addict," but Arnold assured his son Lorre was a "different man." "When he left the sanitarium he said he wouldn't ever touch the stuff," said Fred, "but I don't think that lasted very long." Lorre himself reassured Fred that he had the upper hand on his habit, "saying that when you use drugs you have to space yourself, otherwise you will just be lost." To those close to him, his dependence was very evident. "Although he never complained about it," said Rausch, "it never remained hidden from us." After late-night consultations with his writers, he often arrived in the morning unshaven. "He didn't want to see himself in the mirror," said Bartning, who scrambled to line up a barber. The ups and downs of well-being and withdrawal fell into a well-worn pattern. Even those cast and crew members not privy to the secret commented on his apparent sickness and the noticeable presence of a doctor by his side. He rarely ventured out, keeping to his apartment. "He had fully withdrawn himself," recalled Bartning, "and there was no company, besides just a couple, Eggebrecht and Jacobson."

One day, Lorre and Bartning were sitting in his dressing room when, recalled the editor, "in came a ripe blonde lady and theatrically fell down at Lorre's feet." He looked at her in the mirror but didn't get up.

"Oh, yes," Lorre finally whispered.

The blonde was Inge Landgut, who had played Elsie Beckmann in *M* some twenty years earlier. She had stopped by to say hello after learning he was filming in Hamburg. "I was happy, nearly relieved when I shut the door myself and stood outside in the fresh air," she recalled. "My impression was that it wouldn't have made any difference who was standing before him. However, in order to judge something one must know what was going on inside of him. I cannot judge it, but saw at that time only the eerie one before me."

Lorre needed money for drugs. "He wanted money, money, money, and he would do anything to get it," recalled a frustrated Fred Pressburger, who blamed financial pressures for pushing his father over the edge. Lorre put the bite on almost anyone who would listen. His ability to buy a fix often depended on the success of his line. "I remember still a Saturday I brought him from the firm two or three thousand marks," said Bartning, "and on the next Monday he asked me if I could loan him money. I gave him 200 marks." Pressburger recalled that Lorre then approached Mainz. "Look, you have nothing to do with this picture," he told the credulous producer, "but I bet you could make money if you could distribute it abroad. Lend me $5,000 and you can have the rights because I am a partner." When Mainz learned that Lorre did not own the foreign distribution rights, he wanted his money back. He appealed to Pressburger, who told him, in short, he was out of luck, and pocket.[16] "How he did that, I don't know," marveled Bartning. "Anything was possible with Lorre. Anyway, we were amazed. This occurred on a Sunday. On Monday I came to him and he came smiling toward me and reached into his pants pocket and gave me the 200 marks. In such matters, he would not have let me down. Apparently, he had let other people down." In addition to finagling a fifty-thousand-deutsche-mark loan "on condition he repay the sum twenty-four months after the opening of the film," Lorre received a generous expense account. "He had, I believe," recalled Bartning, "about 200 marks for expenses per day. I still remember that we had the feeling this was unheard of, but the money was always gone."[17]

Lorre made no attempt to hide his other addiction from either his co-workers or filmgoers. By now, the cigarette—and its attendant smoke—had become indivisible from his screen image, as suggestively sinister as his menacing purr and globular eyes. "Without it, he couldn't function," said Jerry Lewis, who later directed Lorre in two feature films. "His cigarette was his greatest prop . . . how he lit it, when he lit it, how he smoked it and when. It was an adjunct of his personality." When Lewis made *The Patsy* in 1964, he and several actors conspired to concoct a scene in which Lorre's cigarette would be grabbed out of his hand. "Lorre came to me in a panic and said, 'I will do anything you want, but please don't take my cigarette.'"

"He didn't *just* smoke," said Robert Cummings, "he was never without a cigarette, seemingly an endless chain, lit in the dawn and not going out until the next dawn." Or so it seemed both on and off the screen. Behind the scenes, Lorre's cast and crew criticized his chain-smoking, which they found unbearable. It was an unrealistic cinematic accessory, given the scarcity of cigarettes during wartime. They also marveled at his extravagance; American cigarettes cost roughly $2.50 apiece. Critics also took note of Lorre's smoking, pointing out that some viewers laughed at his perceived affectation, while others diagnosed a case of acute nicotine poisoning. If the cigarette symbolized the murderer's "timely nervousness," as one reviewer supposed, for most it simply got on the nerves.

Lorre's state of mind—one minute melancholy, the next rallying at full tilt—not only paced the production by fits and starts but also set the mood of the picture. Fixing his camera on Rothe, Lorre framed his own image, that of a lost and lonely man locked in a dark struggle, looking for a way out. Herbert Timm, writing for the Bremer *Weser Kurier,* described "the tired sadness of his eyes, the resigned twitch of his mouth, which can no longer smile; a lost gesture, a hopeless raising of the shoulders" and noted how "he plays his Dr. Rothe, sparse in his movements, tearing open the abyss with a tossed off word and building a world out of the seemingly unimportant." Lorre's portrayal was a self-portrait of a man who sought to sever his connection with the past, only to learn there is no escape.

Obscuring the thin line between reality and illusion blurred Lorre's artistic vision. His co-workers weren't sure what the film was supposed to say. "The main problem was the script," claimed Pressburger, "because it wasn't quite clear what the film was supposed to be about." What had begun as a simple altruistic note had swelled into a cacophony of discordant sounds. "Lorre wanted just everything," said Bartning, "everything was supposed to be included." De Maupassant was there, winding in and out like a dark undercurrent. Lorre even drew on Friedrich Schiller, further mixing his message. He saw much of the German dramatist's "tragic hero" in Rothe, and perhaps in himself. Lorre believed that the doctor deserved both admiration and pity because, caught in the conflict of irrational forces, he repents of his transgressions and through his self-sacrifice in the refugee camp summons moral resistance to his suffering, invoked by the "stress of circumstances." In keeping with Schiller, after exercising his free will to reach a moral end, Lorre's self-styled "psychopathic hero" conquers fate by acquiescing to it, willing his own destruction. This act of self-liberation shows the sublime and noble human character. In death, Rothe harmonizes free agency and passion, thereby achieving the state of *der schönen Seele* (beautiful soul).

If German politics didn't qualify as a crisis, it certainly fell into the category of a complication. Initially, Lorre had sought to stay out of it. "Peter was until the end of the 1940s an apolitical man," said Eggebrecht, who was once a member of the Kommunistische Partei Deutschlands (German Communist Party) and spent time in a concentration camp. "Then everything changes through conversations with many people—also me, and naturally through the experience of the German postwar world, with its reluctance to understand the criminal regime. I believe Peter eventually came to his political views." In an interview given just before *Der Verlorene* began shooting, Lorre acknowledged the resentments that greeted returned émigrés and found them completely understandable. Others had knocked their heads against the same wall. Douglas Sirk, who briefly returned to Europe after the war, discovered an unwillingness to accept "any kind of interpretation of what life was like in Germany during the war. . . . I meet someone I knew from way back and he keeps telling me how bad things were for them, how they suffered, how they endured, how many examples he could give me of courage, and so on, and how splendid, comfortable and serene the life of an émigré must have been."

Lorre told the press he wanted to extinguish any ill feeling with tact. From the beginning, he claimed that his film would be psychological in nature: "It will not be a political film, that is politics will not be in the foreground, but people." And for the most part, he held that thought. However, his firsthand view of postwar reality put a hard edge on his political sensibilities and turned his inside look out. "Five or six years after 1945," said Eggebrecht, "we were all, naturally also Peter and I, burningly interested in the enlightening of the crimes of the Hitler State. We noticed already there were strong powers resisting the necessary reckoning."

Lorre discovered at close hand that the spirit of fascism was still alive, if not well, and more deeply ingrained than he had ever supposed at a distance. He found a devastated and demoralized but also cynical and self-pitying people who refused to accept responsibility for Nazi war crimes. Orson Welles expressed similar sentiments in a March 1951 issue of the *Fortnightly*. A German girl had told him that the German "feels naked without a uniform. He needs to march with lots of other Germans or he gets sulky. Also he must have somebody to bully." The celebrated filmmaker wrote that far from breaking with the past, "millions of them are incurably Nazi-bent." Like Lorre, Welles had come around to the numbing idea that there was "no cure at all for being German."

But which one, a "good" or a "bad" German? After drunkenly searching his hotel room for a mythical "good German" in *Hotel Berlin* (1945), Lorre's Professor Koenig collapses in a fit of nervous laughter. Thomas Mann had no better luck turning up the "other" Germany. Unlike Brecht, who believed the few had forced their will upon the many, Mann held that the German character and Nazism were one and the same and divisible only by a purging of the national soul, which needed to begin with a decisive and utter military defeat: "Let the hour ripen when the Germans themselves settle accounts with the villains with a thoroughness, such as the world scarcely dares to hope from our unrevolutionary people." There were not two Germanys, "a bad and a good," as Brecht liked to believe, "but only one, whose best side had been turned by diabolic cunning into evil."

Germany's "escape from reality," wrote Hannah Arendt, an exiled intellectual who returned in 1950 to assess the scene, had become "an escape from responsibility." Even the plight of the refugees, she observed, drew only public indifference: "This general lack of emotion, at any rate this apparent heartlessness, sometimes covered over with cheap sentimentality, is only the most conspicuous outward symptom of a deep rooted, stubborn, at times vicious refusal to face and come to terms with what really happened." De-Nazification ran only skin deep, like a cold cream applied to temporarily erase the wrinkles. Old ideologies hung on. "No one ever gave a thought to a 'new' beginning," lamented Henry Pachter. Thanks to the 1951 Act of General Clemency, Nazis walked the streets, taught in the schools, and manned the city governments and business offices.

Nonetheless, from the beginning, Rothe combined elements of both a good and a bad German. After all, it was the mixture of good and evil that gave Lorre's screen characterizations depth and balance. However, if he had once sided with Brecht, he now leaned toward Mann.[18] Only after he discovered that "crimes have been committed which no psychology can help to excuse" did *Der Verlorene* take a political turn and the neurotic doctor who "glided" into murder become a "murderer because the moral chaos of an unfortunate epoch had destroyed his equilibrium."

Shortly after the film's release, Lorre admitted that the story had made it possible to take a critical look at Nazi Germany without direct explanations. How else could he benefit a people who, in Mann's words, "learned nothing, understand nothing, regret nothing?" As his altruism soured into animosity, his focus shifted from the victim to the perpetrator and swept up Dr. Rothe in a political conspiracy reminiscent of the July 1944 mutiny of Reichswehr officers against Hitler.[19] The "kitchen sink," as it were, signified Lorre's growing need to say more, to broaden his base from psychological mission to political platform. "Peter had a lot of hostility towards Germany," said Pressburger. "He resented the Nazis and the crimes they committed and wanted to make *Der Verlorene* a sort of metaphor of Germany. I mean he was Germany. So he said this is me murdering a woman by accident, by anger, and it became a pleasure." Friends who saw him shortly after he returned to the United States recalled that Lorre was deeply disturbed by conditions abroad. As late as 1962, he admitted that he could not swallow Germany's desire for forgiveness and would never forget the lessons learned from the Nazi era.

More than a case of mercy running dry, *Der Verlorene* reflected, however obscurely, Lorre's struggle to come to grips with the issue of personal versus collective accountability. Hoesch's arrival at the refugee camp reminds Rothe that man cannot sidestep his obedience to moral law. After all, debts must be paid. Like Rothe, the German people owed "interest and interest's interest." The film presented a darkly fatalistic correlate to Ludwig Marcuse's conviction that "the rupture between the Fatherland and the émigrés from Hitler will heal only in the day that the last refugee who not only escaped but fought back is dead." Could Germany cleanse itself by simply acknowledging its crimes? Or would it take the passing of a generation? Whatever hope Lorre held out for Rothe—that is, for Germany—seemingly vanishes in the final, foreboding scene when he steps into the path of a speeding locomotive.

Early in 1951, the dark cloud that had been hanging over *Der Verlorene* since autumn burst, deluging the production with problems. As Eggebrecht and Lorre sharpened the story's political edge, Mainz grew increasingly nervous. Whether or not he smelled a flop, as Fred Pressburger suggested, or hitched his star to the heroically happy *Dr. Holl*, FAMA's first film, which was being shot at the same time, the Hamburg producer backed out, citing personal reasons. Despite growing friction with Lorre, Mainz agreed to extend FAMA's "corporate cover." The fractured consortium had no choice but to assume increased liability for the studio contract with Junge Film Union.

Like John Gielgud on *Secret Agent,* Karl John filmed by day and appeared on stage in the evenings. Already stressed by Lorre's loose working methods, the actor felt the additional pressure of getting to Hamburg's Schauspielhaus by curtain time. On January 28, on his way home from a press ball, he broke his leg in a car accident that kept him in bed for six weeks. It was a lucky break for all but the actor, since it postponed outdoor shooting and bought much-needed time to regroup. In addition, payment of insurance claims ended months of frantic scrambling for additional funds. Then on February 19, Arnold Pressburger died of a cerebral hemorrhage that Fred believed had been induced by production worries.

With studio work near completion, tensions between Lorre and Grimm, his assistant director, had reached a boiling point and erupted into a "terrific fight" in early January. In a letter tendering his apologies to Pressburger, Grimm said he had "accepted with joy" the job of collaborating on the script and working on the film, but that Lorre's lack of dramaturgical experience caused him to question his own ability to meet that responsibility. By March things had again heated up. Before citing his reasons for leaving the film, Grimm reminded Fred he had been hired to "assist Mr. Lorre with his first directorial work . . . and to finish the production on time and within the planned budget." Nothing in his "collective experience," however, had prepared him for Lorre's "novel kind of direction." Wholesale improvisation of not only dialogue, but also the order of scenes and story line "meant that the script was . . . no longer a dependable foundation and that the schedule could not be met. Through this situation my work lost the basis for effective collaboration. . . . In this situation, artistic collaboration with Mr. Lorre became impossible."

If the *Sturm und Drang* of directing his first film weren't bad enough, Lorre still faced the problem of naming his picture. The working titles, *Bestie Mensch* and *Das Untier,* would only inflame an already reactive public. *Carl Rothe, Doctor of Medicine* went too far in the other direction. To stir up positive publicity and come up with a suitable title, National decided to put the question to a group of viewers at a special screening of the film in late February 1951. The winner would receive one thousand deutsche marks. Among the 684 suggestions were "*Gott führt uns wunderbar [God Leads Us Wonder-*

fully], *Augen sehen dich an* [*Eyes Look at You*], *Auswurf* [*Outcast*], *Kolportage* [*Rubbish*], *Raserei* [*Rage*], *Katharsis?* . . ., *Mysterium* [*Mystery*], and *Pfui.*" In the end, the reward for the title, *Der Verlorene* (*The Lost One*) went to Eggebrecht. "Naturally this theme," said the writer, "reflected Peter's totally depressed situation."

Lorre had completed filming without a finished script. "We had always improvised with script pages," said Bartning, "and one day I got a weird feeling in my stomach. 'Listen,' I said to Lorre, 'the only thing that we have of the film is the rough-cut copy and otherwise no script. Nothing.'" Bartning recommended that he write a continuity script, which would be "completely without artistry or literary ambition." For several days, he worked alongside a secretary dictating dialogue and recording and numbering takes, which, with the help of a shooting report, they arranged in chronological order. On March 22, or Green Thursday, as he remembered it, Bartning took a taxi to the train station.[20] Climbing aboard, he heard fire sirens but took no special note of them. He sat down and lightly dozed. Suddenly, he heard someone call his name.

"'Is Mr. Bartning here?' shouted a train official.

'Hello, I'm he.'

'You've been called back at once to Hamburg. Your cutting room has burned down.' Yes, that was a wrench in the works," recalled the editor with classic understatement.

Bartning had left his assistants, Margot Schubert and Hanni Schäfer, at the Rhythmoton film synchronization studio on Harvestehuder Weg. When an electric heater shorted, flames shot out and ignited a roll of film. The women cracked the door and yelled for help, then slipped out and closed off the room, robbing the fire of oxygen and preventing its spread. Schubert tore the fire extinguishers off the wall, but the intense heat forced her to retreat. An hour later, firemen had the flames under control, but the editing room had been completely destroyed.

Bartning re-edited the work print from thirty thousand meters of negative film stock that had been stored at a copying facility. "The reconstruction was tedious and boring," he later recalled, "but relatively possible." On Good Friday he and his assistant worked through the charred and soaked shooting report, turning fragile pages that disintegrated on touch. Barely able to read the numbers, they compiled a new list for the copyist, so that *Der Verlorene* could rise again after Easter.

Lorre did not stick around for the resurrection. Having amassed numerous debts, he left Hamburg without good-byes. "He suddenly disappeared," remembered Bartning, "and the grocery where they were getting their groceries was looking behind sadly. He had received a lot of money from the firm and he hadn't paid a single penny in taxes. It is supposed [the tax collector] was after his ass."

Junge Film Union, which had not been paid the last installment for the use of its studio, knew just how the tax collector felt. Facing bankruptcy, National was no longer a player in what turned into a production war. Junge Film Union turned to Fifi, which, in turn, turned on it. Brought in to help sort out the tangled issues of sale, distribution, and foreign rights—and the incessant question of how Lorre could be prevented from taking money out, "because he tried like crazy"—Pressburger called on German producers Erich Pommer and Günther Stapenhorst (as arbitrators) and the requisite number of lawyers, who fed the ongoing negotiations.

Pressburger also saw to it that the film was completed. As a film editor, he had ideas of his own. "Pressburger sat down with me at the cutting room table and was very complaining," said Bartning, who chalked up his distrust—"perhaps he didn't know who had previously been a Nazi"—to "crazy" Jewish complexes against Germans. "He probably found that everything wasn't as good as he expected and that one had to do everything completely differently."

"My suggestions were very minor actually," countered Pressburger. "I thought things were too long and I wanted to edit. I suggested that they should cut certain things shorter."

The German news media added to the problems that plagued the film by giving Lorre a dose of negative publicity. He had quietly gone about the business of filmmaking unaware that his secrecy was alarming the German public.[21] Pulp fiction featuring "murder and violence" as well as "seduction, naive love, sweet life, depravity and unbridled longings" flooded West Germany after 1950, sensitizing citizens to inflammatory themes. Before anyone had screened even a rough-cut print of *Der Verlorene*, the press rumored that the picture showed seven graphic sexual crimes. When the *Münchner Merkur*, in an article titled "Das Untier vor den Toren" ("The Monster before the Door"), stated that the murder of "numerous" women "is committed here continuously psychopathically," publicist Hellmut Schlien directed a reply: "The fact is that the entire film only contains four deaths. Singled out in one case the superficial observer would view the murder of the unknown woman in the overhead railway to be a *Lustmörder*."

Fearful that scenes of violence and willful murder would incite youthful audiences, a "Bonner Dramaturgie" had reportedly warned Lorre to tone down any contentious material.[22] A misinformed press even claimed that the production team had responded to impending censorship by eliminating all but two murders and substituting a subplot about a political conspiracy. Eggebrecht disputed the charge, maintaining that "censors did not force us to make changes, as far as I was involved in the work. I can assure you of that."

On June 21 an "already suspicious" Freiwillige Selbskontrolle der Filmwirtschaft (FSK), a voluntary control board of film administration charged with preventing movies from exerting negative moral, religious, or political influences, actually approved *Der Verlorene* and imposed only two minor restrictions: it could not be shown on designated religious and legal holidays or to viewers below sixteen years of age.[23]

Attempting to stem the tide of supposition, Lorre held a special screening in Munich on June 26, his forty-seventh birthday, for friends and members of the press. They discovered that he had, like Fritz Lang twenty years earlier, left the murders of Renate Mannhardt and Lotte Rausch to the imagination and had very simply staged that of Karl John. However, the little positive publicity that resulted from the preview failed to check the picture's growing notoriety.

Three days before the film's Frankfurt premiere, the *Münchner Illustrierte* ran the first installment of a serialized version of *Der Verlorene* "von Peter Lorre." Its appearance added fuel to the fire. It is hard to say on which side of the argument the publication fell. As publicity, it ushered in and supplemented the run of the film—the twenty-two-chapter serial actually outlasted the showing by nearly two months. It also repaid Lorre's debt to Egon Jameson. If the journalist was to realize anything from the project based on his own research, he might at least earn credit in the press. For purely financial reasons, however, he apparently agreed to drop his byline. The paper undoubtedly preferred to trade on the strength of Lorre's name.

A small note in *Film Press*, August 15, 1951, reported that Jameson was writing a novelization of *Der Verlorene*, loosely based on the film script, for the *Münchner Illustrierte*.[24] Clearly inspired by the original concept of *Das Untier*, the serialized story reinforced rumors that Lorre had indeed reached into the past for the pathological roots of the film. Egon Jameson incorporated dialogue taken verbatim from an early version of the script, indicating either that he contributed to the development of the screenplay or that he had a free hand to plagiarize lines eliminated during the evolution of the story.

After "discovering" Rothe's diary—written in green, red, and black ink—in a leather briefcase, Jameson set up a first-person narrative reminiscent of Maupassant's "The Horla." He presents the doctor as a grown-up *M*, who gives a mature, albeit introspective, voice to his urges. Rothe's love/hate relationship with the fiery Inge, who has caught him on the rebound, thoroughly deranges his rational sensibilities. While resisting his proposals of marriage, she nonetheless steals his research, extorts money from him, and dallies with "Wölfchen" Hoesch. True to the film, his deadly alter ego steps forward to revenge the wrong: "My hand. It doesn't obey me anymore. . . . Fatigue is paralyzing my muscles. . . . The eyes are closing. A rustling is starting. I see colorful circles, which, like color games, dance around each other."

"If I correctly combine all the scribbles and the hints which are on these pages of the diary of Dr. Carl Rothe," analyzes Jameson's narrator, who keeps a clinical distance, "so is the unhappy man chasing through the empty streets without a purpose. In fear of himself. He is not able to think clearly or even to think to the end, as if he had to flee from that unknown which is in him, which grabs him, strangling him, who lets him do things he would never do with a healthy mind. His desperation growing every minute in which his perception becomes clearer. There is no escape."

"I didn't murder because I wanted to," resumes Rothe. "A second strange person living in me strangled her."

To atone for his sin, the doctor puts his own life at risk rescuing people: "I will save people. With the one-hundredth person I will be free again. If I die, all the better." The hero of the burning street earns the nickname "Angel of Rubble." However, the very private side of his public figure continues to kill young women, four more to be precise. And like Beckert, afterward he re-members only that he has "to kill. I must. I can't live anymore without killing. Yes. Yes. I am broken apart into two different beings. Yes, and the one being has to kill."

Finally, Rothe resolves to kill in "full consciousness."

"One piece of dirt less! One piece of garbage of this time! You! Winkler! I! Away with us!"

On a cynical note, Hoesch concludes, "You're not going to accomplish anything, Rothe. In the big picture, it doesn't matter! . . . no rooster is going to crow over us."

He lets the pistol fall.

"I wasn't prepared for so much impertinence," reflects Rothe. "Or didn't I have the strength to pull the trigger?"

After the war, however, he succeeds.

On his deathbed, Hoesch agrees to cooperate with the police only after seeing Rothe. When they refuse, he tells them, "Then I won't talk."

On October 2, 1945, Rothe keeps his rendezvous with the train.

National's propaganda-drumming pressbook was stuffed with meaty text promoting the salutary nature of the film. "No Freely Invented Film" reviewed the factual basis of the story. In "Der unaufgeklärte Mord—ein Zeitproblem!"

("The Unexpected Murder—A Problem of the Time!"), Hamburg's chief state attorney, Gerhard F. Kramer, praised the picture's "enlightened explanation" of the soaring postwar homicide rate and even dragged Schiller out of the closet for literary ballast. Covering all bases—with the rebirth of the German cinema representing home plate—"A Historical Narrative and a Man's Confession" spoke to the universal meaning of the film's "indictment and admonition raised to humanity." The remaining pieces introduced cast and crew and highlighted Lorre's artistic personality, his pursuit of reality before and behind the camera, and his unselfish working methods. All was fodder for the newspapers willing to run it. Few did.

More controversy brewed south of Germany. In clearing *Der Verlorene*, the FSK had paved the way for its entry in the Venice Biennale's 12th International Exhibition of Cinematic Art, which ran from August 20 to September 10, 1951. Although more skeptical observers agreed with American actress Myrna Loy, who considered the Venice Film Festival "essentially a showcase for the burgeoning postwar Italian film industry," it attracted entries from all over the world. Possibly hoping to curry favor with German audiences, Lorre publicly declared that he preferred to premiere the picture in Germany, not Italy. The statement, suggested Pressburger in 1985, should be taken with a grain of salt. Far from resisting the idea of entering *Der Verlorene* in the competition, Lorre was delighted. "We were both for it," reiterated Pressburger. "Submitting a film to a festival is not a premiere, really. It could only help Lorre."

The filmmaker traveled to Venice on September 6, explicitly to request admission to the Biennale. "Rumor-mongers" had already speculated that *Der Verlorene* would be excluded from the program for political reasons.[25] Some apparently feared it might cast Germany in a bad light. The same jury, suggested *Die Welt*'s Ernst v.d. Decken, that sought to publicly acknowledge "those films which testify to a genuine effort toward the progress of cinematography as a means of artistic expression" balked at lending credence to a film that fell short of "spreading civilisation and culture, and of promoting the brotherhood of Nations." Even Fred Pressburger believed there was "a great deal of hostility towards the film, particularly by official or semi-official sources." Decken indicated that Director Antonio Petrucci and a representative from the Bonner Bundeshaus had agreed to schedule only two German entries in Venice, *Lockende Gefahr* (*The Allure of Danger*, 1950), the story of a boy who saves a fisherman from acting on his criminal urges, and *Das Doppelte Lottchen* (*Little Lotty Times Two*, 1950), in which separated twin sisters happily reunite their parents. In the end, a press release from the committee officially quelled the rumors with news that *Der Verlorene* "was not included in the calendar because it was not certain that a good copy could be ready in time, and because it was not known whether the author [Lorre] had decided to enter the competition." Whatever the reasons for its omission, German journalists fought stubbornly for its inclusion.

On September 9, one day before the festival closed, an unsubtitled print of *Der Verlorene* was finally screened. Reporting for *Films in Review,* Robert F. Hawkins wrote that "*Der Verlorene,* seen this afternoon, proved to be one of the best postwar German films. It is splendidly directed and acted (by Peter Lorre), and is marred only by a split script which tries to handle two major themes simultaneously: a man's mental condition and German resistance movements during the Hitler regime." Its entry generated some controversy and, by default, a good measure of publicity, but the film won no prizes. First place went to Akira Kurosawa's *Rashomon* (1950), with *A Streetcar Named Desire* (1951) capturing a Special Jury Prize and the prize for Best Actress for Vivien Leigh.

Der Verlorene premiered at the Turm Palast in Frankfurt am Main on Tuesday, September 18, 1951. Its ten-day run played to scant and restless audiences. Although Lorre accused National of not getting behind the film, he had only himself to blame for not taking up the slack in its marketing campaign. In one of his few promotional appearances, he turned up at the Heidelberg Film Club's evening showing of *Der Verlorene* at the Capitol, where he received public thanks and heartfelt applause for donating the proceeds to the city's building lottery.

Bartning remembered feeling "mad and disappointed" when he saw the film at Berlin's Delphi Theater. "My wife had to hold me down," he angrily recalled, "because I would have run on the stage and proclaimed, 'That is not the film,' so wild was I. . . . I never saw it again." Few Germans even saw it once, and those who did were not enthusiastic. "No one was there," said Bartning. "People went out embarrassed. No applause. Nothing. People simply went out."

Heavy press coverage of the premiere told Lorre that he had struck a nerve. Quite predictably, *Der Verlorene* became an instant focus of controversy, "the hottest iron of the last five years, the lost one in the midst of those who are out of their minds." German reviewers agreed to disagree on almost every aspect of the film. Disgusted with the mediocrity of postwar cinema, Alexandre Alexandre, writing for the Düsseldorf *Der Mittag,* pointed out that "not large sums of money make truly valuable films, not super-modern, technologically equipped studios, nor stars whose salaries often stand in opposition to their performances and their enthusiasm for the art of making movies . . . but poets—film poets." Lorre proved it "possible to escape the pattern which threatened to strangle the German postwar movie." German movie critics apparently agreed because they voted him *Film Revue*'s "Bambi" prize for the "most artistic film" of 1951. For others, however, renewing old forms did not signify new beginnings. *Der Verlorene* brought to mind a time of unparalleled expressiveness in the arts, but its sense of cynicism recalled too strongly a similar trend of the Weimar years.

Der Verlorene's fusing of pathology and politics also raised eyebrows—and hackles. The *Hamburger Echo*'s "St-e" understood how the "regime of inhumanity breaks down the barrier between human and beast." "G-z," however, writing for the *Stuttgarter Zeitung,* argued that one "cannot mix a lust murder with an indictment of a political system." In Munich's *Süddeutsche Zeitung,* Gunter Groll stated that the film didn't clearly explain "how a man becomes a murderer in the witches' cauldron of murderous times." He believed it was wrong to show a "timeless type" as "typical of the times" and "an exception as universal and symbolic." After all, lust murder was not specific to the Third Reich, but could happen anywhere and anytime—wherever conditions are right, Lorre might have added.[26]

The Filmbewertungsstelle der Länder der Bundesrepublik Deutschland (Film Evaluation Office of the States of the Federal German Republic), which stood next in line after the FSK to pass judgment on *Der Verlorene,* found for the critics, who believed that "one cannot touch the nerves with one crime and rouse the flaming moral anger with other crimes." On September 6, 1951, shortly after beginning its rating system, the FBL awarded *Der Verlorene* the *Prädikat* "wertvoll" (valuable), which guaranteed a 50 percent tax reduction and a wider audience. Judging by the criteria—originality and difficulty of the theme, cultural and present value, artistic-technical form, single performances (e.g., direction, acting, photography, and so on)—the Lorre production might well have anticipated the *Prädikat* "besonders wertvoll" (especially valuable).[27]

Dominated by government officials, with minority representation by professionals in private practices, film journalists, representatives from the film industry, and churches, the commission explained that after "long and intensive discussion," it could not give the higher of the two ratings: "The first reason was that, despite the horrible consequences for which the environment is to blame, in the beginning it deals with an act of pathological insanity. It is through this that the first deed is missing a last motivation. It cannot be based directly on the circumstances of our state system in the Third Reich and also not alone from the human aspects. Even if it is recognized that the movie in its further handling shows an ethically and politically positive tendency, the macabre starting point does not allow the granting of a higher *Prädikat.*"

Salvaging what they could, National excerpted another paragraph from the commission's opinion that put a better face on the "*wertvoll*" rating and pushed it into print: "This action, which rests on a true occurrence, has been formed with very unusual forcefulness. The quality of the acting by Peter Lorre and the other actors, and the direction and the camera are from a cinematic power of expression as no other German film of the last years and as almost no foreign film of the postwar period has shown. In addition to this very special artistic performance stands also the tendency of the film, which shows in an extremely necessary and impressive way to what kind of destruction of an individual a dictatorially guided state can lead."

Few newspapers took the bait, however, undoubtedly reluctant to fly in the face of a growing consensus that acknowledging the past meant succumbing to it. "Etched black on black," Lorre's film reputedly shrouded viewers in a "nihilistic fog" that presumed the world is inherently bad and man bestial. *Der Verlorene* "burdens the senses, troubles the heart and suffocates the hopes," warned Manes Kadow in the *Frankfurter Neue Press.* He cautioned audiences to defend themselves against the "smartly shaded excuse of our mental fatigue. It is trapped in analysis. Even in psychoanalysis. Its statue is hatred and revenge, the helplessness and longing. We need more." Setting Lorre's "hopeless hero" against the chaos and confusion of the times, such critics deplored the dark fatalism of a human being "not worth pitying in his passivity, in his soft drifting away." Psychopathic impulses neither merited sympathy nor served a tragic function. However artistically courageous Lorre's walk through the "jungle of art," it belonged to the "boundary zone of life" and Dr. Karl Rothe's pathological excesses in the psychological textbooks.

Alexandre Alexandre, writing for Frankfurt's *Abendpost,* declared that if Lorre had gotten into "the devilish workings of hypocrisy, unconcealed cynicism, easy responsibility, wormy morals, bestiality and unchained madness of our epoch," he had no right to do so, having trespassed on history through which he had not lived. Vocal detractors even took sharp aim at his "small boy's picture of the resistance," which played like a parody of the "July putsch."

While some critics did not like what he was saying, others liked the way he said it. "He alone convinces," wrote Christian Ferber in Munich's *Neue Zeitung,* "a guy like a well-built cello; elegant in the curves, carrying away with each tone; touching, charming, human; terrifying, when the compulsion to murder arises; creaturely poor, when the fear of himself overcomes him; brother Abel and brother Cain in one body; a great actor." Others likewise credited his "brilliantly moderated" acting, which "etches the hell visages of his criminals into our consciousness." Even when the story was not convincing, his "painful impressiveness" put it over "because barely before was one of our film actors so eerily intensive, so economical in means and so suggestive in effect." A few even praised his understanding of form, rhythm, and the language of pictures and predicted that he stood on the brink of a distinguished career as a director.

Looking at Lorre (which is difficult to avoid, given the number of intense close-ups), he seems to be carrying the pain of the world in his face: rage, regret, longing, anguish, isolation, resignation, disgust, apathy. As a landscape of human expression, it had matured into a fretwork of lines, angles, and contours that reflected "the lostness of a human being in the time," wrote Hans Hellmut Kirst in the *Münchner Merkur*. "Convincingly caught in a depressing milieu, expressed by posture and pace, it can be read in helpless facial features which are eaten up by loneliness, longing and restlessness. Peter Lorre as Dr. Rothe above on the screen surrounded by shadow and light, wearily lurking, pursued and resigned, with a twisted smile of the marked one—one of the greatest acting accomplishments which the German film has ever shown."

Lorre knew he could express more with his face than his staff of writers could say in six scripts. For many critics, however, overstating his strength weakened his performance. Placing himself too much in the foreground made him an easy target for accusations of egocentrism. The director Lorre, they maintained, should have reined in the actor Lorre, whose "face doesn't let go." "Even the most expressive countenance cannot hold out continually," pointed out Gerd Schulte in the *Hannoversche Allgemeine Zeitung*. "Artistic usages, which, economically used, have the strongest effect, are worn out in this way. One should not stereotype his own stereotype."

Faint praise came late when the Bundesinnenminister Dr. Lehr declined to award the German Film Prize for the best feature film of 1952. The mostly political committee, whose disregard of artistic criteria caused many to question its judgment, believed, not surprisingly, that movies should serve "the cultural advancement and development of taste." Unable to overlook one of the most important and controversial postwar films, however distasteful, it awarded *Der Verlorene* "lobende Anerkennung" (praiseworthy recognition) and stated that the film "possesses without question high preferences: the acting capability of the main actor Peter Lorre, the cinematography, the music, the bold discussion of the destructive powers of the recent past."

German censors kept audiences looking forward, not back. Tired of "accusatory" films, moviegoers thirsted for escape from their problems. In pictures that portrayed the "idealized pleasures of country life," they drank their fill of *Heimatschnulzen* (homegrown schmaltz), "heather and heartache" daydreams doused in sentimental fatalism.[28] Accustomed to seeing its doctors as self-sacrificing, dedicated heroes, audiences thought ill of Rothe's bedside manner.[29] Instead of saving lives, he took them. Even that sharp contrast, however, faded against the moral ambiguity of the film's postwar backdrop, making it difficult to know where American film noir began and German rubble left off.[30] First-person narrative from a deserted, rundown, and underlit canteen, gloomy basement corridors, cold and lonely city streets, starkly nuanced dialogue, and through it all the hollow echo of gallows humor gave visual and verbal texture to the cynical, disillusioned, and despairing tone of the times. Seemingly swept up with the prevailing postwar pessimism, Lorre turned the lights lower with what a recent essayist labeled his "hardboiled melancholy." It was a bitter pill to take.

Lorre was convinced that German audiences had misunderstood *Der Verlorene*. Fred Pressburger disagreed: "They didn't misunderstand it. The problem was they understood it only too well. They didn't want any part of it. In a way, maybe the film was not good enough to overcome that. . . . The final rejection was that they just didn't go and see it." It wasn't simply a matter of Lorre being out of step with his German viewers. "He wanted to be out of step," said Pressburger. More important, he was also out of time. After the war, the Allies closely monitored cultural reparation of occupied Germany. De-Nazifying the cinema took high priority. Any films that intimated nationalist tendencies were impounded and replaced with innocuous imports. Often escapist, these pictures looked to the future rather than the past and stressed the importance of democratic values to Germany's moral reconstruction.

The Allies also helped put the German film industry back on its feet, with the Soviet Union's state-sponsored DEFA (Deutsche Film Aktiengesellschaft) taking the lead. The first postwar films fell under the heading of *Trümmerfilme* (rubble films), a realist movement that treated contemporary social problems: the assimilation of returned soldiery (*Irgendwo in Berlin* [*Somewhere in Berlin*], 1946), war crimes (*Die Mörder sind unter uns* [*The Murderers Are amongst Us*], 1946), land reform (*Freies Land* [*Free Land*], 1946), anti-Semitism (*Ehe im Schatten* [*Marriage in the Shadow*], 1947). In cold theaters audiences huddled together for commiserative exercises in self-examination, all part of the plan for spiritual recovery. "The Germans must make films which have some connection with the times," said producer Erich Pommer, "and show a way into the future." Too late to be a "rubble" film, *Der Verlorene* fell into the category of generic hybrid. Axel Eggebrecht eventually dismissed it as "a sensational thriller with political shading." Although it rose from the ruins, *Der Verlorene* was no *Trümmerfilm*.

Der Verlorene fell flat with French audiences, but it found its big supporter in French film historian Lotte H. Eisner, who felt the language barrier blocked understanding of Lorre's message. She defended his vision in a review essay for *Cahiers du Cinéma:* "The 'lost one' does not blame the Nazis for his own fall, but for not having acted ruthlessly against him after the murder, for not having judged and executed him. He blames them for disguising a murder victim as a suicide because it serves their own dirty ends. . . . Perhaps the case of Peter Lorre's film is as complex as that of *Limelight,* which had to be re-seen and re-seen before all its layers of hidden beauty could be penetrated and some of its more bewildering aspects could be understood." In her classic work *L'écran demoniaque* (1952), which reached English-speaking audiences (in a revised edition) as *The Haunted Screen: Expressionism in the German Cinema and the Influence of Max Reinhardt* (1969), Eisner further spelled out her critical approval: "Lorre gives evidence of very personal inspiration. He has matured, his physique has improved with his art, he knows how to avoid false pathos and overemphasis, and how to give full weight to silences. . . . There is not a single slip, a single forced contrast, or a single false value." In a postwar cinema stagnated by mechanical comedies and smothering dramas, said Eisner, *Der Verlorene* recalled the best of the past and looked to a brighter future. With its failure, she lamented, "the German cinema lost for some years all its hopes of renewal."

In August 1952, six months after returning to the United States from Germany, Lorre put Jonas Silverstone to work negotiating the American release of *Der Verlorene.* However, sorting out the tangled foreign rights for a film that had little chance of finding an audience at home proved doubly discouraging. Silverstone took a cue from Lorre's growing resignation in the face of commercial reality and lost heart. Armed with ready answers for his reluctance to bring the picture out over here, he expressed concern that it would be "simply treated as a psychological shocker" rather than as "the only anti-Nazi picture made in Germany, a story of times without law." Political considerations, he later elaborated, persuaded him to keep it under lock and key, adding, "I must be out of my mind—I own 60% of it."[31] Putting a public-spirited face on his decision to "not ever bring it out over here," Lorre stated that "it would probably make money too. But there are times when an actor should know enough not to make money. I don't think the State Department would like me to indict any other country's politics."

Although German film clubs dragged *Der Verlorene* out of the closet from time to time, the picture did not reach American audiences until 1983. Centering more on form than content, critics singled out the same strengths and weaknesses as their German counterparts had thirty-two years earlier. Once again, they credited Lorre with delivering one of his best screen performances. "He reached new heights as a master of gesture, mood, symbolic image and significant silences," wrote Prairie Farkus in the *Daily World*, the only Marxist daily newspaper published in the United States. *New York Times* critic Vincent Canby called it "an interesting expression of the frustration of Lorre's creative personality," touching on an aspect of his history that seemed to evoke sympathy from American critics. The *Los Angeles Herald-Examiner* noted that the actor moved through the film "with an almost palpable weariness and despair." He "looks tired, weary of life, drawn," added Shawn Cunningham in the *Villager*. "There's a heaviness in each footstep and in each drag on the chain smoked cigarettes." Despite the "authentic note of internal suffering that cannot be questioned," for most critics, Lorre's "carefully controlled, intense performance" was far more impressive than his film. Critical opinion of *Der Verlorene* ran the gamut from a lukewarm "evocative" to a damning "platitudinous." For all the subtlety of Lorre's "natural" acting style, as a filmmaker he neither resolved the story's moral dilemma nor managed a meaningful political statement.

Comparisons between Lang and Lorre seemed inevitable. Only one reviewer noted the difference between their geometric and allegorical directing styles. Another credited Lorre with breathing "freshness into the expressionist style, while showing a great deal of restraint." Most, however, thought *Der Verlorene* derivative of Lorre's most notable screen success in *M* and suggested that he depended too much on Fritz Lang for inspiration. Twenty years later, they pointed out, he had paid his debt to the past in the deflated currency of an "inwardly tortured psychotic murderer who is really a good guy at heart."

Lorre stayed on in Germany through late fall and early winter of 1951 in hopes that *Der Verlorene* would catch on and generate film offers. "We sat in his small dreary hotel room on Munich's Karlplatz," recalled Manfred George, a reporter for the American German-language newspaper *Aufbau*. "He told of his disappointments. He was tired and depressed and times were far off. . . . Peter Lorre sat and waited for the hotel clerk to call and announce the arrival of film producers, backers and distributors. No one called." Neither the producers, who had taken pot shots at "an outsider and emigrant [who] was already a thorn in the side" because he proved artistic films could be made with limited means, nor National, which he accused of making cuts without consulting him, prompting a knife-twisting clarification that independent production was impossible without independent distribution.

He took it personally. "The defeat of *The Lost One* almost crushed my father," said daughter Catharine. "It was a miscarriage. He felt the film worked. It was every part of his creative ability. A lot of energy was gone." Of his post-partum mood, Irving Yergin remembered that the film's failure left Lorre hurt, bitter, and depressed. His staged comeback in his homeland had backfired. Like Beckert and Rothe, he stood on the outside looking in, a stranger in what had become a strange land.

In an earlier letter to Elisabeth Hauptmann, he had replied, albeit somewhat belatedly, to Brecht's invitations to join his ensemble with veiled overtures indicating that "the winter sleep and swamp time ended long ago." Interested in reestablishing contact, he asked Hauptmann to send him some of Brecht's poetry. However much he wanted the verse, Lorre used the opportunity to put out feelers about a position. "I don't want to be a nobody forever," echoed an actor desperately anxious to renew his options in Germany. "It would mean so much to me if you could dig up something for me—I would be very grateful to you." But Brecht turned over nothing for his friend.

When reporters asked Lorre what he had in mind for his next picture, he called upon "Kaspar Hauser" for a ready answer. He might have put a more definite face on the future had he known of Alfred Neumann's intentions to cast him as the mentally disturbed Zar in a film production of his novel *Der Patriot* (*The Patriot*). In a letter of March 20, 1951, Neumann had informed director William Dieterle that he had optioned their proposed film projects based on *Der Patriot* and *Der Teufel* (*The Devil*) to producer Rudolph Cartier, of Telecine Films Ltd., London.[32] Dieterle accepted Cartier's offer to direct both pictures. But the plans for the Anglo-American-German production fell apart even before they had fallen together. Cartier admitted that although Neumann was a great author, he lacked experience in the film business. Otherwise, said the producer, he would have chosen Orson Welles for the role of Zar. In June Dieterle advised Neumann to cancel the option because of Cartier's undependability.[33]

Like Brecht, Lorre also voiced thoughts of updating Shakespeare. The idea of translating MacDuff, Duncan, and Macbeth into contemporary Germany fascinated him "just as every story fascinates me where inner conflicts and suffering form the center of a human being."

The foreign press reported that RKO had offered Lorre the position of European director for its planned distribution of *Der Verlorene*, which it also intended to produce in an English-language version before the winter theater season began. Press reports also stated that German and Italian producers sought his services for salaries up to seventy-five thousand deutsche marks. If it sounded too good to be true, it was.[34]

Another project at least held the possibility of materializing. German response to Malcolm Lowry's *Under the Volcano* had been very warm. Ernst Klett Verlag, Lowry's German publisher, had sought to obtain the film rights to the novel in fall of 1950. One year later, Clemens ten Holder, his translator, informed Lowry that Klett was interested in negotiating a movie version with a German company, possibly Arnold Pressburger Productions. The financial potential of such a plan, perhaps with Peter Lorre in the main role of the Consul, he added, was great and would increase sales of the book. Although earlier efforts from American film companies had, according to Lowry, fallen through "for fear of censorship," the author attached more importance to a German production. As a student of expressionist cinema, Lowry told Klett he "would rather have it produced in Germany than in any country in the world." That same day, Lowry wrote to ten Holder in "a complete dither of excitement" about the possibility of a film. He felt that the book would make a great picture. Believing that he had "many excellent ideas for its transposition into the cinematic medium, which [he could not] help but feel would be valuable," he stated that he and his wife, Margerie, wanted a hand in writing the scenario. Several weeks later, possibly anticipating Klett's reluctance to involve Lowry in the script development, ten Holder tried to put the brakes on the author's careening enthusiasm with news of *Der Verlorene*'s disappointing show. He also raised the larger, more difficult issue of financing films in postwar Germany.

Lorre and Lowry shared much more in common than names that sounded the same (a fact that fascinated Lowry). Their respective cinematic and literary efforts grew out of "a great hash" concocted from every hidden, repressed, and pigeonholed experience from pasts that haunted presents: exile, isolation, loneliness, despair, damnation, remorse, redemption, tragic self-awareness, and the loss of identity.[35] In a letter to his English publisher, Lowry wrote that his novel was "concerned with the guilt of man, with his remorse, with his ceaseless struggling towards the light under the weight of the past, and with his doom." That "the part [of the Consul] might have been written for him [Lorre]" speaks to a perception that went well beyond admiration.

Darker parallels existed between the two men. Both were addicts whose chemical dependencies stemmed from their own frustration and failure. Tortured by personal demons, many self-inflicted, Lowry and Lorre journeyed into emotional labyrinths and lost their way. Rediscovery became a series of dizzying regressions that spiraled out of control, blurring the line between art and autobiography. Like the scorpion in the story, not wanting to be saved, they stung themselves to death. Form followed theme. If Lowry, who did a stint in Hollywood, wrote in cinematic terms, Lorre thought in them. Both visualized the machinelike qualities of fate, the one in the mechanized, circular image of a carousel, the other in the relentless rotation of the locomotive's wheels. These images are reminders that "the present cannot escape the past, that the impotence of man's present merges with the guilt of his past." It is hardly surprising, then, that novel and film are both circular: prologue is epilogue. The central characters rush downhill toward death and damnation. Likewise, both stories run their course in a day, with frequent use of flashbacks. Using mirrors, staircases, and shadows to achieve a degree of "expressive emphasis and distortion," Lowry and Lorre each paid homage to the German cinema. Interior monologues and metaphoric language also darkened an already "stifling, doom-laden . . . overwhelming and all-encompassing vision of decay, despair and self-destructiveness" that characterized the men and their works. And like Lowry, Lorre (more so in the early script versions) cast "the autobiographic consciousness" as the hero of his story.

Although Lorre apparently still needed to be sold on the idea, Lowry was convinced that they could make a film so great that "God knows what it might lead to eventually." The idea that Lorre, "one of the greatest actors who has ever lived," might play the Consul and possibly even produce the film, kept Lowry's head in the clouds. He confided to Harold Matson, his agent, that he had

> a real regard for Lorre's art, which by the way has rarely been seen here at its highest, not even in "M."—Chaplin said he was the greatest living actor too, by the way, and Chaplin is probably right.—But the point is the public has tended to think of him as a sort of Mr. Yamamoto-cum-horror doctor. There couldn't be a better part for him than the Consul, though an enormous amount depends on his director. Not even Fritz Lang did well enough by him perhaps. And even Paul Fejos—an even greater, if possible, director—did not do right by him, or himself.[36]

By late November, with *Der Verlorene* all but driven out of the theaters, and Lorre looking for another German production, Klett succeeded in interesting the actor in making a film out of *Under the Volcano*. Reportedly "fascinated" with the project, Lorre even read from Lowry over Radio München before returning to New York. Though Klett had offered to strike a fifty-fifty deal on profits from a film version one year earlier, problems arose when the publisher indicated that it preferred to "go around" Matson and deal directly with Lowry, whose "say in the treatment and scenario" remained to be settled to his satisfaction. Although he refused to sign a film contract, Lowry nonetheless nurtured hope that the project would not fall through. In December 1951 he even suggested keeping Lorre's "interest hot" by writing a letter that would be personally delivered by Matson in New York. Matson replied that in his judgment the "whole tangle" seemed "very unlikely of a profitable outcome . . . and I wonder if it's worth pursuing unless there's something persistent and definite forthcoming from Klett." As late as October 1952 Lowry still held out the possibility of a German film starring Lorre.

Broke and without solid prospects, Lorre raised the red, white, and blue flag. Surrendering to America, however, did not mean yielding to Hollywood. According to the German press, he planned to conquer Broadway as the crippled French painter Toulouse-Lautrec in a stage play of Pierre La Mure's novel *Moulin Rouge,* adapted by the author and actor José Ferrer, who would also direct the production for the Plymouth Theater. Lorre reportedly signed a two-year contract for fifteen hundred dollars weekly and 7.5 percent of the earnings and committed to a film version of the play for RKO.[37]

"Strange to say," said José Ferrer, "I know nothing whatever about Peter Lorre being involved with *Moulin Rouge.* I suspect that this is the work of Pierre La Mure, who was apt to say anything to anyone if it suited his mood of the moment. I bought the dramatic stage rights to *Moulin Rouge* with the idea of presenting the play that Mr. La Mure had written. The play was flawed, in my opinion, but I felt that there was enough material in the novel to make a good dramatic presentation. Unfortunately, Mr. La Mure was most intractable and refused to change a word of his play, so I was hopelessly stuck with something I could not seem to be able to manage. It was at this point that John Huston called me up and asked me if I was interested in making the film (*Moulin Rouge,* 1953) and naturally I was, and that was the end of the plan for producing *Moulin Rouge* as a play."

At the first of the year, an American officer in the Special Services offered Lorre a free flight home in exchange for showings of *Der Verlorene* at U.S. Army bases in Italy, Greece, and North Africa. After receiving triple typhoid and tetanus vaccinations at the 18th Field Hospital in Nuremberg, Lorre boarded a DC-4 Air Force transport out of Frankfurt's Rhein Main airport on February 16, 1952. The plane was bound for Westover Air Force Base in Springfield, Massachusetts. He took with him only a toothbrush, a washcloth, a razor, and a 35mm print of *Der Verlorene,* allegedly stolen, since he had no permission from National to keep a copy of the film. Annemarie waved goodbye from the tarmac.

9

ELEPHANT DROPPINGS

With occasional interruptions, I've been
killing my way through life. It's that simple.

—Peter Lorre

I need the hum of the cameras and the illumination
of the spot-light. I will make films until I die.

—Peter Lorre

Disappointment awaited Lorre in America. Wasted and unable to generate interest in *Der Verlorene,* the defeated actor-director-writer returned from his lonely mission empty-handed. He had sought to listen and to learn, and perhaps to help himself by helping others. His countrymen had paid him back in indifference, "with interest and interest's interest." Friends felt that he also wanted to shout down those who doubted he could rise above the studio star system by proving that he could write, direct, and act. No one heard him. Now he picked up where he had left off, as if *Der Verlorene* had never happened.

Back in New York, Lorre visited the Silverstones in Pleasantville, then checked into Beekman Towers at the corner of Forty-ninth Street and First Avenue to be nearer NBC, which guest-spotted him on *The Big Show* on March 9, 1952. Tallulah Bankhead sugarcoated Lorre's reintroduction to the American public: "And now, darlings, making his first appearance in the United States after a year's absence abroad, where his most recent triumph he directed, produced and starred, in one of Europe's most sensational pictures, the distinguished artist, Mr. Peter Lorre." He opened on a familiar note: "I started my career in the theater as a romantic actor (*laughter*), but against my will they put me into horror pictures. I always wanted to be the actor who got the girl, but in my pictures by the time I get the girl, she's dead. Well, I've struggled to get away from playing with monsters, but I guess it is my fate, because here I am today with Tallulah Bankhead."

"Well, that's my fault," riposted Bankhead. "I'm just going to have to enunciate more clearly. I distinctly told them to get me Peter Lawford!" Poe's "The Cask of Amontillado," a comic takeoff on Meredith Wilson's novel *Who Did What to Fadalia?* and a few crooned lines from "May the Good Lord Bless and Keep You" rounded out his return to radio.

Later in the month he sank his teeth into a meatier repast on *Lux Video Theater*'s "Taste." Billed as "Hollywood's Loveable Bogeyman," he played a sinister gourmet who wagers that he can guess the date and vineyard of a rare claret served with dinner, staking his town and country houses against the hand of his host's reluctant daughter.

When friends—and oftentimes strangers—asked something of Lorre, he unselfishly lent a helping hand without cross-examining them or qualifying his response. In May 1952 his generosity earned him one of the most remarkable credits in his spare political résumé. After the war, Jonas Silverstone's commanding officer, Thomas B. Sawyer, had been elected to a Democratic seat in the North Carolina state Senate. Now, in his move to unseat incumbent Representative Carl T. Durham in the May 31 Democratic primary, Sawyer called on Silverstone for a little celebrity backing. Lorre readily agreed to leave Annemarie, who had recently arrived from Hamburg, with Beatrice Silverstone in New York and stump for the candidate through four counties—Durham, Orange, Alamance, and Guilford—making up the 6th Congressional District.

Lorre distanced himself from the political bandwagon by claiming that his chief purpose in coming to North Carolina was to entertain the wounded veterans of the Korean conflict hospitalized at Fort Bragg. Sawyer supporters, however, invented a shared past for the actor and their candidate. Accompanying a photo of the two at the Washington Duke Hotel—warmly pictured with their hands on each other's shoulders—was a brief, and entirely fictional, mention of their first meeting at an army hospital in Casablanca, where Sawyer had been a patient during the war. Nonetheless, Lorre gladly barnstormed on radio and television and appeared—along with circus clown Buzzie Potts, the Duke Ambassadors Dixieland Combo, Texas Jim Hall and his Radio Rangers, Bob Williams and his Cumberland Mountains Boys, and the Singing Blacksmith—at "Tom Sawyer for Congress" rallies in High Point, Greensboro, Burlington, and Durham.

"He didn't say that Jonas was a mutual friend of ours," explained Sawyer. "He made it more direct. He just said he was a friend of mine and that he knew I'd make a good Congressman." After plugging the politician, Lorre drew thunderous applause with his recitation of "The Tell-Tale Heart" and then, with Sawyer and Silverstone, wearily piloted the candidate's old Studebaker Land Cruiser to their next engagement.

If Lorre and politics made strange bedfellows on other occasions, this was no exception. Politically, he generally rallied some form of commitment de facto, under duress, or ex post facto. Giving politics a wide berth, however, did not spare him an inside look at the "good ol' boy" network in North Carolina. Carl Durham saw in the Communist witch-hunt hysteria a chance to pull the plug on his opponent's Hollywood connection. An underling rumored that Sawyer had "C-o-m-m-e-r-n-i-s-t-s" working for him. Though he did not name the actor, Durham even repeated the accusation in a radio ad.

Sawyer was furious and used his military service connections to contact J. Edgar Hoover. "Hoover went into the whole thing," recalled Sawyer, "and said that Peter Lorre's former wife [Karen Verne] had once attended a communist front organization and that was the only link they could ever find, so it was strictly guilt by association." Sawyer believed the allegation "very much shocked" Lorre, but he couldn't say that he was upset, "because he was beginning to understand the mentality of the southern politician." Whether the actor hurt or helped Sawyer's campaign is impossible to assess. Lorre felt that he had done more harm than good, although Sawyer disagreed. Nonetheless, Durham won reelection.

Lorre's unsettled future returned him to his beginnings. He looked to the theater for renewal. "You can stay alive," he said later, "even if you have to go back to a little theater somewhere. . . . If [you're] good in it you will be all fresh and they will take you all over again." He had been trying to get to Broadway for seventeen years but had come no closer than appearing—with Marlene Dietrich—in *Broadway*, "An American Time-Picture in Three Acts" at the Vienna Kammerspiele in September 1927. The right vehicle eluded him, and poor timing plagued him. In 1952 he settled for a summer stock engagement in playwright and screenwriter Edwin Justus Mayer's *A Night at Madame Tussaud's: A Shocker in the Grand Guignol Manner*. Set in Paris in 1794, the bloodiest year in the Reign of Terror, when the fear of being denounced as a rightist hung like a shroud over a nervous citizenry, the play drew obvious parallels to 1947, the year that HUAC began pressing informants to name names.

At Madame Tussaud's Museum, Brutus (Lorre), a long-haired, pock-faced artist and self-styled patriot who knows the benefits of informing, fashions death masks of the enemies of the Revolution who have met their end under the guillotine's blade. When Madame Tussaud shelters a titled couple posing as brother and sister, Brutus denounces the house. Before the Marquis Lomenie de Brienne and Ninon can escape to Calais and on to England, she is forced to endure his macabre advances: "Blood. Blood. It's a funny thing about that, Ninon. I've never told you, have I? I don't understand it myself. I want you. I want you all the time. But never so much as when the blood begins to run over the scaffold. Never so much as then. Why should I want you so much then, Ninon?" When she threatens to inform against him, Brutus replies that the inquisitors will swallow anything he tells them: "Yes, they will! I know it better than anyone! I've told them a thousand lies." In the end, Brutus becomes the unwitting victim of his own treachery, literally losing his head over Ninon, who decapitates him.

A Night at Madame Tussaud's began its five-week tryout on the "straw-hat" circuit, opening at the Norwich (Connecticut) Summer Theatre on August 18, 1952. "Broadway could do with a good horror play with comedy overtones," wrote *Variety*'s Vernon Rice on August 20. "Time and a lot of work will decide whether this can be it." *Madame Tussaud* was in rough shape. Heavy exposition further congested the already airless piece. The critics, guardedly optimistic, advised accelerating the pace, heightening the suspense, and fleshing out the historical setting. "Somebody will have to decide if the play is going to be an out-and-out horror," diagnosed Rice for the *New York Post*'s August 20 evening edition, "or a horror play with comedy overtones. With Lorre around, it should be comedy that's stressed." Lorre—who codirected with Mayer—prescribed a full dose of humor for the play's ailments. In his American stage debut, the actor played, in his own wisecracking words, "a great man, a great artist, and a great patriot." Relishing, as one critic noted, "crime for the fun of it," he became a mischievous prankster gleefully romping through the Reign of Terror. "I don't understand it," Brutus pleads to Ninon. "I'm the best-hearted man in the world. And yet, people always say I frighten them. Or if they don't say it, they look it."

Hiding pixies in his menace had long been part of the act. "The reason I can dare to put humor into a dramatic piece," he boasted, "is because I can get the audience back into it at any moment." As Peck's Bad Boy, he set the production on end, translating the melodrama into a "ghoulish mélange of humor, comedy, blood and paranoia." Lorre conceded toward the end of the Boston run that "the play needs plenty of work, but we're delighted with the response so far."[1]

Behind the scenes, however, conflict undermined *Madame Tussaud's* comic overtones. Producer and stage manager Ben Kranz and actress Miriam Hopkins, who played the part of Ninon, had optioned the play. "Lorre and Hopkins hated each other cordially," said Paul Mayer, Edwin Justus Mayer's son. Accustomed to being "top dog," the actress called the shots. Her habitual hysteria rankled Lorre. For a recreational outlet, he arm-wrestled, taking on all comers, and easily put down actors half his age. Under his breath, however, "you could hear him muttering 'that bitch' and so on," said actor Joseph Warren. "I tell you I wouldn't have wanted to be on the receiving end. He could be rough, rough as a cob." In Boston Hopkins fluttered on stage like a fidgety canary while Lorre stood next to her, flat and sober, obviously amused at the chance to throw his jaded costar into sharp and silly relief. They finally refused to speak to each another.

Things reached a breaking point at York, Pennsylvania, during the final week of the tour. "Hopkins got so angry with Peter," recalled Mayer, "that after the final curtain, she kicked him. He took his bow hopping on one foot, certainly more for effect than from pain. He must have enjoyed that!" Their animosity doomed the play's chances for a major production. The Shuberts had voiced interest in bringing it to Broadway and planned to star Lorre, for whom Mayer had tailored the role, but they emphatically did not want Hopkins, who was twenty years too old for the part of Ninon.[2] Conversely, Hopkins wanted the Shuberts, but not Lorre. Mayer asked her to release the play, which she refused to do. "Hopkins held the rights long enough," said Mayer, "for the Shuberts to cool off, long enough for Peter to go back to Hollywood, long enough for the thing to fall apart."

"It was not a great play," conceded the playwright's son, "but it was an audience-pleaser." In its second week's run, *A Night at Madame Tussaud's* reportedly drew seven curtain calls at the Boston Summer Theater, affirming Rice's early prediction that "the master scarer . . . will prove a draw, if only for curiosity value."

Plans for a long pre-Broadway tour, directed by Rouben Mamoulian and put on by the Playwrights Company, did not come together. Lorre would not give up, but kept after Mayer to revise the play. Eventually the author trimmed and tightened the overwritten piece. In the summer of 1960, eight years after the first run, Lorre made plans for a second theatrical circuit. The sponsors, Jonas Silverstone, Mortimer Rosenthal, and Manning Gurian, projected a West Coast premiere and a cross-country tour, culminating in a fall Broadway debut. However, in September Mayer suffered a stroke at the typewriter while working on a final rewrite of the script. On his deathbed, he made his son promise to finish the work. Completing the play deferred production another year. By then, growing discord between Paul Mayer and Jonas Silverstone had irrevocably crippled their plans.

Reluctant to surrender unconditionally to Hollywood, Lorre hung back and scouted out his options. Wistfully, he mulled over old plans to reassemble his ideal film production team and stage Pierre La Mure's *Moulin Rouge* and chalked out new ones, including a fall Broadway production of *The Happy Ant Hill*, a character comedy with a European background, by Franz Spencer (previously Franz Schulz, coauthor of *Was Frauen träumen*).[3] He needed to stay professionally active, not just for the money it brought in, because he never kept score on that account anyway, but for the work itself.

When casting did not call, Lorre felt unwanted. He fought back with self-mockery, bantering about his bulging eyes and his puckish stature, keeping his perspective at the price of his self-respect. One evening during dinner he looked across the table to John Appleton, the similarly bug-eyed English character actor.

"You know, John," cracked Lorre, "we both have eyes that look like fried eggs."

"John looked literally as if the fried eggs were dripping down his cheeks when he heard that one," recalled screenwriter Ellis St. Joseph.

At Warner Bros., Lorre once told Andrea King that he thought "he looked like a frog. Oh, he hated having to go to the stills gallery and do publicity things. I mean he really loathed it. And he would make the most awful excuses in the world not to do it, but he'd do it. He'd say, 'I'm not somebody that belongs in a movie magazine.' He felt that type of publicity was just for the beautiful people and that it was not his world at all." Lorre began to gain weight that he would never shed after returning from Germany. "Peter was upset, and that's a mild expression," said Jonas Silverstone, "with his size and shape, and because he had so much within him which could have been incorporated into a more attractive physiological being." Rejection sharpened his growing self-consciousness. For the past twenty-five years, the actor had successfully turned his singular appearance to commercial advantage. Now even that asset had become a liability.

When agent Paul Kohner got wind of Lorre's return from Germany—very possibly from John Huston, whom he had represented since the late 1930s—he shot off a letter congratulating him on his "outstanding and successful film in Germany. You know that for years I have been interested in representing you and we have had on occasion conversations about this possibility. I very keenly feel that I could produce very interesting offers for you and I am wondering if you at this time would consider giving me such an opportunity."

Kohner said he was coming to New York in May 1952 and suggested that they could have a chat. Anxious to get the actor under contract—and clearly aware that Huston had Lorre in mind for a film role—he asked Lorre "to let me know whether you are, in principle, interested." He was.

In December 1952 Karen filed a divorce complaint with the New York State Supreme Court, citing a long list of reasons why she should be granted a separation and $250 per week alimony.[4] Still "sultry, shapely," according to one reporter, she drew a poignant contrast between her lifestyle and Peter's. Because her husband resented her success in films, claimed Karen, she had given up her career to take care of the house and him, yet he had left their "happy home" in March 1950. Her letters begging him to reconsider, she stated in her petition, fell on deaf ears. Now, she complained, the studios didn't want her. Grossly exaggerating her privations and Peter's perquisites, she underscored the injustice of living a hand-to-mouth existence while he does "extremely well on his $50,000 a year minimum take from movies and stage. He wears the most expensive clothes, patronizes the best restaurants and night clubs and spends lavishly." Bereft of personal belongings and saddled with failing health, she rested her case for financial support. For whatever reason, Karen shortcut the process and refiled in Nevada several months later.

Huston saw a film in his friend Claud Cockburn's novel *Beat the Devil,* a potboiler about a band of international crooks—"fragrant with imperial decay"— bent on defrauding British East Africa out of rich uranium deposits, and persuaded Humphrey Bogart to pay the author three thousand pounds "for rights and screenplay, or a lesser sum up front, against a greater, but as yet insubstantial reward—the famous 'points'—in the distant future." Cockburn took the lump sum. After the success of *The Maltese Falcon* and *Casablanca,* Bogart had come to think of Lorre as a "good-luck token." In November he wrote to Huston: "We are trying to work out some way to get Peter Lorre in the picture. I presume you want him." Huston did indeed want Lorre for the part of O'Hara, a puckish miscreant more ludicrous than larcenous.

When Cockburn's screenplay proved unsatisfactory, Huston put Tony Veiller and Peter Viertel on the job. Three months later, Bogart arrived in London to find the new script waiting for him. His independent production company, Santana Pictures Corp., had arranged to share cost and credit with Roberto Haggiag on the Italian end and the Woolf brothers' Romulus Films on the English end.[5] If in *Beat the Devil,* with its gallery of rogues and quest for riches, Bogart had anticipated another *Maltese Falcon,* he was sadly mistaken. He told Huston that he couldn't finish reading the script: "It stinks." Huston agreed that, in his associate producer Jack Clayton's words, the screenplay lacked "a certain lightness of touch," and told Bogart he'd see him in Rome.

The Woolf brothers voiced similar reservations. "My brother and I didn't care for the book at all and said we would rather find something else," recalled executive producer Sir John Woolf, "but in the end Huston persuaded us to do it in the same way in which we had persuaded him to do *Moulin Rouge,* telling us that it would be another *Maltese Falcon* which, of course, was his favourite film, with a similar cast—Humphrey Bogart, Peter Lorre, Sidney [*sic*] Greenstreet, etc. . . . We were proposing to shoot it in colour but John Huston, with the *Maltese Falcon* in mind, wanted it to be in black and white which I think was a mistake."

Huston told Bogart in a letter dated November 19, 1952, that he didn't think the picture would be improved by using color, adding, "this is a question that I, a lowly craftsman, am less able to answer than you big corporation guys. Whatever you and Morgan decide is fine by me." Bogart replied on the twenty-sixth, deferring to the Woolf brothers, whom he dubbed "the brains."

Several weeks later, at George's American Bar, Huston and Bogart drowned sorrows that never come too late. On their table lay a copy of *Daily Variety,* which heralded the technical revolution in Hollywood; black and white pictures were out, and 3-D was in. To make matters worse, in a letter of February 13, 1953—ten days before the scheduled start of production—Joseph Breen pronounced the Veiller-Viertel first draft "unacceptable under the provisions of the Production Code." Besides condoning the adulterous relationship between Bogart's and Jennifer Jones's characters, it glamorized a criminal: "This story would seem to indicate that a man of his kind, with a criminal background, is a very dashing, romantic, and heroic character. . . . He should be thoroughly denounced by someone in the story." Foul language, brutality, homosexuality, scanty bathing suits, and a belch rounded out the list of complaints.

Breen was onto something. Huston had wanted to invent a "brand new" Bogart: "Not that old thing that's been haunting raincoats and snap-brimmed hats for God knows how long. I'd like to see you a very Continental type fellow—an extreme figure in a homburg, shoulders unpadded, French cuffs, regency trousers, fancy waistcoats and a walking stick." Neither Breen nor Bogart were buying. "And now we come to the matter of the wardrobe," Bogart wrote Huston. "I've given this a great deal of thought, oh I would say about two or three minutes while I was preparing a highball last night. I agree with you about the trench-coat etc. but as regards your brilliant conception of my wardrobe, may I say that you're full of shit. . . . As regards the cane, I don't have to tell you what you can do with THAT."

Bogart's banter notwithstanding, Huston smelled disaster and proposed they abandon the picture. "Hell, it's only money!" Bogart rallied.

"That stiffened my back," Huston wrote in his autobiography, *An Open Book*. "You can't argue with somebody like that, so we went ahead to do the best we could."

The David O. Selznick production of *Indiscretion of an American Wife* (1954), for which Truman Capote had written dialogue, was wrapping up in Rome when the *Beat the Devil* advance unit arrived. Selznick, whose wife Jennifer Jones was set to costar in the picture, had earlier advised Huston to drop the project and take one of his. Now he urged him to call in the "next-door to penniless" Capote, who was living in an outrageously expensive penthouse on the Via Margutta, "even if it is only for two or three weeks. . . . His is, in my opinion, one of the freshest and *most original* and most exciting talents of our time—and what he would say through these characters, and how he would have them say it, would be so completely different from anything that has been heard from a motion-picture theater's sound box as to give you something completely fresh—or so at least I think."

Huston gave Capote a copy of the book, which the writer claimed he never read, offered him a salary of fifteen hundred dollars a week, and told him he'd see him in Ravello, a remote village perched high above the Mediterranean along the Amalfi coast and the setting for most of the picture.

"When I got there," said Capote, "I found the story impossible as it stood, a straight and rather incredible melodrama. Both John and I felt that the best thing to do was to kid the story as we went along. The only trouble was that shooting had to begin the following week."

Huston answered the stress and strain of filmmaking with a party. "We usually have a party toward the end of the movie," said veteran Huston cinematographer Oswald "Ossie" Morris. "So we have the party and the object was to have a great ceremony of tearing up the script. Now this is the Saturday night before we were due to start the movie on Monday!"

Capote wrote for his own amusement, prompting a friend to ask, "Was it really all a game to you?" Unit publicist Julie Gibson said that he "changed the whole concept" of the film. "He'd write daily and then say, 'Oh, John is going to be surprised tomorrow. I changed the whole ending.' And that's the way it went, so nobody knew what was happening." According to Capote, he managed to stay two or three days ahead of the shooting schedule. Associate producer Jack Clayton called it closer than that, insisting that Capote often wrote the next day's scenes as the unit was out shooting and held anxious consultations with Huston and Bogart in the evenings on their return.

The picture caught up with them. Like Lorre, who had instructed his players on *Der Verlorene* that seeing the script beforehand would interfere with the intuitive development of their dialogue, Huston delivered lines just before shooting a scene, along with an explanation that this new technique would foster more spontaneous performances. "We enjoyed the entire experience," he later joked. "It was, you know, a challenge, but we met it with gaiety and the script really took off and wrote itself after a while. We followed its writing of itself with considerable admiration! (laughter). I didn't know how good it was, or how bad, or anything like that, we all knew that it was something. We just went with it."

Morris recalled that "long before the film started, I talked to John about how we were going to do the film. He said, 'Kid, I'd like this to be a sort of shaggy dog movie.'" A sense of off-set humor openly fed the on-screen fun. "It was all done to keep this sort of feeling of chaos and fun and everything going, because it was mad," explained Morris.

> That was all fostered by Huston; it was done deliberately. One night Huston and Bogart were playing poker and the message came down to Bogie, who was supposed to be producing the film, that Miss [Jennifer] Jones was sitting on top of the wardrobe in her room and wouldn't come down until he, Bogart, went up and got this man out of her bed. And Bogie said it can't be true. They went on playing poker. Finally, Bogie went upstairs and there was Peter Lorre in a bright red flannel nightie in Jennifer Jones' bed, smoking his long cigarette and reading the paper. She had come into the room, seen Peter there, screamed and leapt straight on top of the wardrobe and refused to come down until Bogart came up and got him out of her bed and apologized. So Bogie went up and fished Peter out of the bed. It was all a put-up job. That's the sort of thing that went on.

The reunion of "the unholy three" turned the clock back to happier days, and less lucrative ones, as it turned out. To work with Huston and Bogart again, Lorre had agreed to half his usual salary. Bogart's business manager, Morgan Maree, had offered him fifteen thousand dollars, which Paul Kohner persuaded him to accept, along with first-class living expenses. Just like old times, Huston and Bogart unleashed the mischievous prankster in Lorre. "He was a delight to work with and a joy to have as a friend," said Huston, "as he possessed a rare talent for gaiety. There was not a pompous or even a solemn bone in his body." When Lorre arrived in Ravello, they pretended shock that he had not dyed his hair blond, as his character was described in the script. If

Lorre caught on, he did not show it. Like the seasoned instigator he was, he answered them in kind—and went one step further. "Truman had that crazy little hairdo, the bangs, and the blond hair," said Gibson, "so Peter came down with his hair bleached and bangs cut exactly like Truman's." Lorre quipped, "I thought that this would be good for the character and maybe Truman could play my son."

The mood was infectious. Lorre and Bogart, precariously perched on their bow-bedecked burros, trotted down the steep mountain roads to meet visitors, including Orson Welles, Ingrid Bergman, and Roberto Rossellini. Huston, Bogart, and Lorre hired the town band to serenade recent arrivals into consciousness in the early morning hours. They also very soberly informed a visiting David Selznick that it was customary for British film units to wear full evening dress at dinner. He did not fall for this, and the only victims were the English actor Edward Underdown, who played Harry Chelm, and his new bride, Rose, both of whom turned out in full evening regalia. Lorre also pulled one of his oldest pranks in front of the camera. "He had a famous trick with my camera assistant, which never failed," related Morris. "Gerry Turpin would take the tape measure out to Peter's face—an absolute dead-pan—and time and time again Peter would snap at him like a dog, frightening the life out of him and he would drop the tape. It never failed."

When they could, cast and crew recessed to Amalfi and Positano. However, most of the time they spent in tiny Ravello, billeted at adjoining hotels, where volatile temperaments quickly kindled petty annoyances and hurt feelings. All seemed to be wrapped up in their own problems, except Huston, Bogart, Capote, and Lorre, who, in Gibson's words, "seemed to be completely oblivious to it all and having a ball." Production problems kept the company on edge. Those who worked for Haggiag wondered if and when they would be paid. When his production manager failed to settle accounts with the hotel, they found themselves locked out without their bags. Waiting limousines and buses could not whisk them away until the tab had been settled and their luggage released.

On the Romulus end, Jack Clayton worked to straighten out the financial logistics, while Lorre kept tempers down. Behind the scenes, he assumed the role of psychiatrist, tendering his couch to harangued co-workers. "If anyone had a problem, they'd go to Peter," said Gibson. "He'd say, 'Well now, that isn't a problem. This is the way we will work it out.' He worked everything out for everybody. . . . Peter was way ahead of everyone else. He could see through everything that was happening. That was the interesting thing to me, to find that somebody who had played those evil, sinister roles as he did was in life such a good person. I mean a good human being. I don't think he had a selfish bone in his body."

After hours, the hard-drinking raconteurs posted their burro-bruised posteriors around the poker table or leered at the Ping-Pong-playing form of Gina Lollobrigida. Only Robert Morley, who kept to himself, taking his meals in his room, felt discomforted by the comically chaotic situation. Lorre targeted the Sydney Greenstreet replacement as a stuffed shirt primed for a ruffling. He sat back, watched, listened, and then, at the right moment, he struck. With a look, a carefully chosen word—usually a four-letter rejoinder—or even a nettling impersonation, he scandalized the sniffy Englishman, who failed to appreciate his ribald humor. "I have always thought him an intensely tiresome little chap," carped the disgruntled Morley, "with quite the foulest vocabulary I have ever had the misfortune to listen to." Lorre peppered his social conversation with what columnist Earl Wilson called "Ernest Hemingway words." Being slightly deaf, Morley was spared much of his choice vocabulary. Nonetheless, he heard enough. "I remember an occasion on the set when the continuity lady washed Peter's mouth out with soap," he recalled—wistfully one supposes—"which didn't seem to do much good."

Huston wanted individuality and spontaneity from his players. He walked them on a loose lead and gently tugged them into place. "I get a man for the part," he asserted. "I don't get someone and then train them into it." Gibson confirmed, saying, "John would let Peter do pretty much what he wanted, because whatever he did was better than anything you could tell him." Morris also noticed that Lorre "veered off more toward the comic than I thought he would. I got the feeling that Peter got the buzz it was tongue-in-cheek and he was going to make the most of it. And that Huston approved. . . . Peter got into the character in the morning and he just never dropped it. Now, I've got a sneaking feeling that character carried on in the evenings in the hotel. . . . The person that comes over in the film is my understanding of Peter himself."

Huston, who admitted to Gibson that he had only really come to know Lorre during *Beat the Devil*, considered him "a nimble creature in his mind and in his talents [who] took everything and made it his own and it was extremely personal. He incorporated the role into his own personality, which was a very subtle one indeed, and also supple."

Huston later explained that in *Beat the Devil* "the crooks, ostensibly heroic people, the romance, even virtue, become absurd." Such is the case of O'Hara (Lorre), a whimsically droll bungler who brings up the rear, scuttling behind his cohorts, a cosmopolitan gang of desperados. When Dannreuther (Bogart) derisively refers to him as a "wide-eyed leprechaun," Lorre (in one of the few lines preserved from the novel) defensively points out that "in Chile, the name of O'Hara is a tiptop name. Many Germans in Chile have become to be called O'Hara." Capote got on famously with cast and crew. He enlarged Lorre's role, giving him some of the film's best lines and situations, including the discourse on time: "Time, time, what is time? The Swiss manufacture it. The French hoard it. The Italians squander it. The Americans say it is money. Hindus say it does not exist. You know what I say? I say time is a crook."

In a time-stalling scene that Huston described as "a little vignette, a little jewel in the picture, a delightful interlude," O'Hara prevents Dannreuther from keeping an appointment with Mrs. Harry Chelm (Jennifer Jones), wife of a suspected competitor for the riches of Africa. This allows Peterson (Robert Morley) to keep the rendezvous and nose out their plans. Huston sat Lorre on a chair and centrally framed him in a full shot. The scene simply set, he let the actor go. He began with a few disjointed remarks about age and experience. "It smokes, it drinks, it philosophizes," Bogart cuts in. Midway through his monologue, O'Hara peers through the window and notices that Peterson has finished. Rather than playing the charade to its conclusion, he scampers out and down the hall, his words echoing into silence.

Four years earlier, Lorre had promised audiences a break from his face. *Beat the Devil* delivered what he described as a "healthy departure from my Hollywood roles." Now, United Artists, the film's distributor, parlayed his absence into a publicity campaign aimed at resurrecting the menacing Peter Lorre of Warner Bros. fame: "Peter Lorre has been chafing under the bit of virtue. His knife has been gathering rust, his evil eye turned benign from long disuse. . . . Now, in 'Beat the Devil,' he is back at the old evil stand." It was blatantly false advertising. Lorre capably transcended the past to establish himself as a redoubtable comic presence.

Beat the Devil defies categorization. After reading the Veiller-Viertel script, Huston admitted in a letter to Bogart that "it is hard to tell whether it's a drama, a comedy or an action picture." Bogart, soon after returning stateside, glibly described it as "a sort of satire on the 'Maltese Falcon' private detective" picture. Huston later allowed that the film was "more a lark than a satirical story. . . . It made no points about anything in particular, we just had a very good time." The frenetic mood, a cast unleashed before and behind the camera, and Truman Capote's aberrant sense of humor swarmed into a collage that drew on several film genres but served none of them.

"It was a flop first in New York," Lorre noted. "Why wouldn't it be? It was a delicious sardonic comedy, meant for the art theaters, and they opened it with a blood-and-thunder campaign, on the circuits. People just didn't get it."[6] Either they flowed with the mélange of fresh dialogue and comic situations that roamed the Italian landscape in search of an idea, or they recoiled at the confusion and threw in with Bogart, who ultimately labeled the film "a mess." *Beat the Devil* gave, to one critic's mind, "the air of an expensive house-party joke, a charade which enormously entertained its participants at the time of the playing, but which is too private and insufficiently brilliant to justify public performance."

Only with its re-release in 1964 did audiences appreciate *Beat the Devil* as a screwball classic. The picture's flighty and fractured in-group humor and all-too-apparent improvisation (flubbed lines remain in the final cut) appealed to moviegoers of the 1960s, elevating it to cult status. *Beat the Devil* was conceived as one thing, advertised as another, and finally received accolades as something quite different from either.

Lorre arrived in Ravello in mid-February without Annemarie, who was well advanced in a pregnancy that must have surprised her as much as it did him. When doctors had removed an ovarian cyst eleven years earlier, they had told her it would be difficult for her to become pregnant. Because Peter was not yet divorced from Karen, Annemarie had returned to her family in Hamburg to give birth. After seven weeks of location shooting at Ravello in the spring of 1953 and ten days of wrap-up work at Shepperton Studios in London, Lorre flew to Hamburg to marry Annemarie on July 21 and to see for the first time their daughter, Catharine, born June 22. (Being a nonpracticing Jew, he followed Annemarie's lead and registered his religion as Lutheran.) Only two days earlier a Las Vegas court had granted Karen a divorce on grounds that she and Lorre had "lived separate and apart for more than three consecutive years without cohabitation, to-wit: since March 8, 1950" and awarded her a $13,750 cash settlement.

Now forty-seven, Lorre took on an unlikely role, but one that he slipped into with surprising ease. Annemarie wrote to "Pemsky" (Paul E. Marcus) in Germany that their "miracle child" was "sweet and good, especially when Peter goes to her room in the evening and when she is asleep. Then he is playing his own Emperor of Portugal, you know that beautiful [Selma] Lagerlöf story, which Peter always wanted to produce and film, and one day he eventually is going to do it."[7] He delegated the care of baby Catharine to Annemarie, while he adored and showcased his daughter to friends. Bogart and Lorre jointly introduced her to the press, and Burl Ives sang her folk ballads and lullabies and gave "horseyback" rides. Lorre's relationship with Catharine remained constant for the nearly eleven years they had together. He put his doll-like progeny, who bore a striking resemblance to her father—"She looks like me, but on her it looks good"—on a pedestal and kept her there.

Lorre moved his family to Benedict Canyon in Beverly Hills, where he rented a house whose warm atmosphere and open fireplace made it, in his words, "an ideal *cafehaus*." As Mrs. Peter Lorre, Annemarie confessed that she had "turned strictly housewife. I prefer it that way." Lorre too preferred that nothing distract her from fulfilling—as he saw it—a woman's traditional role.

Annemarie fell in love with California and wrote to friends in Germany that their newfound paradise boasted not only orange trees, hummingbirds, a wondrous variety of flowers, and "a just about English garden," but also a kitchen "with everything electrical, beginning with the dishwasher to the washing machine and the toaster and garbage disposal." Between the lines, Annemarie's letter said much more—that she and her husband stood on the brink of a great new life.

Lorre's new life allowed him little time to consider overtures from Fritz Lang, who was under a two-picture contract at Columbia, to star as a psychotic locomotive engineer in a remake of Jean Renoir's *La Bête Humaine* (1938), based on the novel of the same title by Emile Zola. In an undated treatment titled *The Human Beast*, Lorre (so named) returns from the army after being hospitalized for combat fatigue, which has left him with "momentary fits of madness." He falls in love with the unhappy wife of the "demonically jealous" assistant station-master, who forces her to witness the murder of a wealthy gentleman on the train. After making her an accomplice to the crime, he blackmails her into staying with him. The woman persuades Lorre to kill her husband. When he fails, she refuses to see him. Though he recognizes her for what she is—"an ambitious, heartless, egotistical woman"—Lorre cannot live without her and begs her to go with him. However, when he learns that she plans to run away with another man, he strangles her, leaving the scene of the crime "completely out of his mind" and reports for work. He madly pilots the train toward San Francisco. His frightened friend tries to reason with him, but "Lorre shouts back that he has killed the only being he ever loved, and that he doesn't care what happens." A fight breaks out, and the two men fall from the speeding locomotive, which careens madly toward its doom.

Unable to convince Lorre that he should reunite with him, Lang watched producer Jerry Wald's dissatisfaction with the Zola story, in which "*everybody* is bad," transform the exposure of man's bestial side into just another love triangle in the "present-day American" spirit of *The Big Heat* (1953), again with Glenn Ford and Gloria Graham. Lang did not think the picture, retitled *Human Desire* (1954), worth comparing to the Jean Renoir version.

In 1952 Walt Disney formed WED (Walt Elias Disney) Enterprises to realize his dream of creating a family amusement park. Among the artists he recruited to design and plan what would become Disneyland was Harper Goff, who had worked as an assistant art director on many of the Warner Bros. classics of the 1930s and 1940s. Before Goff got to work on the theme park, Disney assigned him to scale down some live-action footage of sea slugs shot by marine biologist Dr. George E. MacGinitie and work it into an undersea film for his "True-Life Adventure" nature series. Instead of counterposing the colorful animals with inanimate objects, the artist visualized cartoon characters interacting with real sea creatures. Goff worked on the idea of translating live-action "ballet inserts" into several animated sequences from Jules Verne's classic futuristic adventure *20,000 Leagues under the Sea,* one of his favorite stories. He began his storyboard with the tour of Captain Nemo's undersea garden. From there, he created an entire script in rough outline, then integrated larger sketches in more detail and color, along with notes on the use of underwater photography. Since he was not a cartoonist, his storyboard looked like an outline for a live-action film.

Disney had earlier considered animating the Verne tale, but property conflicts and potentially high costs had frustrated his plans. Goff's storyboard rekindled his interest. "Sooner or later," said Disney, "I'm going to have to start making real one-hundred-percent live-action pictures, instead of fifty-fifty." He thought about casting the film and got back to Goff: "If we made a live-action picture of it, instead of a cartoon, what would you say if we cast Kirk Douglas as Ned Land? My daughter has seen this guy in a prize-fighting picture, *Champion* [1949], and she's absolutely crazy about him. He's got wonderful muscles."

Goff was amazed. "I thought we were daydreaming," he said. "I couldn't believe that Walt was even considering making a live-action picture." The question of casting, however, did not catch the set designer off guard. "Whenever I read a book," said Goff, "I cast the people in it in the image of somebody I relate to as an actor." He saw Lorre as Professor Arronax's tractable assistant, Conseil: "I had apparently and unconsciously thought of him as kind of obsequious . . . a gentleman's gentleman, but one who feels he possesses as much horse sense and intelligence as his absentminded boss. . . . When I looked at it, Conseil was a round-faced guy with big eyes, kind of a hat holder the way I had pictured him and drawn him." Disney agreed.

Goff's storyboard next went to Bill Walsh, a supervising writer who saw that the studio's products carried the "Disney touch." Characterized as an extension of Walt Disney's personality, he toned down Verne's political message, softening the insurgent and misanthropic Nemo, and selected sequences from the book to translate into film, finding a careful balance between the human equation and mechanical devices. He then brought in John Tucker Battle to create a screenplay, which Disney labeled the "empirical script." This all-inclusive scenario translated the story into screen form. Walsh next engaged Earl Felton, who produced a final draft—which underwent nine revisions during principal photography—and tailored the roles to the players, adding many comic touches to the picture.

Disney assembled a strong cast, which featured James Mason, Paul Lukas, Kirk Douglas, and Peter Lorre, and offered the job of directing his first live-action feature to Richard Fleischer, whose work on *The Happy Time* (1952) had especially impressed him.[8] To give Verne's glimpse into the future the look and feel of scientific reality, Disney put to work his Special Effects and Processes Department and chose scenic Montego Bay in Jamaica for location shooting.

Jules Verne described Conseil as "fit for any kind of service" with a "strong constitution [that] defied all illness; he had powerful muscles, but no nerves." In the film version, Disney also required him to supply comic relief. Lorre plays the foil for Kirk Douglas, who delights in rubbing his crew cut the wrong way. At one point, Captain Nemo (James Mason) permits the brawny harpooner and the dumpy underworker to join an undersea hunting expedition. Ned and Conseil spot a sunken galleon and wander off in search of hidden treasure. When a hostile shark swoops down on them, Nemo plugs the fish with his spear gun. Back aboard the submarine, Professor Arronax (Paul Lukas) reproaches the reckless adventurers. Ned brazenly admits that booty was their aim, but Conseil innocently protests that he accompanied his friend in the name of science. "Don't look at me with those *soft-boiled eggs*," improvised Douglas. "I saw the glint of gold in them when that chest busted."

"I always had a kind of feeling," said Goff, "that Peter's role was written just about the way he would have done if he had been ad-libbing it." Lorre often discussed his role with Fleischer and suggested additions to the part. "Even things offered extemporaneously were not extemporaneous, but well thought out," said the director. "Peter thought about his role carefully and deeply." Tempering a generalization that Lorre took direction well, Fleischer added, "His screen image was not without validity—he really did have a morbid sense of humor. He knew what his eyes could do and he didn't hesitate to do it. My biggest problem was holding him down. Peter always gave more and was constantly improvising or trying new things." Nonetheless, the actor managed to wedge some bits of business into the final cut. To quiet Esmarelda, Nemo's pet seal, Ned snatches a humidor and feeds her a seaweed cigar, which she gobbles down. When Lorre crawls over the floor in search of more cigars, the seal nudges his backside, earning a hearty guffaw for her effort. "Now eat them slowly," he improvised. "You don't have to inhale them."

Lorre firmly held that he had an aptitude for comedy and regretted he could not convince others of this. In a Disney promotional sheet, studio publicist Joe Reddy wrote: "After all these years, Peter Lorre wants everyone to know that he is, deep down inside, a comedian. The little, round man—who has made a profitable career making little round holes in his movie victims—claims his type casting as a villain was a mistake." On the set Lorre opened up about typecasting with Goff and Fleischer, taking them on a rare excursion over sensitive ground. Fleischer recalled that Lorre had "high hopes" of breaking the pattern with this role. "I thought that he was more hopeful that it would break the mold than convinced it was going to," clarified Goff. "I think he talked about it in a wistful way, like maybe it will, maybe this is the thing that will."

In reply to one of Reddy's questions about the funniest thing that ever happened to him in his career, the actor answered, "That I was cast as a villain. Here I have always wanted to 'kill' people with jokes—and I end up just plain killing them." At the first sight of Disney's mechanical squid, he quipped, "He's got the part I usually play."

Lorre loved to impersonate Kirk Douglas. When the camera rolled, he pinched his chin into a dimple, closed his eyes, and read his lines. "There could be no tension when he was around," said Fleischer. "He exuded humor. His joy was in wringing humor out of every moment he could find." Lorre functioned as a "cohesive factor" whose little services ranged from lifting morale to offering counsel, not as a backseat director, but as a teammate who needed to promote the total effort. "A discussion took place," recalled James Mason, "when we were rehearsing a conversation in the bowels of the 'Nautilus,' one in which Nemo speaks bitterly of events which turned him into such a weirdo. At one moment I seemed to Peter to be pressing too hard, tending to scream before I had generated sufficient emotion internally to justify it. He seemed to be deeply hurt and muttered, 'You're not going to do it like that, are you?' Punctured, I made a supreme effort to render the scene in such a way that it would not cause him any further distress."

An inveterate practical joker, Lorre grew feistier with age, pulling incredibly elaborate, sometimes bizarre practical jokes. At the Roundhill Hotel in

Montego Bay, he met an officious manager who callously berated the black employees in front of the Disney group, including Douglas, Goff, Lorre, and cinematographer Franz Planer, who had worked with the actor on *The Face behind the Mask* (1941) and *The Chase* (1946). The major-domo also scheduled the company's free time without their permission. Each evening, after cast and crew knocked off work, he importuned them to change clothes, go out to one of the cabanas on the beach, and take a swim. "Peter defied him," said Goff. "He just ran out of his room, down across the lawn and jumped into the water and came back and went to his room."

Lorre arranged a "semi-public taking-the-wind-out-of-the-sails," related Goff, "and caught him up in a very hilarious practical joke. This seemed to be something that Peter really enjoyed when he met a pompous ass or insufferable bore. It never was really cruel, but so sophisticated that the guy himself didn't know it happened to him." A nightclub on 1 Downing Street, a two-way mirror, and two exotic dancers—identical twins—provided the setting. Douglas and Lorre arranged for the hotel manager to catch a private performance by one of the dancers. The two pranksters also planned for members of the Disney cast and crew to observe the show through a two-way mirror. "The plan was to get the guy loaded," said Goff. "The women, who had rehearsed all the action and synchronized their movements, would come in and do everything in unison. It was really befuddling to him because he thought he was seeing double. Then all of a sudden one of them would disappear and there would only be one. The next couple of days there was a great deal of laughter. Everyone congratulated Peter, who said, 'I didn't do anything, except suggest it and pay the bill.'"

Bridging two apparently irreconcilable trends in his film career, *20,000 Leagues under the Sea* enjoyed enormous popular acclaim and critical praise and at the same time asked something new of Lorre in a substantive role. Some critics, accustomed to seeing the "merchant of menace" in a more sinister capacity, felt he had been miscast as Conseil, but Lorre did not listen. "Peter wasn't sure it was going to bring him a lot more friends in the viewers because he was a minor hero," said Goff. "But he was not unhappy with what he was doing in *20,000 Leagues under the Sea*." He told Reddy that his fan mail had always been friendly and added, "I've been luckier than a lot of movie villains in that my fans have never confused me with the parts I play."

In a letter to Marcus on March 22, Annemarie wrote that the diving-suit work was hot and strenuous, "a giant agitation [but] he hasn't had so much fun in a film in a long time." Lorre returned from location work "burnt brown" and fired with tales of the lush and beckoning countryside. "Peter thinks one can easily become a beachcomber there, for a period of time," she said, "but between us I believe that Peter can do that almost anywhere."

Invigorated by Hollywood's renewed interest, Lorre took stock of his life. "The people here now know that he is healthy and are happy with him and his work," Annemarie continued, "which expresses itself by a large concrete interest in all fields. What kind of feeling it is to know that they need him. It makes him proud and thankful and crazier for work than previously." The tropical sea breezes put him on a health kick: beer, cheese and his beloved goulash were out. The sunshine also brought out the writer in Lorre. He bought a new typewriter, which, said Annemarie, "fascinates Peter so . . . that one has justified hopes he really will begin to write. He has a working room and hundreds of pencils and a pencil sharpener which hangs on the wall and many cartons and little machines for stapling together old and new papers. It is an empire in itself, his and he likes it so. There he can be alone when he wants."

During the making of *20,000 Leagues under the Sea,* Lorre enthusiastically confided to Fleischer that he was working on a murder-comedy that he wanted to produce. Most likely, this was *The Survivor,* a screenplay by fellow émigré and friend Hans Wilhelm—based on an original story by Peter Lorre and Hans Wilhelm—about a professional pallbearer who ingratiates himself with grieving and vulnerable widows. A sucker for a pretty face, he nearly cons himself out of a handsome legacy when he pushes a pyramid scheme that plays on the time difference between Rome and New York. When the scam backfires, he attempts to murder his patroness. He botches the job and retreats, under the guise of amnesia, to a sanatorium, where, with the happy grin of an accomplished moron, he hatches a plot to win his freedom and enjoy the fruits of his labor.

It is natural to suppose that Lorre also expected to star in this comedy vehicle, which he planned to shoot in Italy with a foreign cast. Wilhelm had captured his collaborator on paper, freeze-framing a mocking and mischievous wit, full of wry charm. It was a role after Lorre's own taste, and likely one of his own design.

From his office sanctuary, he fed the dream of discovering the elusive pivotal role. "There are some really good things going on," Annemarie confided to Marcus. "What do you think of Pancho Villa? Certainly that cannot be played by such a boyish face." Lorre declined to talk about his plans, claiming that he was superstitious, but news of work abounded—a four-picture directorial deal with Disney; an Italian production with Roberto Rossellini and Ingrid Bergman, set for the fall of 1954; and a role in the upcoming *We're No Angels* (1955) with Humphrey Bogart. That spring, Lorre also announced plans to reassemble the crew of *Der Verlorene*—including Egon Jameson and Axel Eggebrecht—for an independent German-American collaborative film venture, which would benefit from the "mutual exchange of fertile ideas on both sides." But nothing materialized. In a letter to the *Hamburger Anzeiger* published March 10, 1954, under the heading, "Ist Peter Lorre vergessen?" ("Is Peter Lorre Forgotten?") the actor lamented that

> every day I am questioned if I would like to make somewhere some kind of movie: the most horrible stories are among these, unfilmable murder stories—but they ask me if I would film them. I receive good and solid offers, occasionally from established movie societies in England, Italy, Egypt, and even—don't laugh—Japan. Not to say offers from U.S. firms. Swedish producers want me to direct and suggestions come from South America: if I were to accept them all I would be working until 1960. But among all the letters there isn't one from Germany. No offer. No inquiry. Would you return to a land that you love, whose language you speak, in which you grew up—without being called?

Little wonder that Lorre retreated to his private domain. Within the walls of his workroom, he could put his life in order and keep the world outside at bay. Hollywood did not storm his office stronghold. His regenerative hiatus lasted more than a year, during which he filled his time with television work.

On October 21, 1954, Lorre appeared on CBS's popular anthology series *Climax!* in "Casino Royale." In the first adaptation of a James Bond spy tale, based on Ian Fleming's novel, Lorre was cast as Soviet agent "Le Chiffre." Reluctant to work in live television, Barry Nelson expressed no interest in playing an American version of the British agent until he learned he would be costarring with one of his favorite actors. Pallid by contemporary standards, "007" appeared more so to Nelson, who came out of a story conference feeling the part was poorly written and rather dull. Much to his surprise, Lorre "went to bat" for the young actor and suggested the part be "repaired." Improving the role, however, did not mitigate the pressures of shooting live. When the director discovered that the show ran three minutes overtime, he ordered lines trimmed rather than cut a scene, setting off Nelson's "body tic." Offscreen, Lorre teased the actor, "Barry, stand still so I can kill you."

The *Climax!* episode is famous for a scene described by screenwriter Charles Bennett, who coscripted the teleplay, in which "Peter expired as the camera sent the show across the nation live. But then, the director failed to push the right button, and instead of this scene jumping to the next, the cameras remained on 'dead' Peter. Rightfully concluding that his job was done, he rose and quietly departed to his dressing room, smiling whimsically, to the utter bewilderment of possibly thirty million viewers." As Bennett watched the show, he "was appalled, so was Peter when he learned what had happened."

Believed lost, an incomplete telerecording of the show surfaced in the 1980s. The closing minute materialized some years later. In the commercially available video, one sees Lorre take a bullet, stumble, wheeze, and then break character as he furtively steals to the next set, where a second bullet dispatches him.

Lorre kicked off 1955 as Dr. Einstein in *The Best of Broadway*'s January 5 broadcast of "Arsenic and Old Lace," costarring Helen Hayes and Boris Karloff and adapted by Howard Lindsay and Russel Crouse, who had produced the original stage play. Nicknamed "the morticians" by Hayes, the long-faced duo gravely suggested daily changes during the script readings. In one of the biggest comedy hits of the year, Karloff and Lorre, wrote *Variety*, "made the perfect murderous pair, relishing every line and turning them out beautifully."

Lorre received a letter from Paul Kohner in March asking if he would be interested in starring in Robert Thoeren's *Autobanditen* (released as *Banditen der Autobahn*, 1955), scheduled for shooting in May (it didn't get under way until fall) under the direction of Géza von Cziffra, who had specialized in comedies at UFA during the late 1930s. However, back-to-back television commitments—he appeared in nine shows by the end of the year—confined the actor to the small screen.

One of the more memorable but least remembered roles was that of a beleaguered complaint department clerk whose morbid outlook discourages refunds in "The Sure Cure," an episode of *The Eddie Cantor Comedy Theatre*, broadcast May 2, 1955. When his doctor diagnoses a fear of humor and prescribes a course of smiling, Lorre counters, "Wouldn't surgery be easier?" He reads and tells jokes, both ineptly, and wears a Hitler moustache. Nothing works, until he overhears his ex-girlfriend tell her new husband that her mother is going to live with them. A cheered Lorre lets out a hearty laugh.

By now, Lorre's movie persona provided a point of reference, giving visual context for a string of pejorative images—scary, horrific, sinister. In J.D. Salinger's *Catcher in the Rye* (1951), a young woman sees Peter Lorre, "The movie actor. In person. He was buyin' a newspaper." Her idea that he is cute invites the obvious rebuttal that she is a moron.

In Richard Matheson's science fiction tale "Shipshape Home," a three-eyed janitor who looks and sounds like "Peter Lorre" conspires to rocket a city block of young couples to another planet. "The man is a creep," intones a suspicious wife, prompting an understanding husband to reply, "Hon, what can the poor guy do about his face? . . . Heredity. Give him a break." When the story made its way to television as *Studio 57*'s "Young Couples Only," who better to play the janitor than Peter Lorre himself (outfitted with a none-too-convincing third eye in the back of his head)?[9] Afterward, a small production company at Republic Pictures hired Matheson to expand the concept into a feature film that would star Lorre. "I tried," said the writer, "but it was literally impossible. At the end, he was going to get on the rocket ship with the aliens and go to their planet and all that stuff. It didn't seem to work and never got made."

During this period of yawning gulfs in his film career, television afforded more substantive roles—and often higher billing—than movies. *Climax*'s "A Promise to Murder," which aired in November, got its start as Oscar Wilde's "Lord Arthur Saville's Crime." In the one-hour drama, Lorre played Mr. Vorhees, a palm reader whose prophecies bear a sinister fulfillment. His scenes in a boy's playroom, where he dreamily retreats into memories of his own deprived childhood and rediscovers the magic of youth, display the sort of hand-to-glove fit that characterizes the actor's best performances. Regrettably they are all but forgotten today, overshadowed by mediocre films that enjoy years of endless repetition on television.

On December 10, 1955, he returned to NBC for *Rheingold Theatre*'s "The Blue Landscape," in which "for a welcome change, I play a gentleman who is on the side of the law. In fact, he is the law." Lorre also welcomed the opportunity to work with the fifth-billed Celia Lovsky, with whom he had last shared the spotlight in 1932.

When Hollywood finally called on Lorre—nearly two years after the release of *20,000 Leagues under the Sea*—it asked the actor to play himself in an unbilled guest appearance in *Meet Me in Las Vegas* (1956), an MGM musical-comedy. At a blackjack table, opposite dealer Oscar Karlweis, Lorre intoned his one and only line—"Hit me, you creep"—with faint malevolence.

During the 1950s the American film industry underwent enormous change. In 1944 the Justice Department reactivated the *Paramount* case, which had charged the five major studios—Paramount, MGM-Loew's, RKO, Warner Bros., and 20th Century–Fox—with conspiring to restrain trade and monopolize production, distribution, and exhibition. A three-judge panel of the Federal District Court in the Southern District of New York ruled that vertical distribution violated the Sherman Act but found divorcement unnecessary and ordered a system of competitive bidding for films. Both sides appealed to the Supreme Court, which affirmed divestiture but remanded the case to the District Court to reconsider its decision about breaking up the vertical integration of the motion picture industry. In July 1949 the lower court found divorcement of exhibition from the production-distributions branches of the industry a necessary remedy.

The domestic picture grew dimmer. Wage and price regulations of the early and middle 1940s gave way to postwar inflation at the end of the decade and recession in the early 1950s. Annual theater attendance dropped off from 90 million in 1946 to an estimated 45 million by 1953. With block-booking and blind bidding struck down, extended runs fell off and output dwindled. As box-office returns steadily fell, the consumer price index pushed higher. The majors retrenched, cutting production, pruning staffs, and renegotiating salaries; stars became an unaffordable luxury. When contract options ran out, unemployed actors moved on to other studios, freelanced, or formed their own companies.

The industry also lost its foothold abroad. In 1947, as part of a larger program of protectionist measures, Britain had levied an import duty on American films, trimming foreign earnings.

And then came television. Soon the public of Milton Berle, Howdy Doody, and Lucille Ball rivaled that of the cinema's top-ranking stars. Competing with television put the film industry in a desperate battle for survival. It was time to try something new. Hollywood fought back with technology, capitalizing on the medium's strongest asset—the sheer size of the movie. The studios garnished tried and true recipes with technical innovations such as CinemaScope, Panavision, VistaVision, Cinerama, and 3-D that stressed the physical limitations of television and the spatial potential of the cinema. The trend nurtured some important scientific advances, but too often filmmakers depended on gimmicks to compensate for a lack of content.

Postwar inflation, labor unrest, and the festering cold war with the Soviet Union fragmented the unity fostered during the 1940s. Blacklisting also continued to cast a shadow over the entertainment world, barring many artists from work. As a whole, the nation became more serious, its perspective more contemporary. An awakened public looked to an introspective cinema that tackled controversial subjects (*A Hatful of Rain*, 1957) and probed human feelings (*A Streetcar Named Desire*, 1951). Independently produced "small films" shot in black and white and adapted from teleplays offered lifelike characters with everyday problems (*Marty*, 1955; *The Bachelor Party*, 1957).

Expediency demanded that Hollywood shed its clichés. As the film industry replaced its stereotyped properties with unconventional ones, it relegated character actors to walk-ons in formula blockbusters. Being a star was no longer enough. Independent filmmakers sought fresh faces and new modes of thought and expression. When images gave way to individuality, Hollywood's stock and staple went by the boards. Not wanting to display him in roles divorced from his screen persona as a bogeyman, Hollywood banished Lorre to the "lowbrow bonanzas" and bid him parade through like an everyday vaudevillian stuffed between the bigger numbers. Cinema with a social conscience— what the actor had sought in his own career—had finally come of age in America. He wanted in, to be part of the new trend, but he was not invited. The closed door was hard to take.

Another entrance remained open, the trapdoor that dropped him into the role of Colonel Arragas, the local chief of police of "Congotanga . . . savage Africa's city of outcasts!" Universal-International's thirty-second radio spot for *Congo Crossing* (1956) promised "the renegade and the Tangier woman, each with a sin to hide, each with a crime to flee, each with a date they must keep in a rendezvous with terror!!" It delivered a plot as sluggish as the Nile, the undergrowth brimming with stock characters, a jungle repertoire of decrepit crocodiles, and an animated swarm of tsetse flies. There to lighten and amuse, as well as lend a mock sinister presence, Lorre fell back on an offhand duality, obligingly adding his stamp in a hastily mounted salvage operation. Behind the guise of a toughly officious would-be menace, he is artless and well-disposed, more vacillating than villainous, casting a benign eye on all human foibles.[10]

After putting in a cameo appearance as a Japanese steward in Michael Todd's *Around the World in Eighty Days* (1956), Lorre accepted a slightly larger role in Paramount's *The Buster Keaton Story* (1957), a specious film biography of the deadpan clown directed by Sidney Sheldon, in which the actor figured as a brutally sadistic film director.

Lorre's appearances on television now outnumbered those in feature films. Between game and talk shows and among the crooks, robbers, and thugs, he still had time for drama and it for him, but in a small way. In October 1956 he earned high marks for his performance as a rebellious garment worker in *Playhouse 90*'s "Sizeman and Son." Jack O'Brian, writing for the New York *Journal-American,* saw a Lorre audiences had forgotten: "Peter Lorre played a presser with the sort of rich deep delicious and endearing implied power of the roles which first brought him to America, not the low-comedy horror nonsense which made every cheap night-club imitator feast on the more vulgar nuances of his broad delivery. This was the old Lorre of great feeling and intelligence and the very best practice of his more sensitive craft. Lorre was, in a word, great."

The following March, the actor appeared as a drunken has-been director in the *Playhouse 90* production of F. Scott Fitzgerald's *The Last Tycoon*. "The ultra-reliable Keenan Wynn and veteran character thesp[ian] Peter Lorre were in there," wrote *Variety*, "but they were mostly stock figures—or even caricatures—to give the Hollywood 'production chief'[Jack Palance] a backboard from which to bounce in one of Fitzgerald's most brooding works."

In 1957 the producers of *Climax!* engaged Ellis St. Joseph to update Barre Lyndon's "The Amazing Dr. Clitterhouse" for Michael Rennie and Peter Lorre. The actor invited St. Joseph to dinner to discuss the teleplay, which had been sent to him for his approval.

"I'm grateful you accepted it," said the writer, anxious for a word of praise. "What did you think?" Lorre admitted he hadn't read it. "When you are asked to jump into a barrel of shit," he bluntly added, "you don't ask if it's feet first or head first." St. Joseph recalled that he "crumbled" under Lorre's critcism: "My ego fell apart. I just stared at him in dismay."

In an interview for *TV Guide*, November 2–8, 1957, Lorre observed that "television came into being before people knew what to do with it. Today it's an industry and nobody has time to *think* about it." However disparaging he was about the new medium, the actor jumped into a barrel of something far less odious than he supposed in St. Joseph's "A Taste for Crime," which gave him "a chance to say ironic lines, the kind that I liked to write and the kind that he could say." In what turned out to be one of the highlights of his television career, Lorre played an elusive master criminal to Michael Rennie's eminent scientist, who sets out to prove that glandular disturbances create the criminal mind.

The actor's availability and recognizability suggested him for a number of projected television series. The first, *The Getter and the Holder*, coproduced by Peter Lorre's Falcon Productions and Sam Neumann from his own plays, and starring the actor and Francis L. Sullivan, yet another Sydney Greenstreet replacement, was reportedly—prematurely, as it turned out—scheduled to begin shooting in April 1953. The second, a comedy-horror show written by cartoonist Charles Addams and projected for the 1953 fall season, died on the drawing board. In early 1957 Hunt Stromberg Jr., an assistant program director at 20th Century–Fox, who had conceived the idea of *Collector's Item*, a television series about two intrepid antiquarians, assigned screenwriter Herb Meadow to develop the concept and produce a pilot for the 1958–59 season. Meadow recalled reading a fanciful tale about golden horseshoes encased in black paint. From this germ, he developed "The Left Fist of David," a story about an art collector and his assistant, a rehabilitated forger, who foil the theft of a priceless relic.

Meadow found his leads by paging through a casting directory. Steady money, a dry spell of movie offers, and the chance to work with Vincent Price persuaded a reluctant Peter Lorre to have a go. The same could not be said of 20th Century–Fox, which, according to the writer, gave the new medium a cold shoulder. Stromberg drafted a first-time producer, who, in turn, hired a live television director whose inexperience in film left the actors in the position of having to direct themselves. Even the secretary complained that her sister mocked her because she had been demoted to the nadir of entertainment. Fox allocated a property storeroom for the principal set, scheduled shooting during the intense heat of the day—without a blower—because evening filming cost more, and failed to hire a policeman to maintain order. When a hysterical assistant executive-producer began calling the set every half hour for a progress report, Meadow had the telephone removed. Chaos reigned.

Add to this Lorre's and co-worker Thomas Gomez's poor health. In a wrestling scene, the rotund actors looked to Meadow like two balloons clinging to each other: "They were laughing until suddenly they stopped, both of them, because they had both lost their wind and were so distressed we had to stop. Lorre was very quiet. He just sat, looking off into space, recovering his breath. Gomez was terribly red in the face. I was afraid he was going to have an attack of some kind."

Faced with the option of shrugging off the fiasco and collecting his check, or of giving his professional best, the actor dug in. "I think he had an innate artistic intelligence," said Cliff Robertson, who worked with Lorre in "The Cruel Day" on *Playhouse 90*. "He was so good he seemed to have that security and ease only an experienced, usually older actor displays. You had a feeling that it was kind of rolling off his back."

"Almost all of his lines in the script," said Herb Meadow, "are his suggestions. He knew what he was best at, and while the lines themselves did not come out as brilliant lines—because they couldn't, since he was not the star—they came out as an expression of personality which was slowly building into something that was Lorre's best."

Behind the scenes, the actor played a more challenging role, that of peacekeeper. Location shooting took the company to a palatial Bel-Air estate bristling with statuary. "We were standing near the Greek Classic, 'The Wrestlers,'" related Meadow.

Price, Lorre, the director, the cameraman and I were having quite an argument. I was ready to fight because the thing had gotten completely out of hand. Everybody was doing what he wanted to do and I had lost control of my company. At the peak of this thing, there was one of those inexplicable silences as everybody tried to decide who was going to hit whom first. Pointing to the statue, Lorre said wonderingly, absolutely straight, as though he really meant it, "Do you know, the last time we passed here the other one was on top." Now it was typical of what he would do. His funnies always had a purpose. It struck us as terribly funny, and that's all that was necessary. So he saved us for another few hours.

What Meadow expected would take a few weeks ran nearly four months: "We were wading through a mess and all of us were terribly relieved when it was over. We were all sick of it. . . . The pilot was no damned good. We knew it wouldn't sell [and] that we had not been allowed somehow to do our best."

While Price praised the pilot episode, he damned a second one ("Appraise the Lady") without faint praise: "It had a very bad script and character and structural problems. Both Peter and I told the producers that we didn't know why they were wasting their money."

Although the series was not sold and never aired, "The Left Fist of David" began turning up in the fine print of mail-order video catalogs in the 1980s. The production has a last-stand look about it. With no time for heroic measures, the actors determinedly squared off against the labored script and disjointed direction. Serving the right wine, as it were, Lorre insinuated mock irony into his throw-away lines, but it was not enough to ease a painful situation. Even Bernard Herrmann's gothic music score sounds hauntingly suspicious of the proceedings.

On May 25, 1961, Lorre signed with Moffett Enterprises Inc. to host and possibly appear in *Peter Lorre Playhouse*, thirty-nine half-hour—later changed to one-hour—mystery telefilms scripted by actor-writer John Trayne.[11] Producer-director Phil Tucker created the series format, but Trayne took credit for introducing the actor, whom he sat behind a desk, back to the camera, wearing a bowler hat and facing a giant spider web. Looking like a plump arachnid, Lorre slowly turned toward the audience as he spoke his lines.[12] One month earlier Moffett Enterprises had arranged for the use of the production and editing facilities at KTTV in Los Angeles. With the pilot completed and production scheduled to resume in August, Moffett negotiated with Paramount—unsuccessfully, as it turned out—to finance the series for syndicated release.

Time and uninterrupted appearances on quiz shows, comedy-varieties, and dramas did not soften the actor's attitude toward television, which, he told the Canadian Broadcasting Corporation's Elwood Glover in 1962, was a medium without an apparent need for expression: "One criticism that I have to make, that is seldom made, is that you should go the other way around. You should now try to find out what can we express in that instead of imitating theater, which we still do."

In short, he did it for the money. Or so he made believe.

Co-worker Cliff Robertson felt that Lorre survived TV "in spite of fine talent through a delightful philosophy of irony and good humor." Loath to turn in anything clichéd or hackneyed, and feeling that the bits of business he delighted in creating might amuse audiences, he instinctively added, embellished, and enriched his performances. If his director rebuffed him, he shrugged his shoulders as if to say, "Well, I tried."

"He was a buoyant little cork," said Robertson, "that just went over those big waves, troubles, aches and turmoil and just bobbed right over them. He didn't try to go crashing head on into things. You got the feeling that if there was any kind of heavy discussion about the character, he'd be the first to say, 'Well, O.K., if that's the way you want it,' which was in one way charming and in another way rather sad, because more times than not he was right."

Acting triggered an apparent cleft in Lorre's personality. When the cameras rolled, self and image separated, the one receding into the background, the other moving into sharp focus. Most directors wanted what the screen personality, with its tools of the trade—the bulging eyes, the baby-faced innocence, the diffident whine—could bring to the role, not what the actor could bring of himself. Far more willing to bank on the ephemeral shadow-image than on its flesh and blood counterpart, they incanted, "Just be Peter Lorre." For the actor, filmmaking had become a revolving door, with his double, the dark insider, being ushered in, while he was escorted out. At times he gave up waiting for something better and wearily resigned himself to lending the "Peter Lorre" stamp. At other times, he asked audiences not to confuse him with his screen image. In a 1957 newspaper piece titled "Bin ich noch ein Mensch?"— "Am I Still a Human Being?"—he confided:

It is horrible to be a monster! If I had been able to foresee, when they offered me the part in "M," what direction my career and my life would take—believe me, I wouldn't have taken the role for all the money in the world.

Look at me. I'm the most frightening and despised villain ever shown on the screen. Whenever a producer needs a detestable film villain, you can be sure that they say: "Get Peter Lorre, he's a real monster!" And when I stand in front of the camera, they say: "Play it really mean, Peter! Play it like you are!"

I have played so many villains through the years, that I have to look in the mirror three times daily to convince myself that I'm still a human being.

It wouldn't be half so bad if my roles didn't influence my private life. They do. Of others I always read in the papers that they are happy, cheerful and that they have an ideal family life. No one writes that about me, although I have a real nice wife and my cute little Catharine, who is three years old. When they want to take my picture for a story about my private life and I try to smile, they laugh at me: "Come on, Peter, try to look a little wicked—as if you just killed somebody!" Sometimes I think that other people think I really do that. How would you feel when you meet somebody and from the first moment you have the uncomfortable feeling that he will ask you in the next moment whose throat you cut? And he will ask, you can be sure of that!

Lorre didn't want to be typecast at all. "I don't want to be typed as a villain or a comedian," he emphasized. "One would be as bad as the other. I had to fight that sort of thing several times in my life. And it's a painful fight because it consists of turning down money to do a role." Keeping his options open, he mediated, "Let us say that in the future, I want to do whatever is human."

The actor wanted to work with directors willing to run the risk of turning the camera on Peter Lorre, that side of him seldom captured on-screen but so familiar in private life. In Rouben Mamoulian he found his director. "Character actors," explained the filmmaker, "don't have to be typed at all because character actor means he can play a variety of characters. But a character actor frequently is artificially typecast because he does one part and he's good in it, so everybody wants him for the same kind of part and the guy becomes very unhappy, naturally."

Mamoulian drew the most original performances from artists whose screen images he redefined. In his first sound film, *City Streets* (1931), he cast the benevolent Guy Kibbee in the unexpected role of a murderer. Later, he met a young freckle-faced girl with an upturned nose at a Hollywood party. "You're not Myrna Loy?!" he burst out. "What about all this Oriental stuff? What about your own personality?" When she complained of being typecast as a Far Eastern beauty, he transported her to the musical *Love Me Tonight* (1933), relaunching her career. Convinced that Irving Pichel would make a fitting Hyde, Paramount Pictures planned to star the middle-aged actor in *Dr. Jekyll and Mr. Hyde* (1932). Mamoulian balked and insisted on the young and attractive light comedian Frederic March, fresh from his triumph in *Laughter* (1930). He remained adamant: "I said he can do it. I want him." The rest is film history.

Mamoulian knew Lorre personally and was

fascinated by the very interesting combination which doesn't happen frequently in life. The person had a totally different image in his profession from that in his life. "Now Peter Lorre," everybody said, "Oh, well, he's for these mystery stories and these strange people." Actually Peter was a very cultured man, a very sensitive person, a very lovable man, and with a great sense of humor. He said to me that he was doing something in London and was in a very first-class restaurant and everybody was staring at him. So mischievous as he was, he took one of those little paper things a drinking straw is wrapped in, compressed it, and when nobody was looking he stuck it in his nostril. Then he did something and everybody's attention was on him. He just sat on the chair and started taking it out of his nose. He wanted to shock these people—they were so stiff. They threw him out and he was never allowed to come back.

At a dinner party given by the Lorres, Mamoulian watched the actor greet his guests, some of whom he had never met, with the face of a blithe cherub. He extended his right—apparently paralyzed—hand, clenched into a rigid claw. Mamoulian stifled a chuckle as the visitors recoiled, threw sidelong glances, and stammered in acute embarrassment before quietly melting away.

He didn't recognize his friend on-screen. The clashing contradiction overwhelmed him: "My God, in this man, who played all these villains and all of these exaggerated, same type of murderer, there is so much innocence in him in life. He's a child in a way, and yet with it there is a sophistication, and there is good will. None of that is being utilized." Lorre's obvious worldliness, set against his childlike captivation with gadgets—including a slot machine in his home—intrigued Mamoulian. "Most of the time he seemed to be enjoying life hugely," he said. "He had a great kind of gusto when he felt happy. He was overflowing with feeling, and he was gay and happy, so that when I started *Silk Stockings* I thought he'd be perfect."

Mamoulian cast Lorre as Brankov, a comically innocent and easily corrupted Russian commissar seduced by the pleasures of Paris, in Metro's *Silk Stockings* (1957), a lavish musical remake of Ernst Lubitsch's *Ninotchka* (1939). It was produced by Arthur Freed and starred Fred Astaire and Cyd Charisse. On a very happy set, comrades Peter Lorre, Joseph Buloff, and Jules Munshin enjoyed an easy understanding open to a little playful recreation. Each of them subtly maneuvered to upstage the others, taking scenarist Leonard Gershe aside and suggesting business to increase their parts. Soon their little games escalated into major script changes. Mamoulian tells the story:

On every film that I've done they always play some huge practical joke on me and yet I'm very strict on the set. But I appreciate them. So I must tell you what Peter Lorre cooked up during *Silk Stockings*. I had just finished a scene with Fred Astaire and Cyd Charisse and the next morning I was to shoot the three comedians in a number that follows "Josephine," where they're told that they're all called back and they think they're going to Siberia.

So the three of them are sitting on this big set and they go through a dialogue scene and then they go into this dance-music-singing thing which goes, "When you're sent to sweet Siberia, Sibeerie-errie-a . . . as long as you don't need ice for cocktails, there's plenty of it around" . . . all those horrors of Siberia. I was going to shoot that next morning and so I came on the set, a big ballroom set and had a camera on the crane, and I saw a whole crowd. Fred was there, Cyd Charisse was there. All the other members were there, every producer in the studio was there and the head of the studio, L.B. Mayer.

So I said to my assistant, "What's going on here?" And he said, "Oh, they just thought they would like a couple of laughs as long as you have those three comedians." I said, "Oh, come on. Don't be silly. I never heard of such a thing." I could understand when I was doing Cyd and her dance; a couple of producers snuck in to see her. She's beautiful to look at, but don't tell me they're coming to see . . . My assistant says, "They're interested in seeing those three comedians." So, okay, I let it go. I rehearsed for an hour and they were still there. And finally I said alright and they did the scene. They did the song and the dance.

Finally, I said, "Alright, we'll make a take." As they go into the number I hear, "When you're working for Mamoulian, it's like working for Napoleon . . ." and so on—a whole new lyric! Now when they started this, I said I'm going crazy, it can't be! So I look at the people and they're watching me instead of watching the comedians.

Well, it turned out that Peter Lorre got this idea about rewriting this number and doing it as a surprise on the set for me. So they told him, "Well, you can't do that because it would take an hour—it's a Technicolor film and that's at least $5,000–10,000 cost to the studio." So they went to the producer Arthur Freed and he said, "Well, I'm telling you I can't approve this. You'll have to go to Mr. Mayer." So they went to Mr. Mayer and he approved it. So having approved it, he wanted to see just what he was paying $10,000 for, so they all came in to see it.

Mamoulian later discovered that Lorre and his compatriots had spent two weeks organizing the prank and writing the lyrics. Of course, they kept their plans a secret. At the end of filming, the trio presented a recording of the song and a framed copy of the text to Mamoulian. "I would almost bet that Peter engineered it," he reflected twenty years later. "It was very much like him."

Dance director Hermes Pan choreographed the "Too Bad (We Can't Go Back to Moscow)" number with Munshin, Buloff, and Lorre. "I'm not a dancer," Lorre honestly admitted to Pan at their first meeting. Although he was shuffled to the side in the more complicated dance routines, his ineptitude did not stem his enthusiasm to try something new. "He was sort of elated by doing these dances," recalled the veteran choreographer. "He had a lot of inspirational things that he would suggest to make it funny. He said, 'Okay, I'm going to hold on to the chair and I'll do a kazatski.'[13] And I said, 'Great!'" Precariously balanced between table and chair, with a butter knife clenched between his teeth, Lorre executed his own version of the demanding Ukrainian dance. For nearly a minute, he pressed the movement, overtaxed yet obviously pleased with himself. "I don't like to impose on people and try to make them do things they can't do," added Pan, "so he came up with these ideas and I think it was wonderful."

Lorre shared a dressing room with his Russian comrades. He had little to do with the vivacious Munshin but was quickly drawn to the old-world charm of Joseph Buloff. After closing the day with a drink in their dressing room, Buloff often chauffeured Lorre to his home across the valley. As they drove along, he regaled Lorre with stories of the Jewish theater. Lorre listened and laughed, content to keep the conversation one-sided. Buloff probed, but his co-worker warded off intrusions into his personal life. A shadow would fall across his face, bringing the slow, silent, and restrained aspect of Lorre's screen persona to mind. Buloff wondered if he simply hated the picture and his role. He only knew for certain that Lorre carried a secret that, after hours, plunged him into deep depression. Lorre volunteered no explanation until one evening, during their ride home, when he suddenly interrupted, "I am a very sick man." Buloff did not understand or press him about it. It was a desperate little confession, completely out of character.

No one realized that Lorre was physically used up. It was a grand cover-up. He had become a chronic complainer, beset with everyday ailments, habitually rummaging through his bagful of medicines for instant remedies. According to Charisse, "he was taking a little something he shouldn't have [most likely Cheracol, a codeine-based cough medicine] . . . and we saw little drops of it fall to the ground as he walked across the stage." Some chalked him up as a hopeless hypochondriac. The actor's fragile health and constant pill-popping did not slow him down (although he did injure his leg rehearsing one of the dance numbers). "During *Silk Stockings* he seemed full of joy and vigor," said Mamoulian. "I never knew about his health because he was always sliding through like a kid, mischievous, but always serious. He was a fun, colorful guy, if you could get that out of him." Lorre seemed so altogether content that he even faithfully stuck to the script. He did not grab the moment because it was freely given to him by a filmmaker who had engaged Peter Lorre to be himself.

"In his first big comedy role," advertised the film's trailer, the actor earned more money as a hoofer than he ever made as a homicidal maniac. He reported to work October 29, 1956, and checked out January 23, 1957, taking with him twenty-seven thousand dollars for fifty-eight days' work. Lorre fully realized that Mamoulian had plucked him from the swamp, risking, in Hollywood's view, a less commercial use of his talents. He applauded the bold move—it meant more to him than anyone knew. He felt renewed, anxious to arrest his slow deflation with further ventures into comedy.[14]

He got something else instead. There is a fine distinction between caricature—the nonsensical imitation of a characteristic style—and self-parody—a deliberate distortion of that style for comic effect. In many of his last roles, Lorre warily seesawed between the two, but when pushed off balance, he fell headlong into one, the other, or both. Once upon a time, the actor had chilled audiences with rampaging flights into the twisted brain. Now he played the clown. Directors, producers, studio executives, screenwriters, publicists, and casting agents all took part in making a mockery of the actor at a heavy cost to the man. "Peter didn't want to be a standard character," said Lester Salkow, his agent and business manager after 1956. "He was remorseful at the thought of the typecast. He didn't want to be a caricature. He loved new facets and was saddened by the thought that there was limited use made of his talents."

Lorre supposed he was no longer taken seriously as an actor. On talk shows, he sidestepped audience expectations by reminding them that he had been paid to play these roles: "I can do Japanese pretty well. It's easy, but for no money, no Japanese. . . . I don't think I'm very morbid for no money." The actor occasionally leveled blame, shooting his barbs at nebulous targets—a mogul, a studio executive, the Front Office—but more often he dismissed the phenomenon with a shrug of his shoulders, as if to say, "That's how the system works." One friend chalked it up to a "European kind of fatalistic view." He never groused about his lot or bored his co-workers with harangues about Hollywood's misuse of his talents. "That would have been too common an opinion to even bother with," voiced co-worker Keenan Wynn. "Peter would do whatever job you hired him for and he would do it well, but he knew it was shit." The trend also found its counterpart in television, usually in comedy-variety shows. A frequent guest on *The Red Skelton Show*, "the perennial bad man Peter Lorre" most often turned up in comedy sketches that lampooned his popular screen image. In a 1959 show, he played a mad scientist anxious to recruit Clem Kadiddlehopper as a guinea pig for his experiments.

The Lorre image had become so crystallized that impressionists began to mimic his style and mannerisms. Before audiences well versed in Lorre's lingo, they went goggle-eyed and rhythmically purred with faint malevolence. Impressionists, Lorre claimed—none too convincingly—gratified him. "I am without a question the most imitated man in nightclubs," he marveled. "Once when I appeared on a *Milton Berle Show* there were 10 people who tried to tell *me* how to sound like Peter Lorre." Actually, he loved to impersonate the impressionists impersonating him, and he claimed that by pinching his nose between his fingers, he could do a better "Peter Lorre" than anyone.

The actor no longer went "first class," on- or offscreen. When he learned he owed more than four hundred dollars in accumulated dues to the Screen Actors Guild, Lorre addressed an apologetic note to former British stage and film actor Pat Somerset, the head of Membership Services, explaining that when he left for Europe in 1949, he had forgotten to withdraw his membership. "Let me assure you," he wrote, "that my neglect at the time was due to a long siege of serious illness. I am not to [*sic*] well off at the moment financially. Therefore I . . . would be grateful for an adjustment."[15] In her letters home, Annemarie complained of being habitually short of money. Holiday travel, she lamented, was out of reach. Peter's philanthropic nature, a backlog of medical bills, and Annemarie's growing dependence on alcohol, coupled with too little work and a reckless disregard for day-to-day money management, undid them financially.

Lorre's private life became a closed book. Talking about his marriage upset him so much that when the subject was broached, he clammed up and quietly retreated to his dressing room. He drew from others the care and understanding he did not get at home. If, as his brother Andrew believed, Peter had married all of his wives after he had fallen out of love with them, then his marriage to Annemarie was indeed born under a cloud of duress. Nonetheless, their relationship appears to have held steady the first few years. In early 1956 Annemarie was again pregnant, renewing Peter's long-standing hopes for a son. On June 6 she suffered a miscarriage—rearranging furniture, according to family history—and lost their boy and nearly her life in the resultant hemorrhaging.

"We have to thank God—that everything went so well," Peter wrote Annemarie's parents in Germany. "I can think of nothing else than gratitude that Annemarie is still alive and out of danger. It was close—very close. It was a question of minutes—but God did everything right, so he must love her very much."

Peter's letter, written in the wake of near catastrophe, belied the tone of their marriage. His failing relationship with Annemarie wore on him physically and emotionally. Peter's "nerves shot up," said Celia, along with his blood pressure, already elevated by years of chain-smoking. On December 8, 1956, she had "dinner at Peter's. He is so tired and sad. He said to me: 'I don't like to go home. I won't be abused.'" Whether Annemarie's drinking fed her instability or stemmed from it is impossible to diagnose at this point. Publicly, she flaunted her status as Mrs. Peter Lorre, embarrassing her husband with her egotism and strident insensitivity. At home, she opened his mail. Like the press agent she claimed to have been, she regurgitated for public consumption tales of her husband's mentorship with Freud and of his promising future as a doctor. "If the theater hadn't entered his life," bragged Annemarie, "Peter would probably be a famous psychoanalyst today." Coming from her mouth, his dreams sounded ridiculous.

The downhill run had gained more momentum than Lorre knew. On January 16, 1956, the *Hollywood Reporter* announced that *The Black Sleep* would star Basil Rathbone, Peter Lorre, Lon Chaney, John Carradine, and Bela Lugosi. According to its director, Reginald LeBorg of Bel-Air Productions tried to get Lorre for the part of Odo, the gypsy, who "was supposed to act as comic relief from the horror. . . . but he wanted too much money. If Lorre had been in it, we would have built the part up."[16]

Remembering how well Peter Lorre and Edward Arnold had clicked in *Crime and Punishment,* AIP producer Alex Gordon thought to pair them as an evil hypnotist and a money-hungry promoter in *The She-Creature* (1956), about a beautiful woman who is regressed to a past life as a whiskered, horned, and armor-plated prehistoric monster. Director Eddie Cahn, who had worked with Arnold in *Main Street after Dark* at MGM and *Afraid to Talk* at Universal, seconded the idea. Gordon kicked around figures with the William Morris Agency, which chose to consult Arnold before committing him to appear in a small independent production. On good terms with the actor, Cahn felt a personal pitch would be more persuasive, allowing him to trade on their pleasant working relationship. When he tried to contact Arnold, he learned that the sixty-six year-old actor had died only days earlier. In Lorre's case, the Sam Jaffe agency shortcut the process, committing him before he had read the script, which he dismissed, in Gordon's sugarcoated words, as "a piece of junk."

"He hated it," recalled Gordon. "He wouldn't act in such a cheap film."

Jaffe was having none of it. "If they'll pay your fee," he told his client, "you'll do it." Rather than accept the assignment, Lorre left the agency.[17]

At a party for Lester Salkow, the actor once hung up a skeleton with a note that read, "This is what you would look like if Lester Salkow were your agent." Salkow did his best to keep Lorre working during these lean years, although it inevitably required him to recycle the actor's threadbare image in secondhand parts. In *The Sad Sack* (1957), a zany Jerry Lewis feature, Lorre, as an Arab heavy, was obliged to push his villainous screen persona to the limit. With requisite understatement, he comforts his knife, "Patience, my angel. We will not lose him." In another of his few scenes, he softly queries, "Please, can I kill him now?"

The same year he appeared as a greedy, dissolute French commissioner in *Hell Ship Mutiny* (originally titled *Captain Knight of the South Seas*), an obvious attempt to resurrect the menacing Lorre of earlier days. The actor ran the gauntlet, yielding to audience expectations and salvaging what he could from an uncertain career.

As television displaced radio, Lorre's performances over the airwaves had dwindled to a trickle until 1953, when he stepped into the role of host, or rather "exciting guide to terror," of Mutual's *Nightmare*, a poorly plotted horror series, which aired weekly from October 1, 1953, to September 29, 1954. On April 27, 1958, the actor stood before the mike a final time, joining Boris Karloff, Alfred Hitchcock, and singer Julienne Marie on *Easy as ABC*'s "O is for Old Wives' Tales." Presented by United Nations Radio and broadcast by CBS, the thirteen-week series celebrated the work of UNESCO (United Nations Educational, Scientific and Cultural Organization).

Although he is regarded as "one of the worst things that ever happened to filmed science fiction," producer and director Irwin Allen was perhaps one of the best things that happened to character actors who could not afford to be choosy. In his nearly thirty years of film and television production, he claimed to have hired virtually everyone in the industry, including Peter Lorre. Besides finding him a warm and compassionate person, the kind of man he was interested in knowing better, Allen considered Lorre a "cinema genius," a master of timing, and stood in awe of that remarkable face, over which the actor exercised uncanny control. Nevertheless, he asked nothing new of Lorre when he cast him in four of his "all-market" Cinema-Scope-Deluxe movies. The first, *The Story of Mankind* (1957) brought to the screen Hendrik Van Loon's bestselling children's history of the human race. Through his independently owned Cambridge Productions, in cooperation with Warner Bros. (whose vault he drew on for stock footage), Allen promised to put the punch back into history.

He selected key characters from the past—both good and bad—and matched them with giants in the film world—Hedy Lamarr as Joan of Arc, Harpo Marx as Isaac Newton, Edward Everett Horton as Sir Walter Raleigh, and Dennis Hopper as Napoleon. Working with Charles Bennett, he slapped a contemporary outlook over the juvenile narrative, vulgarizing Van Loon with gags and gimmicks in a tongue-in-cheek charade.

Allen cast Lorre on the debit side of history as Nero: "twisted by endless orgies, this madman knew no end of violence, no limit to lunacy. He arranged the suicides of most of his closest friends, had his mother clubbed to death . . . poisoned a lot of the people he knew and sought out similar amusements." Belted by bacchanalia, Lorre sits, head in hand, depraved and woeful by turns. "Let the wine flow," he exhorts, "for tonight, tonight Nero celebrates his greatest triumph!" Dropping his goblet, he wearily shuffles to the balcony and strums a lyre while Rome burns.

Sketches and caricatures had suggested Lorre as Nero's contemporary likeness. If so, it flattered neither of them. The actor looked in poor health. Like tallow melting from a stubby candle, his flesh drooped from his bones; his bloated face and foreshortened figure physically expressed the deformity of the character he portrayed.

By this time, Allen and Lorre saw a good deal of each other socially. On Sundays, Peter often brought Annemarie and Catharine over for brunch and a swim. One day, the conversation turned to Allen's new circus picture. Lorre loved clowns. His discourses about the dramatic possibilities of the funnyman underlined the serious thought he had given the subject. "Playing a clown, a real facemaker, fascinated him," said Vincent Price. "It was his definition of acting." Lorre enthusiastically read the script and told Allen, "Hey, this is something I should do."[18]

"I thought it was simply marvelous to have this man," recalled Allen, "this great, pathetic face, this great villainous face, to play a clown. It was the coup of all time to me."

Lorre had not played a clown since the ill-fated stage production of *Der Dompteur* at the Theater am Schiffbauerdamm in 1931. As Skeeter in *The Big Circus* (1959), his globular eyes and melancholy expression form a natural mask that appears all the sadder because it has nothing to do. In makeup, he is just part of the scenery. Out of makeup, he is crusty but benign, his frustration subsiding into boredom. Certainly, his poor health posed an obstacle to the performance of physical, clownlike antics. Little wonder that friend and co-worker Gilbert Roland found Lorre as apathetic on-screen as off. The actor seemingly saved the best of his clown characterization for publicity shots, which gave him more time for development than the few fleeting moments on-screen.

When Lorre wanted to add something to his role, he would direct his comments to Victor Mature, who, besides having script approval, "had 10% of the gross, plus a bunch of money up front." These the actor forwarded to Allen, who, in turn, passed back the word, "Fine, tell him to do it." After coming up with a coat and hat for Skeeter, costume designer Paul Zastupnevich tried to think of a little gimmick that would give Lorre something to work with. "Could I have a little yellow bird?" asked the actor. Zastupnevich not only perched a yellow canary atop the hat, but also put three eggs beneath it. Like a child with a new toy, Lorre was delighted with the simple prop.

Charles Bennett, who scripted the picture, described a Peter Lorre who perhaps did his best work behind the scenes: "To me he was a great performer, somebody who enjoyed his work immensely, gleeful, and always eager to come up with gags, ideas, constructive comedy suggestions, not only for his own part but for the other parts around him. In *The Big Circus* it was Peter Lorre who suggested that a nice comedian (Howard McNear, now famous as Mayberry's Floyd the Barber) should be trapped in a cage directly alongside a wildly fierce lion; one of the best laughs in the movie and nothing to do with Peter's part." Lorre took obvious delight in the situation, borrowing his best line—"Softly, softly, catchee monkey"—from *Mysterious Mr. Moto*.

Not all of the technical innovations that Hollywood employed to keep moviegoers coming back were qualified successes. In the 1930s Hans Laube, a Swiss osmologist who had devised a method for cleansing the air in large auditoriums, was struck with the notion of putting odors back into the air. He worked on the idea of adding scents to movies and in 1939 exhibited a film accompanied by a variety of smells at the New York World's Fair. In cooperation with several companies pioneering in American television, Laube worked to bring "smell-action" to the small screen. However, when the process proved impractical, it was abandoned.

In 1954 producer Michael Todd and his son Michael Jr. first witnessed a similar process designed to synchronize the projection of odors with the action on film. The Todd Company financed further experiments to inject odors into theater auditoriums in hopes that the process would be ready for *Around the World in Eighty Days* (1956), but their expectations were premature. Convinced of the superiority of Laube's design, Todd Jr. contracted with his company, Scentovision Inc., and provided the scientist with a laboratory at the Todd Cinestage in which to further develop his process.[19]

Laube called his device a "smell-brain." Each unit consisted of more than thirty metal vials containing 400 cc of highly concentrated synthetic odors, or enough for 180 performances. A plastic pipe connected to an outlet at each seat. On cue, about 2 cc of a specified essence was released, reaching one thousand viewers. The "smell-brain" exposed moviegoers to a wide range of odors: roses, perfume, tobacco, wine, peppermint, lemons, leather, gunpowder, garlic, shoe polish, and more.

In January 1959 with Laube's machine tested and proven, Todd planned for its commercial use in a feature film titled, appropriately, *Scent of Mystery* (1960). He strove for maximum effect and arrayed an arsenal of technical innovations with which to assault the senses, including a 70 mm Todd Process Camera with distortion-free lenses and a refined depth of field and an eight-channel Todd Belock sound system with a 360-degree projection area and a new wider frequency. Believing that odors could titillate audiences and supply clues for solving the mystery, Todd assigned William Roos to tailor his screenplay as much to "smell-action" as to the Spanish landscape. Enamored of the gorgeous locales, he chose to shoot *Scent of Mystery* entirely on location, meshing the scenery with special effects.

Throwing money at the screen, however, did not compensate for the film's inherent shortcomings. *Scent of Mystery* is a film out-of-balance that reads better than it plays, something the television premiere of this "lost" film in 1986—complete with scratch-and-sniff clue cards supplied at local convenience stores—so strikingly underlined. The working script is an innocuous and amusing whodunit whose crooked characters and plot twists and turns gel into tangible comedy-suspense. However, comparisons to a Hitchcock thriller—a notion planted by the publicists—caused *Scent of Mystery* to suffer miserably by comparison. Jack Cardiff directed with an eye to scenery rather than substance, with the Spanish locales and the Smell-O-Vision cues pushing the story and characters into the background. Hitchcock intensified his suspense with humor; Cardiff diffused his mystery with holiday charm. The result is a pedestrian travelogue paced by an olfactory sense instead of a cinematic one. "It is an artless, loose-jointed 'chase' picture," blasted the *New York Times*'s Bosley Crowther, "set against some of the scenic beauties of Spain, which, indeed, are the most attractive and rewarding compensation of the show."

Lorre's role as Smiley, the sardonic cabby, is a study of the film in microcosm. His part was "an intentional light-hearted caricature of his typical screen image," claimed Todd. "A possibly sinister, shadowy figure who may be in league with the bad guys while appearing to help the hero. . . . he is only projecting a facade of mystery and underworld connections to maintain an image." Reading the script it is easy to imagine Lorre scratching at the already thin veneer of villainy and exposing the humor in Smiley's inane gabble. "Fifteen years ago in Marrekesh [*sic*] when I was still driving a camel, there was a girl," he blathers. "Lucky for me I came to my senses. I sold my camel . . . and I have not been back to Marrekesh since. Otherwise today . . . and I shudder to think of it . . . today I would be a happily married man. And it could happen to you. . . . it can happen to anyone if he isn't careful. You must have friends who got married. . . . Let them be a lesson to you. [a short time later] . . . Every man should have a wife. I once stole the wife of a friend of mine in Casablanca. . . . He had two. I only took the small one." But these scenes are gone in the finished film, as are many others whose dialogue ideally suited the artless and off-center waggery of the "Good Soldier Svejk."

Instead of emerging as a mischievous rogue, Smiley merely supplies a touch of local color. His taxi transports the hero—and thereby moves the plot—while he kills time with laborious one-liners. He is more catalyst than character; time didn't allow for more. Denholm Elliott, the star of the picture, described Lorre as "very jokey, very amiable, not in the least bit grand or upstaging . . . who told jolly little stories about the early days of Hollywood." But this Lorre is hardly visible on the screen. In those few moments, he offered some bits of business welcomed by his director. "If you put in an idea," said Elliott, "he'd keep level with you. In the Malaga night fiesta scene, I caught some streamers in my mouth, so Peter followed along—if you'll gag, I'll gag—and caught them under his nose."

Picking up the baton was an exception in a performance as unsound as the actor himself. "He looked like Tweedle-Dee or Tweedle-Dum," said Elliott of the overweight actor. To cast and crew, he appeared ill during filming. When Elliott called to collect him for a dinner party, he discovered Lorre in an antique nightdress and cap, draped across the bed, snoring fitfully and obviously unwell. He summoned the doctor, who recklessly awakened him with a lumbar punch. The actor sat bolt upright. "Oh, no, Monsieur!" he squawked in pained disapproval.

Most of all, he complained about the heat. As spring turned into summer, temperatures rose above one hundred degrees, with the lights and reflectors adding to the discomfort. In June he suffered from what was later diagnosed as a sunstroke. "One evening in Cordoba, when I was having dinner in a local restaurant," recalled Jack Cardiff in his autobiography, *Magic Hour,* "my assistant director dashed in, breathless with panic: 'Jack, Peter Lorre is dying.' There he was, unconscious, lying on a table in his hotel room, his face a pale grey and his belly weirdly enormous. His breathing was shallow, but every few seconds his body shuddered from huge spasms like colossal hiccups."

According to Cardiff, five heart specialists all shook their heads and agreed that death was imminent. "No one," said Mike Todd, "could diagnose the trouble or prescribe any treatment or medicine that produced any improvement in Peter's condition, when another highly respected local doctor was called in and much to everyone's dismay put leeches on Peter, who responded almost immediately and quickly and dramatically recovered. My staff and associates objected to the leech treatment but Peter [who later claimed the doctor had cut a vein and bled him] wanted to try it and the doctor proved right." "Of course, he could no longer run in the chase scenes," added Cardiff. "We advertised in the Spanish press for a double and luckily found a most realistic Peter Lorre II to do the running for him."

One of the first persons to hear of the near-fatal tragedy was Lauren Bacall, who flew in from London to sit at Lorre's bedside and administer a soothing sweetness that deeply touched him. Annemarie and Catharine arrived soon after, putting a crimp in Peter's busy schedule of nightly dinners with young Spanish ladies. Asked later if his brush with death had changed his outlook on life, Lorre insouciantly said, "I didn't die, so it didn't change my outlook." In less than two weeks, he was back before the cameras.

Despite his collapse, Lorre enjoyed what he described as a break from caricature roles and fed the press an enriched picture of Smiley: "I play a very nice man. . . . On one hand I can count the times I've been a nice man. I enjoy being normal." Lorre said he liked himself in *Scent of Mystery.* "That is most unusual, because I not only don't like myself in many pictures; I don't like many pictures." His performance garnered a few accolades from the critics, including one from the caustic Bosley Crowther, who singled him out for faint praise: "Except for the job of Peter Lorre as a bored taxi-driver . . . the acting is downright atrocious."

Smell-O-Vision fared less well than the movie itself. With inadequate ventilation and an ineffective air cleaner, aromas piled up in the theaters, triggering waves of nausea. "Whiff gags" (including the smell of booze Lorre puts in his coffee), as Cardiff called them, fell under sharp attack and an onslaught of puns and insults—"the Muzak of the olfactory system . . . this all-out attack on the public's nose . . . assaults the nose as a mixture of paint thinner and dimestore perfume . . . a purifying agent . . . leaves a sweet, cloying smell reminiscent of an undertaking parlor." Almost before the odors had time to dissipate from movie theaters, *Scent of Mystery* was forgotten, destined for obscurity. Plans to release an unscented version of the film under the title *A Holiday in Spain* never materialized.

In 1960 Lorre renewed, rather indirectly, his association with Alfred

Hitchcock. Three years earlier he had appeared—with curled locks, looking like a plumped up version of the General in *Secret Agent*—on *Alfred Hitchcock Presents* as a wily detective in a black comedy titled "The Diplomatic Corpse." Far more memorable is "Man from the South," telecast January 3, 1960, in which Lorre wagers his shiny new convertible against Steve McQueen's little finger that his cigarette lighter will fire ten times in a row. Cleaver in hand, the actor's expressions of glee and disappointment rise and fall with his own expectations and the metallic song of the lighter.[20]

Hitchcock delegated most of the work on the series to trusted associates. Paul Henreid directed "The Diplomatic Corpse" and Norman Lloyd (who also co-produced the series from 1957 until 1965) helmed "Man from the South." A gap in his schedule, the right story, or the opportunity to work with a favorite actor put Hitchcock in the director's seat on 20 of the 365 episodes. However, he exercised only script approval for the episodes that starred Lorre.

If the commercial application of Peter Lorre had become commonplace, his use in commercials had not. Celebrity selling had taken an upswing in the 1940s. Joe E. Brown pushed Calox Tooth Powder in 1944. Harold Peary backed Blackstone Cigars that same year. In 1949 Pat O'Brien and Humphrey Bogart sold A-S-R lighters, while Basil Rathbone peddled Fatima Turkish cigarettes. Lorre, too, got in on the advertising act. Far from featuring his "forbidding" screen image, however, Regent Cigarettes magazine ads promoted a practical person who enjoyed badminton, Ping-Pong, and crushproof cigarette cases. In 1954 Virginia Dare cleverly played both sides of the Lorre label by contrasting his "reputation for international wickedness" with his down-to-earth taste in wine. "Fancy wine experts slay me," says an offended Peter Lorre, as he scornfully looks over his shoulder at a wealthy wine connoisseur and his valet tasting from their well-stocked table. "There's no boring, pompous talk about *good years* and *bouquets* in my house," he assures his fans. "All I know is Virginia Dare Wine *sure tastes good!*"

Magazine advertisers apparently credited their readers with enough intelligence to cope with other sides of Lorre's personality, but television ad men did not. In the early 1960s, the actor did for Speidel what he had done for directors since 1931—menace his victim with glee. "I get tremendous satisfaction destroying things," purrs Peter Lorre the destroyer. "Doesn't everybody?" Lorre twists, turns and ties the seemingly indestructible watchband into a knot. "But I can't destroy it," he laments, looking adorably sad. "Twist-O-Flex, by Speidel."

Credited with outdoing DeMille with his disaster spectacles, Irwin Allen pioneered catastrophe kitsch on a global scale in *Voyage to the Bottom of the*

Sea (1961), a highly improbable sci-fi adventure about two navy scientists (Walter Pidgeon and Peter Lorre) who save the world from being charbroiled by snuffing out the Van Allen Belt of radiation with a Polaris missile fired from the atomic submarine *Seaview.*

"It was just a job," recalled actor Frankie Avalon of Lorre's performance as Commodore Lucius Emery. "He was just there. Peter was definitely a frustrated man at that point, knowing he had to do this film and there was really nothing there for him to do. I think at that point he was just having fun with himself. He would do little things that weren't in the script and add little things to his character, and he would get a kick out of it."

As Emery, Lorre created an intense hostility toward Zucco, a rival scientist played by Henry Daniell. "Any time they mentioned the name Zucco, he went crazy," said Avalon. "That was his fun." When Zucco challenges Emery at an international congress, the Commodore growls in a vaguely threatening tone, "Oh, he irritates me!"

One thing he didn't invent was the sweat-soaked look of his clothing, which was achieved with a finely-tuned seltzer bottle. Resentful of being misted for verisimilitude, Lorre grumbled, "The hell with realism" and led a crew member on a chase through the *Seaview* sets. Given the actor's poor health, one imagines that he was easily run aground and sprayed. He also reportedly— one supposes somewhat belligerently—refused to extinguish his cigarettes, which he smoked throughout the picture. That, along with Pidgeon's cigars, clouded the issue of the picture's scientific accuracy.

A stiff and rambling script soaked with plot contrivances and stock characters fatally flawed *Voyage to the Bottom of the Sea.* Critic Howard Thompson aptly noted in the *New York Times* that "Mr. Lorre, as the world's foremost physicist, keeps growling, 'Now wot?' and making the most sense." Lorre mustered even less enthusiasm for 20th Century–Fox's publicity department when he politely told them that *Voyage to the Bottom of the Sea* was one of his favorite films: "I get to play a good guy. After playing top brass in every enemy army in the world I get to play a United States Commodore in this. Also, I have a leading lady all to myself. Her name is Bessie. She's a shark, it's true, but she's all mine."

Lorre looked for something to do, something to break the monotony, something to insulate himself from the sad truth. He was often the first to arrive on the set and the last to leave. Within a few days, he got to know the cast and crew. He extended the gift of friendship and soon moved into their lives. Around him he gathered an audience to lend an ear to his repertoire of anecdotes about a time when making "family" pictures was fun. His personality was infectious, his approach disarming. "He had a unique sense of humor in that it was very quiet humor," said director Joseph M. Newman, who had worked with Lorre on *The Big Circus*. "His voice was soft and musical. His eyes would dance with merriment and at the most tense moments, he would invariably lift the bleak atmosphere with a delightful utterance." Part of Lorre's daily routine during the making of *Voyage to the Bottom of the Sea* was lunch with co-workers Barbara Eden and Walter Pidgeon. He fought for the check after every meal, practically to the floor. "He had a little bit of the devil in him, with kindness," said Eden, "and every square inch of him laughed when he laughed, every round inch."

Behind the elfin twinkle lurked the glint of insurgency. The fear of being wasted motivated Lorre to salt and pepper his bland roles. As best he could, within the guidelines of the stories, he sabotaged dreary, dead-end parts and brought to them something of himself, some bit of unorthodoxy to fracture the dull uniformity of his situation. A shrug, a frown, or a bounce wrought life from tired dialogue. Turned corners of the mouth or just a faraway look said that he was listening and reacting. He was full of creative and constructive ideas, making him, in Joseph Newman's opinion, "a director's actor."

In 1951 Newman had looked to cast Lorre as Massine, an Italian investigator, in *Lucky Nick Cain*, based on William James Hadley Chase's novel *I'll Get You for This* and starring George Raft. For whatever reason, the British actor Charles Goldner played the part. Said Newman: "Goldner . . . was quite a well-known actor on the British stage, and gave an adequate performance, and [was] an interesting guy, but he wasn't Peter Lorre! I mean, you know, there was just ONE Peter Lorre, and Peter Lorre would have made a great difference in the film, because there was that PARTICULAR character."

"Peter believed in the spirit of man," said Allen, "and to that end he was interested in how normal human beings respond and act and if it didn't smack of reality, the reality of human emotions under specific conditions, then he would think of that as fraudulent and would not want to do that or at least gently suggest we do something else." With "great feeling and great good voice," and without being offensive, the actor logically, softly, and intelligently registered his ideas. Allen noted that he responded to Lorre's suggestions and advice during read-throughs of the scripts and during production "with warmth, with thanks, with open ears, with open heart."

Asked if he liked being an actor, Lorre told Mike Wallace that he could not live without it. "And I think that is about the only excuse to be an actor, when you are a grown up man," he explained. The need to work, to keep busy, was a narcotic to which he was desperately addicted. "I think [acting] carries a certain obligation to work at it," said Lorre, "and this is one of the reasons why I don't agree with most actors, or don't like their way of doing things, because talent alone to me doesn't mean a thing." In their bedroom he kept a large blackboard. "Before Peter shoots the next morning," Annemarie explained to Ludwig Veigel, "he puts his lines down there. Then he wakes up and reads the blackboard. He falls asleep again and then he reads it again and the next morning he is ready for his lines." What mattered most went on behind the scenes: planning, preparation, production. "I'll grab a project and work at it, not feeling very sure whether it can be realized or not," said Lorre. "I am perfectly willing to throw it away if it doesn't work out. But it keeps me busy. . . . As long as you can work at a thing, it interests me. Once it's finished, it doesn't interest me at all." Listening to him, one might think the final product was incidental to the effort that went into its creation. He wanted no baggage, only the exercise in carrying it. His film roles were precious parts of himself, which, in the end, he disowned.

Lorre made Irwin Allen laugh. Warmly willing to let him delight others, he offered the actor a comedy role in *Five Weeks in a Balloon* (1962). Lorre got caricature instead, humor at his own expense. In this loose telling of Professor Fergusson's (Sir Cedric Hardwicke's) hot air balloon expedition to plant the Union Jack on the East Bank of the Volta River and lay claim to a vast area of West Africa, the actor played Ahmed, a roguish slave trader. Along with fez, billowing pantaloons, and Muslim slippers, he wears a mortified grimace as he delivers his witless dialogue: "What about breakfast? Don't you see I'm fading away!" As a "caricature of a slave trader," wrote A.H. Weiler for the *New York Times*, "Peter Lorre is simply tired." Sensitive to the very perceptible toll on his figure, the actor sweetly suggested to Paul Zastupnevich, "I know my back is not perfect. If you can give me a little jacket or a little vest." Nothing else was said. The costume designer tailored Lorre's outfit to disguise his rounded shoulders.

"From an actor's viewpoint, the dealer wasn't exactly an endearing character," wrote screenwriter Charles Bennett in a profile for *Close-Ups*. "Yet in spite of his viciousness, Peter immediately established himself as 'Mr. Adorable' and remained so until the movie's fade out. Looking back, I'm not sure that the screenplay intended it that way."

The creative spark flickered, but it never went out. Lorre knew exactly what he was doing and why. He girded his sense of reality and pitted his professional best against the inconsequential parts. Red Buttons observed:

> There was a serious artist under all that, but he put it in perspective. His attitude was that all of this was childish nonsense. He was funny on the set, saying

some outrageous thing . . . like Peck's Bad Boy, mischievous, with a twinkle in his eye, clowning his way through life, but underneath it I felt the turmoil. What he said and how he said it was always shocking. He tackled everything with an amusing and jaundiced eye. I think he missed his calling. He had a fantastic sense of humor, a comedy in his attitude that he carried along with him, a nonchalant attitude. He was a very iconoclastic person. I think they misused his talents. Had he been given the opportunity, he would have been known as a first-rate comedic talent. No doubt about it.

In 1959 Samuel Z. Arkoff and James H. Nicholson, cofounders of American International Pictures (AIP), an independent production company specializing in low-budget exploitation films, decided to discontinue the "small" black and white horror pictures—*The Phantom from 10,000 Leagues* (1956), *Voodoo Woman* (1956), *I Was a Teenage Werewolf* (1957), and so forth—which they had parleyed into a successful staple. By the early 1960s, scores of horror movies flooded the market once cornered by AIP. Double-billing was scrapped. "Just the mere appearance of a combination in the newspapers," said Arkoff, "made it obvious that these were not expensive pictures." Arkoff, Nicholson, and independent producer and director Roger Corman sat down and kicked around new and different concepts of horror. "We came across the name of Poe," recalled Arkoff, "a writer who was universally known, and didn't—like the new writers still alive—cost us a hundred thousand, or more." A fan of Edgar Allan Poe's tales of mystery and imagination, Corman suggested they film "The Fall of the House of Usher" in color and CinemaScope, double the budget, and triple the shooting schedule to three weeks. Arkoff and Nicholson gave him nearly three hundred thousand dollars—by far the biggest budget to date for an AIP picture—and fifteen days.[21]

AIP has not won much respect. "In one of its less charitable moments," Arkoff related in his autobiography, *Flying through Hollywood by the Seat of My Pants*, the *New York Times* "referred to the early days of AIP as having about as much status in the American film industry as the fellow who sweeps up the elephant droppings after a circus parade." Accustomed to ignoring reproachful critics, Arkoff and Nicholson preferred to read audience reaction at the box office. But the "pseudointellectual" axe never fell. *House of Usher* (1960) was a commercial and critical hit, touching off a cycle—eight pictures between 1961 and 1965—of Poe adaptations directed by Corman, who reinvigorated the waning genre of the American horror film, imbuing it with a sense of the *fantastique*. His vision served the allegorical dimensions of the stories as well as their gloomy gothic beauty. On a more practical level, he stretched the production dollar, giving better than he got. Stylizing the Poe canon, however, involved a four-way collaboration. Richard Matheson, best known for his extensive science fiction and fantasy credits, including novels *I Am Legend* (1954) and *The Shrinking Man* (1956) and numerous teleplays for *The Twilight Zone*, adapted Poe's stories for the screen, preserving the author's conception as well as his narrative form. Working on a shoestring budget, art director Daniel Haller created fitting ambiences with his macabre and eerie backgrounds. And using a repertoire of sensuously warm sepulchral tones courtesy of Pathecolor ("Pepsi Cola Gothic," said film critic Vincent Canby), cinematographer Floyd Crosby, who in 1931 had won an Academy Award for his work on the Murnau-Flaherty semidocumentary *Tabu*, added the final atmospheric touches.

The decision, in Arkoff's words, to "lighten up" the Poe adaptations was mutual. "After you did a certain number of them," he explained, "you almost had to because you can't go along on any group of pictures without changing your direction. You can do that on television week after week, but you can't do that in the theater. And we all liked humor. . . . it gave extra strength, an extra factor." Matheson recommended adapting three short stories, each drawn from Poe, to be presented together as *Tales of Terror* (1962). So as not "to be consistently down-beat," he wedged a mock-horror tale between the more or less straightforward retelling of "Morella" and "The Facts in the Case of M. Valdemar." In 1962 Lester Salkow negotiated a one-film commitment for Lorre to appear in "The Black Cat," the middle episode of *Tales of Terror*, loosely based on the story of the same title and "The Cask of Amontillado."

Matheson cast Lorre as Montresor Herringbone (originally Montresor Lushingham), a swollen pixie of a man with a maniacal temper, who drives his long-suffering wife, Annabel (Joyce Jameson), into the arms of wine connoisseur Fortunato Luchresi (Vincent Price). Herringbone repays this effrontery to his pride by entombing them behind a cellar wall. His perfect crime is foiled when Annabel's black cat, unwittingly walled in with the victims, begins to wail, betraying the murderer.

Presuming that audiences wanted to see the actor as they remembered him, as a menace, AIP purposely perpetuated Lorre's screen image as a member of the horror elite. "Even though there might be a section in there that was played light," said Milton Moritz, National Director of Advertising and Publicity for American International, "we would never really attach a tongue-in-cheek approach to the merchandising of the film. Once people came in and Peter used a little tongue-in-cheek or goo-goo'ed the eyes it was acceptable, but they would not necessarily come in on the pretense that he was going to be a comedy character, so more or less everything we prepared in that direction played upon the villain of the past."

AIP promised a faithful retelling of Poe. It was never meant to be, either in concept or execution. "I wanted to make good-humored comedy within the framework of Poe," said Corman, stressing a point that must have seemed obvious even then. For this he depended on the cooperation of his cast, which "jointly entered into the creative process." According to Jameson, "all of the actors had an independent hand in developing their own characters." Being "more of a camera director [who] never worked with the actors or fashioned their roles," Corman encouraged them to stick to the basic story line and build as a team, with the result that many of the ideas sprang from their dialogue. As the "most spontaneous and immediately inventive of the three actors," Lorre enjoyed, in Vincent Price's words, "lots of independence to improvise." Restraining him was a lost cause anyway. "Peter abhorred dullness," said Salkow. "If he could amuse or put mystery into anything, he was for that. He was always scheming to squeeze the most out of a scene. He always got away with it."

"Peter said he wanted to work more in this type of comedy film," confirmed Corman, "that he had gotten away from it and wanted to get back to it." The young director gave him free rein to crawl out from beneath the weight of his creation and stop being "Peter Lorre." The actor throttled his screen image in a comedy-hold, trading upon it as it had traded upon him. Arkoff counted on him to supply the broader laughs in the Poe picture. The actor had something more polished in mind. A "Poe type of sardonic humor," he claimed, came naturally. "But don't think that it is easy to mix fright and fun," explained Lorre. "Not every type of comedian or actor can make it, it takes a fellow well versed in both laughter and violence. . . . It has an inbred difficulty consisting of the fact that if you get an audience laughing, then it takes something to make them stop. I don't want to brag, but I can make people laugh and then be terrified."[22]

"Cast as a villain, he plays his roles for comedy," wrote Rose Pelswick, of the *New York Journal-American,* who interviewed Lorre in September 1962. "Given a comic part, he injects a serious note into the goings-on . . . because that, as he puts it, 'is what makes the character human.'"

"Peter took a part and changed it so that it fit him better," said Price. Careening between the sets and story framework, Lorre amplified the comic possibilities of his character, bringing, in critic James Powers's words, an "elfin Thurber touch to the murderous tale." In a tasting contest at a wine sellers' convention, Lorre and Price square off, one as a rank tosspot, the other as a preening sissy. "There was so much hamming in the scene," added Matheson.

"It came out of them." Coached by a professional wine tester, Price found humor in the elaborate, often extravagant, ritual of wine tasting. He sniffed the bouquet, studiously swished and swallowed, and then robustly inhaled, releasing the aroma, while Lorre just guzzled, belched, and slurred, "It's very good!"

Knowing that Lorre and Price had been cast in the principal roles, Richard Matheson tailored parts to players, unconsciously figuring on "Peter's mad background" to sharpen the comic edge of *Tales of Terror*. When Herringbone discovers his wife is having an affair with Luchresi, he returns home in time to see them passionately bid adieu after an evening's tryst. Standing in the shadows, Lorre composed his face "into a mask of deadly containment," following Matheson's script note. The screenwriter also gave Lorre the lines, "Oh. Oh. I'll strangle her. I'll break her neck. I'll cut off her head. I'll dismember her. I'll—I'll—do something nasty." But they are not in the film. Sensitive to the suggestion of caricature, the actor possibly balked at saying them. Other lines in subsequent Matheson horror-comedies featuring Lorre are also missing. What lay behind such omissions is difficult to say. Perhaps, as Price contended, the actor thought that he could write better lines for himself than Matheson could. For whatever reason, his dialogue adjustments carried a kind of Lorre logic. Mixing malevolent rage with puckish humor, he seemed bent on portraying Herringbone as an irascible drunk rather than a cold-blooded murderer.

Despite the pleasure he took in his work, co-workers noticed that Lorre walked and talked more slowly. He fatigued easily and at times his control of the acting process faltered. With his health giving way under a shell of weight, friends—and doctors—chided, scolded, cajoled, and teased, but failed to stem his appetite for fattening treats or stimulate his desire for nutritious ones. ("I don't eat that grass," he chastised waiters who served him salads. "I'm not a cow.") Protests duly noted, he sipped a forbidden glass of wine at lunch and defiantly ate foods prohibited by his doctor. Herb Meadow had noted Lorre's ungovernable eating habits during the filming of "The Left Fist of David":

> He ate everything. He gorged on everything. There was a contest between him and Tommy Gomez, as to which one could become more vast, more round, or gorge more at lunch. We were on location and being catered by Brittingham's, so the lunches were rather on the posh side. Lorre and Gomez would load their dishes—these were the very large service plates—until they were brimming over, go off and sit down and start pushing this stuff down their gullets, and then to everybody's horror, because after a while it passed the point of a joke, they would go back and have their plates filled again.

"I think it was Gomez," continued Meadow, "who warned him against sweets, Gomez who was addicted to them himself, and Peter said something to the effect that it would take more than that to sweeten his nature, but he was trying, which was a funny little confession."

Lorre typically made light of comments about his size: "I'm very little, but I'm solid." And so did others. When he mentioned his upcoming appearance in *Five Weeks in a Balloon* on *Tell It to Groucho* in May 1962, the acerbic comedian jibed, "And are you playing the part of the balloon?" Posing what he cautioned was "a rather rude question" in a 1960 interview, Mike Wallace pointed out that Lorre seemed to have gained maybe twenty-five, thirty pounds. "Since the death of Sydney Greenstreet," the actor retorted, diffusing the hurt with humor, "I have to make the weight of both of us." In his in-your-face style, Wallace persevered: "You have put on considerable weight. Why?"

"I feel good this way or that way," explained Lorre. "It doesn't bother me. . . . Right at this moment I am going to take it off again, because that feels good."

Privately, however, he dropped his carefree attitude about his weight and revealed his concern. Over a bottle of Coca-Cola on Hollywood's Sunset Boulevard, he assured actress Blandine Ebinger, the wife of composer Friedrich Hollaender, that he would improve his health. "I have to," he said. "For all who love me. Also for my child." But the pounds stayed on.

"Do I look like that?" Lorre cracked when stuntman Harvey Parry came on to the set of *The Comedy of Terrors* (1964) wearing a large pad around his middle.

"Yes, Peter," he answered, "you're pretty fat."

He now avoided all forms of exercise and scoffed at those who did not. Lorre told Hal Kanter that he had once gone to the top of a mountain in Switzerland, where he had met an old Jewish man.

> "How long have you worked up here?" Peter asked him.
> He said, "About forty years."
> "Well, do you ever go skiing down the mountain?"
> "Skiing, certainly not, that's *goyishe nachas* [Gentile happiness or non-Jewish joy]. Only Gentiles are happy skiing."
> Peter thought that was absolutely wonderful, because he shared the same view. Only Gentiles are stupid enough to enjoy rushing down a mountain on two pieces of wood.

By his middle fifties, Lorre's poor health had begun to impose a new set of constraints on his private as well as his professional life. The accident-prone actor became increasingly susceptible to injury, incurring more than his share of mishaps. In May 1963 he even suffered a bloody nose when he lost control of his car on Sunset Boulevard and struck a parked truck.

With the renewed interest in Brecht in the early 1960s, the actor received invitations to present what he described as programs on the playwright. Easily the most successful of these was "Brecht on Brecht: An Improvisation," a staged reading of "his poems, songs, ballads, memories, observations, questions and answers," arranged by George Tabori and presented by the Greater New York Chapter of the American National Theatre and Academy at the Theatre de Lys in 1961. Asked to appear with Lotte Lenya, Viveca Lindfors, Dane Clark, and others, Lorre declined on the grounds that Brecht had not yet been satisfactorily translated: "For instance, the term 'Epic Theater,' which is used to describe his plays. Brecht would never call what he was doing 'Epic.' But in being translated from the German its meaning was lost." Lorre's excuses were academic. His poor health simply got in the way. While the indomitable Lenya belted out "Pirate Jenny" in "Brecht on Brecht," Lorre was no match for the rigors of live stage.

His most attractive offer came from University of Southern California theater professor Andrew Doe, who approached the actor about collaborating on a student production of *Mann ist Mann*. Lorre responded warily, cautioning that he would open up about Brecht, but only in an academic setting. Regrettably, it never worked out.

Like Brecht, who "had a wonderful habit with girlfriends, of maintaining their allegiance after the essential union was over," Lorre still enjoyed the loyalty of his first two wives. Indeed, his relationships with Celia and Karen proved far more amicable than his marriage to Annemarie. His friendship with the first and only Mrs. Peter Lorre, as she came to think of herself, remained a constant in his life, as immutable as her devotion to him. Hardly a day went by that Peter did not see or talk with her. Celia chronicled the overlapping of their lives in her diaries, following his career as closely as her own. Using his connections, he helped her land acting jobs and occasionally coached her with her parts. Sometimes he even accompanied her to the television studio, where he offered moral support to the actress, who was ill at ease performing before a live camera. After Peter and Annemarie lost their baby in 1956, he confessed to Celia, "Now I'm doing better because I can talk with you. It's good that you're there." Celia dined at the Lorres' several nights a week. She babysat Catharine and cared for Peter in many ways as well. Knowing that roles didn't come so often to older actresses—Lovsky was in her sixties—he regularly slipped five dollars into her hand. Occasionally, she returned the favor. Believing that an extended family that votes together stays together, Celia proudly recorded in her diary, "We voted—for Adlai Stevenson of course—and then went to Peter's house. I got $3.50 from Annemarie." Among her Christmas gifts Lorre stuck a card that summed up his feelings: "Stay as sweet as you are. Peter."

All things considered, Lorre's ex-wives got along famously. Celia's diaries for these years reinforce the impression that her social contact stretched barely beyond the circle of her husband's wives. When not at Peter and Annemarie's, Celia often kept company with Karen, with whom she lunched and attended premieres. Karen even helped Celia study her lines and nursed her when she was sick. Strapped for money, Karen sold Celia her mink coat on the installment plan. One evening Celia and Karen were having dinner at a Beverly Hills delicatessen when Peter, Annemarie, and baby Catharine unexpectedly dropped in and joined them. Celia reported that "Annemarie was very gracious to Karen, and Peter for [the] first time in six years looked her in the eyes and gave her his hand."

When Peter spoke of Karen, his eyes lit up and his tone changed. People came away with the feeling that she had been the love of his life and that he deeply regretted the marriage had not lasted. Nonetheless, it was Celia's exalted position in the Lorre family that nettled Annemarie. She sent his first wife packing, though not for long. While Celia simply stayed away until the storm blew over, Peter found escape in cruising Hollywood in his Buick sedan—driven by a friend—and racing Cadillacs.

When Annemarie's psychiatrist, or as Lorre put it, "opposing counsel," took her side, the lines were drawn; they separated on October 15, 1962. Being apart from his wife was bearable, even preferable, but he missed his nine-year-old daughter and feared for her health. With Annemarie's alcoholism and Catharine's diabetes, he rightly worried that his estranged wife would not care for her properly. Lorre moved out of the rented home on Rodeo Drive and into a small, modestly furnished one-bedroom apartment at the rear of a large red brick building at 7655 Hollywood Boulevard, with a private entrance off Stanley Street. He decorated it with small American antiques, colonial glass, and photos and relics of his years on the Berlin stage. Only minutes away, Celia lived on Crescent Heights just above Sunset Boulevard. Here, Lorre found peace and quiet, and much needed respite from Annemarie. He also became socially reclusive. "Peter was very closed mouth, very closed in," observed Arthur Kennard, who headed the television department at Lester Salkow's agency. "If you wanted to see him, you met him somewhere. As a matter of fact, I think Peter maybe came to the office once."

By his own account, Lorre turned down invitations "all over the place." It didn't have anything special to do with Hollywood, he told Helen O'Connell. He just thought that all parties were a bore. In Hollywood, he actually enjoyed a "bigger" freedom to just say no: "I am completely independent and there I live my life in my house, have a few friends come over. We talk a little, or go to their house . . . and somehow you have a sort of more *lebensraum* [living space], as Mr. Hitler used to say. Maybe he meant California, I don't know. But, something they also say, it gets in your blood."

Around this time, Hollywood cemented its connection with a Star—located at 6619 Hollywood Boulevard—on its legendary Walk of Fame. Peter Lorre was among the first of 1,558 artists to receive such recognition of his contribution to motion pictures by the Hollywood Chamber of Commerce, which spread the honors over a period of sixteen months, beginning with ground-breaking ceremonies on February 8, 1960.

Away from the studio, Lorre read and slept away the stillness between guest spots. At close hand were his German-language editions of Brecht and Poe. "He read from one to three books daily," noted Catharine, "with a wide range— everything from Dostoevsky and psychology handbooks to Agatha Christie. I think a character my father greatly identified with was Agatha Christie's Hercule Poirot. The dialogue, accent, pattern of thinking were much like him. Poirot never took anything at face value. He used, as my father would say, 'the little gray cells.' It was the perfect character because of the sense of drama and comedy."

Here a few of his closest friends came to visit him, to chew over film plans or simply offer companionship to the obviously lonely actor. Harvey Parry, who had stunted for Lorre since the Moto days at Fox, stopped by to play cards and have a drink: "I felt that I was doing him some good by going over and talking with him. He'd tell me some of his troubles, personal things . . . people hurt his feelings. He was a sensitive little guy, but never to the point where he'd get revengeful." Along with his maid, Beatrice Lane, a surrogate mother who saw to it that he ate properly, Lorre's friends took a hand in looking after him. Celia made sure his daily needs were being met. Robert Shutan slipped him a few dollars and discharged some of his overdue debts. Fritz Lang even popped in and prepared lunch for him. The living legend and the faded film star met in a setting as remote from Berlin's frenzied heyday and their triumphs in the German cinema as anyone could conceive. In a dusty gray film can rested the 35mm nitrate print of *Der Verlorene,* which Lorre had brought from Germany, forgotten by its director, who clung to his dream of again forming his own independent production team. No one asked to see the film—and no one did see it—until its American release in 1983.

On August 15, 1963, Annemarie filed for divorce, charging her husband with extreme cruelty and wrongfully inflicting upon her grievous mental suffering. The formal complaint was nothing less than a written version of her verbal harangues. She stated that Lorre rarely made less than $70,000 per year, a gross exaggeration of his last lean ten years, "all of which sums he has irresponsibly wasted and squandered or secreted," and also charged him with failing to provide adequate financial support for her and Catharine. Annemarie accused her husband of sitting on a valuable asset, "Lady Macbeth of the Yards"—hardly a salable property at that point—saying that he refused to produce or capitalize on it. The *Los Angeles Times* reported that Annemarie asked for $1,150 monthly in temporary alimony and $525 for child support.[23] The formal complaint makes no reference to any figures, however, and Shutan did not recall money sums being mentioned. For the time being, Lorre simply continued to pay the bills, as best he could.[24]

After the successful tempering of horror with humor in *Tales of Terror,* Lester Salkow, who also represented Vincent Price and Boris Karloff, negotiated "multiple deals" binding the actors to back-to-back horror-comedies at AIP. "There was always talk of more with the four actors in that genre," said Salkow, "but, as it was, we just planned them two at a time." Lorre's exclusive contract with American International Pictures prohibited him from performing in any other pictures that fell into the categories of horror, terror, or science fiction, or in films based on the works of Edgar Allan Poe.

In January 1962 AIP had signed Richard Matheson to write two costarring vehicles for Vincent Price and Peter Lorre, the first a full-length horror-comedy based on Edgar Allan Poe's poem "The Raven," and the second an untitled comedy. This suited Matheson, who admitted never having any particular interest in the gothic storyteller. In fact, the prospect of adapting another of the author's stygian tales distressed him. Corman likewise winced, uneasy with the thought of repeating himself. "It was tongue-in-cheek from the very beginning," admitted Matheson. From the eighteen six-line stanzas of the poem lamenting the lost Lenore, he created a screenplay that spoofed itself and the Poe series altogether, behaving every bit like a mischievous child mocking its overweening parents. By now, Lorre's appearance in horror-comedies had come to outnumber his appearances in the genre they parodied.

Again, the studio played it straight, taking audiences by surprise. Publicity went all out, overplaying its hand with horror hype that invited moviegoers to "step through the darkness, along touchstones of terror with the raven tapping evermore." Lending the picture far more literary merit than it deserved,

Lorre even maintained that the Poe team worked the author's satirical sense of humor and dead wit into the picture. Although AIP claimed to have brought to the screen "the basic element of Poe's great work," *The Raven* bore almost no resemblance to its namesake. The publicity department capitalized on Price, Karloff, and Lorre's first screen collaboration and fostered the idea that their collective power to horrify outweighed their individual efforts: "Now it lives on the giant motion picture screen in color and Panavision, starring the trio that make up the great TRIUMVIRATE OF TERROR—Vincent Price, Peter Lorre, Boris Karloff—greater than Dracula, Werewolf and Frankenstein together. Come on an adventure into monstrous terror, as gruesome, as great as the genius who created it." A promotional recording for the film included Lorre reading portions of the poem, with Karloff telling moviegoers that "this is a sample of what happens in Edgar Allan Poe's 'The Raven' . . . before the picture ends, I guarantee your blood will run cold. . . . Have I disturbed you? Oh, I didn't mean to. I want you to see Edgar Allan Poe's *The Raven*. You see, I share in the box office receipts."

In *The Raven,* Lorre appeared as a rain-soaked raven that regains his human form in the gnomish figure of Dr. Bedlo, a medieval sorcerer, only to be reduced to a pool of raspberry jam before once more changing into a bird. After reading the script and agreeing that it made no sense, Price, Lorre, and Karloff wrote some additional jokes and brought them to Corman. "Roger just let the thing roll," said costar Hazel Court. "He let the three of them have a go." To set the mood, Price, who later said he played the role of Dr. Craven with his tongue in both cheeks, walked across his study, bumping his head on the end of a telescope, tipping off the audience right away.

"Are you some dark-winged messenger from beyond?" Price solemnly declaimed to his feathered visitor. "Shall I ever hold again that radiant maiden whom the angels call Lenore?"

Rather than "quoth . . . Nevermore," Lorre, as the bird, cracked, "How the hell should I know? What am I, a fortune teller?"

Lorre custom-fit the role after Matheson laid out the pattern. "He's the only actor who sort of winged my lines and it didn't bother me," said the screenwriter. "In every other case, it aggravates the hell out of me when somebody blats out a carefully worked line any way they feel like it." Corman also remembered that Lorre "didn't spend much time learning his lines, but he knew his great strength was the vitality and humor and energy he brought to his scenes."

"I felt that he was enjoying every moment of playing comedy," recalled Court. "It was like another window had opened up for him. That was a joyous thing."

"Peter loved to improvise," said Price. "His acting technique was improvisation." Lorre stretched the point in an interview published in the *San Francisco Chronicle* in February: "Often on a script he [Matheson] merely writes 'Lorre speaks' and I then supply the line. I'm in the situation. It works out well." Leaving "enough blank space either side" of the script pages, indicated Lorre, gave him room to spread out. Adjusting to the actor's looseness stressed old friendships. "With Boris and Peter," explained Corman, "there was tension and an incredible clash of acting methods. Boris frankly did not like Peter's way of doing things. It made him nuts and threw off his memorized reading of the lines. He told me a couple times he was not happy with his scenes with Peter." At one point, Lorre made a shambles of a scene with his extemporizing. Price became exasperated and sharply scolded, "For Christsake, Peter, just say the lines!"

"You want me to say the lines, old boy?" uttered a stung Lorre.

"Yes, say them," implored Price, "let's get on with it." Lorre said the lines, which he knew perfectly. Before long, however, the actor had rallied and struck off on his own once again.

"You would do a scene," commented Court on Lorre's playful behavior before the camera, "and it wouldn't be quite the same when you did the take. You had to be just one jump ahead of him, knowing that he might do something different. He wouldn't necessarily stick to the camera techniques of being exactly on the spot. It didn't appear to worry him whether he'd get his lines or not, and yet I guess he always did."

She had to stay one jump ahead of him behind the camera as well. Court laughingly told Vincent Price biographer Lucy Chase Williams that Lorre "was always pinching me on the behind! Today, he'd be sued." Asked if she minded, "No-o-o-o, of course not!"

Lorre's "bits of business" are easy to pick out, even without reading the script. Inquiring after the ingredients of the recipe that will restore him to his rightful form, Dr. Bedlo asks for "Dried—*or evaporated*—bat's blood!" At another point, he follows Dr. Craven through a cellar corridor encrusted with cobwebs. "Hard place to keep clean, huh?" he offhandedly ad-libs. When Craven offers him a glass of warm milk, the actor comes back with one of his favorite expressions—"How vomitable!" In another scene, Craven warns Bedlo, "You'll need something to protect you from the cold." Bedlo scurries to fetch another glass of wine, prompting Craven to chide, "No, I meant clothes!"

A young Jack Nicholson played Lorre's son Rexford. Between scenes, he listened with rapt attention to the old master's stories of Bogart, Brecht, and Nazi Germany. Lorre must have sounded like little more than a ghost haunting the past, yet Nicholson found him "one of the most sophisticated men I ever knew." He no doubt also noticed, even admired, the liberties Lorre took with his lines. Instead of squealing the scripted "Now will you kindly get off my chest" when Nicholson wrestles him to the floor, Lorre extemporized, "Don't sit on my chest. I'm not an armchair, you idiot!"

During a duel of magic with Scarabus (Boris Karloff), Bedlo invokes the power of his wand to cast a spell. As he nears his rival, Scarabus zaps him with an electric charge. "You're defending yourself, you coward!" retorts Bedlo. After a second thrust, Scarabus melts the weapon, provoking him to ad-lib, "Oh, you! You dirty old man!"

By now, the tailoring of part to player had become part of the formula. Matheson understood Lorre better than he knew, scripting a "more grotesquely droll than menacing" character that came very close to bringing the private figure into public view. In *The Raven,* and possibly more so in the screenplay, the phlegmatic sorcerer is a pitiable clown, hounded by the specter of failure in his professional life as a magician and tormented by overbearing women in his private life, situations that he seeks to escape through drink. "All my life I've been of little consequence," Dr. Bedlo reproaches himself in a working copy of the script. "Everything I ever tried—I failed at. That's why I turned to magic; hoping to find, in it, an answer to my lack of purpose; a meaning to my life." Bedlo's melancholy confession, which Lorre trimmed and softened, is out of keeping with the mood of the picture. Perhaps it struck a personal chord. If he saw a connection, however, he didn't show it. He was having too much fun playing out Bedlo as a cherubic imp, innocuously pathetic. "I'm too sweet and gentle, that's my trouble," the actor whimpers in the film's last line. "There was something very soft and nice about him at that age," Matheson later reflected, "so you couldn't make him vicious in the pictures he was in." As comedy masked tragedy, so art imitated life.

Lorre's sense of humor said a lot about his attitude toward the Poe pictures. "As a serious actor" who could "appreciate the ridiculous of the profession," said Price, Lorre attached little importance to the AIP "quickies," as he termed them. Privately, he even dismissed the pictures as "awful" and reluctantly made promotional appearances, preferring to leave that to Price: "I don't have the talent Vincent does. He knows how to chat with the ladies." Arkoff said that Lorre "used to be quite jovial about the fact that some of our Poes weren't as pure as they might have been. He had kind of a wicked sense of humor in that respect." It wasn't that Lorre thought he was too good for horror films; he simply didn't care for them, at least until, like *The Raven,* he and Price had turned them into comedies. What bothered him were the "frequent calls by people looking to get somebody who had name value for a horror picture that wouldn't cost too much." Such offers called into question his credibility as an actor.

Generously—for AIP—budgeted at $350,000, *The Raven* won favor with critics and moviegoers alike, who enthusiastically shared the sense of fun enjoyed by the players. Perhaps, as some reviewers suggested, Poe might turn over in his grave. Even he was not above parodying his own popular horror tales in "The Sphinx" and "Some Words with a Mummy." Commercial acceptance was, as it is now, the order of the day. With characteristic wit, the *New York Times'* Bosley Crowther wrote, "Strictly a picture for the kiddies and the bird-brained, quote the critic." That's all it was meant to be, "low grade" fun, unpretentious and entertaining. Film and theater critic James Powers, then married to Karen Verne, wrote in the *Hollywood Reporter:* "Price, Lorre and Karloff perform singly and in tandem like what they are, three seasoned pros who can take a gentle burlesque and play it to the end of its value without stretching it past the entertainment point. They are performances, in their way, that are virtuoso." With some makeshift slapstick comedy and imaginative special effects in the duel of magic, AIP created an ingenuous picture well suited to the studio's mainstay—the younger moviegoing audience.

If the "Triumvirate of Terror" had tripled the terror (and humor), it had also tripled the theater returns. Pandering to public taste, AIP planned more pictures with "production values and a comedy slant in keeping with current audience response." The studio would go to the well as long as Price, Lorre, and Karloff appealed to audiences or, as it turned out, until the actors passed from the scene. The trades rumored term contracts for its horror roster—Vincent Price, Boris Karloff, Elsa Lanchester, Basil Rathbone, and Peter Lorre—"all with the talent and stature to impart class and prestige to chill-and-thrill entertainment." In January 1963, just after the release of *The Raven,* Lorre reportedly signed for eight more films over the next four years.[25] Sam Arkoff, however, remembers it differently. Largely dependent upon the teenage trade, "we were always ready to shift gears." With the exception of Vincent Price, AIP preferred signing its players to short-term agreements rather than binding them—and the studio—to multipicture commitments.

For the second of his two-picture agreement with AIP, Matheson decided to develop the comic possibilities of a rascally undertaker who was "so bad at what he did, the only way he could get customers was to kill them off himself." He told his idea to James Nicholson and that, said Matheson, sold it. "Your Favorite Creeps Are Together Again," advertised AIP. Matheson wrote *The Comedy of Terrors* with Price, Lorre, Karloff, and Rathbone in mind for the leads.

On the writer's recommendation, Arkoff and Nicholson hired Jacques Tourneur, whose polished direction of the Val Lewton productions *Cat People* (1942) and *I Walked with a Zombie* (1942) had earned him an exalted standing in the horror and fantasy genre.

In *Comedy of Terrors*, Amaryllis (Joyce Jameson) credits her unhappy marriage to Waldo Trumbull (Vincent Price), a crooked undertaker, with thwarting a brilliant operatic career. When the mortuary business falters, Trumbull presses his unwilling assistant, Felix Gillie (Peter Lorre), into helping him recruit new clients, namely his stuffy landlord, John F. Black (Basil Rathbone). The diffident and tone-deaf Gillie grieves for Amaryllis. She will sing for him, he tells her, like the nightingale. When he presses his affection, she entreats him to forbear. "I don't know what that word means," ad-libbed an overwrought Lorre, "but I can't take it anymore." Beneath a table, he draws Amaryllis close, but she pulls free. When he tries to stand, he hits his head.

"I'm so sensitive," Lorre whimpers, improvising, so close to the end, a fitting epitaph.

Gillie hastily scrawls a farewell note telling Trumbull that he and Amaryllis "have fled into the night, driven onward by the madness of our all-consuming passion."

In the pressbook for *Comedy of Terrors*, a studio publicist noted that "it took Peter over thirty years, but he's finally made it as a screen lover after all those years as a menace."

Reportedly "fierce and dogmatic," Tourneur did not check Lorre, who stamped his portrayal with personal charm. Part and player made a good pair, like friends becoming reacquainted after a long separation. Their reunion called for plain speaking. The actor put away the nasal purr and dropped the grimace. Behind the mannerisms stood the man, full of warm and wistful humor. Gillie builds a lopsided, cross-slanted coffin out of old boards. "Pretty close," ad-libbed Lorre, eyeing the unsightly handiwork. "Anybody would be proud to rest in this coffin. . . . I don't like to see anyone buried naked." Later, when Lorre and Price carry Rathbone's body into the mortuary cellar, the actor extemporizes, "He's pretty heavy for such a skinny bird."

Richard Matheson dubbed Price and Lorre the "Laurel and Hardy" of black comedy. At one point, believing that Gillie has exposed their hand, Trumbull snaps, "A fine mess you've made of things again." Their comic instincts formed an easy complement. By now, however, Matheson believed that Lorre "just sort of generalized his dialogue because he didn't have any memory. That's what they told me, that he just could not remember. But he was so charming as a person you just couldn't get angry."[26] Whatever the reason for his improvising, Price sensed Lorre's need to shed his horror image and "kept an open mind because he knew it was going to happen and he liked Peter. He just didn't make an issue of it."

Unhappy with *Comedy of Terrors,* Tourneur later skirted discussion about it. Having preordered a jaunty British comedy with brisk performances and clipped dialogue, he undoubtedly applauded the frail Boris Karloff's suggestion that he exchange roles with the surprisingly robust Basil Rathbone. Whatever acceleration the British veteran lent the picture Lorre slowed with his relaxed delivery. "It probably bothered Tourneur," said Matheson, "but I think he pretty quickly saw that it wasn't something Lorre was doing to be nasty, so what could you do?" What Tourneur did not do, in Matheson's words, was make enough use of Lorre's "tremendous sense of comedy timing" or, according to Jameson, the camaraderie born of freedom given by Corman. Despite Tourneur's heavy hand, the picture took on a life of its own through the easy ensemble spirit of its contract players.

Comedy of Terrors ran a poor second to *The Raven* at the box office and in the columns. A little baffled by this, Matheson believed that the juxtaposition of "comedy" and "terror" tended to work at cross purposes. Victorian grandiloquence and macabre drollery found a cool reception with critics and audiences alike. Rather than accept the film as a precocious spoof, they passed it off as an empty joke. Howard Thompson, writing for the *New York Times,* thought the picture should have been billed as a "chillerdiller—dill as in pickle" rather than as a "horroromp." On the other coast, the *Los Angeles Times*'s Philip K. Scheuer said he felt "ashamed to watch once reputable actors hamming it up all over the place, making a mockery of whatever is left of their poor images."

Behind the camera, Lorre once again cast himself in the role of teacher, confidant, and philosopher, always ready to give more of himself. People listened to him, to the soft strength in his voice. He summoned authority and attention. "The world isn't going to end just because you didn't get that particular picture," Lorre told a disappointed William Campbell, who crossed paths with the actor at Schwab's Drugstore on Sunset Boulevard. "You've got to put things in their proper perspective. You know what I do. I always remember that in the motion picture business, you're in the toy department. You got a toy, you play with it, you put it aside and you go on to the next toy." Arkoff said that he and Lorre shared the same attitude, that "this is a whore's business in part and really a very amusing business as long as you keep your sense of humor."

"Peter was very gentle, always the charmer, very sweet," remembered Court. "He was always kind of above the moment, so knowledgeable. I found him much more intelligent than one really thought of him. . . . He had a need for other things in life besides just coming on set and doing his work. He seemed to care very deeply about everything in the world, but not in a boring way. Every day we learned something from him. . . . He always made you feel good." Price felt that "he was a magnet" who "drew people to him with his sad eyes. There was a great sadness about him, like a sad, cuddly teddy bear. The crew especially adored him—he was just fun to be with."

Often the actors gathered round to reminisce about the past. One day, between takes on *Comedy of Terrors*, Price, Karloff, and Salkow listened to Lorre talk about his days at UFA. Rathbone approached the group. "Peter always threw out little shockers for Basil," Salkow reminisced, "which he didn't realize were for him. 'For a while, it was very tough making films in Germany,' said Peter. 'Of course, after Hitler came to power, may he rest in peace, . . .'" Rathbone declared that he could not remain present and stormed off. Lorre seamlessly sandwiched throw-away lines between the meat and cheese of his stories. He pulled the same trick on reporters, who cleared their ears with the eraser end of their pencils and muttered, "What'd he say?" But Lorre had moved on.

All of the Poe features were shot at Producers Studio on Melrose Avenue with pretty much the same crew carrying over to each picture. AIP offered the veteran actors the respect and dignity they felt for each other, fostering a happy, healthy, family atmosphere. "It was kind of old home week," Matheson said of the feeling of camaraderie on the set of *Comedy of Terrors*. "They were all delighted to be together. They were all pros, congenial, charming—nothing egotistical about them." The shared feelings of comradeship enfolded Lorre in a warm embrace, drawing him into the team. When production drew to a close, Arkoff and Nicholson always threw a big party for which everyone turned out, from the biggest star to the lowest grip. They stayed on late into the night, reluctant to leave, knowing that tomorrow the household would break up and go its own way.

In March 1963 Lorre appeared on *The Hy Gardner Show*. Asked how he liked himself in the movies, the actor repeated the question: "How do I like myself in the movies? I have to like myself. I have to feed a daughter." Such nonsequiturs came easily to one who just wanted to change the subject. Lorre coldly declined to do the "opening-night bit," as he called it, "because I only get paid for making [movies], not for looking at them." The actor had felt this way, he told Gardner, since the first time he entered a projection room: "I don't like to look at myself on the screen, as beautiful as I am. I find that completely narcissistic. I don't understand actors that see rushes and dailies. . . . It doesn't apply to all actors, but some actors; it pertains to me. Bogart was that way, for instance. We are bad audiences. And I have a feeling there is some chemistry that makes some people act and some other people watch it." In fact, he confided that he rarely went to the movies. When, in 1960, had he last seen a movie? "I hate to tell you the truth," he admitted to Mike Wallace. "I might never get a job again. I think the last movie I saw, altogether, in one compact session, was *Gone with the Wind*. It was a rainy day in Palm Springs and some friends dragged me there." For the actor, movies had become a mind-set: "This is one of the good things about our profession, that it keeps you young. Maybe it's because you make up your mind to be childish and not to grow up, so you don't age."

Nevertheless, Lorre seemed to have wound down, permanently. "Peter was very sick" during filming of *The Raven*, recalled Hazel Court. "He perspired all the time, and his eyes were always teary, but the moment the camera started to roll, there was no sign of being ill." And, to the untrained eye, there were no signs of a cover-up. Friends believed that Lorre had held out against morphine, winning his final bout with addiction years earlier. Now, they supposed, he shot up with vitamins instead of narcotics. The pattern, however, was suspiciously reminiscent of his earlier drug abuse. On the set of *Rawhide* in 1960, Lorre had told director Ted Post that

> he wasn't feeling well, that he had a huge headache and didn't feel as if he could do the scene. I said, "I'll jump to another scene while you rest up a bit, and we'll see whether you feel better." He said, "No, no. I'll tell you what I'll do ... give me a few minutes, and I'll be right back." "Okay," I said, "take whatever you need." He came back about ten to fifteen minutes later and said, "I feel better." Then the next day, the same thing happened again. So I got suspicious. And when he said, "I'll be back in ten minutes," I followed him. He had drugs— took a shot of heroin, or coke, or whatever it was he used.[27] Then he vomited. I was watching him. Then I rushed back to work, and a few minutes later he came back and he said, "I feel better now" and he did the scene!

AIP had sent Lorre and Karloff to New York City on a scheduled one-week circuit of RKO theaters to promote *The Raven* in January 1963. Until a blizzard paralyzed the city and forced the cancellation of the tour, the actors made three personal appearances daily. They entered through the front door, parted the sea of adoring fans, and mounted the stage one at a time. Around the middle of the afternoon, recalled Arthur Kennard, who headed the television department at the Lester Salkow Agency and accompanied the junket, Lorre would wind down. On one occasion, he even came close to falling off the stage. A physician was scheduled to arrive at selected theaters and administer an injection. "It was all very hush, hush, very private," said Kennard, who stood guard and asked no questions (nor did Lorre offer any explanation). "When the doctor showed up, they would disappear in one of the backstage rooms or behind a drape. Nobody was to go near."

Several months later, Lorre met Wendy Sanford, a young, attractive, energetic CBS associate producer assigned to "Diamond Fever," a *Dupont Show of the Week* episode in which the actor played a straight role as a jewel thief. During production, Lorre had difficulty remembering lines and suffered from lack of energy and physical coordination. After rehearsals, he retreated to his room at the Warwick Hotel in Manhattan, where he rested and received his accustomed visit from a physician before he and Sanford sat down to dinner and a seven-to-eleven feeding of his lines.

On *Comedy of Terrors,* he could not hide what everyone knew—that he was dying. Film historian Mark Thomas McGee, who visited the set as a young boy, remembered that "after every scene he would slump back into his chair and wheeze for several minutes." When prop man Bob Burns introduced himself to Lorre as the guy "with his head," a latex rubber "Peter Lorre" mask worn by stuntman Harvey for scenes requiring the actor to perform even modest physical feats, he replied, "Well, it's a good thing, because I'm not well. I can't really DO much in this film."

Lorre graciously agreed to inscribe a movie still for Burns from the *Route 66* episode with Boris Karloff and Lon Chaney Jr. Though his hand shook, his mood perked up: "Oh, THAT was a fun show. That was fun to do, getting together with Boris and all the guys."

"He wasn't feeling well at all," remembered Burns. "They had to work with him in the morning, and by the afternoon, he had to go home."

In a wood-splitting scene, Lorre drove an axe into a stump and nearly flung himself to the ground. Harvey Parry stepped in and donned the "head," a prototype for generations of fashionably collectible life masks. Despite the false face and belly stuffing, the sprightly stuntman was not a convincing substitute for the ailing actor. Even keeping Parry in medium shots failed to feed the illusion. Toward the end of the film, Lorre and Joyce Jameson robustly danced round and round in a scene that could not be believably faked. After reshooting the number without a break, the exhausted actor nearly fainted. Tourneur did not read the signs. He pushed on, bringing Lorre to the verge of collapse. His costar saw the pain in his eyes and sensed the sorrow behind them. "I had a deep feeling for Peter as a suffering man, on an emotional parallel for different reasons," said Jameson. "He was the martyr of the picture."

Lorre kept his sense of humor and took the wear and tear on his health in stride, comfortable in the knowledge that the AIP horror-comedies were his means to a financial end. "It was a romp that gave him money which he needed," recalled Sanford. "I remember him saying, 'I'm very happy that I had the opportunity to have a second career because it gives me the money to leave my daughter comfortable.' I think he probably realized that he would not live to see her married. He seemed to be worried about her and not his wife. I don't know whether he knew how ill he was."

10

THE MASK
BEHIND THE FACE

I believe that somewhere within his soul everyone
is an actor. Instinctively, we prefer to dream our life away
in fantasy rather than to face the hard facts of reality.
Dreaming, making a fanciful play out of your life,
is so much more pleasant.

—Peter Lorre

We only saw the tip of the iceberg.

—Wendy Sanford

Facial expression," wrote film critic Béla Balázs, "is the most subjective manifestation of man." Lorre wore the contradiction of person and persona like so
many masks, at times laying bare the inner man, at others obscuring him.
Toward the end of his life, he tore away old disguises and created new ones,
forever confusing the shadowy line between selves, not as an acting art, but as
a survival skill. The face that had expressed the "multiplicity of the human
soul" through the characters he portrayed on screen now betrayed his own
tangled sensibilities. He reckoned his life in twos—horror and humor, art
and commerce, illusion and reality, insider and outsider. Two was the common denominator, though on closer view the dichotomy shattered into a
myriad of broken pieces. In a life gone to quiet extremes, the different Peter

Lorres parted ways. What he said publicly and what he thought privately reflected a man in emotional flux, one who wasn't sure where he had been or where he was going.

His memory did not synchronize with historical events. The actor loved to give advice about young talents tempted by money, based not on his own experiences, but on his reworking of them, reordered into carefully weighed advantages and disadvantages. "It's an amazing thing to be able to retain your integrity in this business of movie-making," he had cautioned in 1955. "You do it with your left hand, so you can still be in the business for something good when it comes along. It's like a doctor—he starts out to help humanity . . . but he's soon working at it as a business. It would be a crazy thing to run away from home to be a face-maker and then not hold to the ideal." Fashioning Brecht's advice to fit the situation, Lorre counseled set designer Daniel Haller to "do what you can do well with your right hand and you'll always be a success within your own self. Once you know yourself, you can always branch out."

The actor now looked back with passive detachment, ignoring the bonds that had held him for thirty years. Suddenly, liabilities had become assets. Being a personality, he intellectualized, is really a great compliment because it cannot be taught. Moreover, he took typecasting by the tail in a deliberate act of defiance: "There comes a time when you have to find the integrity to stand up and refuse to play certain kinds of roles. Of course, you have to allow yourself to be typed for a period of time. I have been typed five or six times in my life." But "after a certain amount of time," he explained, "I have to stop the whole thing. I have to turn down everything that comes my way and start something else." More accurately, Hollywood had turned him down, limiting his options to stark survival. He could not afford a strategic withdrawal or a planned hiatus to regroup. He had to keep going. "For a lazy man," Lorre dissembled shortly before his death, "I work awfully hard."

Lorre said he wished more people were as content as he. The echoes of complacency resounded a false note sweetened by memory. On the Canadian Broadcasting Corporation's *Assignment,* he told interviewer Elwood Glover that after *M* and *Crime and Punishment,* he was box-office poison, which meant that "on top of a great artistic and critical success, no box office." No one knew me, he explained, "so then I made up my mind right then and there that I'm going to go through the rough way and I took on that 'Mr. Moto' series."

It had not happened that way. Casting a myopic eye on a past with which he had not come to grips, Lorre focused on another reality, the one he imagined his life to be. Looking back, he had flown on automatic pilot, relying on

Puck and the Old Man (Lorre and Greenstreet) during filming of *The Mask of Dimitrios*, 1944.

With director Jean Negulesco and costars Zachary Scott and Sydney Greenstreet on the set of *The Mask of Dimitrios*, 1944.

Peter Lorre goes over a radio script with producer and director William Spier before a CBS *Suspense* broadcast, ca. 1944.

Peter at his healthiest:
playing tennis at the
Beverly Hills Tennis
Club *(above)* and
relaxing at the beach
(right), ca. 1943.

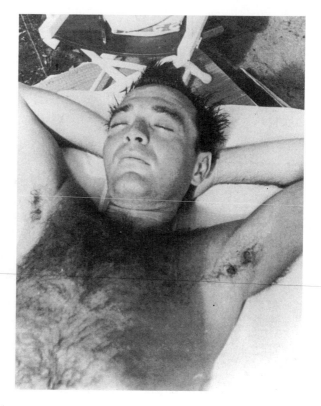

Horseback riding with Karen in Mandeville Canyon, ca. 1945.

Peter Lorre with Karen Verne and his sister-in-law, Zelma (Mrs. Andrew) Lorre, ca. 1945.

Out on the town with Bogart and Lauren Bacall, ca. 1945.

On the set with Bacall preparing for his death scene in *Confidential Agent*, 1945.

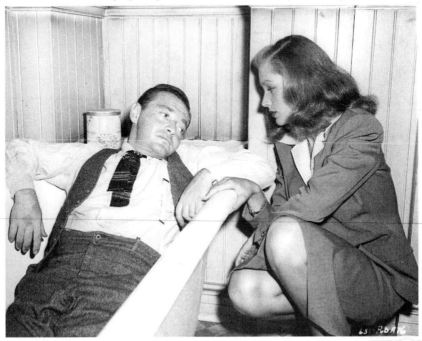

Peter Lorre and Bob Hope on the set of *My Favorite Brunette*, 1947.

"The Touch of Your Hand," *Mystery in the Air* radio series, with Peter Lorre, Hans Conreid (*in sound booth*), and announcer Harry Morgan (*fifth from left*), July 17, 1947.

Annemarie Brenning, at the time Lorre met her, 1950.

Der Verlorene (*The Lost One*), German film poster, 1951.

Turning back the clock in *Der Verlorene* (*The Lost One*), 1951.

Karl Rothe confronts the *Totmacher* (death maker) in the mirror, *Der Verlorene* (*The Lost One*), 1951.

A pensive Peter Lorre during the shooting of *Der Verlorene* (*The Lost One*), 1951.

The defining image of Peter Lorre in *Der Verlorene*. Courtesy of Ronald V. Borst / Hollywood Movie Posters.

Lorre, cameraman
Vaclav Vich (*left*),
and editor Carl O.
Bartning, taking a
break during filming
of *Der Verlorene*.

Lorre and Egon Jameson
at the Frankfurt premiere
of *Der Verlorene*.

On the set of *Beat the Devil*, 1954. *Left to right:* Peter Lorre, Marco Tulli, Robert Morley, Humphrey Bogart, Gina Lollobrigida, and Edward Underdown. Courtesy of National Film Archives / Stills Library, London.

"I'm not a dancer," Peter Lorre told Hermes Pan, who choreographed the "Too Bad (We Can't Go Back to Moscow)" number in *Silk Stockings*, 1957. Joseph Buloff, Jules Munshin, and Peter Lorre.

"Siberia" is simply hilarious as sung and danced by Joseph Buloff, Jules Munshin and Peter Lorre.

M-G-M Presents "*Silk Stockings*" In Cinemascope and METROCOLOR

Peter and Catharine, ca. 1958.

Peter Lorre and Vincent Price in costume for *The Big Circus*, 1959, inscribed to Lester Salkow, their agent.

Final portrait, taken shortly before Lorre's death, 1964.

Catharine Lorre with Devlin, 1978. Photo by Judith Atherton.

his instincts to reach the right decisions, and had made courageous choices, where there were few to make. Time was running out. Putting a good public face on a private defeat, he maintained that his breaks still lay ahead of him. Resolving self and image meant rewriting the past and his part in it, not as a lie, but as a shelter for a vulnerable man who needed to make peace with himself. He never voiced regrets, made excuses, or laid blame, on either the moviemakers or himself. "People say if I had a chance to live my life over again," he told Paul Zastupnevich, "I would do things differently. But you know, if I had not done what I've done, I would not be here today and I would not have worked with some of the wonderful people I've worked with."

By the end of his life, Lorre's celebration of nonconformity had turned into a lament for the lost Hollywood. Recalling the "good old days" for interviewer Bob Thomas, he implied with sad irony that he belonged to the past. "They just don't make drinkers the way they used to," sighed Lorre. "I don't want to sound eulogistic about those times, but dammit, they were great. Today isn't so great. The drinking has slowed down. I don't think it's just age that has done it."

Lorre felt isolated and out of touch. With the eclipse of the studio star system, the stock repertories and the sense of community they fostered likewise faded. Hollywood may have stifled his creativity, his humor, his intelligence, and even his spirit, but it had given him a sense of belonging to a community of professional artists. "I guess I'm one of the last of my group around," he regretted shortly before his death. "I got real mad when Humphrey Bogart died and Sydney Greenstreet passed on. I was mad because they left me alone." He had become a relic of the waning institution that had invited him in and then locked him out. "The movies are no longer an industry," he said. "After all, who ever heard of an industry that offered no loyalty to its employees? The studios offer none at all any more. Making movies used to be fun in the old days. It isn't any longer. It's a cold-hearted business." Lorre now thought of himself as just a working actor, who, said Hal Kanter, "showed up, did his work—sometimes gave a little more—got his check and went home."

"I hate to call myself a star," admitted Lorre. "I'd rather have other people call me a star."

Estranged from the present, Lorre clung to the past. "He loved to tell stories of when Hollywood was Hollywood," said Frankie Avalon, "and particularly about Bogie and Warner Bros. He was kind of reliving that in his mind." Lorre longed for the days of the journeyman, a time when filling the bill took preference over billing. "In Europe," he told Morey Amsterdam, "an actor loves to act. You'll take some of the biggest stars over there who will take a walk-on in another show just for the idea of continually working at their trade. The idea [is] that to become a good actor you only learn through experience, constantly working. And whether it's a big part or a small one is not important, if it's a good part."

Reminiscing often put him in mind of his theatrical roots. "Peter said that those days were especially fulfilling," said Joyce Jameson. "To him, it was a good thing that they, as a group, had the courage to put on anti-Nazi theater. They were creating their own protest theater against the government." Although he occasionally complained of being reminded of *M,* he was now more likely to bring it up. In 1963 he looked back: "First picture I had a starring role in was the first picture I ever made . . . called 'M.' It's still running. . . . And it has one distinction I'm proud of. It's in general release in Europe again, and is beating out every new picture that comes along."

Carrying the torch for his old friend Bogart, Lorre kept the fires of discontent burning with his continued offensive against the studio bureaucrats, the "kreeps" at the top. He had little cause for complaint at AIP, and his struggle remained primarily a symbolic one. Between takes on *The Raven,* the young daughter of William K. Everson, the distinguished film historian, pointed to a supporting player made up as a decaying corpse and asked, "Is that a good monster or a bad monster?"

"Oh, it's a BAD monster," Lorre told the child. "There are NO good monsters at American-International."

He said what he thought; words didn't slip out of his mouth. On promotional tours, which studios rarely asked of him, fulsome comments came hard. In 1960, when a pre-interviewer for Mike Wallace asked the actor, whom he described in his personal notes as a "playful, pixieish, rebellious gnome," if he liked *Scent of Mystery,* Lorre "just looked sad, as if I had twisted his arm." On the subject of actors, he bluntly stated, "People interest me more than facemakers do. . . . I don't like most actors. They're a breed unto themselves. . . . They're all the same bores."

"I have very few friends among actors because I don't like shop talk," Lorre said several years later. "But I like discussing things. That's one of the reasons I liked Bogey so much." He "was my dearest friend, the only facemaker that I have ever known that I really was truly friends with, except for two people that you can't call actors in a pure sense of the word. That's Burl Ives . . . and Joe E. Lewis." Lorre affectionately labeled them, along with Cedric Hardwicke (the only man who could tell theater anecdotes "without chasing [him] out of the window"), "an incongruous bunch of creeps."

The cloud of disconnection that brooded within Lorre condensed with Bogart's lingering death in early 1957. Bogart's life had become full after marrying Lauren Bacall. As husband and father, he settled down and comfortably eased into a domestic routine. In his free time, he sailed, therapy to stabilize his personality, as he put it. Bogart at home, like Bogart on-screen, knew who he was and what he believed in. Form followed content, and his image mellowed and matured with the passing years. Winning the Academy Award for Best Actor in *The African Queen* (1952) heightened Bogart's awareness of the dignity of his profession. He had fought for—and won—recognition as an artist. "I think he was a terribly underrated actor," said Lorre, "not as a star, he wasn't underrated as such, but I think he was a much better actor than most people realized." He felt that "whatever Bogie played you believed him, you believed his toughness, you believed every inch of what he did. If you can cover a person you play so well that you become that person, then you must be a great actor."

Lorre was happy for Bogart. No one, he felt, more richly deserved reward and recognition than his friend. But their paths, which once overlapped, had separated. Lorre's waning film career, together with his marital and drug problems, had gradually distanced the two actors. Lorre's name is missing from the roster of the Holmby Hills Rat Pack, a band of patrons—including Bogart and Bacall—of Romanoff's restaurant dedicated to "the relief of boredom and the perpetuation of independence."

News of Bogart's throat cancer rallied his devoted friend, whose admiration and respect never wavered. Several years after Bogart's death, Lorre looked back with Mike Wallace:

> Toward the end of his life, when that terrible illness befell him, he turned into a great real hero and into the toughest man I have ever seen. . . . His aversion against drama as such was so great that he kept up the pretense of everyday life up until the very last day when he died. They used to prop the man into an elevator. He only weighed about ninety-five pounds at that time. They used to bring him downstairs and he received his friends, he had drinks with them, collapsed around seven o'clock and they carried him upstairs again. But he would never change his way of living and absolutely refused to put any drama into it. And it was the most touching experience and the most heartbreaking one I have ever gone through.

Lorre never found what he was after. He didn't care to admit it, even to himself, but his search had dead-ended in a bankrupt dream. Catharine Lorre sensed that this void haunted and hounded him to the grave. He believed in the no-questions-asked kind of friendship he enjoyed with Bogart and only a few others built on nuts-and-bolts professionalism. Bogart's death removed Lorre one step farther from the past they had shared. "My dearest pal; I still feel the void," he spoke out five years later.

Five months earlier, Lorre had also lost Brecht. Celia's diary entry for August 17, 1956, three days after the playwright's death, records simply, "Brecht is dead." Her understatement underscored the enormity of its implications for Lorre at this point in his life. Another door had shut, closing the opportunity for Lorre to redeem himself in Brecht's eyes.

In 1943 Lorre had walked over to Burl Ives at the Gjon Mili studio in New York and introduced himself: "I would like to shake hands with you. I'm Peter Lorre. You see, I dig the ballad." The meeting sparked an instinctive friendship that was closer than brothers, or as Ives used to say, "a copious kind of relationship that I've had very few of." Friends said they were cut from the same cloth. With Ives, Lorre gave in friendship a graceful charm and humor as good as he got in return.

Several years later, Ives was

over at Peter's one night and had to leave before anyone else. My beard at that time was a tawny color, like my hair. When I left, I went and put on my hat, which was a Borsalino, one of those fuzzy hats, and it was a tawny color. And my topcoat, sometimes called a camel's hair, was also about the same color. So Peter walked with me to the door and I put on my coat and my hat. And, as he usually did, he put his arms around me and kissed me goodnight on each cheek, and said, "Good night, you summer rabbi."

Ives felt he was one of Lorre's few friends to sit at the receiving end of his mind, what he termed his "essence of spirituality." Said the singer: "Peter always had a melancholy something about him. I don't think that he was ever a jolly, happy-go-lucky man. I think he was basically thoughtful and philosophic, and deep. He was a thinking person and concerned himself with much deeper realms of human ambitions, thoughts and desires, all human considerations, than the average person would have suspected. He was a very alive, but controlled man."

At one point, Ives considered abandoning his career and going into the restaurant business. "Of all the germs that came together," said Lorre, intent on dissuading him, "we could have been so many different people. We are actors. We are different. Respect the things we are put here to do." As "vehicles or wires" through which creative energy flows, he added, actors return the gift entrusted to them. That's what sets them apart.

During the last decade of Lorre's life, Scandia Restaurant became a sort of surrogate home that passed for the Vienna coffeehouse of his youth. Ives recalled,

> We were at Scandia Restaurant one time, and that was after I had been in *Cat on a Hot Tin Roof,* and had made a small splash in the movie business. . . . And I had not played the guitar in some time. To whomever we were sitting with I said I thought I was going to tune up the guitar. In the meantime, the revolution in electronic sound had started. Whoever we were sitting with said, "Are you going to come back and sing ballads just like you did before? Have you ever considered studying the classical guitar and really doing more with the guitar instead of just playing the simple accompaniments which you play?" I said, "Yes, I've thought about it, but I don't like to disturb something that's working for me." Peter interrupted and said, "Listen, you don't argue with the way a man signs his name."

Next door to the restaurant on Sunset Boulevard sat Finlandia Baths, another favorite haunt that warmly recalled another time and place, where Lorre worked to sweat off the pounds put on by his beloved goulash, sauerkraut, and liver dumplings. There, at a party catered by Scandia, Lorre met a Bavarian waiter named Ludwig Veigel, whose formal wear—a black tie scotch-taped to his bare chest—delighted him. They struck up a friendship, based partly on nostalgia for the old ways but mainly on Lorre's need for devoted friends: "Peter was a man who needed friends, but not friends for a good time, friends for a sad time. He wanted to empty his heart out. He wanted to talk about his problems." Cloistered in the dark, old-world milieu of Scandia, Lorre hid from view. "Peter was actually an introvert," explained Veigel. "He was very shy. He loved his friends very dearly, but he wasn't outgoing to strangers. When someone would come in and say, 'Are you Peter Lorre?' he would say no."

One time Veigel invited Lorre for drinks. They listened to recordings of Viennese *Volkslieder,* most memorably a song about a carriage driver whose forty-year-old horse dies and cannot be buried. The actor suddenly started crying, tears "rolling down his face," said Veigel.

"What's the matter with you?" asked Lorre. "Don't you like the music?"

"Peter, I heard it before," replied Veigel. "I cried once. I don't have to cry again, do I?"

"O.k., fine," conceded Lorre, "then it's my cry."

Lorre's disaffection with the film industry pressed him to seek out those who also remembered an earlier era, journeymen actors such as Cedric Hardwicke and Burl Ives. Moviemaking had grown too flashy, as he used to say; the dream factory had become a circus. He abhorred the phoniness and narcissism nurtured in the new Hollywood. Sitting by himself, he would sometimes go "into a shell," said Veigel. "He became a strange Peter Lorre, almost a child who hated his mother or father. He withdrew completely. He could change his image so much . . . not silent, but sphinx-like; he didn't look right, he didn't look left, just sat there. . . . But you could almost see the transfiguration of his mind to his body. . . . Either he was oblivious to the fact that this was going on or he was so hurt that he was practically bleeding inside."

"Don't you think I would be more typical," Lorre asked Harper Goff during the making of *20,000 Leagues under the Sea*, "sitting beside a couch and you laying down on it than if I was trying to be an actor?" He told people that he had studied in Vienna to become a psychoanalyst, and from time to time even added that he had been a student of Sigmund Freud. "Peter seemed to be fully sold on the idea that he had trained to do that sort of work," continued Goff, "and that acting was a desperate second choice in his heart."[1] The talk signified his estrangement from the acting life, but he repeated it sincerely and people were convinced.

"I think we respected each other because both of us had the same frustrations," explained director Joseph Pevney. "Secretly we had the scientific bent. The theater was for both of us, I believe, a form of compensation."

Lorre did not merely play at his avocation, but worked at it. "In *The Big Circus*," said Paul Zastupnevich, "Peter played with a chap that had gotten extremely nervous. He was about to blow his lines and Peter took him aside unbeknownst to anyone: 'Well, you know, there is nothing to it. The reason that you are blowing it is because you are hanging yourself up on a word. Why don't you transpose?' So he took one thought and transposed it to the front and put the other to the back and said, 'Nobody will know the difference.' And the guy went right through the sequence without fluffing. But Peter didn't like people to know that he could be helpful."

In *Three Strangers*, the script called for Sydney Greenstreet to hurl Geraldine Fitzgerald against a wall. Naturally apprehensive about managing the physical maneuver without a stuntwoman, she confided in Lorre. To calm her fears, he told her he had once been with a circus: "He said that when the tumblers throw each other, they always go and place themselves in the position in which they wish to end up. So he suggested that I go and position myself against the wall in the exact spot where the cameraman wanted me to end up. Sure enough, when Sydney Greenstreet threw me through the air, I did land on the right spot!"

Lorre reached out to help the inexperienced and insecure June Vincent on the set of *Black Angel*. "He had a scene in which he had to hurt me," she said. "And we did it a couple of times, and I was not a good enough actress to come across with it correctly. He whispered in my ear, 'Now, listen, you think about something else this time. I'm really going to hurt you.' And he did! He didn't hurt me badly, but he physically hurt me enough so that I reacted exactly the way I should. And then I realized what he had done."

Lorre also helped Morey Amsterdam in May 1945 while performing his house act at the Golden Gate Theater in San Francisco. Amsterdam, "San Francisco's own comedian," emceed the show, which included Lorre, billed as "that loveable Boogieman," the dancing Albins, the roller-skating Three Flames, and Irene Manning. When Amsterdam herniated himself on stage, the house doctor told him to put his feet up and rest for a few hours until the swelling went down. Lorre watched quietly. After the doctor left, he told Amsterdam he had studied medicine in Germany and urged him to look after the injury immediately. An ambulance rushed the comedian to the hospital, where another physician confirmed that the hernia might have strangulated and killed him.

Lorre also occasionally turned his percipience to his own advantage. In August 1962 the actor accompanied co-workers Fabian and Chester the chimp on a promotional tour for Irwin Allen's *Five Weeks in a Balloon*. If it were not for Chester, Lorre confided to one reporter, he would be having a good time. After the chimp "had an accident" on a publicist in Denver, Lorre tried to smooth things over by telling her that it was good luck. "Good luck!" she yelled. "With a monkey?" "Especially a monkey," he answered knowingly.

Publicly, most people saw the same Peter Lorre, a man who role-played a give-and-take game with his screen image, becoming both perpetrator and victim of his typecast. Stretching out his hands and begging for acceptance, if not as the person, then as the persona, he had come to feed on welcome scraps of affection. The first time Wendy Sanford arrived at the Warwick Hotel and called up from the lobby, Lorre joked into the phone, "Tell those undertakers to send you right up." Such cracks readily slipped out; it had become part of the act. In the spotlight, Lorre quickly slipped into his movie persona and became the "Peter Lorre" audiences wanted him to be.

On television comedy-variety shows, Lorre played both sides of the net with professional agility. In 1963 Jack Benny introduced the actor as "one of the most frightening, ruthless, cold-blooded and meanest individuals of all time." Lorre just looked sad and voiced his concern that audiences would misunderstand him. This set up another introduction, one he had written for himself, as "one of the sweetest men in show business, a man whose emotional sensitivities are touched equally by the cry of a lost child, the chirp of a wounded sparrow, or the silent protest of a crushed petunia. That's the way I really am." He later sings an old-time favorite: "I want a girl, just like the girl that murdered dear old dad. She was a ghoul, the only ghoul, that daddy ever had." When Benny stops him, Lorre pulls out a stiletto as long as his arm.

Hollywood's teaming of so-called "horror" personalities soon trickled down to TV. The small-screen world of compressed story lines and commercial breaks cashed in on the instant recognition of Boris Karloff, Vincent Price, Lon Chaney, and Peter Lorre, who crisscrossed the two mediums with ease. In *Route 66*'s "Lizard's Leg and Owlet's Wing," in which "some of the creepiest characters who ever chilled the marrows of old-time horror movie fans will come to life again," Lorre, Chaney, and Karloff were asked to go one better—to play themselves. The three meet incognito at a convention of executive secretaries to test various disguises they intend to use on a forthcoming television series. Lorre and Chaney want to stick with the "old, time-tested monsters," but Karloff insisted on trying "a new, modern approach to horror." The studio promised that "Karloff will re-create his legendary role as Frankenstein's frightening monster, and Chaney will do a trio of terrifying characters—the Hunchback of Notre Dame, the Wolf Man and the Mummy. Lorre will supply his inimitable brand of horror sans makeup." In this case, "sans makeup" meant top hat and cape, a costume ridiculously out of character with his bogeyman image. The actor did better kidding his image than submitting to it. When a hotel clerk tells him he bears a striking resemblance to Peter Lorre, he replies, "That's pretty insulting, isn't it?"

Andrew Lorre knew just how his brother felt: "There was a strong family resemblance in appearance and voice, even our father never knew which one of us called. Often I was told that I talked 'just like Peter Lorre,' to which my reply was, 'Yes, but he is getting paid for it.' Twice, once in Amsterdam and again in Australia, I was mobbed by reporters who mistook me for him."

Wherever he dined, Lorre visited the kitchen, chatted with the chef, and came back with a butcher knife, a souvenir of his visit. It was an innocent hobby, but the sight of the knife-wielding actor amply reinforced his popular screen persona as a homicidal maniac. The actor assumed his on-screen guise even when denying that he was "Peter Lorre." One day he and friend and attorney Robert Shutan dined out. A woman nervously passed by their table, turned and walked by again.

"Aren't you Peter Lorre, the actor?" she cautiously asked.

Lorre stood up, his eyes swelled, and his napkin hit the table. Mock menace seeped into his voice. "Do you know what a scoundrel he is?" fumed the actor. "You just can't go around telling people that." Embarrassed, she apologized and slipped away.

Lorre likewise fed and fell behind his sardonic screen image with the press as well, not as an alibi to excuse his unrealized potential, but as a refuge from his own vulnerability. Although he occasionally complained of being called "Mr. Murder" and wished that people would stop reminding him of *M*, more often he wouldn't let them forget. "In my first picture (*M*) I was a child killer," he explained to one interviewer. "You can't be worse than that. Since then, I've graduated to grownups." Giving vent to the one-sided love affair that arose between him and Chester the chimp, Lorre drolly groused, "I have no feeling whatsoever for him, but he is crazy about me. All degenerates are."

In an article titled, "The Peter Lorre Nobody Knows," a journalist for the *New York Mirror* recounted a conversation with the actor: "But he didn't want to talk about pictures. 'What are you going to do when young men come calling on your daughter?' he hissed. I said I reckoned I'd open the door real polite-like and ask them in. He shook his head from side to side. His eyes went glassy, the famous sneer-smile twisted his cruel mouth and he said, dreamily, 'No. No, I won't do that. I think I'll just kill them.' He savored the idea. As I tiptoed out he was lost in thought. I could read those thoughts . . . 'No guns, too noisy . . . stab a few perhaps . . . but poison is best . . . it hurts the most . . .'"

"I think he hid behind that a lot," explained Sanford.

He had fun with his image and used it, putting on the Peter Lorre voice because he knew that it would amuse them, but he did it tongue-in-cheek. . . . When he was hurt or disappointed he would go into his Peter Lorre song and dance, saying, "This is the Peter Lorre you want, so okay, I'll give it to you." He seemed to feel that it was expected of him. And at those times I don't think that he wanted people to see that he was a caring, charming, lovable guy. He felt that the other was more interesting and more fun for them, so he danced to the piper.

When working with young directors, he would ask, in a telling sort of way, "What you want me to be is Peter Lorre, don't you?" He wanted to give of himself, his warmth, his feeling and his fellowship, but he feared it wasn't enough, that he wasn't enough. The public, he believed, expected more of him. "I've played mostly bad men—killers—but the audience loves me," Lorre liked to point out. "You know, I can get away with murder."

Being "Peter Lorre" did have its rewards, not the least of which, he joked, was not losing a part to William Holden. During production of "Diamond Fever," cast members attended a screening of *M* at a downtown art theater and came back with glowing reports. Lorre thrived on this adulation. It validated his self-image as a star, maintaining his celebrity status in full regalia, as if the wave of success had never set him down. When he walked into restaurants, a parade of security men and newfound friends trailed behind his recognizable face and portly frame. "I had never seen such an outpouring of affection and admiration," said Sanford. "These were cab drivers and people in restaurants, not just fans, but people who felt a personal connection. Peter had a talent for getting to people, for getting to the core. I mentioned it to him, that this had never happened to me before with anyone else I'd been with and he said, yes, he felt that too, and that he cared about them." Lorre made the people around him feel important, not least of all by remembering their names. In his company, they also became personalities in their own right.

Playing the philanthropist also became part of the treatment. As soon as the plane landed in New York City for *The Raven*'s promotional tour in 1963, Lorre asked Arthur Kennard to get him a roll of five-dollar bills. He liberally disbursed the cash in tips, dropping twenty-five dollars before he even stepped inside the Hampshire Hotel. Every time the actor went up or down the elevator, he tipped the operator five dollars. Soon, the hotel employees fought to serve him.

His closest friends during these last few years described him as a shy, sensitive man who needed recognition. He either occupied center stage or faded into the background, as conspicuous one moment as he was inconspicuous the next. "If autograph people came up to him," noted Zastupnevich, "he couldn't understand why they wanted his autograph. He would say, 'Well, I'm not that important. I'm not that important now.'" Lorre told his pharmacist that he really didn't need his regular dose of cherry-flavored Cheracol, a codeine-based cough medicine, adding, "I come here because you're the only one left who asks for my autograph."

Screenwriter Edwin Blum suggested that although Lorre frequented the Beverly Hills Tennis Club, he didn't quite fit in with

the gang. It was as if we all took him in because somehow, in a way we didn't understand, we felt sorry for him. He wasn't asking to be pitied or taken on because we felt sorry. Had he known that, he would have walked right out. But I, at least, sensed in him some unknown tragedy in his youth—a Kafka-like tragedy. It was as if the monstrous de-personalized forces of Central Europe had sought in a mechanistic way to turn him into an anonymity. And, to conclude my surmise, I really do believe he became the Lorre of "M" as an attempt to escape that anonymity. It was as if he sensed that such anonymity can only result in the death of the living spirit—or in a paranoid response. Thus, in an intuitive creative act, he brought forth the Lorre who still looms before us as the archetype—the expressionist archetype—of the psychotic killer.

Caught between the present and the reinvented past, Lorre had lost his way. Asked what his reaction was to seeing himself on-screen, he once replied, "I look at the man before me and wonder where I've seen him!" Every person is three people: the person people say we are, the person we think we are, and the person we really are. With Wendy Sanford, Peter Lorre also became a fourth, the person he wanted to be, someone who succeeded where he had failed. He cast himself as a Brechtian hero cut from Warner Bros. stock. "He trusted me enough to talk about his life," she said, "and about things that had been important to him, even though at times obviously he had fantasized about them." In her company, he recast himself in the role of activist-agent. When Hitler came to power, he told her, he had two strikes against him; first, he had politically opposed the new regime, and second, he was Jewish. After he had fled Berlin and thrown in with fellow exiles in Paris, he secretly joined an underground movement:

> He said that they would make underground forays into Germany and bring out people who had brilliant minds—scientists and intellectuals. (I got a very strong impression that Peter fancied himself an intellectual.) He said that they didn't bring out loved ones. One of the last times he went in, which was about the twelfth time, they were ambushed. They had been betrayed, he said, and he had gotten away; but he had lost his nerve and never went back again. He also realized that because his face was so well-known, it would be a danger to everyone else.

In another version of an old story, Lorre told how, after exiting Berlin, he had received a wire from Goebbels offering him honorary Aryan status in exchange for his promise to return and make propaganda pictures.

Padding his scant political profile, he also loved to tell of the eight Nazi saboteurs landed by German submarines off Florida and Long Island on the night of June 12, 1942, and apprehended by the FBI just fourteen days later. Ordered to destroy hydroelectric and aluminum plants, rail lines, reservoirs, and locks on the Ohio River, they carried explosives and incendiaries, fuses, timing devices, forged documents, $174,000 in American currency, and the names and addresses of their contacts in the United States written on a handkerchief in an ink that only ammonia fumes would expose. Lorre claimed, with a surprisingly straight face, that his name ranked third on their list of one hundred enemies of the Reich to be polished off.

"I think he embroidered his past for the sake of being an interesting and amusing companion," said Sanford. "He felt that he was not being used properly and wanted everyone to know that there was more to him than what was on the screen." The "tubby little Buddha" who often retreated behind his boogeyman image became attractive to her "because of what was inside him: I never voiced it, but he must have sensed it or seen it on my face; when I realized that he had a very civilized mind and he was actually a very charming companion, I thought, 'Oh, Peter, how could you have done this. You're not like that at all.' And I think he must have sensed that. He felt he could trust me. And that's why he wanted to show me yes, I was right, he wasn't like that."

At the same time, however, he also wanted her to know he wasn't as harmless as he appeared. Sanford recalls that, after they had wrapped up production on *Diamond Fever*,

> He said, "I've been a perfect gentleman with you, haven't I?"
> I said, "Yes, you have been."
> "I just want you to know if things were different, I wouldn't have been."
> He said it with such a sweet way, I took it as a compliment.

After he returned to Hollywood, he followed up what she described as a "personal relationship without being intimate" with telephone calls until shortly before his death.

Who and what did Lorre want to be? "Peter wanted to be thought of as a 'heavy' actor," said Ludwig Veigel. "He wanted his portrayals to be the real thing—reality, juicy. He wanted people to know what life is, not the pretty things, but the sad things." Interviewed by film historian Joel Greenberg during the making of *Comedy of Terrors*, Lorre eagerly brought the conversation around to Brecht's epic theater. "He thought of himself as an intellectual and a serious actor," said friend James Powers, who Lorre confessed to Celia came closest to replacing Brecht as his intellectual touchstone. "But he couldn't make up his mind whether to be a serious artist or a popular guy. He wasn't taking it [his career] seriously himself. He never made the choice. As he grew older, his choice of options diminished."

"When I met Peter," said Kirk Douglas, "I think he felt it was all over and he was just marking time making a living . . . that he had not done as much with his talents as he could have, but then one has to make a living."

Television director Buzz Kulik detected a "goodly amount of cynicism" in Lorre's attitude toward the film business. He talked little about current projects and much more about his early days in Germany and America. He now took the roles as they came, with little concern about typecasting or quality. Blandine Ebinger remembered that his "strange, tired, sensual-mysterious" eyes looked at you as if they wanted to say: "Oh, go. I've known you for a long time. You tell me nothing new. You bore me."

At what point had his career derailed? "I think he felt had Hitler not happened and had he gone on as Bertolt Brecht's actor," said Sanford, "he would have been himself and been appreciated for what he really was. I don't think he ever found himself again after that." And who would he have become? Fearing the illusion earned greater acceptance than the reality, the actor play-acted a game of wish-fulfillment to the end. Lorre toyed and wisecracked, his gentle amiability shining through a cloud of remorse. After swinging a television deal for Lorre, Arthur Kennard handed him the contract. "I don't sign contracts," Lorre dryly intoned. "I make the faces, you make the deals." He then showed Kennard how to forge his signature, which the agent polished to perfection. Few saw through the guise, the shield that warded off the melancholy and softened the blow. Whatever was left of the good soldier Švejk drew on depleted reserves.

"I have to return to latrine duty," he told his brother Andrew after one of his last visits. Reconciling himself to the commercial reality of Hollywood meant giving in to public expectations. To Ebinger, he complained that filmmakers could come up with nothing new for him.

"It's always the same. A murderer. A criminal."

"But you can choose," she challenged.

"No, Blandine," said Lorre. "I cannot choose. I am stamped."

Too weary to squeeze through the bars, the actor walked through his last roles. "I think toward the end there still was an anger in him and also of course a loss of self-esteem and self-worth," summed up Sanford, "and sadness at his inability to get through. I got a feeling of, 'I'm enjoying what there is, but isn't it a shame that I wasn't allowed to do more.'"

"There was a sadness about him that was inescapable," said Hal Kanter. "If not for his sense of humor, Peter would have destroyed himself much earlier." Clearly, it smoothed out the wrinkles in a crumpled life. However, he did not think it funny when someone tried to steal what little he had left—his name. The last thing Lorre needed—another impersonator—stepped into his life in

1962. Allegedly born April 1, 1934, in Karlsruhe, Germany, to an unmarried factory worker, Eugene Weingand had been adopted by foster parents. In 1954 he immigrated to New York and four years later made his way to southern California, where he worked as a real estate salesman and attended the Loretta Young Acting School, performing in small theaters on the side. Weingand claimed that people thought he looked like the famous movie villain and even began calling him "Peter Lorie." He adopted the name, introducing himself as "Peter Lorie" or "Peter Lorie, Jr." Most of the time, Weingand let those he met assume the rest.

In July 1963 he applied for a change of name to Peter Lorie, citing two reasons: "Because everybody calls me Peter Lorie . . . [and] . . . Because my name is too hard to pronounce." The real Peter Lorre objected in the press and in the courtroom. "I am without a question of a doubt the most imitated man in night clubs," stated the actor. "I have never sued anybody who imitated me. But it's a different story to use my name. . . . My special relationship to an audience is a deep satisfaction to me. . . . When I come on a screen in a theater there is a silence. That means there is a contact. My name to me is a reward. It means to me everything that encompasses me in relationship to others."

Robert Shutan took Weingand's deposition on September 10. He was determined to learn all he could about the man who wanted to carry the name "Peter Lorie."

Q Have you any idea, any idea at all, as to who your father was?

A I don't know . . .

Q In other words, you actually have no idea who your father was, therefore could not possibly know whether that person was alive or dead; is that a fair statement?

A Yes . . .

Q Are you in any way related to Peter Lorre, the actor?

A I don't know. I don't think so.

Q Do you have any reason to believe that you are?

A No reason was given to me yet to believe so.

Q Do you have any reason whatsoever of any kind to believe that in any way you are related to Mr. Peter Lorre, the actor?

A I don't have no reason now, no. . . .

Q May I ask you to explain that answer, when you say you don't have any reason now; what do you mean by now?

A At this particular moment I don't have any reason to believe that I'm related to him.

Q Have you ever in the past had any reason to believe that you're related to him?

A No, I don't think so.

Q Do you expect in the future to have any reason to believe that you are related to him?

A No.

Q Was there any particular reason for you to qualify your answer then and say you don't have any reason now?

A I don't believe that I'm related to Peter Lorre, the actor. Would that clear it up?

Q Let me ask the questions. In addition to your not having any reason, in addition to your telling me that you don't believe that you're related to Peter Lorre, I would like you to answer the question: do you have any reason of any kind whatsoever to believe that you might possibly be related to Peter Lorre, the actor?

A I have no reason to believe that.

Shutan's patience wore thin, but not his sense of humor. Asked why he wanted to introduce himself as Peter Lorie Jr., Weingand replied:

A Well, I want to have my name changed to Peter Lorie, so I don't want to have no confusion of any kind that people might take me for a 65 year old man, so I figure well, I'll tell them I'm Junior. What's wrong with that?

Q I see, you figure that the best way to avoid confusion so that nobody will think that you're related to Peter Lorre, or are Peter Lorre, is to call yourself Peter Lorie, Jr.?

A Perhaps.

Q Did it occur to you that there might be less confusion if you introduced yourself as Eugene Weingand?

A Perhaps.

The Superior Court of Los Angeles County considered Weingand's petition on October 3, 1963. The players in what had the comic overtones—and punch lines—of a television sitcom were Robert Shutan, representing the Objector Peter Lorre; Curtis L. Gemmil, counsel for the Petitioner Eugene Weingand; Superior Court Judge Burnett Wolfson; Eugene Weingand; and Peter Lorre.

Judge Wolfson did not find Weingand's reasons for the petition for a change of name convincing:

Q Anyone ever call you Bob Hope?

A Not yet.

Q Jack Benny?

A No.

Q Danny Thomas?

A No.

Q George Jessel?

A No. . . .

Q The only reason you want your name changed is because people call you
    Peter Lorie?

A That's one of them, yes.

Q What's the other reason?

A Because my name is too hard to pronounce.

Q What's hard to pronounce about Eugene Weingand?

A (No response.)

Even Lorre got in on the act:

Q COURT: Be seated, please and state your name.

A My name is Peter Lorre. I hope you believe me. . . .

Q BY THE COURT: Do you ever do a Jack Paar show?

A I did, I admit to that.

Q Johnny Carson Show? Did they only pay you $320?

A They didn't pay it to me, but they paid it to somebody.

Weingand privately admitted that his petition for a change of name was
only a publicity stunt. On the stand, however, he denied laying plans to launch
a career in show business. Acting, he claimed, was just a hobby. Lester Salkow
testified that a soundalike in the entertainment field would compromise the
"considered box-office value" of his client and create confusion in the minds
of producers, exhibitors, and the public. Likewise, Milton Moritz pointed out
that AIP had hired Lorre as an "exclusive" and that a bogus imitator would
reduce the value of their contract with the actor and materially affect his earning capacity.

Believing Weingand had sought only "to cash in on the reputation established over a period of years by Peter Lorre," Judge Wolfson denied the petition and permanently restrained him from using the name "Peter Lorie," spelled
in any fashion, without the written consent of the actor.

In December 1964, eight months after Lorre's death, Weingand appealed the judgment of the Superior Court on the grounds that Judge Wolfson had exceeded his jurisdiction "in permanently restraining petitioner from using the name Peter Lorie . . . unless (he) first obtains in writing the express written consent of Peter Lorre."[2] He won his point and the Second District Court of Appeals modified the judgment, dropping the permanent injunction.

In his deposition and on the stand, Weingand had denied any familial relationship to Lorre. After the actor's death, however, he brazenly began passing himself off as Lorre's son, repeatedly contradicting his earlier testimony. His driver's license and social security card even bore the name "Peter Lorre, Jr." Although they never met outside the courtroom, Weingand concocted a reunion with Lorre in London. In interviews, he cited Rosenberg, Lorre's birthplace, as the actor's original name. Asked by a prospective client if his father suffered from a liver ailment, Weingand slandered, "No, he has another ailment. . . . Alcohol."

In November 1971, claiming that he was "the surviving son of Peter Lorre, who married my mother in Germany in 1932," Weingand filed a petition for a change of name to "Peter Lorre, Jr.," which stated that "no previous application for change of name had been made on behalf of the petitioner." On December 15, two weeks before the scheduled hearing, Martin Hersch, Weingand's attorney, suddenly filed for dismissal.

In the coming years Weingand eventually landed several small roles in television productions and appeared under the name Peter Lorre Jr. in a low-budget horror title, *The Cat Creature* (1973), in which he leaned heavily on the actor's familiar screen style, even affecting—and wildly exaggerating—his soft, menacing delivery.

A decade later found Weingand impersonating Lorre—as "Booberry"—in a popular television advertisement for General Mills's "Frankenberry," "Count Chocula" and "Booberry" cereals, until Andrew Lorre stepped in and pulled the plug on his commercial exploitation of the family name. Nonetheless, Weingand continued to play out the charade, turning Lorre's life upside down and inside out.

There were no appointments at AIP. Sam Arkoff kept his door open to anyone who wanted to drop by. Lorre appreciated the ready availability of a responsive ear to bend. He typically wandered in with a bit of business or a story idea and softly brought the conversation around to the past, to parts he had wished to play and projects he still hoped to realize, always with the thought of discovering that elusive pivotal role, the one to fan the creative spark and recoup the lost opportunity. Among them was an American remake of *M,* something he had earlier dismissed as artistically infeasible. "One of the things he was a little sad about," recalled Arkoff, "was that so few people in this country had really seen the picture." The studio head listened sympathetically but expressed some reservations about the idea. "Many of our Poe pictures," he later explained, "would do well in the English-speaking countries, but they would not do too well in some of the non-English-speaking countries. . . . In the rest of the European market, when one had a horror picture, it was normally adult only because of the concept of horror being adult and it should be kept away from the kids. And M, in that sense, was an adult picture." Arkoff did not see a large market for a faithful remake of M and cautioned Lorre there probably would have to be some humor in it. The actor nodded in agreement, doubtlessly wondering if he should have stayed in Europe and faced Hitler.

Just as unlikely was Hy Gardner's suggestion that Lorre might make a good "younger edition of Winston Churchill." Lorre told him that he doubted very much if audiences would have accepted him in such a role, "but I would loved to have played Churchill. Many a man had that bright idea, but the trouble is, I can't speak English."

AIP had other plans for Lorre. In *Muscle Beach Party* (1964), a picture geared for the teen trade, the actor made a pro bono appearance. Lorre paraded out Dr. Strangdour, the strongest man in the world, as a quiet thug, a gentle heavy. If he felt the minute of self-parody was made at his own expense, he didn't seem to care.

Roger Corman had hired Chuck Griffith to adapt Edgar Allan's Poe's "The Gold Bug" for Price, Lorre, and Rathbone. The screenwriter turned the tale into a horror-comedy along the lines of *A Bucket of Blood* (1959) and set it in the South after the Civil War, with Price as a decayed planter who turns his burned-out mansion into a hock shop to maintain appearances. Lorre, a "servant in the house whose uncle was an admiral in the Transylvanian navy," carries a gold bug around in a snuffbox and lets it out at night to dance the gold bug rag on the keys of a harpsichord. The actor died before Griffith finished his script.

Happy with *Comedy of Terrors*, Arkoff had also signed Richard Matheson for another horror-comedy with "all four of them"—Vincent Price, Peter Lorre, Boris Karloff, and Basil Rathbone—plus Tallulah Bankhead. The writer tailored *Sweethearts and Horrors* to Price as a ventriloquist, Karloff as a child-hating host of a kiddie show, Rathbone as an aging musical comedy star, and Lorre as an inept magician whose fire act gets out of hand, burning down every theater in which he plays. "They're all called back to their father's home, after he dies, for the reading of the will," said Matheson. "The father manufactured gags, and the whole house is booby-trapped with gags. Then they start getting murdered off, one by one. It would have been a ball, because it was a very funny script." But the actors began "popping off" at the rate of nearly one per year, leaving only Price.

Up to two days before his death, Lorre worked closely with Daniel Haller on the script for a black comedy titled *It's Alive.* Lorre would have been featured as a desert snake farmer, whose wife (Elsa Lanchester) evolved into a serpent in the course of the story. "It was a psycho picture," said Haller, "but more of a comedy. Peter was going to be a pleasant murderer."[3] AIP had given the go-ahead for the project, which had only reached the story-outline stage when the actor died. Had the film been made, it would have marked Haller's directorial debut and would have given Lorre his second credit as screenwriter.

During this time, Lorre and Price's friend Charles Bennett also wrote a screenplay capturing a personal side of their private lives,

> in which Peter would have played a very gentle, very kind, deeply devout old Spanish priest . . . combating the lovely, suave "villainy" of Vincent Price. It never crossed my mind (nor anyone else's) that Peter would come over as a heavy; his gentle amiability would have come through one thousand percent. A lovely kindly priest.
>
> In any case, the movie wasn't made . . . mainly because Vincent decided, perhaps rightly but I think sadly, that his image as a "heavy" had to be changed. . . . But Peter would have been wonderful as this wily old priest, with a sense of humor worthy of his devotion. . . . If the movie is ever made, I will find it hard to find as gloriously simple, amusing [an] actor who could take Peter's place.

Lorre also voiced definite plans for two independent films, a fantasy and a drama: "To be really independent, you must work by yourself from scratch, not imitate a major company on a lower budget." Nor had he apparently given up on filming Edgar Lee Masters's *Spoon River Anthology.* "It is great," lauded Lorre, "but they have never interpreted it right."

Long after Lorre believed his radio career was dead and buried, a small and short-lived company set up shop at General Service Studios in Hollywood and proclaimed a new Golden Age of the airwaves. Master Artists Corporation promised to put "the world's most engaging personalities" within range of local radio stations with a series called "Star-Essence." Concepts scaled to published rates included 260 five- and ten-minute radio shows: "Liberace on Love," Mel Tormé's "Words on Music," Jim Rodgers's "Tales of a Balladeer," and a "BONANZA of superb SUSPENSE and TERROR created by Mr. Peter Lorre's

'Treasury of Terror!'" Shows for Vincent Price, Hayley Mills, and Sir Cedric Hardwicke were also in preparation. To promote the future of radio as a "prime entertainment," MAC distributed sample shows with commercial breaks on 45 rpm long-playing records. Lorre narrated a title-less tale about a police inspector whose unforgiving ex-girlfriend sends him amputated fingers he believes to be her own. "Star-Essence" did not catch on, fading out before it had time to shine.

On Lorre's desk also lay the script for 20th Century–Fox's *John Goldfarb, Please Come Home* (1965), a fatuous comedy that would have cast the actor as an Arab potentate, a role ultimately played by Peter Ustinov. Earlier in the year, the *Berliner Tageblatt* had detailed the actor's plans to return to Europe and join up with French comedian Bourvil in *Citizens of Fear*.[4] He never made the trip. And in April Lorre was set to make a guest appearance in *Bikini Beach* (1964).

As the project files grew, Lorre's health ebbed. He had always drawn strength from his work. Near the end, there was none to give or take. "For Peter," said co-worker Joyce Jameson, "acting was reality. There was no reality in terms of life. If he couldn't act, there was nothing."

In his final screen performance, Lorre glumly portrayed an acrid Hollywood director in *The Patsy* (1964), originally titled *Son of Bellboy*, a Jerry Lewis comedy about a group of show business professionals who attempt to turn a bumbling bellboy into a star. Coauthor and director Lewis wanted authentic types, players instantly recognizable to the public. Never was the transience of fame more apparent to Lorre. A younger Lorre might have worked around the strident, egotistical Lewis with subtle defiance. Now, he just ignored him. "There was no conflict with Peter," said actor Keenan Wynn, "because Peter was more intelligent than any of those people. He didn't pay any attention to Jerry." Nor did Lewis impose himself on Lorre, whom he later described as "a scene thief beyond compare," but left him alone. It suited the actor's mood. Lorre checked out at Paramount on March 19, 1964. Although he could not have afforded to turn down his role in *The Patsy*, he avoided conversation about the picture and swore he would never see it. Friends supposed it put the last nail in his coffin. "If he could have had his choice," said his daughter Catharine, "he would have cut his part out of the film."

Lorre knew he was failing. "Peter was afraid to exert himself too much," recalled Paul Zastupnevich, "because he tired very easily and he wanted to try to save himself for the scene. Once or twice, when he was extremely tired and would fluff his lines, he got very angry with himself because he did not like to hold up his fellow actors."

The tight six-day schedule on *Kraft Suspense Theatre*'s "The End of the World, Baby," telecast October 24, 1963, had overwhelmed the already spent actor, turning his final television appearance into an unbearable chore. When Lorre admitted he could no longer drive, director Irvin Kerschner arranged for ropes to pull his car out of frame in one scene. Ascending a flight of stairs in another shot was flatly impossible. Nor could he remember more than one line of dialogue at a time. "He just couldn't sustain it," said Kerschner, who worked around Lorre's illness with skill and patience. "He just kept saying, 'Well, I'll be alright. I'll get it,' but he didn't. It was really sad." Kerschner finally decided to give Lorre one line, cut away, and so intercut the rest of the scene. To compensate for his inadequacy, the actor lapsed into storytelling, recounting the good old days at UFA. "It was his way of showing us that he was somebody once," explained Kerschner. "Every actor will fall back on a way of doing something that they've done before. If you don't do your homework and you don't get into a character, you have shtick that you do, and I felt that Peter was by then depending a lot on the shtick to get him out of trouble. . . . I was worried for him. I was embarrassed for him. I felt sorry for him."

At AIP, Lorre had carried a satchel of medicines around the set. His use of prescription drugs was symptomatic of more than poor health. It told his friends he was giving in and giving up. They worried for his life. Although he shrugged off their concern, others felt the likelihood of an early death deeply troubled him. "His health was poor," noted writer Herb Meadow, who had worked with him on "The Left Fist of David." "We started to bet on whether or not he'd outlast the picture, all of us betting against him, giving him anywhere from ten minutes to an hour. He responded with funnies, but the funnies were only spoken; his eyes were not laughing, and we quit because we realized that we were not being funny, we were only frightening him. He did not enjoy death, he did not enjoy jokes about it. I remember now thinking that he must have had it on his mind a great deal, because he took it in a very troubled way."

Jonas Silverstone thought that many of Lorre's pranks were forced: "Basically, Peter was a very serious man. I think he was playing a point-counterpoint of his own direction. Peter gave the appearance of loving fun and he did like fun very much, but I do think he was driving himself to have fun, particularly toward the end. But above all, I think Peter was and remained a very serious man, full of tragedy. I think he was very aware of it." Joel Greenberg came away with the impression "of someone utterly jaded and exhausted. Creatively, one felt, he was already dead, and had been for a long time."

"He didn't like being Peter Lorre the clown," expanded Meadow. "He didn't like doing what was expected of him. He went along with it because that was the way the dice had rolled. He didn't have much choice anymore. I think probably that killed him more than anything else. I think that when people as strong-minded as Peter Lorre decide they've had enough, they can just turn their faces to the wall and die." "Peter got more down," concluded Harvey Parry, "until it finally worked him into the ground."

Perhaps, as he had symbolized in *Der Verlorene*, fate is an onrushing locomotive, an unstoppable force. The engine had gathered too much momentum to be sidestepped so near the end of its journey. Lorre knew the machine's path and met it with open eyes. On the evening before his death, Peter saw—collectively—his two ex-wives and Annemarie for a final time. Karen, who noticed the whiteness of his face and hands, even remarked on his deathly pallor. Annemarie rubbed some warmth into his cold feet.

On Sunday, March 22, he slept most of the day. As she often did, Celia drove to his apartment to prepare lunch for him. Afterward, she went home and telephoned him at about four o'clock. When he did not answer, she returned to his apartment, where she found him in a deep sleep. He awakened and asked her to call his friend and doctor Joe Golenternak. The physician could not be reached, so Golenternak's associate came instead, took Lorre's pulse, shrugged, and left. Celia stayed with him until ten-thirty that night. The next morning, Beatrice Lane discovered his body on the bedroom floor. Thinking that he might only be unconscious, she called Celia, who rushed over. Golenternak, who had never received the message from the previous day, arrived at noon and pronounced Lorre dead. By the location of the body, it appeared as if he had gotten up, perhaps to open or close the window, and suffered a cerebral hemorrhage. According to Shutan, who arrived soon after, Lorre wore the face of gentle sleep.

To Lester Salkow fell the sad charge of finding a friend to deliver a eulogy. When Vincent Price asked if there was anything he could do, the agent accepted his offer. During a rehearsal for *The Red Skelton Show*, Price asked for an extra hour at lunch to speak at Lorre's funeral. Skelton, on whose show the actor had appeared at least eight times, closed the set while he and his cast and crew attended the services.

At one o'clock on March 26, 1964, Rabbi William Sanderson conducted brief rites for Peter Lorre at Pierce Brothers' Hollywood Chapel. Among the honorary pallbearers were both friends and co-workers, including Irwin Allen, Samuel Z. Arkoff, Sir Cedric Hardwicke, Burl Ives, Joe E. Lewis, Lester Salkow, Robert Shutan, Jonas Silverstone, and Irving Yergin.

Then Price, who understood Lorre better than he knew—indeed, perhaps, better than Lorre knew himself—spoke of the actor, of the man:

A great actor of another era said of our calling that we are sculptors in snow and yet at the final dissolution of this ephemeral image the whole world mourns. Something irreplaceable has disappeared, but if there is immortality, surely it is in the remembrance of man, and what the actor creates is a lasting memory however unsubstantial the material of which it is made. The memory of a great performer is elemental, and the elements are life.

Peter had no illusions about our profession. He loved to entertain, to be a face maker, as he said so often of our kind. But his was a face that registered the thoughts of his inquisitive mind and his receptive heart, and the audience, which was his world, loved him for glimpses he gave them of that heart and mind.

If the admonition that it is more blessed to give than to receive is to be believed, surely the actor is blest, for he succeeds only in so far as he gives and what he receives can never compensate for what he gives, for he gives fully of himself and receives at best only a part of others . . . and yet in touching the lives of others, if only in passing, he can never wholly know what great and unexpected good he may have done—relieved some living pressure in making one man laugh, or through interpretation of the great truths of poetry or prose made another think and mend his mind. This is enough and any actor knows it is enough, for talent is the rarest gift, and even if it is given greatly only to a precious few, that talent must be greatly given always . . . to all.

Peter held back nothing of himself. He shared his wit, his curiosity, and yet he always seemed to be exploring you. The aura of devotion that surrounded him made all men glad to be his friend, to feed him and be fed by him in turn.

One of the greatest experiences in our profession, and one that too seldom happens, is the chance to work with another player many times over the years. It makes the contest keener—for acting is an art and the greatest art of it is one actor's relationship to another—interplay—counterpoint—conflict. Good actors have a thousand faces and one must know them all to be the proper mirror—one for the other. Reaction is the language of the theatre.

I have had the excitement, the challenge of doing many entertainments with Peter and I say entertainments because that was our concern. In the theatre one can teach and preach, hold up for view the problems of all life, but always for me the primal purpose of our art will be to entertain—to set in motion the chances of escape.

Peter believed this too and brought to entertainment the veteran's verve to make it right. No way to bring this about went unexplored and he could map the perfect path to leave no person lost along the way.

The something sad about him and a certain necessary madness went together to capture hearts and give his fellow players pause lest they be unprepared to match his winsomeness. This was a man to be aware of at all times for he was well aware of all who shared the stage with him and working with him never failed to fulfill the seventh and perhaps most sacred sense—the sense of fun.

The snow statue of his work perhaps will melt away, but the solid substance of his self must last. Man's immortality is man, his family, his friends and in the actor's dream of life, the audience—his identity with them . . . and this man was the most identifiable actor I ever knew. No part of him was other than himself—his voice, his face, the way he moved—his laugh . . . perhaps the grief that winters us in losing him may keep his statue whole—if not the image of the actor, at least the stature of the man.

Afterward, Price recounted anecdotes and incidents that marked the course of their working friendship. He had the small group laughing and crying. "I guess that's the way Peter would have wanted it," he concluded. "Thank you for coming."

As much as those close to him may have anticipated his death, it seemed lamentably unfair, and many were shocked to learn that he was only fifty-nine years old. "Peter never got his just rewards," said Daniel Haller, "what he deserved from his career and life." Those who shared Lorre's dreams and disappointments knew he was capable of much more than was asked of him. "He always had the feeling he could find the right combination of people," said Lester Salkow, "a unison where he might be the pivotal person in a real artistic film." Three days before his death, Lorre had reportedly signed a new contract with AIP that renewed his option for two more pictures.

Peter and Annemarie had been scheduled to attend a divorce hearing on March 23. Because they had not completed a property settlement, Superior Judge Wolfson had postponed the hearing until April 6. Superior Judge Clarke E. Stephens appraised the actor's estate at thirteen thousand dollars, but Lorre, who left no will, actually died insolvent, having never fully discharged his back income taxes after declaring bankruptcy in 1949.[5] Sadly, he left young Catharine nothing in the way of financial security, which had been one of his greatest fears.

Peter Lorre's body was cremated and inurned privately in the Abbey of the Psalms at Hollywood Memorial Park Cemetery.

EPILOGUE

MIMESIS

The good actor is characterized by
the high multiplicity of his "phantoms."

—Otto Fenichel

Three months after Peter Lorre's death in March 1964, police officers in Elk City, Oklahoma, arrested nineteen-year-old Larry McLean for counseling a devil-worshipping cult allegedly responsible for vandalizing a string of local churches. Dedicated to destroying all emblems of God, the secret society also planned to exhume the body of its idol, Peter Lorre, and restore it to life.

As a pop icon, Lorre had arrived. Merchandisers found the image far more marketable than the actor. Little wonder that he was busier in death than he had been in life. Ironically, it was Eugene Weingand who kicked off the postmortem commercialization of Lorre's screen image in 1965. Billed as "Peter Lorre, Jr.," he played a suspected K.A.O.S. agent who had infiltrated C.O.N.T.R.O.L.'s spy school on a television episode of *Get Smart*. During the mid-to-late 1960s, Paul Frees reproduced Lorre's distinctive voice for a recurring role as Morocco Mole—opposite Sydney Greenstreet as Yellow Pinky—in *The Atom Ant/Secret Squirrel Show*. In 1967 a puppetized Peter Lorre assisted Boris Karloff's voice-acted Baron von Frankenstein in *Mad Monster Party*. Another Lorre legatee teamed a Joel Cairo clone with "Sydney Street" in a 1969 episode of *The Avengers*, titled "Legacy of Death." That same year, Lorre returned to Casablanca on *Get Smart*. Along with incarnations of Boris Karloff and Bela Lugosi, he also gave voice to a talking tree in the witch's forest on behalf of the 1969 children's series *H.R. Pufnstuf*. As Igor, he assisted a mad scientist on *The Electric Company*. In 1970

Scooby-Doo, Where Are You? teamed him with Mr. Greenway in "That's Snow Ghost." The Lorre persona even took a religious turn in *Godspell* (1973), a musical version of the Gospels, in which actor Jerry Sroka impersonated Lorre for the telling of a parable about forgiveness. In a scene from *The Return of the Pink Panther* (1975), a jewel thief (Christopher Plummer) forces Pepi (Graham Stark) to reveal the whereabouts of the "Fat Man" while the notes of "As Time Goes By" hang in the air. In Hanna-Barbera's *Secret Lives of Waldo Kitty* (1975–76), Lorre was cast as a villainous cocker spaniel called Peter opposite a bulldog named Sidney Greenalley. As a Boston terrier, he enjoyed the canine companionship of a bloodhound (Humphrey Bogart), a boxer (Edward G. Robinson), a terrier (James Cagney), and a poodle (Mae West), who plan to break out of the dog pound in Disney's *The Shaggy D.A.* (1976). Two years later, a curly-locked Dom DeLuise gave his updated Joel Cairo a Lorre-like twist in *The Cheap Detective*, a parody of *The Maltese Falcon* that starred Peter Falk as a Sam Spade spin-off. The animated *Drak Pack* featured three do-gooding teenage boys capable of transforming themselves into Dracula, Frankenstein, and the Werewolf. Assisting their archenemy, Dr. Dred, were Fly, Mummy Man, Vampira, and Toad, a small, squat, round-faced, pop-eyed creature with a high-pitched voice.

Robin Williams turned his comic genius in Lorre's direction in 1993 as the Genie in *Aladdin*. The actor has long been fodder for Williams's comedic canon. In the late 1970s, Home Box Office looked in on *The Comedy Store*, where Williams whistled a few bars from "In the Hall of the Mountain King" as he approached a young woman in the audience. "You don't find me unattractive, do you?" he softly purred. Possibly the only impersonator conversant with Lorre's credits, he is also the best, always ready to take caricature to the next level.

On *Dinah and Friends*, another comedian impersonated Lorre opening a Christmas present, the indestructible Mr. Armstrong. Stretching it out of shape, he comforts it, saying, "I bet that feels good, Mr. Armstrong."

Advertisers plugged an animated Lorre into a commercial socket. The Dairy Council had him pushing milk instead of mayhem. For the American Heart and Lung Association's "It's a Matter of Life and Breath" campaign, he joined Sydney Greenstreet, Humphrey Bogart, Boris Karloff, Jimmy Cagney, and Edward G. Robinson, who made up the "Half a Dirty Dozen." Not unexpectedly, Lorre was cigarettes ("I'm little, but I'm deadly"), while Greenstreet represented overeating. In a subsequent spot, the "Fat Man" tells audiences that his doctor has put him on a strict diet of mustard, ketchup, and pepper. Suddenly, a goggle-eyed Lorre jumps out from behind his chair and giggles, "Yes, but he went back for seconds!" In another plug for good health, Lorre assisted a mad doctor in building a beautiful girl out of milk, meat, and vegetables, foods one needs to stay healthy. General Mills's "Booberry," whose voice-over was furnished by Eugene Weingand, sported a hat (à la Toady in *Rope of Sand*), a bow tie, and a chain around his waist with a bowl and spoon attached to one end and a box of cereal on the other. He competed with Boris Karloff and Bela Lugosi, each of whom insisted his cereal was best. Lorre's soft purr has even been heard rattling off the names of bugs on the hit list of Arab Termite and Pest Control.

The actor moved into the medium of pop music in the 1980s with The Jazz Butcher's "Peter Lorre" and Tom Smith's "I Want to be Peter Lorre." In 1992 singer Kate Westbrook released an album titled "Goodbye Peter Lorre," which featured a song of the same name with the subtitle "If Brecht Could See Me Now."

Younger generations unfamiliar with his movies know Lorre's voice as that of Ren, the mildly malevolent, pop-eyed Chihuahua patterned after Joel Cairo, who denounces an obese cat named Stimpy as an "eediot." In 1995 Warner Bros. reassembled the cast of *Casablanca* for *Carrotblanca,* with Bugs Bunny as Bogie, Daffy Duck as Dooley Wilson, Yosemite Sam as Conrad Veidt, Penelope the cat as Ingrid Bergman, Sylvester as Paul Henreid, and Tweety Bird as a heavy-lidded Lorre. Three years later Lorre, turned out in a tux and clutching a bottle of wine, met Homer Simpson on a ship of "lost souls" in an episode titled "Kidney Trouble."

Even the Ferengi, small, large-eared, sharp-toothed aliens, who believed that "the bigger the smile, the sharper the knife," were labeled "Peter Lorres of space" by the production staff of *Star Trek.*

The Lorre image carried over to the new century in the cartoon series *Jackie Chan Adventures.* In an episode titled "Enter the Cat," a Lorre soundalike gives voice to a villainous Moroccan who assists a sinister fat man dressed in a white suit and a Panama hat.

Lorre once said that when he portrayed a character, he ceased to exist for a time. Some seventy years after Fritz Lang introduced him to audiences as a dark presence and a disembodied voice, he remains lastingly insinuated in the public mind as an image of shadowy substance. Such caricatures continue to celebrate the legacy of an actor who walked away leaving only a ghostly reflection in the mirror.

APPENDIX

PETER LORRE CREDITS AND BROADCAST APPEARANCES

Credits are only complete until they are not, which is another way of saying that documenting the stage, film, radio, and television performances of an actor is a work in progress. Special appearances, guest shots, and commitments made but not met are just a few of the wide variety of variables that prevent closure. While these credits don't pretend to be complete, they do represent the most comprehensive and accurate inventory to date. Dates cited represent opening nights in the case of theater, release dates in the case of films, and original air dates in the case of radio and television.

Radio shows on which Lorre was scheduled but did not appear include *Arch Oboler's Plays,* "Home Town," Dec. 9, 1939, NBC, 8:00–8:30 p.m.; *Arch Oboler's Plays,* "Nobody Died," Dec. 16, 1939, NBC, 8:00–8:30 p.m.; *Over Here,* Dec. 5, 1942, NBC-Blue, 8:30–9:30 p.m.; and *Deliver Us from Evil,* Dec. 6, 1942, NBC-Blue, 2:00–3:00 p.m.

I am grateful to Haris Balic, at the Austrian Theater Museum in Vienna, who generously provided theater programs, reviews, and articles helpful in chronicling Lorre's stage work. Stephan Dörschel did the same from the Akademie der Künste in Berlin. I have also drawn from Brigitte Mayr's "Lorre auf der Bühne" in *Peter Lorre: Ein Fremder im Paradies,* edited by Michael Omasta, Brigitte Mayr, and Elisabeth Streit. Cheryl Morris compiled the actor's American stage credits as well as those for film, radio, and television.

STAGE

Die lustigen Weiber von Windsor (*The Merry Wives of Windsor*). Director: Leo Mittler; from the play by William Shakespeare; Thalia Theater, Breslau; Nov. 22, 1924. Cast: Ludwig Stössel, Edgar Flataus, Peter Lorre (a servant).

Die Journalisten (*The Journalists*). Director: Hans Peppler; written by Gustav Freytag; Lobe Theater, Breslau; Nov. 22, 1924. Cast: Hans Peppler, Margarethe Wolf, Peter Lorre (bit part).

Die Bremer Stadtmusikanten (*The Bremen Town Musicians*). Director: Julius Arnfelds; from the story by the Brothers Grimm; Lobe Theater, Breslau; Dec. 21, 1924. Cast: Peter Lorre (Esel, a donkey), Carl Behr, Clare Felber, Rolf Dreves.

Romeo und Julia (*Romeo and Juliet*). Director: Paul Barnay; from the play by William Shakespeare; Lobe Theater, Breslau; April 25, 1925. Cast: Hans Brausewetter, Hertha Pauli, Therese Giehse, Hans Peppler, Sigurd Lohde, Peter Lorre (apothecary).

Wie es euch gefällt (*As You Like It*). Director: Franz Wenzler; from the play by William Shakespeare; Schauspielhaus, Zurich; Sept. 19, 1925. Cast: Hans Peppler, Friedl Haerlin, Else Rambausek, Hans Spallart, Sigurd Lohde, Franz Schafheitlin, Peter Lorre (2 roles: Sir Olivarius Textdreher [Sir Oliver Martext] and Wilhelm, a farm boy in love with Käthchen [Audrey]).

Gesellschaft (*Loyalties*). Director: Franz Wenzler; from the play by John Galsworthy; German by Leon Schalit; Schauspielhaus, Zurich; Sept. 22, 1925. Cast: Karl Marx, Friedl Haerlin, Sigurd Lohde, Fritz Ritter, Hans Peppler, Hans Spallart, Peter Lorre (Gilmann the grocer), Franz Schafheitlin.

Der Mann, das Tier und die Tugend (*The Man, the Animal, and Virtue*). Director: Hans Peppler; written by Luigi Pirandello; Schauspielhaus, Zurich; Sept. 30, 1925. Cast: Franz Schafheitlin, Hans Peppler, Peter Lorre (Mr. Totó, the apothecary and brother of Dr. Pulejo), Hans Spallart, Else Rambausek.

Der Kreidekreis (*The Chalk Circle*). Director: Franz Wenzler; from the Chinese by Klabund; Schauspielhaus, Zurich; Nov. 8, 1925. Cast: Friedl Haerlin, Sigurd Lohde, Karl Marx, Hans Peppler, Peter Lorre (first coolie), Franz Schafheitlin, Hans Spallart.

Das Paketboot Tenacity (*The Package-Boat Tenacity*). Director: Hans Raabe; from the play by Charles Vildrac; German by Theodor Däubler; Schauspielhaus, Zurich; Nov. 14, 1925. Cast: Karl Marx, Hans Spallart, Hans Raabe, Hans Peppler, Peter Lorre (a worker).

Im Weissen Rössl (*In the "White Horse"*). Director: Hans Peppler; written by Oskar Blumenthal and Gustav Kadelburg; Schauspielhaus, Zurich; Nov. 15, 1925; Stadttheater, Zurich; Nov. 21, 1925. Cast: Friedl Haerlin, Franz Schafheitlin, Else Rambausek, Peter Lorre (Loidl, a beggar), Hans Spallart, Hans Peppler, Fritz Ritter.

Napoleon oder die hundert Tage (*Napoleon or the Hundred Days*). Director: Hans Peppler; written by Christian Dietrich Grabbe; Schauspielhaus, Zurich; Nov. 25, 1925. Cast: Hans Raabe, Friedl Haerlin, Franz Schafheitlin, Sigurd Lohde, Peter Lorre (2 roles: King Ludwig XVIII and Ephraim), Karl Marx, Hans Spallart.

Dr. Knock oder "Der Triumph der Medizin" (*Dr. Knock or "The Triumph of Medicine"*). Director: Hans Peppler; written by Jules Romains; German by Benno Vigny; Schauspielhaus, Zurich; Dec. 2, 1925. Cast: Sigurd Lohde, Peter Lorre (the apothecary Mousquet), Franz Schafheitlin, Hans Peppler, Hans Spallart.

Der heilige Johanna (*St. Joan*). Director: Franz Wenzler; written by G.B. Shaw; Schauspielhaus, Zurich; Dec. 9, 1925. Cast: Else Rambausek, Hans Peppler, Karl Marx, Franz Schafheitlin, Sigurd Lohde, Peter Lorre (a castle manager), Hans Raabe, Fritz Ritter.

Das tapfere Schneiderlein (*The Brave Little Tailor*). Director: Fritz Ritter; adapted from the Grimm fairy tale by Peter Lorre and Fritz Ritter; Schauspielhaus, Zurich; Dec. 12, 1925. Cast: Peter Lorre (the tailor), Fritz Ritter, Else Rambausek, Hans Spallart, Franz Schafheitlin, Hans Peppler, Sigurd Lohde.

Heinrich IV (*Henry the Fourth*). Director: Hans Peppler; written by Luigi Pirandello; German by Hans Feist; Schauspielhaus, Zurich; Dec. 18, 1925. Cast: Alexander Moissi, Margarete Hopf, Else Rambausek, Franz Schafheitlin, Hans Peppler, Fritz Ritter, Hans Spallart, Peter Lorre (first lackey in uniform).

Faust 1. Teil (*Faust, Part 1*). Director: Hans Peppler; written by Johann Wolfgang von Goethe; Schauspielhaus, Zurich; Dec. 22, 1925, and Jan. 9, 1926. Cast: Alexander Moissi, Hans Peppler, Franz Schafheitlin, Peter Lorre (Siebel, one of the merry fellows in Auerbach's cellar), Else Rambausek, Sigurd Lohde, Fritz Ritter.

Die schlimmen Buben in der Schule (*The Bad Boys in the School*). Director: Hans Peppler; written by Johann Nestroy; Schauspielhaus, Zurich; Dec. 31, 1925. Cast: Alexander Moissi, Karl Marx, Sigurd Lohde, Else Rambausek, Peter Lorre (Stanislaus, son of Mr. Wichtig), Hans Spallart.

Er ist an allem schuld (*It's His Fault*). Director: Fritz Ritter; written by Leo Tolstoy; Schauspielhaus, Zurich; Jan. 16, 1926. Cast: Alexander Moissi, Rosa Wohlgemuth, Sigurd Lohde, Peter Lorre (Taras, assistant to the village mayor).

Peer Gynt. Director: Hans Peppler; written by Henrik Ibsen; Schauspielhaus, Zurich; Jan. 19, 1926, and Jan. 21, 1926; Stadttheater, Zurich; Feb. 8, 1926. Cast: Therese Bellau, Sigurd Lohde, Hans Peppler, Friedl Haerlin, Franz Schafheitlin, Peter Lorre (2 roles: Bridegroom of Ingrid, daughter of the Haegstadtbauers, and Prof. Begriffenfeldt, director of the lunatic asylum), Fritz Ritter, Karl Marx, Else Rambausek, Hans Raabe, Hans Spallart.

Potasch und Perlmutter als Filmcompagnie (*Potasch and Perlmutter as a Film Company*). Director: Hans Peppler; written by Montague Glass and Jules Eckert Goldman; Schauspielhaus, Zurich; Jan. 24, 1926. Cast: Alexander Starke, Hugo Welle, Therese Bellau, Karl Marx, Franz Schafheitlin, Sigurd Lohde, Friedl Haerlin, Peter Lorre (film actor Lionel Brandon), Hans Peppler.

Potasch und Perlmutter als Filmcompagnie (*Potasch and Perlmutter as a Film Company*). Director: Hans Peppler; written by Montague Glass and Jules Eckert Goldman; Schauspielhaus, Zurich; Jan. 27, 1926. Cast: Alexander Starke, Hugo Welle, Therese Bellau, Karl Marx, Franz Schafheitlin, Sigurd Lohde, Friedl Haerlin, Peter Lorre (film actor Viktor Curzon), Hans Peppler.

Nachtasyl (*Night Refuge*). Director: Hans Raabe; written by Maxim Gorky; Schauspielhaus, Zurich; Feb. 3, 1926; Stadttheater, Zurich; March 9, 1926. Cast: Sigurd Lohde, Else Rambausek, Karl Marx, Fritz Ritter, Friedl Haerlin, Peter Lorre (Bubnow, the cap maker), Franz Schafheitlin, Hans Peppler, Hans Spallart.

Faust 1. Teil (*Faust, Part 1*). Director: Hans Peppler; written by Johann Wolfgang von Goethe; Schauspielhaus, Zurich; Feb. 10, 1926. Cast: Albert Bassermann, Hans Peppler, Franz Schafheitlin, Peter Lorre (Siebel), Else Rambausek, Sigurd Lohde, Fritz Ritter.

Die Stützen der Gesellschaft (*The Pillars of Society*). Director: Hans Raabe; written by Henrik Ibsen; Schauspielhaus, Zurich; Feb. 11, 1926. Cast: Albert Bassermann, Therese Bellau, Margarete Hopf, Karl Marx, Peter Lorre (Viegeland, a merchant), Else Rambausek, Hans Peppler.

Wallensteins Tod (*Wallenstein's Death*). Director: Hans Peppler; written by Friedrich von Schiller; Schauspielhaus, Zurich; Feb. 18, 1926. Cast: Albert Bassermann, Karl Marx, Fritz Ritter, Sigurd Lohde, Peter Lorre (Seni, an astrologer), Hans Spallart, Franz Schafheitlin, Friedl Haerlin, Leonie Peppler.

Das grosse Rad (*The Large Wheel*). Director: Franz Wenzler; written by Max Pulver; Schauspielhaus, Zurich; Feb. 18, 1926. Cast: Alexander Starke, Friedl Haerlin, Sigurd Lohde, Peter Lorre (Höllenstein, a literati), Else Rambausek, Hans Spallart, Franz Schafheitlin, Hans Peppler, Karl Marx, Fritz Ritter.

Schweiger. Director: Hans Peppler; written by Franz Werfel; Schauspielhaus, Zurich; March 4, 1926. Cast: Hans Peppler, Lore Busch, Hans Raabe, Franz Schafheitlin, Fritz Ritter, Peter Lorre (S. Topas, Chief Editor of the *Arbeiterwillens* [*Workers' Will*]), Karl Marx, Therese Bellau.

Schloss Wetterstein (*Castle Wetterstein*). Director: Herr Salzmann; written by Frank Wedekind; Schauspielhaus, Zurich; March 6, 1926. Cast: Karl Marx, Margarete Hopf, Erika Thimm, Franz Schafheitlin, Hans Spallart, Peter Lorre (Schigabek), Fritz Ritter, Hans Peppler.

Fannys erstes Stück (*Fanny's First Play*). Director: Franz Wenzler; written by G.B. Shaw; Schauspielhaus, Zurich; March 18, 1926; Schauspielhaus in "Zur Kaufleuten," Zurich; April 5, 1926. Cast: Friedl Haerlin, Franz Schafheitlin, Peter Lorre (an actor), Karl Marx, Else Rambausek, Therese Bellau, Hans Peppler.

Judith und Holofernes (*Judith and Holofernes*). Written by Johann Nestroy; Schauspielhaus, Zurich; March 30, 1926. Cast: Peter Lorre (Holofernes), Hugo Welle.

Egmont. Director: Hans Peppler; written by Johann Wolfgang von Goethe; Stadttheater, Zurich; April 3, 1926. Cast: Erika Thimm, Hans Peppler, Karl Marx, Hans Raabe, Hans Spallart, Fritz Ritter, Peter Lorre (Seifensieder, a citizen of Brussels), Sigurd Lohde, Franz Schafheitlin.

Jettchen Gebert. Written by Georg Hermann; Schauspielhaus in "Zur Kaufleuten," Zurich; April 14, 1926; Stadttheater, Zurich; April 25, 1926. Cast: Franz Schafheitlin, Margarete Hopf, Hans Raabe, Hans Peppler, Friedl Haerlin, Fritz Ritter, Peter Lorre (Julius Jacoby), Hans Spallart.

Weisse Fracht (*White Cargo*). Director: Hans Peppler; written by Leon Gordon; German by Arnold Korff; Schauspielhaus in "Zur Kaufleuten," Zurich; April 22, 1926. Cast: Arnold Korff, Hans Spallart, Hans Raabe, Sigurd Lohde, Hans Peppler, Peter Lorre (Jim Fish, a native).

Hans Jacob Suler. Director: Hans Peppler; written by Erika Wettstein; Schauspielhaus, Zurich; June 30, 1926. Cast: Friedl Haerlin, Franz Wenzler, Peter Lorre (Rudolf Sprungli).

Faust. Directors: Franz Wenzler and Robert Lohan; written by Nicolaus Lenau; Kammerspiele, Vienna; Sept. 29, 1926. Cast: Hans Peppler, Leonard Steckel, Margarete Hopf, Max Wittmann, Friedl Haerlin, Heinz Leo Fischer, Paul Verhoeven, Trude Brionne, Peter Lorre (2 roles: second doctor and second lad).

Die Nacht ist unser (*The Night Is Ours*). Director: Robert Lohan; written by Henry

Kistemaeckers; Kammerspiele, Vienna; Oct. 8, 1926. Cast: Charlotte Klinder, Trude Brionne, Therese Bellau, Hanne Dorian, Olga Diora, Hans Zesch-Ballot, Hans Peppler, Theodor Grieg, Peter Lorre (William Burtley), Paul Verhoeven.

Kopf oder Schrift (*Heads or Tails*). Director: Robert Blum; written by Louis Verneuil; Kammerspiele, Vienna; Oct. 16, 1926. Cast: Friedl Haerlin, Hans Peppler, Paul Verhoeven, Max Wittmann, Hans Zesch-Ballot, Theodor Grieg, Peter Lorre (Prince Silif Erzeroum).

Die fleissige Leserin: Das Neueste Magazin (*The Diligent Reader: The Newest Magazine*). Director: Leonard Steckel; written by Marcellus Schiffer; Kammerspiele, Vienna; Oct. 22, 1926. Cast: Rosy Werginz, Friedl Haerlin, Margarete Hopf, Olga Diora, Trude Brionne, Max Wittmann, Paul Verhoeven, Hans Peppler, Peter Lorre, Hans Zesch-Ballot. In this revue, Lorre appeared in the following sketches: *Novelle—Der Schrei aus dem Nord-Süd-Express* (*Novella—The Cry from the North-South-Express*), as A Hi Hung; *Interview*, as a reporter; *Rätselecke* (*Mystery Corner*), as Amerika; *L'Aiglon-Theater* (*The Eaglet Theater*), as a director; *Valencia*, as Kellner; *Tanzgruppe* (*Dance-Group*), as one of the dancing girls.

Galante Nacht (*Gallant Night*). Director: Ernst Ludwig Matthy; written by Hans Bachwitz; Kammerspiele, Vienna; Oct. 28, 1926. Cast: Charlotte Klinder, Hans Zesch-Ballot, Olga Diora, Peter Lorre (the waiter), Theodor Grieg.

Die Mädchen auf dem Diwan (*The Girls on the Couch*). Director: Hans Peppler; written by Andrée Birabeau and Lucien Monseigneur; Kammerspiele, Vienna; Nov. 4, 1926. Cast: Hans Zesch-Ballot, Hans Peppler, Friedl Haerlin, Trude Brionne, Peter Lorre (the commissar), Max Wittmann.

Marlborough zieht in den Krieg (*Marlborough Goes to War*). Director: Franz Wenzler; written by Marcell Achard; Kammerspiele, Vienna; Nov. 10, 1926. Cast: Hans Peppler, Heinz Leo Fischer, Hans Zesch-Ballot, Paul Verhoeven, Max Wittmann, Peter Lorre (Lafleur).

Das Haus in Altona (*The House in Altona*). Director: Ernst Ludwig Matthy; written by Imre Fazekas; Kammerspiele, Vienna; Jan. 31, 1927. Cast: Margarete Hopf, Hans Peppler, Hanne Dorian, Theodor Grieg, Peter Lorre (Ratte, a piano-player), Therese Bellau, Eddie Peppler, Olga Diora, Paul Verhoeven.

Amor in Nikolsburg (*Cupid in Nickolsburg*). Director: Sigi Hofer; written by Armin Friedmann and Hans Kottow; Kammerspiele, Vienna; Feb. 17, 1927. Cast: Sigi Hofer, Lili Fröhlich, Hanne Dorian, Hans Moser, Paul Verhoeven, Peter Lorre (Max Schönau, an employee with Wellisch).

Venus im Völkersbund (*Venus in the League of Nations*). Director: Franz Wenzler; written by Gegenwart von Rolf Lauckner; Kammerspiele, Vienna; Feb. 25, 1927. Cast: Max Wittmann, Margarete Hopf, Eva Fiebig, Theodor Grieg, Paul Verhoeven, Hans Peppler, Therese Bellau, Olga Diora, Peter Lorre (Cesar Vauscher, a municipal civil servant).

Die Stunde des Absterbens (*The Hour of Dying Off*). Director: Herbert Waniek; written by Franz Theodor Csokor; Theater in the Josefstadt, Vienna; Feb. 27, 1927. Cast: Carl Goetz, Paula Janower, Aurel Nowotny, Grete Witzmann, Lina Woiwode, Peter Lorre (the son of the Hauptmanns), Frau Wurm, Herbert Dirmoser, Herr Hilbert, Wilhelm Voelcker.

Nr. 17. Director: Robert Wiene; written by Jefferson Farjeon; Kammerspiele, Vienna; March 25, 1927. Cast: Hans Moser, Hans Zesch-Ballot, Heinz Leo Fischer, Peter Lorre (Smith, a man with a humpback), Max Wittmann, Olga Diora, Theodor Grieg, Eva Fiebig, Paul Verhoeven.

Ein Abend der Überraschungen (*An Evening of Surprises*). Director: Rudolf Beer; written by Max Brody; Theater in the Josefstadt, Vienna; April 9, 1927. Cast: Gisela Werbezirk, Karl Ehmann, Egon Friedell, Victor Kutschera, Peter Lorre, Fritz Strehlen, Hans Ziegler, Alma Seidler, Lily Darvas, Hans Thimig, Hansi Niese. In this revue, Lorre appeared in the sketch "Die Ohrfeige" ("Box on the Ear").

Alles verkehrt! (*Everything Upside Down!*). Director: Leo Strassberg; written by Wilhelm Sterk and Fritz Liebstoeckl; Kammerspiele, Vienna; April 20, 1927. Cast: Heinz Leo Fischer, Hans Peppler, Peter Lorre, Therese Bellau, Hans Lackner, Sigi Hofer, Paul Verhoeven, Max Wittmann, Olga Diora, Eva Fiebig, Eddie Peppler, Hanne Dorian, Margarete Hopf. In this revue, Lorre appeared in the following sketches: *Generalprobe* (*Dress Rehearsal*), as the librettist; *Jugendliche haben Zutritt* (*Young People Allowed Admission*), as Max; *Endlich ein bisschen Geist* (*Finally a Little Wit*), as a spirit voice; *Fussballmatch* (*Soccer Match*), as a referee; *Weltgeschichte* (*World History*), as Ivan Bolschevikow; *Das Klavier* (*The Piano*), as an unnamed character.

Lissy, die Kokotte (*Lissy, the Coquette*). Director: Erika Glaessner; written by Erika Glaessner; Kammerspiele, Vienna; April 28, 1927. Cast: Erika Glaessner, Heinz Leo Fischer, Paul Verhoeven, Hanne Dorian, Max Wittmann, Olga Diora, Peter Lorre (sheriff).

Die Nackten kleiden (*To Dress the Naked Ones*). Director: Ernst Ludwig Matthy; written by Luigi Pirandello; Kammerspiele, Vienna; June 4, 1927. Cast: Maria Orska, Heinz Leo Fischer, Robert Valberg, Jakob Feldhammer, Peter Lorre (Alfredo Cantavalle, journalist), Therese Bellau.

Sie darf keinen Sohn haben: Mademoiselle Flûte (*She Shouldn't Have a Son: Miss Flûte*). Director: Robert Blum; written by Louis Verneuil; Kammerspiele, Vienna; Aug. 16, 1927. Cast: Poldi Müller, Hans Lackner, Käthe Franck-Witt, Hertha Pauli, Peter Lorre (Mignottet, the brother of the court president), Therese Bellau.

Bitte, wer war zuerst da? (*Please, Who Was Here First?*). Director: Ernst Ludwig Matthy; written by Yvês Mirande and Monézy-Éon; German by Julius Elias; Kammerspiele, Vienna; Sept. 3, 1927. Cast: Theodor Grieg, Ilde Overhoff, Willy Hendrichs, Peter Lorre (Renard de Leuclume), Grete Wagner, Harald Paulsen, Käthe Franck-Witt, Martin Berliner.

Wenn Man zu Dritt . . . (*If You Go as a Trio . . .*). Director: Max Brod; written by Pierre and Serge Veber; Kammerspiele, Vienna; Sept. 16, 1927. Cast: Harald Paulsen, Eugen Günther, Max Brod, Marlene Dietrich, Clara Karry, Käthe Franck-Witt, Peter Lorre (Felix Kellner).

Broadway. Director: Franz Wenzler; written by George Dunning and Philip Abbott; Kammerspiele, Vienna; Sept. 20, Dec. 6, 1927; Jan. 4, 1928. Cast: Arthur Peiser, Harald Paulsen, Emmy Schleinitz, Peter Lorre (Joe, the waiter), Marlene Dietrich, Friedl Haerlin, Theodor Grieg.

Die Kleine vom Varieté (*The Little One from the Varieté*). Director: Theodor Grieg; written by Alfred Möller; Kammerpiele, Vienna; Dec. 4, 1927. Cast: Camillo Triembacher, Kitty Rösler, Wilhelm Voelcker, Theodor Grieg, Peter Lorre (Paul Semmelmann, hairdresser).

Pst! Madame Republik. Written by Fritz Löhner-Beda and Florian; Kammerspiele, Vienna; Dec. 23, 1927. Cast: Gisela Werbezirk, Elsie Altman, Willi Forst, Theodor Grieg, Peter Lorre, Fritz Heller, Hertha Hansen. In this revue, Lorre appeared in the following sketches: *Schule der Zukunft* (*School of the Future*), as the teacher; *Das Phantom der Oper* (*Phantom of the Opera*), as the flutist; *Das Fenster des Kaisers* (*The Window of the Emperor*), as Director Neger; *Girl-Dämmerung* (*Twilight of the Girl*), as the director; *Protest!* as someone who takes complaints; *Koalition!* (*Coalition!*), as a Socialist.

Maya. Director: Franz Wenzler; written by Simon Gantillon; German by Robert Blum; Kammerspiele, Vienna; Jan. 1, 1928. Cast: Theodor Grieg, Annemarie Seidel, Trude Brionne, Grete Keller, Otto Hartmann, Therese Bellau, Theodor Grieg, Peter Lorre (a young steward), Oskar Beregi.

Schloss Wetterstein (*Castle Wetterstein*). Director: Franz Wenzler; written by Frank Wedekind; Kammerspiele, Vienna; Feb. 7, 1928. Cast: Maria Orska, Theodor Grieg, Else Schilling, Franz Kammauf, Walter Doerry, Peter Lorre (Schigabek).

Die Schwester (*The Sister*). Director: Franz Wenzler; written by Hans Kaltneker; Kammerspiele, Vienna; Feb. 14, 1928. Cast: Maria Orska, Friedl Haerlin, Edwin Jürgensen, Willy Hendrichs, Theodor Grieg, Walter Doerry, Peter Lorre (2 roles: the sexual researcher and a street-ghost).

König der Diebe (*King of Thieves*). Director: Franz Wenzler; written by Jean Guitton; Kammerspiele, Vienna; March 10, 1928. Cast: Hans Moser, Theodor Grieg, Oskar Hugelmann, Gusta Karma, Käthe Franck-Witt, Peter Lorre (2 roles: Levy and the gentleman in the black frock coat), Wilhelm Voelcker, Fritz Heller.

Der Abenteurer von dem Tor (*The Adventurer at the Gate*). Director: Ernst Ludwig Matthy; written by Milan Begović; from the Croatian by Peter vom Preradović; Kammerspiele, Vienna; April 24, 1928. Cast: Friedl Haerlin, Käthe Franck-Witt, Julius Haller, Willy Hendrichs, Hans Spallart, Trude Brionne, Peter Lorre (the well-bred young man), Theodor Grieg.

Schnucki. Director: Adolf Glinger; written by Adolf Glinger and Otto Taussig; Kammerspiele, Vienna; April 27, 1928. Cast: Hans Moser, Anny Evera, Theodor Grieg, Hans Spallart, Grete Keller, Peter Lorre (Dr. Katz, lawyer), Fritz Heller.

Der Brief (*The Letter*). Director: Franz Wenzler; written by W. Somerset Maugham; Kammerspiele, Vienna; May 16, 1928. Cast: Tilla Durieux, Theodor Grieg, Edwin Jürgensen, Willy Hendrichs, Peter Lorre (Ong Chi Seng), Wilhelm Voelcker, Hans Spallart.

Lenin. Director: Hans Abrell; written by Ernst Fischer; Carltheater, Vienna; Sept. 26, 1928. Cast: Eduard Rothauser, Hans Schultze-Wendel, Arthur Fischer-Streitmann, Peter Lorre (Kamenew, one of the Soviet commissars), Paul Camill Tyndall, Max Wittmann, Eduard Spiess, Eddie Peppler.

Scherz, Satire, Ironie und tiefere Bedeutung (*Comedy, Satire, Irony, and Deeper Meaning*). Director: Carl Behr; written by Christian Dietrich Grabbe; Carltheater, Vienna; Oct. 26, 1928. Cast: Eduard Rothauser, Hertha Pauli, Josef Schaper, Hans Schulze-Wendel, Max Wittmann, Franz Berisch, Peter Lorre (the village schoolmaster), Eddie Peppler, Arthur Fischer-Streitmann.

Pioniere in Ingolstadt (*Engineers in Ingolstadt*). Director: Jacob Geis; written by Marieluise Fleisser; Theater am Schiffbauerdamm, Berlin; March 30, 1929. Cast: Albert Hoerrmann, Marcel Mermino, Henrich Mathies, Heinrich Gretler, Franz Weilhammer, Peter Lorre (Fabian), Ludwig Stössel, Hilde Körber, Lotte Lenja, Leo Reuss, Fritz Ritter, Kurt Gerron.

Happy End. Directors: Erich Engel and Bertolt Brecht; written by Elisabeth Hauptmann; Theater am Schiffbauerdamm, Berlin; Aug. 31, 1929. Cast: Carola Neher, Oskar Homolka, Helene Weigel, Peter Lorre (Dr. Nakamura, called the "Governor"), Kurt Gerron, Theo Lingen, Albert Hoerrmann, Karlheinz Carell, Paul Günther, Marianne Oswald, Karl Huszar-Puffy, Erna Schöller.

Dantons Tod (*Danton's Death*). Director: Karl Heinz Martin; written by Georg Büchner; Volksbühne, Theater am Bülowplatz, Berlin; Aug. 31, 1929. Cast: Hans Rehmann, Peter Lorre (Saint-Just), Walter Franck, Ernst Karchow, Hans Peppler, Helene Sieburg, Lotte Lenja.

Frühlings Erwachen (*Spring's Awakening*). Director: Karl Heinz Martin; written by Frank Wedekind; Volksbühne, Theater am Bülowplatz, Berlin; Oct. 14, 1929. Cast: Helene Eisenstaedt, Helene Sieburg, Hans Peppler, Grete Bäck, Carl Balhaus, Josef Almas, Peter Lorre (Moritz Stiefel), Gerda Schaefer, Ellen Schwanneke, Lotte Lenja, Ernst Ginsberg.

Die Unüberwindlichen (*The Unconquerable*). Director: Heinz Dietrich Kenter; written by Karl Kraus; Volksbühne, Theater am Bülowplatz, Berlin; Oct. 20, 1929. Cast: Peter Lorre (Barkassy, publisher of *The Whistle*), Hans Peppler, Leonard Steckel, Josef Almas, Kurt Gerron, Cäcilie Lvovsky, Heinrich Gretler, Ernst Ginsberg, Armin Schweizer.

Der Kandidat (*The Candidate*). Director: Hans Hinrich; written by Carl Sternheim; from the play by Gustave Flaubert; Deutsches Theater, Kammerspiele, Berlin; Jan. 27, 1930. Cast: Otto Wallburg, Maria Fein, Toni van Eyck, Peter Lorre (Bach, editor of *The People's Voice*), Cäcilie Lvovsky, Paul Hörbiger, Willi Forst, Victor de Kowa, Hans Deppe.

Voruntersuchung (*Preliminary Investigation*). Director: Hans Hinrich; written by Max Alsberg and Otto Ernst Hesse; Renaissance Theater, Berlin; Oct. 14, 1930. Cast: Max Paulsen, Mathias Wiemann, Ludwig Stössel, Annemarie Steinsieck, Hans Brausewetter, Karin Evans, Peter Lorre (Bruno Klatte, reciter), Sylvia von Rodenberg, Erwin Faber, Julius Falkenstein, Trude Brionne.

Die Quadratur des Kreises (*Squaring the Circle*). Director: Francesco von Mendelssohn; written by Valentin Katayev; Theater am Schiffbauerdamm, Berlin; Dec. 4, 1930. Cast: Heinz Rühmann, Peter Lorre (Kosomol Wasja), Lotte Lenja, Hilde Körber, Theo Lingen.

Mann ist Mann (Man Equals Man). Director: Bertolt Brecht; written by Bertolt Brecht; Staatstheater, Berlin; Feb. 6, 1931. Cast: Peter Lorre (Galy Gay, an Irish packer), Helene Weigel, Theo Lingen, Wolfgang Heinz, Alexander Granach, Leo Reuss, Paul Bildt.

Der Dompteur (*The Lion Tamer*). Director: Günther Haenel; written by Alfred Savoir; Theater am Schiffbauerdamm, Berlin; March 6, 1931. Cast: Fritz Kampers, Carola Neher, Gustaf Gründgens, Peter Lorre (Pipi the Clown), Theo Lingen, Karlheinz Carell.

Nebeneinander (*Side by Side*). Director: Karl Heinz Martin; written by Georg Kaiser; Volksbühne am Bülowplatz, Berlin; Sept. 16, 1931. Cast: Peter Lorre (the Pawnbroker), Ernst Busch, Luise Ullrich, Inge Konradi, Ernst Karchow, Josef Dahmen, Lotte Lievan.

Geschichten aus dem Wiener Wald (*Tales from the Vienna Woods*). Director: Heinz Hilpert; written by Ödön von Horváth; Deutsches Theater, Berlin; Nov. 2, 1931. Cast: Lina Woiwode, Peter Lorre (Alfred), Frida Richard, Willy Trenk-Trebitsch, Lucie Höflich, Heinrich Heilinger, Josef Danegger, Paul Hörbiger, Carola Neher, Hans Moser, Paul Dahlke, Cäcilie Lvovsky, Grete Jacobsen, Karl Huszar-Puffy, Hermann Wlach, Elisabeth Neumann.

Die Nemo Bank. Director: Louis Verneuil; written by Louis Verneuil; German translation by Alfred Polgar; Komödienhaus, Berlin; Dec. 23, 1931. Cast: Max Pallenberg, Edith Edwards, Peter Lorre (a crooked teller), Herbert Hübner, Else Bassermann, Hans Deppe, Herman Wlach, Ferdinand von Alten, Fritz Alberti, Carl Jönson, Hans Schirmeisen, Rudolf Amendt, Erhart Stettner, Walter Schramm-Dunckner, Wolfgang Frees, Erich Walter, Friedrich Ettel.

Golgotha. Director: Aurel Nowotny; written by B.D. Ludwig; Zirkus-Renz, Vienna; April 16, 1933. Cast: Hans Schweikart, Ebba Johannsen, Peter Lorre (Judas), Dagny Servaes, Margarete Schell-Nöe, Nico Habel.

Bertolt Brecht Evening. Director: Erwin Piscator; Studio Theater of the New School for Social Research, New York City; March 6, 1943. Guests: Peter Lorre, Lotte Lenya, Wieland Herzfelde, Elisabeth Neumann, Theo Goetz, Ludwig Roth, Ernst Roberts, Elisabeth Bergner, and others. Lorre read six poems from *Deutschen Satiren* (*German Satires*); four poems from *Svendborger Gedichte* (*Svendborg Poems*), including "Schwierigkeit des Regierens" ("Difficulties of Governing"), "Über die Bezeichnung Emigranten" ("On the Designation 'Emigrants'"), "Legende von der Entstehung des Buches Taoteking auf dem Weg des Laotse in die Emigration" ("Legend of the Origin of the Book Taoteking on Lao-tse's Journey into Emigration"), and "An die Nachgeborenen" ("To Posterity"); and "An die deutschen Soldaten im Osten" ("To the German Soldier in the East").

Alfred Döblin's 65th birthday celebration. El Pablo Rey Playhouse, Santa Monica, CA; Aug. 14, 1943. Guests: Berthold Viertel, Heinrich Mann, Fritz Kortner, Peter Lorre, Alexander Granach, Ludwig Hardt, Eduard Steuermann, Ernst Toch. Lorre recited from Döblin's works.

The Man with the Head of Glass. Written by Frank Wilson. Lorre toured the following movie theaters, all in 1944: The Earle, Philadelphia, PA, Aug. 18; The Palace, Cleveland, OH, Aug. 25; Hamid's Pier, Atlantic City, NJ, Sept. 2; The RKO, Boston, Sept. 7; The State, Hartford, CT, Sept. 22; The Palace, Columbus, OH, Sept. 26; The Oriental, Chicago, Sept. 29; St. Charles, New Orleans, Oct. 12; The National, Louisville, KY, Oct. 20. Cast: Peter Lorre.

The Man with the Head of Glass. Written by Frank Wilson; 3 additional engagements, all in 1945: The Strand, New York City, March 2; Golden Gate Theater, San Francisco, May 16; The Adams, Newark, NJ, Oct. 10. Cast: Peter Lorre.

The Tell-Tale Heart. Adapted by Frank Wilson from the story by Edgar Allan Poe; The Roxy, New York City; Feb. 11, 1947. Cast: Peter Lorre.

Nacht der Prominenten (*Night of Prominent People*), Kabarett der Komiker . Town Hall, New York City; March 1, 1947. Cast: Peter Lorre, Oscar Karlweis, Señor Wences, The Barry Sisters, Hermann Leopoldi, Kurt Robitschek, Calgary Brothers, Kitty Mattern, John Kolischer, Cardini, Walter Joseph, and others. In this revue, Lorre appeared in the sketch *Der letzte Österreicher* (*The Last Austrian*), written by Kurt Robitschek.

The Tell-Tale Heart. Adapted by Frank Wilson from the story by Edgar Allan Poe. Lorre toured the following movie theaters: The Chicago, Chicago, Nov. 5, 1948; The Albee, Cincinnati, OH, Dec. 23, 1948; The Palace, Columbus, OH, Jan. 10, 1949; The Olympia, Miami, FL, Jan. 19, 1949; The Hippodrome, Baltimore, March 3, 1949; The Earle, Philadelphia, April 22, 1949. Cast: Peter Lorre.

The Tell-Tale Heart. Adapted by Frank Wilson from the story by Edgar Allan Poe; The Paramount, New York City; May 11, 1949. Cast: Peter Lorre.

The Tell-Tale Heart, The Bells. Adapted by Frank Wilson from the stories by Edgar Allan Poe. Lorre toured the following movie theaters in England, all in 1949: The Grand, Derby, July 4; The Empire, Wood Green, July 18; The Hippodrome, Manchester, July 25; The Empire, Chiswick, Aug. 1; The Palace, Leicester, Aug. 8; The Empire, Hackney, Aug. 15; The Hippodrome, Bristol, Aug. 29; The Empire, Chatham, Sept. 5; The Empire, Shepherd's Bush, Sept. 12. Cast: Peter Lorre.

The Tell-Tale Heart. Adapted by Frank Wilson from the story by Edgar Allan Poe; Amerika-Haus, Hamburg; Aug. 10, 1950. Cast: Peter Lorre.

The Tell-Tale Heart. Adapted by Frank Wilson from the story by Edgar Allan Poe. Lorre toured the following venues, all in 1952: The Armory, High Point, NC, May 22; The Armory, Greensboro, NC, May 23; Walter Williams High School, Burlington, NC, May 23; City Armory, Durham, NC, May 24; Danceland, Greensboro, NC, May 24. Cast: Peter Lorre.

A Night at Madame Tussaud's: A Shocker in the Grand Guignol Manner. Directed by Peter Lorre and Edwin Justus Mayer; written by Edwin Justus Mayer. Lorre, Hopkins, Clanton, Frayne, and Watson toured the following theaters, all in 1952: Summer Theatre, Norwich, CT, Aug. 18; Boston Summer Theater, New England Mutual Hall, Boston, Aug. 25; Grist Mill Playhouse, Andover, NJ, Sept. 1; Kenley Theater, Lakewood Park, Barnesville, PA, Sept. 8; Kenley Players, York, PA, Sept. 15. Cast: Miriam Hopkins, Peter Lorre (Brutus), Ralph Clanton, Viola Frayne, Rudulph Justice Watson; Additional Cast: Norwich—Barry Alan Grael, Joseph Warren, Geoffrey Brown, A. Serli Peary, Sidney Antebi, Harriet Tecot; Boston—Alan Tower, Paul Clarke, Joe Graham, Arthur Wenzel, George Birt, Matt Connolly Jr., Helen Dayton; Barnesville—Leslie Cutler, John Himes, Russ Anderson, Ted Atwood, Francis McMenamin, Janet Stanaland.

FILM

Die verschwundene Frau (*The Missing Wife*) (Österreichisches Filmindustrie, 1929). Director: Karl Leiter; screenplay: Franz Pollak, based on the novel by Max Dürr; cinematography: Eduard von Borsody; 2,500 meters. Cast: Harry Halm, Iris Arlan, Mary Kid, Peter C. Leska, Richard Waldemar, Reinhold Häussermann, Peter Lorre (dental patient).

M (Nero-Films, 1931). Director: Fritz Lang; producer: Seymour Nebenzal; screenplay: Thea von Harbou, based on an article by Egon Jacobson; cinematography: Fritz Arno Wagner; murderer's theme by Edward Grieg: extract from *Peer Gynt*; 110 min. Cast: Gerhard Bienert, Rudolf Blümmer, Fritz Gnass, Gustaf Gründgens, Peter Lorre (Hans Beckert), Fritz Odemar, Karl Platen, Ernst Stahl-Nachbaur, Georg John, Paul Kemp, Inge Landgut, Theo Lingen, Theodor Loos, Franz Stein, Hertha von Walther, Otto Wernicke, Rosa Valetti, Ellen Widmann.

Bomben auf Monte Carlo (Bombs on Monte Carlo) (UFA, 1931). Director: Hanns Schwarz; executive producer: Erich Pommer; producer: Max Pfeiffer; screenplay: Hans Müller and Franz Schultz; based on the novel by Fritz Reck-Malleczewen and a story by Jeno Heltai; cinematography: Günther Rittau; music: Werner R. Heymann; lyrics: Robert Gilbert; 108 min. Cast: Hans Albers, Anna Sten, Heinz Rühmann, Ida Wüft, Rachel Devirys, Kurt Gerron, Karl Etlinger, Peter Lorre (Pawlitchek), Otto Wallburg, Charles Kuhlmann, Bruno Ziener, Lydia Potechina, Gertrud Wolle, Fritz Behmer, Paul Henkels, Comedian Harmonifts, Kapelle Carlo Minari.

Die Koffer des Herrn O.F. (The Luggage of Mr. O.F.) (Tonbild-Syndikat AG, 1931). Director: Alexis Granowsky; producers: Hans Conradi and Mark Asarow; screenplay: Leo Lania and Alexis Granowsky; based on an idea by Hans Homberg; cinematography: Reimer Kuntze and Heinrich Balasch; music: Karol Bethaus; songs: Erich Kästner; 80 min. Cast: Alfred Abel, Harald Paulsen, Peter Lorre (Stix, the editor), Ludwig Stössel, G.W. von Nello, Margo Lion, Hedy Kiesler, Ilse Korsek, Liska March.

Fünf von der Jazzband (The Jazz Band Five) (UFA, 1932). Director: Erich Engel; screenplay: Hermann Kosterlitz and Curt Alexander; cinematography: Reimer Kuntze; 88 min. Cast: Jenny Jugo, Rolf von Goth, Fritz Klippel, Karl Stepanck, Günther Vogdt, Theo Shall, Werner Pledath, Arthur Mainzer, Heinrich Gretler, Walter Steinbeck, E. Helmke-Dassel, Fritz Melchoir, Vera Spohr, Frida, Robert Klein-Lörk, Peter Lorre (car thief).

Schuss im Morgengrauen (A Shot at Dawn) (UFA, 1932). Director: Alfred Zeisler; executive producer: Erich Pommer; producer: Alfred Zeisler; screenplay: Rudolf Katscher, Otto and Egon Eis; based on the play *Die Frau und Der Smaragd (The Woman and the Emerald)* by Harry Jenkins; cinematography: Konstantin Tschet and Werner Bohne; 73 min. Cast: Heinz Salfner, Ery Bos, Karl Ludwig Diehl, Theodor Loos, Fritz Odemar, Peter Lorre (Klotz), Gerhard Tandar, Kurt Vespermann, Ernst Behmer.

F.P.1 antwortet nicht (F.P.1 Doesn't Answer) (UFA, 1932). Director: Karl Hartl; executive producer: Eric Pommer; producer: Eberhard Klagemann; screenplay: Walter Reisch; based on the novel by Kurt Siodmak; cinematography: Günther Rittau, Konstantin Tschet, and Otto Baecker; music: Allan Gray; lyrics: Walter Reisch; 114 min. Cast: Hans Albers, Sybille Schmitz, Paul Hartmann, Peter Lorre (Johnny), Hermann Speelmans, Paul Westermeier, Arthur Peiser, Gustav Püttjer, Georg August Koch, Hans Schneider, Werner Schott, Erik Ode, Philipp Manning, Georg John, Rudolf Platte, Friedrich Gnas.

Der weisse Dämon (The White Demon) (UFA, 1932). Director: Kurt Gerron; executive producer: Erich Pommer; producer: Bruno Duday; screenplay: Lothar Mayring and Friedrich Zeckendorf; cinematography: Carl Hoffmann; 106 min. Cast: Hans Albers, Lucie Höflich, Gerda Maurus, Trude von Molo, Alfred Abel, Hans Joachim Schaufuss, Raoul Aslan, Peter Lorre (hunchback), Hubert von Meyerinck.

Stupéfiants (Narcotics) (UFA, 1932). Directors: Kurt Gerron and Roger Le Bon; executive producer: Erich Pommer; producer: Bruno Duday; screenplay: Lothar Mayring and Fritz Zeckendorf; French dialogue: Georges Neveux; cinematography: Carl Hoffmann. Cast: Jean Worms, Jean Mercanton, Jean Murat, Danièle Parola, Jeanne Marie-Laurent, Monique Roland, Raoul Aslan, Peter Lorre (hunchback), Roger Karl, Gaston Mauger, Lucien Callamand, Henry Bonvalet. Note: This is the French version of *Der weisse Dämon*.

Was Frauen träumen (What Women Dream) (Super Film GmbH, 1933). Director: Géza von Bolvary; producer: Julius Haimann; screenplay: Franz Schulz and Billie Wilder; cinematography: Willy Goldberger; music: Robert Stolz; lyrics: Robert Gilbert; 81 min. Cast: Nora Gregor, Gustav Fröhlich, Kurt Horwitz, Otto Wallburg, Peter Lorre (Otto Füssli).

Unsichtbare Gegner (*Invisible Opponent*) (Pan-Film, 1933). Director: Rudolf Katscher; producer: Sam Spiegel; screenplay: Lothar Mayring, Heinrich Oberländer, and Richard Steinbicker; based on an idea by Ludwig von Wohl; cinematography: Eugen Schüfftan and Georg Bruckbauer; 87 min. Cast: Gerda Maurus, Paul Hartmann, Oskar Homolka, Peter Lorre (Henry Pless), Paul Kemp, Raoul Aslan, Leonard Steckel, H. Kyser, Eva Schmidt-Kaiser.

Les requins du Pétrole (*The Oil Sharks*) (Pan-Film, 1933). Director: Henri Ducoin; producer: Sam Spiegel; screenplay: Lothar Mayring, Heinrich Oberländer, Richard Steinbicker; French dialogue: Fred Ellis; based on an idea by Ludwig von Wohl; cinematography: Eugen Schüfftan and Georg Bruckbauer; 87 min. Cast: Arlette Marchal, Vivian Grey, Gabriel Gabrio, Jean Galland, Raymond Cordy, Robert Ozanne, Raoul Aslan, Peter Lorre (Pless). Note: This is the French version of *Unsichtbare Gegner.*

Du haut en bas (*From Top to Bottom*) (Tobis-Klangfilm, 1933). Director: G.W. Pabst; producer: Georges Root; screenplay: Anna Gneyner; based on a play by Ladislaus Bus Fekete; cinematography: Eugen Schuefftan; song "Chaque semaine a sept jours" ("Each Week Has Seven Days") by Herbert Rappoport; 80 min. Cast: Jean Gabin, Jeannine Crispin, Michel Simon, Mauricet, Wladimir Sokoloff, Leon Morton, Milly Mathis, Margo Lion, Catherine Hessling, Peter Lorre (beggar), Pauline Carton.

The Man Who Knew Too Much (Gaumont-British, 1934). Director: Alfred Hitchcock; producer: Michael Balcon; associate producer: Ivor Montagu; screenplay: Edwin Greenwood and A.R. Rawlinson; written by Charles Bennett and D.B. Wyndham Lewis; additional dialogue: Emlyn Williams; cinematography: Curt Courant; 75 min. Cast: Leslie Banks, Edna Best, Peter Lorre (Abbott), Frank Vosper, Hugh Wakefield, Nova Pilbeam, Pierre Fresnay, Cicely Oates, D.A. Clarke-Smith, George Curzon.

Mad Love (MGM, 1935). Director: Karl Freund; producer: John W. Considine Jr.; screenplay: P.J. Wolfson and John L. Balderston; based on the novel *Les Mains d'Orlac* (*The Hands of Orlac*) by Maurice Renard; translated and adapted by Florence Crewe-Jones; adapted by Guy Endore; cinematography: Chester Lyons and Gregg Toland; 67 min. Cast: Peter Lorre (Dr. Gogol), Frances Drake, Colin Clive, Ted Healy, Sarah Haden, Edward Brophy, Henry Kolker, Keye Luke, May Beatty.

Crime and Punishment (Columbia, 1935). Director: Josef von Sternberg; producer: B.P. Schulberg; screenplay: S.K. Lauren and Joseph Anthony; based on the novel by Fyodor Dostoyevsky; cinematography: Lucien Ballard; 88 min. Cast: Edward Arnold, Peter Lorre (Roderick Raskolnikov), Marian Marsh, Tala Birell, Elisabeth Risdon, Robert Allen, Douglass Dumbrille, Gene Lockhart, Charles Waldron, Thurston Hall, Johnny Arthur, Mrs. Patrick Campbell.

Secret Agent (Gaumont-British, 1936). Director: Alfred Hitchcock; producer: Ivor Montagu; screenplay: Charles Bennett; additional dialogue: Jesse Laskey Jr.; based on the play by Campbell Dixon and on the novel *Ashenden* by W. Somerset Maugham; cinematography: Bernard Knowles; 75 min. Cast: John Gielgud, Peter Lorre (the General), Madeleine Carroll, Robert Young, Percy Marmont, Florence Kahn, Charles Carson, Lilli Palmer.

Crack-Up (20th Century–Fox, 1937). Director: Malcolm St. Clair; producer: Samuel G. Engel; screenplay: Charles Kenyon and Sam Mintz; original story: John Goodrich; cinematography: Barney McGill; song "Top Gallants" by Sidney Clare and Harry Akst; 70 min. Cast: Peter Lorre (Colonel Gimpy / Baron Rudolf Maximilian Taggart), Brian Donlevy, Helen Wood, Ralph Morgan, Thomas Beck, Kay Linaker, Lester Matthews, Earl Foxe, J. Carroll Naish, Gloria Roy, Oscar Apfel, Paul Stanton, Howard C. Hickman.

Nancy Steele Is Missing (20th Century–Fox, 1937). Director: George Marshall; producer: Darryl F. Zanuck; screenplay: Hal Long and Gene Fowler; based on a story by Charles Frances Coe; cinematography: Barney McGill; 86 min. Cast: Victor McLaglen, Walter Connolly, Peter Lorre (Professor Sturm), June Lang, Robert Kent, Shirley Deane, John Carradine, Jane Darwell, Frank Conroy, Granville Bates, George Taylor, Kane Richmond, Margaret Fielding, De Witt Jennings, George Chandler, George Humbert, Robert Murphy, Ed Deering, Frederic Burton, Stanley Andrews, Guy Usher.

Think Fast, Mr. Moto (20th Century–Fox, 1937). Director: Norman Foster; producer: Sol M. Wurtzel; screenplay: Howard Ellis Smith and Norman Foster; based on the story "That Girl and Mr. Moto" by John P. Marquand; cinematography: Harry Jackson; song "The Shy Violet" by Sidney Clare and Harry Akst; 66 min. Cast: Peter Lorre (Kentaro Moto), Virginia Field, Thomas Beck, Sig Rumann, Murray Kinnell, John Rogers, Lotus Long, George Cooper, J. Carroll Naish, Frederik Vogeding.

Lancer Spy (20th Century–Fox, 1937). Director: Gregory Ratoff; producer: Darryl F. Zanuck; screenplay: Philip Dunne; based on the novel by Marthe McKenna; cinematography: Barney McGill; 78 min. Cast: Dolores Del Rio, George Sanders, Peter Lorre (Major Sigfried Gruning), Joseph Schildkraut, Virginia Field, Sig Rumann, Maurice Moscovich, Lionel Atwill, Luther Adler, Fritz Feld, Holmes Herbert, Lester Matthews, Carlos J. de Valdez, Gregory Gaye, Joan Carol, Claude King, Kenneth Hunter, Frank Reicher, Leonard Mudie, Lynn Bari.

Thank You, Mr. Moto (20th Century–Fox, 1937). Director: Norman Foster; producer: Sol M. Wurtzel; screenplay: Willis Cooper and Norman Foster; based on a story by John P. Marquand; cinematography: Virgil Miller; 68 min. Cast: Peter Lorre (Kentaro Moto), Thomas Beck, Pauline Frederick, Jayne Regan, Sidney Blackmer, Sig Rumann, John Carradine, William von Brincken, Nedda Harrigan, Philip Ahn, John Bleifer.

Mr. Moto's Gamble (20th Century–Fox, 1938). Director: James Tinling; producer: Sol M. Wurtzel; screenplay: Charles Belden and Jerry Cady; based on the character "Mr. Moto" created by John P. Marquand; cinematography: Lucien Andriot; 71 min. Cast: Peter Lorre (Kentaro Moto), Keye Luke, Dick Baldwin, Lynn Bari, Douglas Fowley, Jayne Regan, Harold Huber, Maxie Rosenbloom, John Hamilton, George E. Stone, Bernard Nedell, Charles Williams, Ward Bond, Cliff Clark, Edward Marr, Lon Chaney Jr., Russ Clark, Pierre Watkins, Charles D. Brown, Paul Fox.

Mr. Moto Takes a Chance (20th Century–Fox, 1938). Director: Norman Foster; producer: Sol M. Wurtzel; screenplay: Lou Breslow and John Patrick; based on the original story "Look Out, Mr. Moto" by Willis Cooper and Norman Foster; based on the character "Mr. Moto" created by John P. Marquand; cinematography: Virgil Miller; 57 min. Cast: Peter Lorre (Kentaro Moto), Rochelle Hudson, Robert Kent, J. Edward Bromberg, Chick Chandler, George Regas, Fredrik Vogeding.

I'll Give a Million (20th Century–Fox, 1938). Director: Walter Lang; producer: Darryl

F. Zanuck; associate producer: Kenneth Macgowan; screenplay: Boris Ingster and Milton Sperling; based on a story by Cesare Zavattini and Giaci Mondaini; cinematography: Lucien Andriot; 90 min. Cast: Warner Baxter, Marjorie Weaver, Peter Lorre (Louie), Jean Hersholt, John Carradine, J. Edward Bromberg, Lynn Bari, Fritz Feld, Sig Rumann, Christian Rub, Paul Harvey, Charles Halton, Frank Reicher, Frank Dawson, Harry Hayden, Stanley Andrews, Lillian Porter, Luis Alberni, Rafaela Ottiano, Georges Renavent, Rolfe Sedan, Eddy Conrad, Egon Breecher, Frank Puglia, Michael Visavoff, Alex Novinsky, Armand Kaliz.

Mysterious Mr. Moto (20th Century–Fox, 1938). Director: Norman Foster; producer: Sol M. Wurtzel; screenplay: Philip MacDonald and Norman Foster; based on the character "Mr. Moto" created by John P. Marquand; cinematography: Virgil Miller; 65 min. Cast: Peter Lorre (Kentaro Moto), Mary Maguire, Henry Wilcoxon, Eric Rhodes, Harold Huber, Leon Ames, Forrester Harvey, Fredrik Vogeding, Lester Matthews, John Rogers, Karen Sorrell, Mitchell Lewis.

Mr. Moto's Last Warning (20th Century–Fox, 1939). Director: Norman Foster; producer: Sol M. Wurtzel; screenplay: Philip MacDonald and Norman Foster; based on the character "Mr. Moto" created by John P. Marquand; cinematography: Virgil Miller; 71 min. Cast: Peter Lorre (Kentaro Moto), Ricardo Cortez, Virginia Field, John Carradine, George Sanders, Joan Carol, Robert Coote, Margaret Irving, Leyland Hodgson, John Davidson.

Danger Island (20th Century–Fox, 1939). Director: Herbert I. Leeds; producer: Sol M. Wurtzel; screenplay: Peter Milne; based on story ideas by John Reinhardt and George Bricker; based on the novel *Murder in Trinidad* by John W. Vandercook; cinematography: Lucien Andriot; 70 min. Cast: Peter Lorre (Kentaro Moto), Jean Hersholt, Amanda Duff, Warren Hymer, Richard Lane, Leon Ames, Douglass Dumbrille, Charles D. Brown, Paul Harvey, Robert Lowery, Eddie Marr, Harry Woods.

Mr. Moto Takes a Vacation (20th Century–Fox, 1939). Director: Norman Foster; producer: Sol M. Wurtzel; screenplay: Philip MacDonald and Norman Foster; based on the character "Mr. Moto" created by John P. Marquand; cinematography: Charles Clarke; 61 min. Cast: Peter Lorre (Kentaro Moto), Joseph Schildkraut, Lionel Atwill, Virginia Field, John King, Iva Stewart, George P. Huntley Jr., Victor Varconi, John Bleifer, Honorable Wu, Morgan Wallace, Anthony Warde, Harry Strang, John Davidson.

Strange Cargo (MGM, 1940). Director: Frank Borzage; producer: Joseph L. Mankiewicz; screenplay: Lawrence Hazard; based on the novel *Not Too Narrow . . . Not Too Deep* by Richard Sale; cinematography: Robert Planck; 111 min. Cast: Joan Crawford, Clark Gable, Ian Hunter, Peter Lorre (M'sieur Cochon), Paul Lukas, Albert Dekker, J. Edward Bromberg, Eduardo Ciannelli, John Arledge, Frederick Worlock, Bernard Nedell, Victor Varconi.

I Was an Adventuress (20th Century–Fox, 1940). Director: Gregory Ratoff; producer: Darryl F. Zanuck; associate producer: Nunnally Johnson; screenplay: Karl Tunberg, Don Ettlinger, and John O'Hara; based on an original production by Gregor Rabinovitsch and the French film *J'étais une aventurière* (*I Was an Adventuress*), written by Jacques Companeez, Herbert Juttke, Hans Jacoby, and Michel Duran; cinematography: Leon Shamroy and Edward Cronjager; dances staged by George Balanchine; musical direction: David Buttolph; 80 min. Cast: Vera Zorina, Richard Greene, Erich von Stroheim, Peter Lorre (Polo), Sig Rumann, Fritz Feld.

Island of Doomed Men (Columbia, 1940). Director: Charles Barton; producer: Wallace

MacDonald; screenplay: Robert D. Andrews; original story: Robert D. Andrews; cinematography: Benjamin Kline; 68 min. Cast: Peter Lorre (Stephen Danel), Rochelle Hudson, Robert Wilcox, Don Beddoe, George E. Stone, Kenneth MacDonald, Charles Middleton, Stanley Brown, Earl Gunn.

Stranger on the Third Floor (RKO, 1940). Director: Boris Ingster; producer: Lee Marcus; screenplay: Frank Partos; story by Frank Partos; cinematography: Nicholas Musuraca; 67 min. Cast: Peter Lorre (Stranger), John McGuire, Margaret Tallichet, Charles Waldron, Elisha Cook Jr., Charles Halton, Ethel Griffies, Cliff Clark, Oscar O'Shea, Alec Craig, Otto Hoffman.

You'll Find Out (RKO, 1940). Director: David Butler; producer: David Butler; screenplay: James V. Kern; story by James V. Kern and David Butler; special material by Monte Brice, Andrew Bennison, R.T.M. Scott; cinematography: Frank Redman; music: James McHugh; lyrics: John Mercer; musical director: Roy Webb; special sound and musical effects: Sonovox; 95 min. Cast: Kay Kyser; Peter Lorre (Prof. Carl Fenninger); Boris Karloff; Bela Lugosi; Helen Parrish; Dennis O'Keefe; Alma Kruger; Joseph Eggenton; Kay Kyser's band, featuring Ginny Simms, Harry Babbitt, Ish Kabibble, Sully Mason, and "The Kollege of Musical Knowledge."

The Face behind the Mask (Columbia, 1941). Director: Robert Florey; producer: Wallace MacDonald; screenplay: Allen Vincent and Paul Jarrico; story: Arthur Levinson; based on a radio play by Thomas Edward O'Connell; cinematography: Franz Planer; 69 min. Cast: Peter Lorre (Janos Szabo), Evelyn Keyes, Don Beddoe, George E. Stone, John Tyrrell, Stanley Brown, Al Seymour, James Seay, Warren Ashe, Charles Wilson, George McKay.

Mr. District Attorney (Republic, 1941). Director: William Morgan; producer: Leonard Fields; screenplay: Karl Brown and Malcolm Stuart Boylan; based on the radio program created by Phillips H. Lord; cinematography: Reggie Lanning; 69 min. Cast: Dennis O'Keefe, Florence Rice, Peter Lorre (Mr. Hyde), Stanley Ridges, Minor Watson, Charles Arnt, Joan Blair, Charles Halton, Alan Edwards, George Watts, Sarah Edwards, Helen Brown, Ben Welden.

They Met in Bombay (MGM, 1941). Director: Clarence Brown; producer: Hunt Stromberg; screenplay: Edwin Justus Mayer, Anita Loos, and Leon Gordon; based on a story by John Kafka; cinematography: William Daniels; 92 min. Cast: Clark Gable, Rosalind Russell, Peter Lorre (Captain Chang), Jessie Ralph, Reginald Owen, Matthew Boulton, Edward Ciannelli, Luis Alberni, Rosina Galli, Jay Novello.

The Maltese Falcon (Warner Bros., 1941). Director: John Huston; producers: Hal B. Wallace (executive) and Henry Blanke (associate); screenplay: John Huston; based on the novel by Dashiell Hammett; cinematography: Arthur Edeson; 100 min. Cast: Humphrey Bogart, Mary Astor, Gladys George, Peter Lorre (Joel Cairo), Barton MacLane, Lee Patrick, Sydney Greenstreet, Ward Bond, Jerome Cowan, Elisha Cook Jr., James Burke, Murray Alper, John Hamilton.

All Through the Night (Warner Bros., 1942). Director: Vincent Sherman; producers: Hal B. Wallis (executive), Jerry Wald (associate); screenplay: Edwin Gilbert and Leonard Spigelgass; based on a story by Leonard Q. Ross and Leonard Spigelgass; cinematography: Sid Hickox; song "All Through the Night," lyrics: Johnny Mercer; music: Arthur Schwartz; 107 min. Cast: Humphrey Bogart, Conrad Veidt, Kaaren Verne, Jane Darwell,

Frank McHugh, Peter Lorre (Pepi), Judith Anderson, William Demarest, Jackie C. Gleason, Phil Silvers, Wally Ford, Barton MacLane, Edward Brophy, Martin Kosleck, Jean Ames, Ludwig Stössel, Irene Seidner, James Burke, Ben Weldon, Hans Schumm, Charles Cane, Frank Sully, Sam McDaniel.

Invisible Agent (Universal, 1942). Director: Edwin L. Marin; producer: Frank Lloyd; associate producer: George Waggner; screenplay: Curtis Siodmak; suggested by *The Invisible Man* by H.G. Wells; cinematography: Leo White; special photographic effects: John P. Fulton; 79 min. Cast: Ilona Massey, Jon Hall, Peter Lorre (Baron Ikito), Sir Cedric Hardwicke, J. Edward Bromberg, Albert Basserman, John Litel, Holmes Herbert, Keye Luke.

The Boogie Man Will Get You (Columbia, 1942). Director: Lew Landers; producer: Colbert Clark; screenplay: Edwin Blum; based on a story by Hal Fimberg and Robert B. Hunt; adaptation: Paul Gangelin; cinematography: Henry Freulich; 66 min. Cast: Boris Karloff, Peter Lorre (Dr. Lorentz), Maxie Rosenbloom, Larry Parkes, (Miss) Jeff Donnell.

Casablanca (Warner Bros., 1943). Director: Michael Curtiz; producer: Hal B. Wallis; screenplay: Philip G. and Julius J. Epstein and Howard Koch; based on the play *Everybody Comes to Rick's* by Murray Burnett and Joan Alison; cinematography: Arthur Edeson; songs: M.K. Jerome and Jack Scholl; 112 min. Cast: Humphrey Bogart, Ingrid Bergman, Paul Henreid, Claude Rains, Conrad Veidt, Sydney Greenstreet, Peter Lorre (Ugarte), S.Z. Sakall, Madeleine LeBeau, Dooley Wilson, Joy Page, John Qualen, Leonid Kinskey, Curt Bois.

Background to Danger (Warner Bros., 1943). Director: Raoul Walsh; producer: Jerry Wald; screenplay: W.R. Burnett; based on the novel by Eric Ambler; cinematography: Tony Gaudio; 80 min. Cast: George Raft, Brenda Marshall, Sydney Greenstreet, Peter Lorre (Nikolai Zaleshoff), Osa Massen, Turhan Bey, Williard Robertson, Kurt Katch.

The Constant Nymph (Warner Bros., 1943). Director: Edmund Goulding; producer: Henry Blanke; screenplay: Kathryn Scola; based on the novel by Margaret Kennedy and the play by Margaret Kennedy and Basil Dean; cinematography: Tony Gaudio; 112 min. Cast: Charles Boyer, Joan Fontaine, Alexis Smith, Charles Coburn, Brenda Marshall, Dame May Whitty, Peter Lorre (Fritz Bercovy), Joyce Reynolds, Jean Muir, Montague Love, Edward Ciannelli, Jeanine Crispin.

The Cross of Lorraine (MGM, 1943). Director: Tay Garnett; producer: Edwin Knopf; screenplay: Michael Kanin and Ring Lardner Jr.; based on a story by Lilo Damert and Robert Aisner and on the novel *A Thousand Shall Fall* by Hans Habe; cinematography: Sidney Wagner; 89 min. Cast: Jean-Pierre Aumont, Gene Kelly, Sir Cedric Hardwicke, Richard Whorf, Joseph Calleia, Peter Lorre (Sergeant Berger), Hume Cronyn, Billy Roy, Tonio Selwart, Jack Lambert, Wallace Ford, Donald Curtis, Jack Edwards Jr., Richard Ryen, Frederick Giermann.

Passage to Marseille (Warner Bros., 1944). Director: Michael Curtiz; producer: Hal B. Wallis; screenplay: Casey Robinson and Jack Moffitt; based on the novelette *Men without a Country* by Charles Nordhoff and James Norman Hall; cinematography: James Wong Howe; 110 min. Cast: Humphrey Bogart, Claude Rains, Michele Morgan, Philip Dorn, Sydney Greenstreet, Peter Lorre (Marius), George Tobias, Helmut Dantine, John Loder, Victor Francen, Vladimir Sokoloff, Edward Ciannelli, Corinna Mura.

The Mask of Dimitrios (Warner Bros., 1944). Director: Jean Negulesco; producer: Henry

Blanke; screenplay: Frank Gruber; based on the novel *A Coffin for Dimitrios* by Eric Ambler; cinematography: Arthur Edeson; 95 min. Cast: Sydney Greenstreet, Faye Emerson, Zachary Scott, Peter Lorre (Cornelius Latimer Leyden), Victor Francen, Steven Geray, Florence Bates, Edward Ciannelli, Kurt Katch, Marjorie Hoshelle, Georges Metaxa, John Abbott, Monte Blue, David Hoffman.

Arsenic and Old Lace (Warner Bros., 1944). Director: Frank Capra; producer: Frank Capra; screenplay: Philip G. and Julius J. Epstein; based on the play by Joseph Kesselring; produced for the stage by Howard Lindsay and Russel Crouse; cinematography: Sol Polito; 118 min. Cast: Cary Grant, Priscilla Lane, Raymond Massey, Jack Carson, Edward Everett Horton, Peter Lorre (Dr. Einstein), James Gleason, Josephine Hall, Jean Adair, John Alexander, Grant Mitchell, Edward McNamara, Garry Owen, John Ridgely, Vaughan Glaser, Chester Clute, Charles Lane, Edward McWade.

The Conspirators (Warner Bros., 1944). Director: Jean Negulesco; producer: Jack Chertok; screenplay: Vladimir Pozner and Leo Rosten; additional dialogue: Jack Moffitt; based on the novel by Frederic Prokosch; cinematography: Arthur Edeson; 100 min. Cast: Hedy Lamarr, Paul Henreid, Sydney Greenstreet, Peter Lorre (Jan Bernazsky), Victor Francen, Joseph Calleia, Carol Thurston, Vladimir Sokoloff, Edward Ciannelli, Steven Geray, Kurt Katch.

Hollywood Canteen (Warner Bros., 1944). Director: Delmer Daves; producer: Alex Gottlieb; original screenplay: Delmer Daves; cinematography: Bert Glennon; 125 min. Cast: Andrews Sisters, Jack Benny, Julie Bishop, Betty Brodel, Barbara Brown, Joe E. Brown, Eddie Cantor, Kitty Carlisle, Jack Carson, Dane Clark, Joan Crawford, Helmut Dantine, Bette Davis, Faye Emerson, Victor Francen, John Garfield, Mary Gordon, Sydney Greenstreet, Alan Hale, Paul Henreid, Robert Hutton, Andrea King, Joan Leslie, Peter Lorre (himself), Ida Lupino, Irene Manning, Eddie Marr, Nora Martin, Joan McCracken, Chef Milani, Dolores Moran, Dennis Morgan, Janis Paige, Eleanor Parker, William Prince, Joyce Reynolds, John Ridgely, Roy Rogers and Trigger, S.Z. Sakall, Zachary Scott, Robert Shayne, Alexis Smith, Barbara Stanwyck, Craig Stevens, Joseph Szigeti, Donald Woods, Jane Wyman, Jimmy Dorsey and Band, Carmen Cavallaro and Orchestra, Golden Gate Quartet, Rosario and Antonio, and Sons of the Pioneers.

Hotel Berlin (Warner Bros., 1945. Director: Peter Godfrey; producer: Louis F. Edelman; screenplay: Jo Pagano, Alvah Bessie; based on the novel by Vicki Baum; cinematography: Carl Guthrie; 98 min. Cast: Faye Emerson, Helmut Dantine, Raymond Massey, Andrea King, Peter Lorre (Prof. Johannes Koenig), Alan Hale, George Coulouris, Henry Daniell, Peter Whitney, Helene Thimig, Steven Geray, Kurt Kreuger.

Confidential Agent (Warner Bros., 1945). Director: Herman Shumlin; producer: Robert Buckner; screenplay: Robert Buckner; based on the novel by Graham Greene; cinematography: James Wong Howe; 115 min. Cast: Charles Boyer, Lauren Bacall, Katina Paxinou, Peter Lorre (Contreras), Victor Francen, George Coulouris, Wanda Hendrix, John Warburton, Dan Seymour, George Zucco, Miles Mander.

Three Strangers (Warner Bros., 1946). Director: Jean Negulesco; producer: Wolfgang Reinhardt; original screenplay: John Huston and Howard Koch; cinematography: Arthur Edeson; 92 min. Cast: Sydney Greenstreet, Geraldine Fitzgerald, Peter Lorre (Johnny West), Joan Lorring, Robert Shayne, Marjorie Riordon, Arthur Shields, Rosalind Ivan, John Alvin, Peter Whitney, Alan Napier, Clifford Brooke, Doris Lord, Lumsden Hare.

Black Angel (Universal Pictures, 1946). Director: Roy William Neill; producers: Roy

William Neill and Tom McKnight; screenplay: Roy Chanslor; based on the novel by Cornell Woolrich; cinematography: Paul Ivano; musical score: Frank Skinner; songs: Jack Brooks and Edgar Fairchild; 80 min. Cast: Dan Duryea, June Vincent, Peter Lorre (Mr. Marko), Broderick Crawford, Constance Dowling, Wallace Ford, Hobart Cavanaugh, Freddie Steele, John Phillips, Ben Bard, Junius Matthews, Marion Martin, Michael Brandon, St. Clair and Vilova, Robert Williams.

The Chase (United Artists, 1946). Director: Arthur D. Ripley; producer: Seymour Nebenzal; screenplay: Philip Yordan; based on the novel *The Black Path of Fear* by Cornell Woolrich; cinematography: Franz Planer; 86 min. Cast: Robert Cummings, Michele Morgan, Steve Cochran, Peter Lorre (Gino), Lloyd Corrigan, Jack Holt, Don Wilson, Alexis Minotis, Nina Koschetz, Yolanda Lacca, James Westerfield, Jimmy Ames, Shirley O'Hara.

The Verdict (Warner Bros., 1946). Director: Don Siegel; producer: William Jacobs; screenplay: Peter Milne; based on the novel *The Big Bow Mystery* by Israel Zangwill; cinematography: Ernest Haller; 86 min. Cast: Sydney Greenstreet, Peter Lorre (Victor Emmric), Joan Lorring, George Coulouris, Rosalind Ivan, Paul Cavanagh, Arthur Shields, Morton Lowry, Holmes Herbert, Art Foster, Clyde Cook.

The Beast with Five Fingers (Warner Bros., 1946). Director: Robert Florey; producer: William Jacobs; screenplay: Curt Siodmak; based on the short story by William Fryer Harvey; cinematography: Wesley Anderson; special effects: William McGann (director), H. Koenekamp; 90 min. Cast: Robert Alda, Andrea King, Peter Lorre (Hilary Cummins), Victor Francen, J. Carroll Naish, Charles Dingle, John Alvin, David Hoffman, Barbara Brown, Patricia White, William Edmunds, Belle Mitchell, Ray Walker, Pedro de Cordoba.

My Favorite Brunette (Paramount, 1947). Director: Elliott Nugent; producer: Daniel Dare; original screenplay: Edmund Beloin and Jack Rose; cinematography: Lionel Lindon; song "Beside You" by Jay Livingston and Roy Evans; 87 min. Cast: Bob Hope, Dorothy Lamour, Peter Lorre (Kismet), Lon Chaney, John Hoyt, Charles Dingle, Reginald Denny, Frank Puglia, Ann Doran, Williard Robertson, Jack La Rue, Charles Arnt; unbilled guest stars: Alan Ladd, Bing Crosby.

Casbah (Universal International, 1948). Director: John Berry; producers: Nat C. Goldstone (executive) and Erik Charell (associate); screenplay: L. Bush-Fekete and Arnold Manoff; based on the novel *Pepe Le Moko* by Detective Ashelbe (Henri La Barthe); cinematography: Irving Glassberg; musical story: Erik Charell; music: Harold Arlen; lyrics: Leo Robin; choreography of Dunham Group: Katherine Dunham; 93 min. Cast: Yvonne De Carlo, Tony Martin, Peter Lorre (Inspector Slimane), Marta Toren, Hugo Haas, Thomas Gomez, Douglas Dick, Katherine Dunham, Herbert Rudley, Gene Walker, Curt Conway, André Pola, Barry Bernard, Virginia Gregg, Will Lee, Harris Brown, Housley Stevenson, Russell Johnson.

Rope of Sand (Paramount, 1949). Director: William Dieterle; producer: Hal B. Wallis; screenplay: Walter Doniger; additional dialogue: John Paxton; story: Walter Doniger; cinematography: Charles B. Lang Jr.; 104 min. Cast: Burt Lancaster, Paul Henreid, Claude Rains, Peter Lorre (Toady), Corinne Calvet, Sam Jaffe, John Bromfield, Mike Mazurki, Kenny Washington, Edmond Breon, Hadyn Roarke, David Thursby, Josef Marais and Miranda.

Quicksand (United Artists, 1950). Director: Irving Pichel; executive producer: Sam H.

Stiefel; producer: Mort Briskin; screenplay: Robert Smith; cinematography: Lionel Lindon; 79 min. Cast: Mickey Rooney, Jeanne Cagney, Barbara Bates, Peter Lorre (Nick Dramoshag), Taylor Holmes, Art Smith, Wally Cassel, Richard Lane, Patsy O'Connor, John Gallaudet, Minerva Urecal, Sidney Marion, Jimmy Dodd, Kitty O'Neil, Frank Marlowe, Alvin Hammer, Ray Teal, Tom Munroe, Red Nichols and His Five Pennies.

Double Confession (Associated British-Pathé, 1950). Director: Ken Annakin; producer: Harry Reynolds; screenplay: William Templeton and Ralph Keene; based on the novel *All on a Summer's Day* by John Garden; cinematography: Geoffrey Unsworth; 85 min. Cast: Derek Farr, Joan Hopkins, Peter Lorre (Paynter), William Hartnell, Kathleen Harrison, Naughton Wayne, Ronald Howard, Leslie Dwyer, Edward Rigby, George Woodbridge, Henry Edwards, Vida Hope, Esma Cannon.

Der Verlorene (*The Lost One*) (National Film GmbH, 1951). Director: Peter Lorre; producer: Arnold Pressburger; screenplay: Peter Lorre, Benno Vigny, and Axel Eggebrecht; cinematography: Vaclav Vich; 98 min. Cast: Peter Lorre (Dr. Karl Rothe), Karl John, Helmut Rudolph, Johanna Hofer, Renate Mannhardt, Eva-Ingeborg Scholz, Lotte Rausch, Gisela Trowe, Hansi Wendler, Kurt Meister, Alexander Hunzinger.

Beat the Devil (United Artists, 1954). Director: John Huston; producer: John Huston; screenplay: Truman Capote and John Huston; based on the novel *Beat the Devil* by Claud Cockburn (James Helvick); cinematography: Oswald Morris. Cast: Humphrey Bogart, Jennifer Jones, Gina Lollobrigida, Robert Morley, Peter Lorre (Julius O'Hara), Edward Underdown, Ivor Barnard, Marco Tulli, Bernard Lee, Mario Perrone, Guilio Donnini, Saro Urzi, Juan De Landa, Aldo Silvani.

20,000 Leagues under the Sea (Buena-Vista, 1954). Director: Richard Fleischer; producer: Walt Disney; screenplay: Earl Felton; based on the novel by Jules Verne; cinematography: Franz Planer; 120 min. Cast: Kirk Douglas, James Mason, Paul Lukas, Peter Lorre (Conseil), Robert J. Wilkie, Ted de Corsia, Carleton Young, J.M. Kerrigan, Percy Helton, Ted Cooper.

Meet Me in Las Vegas (MGM, 1956). Director: Roy Rowland; assistant director: George Rhei; producer: Joe Pasternak; screenplay: Isobel Lennart; cinematography: Robert Bronner; choreography: Hermes Pan and Eugene Loring; music: Nicholas Brodszky; lyrics: Sammy Cahn; 112 min. Cast: Dan Dailey, Cyd Charisse, Agnes Moorehead, Lili Darvas, Jim Backus, Oscar Karlweis, Liliane Montevecchi, Cara Williams, George Kerris, Betty Lyn, the Slate Brothers, Pete Rugolo, John Brascia, John Harding, Benny Rubin, Jack Daly, Henny Backus; guest stars: Jerry Colonna, Paul Henreid, Lena Horne, Frankie Laine, Mitsuko Sawamura; unbilled guest stars: Peter Lorre (himself), Tony Martin.

Congo Crossing (Universal, 1956). Director: Joseph Pevney; producer: Howard Christie; screenplay: Richard Alan Simmons; based on a story by Huston Branch; cinematography: Russell Metty; 85 min. Cast: Virginia Mayo, George Nader, Peter Lorre (Colonel John Miguel Orlando Arragas), Michael Pate, Rex Ingram, Tonio Selwart, Kathryn Givney, Tudor Owen, Raymond Bailey, George Ramsey, Bernard Hamilton, Harold Dyrenforth.

Around the World in Eighty Days (United Artists, 1956). Director: Michael Anderson; producer: Michael Todd; screenplay: James Poe, John Farrow, and S.J. Perelman; based on the novel by Jules Verne; cinematography: Lionel Lindon; 173 min. Cast: Cantinflas, David Niven, Shirley MacLaine, Robert Newton; guest stars: Finlay Currie, Robert Morley, Ronald Squire, Basil Sidney, Noel Coward, Sir John Gielgud, Trevor Howard,

Harcourt Williams, Martine Carol, Fernandel, Charles Boyer, Evelyn Keyes, Jose Greco and troupe, Luis Dominguín, Cesar Romero, Gilbert Roland, Alan Mowbray, Sir Cedric Hardwicke, Melville Cooper, Reginald Denny, Ronald Colman, Robert Cabal, Charles Coburn, Peter Lorre (Japanese steward), George Raft, Red Skelton, Marlene Dietrich, John Carradine, Frank Sinatra, Buster Keaton, Colonel Tim McCoy, Joe E. Brown, Andy Devine, Edmund Lowe, Victor McLaglen, Jack Oakie, Beatrice Lillie, John Mills, Glynis Johns, Hermione Gingold, Edward R. Murrow, A.E. Matthews, Ronald Adam, Walter Fitzgerald, Frank Royde.

The Buster Keaton Story (Paramount, 1957). Director: Sidney Sheldon; producers: Robert Smith and Sidney Sheldon; screenplay: Sidney Sheldon and Robert Smith; cinematography: Loyal Griggs; technical adviser: Buster Keaton; 91 min. Cast: Donald O'Connor, Ann Blyth, Rhonda Flemming, Peter Lorre (Kurt Bergner), Larry Keating, Richard Anderson, Dave Willock, Claire Carleton, Larry White, Jackie Coogan.

Silk Stockings (MGM, 1957). Director: Rouben Mamoulian; producer: Arthur Freed; screenplay: Leonard Gershe and Leonard Spigelgass; suggested by *Ninotchka* by Melchoir Lengyel; cinematography: Robert Bronner; music and lyrics: Cole Porter; book of the original musical play: George S. Kaufman, Leueen McGrath, and Abe Burrows; produced for the stage by Cy Feur and Ernest H. Martin; music supervised and conducted by André Prévin; all dances in which Fred Astaire appeared choreographed by Hermes Pan; all other dances choreographed by Eugene Loring; 117 min. Cast: Fred Astaire, Cyd Charisse, Janis Paige, Peter Lorre (Comrade Brankov), George Tobias, Jules Munshin, Joseph Buloff, Wim Sonneveld.

The Story of Mankind (Warner Bros., 1957). Director: Irwin Allen; producer: Irwin Allen; screenplay: Irwin Allen and Charles Bennett; based on the novel by Hendrik Van Loon; cinematography: Nick Musuraca; 99 min. Cast: Ronald Colman, Vincent Price; guest stars: Hedy Lamarr, Groucho Marx, Harpo Marx, Chico Marx, Virginia Mayo, Agnes Moorehead, Peter Lorre (Emperor Nero), Charles Coburn, Cedric Hardwicke, Cesar Romero, John Carradine, Dennis Hopper, Marie Wilson, Helmut Dantine, Edward Everett Horton, Reginald Gardner, Marie Windsor, George E. Stone, Cathy O'Donnell, Franklin Pangborn, Melville Cooper, Henry Daniell, Francis X. Bushman, James Ameche, Toni Gerry, David Bond, Austin Green, Nick Cravat, Eden Hartford, Dari Crayne, Alex Lockwood, Richard Cutting, Melinda Marx, Anthony Dexter, Bart Mattson, Don Megowan, Ziva Rodann, Marion Miller, Henry Ruby, Nancy Miller, William Schallert, Leonard Audie, Reginald Scheffield, Burt Nelson, Abraham Sofaer, Tudor Owens, Bobby Watson.

Hell Ship Mutiny (Republic, 1957). Directors: Lee Sholem and Elmo Williams; executive producer: Jon Hall; associate producer: George Bilson; screenplay: De Vallon Scott and Wells Root; cinematography: Sam Leavitt; 66 min. Cast: Jon Hall, John Carradine, Peter Lorre (Lamouet), Roberta Haynes, Mike Mazurki, Charles Mauu, Stanley Adams, Danny Richards Jr., Felix Locher, Peter Coe, Michael Barrett, Salvador Bagues.

The Sad Sack (Paramount, 1957). Director: George Marshall; producer: Hal B. Wallis; screenplay: Edmund Beloin and Nate Monaster; based on the cartoon character created by George Baker; cinematography: Loyal Griggs; music scored and conducted by Walter Scharf; musical numbers staged by Charles O'Curran; 98 min. Cast: Jerry Lewis, David Wayne, Phyllis Kirk, Peter Lorre (Sergeant Abdul), Joe Mantell, Gene Evans, George Dolenz, Liliane Montevecchi, Shepperd Strudwick, Abraham Sofaer, Mary Treen.

The Big Circus (Allied Artists, 1959). Director: Joseph M. Newman; producer: Irwin Allen; screenplay: Irwin Allen, Charles Bennett, and Irving Wallace; based on a story by Irwin Allen; cinematography: Winton Hoch; title song by Sammy Fain and Paul Francis Webster; 108 min. Cast: Victor Mature, Red Buttons, Rhonda Fleming, Kathryn Grant, Gilbert Roland, Vincent Price, Peter Lorre (Skeeter the Clown), David Nelson, Adele Mara, Howard McNear, Charles Watts, The World's Greatest Circus Acts, Steve Allen.

Scent of Mystery (Michael Todd Jr., 1960). Director: Jack Cardiff; associate director: Piero Musetta; producer: Michael Todd Jr.; screenplay: William Roos; original story by Kelley Roos; additional situations: Gerald Kersh; cinematography: John Von Kotze; osmologist: Hans Laube; 125 min. Cast: Denholm Elliott, Peter Lorre (Smiley), Liam Redmond, Beverly Bentley, Paul Lukas, Mary Laura Wood, Leo McKern, Peter Arne, Juan Olaguivel, Maurice Marsac, Diana Dors, Judith Furse, Billie Miller, Michael Trubshawe.

Voyage to the Bottom of the Sea (20th Century–Fox, 1961). Director: Irwin Allen; producer: Irwin Allen; screenplay: Irwin Allen and Charles Bennett; story by Irwin Allen; cinematography: Winton Hoch; song "Voyage to the Bottom of the Sea" by Russell Faith; 105 min. Cast: Walter Pidgeon, Joan Fontaine, Barbara Eden, Peter Lorre (Commodore Lucius Emery), Robert Sterling, Michael Ansara, Frankie Avalon, Regis Toomey, John Litel, Howard McNear, Henry Daniell, Skip Ward, Mark Slade, Charles Tannen, Delbert Monroe, Anthony Monaco, Michael Ford, Robert Easton.

Tales of Terror (American International Pictures, 1962). Director: Roger Corman; producer: Roger Corman; screenplay: Richard Matheson; based on three Edgar Allan Poe stories; cinematography: Floyd Crosby; photographic effects: Butler-Glouner, Inc; technical adviser for wine-tasting sequence in "The Black Cat": Harry W. Waugh, John Harvey and Sons, Ltd., Bristol, England; technical adviser for hypnotism sequence in "The Case of M. Valdemar" segment: William J. Bryan Jr., M.D., executive director of American Institute of Hypnosis; 90 min. Cast: "Morella" segment: Vincent Price, Maggie Pierce, Leona Gage; "The Black Cat" segment: Vincent Price, Peter Lorre (Montresor Herringbone), Joyce Jameson; "The Case of M. Valdemar" segment: Vincent Price, Basil Rathbone, Debra Paget, David Frankham; also: Lennie Weinrib, Wally Campo, Alan DeWitt, John Hackett, Ed Cobb, Scott Brown.

Five Weeks in a Balloon (20th Century–Fox, 1962). Director: Irwin Allen; producer: Irwin Allen; screenplay: Charles Bennett, Irwin Allen, and Albert Gail; based on the novel by Jules Verne; cinematography: Winton Hoch; The Brothers Four sing "Five Weeks in a Balloon" by Jodi Desmond; 101 min. Cast: Red Buttons, Fabian, Barbara Eden, Cedric Hardwicke, Peter Lorre (Ahmed), Richard Haydn, Barbara Luna, Billy Gilbert, Herbert Marshall, Reginald Owen, Henry Daniell, Mike Mazurki, Alan Caillou, Ben Astar, Raymond Bailey, Chester the Chimp.

The Raven (American International Pictures, 1963). Director: Roger Corman; producer: Roger Corman; screenplay: Richard Matheson; based on the poem by Edgar Allan Poe; cinematography: Floyd Crosby; special effects: Butler-Glouner, Inc., and Pat Dinga; raven trained by Moe DiSesso; 86 min. Cast: Vincent Price, Peter Lorre (Dr. Bedlo), Boris Karloff, Hazel Court, Olive Sturgess, Jack Nicholson, Connie Wallace, William Baskin, Aaron Saxon.

The Comedy of Terrors (American International Pictures, 1964). Director: Jacques Tourneur; producers: James H. Nicholson and Samuel Z. Arkoff; screenplay: Richard Matheson; cinematography: Floyd Crosby; special photographic effects: Butler-Glouner,

Inc.; 88 min. Cast: Vincent Price, Peter Lorre (Felix Gillie), Boris Karloff, Basil Rathbone, Joyce Jameson, Joe E. Brown, Beverly Hills, Rhubarb, Alan DeWitt, Buddy Mason, Douglas Williams, Linda Rogers, Luree Holmes.

Muscle Beach Party (American International Pictures, 1964). Director: William Asher; producers: James H. Nicholson and Robert Dillon; screenplay: Robert Dillon; story by Robert Dillon and William Asher; cinematography: Harold Wellman; songs: "Beach Party," "Runnin' Wild," "Muscle Bustle," "My First Love," "Surfin' Woodie," and "Surfer's Holiday" by Roger Christian, Gary Usher, and Brian Wilson; "Happy Street" and "A Girl Needs a Boy" by Guy Henrick and Jerry Styner; 94 min. Cast: Frankie Avalon, Annette Funicello, Luciana Paluzzi, John Ashley, Don Rickles, Peter Turgeon, Jody McCrea, Dick Dale and the Del Tones, Candy Johnson, Rock Stevens, Valora Noland, Delores Wells, Donna Loren, Bob Seven, Larry Scott, Steve Merjanian, Chester Yorton, Dan Haggerty, Gene Shuey, Gordon Case, Alberta Nelson, Amedee Chabot, Duane Ament, Gary Usher, Guy Henrich, Roger Christian, Laura Lynn, Luree Holmes, Lorie Sommers, Darlene Lucht, Maureen O'Connor, Mike Diffenderfer, Mike Neder, Ed Garner, Charles Hasley, Micky Dora, John Fain, Bill Graham, Larry Shaw, Duane King, Charles Van Artsdlen, Linda Opie, Sally Sache, Patricia Rane, Kathy Kessler, Mary Hughes, Linda Benson, Morey Amsterdam, Buddy Hackett; introducing Little Stevie Wonder; special thanks to Peter Lorre (Mr. Strangedour).

The Patsy (Paramount, 1964). Director: Jerry Lewis; assistant director: Ralph Axness; producer: Ernest D. Glucksman; screenplay: Jerry Lewis and Bill Richman; cinematography: Wallace Kelley; 100 min. Cast: Jerry Lewis, Ina Balin, Everett Sloane, Phil Harris, Keenan Wynn, Peter Lorre (Morgan Heywood), John Carradine, Hans Conreid, Phil Foster, Richard Deacon, Neil Hamilton, Jerry Dumphy, Jerry Dexter, Scatman Crothers, Del Moore, Nancy Kulp, Fritz Feld, Benny Rubin, Jerome Cowan, Ned Wynn, Henry Slate; guest stars: Rhonda Fleming, Hedda Hopper, George Raft, The Step Brothers, Mel Torme, Ed Wynn.

RADIO
Compiled by Cheryl Morris

Funkstunde Berlin, "Die Seufzerbrücke" ("The Bridge of Sighs") (Funk-Stunde A.G. Berlin, Oct. 5, 1930). Cast: Julius Kuthan, Eugen Rex, Josef Burgwinkel, Peter Lorre (counselor), Käte König, Cäcilie Lvovsky, and others.

Funkstunde Berlin, "Blaubart" ("Bluebeard") (Funk-Stunde A.G. Berlin, May 25, 1931). Cast: Leo Reuss, Jenny Marba, Cäcilie Lvovsky, Arthur Hell, Julius Kuthan, Peter Lorre (Alvarez, a courtier), Alice Hechy, and others.

Funkstunde Berlin / Radio Wien, "Fortunios Lied" ("Fortunio's Song") (Funk-Stunde A.G. Berlin, Dec. 12, 1931). Cast: Peter Lorre (Fortunio, attorney and notary of the Supreme Court in Paris), Cäcilie Lvovsky, Joseph Schmidt, Dolly Haas, Marianne Thalau, Elsa Glass-Sant, Helene Weigel, and others.

Funkstunde Berlin, "Vert-Vert" (Funk-Stunde A.G. Berlin, Jan. 14, 1932). Cast: Bozena Bradsky, Blandine Ebinger, Margret Pfahl, Else Stutz-Budde, Leo Reuss, Cäcilie Lvovsky, Peter Lorre (Bellecour, a singer), and others.

Funkstunde Berlin, "Das Notwendige und das Überflüssige" ("The Necessary and the Unnecessary") (Funk-Stunde A.G. Berlin, Jan. 20, 1932). Cast: Arthur Kraussneck, Roma

Bahn, Paul Wagner, Karl Kraus, Leo Reuss, Cäcilie Lvovsky, Peter Lorre (Schnell, a swindler), and others.

Funkstunde Berlin, "Die heilige Johanna der Schlachthöfe" ("St. Joan of the Stockyards") (Funk-Stunde A.G. Berlin, April 11, 1932). Cast: Fritz Kortner, Carola Neher, Helene Weigel, Peter Lorre (Sullivan Slift and Graham), Ernst Busch, Paul Bildt, Otto Kronburger, Friedrich Gnass, and others.

The Fleischmann Yeast Hour (NBC, May 7, 1936). 60 min. Rudy Vallee, host. Guests: Hildegard Halliday, Peter Lorre (Dr. Mallaire, "The Creation of Dr. Mallaire"), Jean Hersholt, David Oliver, Todd Duncan, Howard University Glee Club.

The Lux Radio Theater, "Trilby" (CBS, Sept. 21, 1936). 60 min. Cecil B. DeMille, host. Guests: Walt Disney, Grace Moore, Peter Lorre (Svengali), Ralph Forbes, Vernon Steele, Ralph Kellard, Grace Hampton, John Deering, Richard Abbott.

The Royal Gelatin Hour (NBC, Nov. 5, 1936). 60 min. Rudy Vallee, host. Guests: Peter Lorre (Alexis Nadova, "Prelude to Murder"), Olivia de Havilland, Eddie Conrad, Swing Kids Quartet, Shelia Barrett, Tom Howard, George Shelton.

The MGM Radio Movie Club (WHN, Nov. 20, 1936). 30 min. George Know, host. Guests: Peter Lorre, Volney Pfeifer.

Hollywood Hotel (CBS, March 5, 1937). 60 min. Louella Parsons, host; Fred MacMurray, MC; Frances Langford. Guests: George Burns, Gracie Allen, Victor McLaglen, June Lang, Peter Lorre (Prof. Sturm, *Nancy Steele Is Missing*), Warden Lewis Lawes of Sing Sing Prison.

Hollywood Hotel (CBS, Oct. 8, 1937). 60 min. Louella Parsons, host; Frances Langford, Jerry Cooper, Anne Jamison, Igor Gorin, Ken Murray. Guests: Dolores del Rio, Peter Lorre (Major Gruning, *Lancer Spy*), Gregory Ratoff, George Sanders, Sig Rumann.

The Royal Gelatin Hour (NBC, Jan. 20, 1938). 60 min. Rudy Vallee, host. Guests: Peter Lorre (photographer, "Picture Man"), Lila Lee, George Barnes, Playboys Vocal Group, Tommy Riggs, Val and Ernie Stanton.

Carthay Circle Theatre Broadcast, premiere of *Marie Antoinette* (NBC-Blue, July 8, 1938). 30 min. Cary Wilson, host; Don Wilson, interviewer. Guests: Judy Garland, Peter Lorre, Robert Young, Pete Smith, Fanny Brice, Hanley Stafford, Adrian, Florence Rice, Clark Gable, Norma Shearer, Basil Rathbone, James Stewart, Paul Muni, L.B. Mayer, Tyrone Power, John Barrymore, Helen Hayes, and others.

Camel Caravan (CBS, Oct. 24, 1938). 30 min. Eddie Cantor, host; Sid Fields. Guest: Peter Lorre. As "Mr. Moto," Lorre investigates the disappearance of Cantor's guest Martha Raye.

The Lifebuoy Program (CBS, Dec. 27, 1938). 30 min. Al Jolson, host; Harry Einstein ("Parkyakarkus"), Martha Raye. Guest: Peter Lorre.

The Royal Gelatin Hour (NBC, Aug. 10, 1939). 60 min. Rudy Vallee, host. Guests: Joe Cook, Peter Lorre (Kosky, "The Execution of Kosky"; Mr. Moto, mystery sketch), Lou Holtz, Carmen Miranda.

George Jessel's Celebrity Program (NBC, Aug. 16, 1939). 30 min. George Jessel, host.

Guests: Mrs. Theodore Roosevelt Jr., Peter Lorre (Mr. Moto, mystery sketch), Frank Crummit.

The Texaco Star Theater (CBS, Oct. 4, 1939). 30 min. Ken Murray, host (in Hollywood); Kenny Baker, Frances Langford, Irene Ryan. Guest: Peter Lorre (Mr. Moto, mystery sketch).

Kay Kyser's Kollege of Musical Knowledge (NBC, Sept. 25, 1940). 60 min. Kay Kyser, host; Kollege of Musical Knowledge orchestra. Guests: Peter Lorre, Boris Karloff, Bela Lugosi.

The Jell-O Program, "Murder at the Racquet Club" (NBC, March 9, 1941). 30 min. Jack Benny, Mary Livingstone, Eddie Anderson ("Rochester"), Dennis Day, Don Wilson, Phil Harris. Guests: Peter Lorre, Charles Farrell, Charles Butterworth, The Guadalajara Trio.

Three Ring Time (NBC-Blue, March 6, 1942). 30 min. Milton Berle, host; Shirley Ross, Crosby Orchestra. Guests: Peter Lorre, Bela Lugosi.

Towards the Century of the Common Man (NBC, June 14, 1942). 30 min. Guests: Charles Boyer, Ronald Colman, Joseph Calleia, Ray Collins, Melville Cooper, Donald Dixon, Peter Lorre, Thomas Mitchell, Alla Nazimova, George Faulkner, Maria Ouspenskaya, Stephen Vincent Benet, Robert Armbruster, Kurt Weil, President Franklin D. Roosevelt.

Inner Sanctum Mysteries, "The Murders in the Morgue" (NBC-Blue, Nov. 29, 1942). 30 min. Raymond Edward Johnson ("Raymond"), host. Cast: Peter Lorre (Franz Webber).

The Philip Morris Playhouse, "Crime and Punishment" (CBS, Dec. 11, 1942). 30 min. Charles Martin, host. Cast: Peter Lorre (Raskolnikov), Anne Rutherford.

Inner Sanctum Mysteries, "The Man Who Returned from the Dead" (NBC-Blue, Dec. 13, 1942). 30 min. Raymond Edward Johnson ("Raymond"), host. Cast: Peter Lorre (Nobel Prize winner).

Suspense, "Till Death Do Us Part" (CBS, Dec. 15, 1942). 30 min. Joseph Kearns ("The Man in Black"), host. Cast: Peter Lorre (Prof. Irwin Kraft), Alice Frost, David Gothard, Mercedes McCambridge.

Stage Door Canteen (CBS, Dec. 17, 1942). 30 min. Bert Lytell, host. Guests: Mrs. Franklin D. Roosevelt, Peter Lorre ("Footnote for Tomorrow"), Grace Moore, Jane Cowl.

Al Jolson Colgate Show (CBS, Dec. 22, 1942). 30 min. Al Jolson, host; Monte Woolly, Carol Bruce. Guest: Peter Lorre.

Inner Sanctum Mysteries, "Dig My Grave" (NBC-Blue, Dec. 27, 1942). 30 min. Raymond Edward Johnson ("Raymond"), host. Cast: Peter Lorre.

The Texaco Star Theater (CBS, Jan. 3, 1943). 30 min. Fred Allen, host; Portland Hoffa. Guests: Peter Lorre (Mr. Moto, "The Missing Shot or Who Killed Balsam Beamish?"), Lois January.

The Kate Smith Show (CBS, Jan. 8, 1943). 30 min. Kate Smith, host; Ted Collins,

Henny Youngman. Guests: Peter Lorre ("The Cask of Amontillado"), Jean Muir, Blaine Cordner.

Inner Sanctum Mysteries, "The Bell Tolls Death" (NBC-Blue, Jan. 17, 1943). 30 min. Raymond Edward Johnson ("Raymond"), host. Cast: Peter Lorre.

Suspense, "The Devil's Saint" (CBS, Jan. 19, 1943). 30 min. Joseph Kearns ("The Man in Black"), host. Cast: Peter Lorre (Count Stefan Kohari).

Radio Reader's Digest, "Education for Death" (CBS, Jan. 31, 1943). 30 min. Conrad Nagel, narrator. Guest: Peter Lorre.

Stage Door Canteen (CBS, Feb. 4, 1943). 30 min. Bert Lytell, host. Guests: Peter Lorre, Phil Baker, Jane Froman, Beatrice Kay.

The Bud Abbott and Lou Costello Show (NBC, Feb. 11, 1943). 30 min. Bud Abbott, Lou Costello, hosts. Guest: Peter Lorre. Abbott and Costello visit Lorre's country home.

Treasury Star Parade, "Thirty for One" (various stations, Feb. 23–Oct. 13, 1943). 15 min. Cast: Peter Lorre, Joseph Schildkraut.

The Day of Reckoning, "The People vs. Benito Mussolini," part 2 of 5-part series (NBC, March 6, 1943). 30 min. Martin Gabel, host. Cast: Peter Lorre (Mephisto), Edmund Gwenn.

Inner Sanctum Mysteries, "The Black Seagull" (NBC-Blue, March 7, 1943). 30 min. Raymond Edward Johnson ("Raymond"), host. Cast: Peter Lorre (Richard Blake).

Suspense, "Moment of Darkness" (CBS, April 20, 1943). 30 min. Joseph Kearns ("The Man in Black"), host. Cast: Peter Lorre (George Ravell / Flaumond), Wendy Barrie, George Zucco, Hans Conried.

The Camel Comedy Caravan (CBS, April 30, 1943). 45 min. Jack Carson, host; Connie Haynes, Herb Shriner. Guests: Peter Lorre (Grogan, "Pamela Stumpf, Girl Paperhanger"; all-night radio show sketch), Susan Hayward. Carson and Hayward take shelter in Lorre's house when rain interrupts their picnic.

The Lady Esther Screen Guild Theater, "The Maltese Falcon" (CBS, Sept. 20, 1943). 30 min. Truman Bradley, announcer. Cast: Humphrey Bogart, Mary Astor, Sydney Greenstreet, Peter Lorre (Joel Cairo).

Duffy's Tavern (NBC-Blue, Oct. 19, 1943). 30 min. Ed Gardner, host; Florence Halop, Charlie Cantor, Eddie Green, Johnny Johnston, Paul Weston and His Orchestra. Guests: Peter Lorre ("The Missing Salami Sandwich"), Mrs. Carbett Wells and Raffles the Myna Bird.

The Amos 'n' Andy Show, "The Locked Trunk's Secret" (NBC, Nov. 5, 1943). 30 min. Freeman Gosden ("Amos"), Charles Correll ("Andy"). Guest: Peter Lorre.

Suspense, "Back for Christmas" (CBS, Dec. 23, 1943). 30 min. Joseph Kearns ("The Man in Black"), host. Cast: Peter Lorre (Hubert Schumacher), John McIntire.

The Bud Abbott and Lou Costello Show (NBC, Jan. 13, 1944). 30 min. Bud Abbott, Lou

Costello, hosts; Connie Haines. Guest: Peter Lorre. Abbott and Costello visit Lorre's sanitarium.

The Frank Sinatra Show (CBS, March 22, 1944). 30 min. Frank Sinatra, host; Bert Wheeler. Guests: Peter Lorre, Phil Silvers.

The Kate Smith Hour (CBS, June 2, 1944). 55 min. Kate Smith, host; Ted Collins, Harry Savoy, Count Basie. Guests: Peter Lorre, Lt. Comdr. James Crowley.

The Texaco Star Theater (CBS, June 4, 1944). 30 min. Fred Allen, host; Portland Hoffa, Mighty Allen Art Players, Hi Lo, Jack and a Dame. Guest: Peter Lorre (Mr. Moto, "More Murder on the Fred Allen Program").

Stars for Humanity (NBC-Blue, June 8, 1944). 60 min. Guests: Eddie Cantor, Milton Berle, Jan Peerce, Paul Robeson, Peter Lorre, Bidu Sayao, and others.

You Asked for It (NBC, June 9, 1944). 30 min. Ben Grower, host; Larry Adler, Carmen Cavallero, Lew Lehr, Clem McCarthy, Lulu Bates. Guests: Peter Lorre (Claude, "Villainous Villain Plays a Poor but Honest Hero"), Helen Jepson, Leo Durocher.

Inner Sanctum Mysteries, "Death Is a Joker" (CBS, June 10, 1944). 30 min. Raymond Edward Johnson ("Raymond"), host. Cast: Peter Lorre (Charles), Berry Kroger, Myron McCormick.

Creeps by Night (NBC-Blue, June 13, 1944). 30 min. Boris Karloff, host. Cast: Peter Lorre.

Stage Door Canteen (CBS, June 16, 1944). 30 min. Bert Lytell, host. Guests: Peter Lorre, Fred Waring, Jane Froman, Edward Martin (governor of Pennsylvania).

Inner Sanctum Mysteries, "The Mind Reader" (CBS, June 17, 1944). 30 min. Raymond Edward Johnson ("Raymond"), host. Cast: Peter Lorre.

Lights of New York (Mutual, June 19, 1944). 30 min. Guests: Peter Lorre, Joy Hodges, Allen Drake, Louis Sobol.

Broadway Showtime (CBS, June 19, 1944). 30 min. Johnny Morgan, host; Vic Anthony. Guest: Peter Lorre.

Suspense, "Of Maestro and Man" (CBS, July 20, 1944). 30 min. Joseph Kearns ("The Man in Black"), host. Cast: Peter Lorre (the Maestro), Richard Conti, John McIntire.

G.I. Journal, #53 (AFRS, July 21, 1944; released Aug. 1944). 30 min. Bing Crosby, guest "Editor-in-Chief." Guests: Ransom Sherman, Mel Blanc, Peter Lorre, Lynn Bari, The Music Maids. Lorre places an ad for a missing body in the *G.I. Journal.*

Creeps by Night, "Beyond the Grave" (NBC-Blue, Aug. 8, 1944). 30 min. "Mr. X," host. Cast: Peter Lorre.

Stage Door Canteen (CBS, Aug. 11, 1944). 30 min. Bert Lytell, host. Guests: Peter Lorre, Mildred Bailey, Johnny Burke.

Inner Sanctum Mysteries, "One Foot in the Grave" (CBS, Sept. 16, 1944). 30 min. Raymond Edward Johnson ("Raymond"), host. Cast: Peter Lorre.

Grace Notes, Louisville, KY, local program (WAVE, Oct. 23, 1944). 30 min. Natalie Potter, host. Guest: Peter Lorre.

Birdseye Open House (NBC, Nov. 23, 1944). 30 min. Dinah Shore, host. Guests: Peter Lorre, Sydney Greenstreet.

Mystery Playhouse (AFRS, early 1944–45). 30 min. Episodes hosted by Peter Lorre include
  Series unknown, "Dead Ringer"
  The Big Town, "Murder Sees Red"
  Mr. Dictrict Attorney, "Oil Swindlers"
  Mr. District Attorney, "The Case of the Backstage Murder" (Feb. 3, 1943)
  The Adventures of Nero Wolfe, "The Case of the Last Laugh Murder" (Feb. 1944)
  The Adventures of the Thin Man, "Murder in the Record Shop" (April 1944)
  Mollé Mystery Theater, "Criminal at Large" (April 11, 1944)
  Creeps by Night, "Those Who Walk in Darkness" (April 11, 1944)
  Hermit's Cave, "Mr. Randall's Discovery" (April 30, 1944)
  The Adventures of Sherlock Holmes, "The Adventure of the Superfluous Pearl" (May 22, 1944)
  Inner Sanctum Mysteries, "Death Is a Joker" (June 10, 1944)
  The Whistler, "The Doctor Prescribed Death" (June 11, 1944)
  Creeps by Night, "The Six Who Did Not Die" (July 11, 1944)
  Mr. and Mrs. North, "Gangster Douglas Grant" (July 12, 1944)
  The Whistler, "The Last of the Devereaux" (July 23, 1944)
  Mr. and Mrs. North, "Pam Keeps Out of Trouble" (Aug. 9, 1944)
  The Whistler, "Beloved Fraud" (Oct. 30, 1944)
  Mollé Mystery Theater, "Dilemma" (Nov. 21, 1944)
  Mollé Mystery Theater, "Nightmare" (Nov. 28, 1944)
  Mollé Mystery Theater, "A Crime to Fit the Punishment" (Dec. 5, 1944)
  Inner Sanctum Mysteries, "Color Blind Formula" (Dec. 6, 1944)
  The Big Town, "Death Stalks the Hunter" (Dec. 12, 1944)
  Mollé Mystery Theater, "The Bottle Imp" (Dec. 12, 1944)
  Mollé Mystery Theater, "The Man in the Velvet Hat" (Dec. 19, 1944)
  Mollé Mystery Theater, "The Letter" (Dec. 26, 1944)
  The Saint, "The Simon Templar Foundation" (Jan. 6, 1945)
  Mr. And Mrs. North, "Frisbie Proves His Point" (Jan. 17, 1945)
  Mollé Mystery Theater, "Yours Truly, Jack the Ripper" (Feb. 27, 1945)
  Mollé Mystery Theater, "The Man Who Murdered in Public" (March 6, 1945)
  Mollé Mystery Theater, "The Cask of Amontillado" (April 24, 1945)
  Mollé Mystery Theater, "Lady in the Morgue" (May 15, 1945)

G.I. Journal, #78 (AFRS, Jan. 19, 1945; released Feb. 1945). 30 min. Jack Haley, guest "Editor-in-Chief." Guests: Peter Lorre, Jane Wyman, John Carradine, Mel Blanc, Connie Haines, Elvia Allman, the Pied Pipers. Haley visits Lorre and Carradine's rest home.

Andrews Sisters' Eight-to-the-Bar Ranch (NBC-Blue, Jan. 21, 1945). 30 min. Patty, Maxine, and Laverne Andrews, hosts; Gabby Hayes. Guests: Peter Lorre, Sydney Greenstreet, Foy Willing and The Riders of the Purple Sage. Lorre and Greenstreet plan a Western murder-mystery film.

Let Yourself Go (CBS, Feb. 28, 1945). 30 min. Milton Berle, host. Guests: Peter Lorre, Joe Besser.

The Voice of Broadway (Mutual, March 1, 1945). 15 min. Dorothy Kilgallen, host. Guest: Peter Lorre.

Philco Radio Hall of Fame (NBC-Blue, March 4, 1945). 60 min. Beatrice Lillie, host; Paul Whiteman band. Guests: Bert Lahr, Peter Lorre ("The Tell-Tale Heart," verse of "The Raven"), Jo Stafford, Artie Shaw.

Stage Door Canteen (CBS, March 9, 1945). 30 min. Bert Lytell, host. Guests: Peter Lorre, Hugh Herbert, Ilka Chase, Allan Jones.

Which Is Which? (CBS, April 11, 1945). 30 min. Ken Murray, host. Guests: Bing Crosby, Peter Lorre, Frank McHugh.

The Lady Esther Screen Guild Theater, "The Mask of Dimitrios" (CBS, April 16, 1945). 30 min. Truman Bradley, announcer. Cast: Sydney Greenstreet, Peter Lorre (Cornelius Leyden).

Command Performance, #171 (AFRS, April 19, 1945; released summer 1945). 30 min. Ken Carpenter, host. Guests: Martha Stewart, Jack Carson, Jack Oakie, Peter Lorre, Sydney Greenstreet, Carlos Ramirez, The Sportsmen. Stewart meets Lorre and Greenstreet and others, on Carson's tour of Beverly Hills.

Arch Oboler's Plays, "An Exercise in Horror: A Peculiar Comedy" (Mutual, May 24, 1945). 30 min. Arch Oboler, host. Cast: Peter Lorre, Bruce Elliott, Theodor Von Ells, Will Wright, Bill Christie, George Sorrell, Frances Pasco, Victor Rodman, Harry Lang, Frank Martin, Winifred Wolf, Lisa Golm, Jan Morgan, Bill Shaw.

Suspense, "Nobody Loves Me" (CBS, Aug. 30, 1945). 30 min. Joseph Kearns ("The Man in Black"), host. Cast: Peter Lorre (Joe Reeze), Wally Maher, Joseph Kearns, Bill Johnstone.

The Baby Snooks Show (CBS, Sept. 23, 1945). 30 min. Hanley Stafford, Leone Ledoux, Bob Graham. Guests: Robert Benchley, Peter Lorre, Sydney Greenstreet.

Pabst Blue Ribbon Town (CBS, March 8, 1946). 30 min. Danny Kaye, host; Georgia Gibbs, David Terry. Guests: Peter Lorre, Butterfly McQueen. Kaye rents Lorre's house.

The Lucky Strike Program, "I Stand Condemned" (NBC, March 24, 1946). 30 min. Jack Benny, Mary Livingston, Don Wilson, Eddie Anderson ("Rochester"). Guest: Peter Lorre.

Mail Call, #189 (AFRS, April 3, 1946). 30 min. Hal Peary ("The Great Gildersleeve"), host. Guests: Lina Romay, Bob Mitchell Choir, Peter Lorre, Harry Gibson, Mel Blanc. Gildy vs. Lorre as skipper of the "Mail Call" boat.

Birdseye Open House (NBC, May 9, 1946). 30 min. Dinah Shore, host; Harry Von Zell, Frank Nelson. Guest: Peter Lorre (zombie sketch).

The Drene Show (NBC, June 20, 1946). 30 min. Rudy Vallee, host; Pinky Lee, Marvin Miller, June Foray. Guest: Peter Lorre (Dr. Lorre, "Young Dr. Vallee").

Chesterfield Supper Club (NBC, Oct. 21, 1946). 15 min. Perry Como, host. Guest: Peter Lorre.

The Eddie Cantor Show (NBC, Dec. 26, 1946). 30 min. Eddie Cantor, host; Margaret Whiting, Harry von Zell, Bert Gordon ("the Mad Russian"). Guest: Peter Lorre. Cantor hires Lorre as his business manager.

The Kate Smith Show (CBS, Feb. 9, 1947). 30 min. Kate Smith, host; Ted Collins. Guest: Peter Lorre (Brown, "The Painting").

The Campbell Room (CBS, Feb. 23, 1947). 30 min. Hildegard Loretta Sell, host; Arnold Stang. Guests: Peter Lorre (psychiatrist sketch), Elliott Roosevelt, Faye Emerson.

Kraft Music Hall (NBC, Feb. 27, 1947). 30 min. Eddie Duchin, Eddie Foy, hosts; Mills Brothers, Melena Miller. Guest: Peter Lorre. Foy and Duchin visit Lorre's sanitarium.

Hollywood's Open House (NBC, March 9, 1947). 30 min. Jim Ameche, host. Guests: Peter Lorre ("The Tell-Tale Heart"), Peter Donald.

The Pepsodent Show (NBC, May 13, 1947). 30 min. Bob Hope, host; Barbara Jo Allen ("Vera Vague"), Jerry Colonna, Desi Arnaz and his Orchestra. Guests: Peter Lorre (Hope's version of *Inner Sanctum Mysteries*), Martha Tildon.

The Benny Goodman–Victor Borge Show (NBC, June 2, 1947). 30 min. Victor Borge, Benny Goodman, hosts. Guest: Peter Lorre (Ghost, "Borge's Ancestral Ghost"; Itchy Hyde, "Till the Shrouds Roll By").

Mail Call, #252 (AFRS, June 25, 1947; released July 8, 1947). 30 min. Cathy Downs, host. Guests: Lina Romay, Andy Russell, Rise Stevens, Hal Peary ("The Great Gildersleeve"), Peter Lorre, Mel Blanc, Jimmy Dorsey Orchestra.

Mystery in the Air (NBC, July 3–Sept. 25, 1947). 30 min. Episodes include
   "The Tell-Tale Heart" (July 3, 1947). Harry Morgan ("Voice of Mystery"), host. Cast: Peter Lorre (murderer), Bob Bruce, Lois Corbett, Jack Douglas, Michael Roy, Bob Andersen, Lyle Bond.

   "Leiningen vs. the Ants" (July 10, 1947). Harry Morgan ("Voice of Mystery"), host. Cast: Peter Lorre (Leiningen), Edwin Cooper, Hans Conried, Jack Moyles.

   "The Touch of Your Hand" (July 17, 1947). Harry Morgan ("Voice of Mystery"), host. Cast: Peter Lorre (Francois Blanchard), John Brown, Hans Conried, Jack Edwards Jr., Barbara Eiler, Alan Reed.

   "The Interruption" (July 24, 1947). Harry Morgan ("Voice of Mystery"), host. Cast: Peter Lorre (Spencer Goddard), Mary Lansing, Russell Thorson, Herb Vigran. Guest: Agnes Moorehead.

   "Nobody Loves Me" (July 31, 1947). Harry Morgan ("Voice of Mystery"), host. Cast: Peter Lorre (Joe Reeze), Lurene Tuttle, Conrad Binyon, Ruth Perrott, Frank Nelson, Cyrus Kendall, Horace Willard, Irvin Lee.

   "The Marvelous Barastro" (Aug. 7, 1947). Harry Morgan ("Voice of Mystery"), host. Cast: Peter Lorre (Gregor Barastro), John Brown, Barbara Eiler, Howard Culver, Jane Morgan, Russell Thorson.

"The Lodger" (Aug. 14, 1947). Harry Morgan ("Voice of Mystery"), host. Cast: Peter Lorre (Mr. Sleuth / The Avenger), Barbara Eiler, Eric Snowden, Raymond Lawrence, Rolfe Sidan, Conrad Binyon. Guest: Agnes Moorehead.

"The Horla" (Aug. 21, 1947). Harry Morgan ("Voice of Mystery"), host. Cast: Peter Lorre (narrator), Peggy Webber, Lurene Tuttle, Ken Christie, Ben Wright, Howard Culver, Jack Edwards Jr.

"Beyond Good and Evil" (Aug. 28, 1947). Harry Morgan ("Voice of Mystery"), host. Cast: Peter Lorre (Philip Gentry), Peggy Webber, John Brown, Howard Culver, Jack Edwards Jr., Russell Thorson.

"The Mask of Medusa" (Sept. 4, 1947). Harry Morgan ("Voice of Mystery"), host. Cast: Peter Lorre (murderer), Peggy Webber, Lucille Meredith, Stanley Waxman, Russell Thorson, Ben Wright, Phyllis Christine Morris.

"The Queen of Spades" (Sept. 11, 1947). Harry Morgan ("Voice of Mystery"), host. Cast: Peter Lorre (Lieutenant Hermann), Lurene Tuttle, Peggy Webber, Ben Wright, Louis Van Rooten, Stanley Waxman, Jack Edwards Jr., Rolfe Sidan.

"The Black Cat" (Sept. 18, 1947). Harry Morgan ("Voice of Mystery"), host. Cast: Peter Lorre (Charles), Lurene Tuttle, Jerry Hausner, Howard Culver, Russell Thorson, Jack Edwards Jr.

"Crime and Punishment" (Sept. 25, 1947). Harry Morgan ("Voice of Mystery"), host. Cast: Peter Lorre (Roderick Raskolnikov), Peggy Webber, Joe Kearns, Ben Wright, Louis Van Rooten, Gloria Ann Simpson, Herbert Butterfield.

Hollywood Fights Back (ABC, Oct. 26, 1947). 30 min. Charles Boyer, host. Guests: Judy Garland, Gene Kelly, Lauren Bacall, Joseph Cotton, Peter Lorre, June Havoc, John Huston, Danny Kaye, Marsha Hunt, Walter Wanger, Cornel Wilde, Melvyn Douglas, and others.

Hollywood Fights Back (ABC, Nov. 2, 1947). 30 min. Guests: Frederic March, Myrna Loy, Douglas Fairbanks Jr., Rita Hayworth, Florence Eldridge, Lauren Bacall, Anne Revere, Burt Lancaster, Danny Kaye, Evelyn Keyes, Paul Henreid, June Havoc, Peter Lorre, and others.

Philco Radio Time (NBC-Blue, Nov. 12, 1947). 30 min. Bing Crosby, host; the Rhythmaires. Guests: Peter Lorre (psychiatrist sketch), Kay Thompson, Williams Brothers.

The Camel Screen Guild Players, "Casbah" (CBS, May 24, 1948). 30 min. Michael Roy, announcer. Cast: Tony Martin, Marta Toren, Peter Lorre (Inspector Slimane), Yvonne DeCarlo.

Command Performance, #328 (AFRS, summer 1948; released June 22, 1948). 30 min. Betty Rhodes, host. Guests: Sara Berner, Lenny Sherman, Joey Preston, Bud Widmon, Peter Lorre, AFRS Orchestra.

Spotlight Revue (CBS, Dec. 10, 1948). 30 min. Spike Jones, host, and the City Slickers, Dorothy Shay, Doodles Weaver, George Rock. Guest: Peter Lorre (doctor sketch).

Theater U.S.A. (NBC-Blue, Jan. 13, 1949). 30 min. Vinton Freeley, host. Guests: Mary McCarthy, Rudy Vallee, Peter Lorre (Marc, "If Men Played Cards as Women Do"), Roland Young, Mischa Auer, Andrea Segovia.

The Henry Morgan Show (NBC, March 20, 1949). 30 min. Henry Morgan, host; Arnold Stang, Lisa Kurt, Patsy Kelly. Guests: Peter Lorre (Der Pfeifer, "Der Pfeifer"), Fred Allen, Victor Moore.

We, the People (CBS, March 22, 1949). 30 min. Dan Seymour, host. Guests: Peter Lorre, Spyros Skouras, George Hackenschmidt, Lois Hunt, Stan Rochinski.

Skippy Hollywood Theater, "Mr. God Johnson" (synd., April 5, 1949). 30 min. Les Mitchell, host. Cast: Peter Lorre ("God" Johnson), Fred Howard, Earl Lee, Gwen Dellano, Herb Butterfield, Charlie Lund.

The Martin and Lewis Show (NBC, May 8, 1949). 30 min. Dean Martin, Jerry Lewis, hosts; Paul McMichael, Roger Price, Ed Herlihy, Dick Stabile and his Orchestra. Guest: Peter Lorre. Lorre suggests the boys do a disc jockey program instead of a mystery series.

Dokumentationsband Zeitfunk (Hessischer Rundfunk [Frankfurt], Sept. 18, 1951). 7 min. Martin Jente von Lossow, interview with Peter Lorre and Egon Jameson at the premiere of *Der Verlorene* in Frankfurt.

Echo des Tages (Westdeutscher Rundfunk [Cologne], Sept. 20, 1951). 6 min. Hans Jesse, 2-part interview with Peter Lorre about his role as an "eternal bad guy in films," *Der Verlorene,* and the situation of German films.

The Big Show (NBC, March 9, 1952). 90 min. Tallulah Bankhead, host. Guests: Richard Eastland, Phil Foster, Joe Frisco, Peter Lorre ("The Cask of Amontillado," sequel to "Who Did What to Fadalia," "Writer Meets the Readers"), Ethel Merman, Shepperd Strudwick.

The Philip Morris Playhouse, "We Strangers" (CBS, July 13, 1952). 30 min. Art Ballinger, announcer. Cast: Peter Lorre (ballet instructor), Carroll Conroy.

The Philip Morris Playhouse on Broadway, "The Night Has a Thousand Eyes" (CBS, Aug. 19, 1953). 30 min. Charles Martin, producer, host. Cast: Peter Lorre (John Triton), Everett Sloane, Jewel Lane, Ed Begley, Mandel Cramer.

Nightmare (Mutual, Oct. 1, 1953–Sept. 29, 1954); 30 min. Episodes include
    "Coincidence"
    "Fear of Heights"
    "The Chance of a Ghost"
    "The Hybrid"
    "The Leech"
    "The Purple Cloud"
    "Food for Thought" (Dec. 10, 1953)
    "The Frightened Frenchman" (Dec. 31, 1953)

"The Invaders" (Jan. 13, 1954)
"Hollow Footsteps" (Feb. 3, 1954)
"The Strange Voyage of Capt. Mundsen" (March 17, 1954)
"The Softer Voice" (April 28, 1954)
"Quorum for Death" (May 5, 1954)
"The Lucky Stretch" (May 12, 1954)
"The Brain Wash" (June 16, 1954)
"Dig the Grave Deep" (June 23, 1954)
"The Last Laugh" (June 30, 1954)
"Desert in the Sky" (July 14, 1954)
"The Face" (July 21, 1954)
"The Hammer Killer" (July 28, 1954)
"Forget Me Not" (Aug. 4, 1954)
"The Abyss" (Aug. 11, 1954)
"The Alien" (Aug. 18, 1954)
"If I Should Die Before I Wake" (Aug. 25, 1954)
"The Coils of Fear" (Sept. 1, 1954)
"Bread and Butter" (Sept. 8, 1954)
"The Rose Has Thorns" (Sept. 15, 1954)
"Grave for Rent" (Sept. 22, 1954)
"H Hour" (Sept. 29, 1954)

Stage Struck (CBS, March 14, 1954). 60 min. Mike Wallace, host. Guests: Noel Coward, Vernon Duke, Kirk Douglas, Maria Riva, Cedric Hardwicke, Peter Lorre, Clive Brooks, Kaye Ballard, Jack Whiting, Charles Goldner, Jeanmaire. Howard Barnes interviews Lorre in Jamaica during filming of *20,000 Leagues under the Sea*.

House Party (CBS, Dec. 6, 1954). 30 min. Art Linkletter, host. Guest: Peter Lorre.

The Amos 'n' Andy Music Hall (CBS, Dec. 16, 1954). 30 min. Freeman Gosden ("Amos"), Charles Correll ("Andy"). Guest: Peter Lorre.

The Dennis Day Show (Feb. 13, 1955). 30 min. Dennis Day, host. Guests: Peter Lorre, Carol Richards.

The Hy Gardner Show (BBC, 1956; never aired). Hy Gardner, host. Guest: Peter Lorre.

Easy as ABC, "O is for Old Wives' Tales" (CBS, April 27, 1958). 25 min. Guests: Alfred Hitchcock, Boris Karloff, Peter Lorre, Julienne Marie.

Assignment (CBC, May 29–31, 1962); 15 min. Elwood Glover, host. Guest: Peter Lorre. Three-part interview.

Sandy Lesberg's World (WBFM, Sept. 20, 1962). 30 min. Sandy Lesberg, host. Guest: Peter Lorre.

Treasury of Terror! (pilot episode, synd., 1963). 15 min. Peter Lorre, host, narrator.

The Barry Gray Show (WOR, Jan. 26, 1963). 120 min. Barry Gray, host. Guests: Peter Lorre, Boris Karloff.

Hollywood Profiles (1963). 3 min. Dick Strout, host. Guest: Peter Lorre.

TELEVISION
Compiled by Cheryl Morris

The Texaco Star Theater (NBC, March 15, 1949). 60 min. Milton Berle, host. Guests: Peter Lorre ("The Man with the Head of Glass"; Dr. X, "Cabinet of Dr. X"), Joan Roberts, Phil Regan, Stewart Morgan Dancers, McNulty Family.

The Arrow Show (NBC, March 24, 1949). 30 min. Jack Gilford, Joey Faye, Jack Diamond, Danny Dayton. Guests: Peter Lorre (babysitter sketch), Mack Triplets, Betty George, Mavis Nims.

Cavalcade of Stars (DuMont, June 4, 1949). 60 min. Jack Carter, host. Guests: Joan Edwards, Peter Lorre ("The Tell-Tale Heart," mad doctor sketch), McCarthy and Farrell, Arnaut Brothers' bird act, The Fontaines.

Variety (BBC, Aug. 27, 1949). 60 min. Charles Heslop, host. Guests: Georgie Wood, Dolly Harmer, The Ballet Montmarte, Kathleen Moody, Rob Murray, Eric Robinson and his Orchestra, Peter Lorre ("The Man with the Head of Glass").

The Texaco Star Theater (NBC, March 18, 1952). 60 min. Milton Berle, host. Guests: Peter Lorre, Connie Haines, Snooky Lansen.

Celebrity Time (CBS, March 23, 1952). 30 min. Conrad Nagel, host. Guests: Peter Lorre, Patricia Morrison.

Lux Video Theater, "Taste" (CBS, March 31, 1952). 30 min. Cast: Peter Lorre (Richard Pratt).

Ford Festival (NBC, April 3, 1952). 30 min. James Melton, host. Leonard Stone. Guests: Peter Lorre (knife salesman, "Room for Two"), Francis Craig.

What's My Line? (CBS, May 4, 1952). 30 min. John Daly, host. Panel: Dorothy Kilgallen, Bennett Cerf, Arlene Francis, Hal Block. Mystery Guest: Peter Lorre.

Suspense, "The Tortured Hand" (CBS, Dec. 16, 1952). 30 min. Cast: Peter Lorre (Count Laszlo Kolalyi), Christiane Selsmann, Will Kuluva, Paul Dehelly.

The All-Star Revue (NBC, Jan. 17, 1953). 60 min. Cast: Martha Raye, Boris Karloff, Peter Lorre, Charyl Sue Fong.

The Dave Garroway Show (NBC, Oct. 9, 1953). 30 min. Dave Garroway, host. Guests: Patsy Kelly, Peter Lorre.

The Paul Winchell–Jerry Mahoney Show (NBC, Nov. 22, 1953). 30 min. Paul Winchell, host. Guest: Peter Lorre (espionage sketch).

The U.S. Steel Hour, "The Vanishing Point" (ABC, Dec. 22, 1953). 60 min. Cast: Viveca Lindfors, Peter Lorre, Claude Dauphin.

The Red Skelton Show (CBS, June 15, 1954). 30 min. Red Skelton, host. Guests: Peter Lorre (mad scientist sketch), Lon Chaney Jr.

Schlitz Playhouse of Stars, "The Pipe" (CBS, Sept. 24, 1954). 30 min. Cast: Peter Lorre

(Lestrova), Michael Pate, Lowell Gilmore, Anthony Eustrel, Trevor Ward, Kay Kuter.

The Betty White Show (NBC, Oct. 7, 1954). 30 min. Betty White, host. Guests: Richard Arlen, Marie Windsor, Peter Lorre, Dan O'Herlihy.

Climax! "Casino Royale" (CBS, Oct. 21, 1954). 60 min. William Lundigan, host. Cast: Barry Nelson, Linda Christian, Peter Lorre (Le Chiffre), Michael Pate, Eugene Borden, Jean DeVal, Gene Roth, Kurt Katch.

Disneyland, "The Disneyland Story" (ABC, Oct. 27, 1954). 60 min. Walt Disney, host. Guests: James Mason, Kirk Douglas, Peter Lorre. Visit to the set of *20,000 Leagues under the Sea.*

I've Got a Secret (CBS, Jan. 5, 1955). 30 min. Gary Moore, host. Panel: Henry Morgan, Bill Cullen, Jayne Meadows, Faye Emerson. Guest: Peter Lorre.

The Best of Broadway, "Arsenic and Old Lace" (CBS, Jan. 5, 1955). 60 min. Cast: Helen Hayes, Billie Burke, Boris Karloff, Peter Lorre (Dr. Hermann Einstein), Orson Bean, John Alexander, Bruce Gordon, Pat Breslin, Allan Tower, King Calder, Richard Bishop, Edward Everett Horton.

The Red Skelton Show (CBS, Jan. 18, 1955). 30 min. Red Skelton, host. Guest: Peter Lorre (haunted house sketch; Ralph Kramden, "The Honeymooners").

Disneyland, "Monsters of the Deep" (ABC, Jan. 19, 1955). 60 min. Walt Disney, host. Guests: Kirk Douglas, Peter Lorre. Douglas and Lorre discuss the giant squid sequence in *20,000 Leagues under the Sea.*

Producer's Showcase, "Reunion in Vienna" (NBC, April 4, 1955). 90 min. Cast: Greer Garson, Brian Aherne, Robert Flemyng, Peter Lorre (Poffy), Cathleen Nesbitt, Lili Darvas, Herbert Berghof, George Vokvovec, Tamara Daykarhanova, Frederick Worlock, Nehemiah Persoff, Gene Saks, Boris Marshalov, Horace Cooper, Edith Meiser, Donald Marye.

Hollywood's Best, Los Angeles, local program (KNBC, April 22, 1955). 30 min. Bob Paige, host. Guests: Peter Lorre, Barbara Lawrence, Dinah Washington, Lester Horton Dancers.

The Eddie Cantor Comedy Theatre, "The Sure Cure" (synd., May 2, 1955). 30 min. Eddie Cantor, host. Cast: Peter Lorre (Ambrose Dodson), Vida Ann Borg, Nestor Paiva.

The George Gobel Show (NBC, June 18, 1955). 30 min. George Gobel, host. Guests: Peter Lorre (Department Chief, mystery sketch), Nat Pendleton.

Star Time Playhouse, "The Pipe" (CBS, Aug. 2, 1955). 30 min. Cast: Peter Lorre (Lestrova), Michael Pate, Lowell Gilmore, Anthony Eustrel, Trevor Ward, Kay Kuter. Repeat of *Schlitz Playhouse of Stars* episode, Sept. 24, 1954.

Studio 57, "Young Couples Only" (DuMont, copyright date Sept. 3, 1955; never aired). 30 min. Cast: Peter Lorre (Mr. Grober, the janitor), Barbara Hale, Bill Williams, Dani Nolan, Robert Quarry, Paul Bryar.

Climax! "A Promise to Murder" (CBS, Nov. 17, 1955). 60 min. William Lundigan, host. Cast: Louis Hayward, Peter Lorre (Maximilian Vorhees), Ann Harding.

The Red Skelton Show (CBS, Nov. 29, 1955). 30 min. Red Skelton, host. Guest: Peter Lorre (Phantom, "Phantom of the Ballet").

The Rheingold Theatre, "The Blue Landscape" (NBC, Dec. 10, 1955). 30 min. Henry Fonda, host. Cast: Hillary Brooke, John Hubbard, Peter Lorre (Inspector Andre Mondeau), Walter Kingsford, Celia Lovsky, John Mylong, Irene Seidner.

Screen Director's Playhouse, "No. 5 Checked Out" (NBC, Jan. 18, 1956). 30 min. Cast: Theresa Wright, Peter Lorre (Willy), William Talman, Ralph Moody.

Studio 57, "The Finishers" (DuMont, Jan. 29, 1956). 30 min. Cast: Peter Lorre (Heitzer), Carmen Mathews, Gordon Mills.

Climax! "The Fifth Wheel" (CBS, Feb. 9, 1956). 60 min. William Lundigan, host. Cast: Hume Cronyn, Peter Lorre (Normie), Bonita Granville, James Gleason, Arthur Treacher, Buddy Baer, John Lupton.

The Ed Sullivan Show, "The John Huston Story" (CBS, July 1, 1956). 60 min. Ed Sullivan, host. Guests: John Huston, Gregory Peck, Edward G. Robinson, Jose Ferrer, Peter Lorre, Mary Astor, Lauren Bacall, Burl Ives, Vincent Price, Billy Pearson.

Climax! "The Man Who Lost His Head" (CBS, July 26, 1956). 60 min. William Lundigan, host. Cast: Cedric Hardwicke, Peter Lorre (Ho), Debra Paget, John Ericson.

Encore Theater, "Queen's Bracelet" (NBC, Sept. 15, 1956). 30 min. Cast: Victor Jory, Mari Aldon, Peter Lorre (Emil Murdock), Ralph Clanton.

The Jackie Gleason Show (CBS, Sept. 29, 1956). 60 min. Jackie Gleason, host; Art Carney, Audrey Meadows, Joyce Randolph. Guests: Charles Laughton, Peter Lorre (cameo), Rudy Vallee, Edward G. Robinson, ZaSu Pitts, Bill Boyd ("Hopalong Cassidy").

Playhouse 90, "Sizeman and Son" (CBS, Oct. 18, 1956). 90 min. Cast: Eddie Cantor, Farley Granger, Mona Freeman, Peter Lorre (Karp), Larry Dobkin, Carol Morris.

20th Century–Fox Hour, "Operation Cicero" (CBS, Dec. 26, 1956). 60 min. Cast: Ricardo Montalban, Maria Riva, Peter Lorre (Moyzisch), Edward Fronz, Alan Napier, Romney Brent, Gregory Gay, Gavin Muir, Leon Ashin, Ivon Triesault.

Playhouse 90, "Massacre at Sand Creek" (CBS, Dec. 27, 1956). 60 min. Peter Lorre, host. Cast: John Derek, Everett Sloane, Gene Evans.

Collector's Item, "The Left Fist of David" (pilot episode, Feb. 1957). 30 min. Cast: Vincent Price, Peter Lorre (Mr. Munsey), Whitney Blake, Thomas Gomez, Eduard Franz, Dick Ryan, Dick Winslow, Harvey Parry.

The Red Skelton Show, "Clem's Oil" (CBS, March 5, 1957). 30 min. Red Skelton, host. Guests: Carol Channing, Peter Lorre ("Small Boy," unbilled cameo).

Playhouse 90, "The Last Tycoon" (CBS, March 14, 1957). 90 min. Cast: Jack Palance,

Keenan Wynn, Peter Lorre (Pete Zavras), Viveca Lindfors, Lee Remick, Robert Simon, John Hudson, Reginald Denny, Art Batanides, Tom Laughlin.

Climax! "A Taste for Crime" (CBS, June 20, 1957). 60 min. Bill Lundigen, Mary Costa, hosts. Cast: Michael Rennie, Peter Lorre (Benny Kellerman), Beverly Garland, Marsha Hunt.

Playhouse 90, "The Fabulous Irishman" (CBS, June 27, 1957). 60 min. Cast: Art Carney, Katharine Bard, Michael Higgens, Eli Mintz, Charles Davis, Peter Lorre.

Collector's Item, "Appraise the Lady" (second pilot, Nov. 1957). 30 min. Cast: Vincent Price, Peter Lorre (Mr. Munsey), Eva Gabor, Susan Morrow, Andrew Duggan, Gladys Hurlbut, William Schallert, Ted Marcuse, Colin Campbell, Mack Williams.

The Red Skelton Show (CBS, Nov. 5, 1957). 30 min. Red Skelton, host. Guest: Peter Lorre (next-door neighbor, Appleby's backyard barbecue sketch).

Playhouse 90, "The Jet-Propelled Couch" (CBS, Nov. 14, 1957). 90 min. Cast: Donald O'Connor, David Wayne, Peter Lorre (Dr. Ostrow), Gale Gordon, Phyllis Avery.

Alfred Hitchcock Presents, "The Diplomatic Corpse" (CBS, Dec. 8, 1957). 30 min. Alfred Hitchcock, host. Cast: George Peppard, Mary Scott, Peter Lorre (Tomas Salgado), Isobel Elsam.

Playhouse 90, "Turn Left at Mt. Everest" (CBS, April 3, 1958). 90 min. Cast: Fess Parker, Peter Lorre (Tenzing Phillips), Paul Ford, Patricia Cutts, Arnold Stang.

Milton Berle Starring in the Kraft Music Hall (NBC, Dec. 24, 1958). 30 min. Milton Berle, host. Guests: Peter Lorre (Santa Claus), Anne Jeffreys, Robert Sterling, George Arnold Ice Revue.

The Red Skelton Show (CBS, May 12, 1959). 30 min. Red Skelton, host. Guests: Peter Lorre (scientist, mad scientist sketch).

The Red Skelton Show (CBS, Nov. 17, 1959). 30 min. Red Skelton, host. Guests: Peter Lorre (Appleby the Weatherman), Mercedes McCambridge.

Five Fingers, "Thin Ice" (NBC, Dec. 19, 1959). 60 min. Cast: David Hedison, Luciana Paluzzi, Paul Burke; Guests: Peter Lorre (Colonel), Alan Young, Brett Halsey, Alan Napier.

Alfred Hitchcock Presents, "Man from the South" (CBS, Jan. 3, 1960). 30 min. Alfred Hitchcock, host. Cast: Peter Lorre (South American gambler), Steve McQueen, Neile Adams, Tyler McVay.

What's My Line? (CBS, Feb. 14, 1960). 30 min. John Daley, host. Panel: Steve Allen, Martin Gabel, Arlene Francis, Dorothy Kilgallen. Mystery Guest: Peter Lorre.

The Tonight Show Starring Jack Paar (NBC, Feb. 15, 1960). 105 min. Hugh Downs, guest host. Guests: Peter Lorre, Helena Carroll, Lester James, Dody Goodman, Alexander King.

I've Got a Secret (CBS, Feb. 17, 1960). 30 min. Gary Moore, host. Panel: Bill Cullen, Betsy Palmer, Henry Morgan, Bess Myerson. Mystery Guest: Peter Lorre.

Playhouse 90, "The Cruel Day" (CBS, Feb. 24, 1960). 90 min. Cast: Van Heflin, Cliff Robertson, Phyllis Thaxter, Raymond Massey, Peter Lorre (Algerian café owner), Nehemiah Persoff, Charles Bronson, Miko Oscard, Thano Rama.

Mike Wallace Interviews (WNTA-TV, March 8, 1960). 30 min. Mike Wallace, host. Guest: Peter Lorre.

Wagon Train, "The Alexander Portlass Story" (NBC, March 16, 1960). 60 min. Cast: Robert Horton. Guests: Peter Lorre (Alexander Portlass), Morgan Woodward, Sherwood Price, Bern Hoffman.

The Red Skelton Show (CBS, May 24, 1960). 30 min. Red Skelton, host. Guests: Peter Lorre (Zurium, "Clem and the Beanstalk"), Mamie Van Doren.

Rawhide, "Incident of the Slavemaster" (CBS, Nov. 11, 1960). 60 min. Cast: Eric Fleming, Clint Eastwood, Sheb Wooley. Guests: Peter Lorre (Victor Laurier), John Agar, Theodore Newton, Lisa Gaye.

Checkmate, "The Human Touch" (CBS, Jan. 14, 1961). 60 min. Cast: Anthony George, Doug McClure, Sebastian Cabot. Guests: Peter Lorre (Alonzo Pace-Graham), June Vincent, Ronald Long, Rebecca Welles, Ken Lynch.

The Best of the Post, "The Baron Loved His Wife" (synd., Jan. 21, 1961). 30 min. Cast: Peter Lorre (Baron), Ingrid Goude.

Peter Lorre Playhouse (pilot episode, June 1961). 30 min. Peter Lorre, host.

Here's Hollywood (NBC, July 21, 1961). 30 min. Helen O'Connell, host. Guests: Peter Lorre, Bobby Rydell.

Mrs. G. Goes to College, "First Test" (CBS, Oct. 11, 1961). 30 min. Cast: Gertrude Berg, Cedric Hardwicke, Skip Ward. Guest: Peter Lorre (Dr. Kestner).

The Tonight Show Starring Jack Paar (NBC, Nov. 16, 1961). 105 min. Jack Paar, host. Guests: Peter Lorre, Cedric Hardwicke, Les Paul, Mary Ford, Leona Anderson.

Mrs. G. Goes to College, "The Trouble with Crayton" (CBS, Dec. 6, 1961). 30 min. Cast: Gertrude Berg, Cedric Hardwicke, Mary Wickes, Skip Ward. Guests: Peter Lorre (Dr. Kestner), Karyn Kupcinet, Philip Coolidge, Robert Emhardt.

Tell It to Groucho (CBS, May 3, 1962). 30 min. Groucho Marx, host. Guests: Peter Lorre, Bonnie Pruden.

Route 66, "Lizard's Leg and Owlet's Wing" (CBS, Oct. 26, 1962). 60 min. Cast: Martin Milner, George Maharis. Guests: Peter Lorre (himself), Boris Karloff, Lon Chaney Jr., Martita Hunt, Conrad Nagel, Sally Gracie, Bill Berger, Jeannine Riley, Ralph Stanley.

The Steve Allen Show (synd., Jan. 14, 1963). 90 min. Steve Allen, host. Guests: Jennie Smith, Peter Lorre, Stan Getz, Lee Roy Minaugh.

The Jack Benny Show (CBS, Jan. 22, 1963). 30 min. Cast: Jack Benny, Mary Livingstone, Eddie Anderson, Don Wilson. Guests: Peter Lorre (Luverne Goodheart), Joanie Summers.

The Tonight Show Starring Johnny Carson (NBC, Jan. 25, 1963). 105 min. Johnny Carson, host. Guest: Peter Lorre.

The Tennessee Ernie Ford Show (ABC, Feb. 20, 1963). 30 min. Tennessee Ernie Ford, host. Guest: Peter Lorre.

The Hy Gardner Show (WOR, March 3, 1963). 60 min. Hy Gardner, host. Guests: Peter Lorre, Boris Karloff.

The Merv Griffin Show (NBC, March 4, 1963). 55 min. Merv Griffin, host. Guests: Peter Lorre, Jack Benny, Dr. Joyce Brothers, Bobby Breen.

The Dupont Show of the Week, "Diamond Fever" (NBC, March 24, 1963). 60 min. Cast: Theodore Bickel, Peter Lorre (Archie Lefferts), Sidney Blackmer, Martin Brooks, Jeri Archer, Katharine Sergava, Ted D'Arms, Val Bisoglio, Lani Miyazaki.

77 Sunset Strip, "5," part 1 of a 5-part episode (ABC, Sept. 20, 1963). 60 min. Cast: Efrem Zimbalist Jr. Guests: Burgess Meredith, Richard Conte, Walter Slezak, Patricia Rainier, Diane McBain, Lawrence Mann, Jimmy Murphy, Wally Cox, Herbert Marshall, Ed Wynn, Peter Lorre (gypsy), Keenan Wynn, William Shatner, Joseph Schildkraut.

Kraft Suspense Theatre, "The End of the World, Baby" (NBC, Oct. 24, 1963). 60 min. Cast: Gig Young, Nina Foch, Peter Lorre (Frederick Bergen), Katherine Crawford.

NOTES

ABBREVIATIONS

ALSC UCLA	Arts Library Special Collections, Charles E. Young Research Library, University Research Library, Univ. of California, Los Angeles
BFINL	British Film Institute National Library, London
CDM BYU	Cecil B. DeMille Archives, Special Collections and Manuscripts, Brigham Young Univ., Provo, Utah
DSC UCLA	Department of Special Collections, Charles E. Young Research Library, Univ. of California, Los Angeles
EHA	Elisabeth-Hauptmann-Archiv, Stiftung Archiv der Akademie der Künste, Berlin
FLC USC	Fritz Lang Collection, Cinema-Television Library, Univ. of Southern California, Los Angeles
FML USC	Feuchtwanger Memorial Library, Specialized Libraries and Archival Collections, Univ. of Southern California, Los Angeles
HR	*Hollywood Reporter*
HWS	Handschriftensammlung, Wiener Stadtbibliothek, Austria
JHC	John Huston Collection, Margaret Herrick Library, Academy of Motion Pictures Arts and Sciences, Los Angeles
JWC USC	Jack L. Warner Collection, Cinema-Television Library, Univ. of Southern California, Los Angeles
LAT	*Los Angeles Times*
MHL AMPAS	Margaret Herrick Library, Academy of Motion Pictures Arts and Sciences, Los Angeles
MPAA PCA	Motion Picture Association of America, Production Code Administration Files, Margaret Herrick Library, Academy of Motion Pictures Arts and Sciences, Los Angeles
MWC HRHRC	Mike Wallace Interviews Collection, Harry Ransom Humanities Research Center, Univ. of Texas, Austin
NYT	*New York Times*

PKC AMPAS	Paul Kohner Collection, Margaret Herrick Library, Academy of Motion Picture Arts and Sciences, Los Angeles
PL FBI	Peter Lorre FBI file
PLS	Peter Lorre scrapbook, author's collection
TCFC USC	20th Century–Fox Collection, Cinema-Television Library, Univ. of Southern California, Los Angeles
TCFLF UCLA	20th Century–Fox Film Corporation, Legal File, Collection 95, Arts Library Special Collections, Charles E. Young Research Library, Univ. of California, Los Angeles
TCLC	Theater Collection of the Lincoln Center for the Performing Arts, New York
UAC WCFTR	United Artists Collection, Wisconsin Center for Film and Theater Research, Madison
USPHS DHHS	U.S. Public Health Service, Department of Health and Human Services, Rockville, Maryland
WBA USC	USC Warner Bros. Archives, School of Cinema-Television, Univ. of Southern California, Los Angeles

PROLOGUE

Epigraphs: Peter Lorre, interview by Elwood Glover, *Assignment,* Canadian Broadcasting Network (CBC), May 29–31, 1962, CBC Archive, Ottawa, Ontario; Otto Fenichel, "On Acting," *Psychoanalytic Quarterly* 15 (1946): 149; *M* (1931).

QUOTATION SOURCES BY PAGE NUMBER

2 "Look what we've got here": Jeff Snyder, "Famed Actor's Daughter Testifies against Buono," *Los Angeles Daily News,* March 4, 1983.

2 "Look, it is . . . am the murderer": Jean Straker, "Such a Modest Murderer," *Film Pictorial,* May 9, 1936.

3 "against the grain . . . amount of inhibition": Peter Lorre, interview by Helen O'Connell, *Here's Hollywood,* NBC-TV, July 21, 1961.

3 "It's a racket . . . wrote a book": Peter Lorre, interview by Jack Paar, *The Tonight Show Starring Jack Paar,* NBC-TV, Nov. 16, 1961.

I. FACEMAKER

Epigraph: Peter Lorre, quoted in "Peter Lorre, 'Horror' King, Quite Willing to Be 'Typed,'" *LAT,* July 28, 1935.

1. Lorre's surname is correctly spelled either with an umlaut (Löwenstein) or without (Loewenstein). Because American-made typewriters and keyboards do not carry the German character, modern usage favors the latter variation, as did Lorre himself.

2. The biographical register contains vital information, personal description, and record of military service.

3. Lorre's first name is often given as Ladislav, the Slovak spelling.

4. After the German *Opa,* meaning Grandpa.

5. Austrian support of Bulgaria aroused resentment toward Emperor Franz Joseph and also very possibly influenced Loewenstein to leave Romania, which declared war on Austria-Hungary on August 22, 1914, siding with Great Britain, Russia, France, and Italy.

6. According to Andrew Lorre, the Czech government also expropriated property held by Loewenstein in the Tatra Mountains near the Russian frontier.

7. All translations from non-English sources are by the author unless otherwise indicated.

8. Franz Theodor Csokor also remembered Lorre working at the Zivnostenkabanka (Unincorporated Business Bank) in the Herrengasse. *Zeuge einer Zeit*, p. 128. Oskar Taussig kept his situation with the Anglo-Österreichischen Bank until 1925, when he stepped into a senior position with the Österreichischen Bundesbahn (Austrian State Railway).

9. In America, Reisch scripted a wide range of films, from *Ninotchka* (1939) to *Journey to the Center of the Earth* (1960).

10. "Little art" is "prose works of short length," including "short stories, sketches, anecdotes, essays, reviews, feuilletons, and aphorisms." Segel, *Vienna Coffeehouse Wits*, p. 29.

11. According to Segel, Sigmund Freud also popped in at Café Herrenhof from time to time. Ibid., p. 27.

12. *Stegreif* means literally "stirred up" or "warming up quickly." Moreno, *Psychodrama*, 1:180.

13. Lorre told co-worker Gustav Fröhlich that he had been "so bitterly poor that he had to sleep with his grandmother in her bed." Fröhlich to author, Jan. 12, 1980.

14. In Moreno's published account, the male actor is identified as Richard. "Peter was the pimp-murderer of the prostitute," wrote Zerka Moreno. "He was not so designated in that book" (Moreno, *Psychodrama*, 1:4). Zerka Moreno to author, July 27, 1977.

15. Alfred Kubin (1877–1959) was an illustrator, painter, and writer who specialized in the macabre. His fantastic and grotesque images of monsters and maimed humans appeared in many books, including German editions of the works of Edgar Allan Poe and Fyodor Dostoyevsky's *Der Doppelgänger*.

16. Lorre also admired Altenberg and frequented one of the poet's favorite haunts, the Café Central. Under the pseudonym Reimerich Kinderlieb, Frankfurt am Main physician Heinrich Hoffmann penned the popular nursery classic *Der Struwwelpeter oder lustige Geschichten und drollige Bilder für Kinder von 3–6 Jahren* (*Struwwelpeter or Amusing Stories and Comical Pictures with Beautiful Color Plates for Children Ages 3–6*), which took a comically instructive look at the consequences of misbehavior.

Both of Lorre's brothers, Andrew and Francis, changed their names. "There is nothing sinister about this," claimed Francis. "We all started out as 'Loewenstein.' In 1936 the Budapest side of the family changed to Lorant. Andrew took on Lorre (following Peter's lead) when he and his wife immigrated to the U.S.A. in 1938." Lorant to author, Nov. 21, 1979.

17. The Lobe Theater closed in 1935. Renamed the Gerhart Hauptmann Theater in 1932, the Thalia Theater closed its doors in 1936. Both theaters were wholly destroyed during World War II.

18. For Celia Lovsky, Peter tacked on the tale of a botched appendectomy at the hands of monks who dosed him with morphine without his knowledge. Lovksy, interview, Oct. 14, 1973.

19. Reference to the casting of Lorre in *Die Dreigroschenoper*, PEM [Paul E. Marcus], "Mein Freund, der Versteller," *Darmstadter Echo*, June 26, 1964.

20. Kosterlitz changed his name to Henry Koster after coming to America.

21. Friend and film critic Lotte H. Eisner recalled that "one day, in Hollywood, in the course of a big dinner, [Lorre] found himself opposite a French director whose table manners were not much appreciated. He ate his soup with such noise that he disturbed everybody. Lorre leaned towards him and politely murmured, 'Don't put yourself to so much trouble, Monsieur. We'll loop you later; for the moment we're shooting silent.'" "Peter Lorre le Meurtrier."

22. Celia Lovsky remembered that Lorre was paid five thousand marks ($1,200) monthly. Lovsky, interviews Oct. 14, 1973.

23. Although casting decisions rested with Aufricht and director Eric Engel, Lorre believed that Brecht brought his influence to bear on his behalf. Brecht scholar Klaus Völker maintained that only very talented beginners were signed for longer than one year at this time. Either Aufricht was mistaken or Lorre so impressed Brecht that he persuaded the theater manager to offer him a long-term contract. After all, it wasn't his money. Völker to author, March 9, 1987.

24. In an apparent effort to minimize the age difference, Lovsky placed Lorre at the Kammerspiele during this time.

25. The *Neuer Theater-Almanach* credits Bratislav Lvovsky with composing *Unter Cirkusleuten* (together with R. Felden), 1905; *Haus Gamineau,* 1907; *Die Irrfahrten des Odysseus,* 1909; and *Elga* (opera libretto, with Richard Battka), 1910.

26. On May 25, 1925, Lovsky wrote Schnitzler that she was a "loyal fan and big admirer of your art" and had been lucky enough to appear in his *Komödie der Worte* (*Comedy of Words*). Later that year, she realized her "dream for years" to play Johanna in the author's *Der einsame Weg* (*The Lonely Way*). According to Schnitzler's diary, Bratislav Lvovksy had sought to cultivate a personal connection with him some twenty years earlier, when he considered adapting one of his plays as an opera. Schiller Nationalmuseum, Deutsches Literatur Archiv, Marbach am Neckar, Germany.

27. As Lotte Lenya's understudy in *Die Dreigroschenoper,* Lovsky had also taken over the role of Jenny when the production moved on to another theater.

28. In May 1919, Lovsky married Heinrich Vinzenz Nowak, a doctor of philosophy who worked as a journalist; she did not obtain a divorce until 1929. She was also romantically linked to Karl Kraus, who called her his "nightingale," German stage director Karl Heinz Martin, and film director Fritz Lang. Engaged to director G.W. Pabst, she failed to show up for the wedding.

29. Nakamura is apparently shot at the end of act 2 and reappears at the very end of act 3.

30. Lovsky believed that "Lang knew perfectly well what the picture was going to be." Lovsky, interview, Oct. 14, 1973.

31. According to Kraus scholar Harry Zohn, he "recognized his age as 'the age of the feuilleton' in which newspaper reports took precedence over events, form eclipsed substance, and the style, the atmosphere, the 'package' were all-important." "Karl Kraus," in Daviau, *Turn-of-the-Century Austrian Literature,* p. 191.

32. Assembling the necessary documents apparently complicated and ultimately postponed their marriage plans. Celia Lovsky maintained that Lorre had been unable to obtain a copy of his birth certificate. Actually, notations on the document indicate that the Bureau of Vital Statistics in Svosovskelic, Slovakia, fielded his request in December 1930. Whether he never received it, or other bureaucratic obstacles blocked their way, is impossible to say. Lovsky, interview, Oct. 14, 1973.

Heimatgefühl is difficult to translate into English; the phrase conveys a strong sense of belonging to place.

33. Radio stations in Stettin, Magdeburg, Breslau, and Königsberg broadcast Lorre's performances for *Funkstunde Berlin* over the eastern part of Germany.

34. While Lorre appeared at the Renaissance Theater, Celia Lovsky performed on *Funkstunde Berlin* as Cupido in Shakespeare's *Timon of Athens.*

35. In a subsequent retelling of the story, Bentley added that Brecht told Lorre to have white paint ready in a bowl upstage. *Brecht Memoir,* p. 55.

5 "different and often . . . of reserve officers": Rothenberg, *Army of Francis Joseph,* pp. 127, 151.

6 "To me, the . . . they were poisonous": Kathy Vern-Barnett to author, Jan. 16, 1999.

6 "spoke of him . . . they needed it": Vern-Barnett, interview.

6 "At home and . . . and so on": Lorant, interview.

6 "extremely pragmatic": Vern-Barnett, interview.

6 "dark mountains": Service, "Women Scream."

7 "taught me what . . . owning many castles": ibid.

7 "To my small . . . further material welfare": "If I Were Santa Claus: Peter Lorre Tells J.M. Ruddy What He Would Do If He Were Given the Role," unidentified manuscript, Peter Lorre file, BFINL.

7 "Unadulterated B.S.": Andrew Lorre to author, Feb. 6, 1978.

7 "not a real . . . was very often": Lorant, interview.

8 "I believe the . . . verge of starvation": Vern-Barnett, interview.

8 "clever . . . from my side": Lorant, interview.

9 "unfeeling and soulless . . . soul out wide": Zweig, *World of Yesterday,* pp. 32, 36, 54, 57, 59.

9 "the nicest time of our youth": Lorant, interview.

9 "enemy officer": A. Lorre, interview by Bigwood.

10 "Practically always on . . . for many years": Lorant, interview.

10 "Opi was an . . . terribly practical man": Vern-Barnett, interview.

10 "a passionate secret . . . journalist Theodor Herzl": A. Lorre, interview, April 6, 1975.

10 "life-saving exercise": Vern-Barnett, interview.

10 "Let's just say . . . a lot longer": Vern-Barnett to author, Dec. 31, 1987.

10 "examine a pregnant . . . to Lauren Bacall": Vern-Barnett, interview.

11 "read a great . . . my many parts": Service, "Women Scream"; Lorant, interview.

11 "I was the . . . and not talk": Lorant, interview.

11 "He had no . . . intended to pursue": Hans Winge, "Mein armer Freund Peter," *Die Presse* (Vienna), March 26, 1964.

11 "expressing yourself and . . . is to it": Peter Lorre, interview by Mike Wallace, *Mike Wallace Interviews,* WNTA-TV, March 8, 1960, MWC HRHRC.

11 "I did not . . . my father's house": Service, "Women Scream."

11 "imagine that anybody . . . as the theater": Vern-Barnett, interview.

12 "some other nuts": W. Ward Marsh, "Lorre's Stage Experience on Continent Brilliantly Flares at the Palace Now," *Cleveland (Ohio) Plain Dealer,* Aug. 25, 1944.

12 "I am amazed . . . of an audience": Reynolds, "Reluctant Menace."

12 "Counting people's money is a thankless business": A.P. Eismann, "Weltberühmter 'Mörder': Ein erfundenes Interview mit Peter Lorre," *Welt am Sonntag* (Berlin ed.), Jan. 28, 1951.

12 "You know . . . me so severely": A. Lorre, interview, June 19, 1973.

13 "wasn't very good . . . I was fired": Peter Lorre, interview by O'Connell.

13 "his boss got . . . to the stage": A. Lorre, interview, June 19, 1973.

13 "We got our . . . away from home": Reisch, interview.

13 "sometimes he was . . . to live on": Lorant, interview.

13 "robbed people out of necessity": Carradine, interview.

14 "little lilac wool jacket for a roll": Lovsky, interview, Oct. 14, 1973.

14 "For a long . . . a sweet-shop": Straker, "Modest Murderer."

14 "I am the . . . really had scurvy": Karsten Peters, "Der Mörder mit der sanften Stimme," *Münchner Abendzeitung,* March 25, 1964.

14 "I know that . . . theater or learning": Lorant, interview.

14 "Peter's great obsession . . . about the theater": Reisch, interview.

15 "petrified formality . . . disciplined conformity": Janik and Toulmin, *Wittenstein's Vienna,* pp. 37, 42.

15 "ersatz totality": Alfred Polgar, "Theorie des Cafe Central," *Kleine Schriften,* vol. 4, *Literatur* (Reibek bei Hamburg: Rowohlt, 1984), pp. 254–59, quoted in Segel, *Vienna Coffeehouse Wits,* p. 267.

15 "asylum for people . . . killed by it": ibid., p. 268.

15 "cosmic uneasiness": ibid., p. 269.

15 "into an irresponsible . . . relationship to nothingness": ibid.

15 "organization of the disorganized": ibid., p. 268.

15 "on the Viennese . . . meridian of loneliness": ibid., p. 267.

15 "solo voice . . . of the chorus": ibid.

15 "as an unmasked . . . not by Gründgens": Dubrovic, *Veruntreute Geschichte,* p. 159.

16 "now and then flashes": Moreno, *Stegreiftheater,* p. 37.

16 "impromptu play . . . extemporaneously": Moreno, *Psychodrama,* p. 3.

16 "science": ibid., p. 12.

16 "he had been . . . impregnated a maid": Zerka Moreno to author, Jan. 8, 1985.

16 "were middle-class . . . evaluate his ability": ibid., July 27, 1977.

17 "ideal school of acting": "Kein Platz für zwei Mörder."

17 "the subject to . . . unlived out dimensions": Moreno, *Psychodrama,* p. 18.

17 "dramatic suicide": "Kein Platz für zwei Mörder."

17 "I don't believe . . . realm of imagination:" Alice L. Tildesley, "Behind the GREASE PAINT," unidentified clipping, TCLC.

17 "the actor must . . . in his performances": Otis L. Guernsey Jr., "Peter Lorre, Who Is Nothing like His Roles," *New York Herald-Tribune,* June 18, 1944.

17 "ecstatic pathos of expression": Dubrovic, *Veruntreute Geschichte,* p. 158.

17 "facial muscle acrobatics . . . spontaneous healing reactions": ibid., pp. 159–60.

17 "He acted particularly . . . was captivatingly infectious": Zerka Moreno to author, July 27, 1977.

17 "bedeviled creature": Moreno, *Psychodrama,* p. 4.

17 "mixture of mockery and kindness": Moreno, "Escape Me Never," p. 6.

17 "news just came . . . in ecstasy": Moreno, *Psychodrama,* p. 4.

18 "moments": Moreno, *Stegreiftheater,* p. 37.

18 "pictures": Herbert Jhering, "*Pioniere in Ingolstadt,*" *Berliner Börsen Courier,* April 2, 1929.

18 "There is little . . . feelings and being": Zerka Moreno to author, Jan. 8, 1985.

18 "peculiar grin . . . mimic behavior": ibid., July 27, 1977.

18 "kitten table for the children": Zohn, "John Kafka," p. 424.

18 "an exploding expression . . . think of Kubin": Kosch, *Deutsches Theater-Lexikon,* 2:1679.

19 "whose hair and . . . of the inspiration": Zerka Moreno to author, July 27, 1977.

19 "that he met . . . from Peter's mouth": Falkenberg, interview.

19 "Moreno did say . . . would not be": Zerka Moreno to author, Feb. 8, 1985.

19 "through a certain . . . enough of it": Lorre, interview by Wallace.

20 "an actor was . . . as a comic": Frazier, *The One with the Mustache,* p. 207. The chapter on Peter Lorre first appeared as "PETER LORRE: I got to go make faces," in *True,* July 1947.

20 "I was on . . . be coming up": Lorre, interview by O'Connell.

20 "dropped my spear . . . promptly fired me": "Biography of Peter Lorre," Publicity Department, RKO Pictures Inc., July 1940, Peter Lorre file, MHL AMPAS.

20 "did not expect . . . his protruding eyes": Sahl, interview.

20 "gave him the . . . to scare others": Sahl, *Memoiren eines Moralisten,* p. 83.

20 "very intelligent, well . . . serious about it": Sahl, interview.

21 "We often went . . . a new dimension": Sahl, *Memoiren eines Moralisten*, p. 83.

21 "dreams of grandeur": Sahl, interview.

21 "When I got . . . was operated on": Statement of Peter Lorre taken in the Office of the Federal Bureau of Narcotics, Feb. 27, 1947, USPHS DHHS. Copies of records relating to Lorre's treatment at the U.S. Public Health Service Hospital in Fort Worth, Texas, are from the author's collection.

21 "excellently": "Schauspielhaus: *Gesellshaft,*" (*Loyalties*), *Neue Zürcher Zeitung,* Dec. 24, 1925.

21 "extremely vivid . . . too much volume": "Schauspielhaus: *Das Tapfere Schneiderlein,*" ibid., Dec. 25, 1925.

22 "His little bit . . . to see you": St. Joseph, interview.

22 "numerous episodes of . . . vomiting, and diarrhea": Dr. D.D. Le Grand, Admission Summary, Personal History, March 24, 1947, Department of Justice, Penal and Correctional Institutions, U.S. Public Health Service Hospital, Fort Worth, Texas, USPHS DHHS.

22 "was not done by the best doctor": Statement of Peter Lorre, Feb. 27, 1947, USPHS DHHS.

22 "no doubt having . . . be the beginning": Lorant, interview.

22 "On and off . . . at that time": Statement of Peter Lorre, Feb. 27, 1947, USPHS DHHS.

22 "My Dear Brother and Kinsman": Peter Lorre to Andrew Lorre, July 1, 1926, author's collection.

23 "was the hit of the evening": F.R., "*Die fleissige Leserin,*" *Arbeiter-Zeitung* (Vienna), Oct. 24, 1926.

23 "Noteworthy is only . . . encouragement and cultivation": F.R., "*Das Mädchen auf dem Diwan,*" ibid., Nov. 6, 1926.

23 "The only one . . . he presented it": F.R., "*Alles verkehrt,*" ibid., April 22, 1927.

23 "Peter Lorre tried . . . for grotesque strangeness": F.R., "*Sie darf seinen Sohn haben,*" ibid., Aug. 18, 1927.

23 "acid-like grotesque humor": F.R., "*Bitte, wer war zuerst da?*" ibid., Sept. 7, 1927.

24 "What was the . . . him more morphine": Lorant, interview.

24 "the most exciting . . . city in Europe": Slezak, *What Time's the Next Swan?* p. 130.

24 "striking mixture of cynicism and confidence": Gay, *Weimar Culture,* p. 2.

24 "sticky, perfumed, sultry": Zweig, *World of Yesterday,* p. 71.

24 "Everything is jam-packed . . . what a scale": Bertolt Brecht to Caspar Neher, Feb. 1920, in Brecht, *Letters,* p. 58.

24 "organically structured": Bruno Taut, quoted in Friedrich, *Berlin between the Wars,* p. 97.

25 "alter ego . . . odd type": Joseph, interview.

25 "big amounts of . . . I became addicted": Statement of Peter Lorre, Feb. 27, 1947, USPHS DHHS.

25 "come out of . . . not at all": Franz Theodor Csokor to Ferdinand Bruckner, Nov. 28, 1936, in Csokor, *Zeuge einer Zeit,* p. 129.

25 "In my forechamber . . . (*Engineers in Ingolstadt*)": Aufricht, *Erzähle,* p. 92.

26 "[Brecht] cast me . . . like an actor": P.K., "Peter Lorre—Fan of Brecht," *San Francisco Chronicle,* Feb. 8, 1963.

26 "hold with beautiful . . . appealed to him": Lenya, interview.

26 "In those days . . . unique, the distinctive": Feuchtwanger, interview.

26 "Whatever he said . . . I really was": Jacobi, interview.

26 "Normally, you don't . . . you don't forget": Alten, interview.

26 "ridiculous . . . was making fun": Rühmann, *Das War's,* p. 48.

27 "making a movie . . . were just soldiers": Charles Bennett to author, April 19, 1975.

27 "He had such . . . asparagus with Vaseline": Koster, interview.

27 "unchained bidet": Ophüls, *Spiel im Dasein,* p. 135.

27 "He showed himself . . . a comedian's melancholy": Lotte H. Eisner, "Sur le procès de Quat'Sous," *Europe,* Special Brecht Number, 35 (Jan.-Feb. 1957): 112.

27 "overpowering": Greenberg, "Peter Lorre."

27 "in that small . . . of our times": Bronnen, *Tage mit Bertolt Brecht,* p. 14.

27 "It was as . . . play I have": David Slavitt, ed., "In the Red," *Newsweek,* Sept. 3, 1962.

28 "Why do you . . . radiates an aura": Peter Lorre, "Ein Aberglaube ist immer dabei," *Berliner Film Anzeiger,* Sept. 28, 1951.

28 "blaze of glory": Lenya, "August 28, 1928," p. ix.

28 "the naked human . . . heard in years": Jhering, "Kritiken aus den zwanziger Jahren," p. 231.

28 "the genius, the . . . master, the creator": Günther Rühle, "Leben und Schreiben der Marieluise Fleisser aus Ingolstadt," in *Gesammelte Werke,* by Marieluise Fleisser, ed. Günther Rühle (Frankfurt am Main: Suhrkamp, 1972), 1:17. (Rühle cobbled together this list of descriptive terms from Fleisser's "Avantgarde" in vol. 3).

28 "You must write like a child": Marieluise Fleisser, "Frühe Begegnung," in *Akzente: Zeitschrift für Dichtung,* ed. Walter Höllerer and Hans Bender (Munich: Carl Hanser, 1966), p. 241.

29 "an epic tableau with different motifs": ibid., p. 19.

29 "change and change . . . they didn't complain": Rühle, *Materialien zum Leben und Schreiben der Marieluise Fleisser,* p. 198.

29 "a half-cretin . . . high school student": Alfred Polgar, "Soldaten und Dienstmädchen," *Das Tagebuch* (Berlin), April 6, 1929.

29 "was aiming for . . . that guaranteed success": Rühle, *Materialien zum Leben und Schreiben der Marieluise Fleisser,* p. 342.

29 "Do you believe . . . allow such things": Aufricht, *Erzähle,* p. 94.

29 "The times had . . . which came afterwards": Fleisser, "Avantgarde," p. 154.

30 "splendid in local stupidity": Alfred Kerr, "*Pioniere in Ingolstadt,*" *Berliner Tageblatt,* April 2, 1929.

30 "Things are ready . . . its political annihilation": Dr. Richard Biedrzynski, "Eine Frau ausgepfiffen! Der Skandal im Theater am Schiffbauerdamm," *Deutsche Zeitung* (Berlin), April 2, 1929.

30 "natural art": Brecht, *Werke, Schriften 4: Texte zu Stücken*(1991), 24:296.

30 "Peter was completely . . . a whole scene": Lenya, interview.

30 "He bills himself . . . slow motion actor": Polgar, "Soldaten und Dienstmädchen."

30 "And a new . . . first-class actor": Kurt Pinthus, "Abermals ein Verbot im Theater am Schiffbauerdamm," *8-Uhr-Abendblatt* (Berlin), April 2, 1929.

31 "I was afraid . . . I will buy a new suit'": Reynolds, "Reluctant Menace."

31 "I was the . . . the Berlin stage": Greenberg, "Peter Lorre."

31 "there were women . . . could say that": Lovsky, interview, Oct. 14, 1973.

32 "I was only . . . and worshiped": Paul Dehn, "Mrs. Lorre says: Peter Is No Monster," *Sunday Referee* (London), Feb. 9, 1936.

32 "love at first sight": Lovsky, interview, Oct. 14, 1973.

32 "I always wanted . . . my private life": Rick du Brown, "Peter Lorre wollte lieber Bösewicht sein als Liebhaber," *Hamburger Echo,* May 9, 1959.

32 "for exemplary and needy students": Hochschule für Musik und darstellende Kunst in Wien, Archiv.

32 "form her parts . . . and her mind": F.R., "*Ein ganzer Mann,*" *Arbeiter-Zeitung,* June 19, 1927.

33 "the city which consumes one totally": Celia Lovsky to Arthur Schnitzler, July 30, 1929, Schiller Nationalmuseum, Deutsches Literatur Archiv, Marbach am Neckar, Germany.

33 "If somebody said . . . to get out": Lovsky, interview, Oct. 14, 1973.

33 "in the same combination": Aufricht, *Erzähle*, p. 96.

33 "middlebrow popular success": Michael Feingold, introduction to Brecht, *Happy End*, p. v.

33 "contained not a . . . or political satire": *Die Rote Fahne* (Berlin), Sept. 4, 1928, reprinted in Monika Wyss, "*Die Dreigroschenoper*," in Wyss, *Brecht in der Kritik*, pp. 82–83.

33 "best": Brecht, *Arbeitsjournal*, vol. 1, *1938–1942*, p. 43.

33 "a couple of nice ideas": Alfred Kerr, "*Happy End?*" *Berliner Tageblatt* (evening ed.), Sept. 3, 1929.

33 "vulgar Marxist provocations": Aufricht, *Erzähle* p. 100.

34 "build your position . . . positions are impossible": Herbert Jhering, "*Happy End*," *Berliner Börsen-Courier*, Sept. 3, 1929.

34 "world-view drama": Günther Stark, "*Dantons Tod*" (theater program), Sept. 22, 1929.

34 "You thought I . . . little bit injured": "Kein Platz für zwei Mörder."

35 "philosopher of terror": Herbert Jhering, "*Dantons Tod*," *Berliner Börsen-Courier*, Sept. 2, 1929.

35 "Hypocritical, mollusk-like . . . to the people": Alexander von Sacher-Masoch, "*Dantons Tod* in der Volksbühne," *Vorwärts* (Berlin), Sept. 2, 1929.

35 "many natural possibilities": Wilhelm Westecker, "Danton in Blau-weiss-rot," *Berliner Börsen-Zeitung*, Sept. 2, 1931.

35 "great histrionic talent": Jhering, "*Dantons Tod*."

36 "the breath of our times": Alexander von Sacher-Masoch, "Wedekinds *Frühlings Erwachen*," *Vorwärts*, Oct. 15, 1929.

36 "gliding togetherness of both children": Max Osborn, "*Frühlings Erwachen*," *Berliner Morgenpost*, Oct. 16, 1929.

36 "a youth to . . . everything a problem": Franz Köppen, "*Frühlings Erwachen* in der Volksbühne," *Berliner Börsen-Zeitung*, Oct. 15, 1929.

36 "Probably no words . . . by Peter Lorre": Walter Benjamin, "Wedekind und Kraus in der Volksbühne," in *Gesammelte Schriften*, ed. Tillman Rexroth (Frankfurt am Main: Suhrkamp, 1972), vol. 4, pt. 2, p. 552.

36 "the quiet Vulcan . . . explodes—and how": Fritz Engel, "*Frühlings Erwachen*," *Berliner Tageblatt*, Oct. 15, 1929.

36 "An extraordinarily capable . . . in technical details": Sacher-Masoch, "Wedekinds *Frühlings Erwachen*."

37 "If he is . . . of the part": Bogdanovich, *Who the Devil Made It*, p. 208.

37 "looked like a . . . and dark eyes": Lang, interview.

37 "I will do . . . star of it": Lovksy, interview, May 12, 1977.

37 "I was really . . . faith in it": Marsh, "Lorre's Stage Experience."

37 "my puss could not be photographed": P.K., "Peter Lorre—Fan of Brecht."

37 "with a face . . . career in films": Bill Slocum, "The Peter Lorre Nobody Knows," *New York Mirror*, Feb. 19, 1960.

37 "belief in miracles . . . this future music": Lorre, "Auf vier Jahre."

38 "frightening occurrence in seven hilarious acts": "Die verschwundene Frau," advertisement, Bundesarchiv/Filmarchiv (Berlin).

38 "cool twilight . . . recluses and eccentrics": Malmberg, *Widerhall des Herzens*, pp. 133–34, quoted in Segel, *Vienna Coffeehouse Wits*, p. 22.

38 "oddly ecclesiastical . . . of cigarette smoke": Werfel, *Pure at Heart*, pp. 319–20, quoted in Segel, *Vienna Coffeehouse Wits*, pp. 23–24.

39 "the great love": Joseph, interview.

39 "pose and pathos": Grimstad, *Masks of the Prophet*, p. 10.

39 "My brother and . . . boy scout troupe": A. Lorre, interview, April 6, 1975.

40 "In reality, Lorre . . . wants to play": *Berliner Börsen Courier*, Nov. 1, 1929.

40 "technical reasons": B.F., "Karl Kraus klagt gegen die Volksbühne," *Berlin am Morgen*, Nov. 2, 1929, reprinted in *Die Fackel*, nos. 827–33, Feb. 1930, XXXI, 35:32–33.

40 "Lorre took the . . . over-exerted himself": Kurt Pinthus, *8-Uhr-Abendblatt*, Oct. 21, 1929, reprinted in *Die Fackel*, nos. 827–33, Feb. 1930, XXXI, 35:29.

40 "He becomes loud . . . self-conscious shouting": Herbert Jhering, "*Die Unüberwindlichen* in Berlin," *Berliner Börsen-Courier*, Oct. 21, 1929.

40 "At a time . . . full of joy": Peter Lorre to Franz Theodor Csokor, Jan. 3, 1930, HWS.

42 "had a chance . . . of the law": Barrett, "Alsbergs Auditorium," *Berliner Zeitung*, Oct. 15, 1930.

42 "proving again and . . . with smallest means": Emik Faktor, "*Voruntersuchung*," *Berliner Börsen Courier*, Oct. 15, 1930.

42 "amusing impudence of the cabaret performer": Paul Wiegler, "Alsberg und Hesse: *Voruntersuchung*," *Berliner Zeitung*, Oct. 15, 1930.

42 "so much laughing . . . people's hands hurt": "*Die Quadratur des Kreises*," *8-Uhr-Abendblatt*, Dec. 5, 1930.

42 "terrific": Erich Burger, "*Die Quadratur des Kreises*," *Berliner Tageblatt*, Dec. 6, 1930.

42 "Peter loved the . . . furthered his talents": Lenya, interview.

43 "a conception of . . . which few understand": Bentley, *Brecht Commentaries*, p. 290.

43 "he was very . . . didn't come through": Roth, interview.

43 "the mentality of our time": Bertolt Brecht, "The Epic Theatre and Its Difficulties," quoted in Willett, *Brecht on Theatre*, p. 23. (Willett cites original German sources for selections from Brecht's notes and theoretical writings.)

43 "sentimental element of a worn out bourgeoisie": Bertolt Brecht, "Kurzer Bericht über 400 junge Lyriker," *Die literarische Welt*, Feb. 4, 1927.

43 "wit sparkles like . . . heart to compassion": "Dialogue about Bert Brecht's Play *A Man's a Man*," in Brecht, *Collected Plays*, 2:238.

43 "Invent a theory . . . will swallow anything": Frank, *Spielzeit meines Lebens*, p. 266.

43 "magnetic sleep by . . . waking them up": Bentley, *Brecht Commentaries*, p. 259.

43 "irrelevant emotion": ibid., p. 58.

43 "not . . . reality": ibid., p. 61.

44 "changes of emphasis": Bertolt Brecht, "The Modern Theatre Is the Epic Theatre (Notes to the opera *Aufstieg und Fall der Stadt Mahagonny*)," in Willett, *Brecht on Theatre*, p. 37.

44 "being . . . pretending": Siebig, "Ich geh' mit dem Jahrhundert mit," p. 128.

44 "realized that you . . . with the actor": Roth, interview.

44 "you never knew . . . Who cares, anyhow?'": ibid.

44 "what Brecht called . . . theater of types": Szczesny, *Case against Bertolt Brecht*, p. 44.

44 "I am so . . . alienation. Later maybe": Lenya, interview.

44 "stopped for a . . . enough for me": Adam, "Lotte Lenya," p. 709.

45 "enigmatic, demonic, full . . . to the point": Siebig, "Ich geh' mit dem Jahrhundert mit," p. 128.

45 "whatever he learned from everywhere": Roth, interview.

45 "strange faces, strange . . . them twelve marks": ibid.

45 "Brecht followed the . . . kind of acting": Bentley, interview.

45 "Brecht found Peter . . . influence is necessary": Feuchtwanger, interview.

45 "other possibilities": Bertolt Brecht, "Short Description of a New Technique of Acting Which Produces an Alienation Effect," in Willett, *Brecht on Theatre*, p. 137.

45 "Brecht was fascinated . . . natural Brecht actor": Bentley, interview.

46 "It might be . . . the parts together": Zerka Moreno to author, Jan. 8, 1985.

46 "natural gestures": Feuchtwanger, interview.

46 "the most objective . . . contradictory internal process": Bertolt Brecht, "The Question of Criteria for Judging Acting (Notes to *Mann ist Mann*)," in Willett, *Brecht on Theatre*, p. 54.

46 "means both gist . . . words or actions": Brecht, "The Modern Theatre Is the Epic Theatre," p. 42.

47 "socially critical . . . the character portrayed": Brecht, "Short Description," p. 139.

47 "He used freedom . . . bare man's cupidity": Joseph Pevney to author, Aug. 21, 1975.

47 "When an actor . . . I take it": Lenya, interview.

47 "recalled how [Brecht's] . . . among its participants": Greenberg, "Peter Lorre."

47 "harmonious cooperation which . . . the European theatre": Manfred George, "Peter Lorre Returns to the German Cinema," *NYT*, Sept. 23, 1951.

47 "If there's not . . . be in there": Roth, interview.

47 "they might well . . . humour and meaning": "Notes on Erwin Strittmatter's Play *Katzgraben*," in Willett, *Brecht on Theatre*, p. 247.

48 "worked hard, but . . . very creative fun": Roth, interview.

48 "into the hands . . . him lying skinless": Bertolt Brecht, "Editorial Notes," in Brecht, *Collected Plays*, 2:246.

48 "human type": Bertolt Brecht, "Introductory Speech (For the Radio)," ibid., 2:237.

48 "a private person . . . in the mass": ibid.

48 "Brecht declare[d] that . . . a classic comedy": Elisabeth Hauptmann, "Notes on Brecht's Works, 1926," in Witt, *Brecht as They Knew Him*, p. 51.

48 "precious ego . . . It's a jolly business": Brecht, "Introductory Speech," 2:237.

48 "monstrous mixture of comedy and tragedy": Brecht, "Editorial Notes," 2:248.

48 "possibly you will . . . person to object": Brecht, "Introductory Speech," 2:238.

48 "socially negative hero . . . powers of attraction": Bertolt Brecht, "On Looking through My First Plays," in Brecht, *Collected Plays*, 2:245.

49 "the only compliment . . . for several pages": Slavitt, "In the Red."

49 "new point of view": Brecht, "The Question of Criteria," p. 53.

49 "clarity and the . . . his meaning clear": Herbert Jhering, "Scandal in the Staatstheater," *Berliner Börsen-Courier*, Feb. 7, 1931.

49 "hallmarks of great . . . interruptions and jumps": Brecht, "The Question of Criteria," pp. 53–55.

50 "They're pale, they're scared, that's what": Benjamin, *Understanding Brecht*, p. 115.

50 "the packer's face . . . the soldier's face": Brecht, "The Question of Criteria," p. 55.

50 "He had put . . . as a sheet": Bentley, interview.

50 "influenced by fear . . . the more profound": Brecht, "The Question of Criteria," pp. 55–56.

50 "Brecht laughed over . . . get the effect": Bentley, interview.

50 "Peter's quietness, subtle . . . Brecht liked this": Feuchtwanger, interview.

50 "the Hitlerite actor . . . a mass meeting": Bentley, *Brecht Commentaries*, p. 59.

50 "the separation of . . . a tragic one": Bertolt Brecht, "Alienation Effects in the Narrative Pictures of the Elder Brueghel," in Willett, *Brecht on Theatre*, p. 157.

51 "There was an . . . very long time": Bentley, interview.

51 "He is a . . . and in us": "Staatliches Schauspielhaus Berlin," B.W. (*Zeitung?*), Feb. 7, 1931, reprinted in Rühle, *Theater für die Republik*, pp. 1071–72.

2. M IS FOR MORPHINE

Epigraphs: King, interview by Katz; Lorre, quoted in unidentified newspaper clipping, ca. 1935, PLS.

1. Carl Balhaus played the part of Moritz Stiefel in the film, which was released in 1929. Some filmographies mistakenly credit Lorre with appearing in *Frühlings Erwachen* (1929) as well as *Der weisse Teufel* (*The White Devil*, 1930), possibly confusing it with

Der weisse Dämon (*The White Demon*), in which he appeared in 1932.

2. Early variations on the same theme included *Eine Stadt sucht einen Mörder* (*A City Searches for a Murderer*) and *Dein Mörder sieht dich an* (*Your Killer Looks at You*).

3. Acknowledged then, but overlooked later, was a series of stories about Kürten's activities supervised by Egon Jacobson, editor-in-chief of the *Berliner Zeitung am Mittag*, who was credited—on-screen—for his article on which Lang based his film.

4. All dialogue from *M*, unless otherwise indicated, is taken from Nicholas Garnham, *Classic Film Scripts: M a film by Fritz Lang* (New York: Simon and Schuster, 1968).

5. Originally cast as Schränker, Hans Peppler died suddenly of appendicitis in mid-December 1930.

6. For further discussion of the sexual significance of Grieg's "In the Hall of the Mountain King," refer to Tatar, *Lustmord*, p. 158.

7. This scene, not contained in the Garnham film script, is taken from the Home Vision Cinema version of *M*, released in 1997.

8. After emigrating to the United States, Kurt Siodmak, who changed his name to Curt Siodmak, became a prolific screenwriter in Hollywood.

9. Lorre, Lang, and Nebenzal attended the Paris premiere of *M* at the Studio des Ursulines on April 18, 1932. The actor, however, did not join his producer and director for the June 5 debut at London's Cambridge Theatre, graced also by members of the English diplomatic corps and officials from the German Embassy. Nonetheless, the trades reported that Lorre had recreated his performance in English for a dubbed version of *M* recorded in England. In his piece "Auf vier Jahre Rückblick und eine Vorschau" (Four Years Looking Backward and Forward), for *Mein Film*, March 17, 1933, the actor claimed to have "played the part in the German and English versions." Since, according to Celia Lovsky, Lorre did not visit England until 1934, when he was invited there by Alfred Hitchcock, it is likely he dubbed his own voice in Berlin. Unfortunately, the English version is now lost.

10. Still unforgiving of Lang's ill treatment during the filming of *M*, Lorre later told an interviewer he did not "know then [in 1929] that Lang was one of the really fine directors of the screen." At the same time that he snubbed the legendary filmmaker, he put Brecht—who was in the United States at the time—on a pedestal. Marsh, "Lorre's Stage Experience."

11. Reference to Lorre's youthful appearance, Erich Burger, "Volksstück 1931? Georg Kaisers 'Nebeneinander' in der Voksbühne," *Berliner Tageblatt*, Sept. 17, 1931.

12. Reference to Alfred Kerr on German fraud, "Verneuil: *Die Nemo-Bank*," *Berliner Tageblatt*, Dec. 24, 1931.

13. After emigrating to America, Hermann Kosterlitz changed his name to Henry Koster.

14. Lorre expressed his regret to Siodmak that his language skills were not up to the task of playing in the French and English versions. Curt Siodmak, "Tribute to Peter Lorre," in Cargnelli and Omasta, *Aufbruch ins Ungewisse*.

15. Examiners specifically objected to showing the profitable possibilities of the drug trade (and what appeared to be a how-to-smuggle guide); the anticipation of a fix; the calming, almost benign nature of morphine; the active involvement of the user; and the authorities' inability to deal with the problem. They recommended making the drug-dependence issue more black and white, emphasizing the dangers inherent in narcotics addiction, and downplaying the soothing, euphoric effects of opiates. The studio simultaneously shot a French version, in which Lorre also appeared, titled *Stupéfiants* (*Narcotics*). The picture was also released as *Rauschgift* (*Dope*) in Austria. "*Der weisse Dämon*," Regierungsoberinspektor Dr. Seeger, Film-Oberprüfstelle, Berlin, Nov. 10, 1932, Staatliches Filmarchiv der DDR.

16. Actor-director Johannes Riemann (1888–1959); actor-playwright Eugen Rex (1884–1943).

17. The "perfect linguist," said Katscher, Lorre "was accepted to play the part also in the French version," *Les requins du Pétrole* (*The Oil Sharks*). Rudolf Katscher to author, Nov. 16, 1980.

18. Reference to the film review by F.B., "*Unsichtbare Gegner*," *Deutsche Allgemeine Zeitung* (Berlin), Sept. 23, 1933.

19. Given the political situation, said Celia, Peter did not consider invitations to perform in vaudeville on stages in Vienna and Zurich. Lovsky, interview, Oct. 14, 1973.

20. This effort marked the first of two incidental story collaborations with Billy Wilder. Asked later why he never used the actor in one of his films, the legendary director replied, "I did think of casting Lorre in one of my films. Somehow the right part never came along." Billy Wilder to author, Aug. 8, 1986.

21. One of the film offers was likely that from Alexis Granowsky, who had directed Lorre in *Die Koffer des Herrn O.F.* and wanted the actor for *Les Nuits Moskovites* (*Moscow Nights*, 1934).

QUOTATION SOURCES BY PAGE NUMBER

52 "virgin": Riess, *Das gab's nur einmal*, p. 306.

52 "I sometimes cursed . . . any film offers": unidentified clipping, PLS.

52 "I never paid any attention to it": Lorre, interview by Glover.

52 "Peter confessed to . . . what Lang wanted": Reisch, interview.

53 "A director should . . . make any movies": Lang, interview.

53 "big canvasses": Fritz Lang, interview by Gretchen Berg, 1965–66, FLC USC.

53 "what makes him . . . makes him tick": Gandert, "Fritz Lang über 'M,'" p. 123.

53 "The first idea . . . to catch [Kürten]": Fritz Lang, "Some Random Notes about *M*," FLC, USC.

53 "every human mind . . . of your peers": Fritz Lang, "Director Tells of Blood Letting and Violence," *Los Angeles Herald-Express*, Aug. 12, 1947.

53 "Let's make a . . . resents very much": "Fritz Lang Seminar," *Dialogue on Film*, April 1974.

54 "This is not . . . everything before me": Riess, *Das gab's nur einmal*, p. 421.

54 "to explain Kürten . . . disintegrating social system": Lang, interview by Berg.

54 "synthesis of facts": Lang, "Some Random Notes about *M*."

54 "habit of sending . . . a sick mind": Lang, interview by Berg.

55 "a two-natured human being": Lenk and Kaever, *Leben und Wirken des Peter Kürten*, p. 83.

55 "fill in some of the gaps": Lang, interview by Berg.

55 "Wordless, he sat . . . at the guests": "*M macht ein Ende*," *Der Spiegel* (Hannover), Aug. 25, 1949.

55 "A director should . . . a cops-and-robbers story": Bogdanovich, *Who the Devil Made It*, pp. 201, 220.

56 "plain thriller": John Grierson, *Everyman* (London), June 16, 1932, reprinted in Hardy, *Grierson on the Movies*, p. 66.

56 "higher instincts": "Berliner Studenten diskutieren mit Fritz Lang," *Film-Kurier* (Berlin), May 23, 1931.

56 "witness to the 30s": Michel Ciment, Goffredo Fofi, Louis Seguin, and Roger Talleur, "Fritz Lang in Venice," *Positif* 94 (April 1968): 9–15, reprinted in Grant, *Fritz Lang Interviews*, p. 100.

56 "looks after the . . . pros and cons": Gandert, "Fritz Lang über 'M,'" p. 124.

58 "gives wordless expression to his inner urges": ibid., p. 126.

58 "Though Peter had . . . to fake it": Lang, interview.

58 "I am a . . . off balance mentally": Gene Phillips, "Fritz Lang Remembers," *Focus on Film* (Spring 1975).

58 "If I play . . . display his symptoms": Marguerite Tazelaar, "Even the Doctors Are Amazed When Lorre Acts Pathological," *New York Herald-Tribune*, Nov. 3, 1935.

59 "Lang wrung him . . . and his best": Falkenberg, interview.

59 "Peter fainted . . . used that shot": Curt Siodmak to author, March 26, 1975.

59 "Stalin of Film": "Fritz Lang's Tonfilm," *Film-Kurier*, May 12, 1931.

59 "Look, if you . . . anything to say": Bogdanovich, *Who the Devil Made It*, p. 228; Lang, interview by Berg.

59 "liked to stir . . . atmosphere of tension": Bienert, interview.

59 "I came upon . . . off the salami": A. Lorre, interview by Bigwood.

59 "A director . . . exists in himself": Lang, interview.

60 "unloosened . . . have done that": Falkenberg, interview.

60 "If you don't . . . injunction against you": Lang, interview.

60 "muttered dire threats . . . a steady keel": Falkenberg, interview.

60 "a genius who . . . of his director": Greene, "Genius of Peter Lorre."

60 "I did not . . . I did understand": Service, "Women Scream."

61 "Create your own . . . work for you": Sonia Moore, *Stanislavski System*, p. xvi.

61 "a very emotional . . . of his emotions": C. Lorre, interviews.

61 "You can't portray . . . in the role": "Hollywood By-The-Way."

61 "Lorre brings a . . . problems Lang avoided": St., "Tonfilme: 'M,'" *Deutsche Filmzeitung* (Berlin) 33 (1931).

61 "contradictions of existence": Benjamin, *Understanding Brecht*, p. 8.

61 "psychological operation": Brecht, "Short Description," p. 137.

61 "interruptions and jumps": Brecht, "The Question of Criteria," p. 55.

61 "never guided actors . . . to overdo it": Bienert, interview.

61 "more simply, in his own way": Lovksy, interview, Oct. 14, 1973.

61 "the feelings of a person": Fritz Lang, "Creating a Motion Picture," in Hochman, *From Quasimodo to Scarlett O'Hara*, p. 386.

61 "the viewpoint of . . . thinks with him": Bogdanovich, *Who the Devil Made It*, p. 217.

62 "sympathetic grasp": Greene, "Genius of Peter Lorre."

62 "If you could . . . an overwhelming pity": Buchanan, "REAL and UNREAL Horror."

62 "In *M* . . . you become weak": C. Barton, interview.

63 "Mr. Lang, this . . . make any cuts": "Fritz Lang Seminar."

63 "a gruesome mockery . . . amusing or satirical": Herbert Jhering, "M," *Berliner Börsen Courier*, May 12, 1931, reprinted in Jhering, *Von Reinhardt bis Brecht*, vol. 3, *1930–1932*, pp. 342–43.

63 "only ever peeps . . . a mere 'sensational'": Hardy, *Grierson on the Movies*, pp. 66–67.

63 "the first film . . . aspects of crime": Lang, "Some Random Notes about *M*."

64 "the film is . . . so we progress": Bruce Blevin, *New Republic*, April 19, 1933.

64 "with delicacy and fine feeling": "Das geheimnisvolle 'M,'" *Filmwelt* (Berlin), no. 21, May 24, 1931.

64 "every attempt to . . . of his punishment": K.E., "Klassiker des Films: Gedanken zur Neuaufführung des Fritz-Lang-Films 'M,'" *Hannoversche Presse* (Hannover), April 16, 1960.

64 "old-fashioned": Marsh, "Lorre's Stage Experience."

64 "remains as fresh . . . of its release": K.E., "Klassiker des Films."

64 "one of the . . . in his life": Lang, interview.

64 "The murderer Peter . . . the moving touch": "Fritz Lang's Tonfilm."

64 "the scarcely comprehensible . . . Unbelievable": Dr. Hans Wollenberg, "M," *Lichtbildbühne* (Berlin), May 12, 1931.

64 "For the crystallization . . . the tragic hero": William Troy, "Tragedy and the Screen," *Nation*, April 19, 1933.

65 "nerve-tickling": Tölle, "'M' Tonfilm von Fritz Lang," *Arbeiterbühne und Film* (Berlin) 6 (1931).

65 "on the whole . . . diminishes the impression": Heinz Pol, "Fritz Langs Film vom Kindermörder," *Vossische Zeitung* (Berlin), May 13, 1931.

65 "physiognomically he is . . . by the beggars": Jhering, *Von Reinhardt bis Brecht,* 3:343.

65 "To show you . . . in Lang's *M*": Marsh, "Lorre's Stage Experience."

65 "Do you realize . . . in that performance": St. Joseph, interview.

65 "My trouble is . . . any other part": Rose Pelswick, *"Crime and Punishment,* His New Film, Due at Radio City Thursday," *New York Evening Journal,* Nov. 19, 1935.

65 "eerie . . . I become uncomfortable": Inge Landgut to author, May 6, 1985.

66 "never before so . . . in the morning": Eggebrecht, *Der halbe Weg,* pp. 255–56.

66 "Terrible letters came . . . I tell you": Rosalind Shaffer, "Star's Success as a Monster Was His Trap!" *New York Sunday News,* Sept. 2, 1934.

66 "Obsessed with the . . . kill the actor": "Lorre's Realism a Danger to His Life," *Secret Agent,* pressbook, 1936.

66 "it was a . . . a tough guy": Fraenkel, interview.

66 "a schoolteacher . . . in the school": Goff, interview, July 31, 1978.

67 "in order to quiet his nerves": Aufricht, *Erzähle,* p. 120.

67 "suggestive voice": Monty Jacobs, "Savoirs *Dompteur,*" *Vossische Zeitung* (Berlin), March 31, 1931.

67 "mask and play, truest circus": Stx, "Spiel um eine Idee," *Berliner Lokal-Anzeiger,* March 31, 1931.

67 "I wanted to . . . to be short": Reynolds, "Reluctant Menace."

67 "cannibalistic innuendo": Falkenberg, interview.

67 "Now people began . . . a horror actor": Reynolds, "Reluctant Menace."

68 "glimmer-magic": Felix Dassel, "Tuchfühlung der Seele," *Deutsche Allgemeine Zeitung,* July 18, 1931.

68 "lyrical frivolity, sexual . . . the right place": Herbert Jhering, *"Bomben auf Monte Carlo,"* Berlin Börsen Courier, Sept. 1, 1931, reprinted in Jhering, *Von Reinhardt bis Brecht,* 3:357.

68 "It is amusing . . . love and guile": unidentified review, Cinémathèque Français, Paris.

69 "Nothing has any . . . in our blood": Kenworthy, *Georg Kaiser,* pp. 66–67.

69 "goes down the . . . historical reminiscence": Norbert Falk, "Georg Kaisers *Nebeneinander,*" *Berliner Zeitung,* Sept. 17, 1931.

69 "too stale, too strange": ibid.

69 "without the shine . . . a life winner": Monty Jacobs, "Kaisers *Nebeneinander,*" *Vossische Zeitung,* Sept. 19, 1931.

69 "hopelessly drowning in . . . empty tragic tirades": Paul Fechter, "Georg Kaisers *Nebeneinander,*" *Deutsche Allgemeine Zeitung,* Sept. 17, 1931.

69 "streaking like a shot out of a gun": Jacobs, "Kaisers *Nebeneinander.*"

69 "the mask of . . . and imposed sentimentality": Max Hochdorf, "Georg Kaiser: *Nebeneinander,*" *Vörwarts,* Sept. 17, 1931.

69 "able, intensive performance . . . a monotone lament": Emil Faktor, *"Nebeneinander,"* Berliner Börsen Courier, Sept. 17, 1931.

70 "Playing more out . . . old clothes shop": Norbert Falk, "Georg Kaisers *Nebeneinander,*" *Berliner Zeitung,* Sept. 17, 1931.

70 "sweet kitsch . . . sour kitsch": Herbert Jhering, *"Geschichten aus dem Wiener Wald,"* Berliner Börsen Courier, Nov. 3, 1931, reprinted in Jhering, *Von Reinhardt bis Brecht,* 3:198.

70 "mistakes and vices": Gregor, *Der Schauspielerführer,* 7:183.

70 "for whose immeasurably . . . borders on innocence": Max Osborn, *"Geschichten aus dem Wiener Wald,"* Berliner Morgenpost, Nov. 3, 1931.

72 "in a time . . . a modern actor": Herbert Jhering, "Peter Lorre," *Berliner Börsen Cou-*

rier, June 24, 1932, reprinted in "Porträts und Charakteristiken," in Jhering, *Von Reinhardt bis Brecht,* 3:19–20.

72 "underwritten . . . any unsuspecting bottom": Rudolph Cartier (Katscher) to author, Dec. 29, 1980.

73 "off the rack": E.H.T., "*Schuss im Morgengrauen,*" *Filmwoche* (Berlin), Aug. 3, 1932.

73 "splendid acting": J.R., "*Schuss im Morgengrauen,*" unidentified review, Bundesarchiv, Berlin.

73 "horribly grotesque": E.H.T., "*Schuss im Morgengrauen.*"

73 "a heavy science . . . with beautiful timing": Reisch, interview.

74 "the human dynamo . . . heart of gold": Kracauer, *From Caligari to Hitler,* p. 214.

74 "Ufa's greatest picture of this year": "*F.P.1 Antwortet Nicht,*" *Variety,* Jan. 17, 1933.

74 "Peter Lorre easily . . . into the background": "*F.P.1 macht das Rennen,*" *Kinematograph* (Berlin), Dec. 23, 1932.

74 "The most complete . . . possible in reality": "*F.P.1 antwortet nicht,*" *Arbeiter-Zeitung,* Jan. 8, 1933.

74 "anti-Semitic accent . . . the back door": Hollstein, *Antisemitische Filmpropaganda,* pp. 30–1.

75 "Lorre creates the . . . a moral imprint": *Der weisse Dämon,* pressbook, 1932.

76 "haunts like a . . . a unique portrayal": Hawa, "*Der weisse Dämon,*" *Lichtbildbühne,* Nov. 27, 1932.

76 "people just demand . . . and over again": Lorre, interview by Paar.

76 "in so singing . . . his enthusiastic intonation": Gustav Fröhlich to author, Jan. 12, 1980.

76 "completely different than . . . funny, happily contented": "*Was Frauen träumen,*" *Lichtbildbühne,* April 21, 1933.

77 "picture [that] makes . . . force look ridiculous": "Was Frauen träumen," *Variety,* April 4, 1933.

77 "strange tale of . . . novel and thesis": George, "Peter Lorre Returns."

77 "He wasn't telling . . . on your forehead": Joseph, interview.

78 "Why not . . . expresses all ages": Eisner, "Peter Lorre le Meurtrier."

78 "similar half-funny, half-sinister part": Rudolph Cartier (Katscher) to author, Nov. 16, 1980.

78 "passionate attention": Mann and Mann, *Escape to Life,* p. 271.

79 "German films must . . . the German people": Hull, *Film in the Third Reich,* p. 23.

79 "a sign of . . . what it could": Jameson, *Wenn ich mich recht erinnere,* pp. 279–81.

80 "better not be . . . suddenly became intractable": Spiegel, interview.

80 "twiddled his hat . . . hear Oscar's lines": Cartier (Katscher) to author, Nov. 16, 1980.

80 "felt no creative joy during work": H.K., "*Unsichtbare Gegner,*" *Lichtbildbühne,* Sept. 19, 1933.

81 "not an extremely . . . extremely interesting character": Spiegel, interview.

81 "was frozen and without interest again": -net., "*Unsichtbare Gegner,*" *Filmwoche,* Sept. 27, 1933.

81 "only a double of his earlier films": H.K., "*Unsichtbare Gegner.*"

81 "completely colorless": S-ch, "*Die Marquise von O,*" *Deutschösterreichische Tages-Zeitung* (Vienna), March 3, 1933.

81 "beautiful in her . . . abyss-deepest silence": Ludwig Ullmann, "Für und gegen Ferdinand Bruckner," *Wiener Allgemeine Zeitung* (Vienna), March 3, 1933.

81 "lead back his homeland into the Reich": speech of April 9, 1938, in Baynes, *Speeches of Adolf Hitler,* 2:1457.

82 "We were under . . . as a monster": Reisch, interview.

83 "to the readers . . . all is good": Lorre, "Auf vier Jahre."

83 "are small, but . . . want, the Ritz": Hollaender, *Von Kopf bis Fuss,* p. 293.

83 "It is necessary . . . become an actor": C.R., "Peter Lorre," quoted in *Cinémonde* (Paris), ca. March 24, 1964.

84 "Emigrant four on . . . also cannot sleep": Hollaender, *Von Kopf bis Fuss*, p. 294.

84 "There's an old . . . to someone else": A. Lorre, interview, March 21, 1980.

84 "Do you remember . . . and the psychoanalyst": George, "Peter Lorre Returns."

84 "Tell me, where . . . that name again": Lovsky, interview, May 12, 1977.

84 "our director one day": Reuth, *Goebbels Tagebücher*, p. 68.

84 "darling actor of . . . room in Germany": DA, "*M* war sein Schicksal," *Der Abend* (Berlin), March 24, 1964.

85 "all the outside . . . Signed, Peter Lorre": Peter Lorre, interview by Hy Gardner, *The Hy Gardner Show*, March 3, 1963, Hy Gardner Celebrity Archive, BBC, London.

85 "each one toying . . . of the kill": Hollander, *Those Torn from Earth*, p. 93.

85 "In an expressionist . . . hungry anymore": Hollaender, *Von Kopf bis Fuss*, pp. 300–303.

86 "Because of my . . . of narcotic drugs": Statement of Peter Lorre, Feb. 27, 1947, USPHS DHHS.

86 "I have to . . . me the money": Falkenberg, interview.

86 "Lorre was at . . . middle of treatment": Joseph, interview.

87 "life-important . . . awful situation": Cecilie Lvovsky to Dr. Oskar Samek, Oct. 10, 1933, in Wiener Stadt- und Landesbibliothek, *Karl Kraus contra . . .*, p. 284.

87 "hummed about like . . . market of illusions": PEM, *Strangers Everywhere*, p. 203.

87 "a mixture of . . . stay-in-bed-disease": Hollander, *Those Torn from Earth*, p. 115.

87 "when the monotony . . . to meet them": Hollaender, *Von Kopf bis Fuss*, p. 312.

87 "form of paralysis, this proneness to hibernation": Hollander, *Those Torn from Earth*, p. 115.

87 "[that stole] from . . . longer kept apart": Hollaender, *Von Kopf bis Fuss*, p. 313.

87 "False! False! . . . some honest labor": Hollander, *Those Torn from Earth*, pp. 116–17, 119.

88 "Sometimes things look . . . right to exist": PEM, *Strangers Everywhere*, pp. 93, 18.

3. ESCAPE TO LIFE

Epigraph: Peter Lorre, 20th Century–Fox press release, 1939, MHL AMPAS.

1. German émigré and Communist International (Comintern) functionary Otto Katz—later known as André Simone—very possibly learned of Lorre's availability from Bertolt Brecht, who had accepted Kurt Weill's invitation to come to Paris in April 1933 to collaborate on a *ballet chante* built around the biblical seven deadly sins.

2. *Der weisse Dämon* (1932) was not Lorre's last, but his third-to-last German film.

3. According to Churchill biographer René Kraus, "At that time London was over-run with international anarchists, chiefly Russian Nihilists. . . . Peter the Painter . . . was roaming the underworld of London, stealing, robbing, and heading a gang of Russian fellow-criminals." *Winston Churchill*, p. 159. In the "Index to the Work of Alfred Hitchcock," *Special Supplement to Sight and Sound*, Index Series no. 18, May 1949, Peter Noble wrote that Lorre "came to England and gave a remarkable study of a character based on the celebrated 'Peter the Painter.'" Charles Bennett denied any connection between Abbott and Peter the Painter of Sidney Street Siege fame and insisted that "the 'heavy' was not only not based on Peter the Painter, it certainly wasn't written for Peter Lorre." Charles Bennett to author, Oct. 30, 1977.

4. According to Hollywood columnist Rosalind Shaffer, Columbia brought Lorre over to "play with Boris Karloff in 'Black Room Mystery.'" Rosalind Shaffer, "La Davis Gives Husband's Pals a Big Surprise," *Chicago Daily Tribune*, July 22, 1934.

5. On April 11 *Variety* reported that the German-language version had been pulled and an English-dubbed version substituted.

6. Reference to the meeting between Chaplin and Lorre, Celia Lovsky, interview, Oct. 14, 1973; Surmelian, "*Sh!* Meet PETER LORRE"; Straker, "Modest Murderer."

7. Reference to Chaplin's direction of a film version of *The Good Soldier Švejk*, Louella O. Parsons, "Charlie Chaplin Would Direct Peter Lorre in Modern Classic," March 20, 1935, unidentified newspaper clipping, PLS.

8. Between 1933 and 1944, 836 émigré actors listed Europe as their last place of residence.

9. Immigration statistics are taken from Morse, *While Six Million Died,* pp. 136, 144.

10. For a discussion of "Reality and Conditions of Exile in the USA," see Wächter, *Theater im Exil,* pp. 134–42.

11. Whether kidding his screen persona or falling behind it, Lorre used his image as it used him. Scene designer Wolfgang Roth remembered one such instance: "We were at Dr. Max Gruenthal's house on West 79th Street and Lorre was visiting there one evening without Celia. The Gruenthals had a wire-haired dachshund. As it passed by, Lorre played this Hollywood acting, like a bogeyman, and said, 'I chop you up into sausages.'" Along with the mock-menace in his voice, he added a mincing gesture with his hands, much to everyone's amusement. Roth, interview. German psychiatrist Max Gruenthal treated Lorre for drug addiction during the 1930s.

12. Reference to Columbia Pictures casting Lorre in "Kasper Hauser," *Variety,* Sept. 11, 1934. (*Caspar Hauser; oder, Die Tragheit des Herzens, Roman,* was first published in Berlin in 1924.)

13. On Feb. 12, 1935, *Variety* reported that Universal planned to make *Crime and Punishment* with Lorre. The availability of Josef von Sternberg, who had signed a two-picture contract with Columbia, likely convinced Cohn to keep the prestige picture at home.

14. In an interview conducted on June 1, 1964, by one of Professor Ralph Freud's students from UCLA's Theater Arts Department, Karl Freund unfavorably compared his filmmaking experience in Hollywood to that in Germany: "The director has most to say in Berlin. Here the producer has more to say. Also, in Germany, I didn't have a picture if I didn't want to. . . . Here you have to make the picture regard [*sic*] you like it or not." Department of Special Collections, Oral History Program, Charles E. Young Research Library, Univ. of California, Los Angeles.

15. Gregg Toland and Chester Lyons shared screen credit as directors of photography. Tying Toland to the "German tradition," Pauline Kael, in *Raising Kane: The Citizen Kane Book* (New York: Bantam Books, 1974), p. 112, credits the cinematographer with breathing Gothic atmosphere into *Mad Love* and later Orson Welles's *Citizen Kane.* Certainly, the films bear visual similarities in lighting and set design. Even "Peter Lorre, bald, with a spoiled-baby face," wrote Kael, looks "astoundingly like a miniature Orson Welles." However, given Frances Drake's observation that "he paid attention mostly to the camera," it is more likely that Toland functioned as middleman between Karl Freund and Welles, passing on German expressionist traditions in which the director-cinematographer was so well grounded. Drake, interview.

16. Reference to Freund and Lorre visiting the Lutheran Hospital, "Rambling Reporter," *HR,* May 2, 1935.

17. Ten years later, when fielding the same question, Lorre used similar language: "In the movies it all depends upon the situation in which an actor finds himself. If the writer and director create the right, sinister atmosphere, a mild-looking, white-haired clergyman could enter the scene and be mistaken for a cold-blooded murderer, and his most innocent gestures and words would take on a homicidal aspect." *Baltimore Sun,* March 6, 1949.

18. Just weeks earlier, Lorre admitted that he had appeared in one horror picture,

The Beast with Five Fingers: "I don't want to go down in history as a monster. I've never played a frog that swallowed a city or something like that." Don Alpert, "Lorre Laughs When It Hurts," *Los Angeles Times,* Jan. 20, 1963.

19. Lorre agreed with Boris Karloff, who received fan mail from youngsters expressing great compassion for the monster in *Frankenstein* (1931), that the word "horror . . . seems to have the wrong meaning." *The Hy Gardner Show,* March 3, 1963.

20. Material relating to Lorre's drug addiction from Dr. D.D. Le Grand, Admission Summary, Personal History, March 24, 1947, USPHS DHHS.

21. Reference to Lorre's frame of mind on set, D.W.C., "'CRIME AND PUNISHMENT'— Behind the Cameras of the Dostoievsky Drama with Lorre and von Sternberg," *NYT,* Sept. 15, 1935.

22. Dr. Ralph R. Greenson took his medical degree from the University of Berne in Switzerland and later taught psychiatry at UCLA from 1951 until his death in 1979. Lorre attracted the friendship of psychiatrists on both coasts sympathetic to his complaints of movie-made stress. Like most doctors, Greenson reluctantly acquiesced to the actor's importunities for narcotic drugs, at the same time hospitalizing him for treatment as the need arose. When he finally said "no more," an argument erupted and Lorre tried to bite him, suspending the friendship for more than ten years. Greenson, interview.

23. Lorre's available medical records contain no reference to exopthalmos. While hyperthyroidism seems the most probable cause, medical texts cite more than one hundred syndromes and diseases associated with the eye condition, as well as chronic drug use. Roy, *Ocular Differential Diagnosis,* pp. 3–19.

24. In his diary, Sept. 3, 1942, Brecht took exception to this generalization: "The Americans too overact all the time and almost all of them are pretty stagey. It is just that theirs is a different staginess, with the result that our people here look stagey while the locals look natural. When you come down to it the American actors are theatricalising a different basic gest, that of the Americans. Our actors strike them as hammy because the muscle that raises the eyebrows is in constant use. In the Americans it is completely out of action. The movements of the Germans are for the most part too abrupt for the screen, too 'angular.' There is something fluid and pliant about the Americans which photographs better. Gesture and facial expression have to be shrunk on a scale of 1 to 10, since the main thing is the head and shoulders—in those giant cinemas the close-ups look tiny." Brecht, *Journals,* p. 256.

25. During the voyage, Wilder and Lorre reportedly collaborated "on a psychological study of a murderer planned by Lorre for a picture subject." "Lorre, Billie Wilder Work on Murder Yarn," *HR,* Oct. 26, 1935.

26. *Secret Agent* "consisted of two of the Ashenden stories by Maugham, 'The Traitor' and 'The Hairless Mexican' and also a play about Ashenden which was written by Campbell Dixon." Alfred Hitchcock, "My Spies," *Film Weekly,* May 30, 1936.

27. Reference to the British Board of Film Censors, "The Mystery of the Secret Agent," May 10, 1946, unidentified newspaper clipping, BFINL.

28. Gielgud, certainly unaware of Lorre's Gründgens ditty (see page 16), would have been equally oblivious to the fact that the comparison may well have been a veiled reference to his own homosexuality.

29. Alfred Hitchcock's article "My Spies," *Film Weekly,* May 30, 1936.

30. The *Hollywood Reporter* grapevined news of Lorre's "return within eighteen months to do one more for G.B., Hitchcock to direct." "Lorre to Hollyw'd: Will Be U.S. Citizen," *HR,* April 20, 1936.

31. Reference to public reaction to *Secret Agent* in Mexico City, "GB 'Secret Agent' Jerked in Mexico to Prevent Riots," *HR,* Dec. 7, 1936.

32. That August, Peter and Celia submitted a Declaration of Intention to become U.S. citizens.

33. A Heller is a bronze Austrian coin of small value.

34. Karl Kraus died on June 12, 1936.

35. Peter Lorre's and Fritz Lang's telegrams are reproduced in Aurich, Jacobsen, and Schnauber, *Fritz Lang*, p. 263.

36. References to "The Monster" in *HR*: "Lorre as 'Monster' before 'Hunchback,'" May 12, 1936; "'Monster' on Skids; To Wash Up Para Deal with H-MacA," May 15, 1936; "Hecht, MacArthur Now Spot 'Monster' for GB," May 19, 1936; "GB 'Monster' Plan Is News to Balcon," June 17, 1936.

37. Reference to the planned production of *Nachtasyl* in *Pariser Tageblatt*, May 22, 1936.

38. Alternate titles included *The Monarch of Russia, The Falcon,* and *The Cossack Czar.*

39. Reference to Universal's plans to star Lorre in *The Hunchback of Notre Dame,* "'U' Set for 'Hunchback'; Lorre Probable as Star," *HR,* Sept. 19, 1936.

40. Reference to Napoleon in Hollywood, Alma Whitaker, "Many Stars Seek Role of Napoleon," *LAT,* July 19, 1936.

41. Sidney Kingsley won the Pulitzer Prize for his play *Men in White* (1933).

QUOTATION SOURCES BY PAGE NUMBER

89 "for conscientious reasons . . . professionally at liberty": Ivor Montagu to author, June 1, 1975.

89 "We wanted him . . . to be engaged": Montagu to author, March 5, 1975.

90 "Hitch and I . . . Hitch had envisaged": Montagu to author, Jan. 16, 1980.

90 "admired him and . . . amount of persuading": ibid., Oct. 8, 1977.

90 "Peter told me . . . opened to him": Falkenberg, interview.

90 "with a single . . . bring good luck": PEM, "Mein Freund, der Versteller."

91 "Now all I . . . got the part": Lorre, interview by O'Connell.

91 "As soon as . . . in the picture": Montagu to author, June 1, 1975.

91 "Your big problem . . . stars are known": quoted in Higham and Greenberg, *Celluloid Muse,* p. 94.

91 "almost in despair . . . to play it": Buchanan, "REAL and UNREAL Horror."

92 "How tall are you": Celia Lovsky, interview, Oct. 14, 1973.

92 "I wasn't the . . . started the picture": "Lorre, European Film Star, Here on Way to Hollywood," *Chicago Daily News,* July 27, 1934.

92 "At that time . . . please, speak English": Bennett to author, April 19, 1975.

92 "a brilliant scenario . . . a tour de force": Truffaut, *Hitchcock,* p. 58.

93 "a musical without music, made very cheaply": ibid.

93 "worked up": Alfred Hitchcock, "My Strangest Year," *Film Weekly,* May 16, 1936.

93 "The door is . . . from the pocket": *The Man Who Knew Too Much,* shooting script, undated, BFINL.

93 "cupboard empty": Montagu to author, Jan. 16, 1980.

94 "little men are . . . are 'walking dynamite,'": Lou Smith, "Peter Lorre—Biography," Universal Studio, May, 1942, Peter Lorre file, BFINL.

94 "getting good actors . . . Understatement is priceless": Alfred Hitchcock, "Some Aspects of Direction," in Hochman, *From Quasimodo to Scarlett O'Hara,* p. 398.

94 "Lorre . . . passion for decorum": Andrew Sarris, "Hitchcock's Les Parents Terribles," *New York Voice,* June 26, 1984.

94 "Peter had the . . . it is delivered": St. Joseph, interview.

94 "a round-faced . . . apparently [his] nurse": *The Man Who Knew Too Much,* shooting script, undated, BFINL.

94 "Mr. Lorre, as . . . placid moon face": Andre Sennwald, "*The Man Who Knew Too Much,*" *NYT,* March 23, 1935.

95 "One of the . . . of the screen": James Shelley Hamilton, "*The Man Who Knew Too Much*," in Hochman, *From Quasimodo to Scarlett O'Hara*, p. 202.

95 "Even Charles Laughton . . . the bad boy": Andrew Sennwald, "Peter Lorre, Poet of the Damned," *NYT*, March 31, 1935.

95 "a brilliant actor . . . into Hitch's conception": Montagu to author, June 1, 1975.

95 "He told some . . . usually did) reciprocate": Montagu to author, Oct. 26, 1984.

96 "the walking overcoat": Truffaut, *Hitchcock*, p. 61.

96 "I regard this . . . the second floor": Montagu to author, Oct. 26, 1984.

96 "We were married . . . dropped the book": Dehn, "Mrs. Lorre says: Peter Is No Monster."

97 "THIS IS A . . . LIVING IN SIN": Lovksy, interview, Oct. 14, 1973.

97 "You will be . . . to impress him": Lorant, interview.

98 "Why so much . . . idea is surprising": "The Düsseldorf Murders," *NYT*, April 6, 1933.

98 "nearest relative or . . . in the U.S.": Records of the Immigration and Naturalization Service, Passenger and Crew Lists Arriving at New York, 1897–1943, RG 85, T-715, vol. 11873, list 46, p. 46, nos. 21 and 22.

98 "countries oftener than our shoes": Bertolt Brecht, "To Those Born Later," in *Poems: 1913–1956*, ed. John Willett and Ralph Manheim with Erick Fried (New York: Methuen, 1979), p. 320.

98 "repellant spectacle . . . Hollywood long ago": "The Murderer of 'M,'" *NYT*, July 29, 1934.

98 "Both of us . . . home at night": unidentified newspaper clipping, PLS.

99 "The links of . . . of our luxuries": quoted in Taylor, *Strangers in Paradise*, p. 95.

99 "In all of . . . the 'genius actor,'": Elisabeth Hauptmann to Walter Benjamin, June 9, 1934, Elisabeth-Hauptman-Archiv, Stiftung Archiv der Akademie der Künste, Berlin.

99 "There is much . . . on the screen": Surmelian, "*Sh!* Meet PETER LORRE."

100 "kindliest of smiles": Hasek, *The Good Soldier: Schweik*, p. 163.

100 "guileless lamb": ibid., p. 56.

100 "is no mere . . . is only simulated": Parrott, *Jaroslav Hasek*, p. 98.

100 "a half-wit for . . . mask of imbecility": Hasek, *The Good Soldier Švejk*, p. 767.

100 "The little man . . . acumen and ingenuity": F.X. Šalda, quoted ibid., pp. 174–75.

100 "idiot of genius": Ivan Olbracht, quoted ibid., p. 167.

100 "epic phlegm": Radko Pytlík, ibid., p. 73.

100 "By seeming to . . . one can fault": Parrott, *Jaroslav Hasek*, p. 119.

101 "shows up the . . . laughed at it": Ivan Olbracht, quoted ibid., p. 166.

101 "It is a . . . Good Soldier Schweik": Reynolds, "Reluctant Menace."

101 "Country of Last Permanent Residence": Peterson, *Refugee Intellectual*, p. 12.

101 "likely to become . . . help from friends": Morse, *While Six Million Died*, pp. 135, 144, 139, 140.

102 "Through its immigration . . . fleeing from Germany": "Hitler Challenges American Protests," *NYT*, April 7, 1933.

103 "Hollywood was still . . . rigid and unchanged": Houseman, *Run-Through*, p. 433.

104 "The experience of . . . breakdown of hope": Pachter, "On Being an Exile," p. 19.

104 "a subdued reflection . . . electric stars below": Mann and Mann, *Escape to Life*, p. 274.

104 "soulless soil": Thomas Mann to Hans Carossa, May 7, 1951, in Mann, *Briefe*, p. 206.

104 "Neither the things . . . any real roots": Hardwicke, *Victorian in Orbit*, p. 210.

105 "a journey of no return": Karl Zuckmayer, *A Part of Myself* (New York: Harcourt Brace Javanovich, 1970), p. 329.

105 "The poor refugees . . . authority and importance": Sakall, *Story of Cuddles*, p. 208.

105 "As long as . . . for some time": 20th Century–Fox press release, MHL AMPAS.

105 "consequential position . . . in this respect": "Peter Lorre Starved and Slept in Park to Get Start as Actor," *New York Herald-Tribune,* Aug. 5, 1934.

106 "we have only . . . nothing but Americans": Max Berges, "There Is No Place for a German Theater," *California Jewish Voice* (Los Angeles), Jan. 24, 1941.

106 "who but a . . . in the garden": Hollander, *Those Torn from Earth,* pp. 299–300.

106 "we have a . . . flowers, many flowers": Service, "Women Scream."

106 "I love everything . . . clothes of Hollywood": Irene Thirer, "Peter Lorre Sails, High in Praise of Hollywood," *New York Post,* Oct. 30, 1935.

107 "I confess that . . . in the world": "Peter Lorre Starved."

107 "Hollywood definitely . . . time to come": unidentified newspaper clipping, PLS.

107 "I am the . . . for a snob": Surmelian, "*Sh!* Meet PETER LORRE."

107 "One of the . . . almost too shy": "Weight Also Important in Playing Sinister Roles," *Secret Agent,* pressbook, 1936.

107 "the constant excitement . . . makes me fidgety": ibid.

107 "meeting people, talking . . . energy for work": "Peter Lorre, Tactician," *NYT,* Nov. 3, 1935.

107 "he still is . . . like a Buddha": Shaffer, "Lorre's Wife Describes Horror Artist."

108 "And where do . . . cold and perfidious": Mann and Mann, *Escape to Life,* p. 267.

108 "Assimilation . . . the absorbing body": Peterson, *Refugee Intellectual,* p. 239.

108 "We were into Americana": Wilder, interview, March 31, 1986.

109 "I was very . . . Mountain Dean wrestle": Lorre, interview by Wallace, pre-interview notes.

109 "Lorre hasn't missed . . . an unofficial second": 20th Century–Fox press release, MHL AMPAS.

109 "He looks like . . . Ted Healy stooge": Cecilia Ager, "Lorre Expounds on the Cinematic Thespic Art Minimizes Make-Up," *Variety,* Nov. 6, 1935.

109 "If I had . . . and faced Hitler": Davie, quoted in *Refugees in America,* p. 90.

109 "hipsters": Ives, interview.

109 "rococo cherub gone slightly astray": B.R. Crisler, "Footnotes on Pictures and People," *NYT,* May 10, 1936.

109 "European stiffness of behavior": Peterson, *Refugee Intellectual,* p. 153.

110 "I am a . . . to act forever": "'M' Star Made Miserable," *New York Post,* July 27, 1934.

110 "I am having . . . signed with Columbia": Rose Pelswick, "PETER LORRE MODEST: 'Crime and Punishment,' His New Film, Due at Radio City Thursday," *New York Evening Journal,* Nov. 19, 1935.

110 "What I would . . . as at home": *Mad Love,* pressbook, 1935.

110 "never played a . . . a funny character": 20th Century–Fox press release, MHL AMPAS.

110 "I am . . . in the mind": Service, "Women Scream."

110 "It is the . . . typed like that": Eileen Creelman, "Picture Plays and Players: Peter Lorre, the Murderer of 'M,' Here to Start Hollywood Career," *New York Sun,* Aug. 2, 1934.

112 "Lorre Saves Dog": "Besuch in Santa Monica," *Mein Film* 499 (1935).

112 "Peter Lorre, expatriate . . . its way home": Philip K. Scheuer, Town Called Hollywood: "BERLIN BURIAL," *LAT,* Jan. 14, 1935.

112 "as quiet and . . . of every party": Lynn, "He'd Rather Act than Eat."

112 "as a sweet . . . a wounded raccoon": Kilgallen, "Ten Knights in My Hollywood Date Book."

112 "I am afraid . . . with no complexes": Service, "Women Scream."

113 "The boy, the . . . 'Crime and Punishment'": *NYT,* Nov. 3, 1935.

114 "There's too great . . . a histrionic gag": Robert Garland, "Hollywood's Mr. Hyde," Nov. 15, 1936, unidentified newspaper clipping, PLS.

114 "You can have . . . great suspense story": Huston, interview.

114 "As a matter . . . go at that": Guernsey, "Peter Lorre, Who Is Nothing like His Roles."

114 "a rather Napoleonic . . . the Hollywood Wellingtons": *NYT,* Nov. 3, 1935.

114 "I can't give . . . in or out": Cecilie Lorre to Dr. Oskar Samek, Feb. 22, 1935, in Wiener Stadt- und Landesbibliothek, *Karl Kraus contra,* p. 287.

114 "It is hugely . . . which everything depends": ibid., pp. 287–88.

115 "specialize in unusual themes:": "Karl Freund Signs as MGM Director," *HR,* Feb. 4, 1935.

115 "a mixture of . . . his eyes protrude": *Mad Love,* draft screenplay, May 22, 1935, Collection of Motion Picture Scripts (Collection 73), ALSC UCLA.

116 "couldn't leave the . . . Peter very well": Drake, interview.

116 "I believe the . . . be perfectly kind": "Peter Lorre, Screen's Most Frightening Villain, Has a Method All His Own," *Mad Love,* pressbook, 1935.

116 "Peter had definite . . . reality and vitality": Keye Luke to author, Aug. 8, 1973.

116 "Make-up's an excuse . . . methods of disguise": Surmelian, "*Sh!* Meet PETER LORRE."

116 "It gives the . . . of personal appearance": "Peter Lorre, Screen's Most Frightening Villain."

116 "They must be . . . a perfect method": "Lorre Employs Light Instead of Grease Paint," *Mad Love,* pressbook, 1935.

116 "I never look . . . believe in imitation": Surmelian, "*Sh!* Meet PETER LORRE—the *Menacing* Man!"

116 "My trick is . . . in the character": "Charlie Chaplin Terms Peter Lorre World's Greatest Character Actor," *Mad Love,* pressbook, 1935.

117 "Peter was a . . . person, easily hurt": Drake, interview.

117 "an explanation of . . . to help others": unidentified newspaper clipping, PLS.

117 "right in the . . . and Box Office": "Personal Triumph for Peter Lorre," *HR,* June 27, 1935.

117 "first American production . . . no mean terms": ibid.

117 "With any of . . . trifle silly": Andre Sennwald, "*Mad Love,*" *NYT,* Aug. 5, 1935.

118 "very good . . . free for it": Thirer, "Peter Lorre Sails."

119 "this offering of . . . all horror films": Whitney Williams, "PETER LORRE Acclaimed the WORLD'S GREATEST ACTOR," *Silver Screen,* Aug. 1935.

119 "The way I . . . frighten the audience": Pelswick, "*Crime and Punishment,* His New Film."

119 "I hold no . . . it in films": Buchanan, "REAL and UNREAL Horror."

119 "How this image . . . or do play": Peter Lorre, interview by Merv Griffin, *The Merv Griffin Show,* NBC-TV, March 4, 1963.

119 "gets his effects . . . from scientific observation": Ager, "Lorre Expounds."

120 "It is a . . . few are aware": P.K., "Peter Lorre—Fan of Brecht."

120 "I cannot find . . . thank him for": Lorre, interview by Hy Gardner.

120 "Poe never heard . . . heart and mind": Donald Kirkley, "Theater Notes," *Baltimore Sun,* March 6, 1949.

120 "perfectly harmless and . . . is psychological horror": Buchanan, "REAL and UNREAL Horror."

120 "I am less . . . portrayal of life": Tazelaar, "Even the Doctors Are Amazed."

120 "Lorre hopes that . . . him to do": Kate Cameron, "Lorre in New Horror Role," *New York Sunday News,* Nov. 24, 1935.

121 "The screen was . . . not the camera": Aeneas MacKenzie, "Leonardo of the Lenses," *Life and Letters Today* (London), Spring 1936.

121 "an irresistible need . . . of his creation": Jean de Baroncelli, "A Formidable Voice," *Le Monde,* March 2, 1966, quoted in Weinberg, *Josef von Sternberg,* p. 223.

121 "In this decelerating . . . a routine one": Josef von Sternberg, *Fun in a Chinese Laundry: An Autobiography* (New York: Collier, 1965), pp. 168, 270.

122 "We were called . . . changing a word": R. Allen, interview.

122 "Oh, yes, he . . . many, many, things": Marian Marsh, interview.

123 "For the first . . . its outer edges": Ager, "Lorre Expounds."

123 "he takes more . . . of the credit": Thirer, Screen Views and News: "Peter Lorre Sails, High in Praise of Hollywood."

123 "It was a . . . was practically unnoticed": Peter Lorre, "The Role I Liked Best . . .," *Saturday Evening Post*, June 11, 1949.

123 "exceptionally handsome . . . dark brown hair": Fyodor Dostoyevsky, *Crime and Punishment*, translated by Constance Garnett (New York: Vintage, 1950), p. 2.

123 "He was attractive . . . friends right away": Marsh, interview.

123 "Everybody warned me . . . helpful and sincere": "News and Gossip of the Week," *Film Weekly*, Nov. 16, 1935.

124 "Joe looked like . . . directs in pictures": Arnold, *Lorenzo Goes to Hollywood*, pp. 272–73.

124 "an actor is . . . idea of his": Sternberg, *Fun in a Chinese Laundry*, p. 113.

124 "Peter tried to . . . worry, it's different'": Marsh, interview.

124 "You see, to . . . things he does": Eleanor Barnes, "British Film Raider," unidentified newspaper clipping, PLS.

125 "When I am . . . a fever pitch": "Inventions of Satan," unidentified clipping, Peter Lorre file, BFINL.

125 "he is overwrought . . . he is working": Rosalind Shaffer, "Lorre's Wife Describes Horror Artist as Charming Husband," *Chicago Daily Tribune*, Aug. 4, 1935.

125 "more readily identified . . . actual physical breakdown": C. Lorre, interviews.

125 "Peter was really . . . back of it": Marsh, interview.

125 "Lorre plays . . . force and finish": Bland Johaneson, "Lorre Dazzling Murderer at Music Hall," *New York Daily Mirror*, Nov. 21, 1935.

125 "Lorre bares the . . . flashes of histrionics": *"Crime and Punishment,"* *Daily Film Renter* (London), Dec. 21, 1935.

125 "Lorre keeps it on a high level": *Star* (London), March 16, 1936.

125 "Mr. Lorre provides a . . . greatest thespic efforts": unidentified newspaper clipping, PLS.

125 "It was a . . . every possible laugh": Graham Greene, "The Genius of Peter Lorre," *World Film News*, July 1936

125 "He has no . . . a detective story": Andrew Sennwald, "'CRIME AND PUNISHMENT'—The French and American Film Versions Are a Study in Contrasts," *NYT*, Nov. 24, 1935.

125 "frequent gleams of . . . into profitable zombies": Joseph Alsop Jr., "Two Versions of 'Crime and Punishment,'" *New York Herald-Tribune*, Dec. 1, 1935.

126 "thought Lorre was . . . the psychotic murderer": Edwin Blum to author, Feb. 26, 1975.

126 "So in this . . . didn't do anything": ibid., March 27, 1975.

126 "Dostoievskian dimension . . . above a mask": Franz Theodor Csokor to Ferdinand Bruckner, Nov. 28, 1936, in Csokor, *Zeuge einer Zeit*, p. 129.

126 "Lorre in New Horror Role": Cameron, "Lorre in New Horror Role."

126 "is by no . . . but great tragedy": Buchanan, "REAL and UNREAL Horror."

126 "a comparatively normal . . . not for pathologists": Pelswick, *"Crime and Punishment*, His New Film."

126 "childlike martyr, radiant in redemption": *"Crime and Punishment,"* *Time*, Dec. 2, 1935.

126 "baleful and spineless by turns": "Dostoievsky Doubled," *Daily Herald* (London), March 13, 1936.

127 "just a good detective story": D.W.C., "'CRIME AND PUNISHMENT'—Behind the Cameras."

127 "butchering . . . character compromise": Joseph Anthony and S.K. Lauren, "Novel into Film," *Film Weekly*, March 21, 1936.

127 "Peter Lorre is . . . the American script": Sennwald, "'CRIME AND PUNISHMENT'—The French and American Film Versions."

128 "within the limits . . . to his audience": Andrew Sennwald, "*Crime and Punishment*," *NYT*, Nov. 22, 1935.

128 "Now Lorre has . . . means of expression": f.s., "*Schuld und Sühne*," *Neue Freie Presse* (Vienna), ca. 1936, PLS.

128 "The difference between . . . wood pulp fictioneer": Sennwald, "'CRIME AND PUNISHMENT'—The French and American Film Versions."

128 "There are many . . . childish, undignified work": "Peter Lorre, Tactician."

128 "though he never . . . knew the answers": Greenson, interview.

129 "There is great . . . his pathological abnormalities": Kennedy, "Monarch of Menace."

129 "An actor . . . the character, utterly": Harry Lang, "He's an INSIDE Actor," *Screen Book*, Dec. 1937.

129 "Acting is like . . . an incurable addict": Maude Cheatham, "Gruesome Twosome," *Movie Show*, March 1946.

129 "the only thing . . . others need stimulants": Surmelian, "*Sh!* Meet PETER LORRE."

129 "was an entrance . . . into the soul": Greenson, interview.

129 "Peter Lorre's mind . . . for his role": Calvet, interview

129 "the appearance of . . . the human soul": Surmelian, "*Sh!* Meet PETER LORRE."

129 "very far apart . . . know the difference": Kanter, interview.

130 "Closely obliged to their spiritual origins": Wächter, *Theater im Exil*, p. 138.

130 "an inborn gift . . . of modern life": Mann and Mann, *Escape to Life*, p. 269.

131 "That was the . . . winging it, innocently": Wilder, interview, March 31, 1986.

132 "In any case . . . looking little animal": Buchanan, "REAL and UNREAL Horror."

133 "When we wanted . . . he could do": Ivor Montagu to author, June 1, 1975.

133 "extremely deceptive": Hitchcock, interview.

134 "waves a comically . . . he's beaten you": *Secret Agent*, shooting script, undated, BFINL.

134 "Mich [Michael Balcon] . . . first 'rougher' alternative": Montagu to author, Dec. 20, 1977.

134 "at the moment . . . it, except ourselves": Montagu to author, Oct. 8, 1977.

135 "this part . . . problems between us": Montagu to author, June 1, 1975.

135 "That Lorre needed . . . was no doubt": John Croydon to author, Feb. 15, 1988.

135 "Shakespearean highbrow": John Gielgud to author, Jan. 2, 1981.

136 "He displayed it . . . left the set": Croydon to author.

136 "Sheer rubbish . . . say no more": Montagu to author, Oct. 26, 1984.

136 "something of Lorre's . . . friends know it": Gottlieb, *Hitchcock on Hitchcock*, p. 20.

137 "rather a jolly . . . a fine art": "Sinister—But with a Difference," *Film Weekly*, Dec. 7, 1935.

137 "plays one of . . . in make-up": B.R. Crisler, "*Secret Agent*," *NYT*, June 13, 1936.

137 "He is one . . . ice within it": Otis Ferguson, "Wings over Nothing," *New Republic*, June 24, 1936.

137 "Dear Untier, for . . . the owl begins": Lovksy, diary, author's collection.

138 "very sick . . . we will pay": Cecilie Lorre to Dr. Oskar Samek, Feb. 8, 1936, in Wiener Stadt- und Landesbibliothek, *Karl Kraus contra*, p. 289.

138 "showed his original . . . Raskolnikov film": Franz Theodor Csokor to Ferdinand Bruckner, Karsamstag, 1936, in Csokor, *Zeuge einer Zeit*, p. 117–18.

138 "Doctor Mallaire . . . are best suited": "Radio Reports," *Variety*, May 13, 1936.

138 "best suited for . . . approaching bedtime hour": "Bogey Lorre on Radio Kiddie Hour," *The Face behind the Mask*, pressbook, 1941.

139 "Dimitri is a . . . nobody knows about": script conference, Aug. 23, 1936, CDM BYU.

140 "I have wanted . . . for many years": Ruth M'Tammany, "Peter Lorre Deserts Horror Roles to Play Napoleon,'" *Indianapolis Times,* Nov. 25, 1936.

140 "for full artistic . . . work in both": Robert Garland, "Hollywood's Mr. Hyde," Nov. 15, 1936, unidentified newspaper clipping, PLS.

140 "Ironically, I was . . . held no surprises": Whitaker, "Many Stars Seek Role of Napoleon."

140 "new angle": "Lorre as 'The Little Corporal,'" undated newspaper clipping, BFINL.

140 "Most Napoleon plays . . . on the screen": M'Tammany, "Peter Lorre Deserts Horror Roles."

141 "If I were . . . myself inside him": Tildesley, "Behind the GREASE PAINT."

4. SOFTLY, SOFTLY, CATCHEE MONKEY

Epigraphs: Peter Lorre in *Crack-Up* (1937); Peter Lorre, quoted in Marsh, "Lorre's Stage Experience."

1. Reference to casting of *Crack-Up,* "Director Sketches the Cast He Wants," *Crack-Up,* pressbook, 1937.

2. On September 10, 1936, the actor had signed a one-picture (*Crack-Up*) commitment with Fox guaranteeing him four weeks' employment at $2,500 per week. Although the *Hollywood Reporter* (Oct. 30, 1936) noted that Lorre had headed east with a term contract in his pocket, according to his "Synopsis of Employment Contract," the agreement didn't officially commence until November 30, 1936. The contract, which carried six one-year options, guaranteed him forty weeks' employment at $1,250 per week the first year. If renewed, his salary would jump $250 per week the first two years, $500 the next two, $750 a fifth, and $1,000 the sixth and final year. The studio reserved the right to lend his services to any other producer of motion pictures and stipulated that Lorre should furnish "all modern wardrobe; producer shall furnish all costumes." He was also required to cancel his verbal agreement with Gaumont-British "to render services in one (1) motion picture," possibly *The Monster.* TCFLF UCLA.

3. Reference to Lorre's health problems, "Peter Lorre's Collapse May Lag Lensing 'Moto,'" *HR,* Feb. 8, 1937.

4. *No Hero* was serialized by the *Post* under the same title, March 30–May 4, 1935.

5. Reference to Warner Bros.' purchase of screen rights to *No Hero,* "Story Buys," *Variety,* Oct. 9, 1935, and Metro's purchase of *Think Fast, Mr. Moto,* "Story Buys," *Variety,* July 29, 1936; under "News of the Screen," Dec. 8, 1937, *Variety* also announced that Fox had purchased Alfred Cohn's *Death at the Artist's Ball* as one of the Mr. Moto series for Peter Lorre.

6. The *Moto* movies were not released in the order they were filmed, which was *Think Fast, Mr. Moto; Mr. Moto Takes a Chance; Thank You, Mr. Moto; Mr. Moto's Gamble; Mysterious Mr. Moto; Mr. Moto's Last Warning; Mr. Moto Takes a Vacation;* and *Danger Island.*

7. A sixth, *Mr. Moto in Baghdad,* by John Reinhardt, had only reached the treatment stage by December 23, 1938.

8. Churchill was visiting the set of *Mr. Moto Takes a Chance* (1938).

9. According to the *Hollywood Reporter,* Nov. 13, 1936, after the "preview click" of *Charlie Chan at the Opera,* which costarred Boris Karloff, the "New 'Chan' Films [would] Have 2 Stars," including a villainous Peter Lorre opposite Warner Oland in the next installment of the series, *Charlie Chan at the Olympics.* However, once successfully established as Mr. Moto, Lorre stepped down only twice during the three-year run into small roles that did not damage his new image as a screen hero.

10. The suspension of services and compensation for reasons of illness were added

to the present term of the actor's employment, pushing back the renewal date of his contract from November to December 1937 and from December 1938 to January 1939. Lorre's unpaid leaves of absence were not always prearranged. He had been advised on February 28, 1938, that *Mysterious Mr. Moto* would begin shooting in the early part of March. When Sol Siegel moved up the date from March 14 to March 11, the studio "tried from March 7th to contact him but were unable to do so; finally his agent located him on March 11th at a Sanitarium and that was the first we knew of his being ill." Lew Schreiber to George Wasson, memo, March 16, 1938, TCFLF UCLA.

11. "Peter contributed absolutely nothing to the characterization of Moto," commented Foster at our interview. When I read his statement back to him, he cringed and looked hurt, not for himself, but for Lorre, whom he had plainly maligned, given the obvious evidence to the contrary on screen.

12. The Mr. Moto adventure described by Parry is *Mr. Moto's Last Warning.*

13. Lorre made Fox's "star" list only once during his three-year tenure there. His situation was not unique. Fox poorly balanced the salaries of its contract players against their actual box-office power. In 1936 Sylvia Sidney took home $225,812 to number one star Shirley Temple's $121,422. If some actors were not paid enough, others were paid too much. The Independent Theatre Owners Association complained, "Practically all of the major studios are burdened with stars—whose public appeal is negligible—receiving tremendous salaries necessitated by contractual obligations." Stars that were "poison at the box office"—Mae West, Greta Garbo, Marlene Dietrich, Joan Crawford, Katharine Hepburn—took "millions out of the industry and millions out of the box office." *Hollywood Reporter,* April 28, 1938; May 3, 1938.

14. Lorre's car reportedly turned over twice when struck by another vehicle. Although Celia sustained a fractured wrist when thrown from the auto, Peter, trapped in the back seat, suffered no injuries. "I owe my good fortune to Harvey Parry, Duke Green and other Hollywood stunt men," he said, explaining his narrow escape. "When they made me an honorary member of their group, I memorized their rules for safety. One rule was: 'In case of an auto crash, lie down immediately on the floor of the car.'" "Stunt Men Avert Mishap to 'Moto,'" *Washington Post,* Dec. 1, 1938.

15. Reference to 20th Century–Fox abandoning four of its seven movie series, Douglas Churchill, "Mr. Goldwyn Storms the Heights," *NYT,* Jan. 8, 1939.

16. "Another reason given for the decline in the popularity of the Peter Lorre series," said *Variety,* "is that the character of Moto could not be made entirely sympathetic, because it would make him too much like Charlie Chan." "Moto Outo," *Variety,* June 28, 1939.

17. In 1957 the Japanese sleuth made his way to television in "The Return of Mr. Moto," a *Pulitzer Prize Playhouse* episode starring Harold Vermilyea and Eva Gabor. He made another appearance some years later when in 1965 Fox released *The Return of Mr. Moto,* an unnoteworthy effort destined for obscurity, starring Henry Silva.

18. According to the first-draft continuity script of *Lancer Spy,* dated April 16, 1937, Lorre had been cast in the small but pivotal role of American agent Captain Spencer van Ryn, who works undercover—as Hauptmann Paul von Gourmach—in the service of the story's principal villain, Count Gottfried Zo von Hollen, played by Sig Rumann. By October, however, all reference to the van Ryn/von Gourmach character had been dropped from the script and Lorre had been elevated from eleventh billing to the third-billed Major Sigfried Gruning. TCFLF UCLA.

19. Reference to Lorre testing for *The Hunchback of Notre Dame,* Louella O. Parsons, "Peter Lorre Will Play Title Role in '*Hunchback of Notre Dame,*'" *LAT,* Oct. 8, 1937.

20. Reference to Lorre turning down starring role in *The Hunchback of Notre Dame,* 20th Century–Fox press release, MHL AMPAS.

21. While film scholars alternately credit both G.W. Pabst and Irish novelist Liam

O'Flaherty with authorship—and for creating the part of the wireless operator with Lorre in mind—*Paramount Unproduced Stories* (Jan. 1966) cites Waclaw Panski as author of the original story, O'Flaherty of a treatment, and Grover Jones of a screenplay. Two additional screenplays list no author. MHL AMPAS.

22. Lorre signed his salary, $2,150, over to William Morris Agency, to which he was indebted "for the purchase of necessaries of life for myself and my immediate family." Assignment, Oct. 18, 1939, private collection.

23. *Stranger on the Third Floor* cost $171,000. RKO defined an A picture as one "for which the budget is $400,000.00 or more or $300,000.00 or more and in connection with which a recognized female star is employed." Mr. Schwab to Mr. Winkler, June 11, 1940, Inter-Department Communication, RKO Radio Pictures Inc. Studio Collection, ALSC UCLA.

24. Lorre actually turned in a total of ten weeks' work for $21,000, with $7,000 allotted to *Stranger on the Third Floor.*

25. Reference to contract between RKO Pictures Inc. and Peter Lorre, May 29, 1940; William Morris Agency Inc. to RKO Radio Pictures Inc., June 13, July 26, 1940, RKO Radio Pictures Inc., Studio Collection, ALSC UCLA.

26. A commercially available video copyrighted and marketed by International Historic Films runs 62 minutes.

QUOTATION SOURCES BY PAGE NUMBER

142 "Colonel Gimpy was . . . to horrify audiences": "Horror of Horror Star Quits Screen," *Crack-Up,* pressbook, 1937.

143 "not got within . . . they ever will": C.A. Lejeune, "*Crack-Up,*" *Observer* (London), Feb. 28, 1937.

144 "marvelously written": Whitaker, "Many Stars Seek Role of Napoleon."

144 "We had anticipated . . . and with Bruckner": Kingsley, interview.

144 "A number of . . . I don't know": "Jinx Pursues Peter Lorre in His Role in Napoleon," *Detroit Evening Journal,* Dec. 31, 1936.

145 "a new Chinese . . . a Chinese background": John P. Marquand to Helen Howe, Feb. 11, 1934, quoted in Millicent Bell, *Marquand: An American Life* (Boston: Little, Brown, 1979), p. 204.

145 "With the ignorance . . . sight is strange": JPM manuscript notebook, quoted ibid., p. 218.

145 "Japanese G Man": "Next Week," *Saturday Evening Post,* Sept. 5, 1936.

146 "carpentry work": Adelaide Hooker Marquand to Blanche Ferry Hooker, March 28, 1936, quoted in Bell, *Marquand,* p. 249.

146 "two stories written . . . upon the same": George Wasson, interoffice correspondence to Sol Wurtzel, W.B. Dover, Julian Johnson, and Clay Adams, Dec. 20, 1937, TCFLF UCLA.

146 "make one picture . . . our staff writers": George Wasson, interoffice correspondence to Sol Wurtzel and John Stone, May 21, 1937, TCFLF UCLA.

146 "sausage factory": Foster, interview.

147 "small man, delicate, almost fragile": John P. Marquand, *Think Fast, Mr. Moto* (New York: Popular Library, 1977), p. 10.

147 "Peter was so . . . except the eyes": Foster, interview.

147 "Acting comes from . . . so you appear": 20th Century–Fox publicity release, MHL AMPAS.

147 "Mr. Moto is . . . as he does": Tildesley, "Behind the GREASE PAINT."

148 "At first it . . . we were kidding": Foster, interview.

148 "'On Your Toes . . . at Mr. Moto's'": "Mr. Moto a la Charlie Chan," *Variety,* Feb. 17, 1937.

148 "Continental horror specialist": ibid.

148 "The first Moto . . . were the rest": Foster, interview.

149 "ridiculous situation": ibid.

150 "unusual sinister quality": ibid.

150 "Menace in nature . . . ally of justice": *Mr. Moto's Gamble,* pressbook, 1938.

150 "Instead of wrecking . . . of his talent": Douglas W. Churchill, "Hollywood Picket Line," *NYT,* April 18, 1937.

151 "shooting is characterized . . . moved the tree": Douglas W. Churchill, "Cleaning and Blocking Hollywood's Old Hat," *NYT,* Aug. 22, 1937.

151 "In those days . . . and that's it": Ames, interview.

152 "poor copy": Lisa, "A Letter from Lisa," in "The Opening Chorus," *Silver Screen,* March, 1938.

152 "95 percent . . . studio publicity departments": Capra, *Name above the Title,* p. 315.

152 "A stickler for . . . movie stunts himself": 20th Century–Fox publicity releases, MHL AMPAS.

153 "came out of it completely cured ": Statement of Peter Lorre, Feb. 27, 1947, USPHS DHHS.

153 "on and off . . . name, Peter Lorre": ibid.

153 "Were you surprised . . . would help me": Parry, interview.

153 "Don't give me . . . hell at that": Sherman, interview.

153 "Though Peter didn't . . . just too expensive": Foster, interview.

154 "Peter was not . . . funny, charming way": Ames, interview.

154 "In the mornings . . . be making faces": Foster, "Hollywood by Roller Coaster."

154 "I'm sorry Peter . . . make a picture": Foster, interview.

154 "Sickness . . . he used to": Parry, interview.

154 "He was a . . . cope with him": Ames, interview.

155 "I would hear . . . put it in": Parry, interview.

155 "brain above brawn": 20th Century–Fox publicity release, MHL AMPAS.

155 "Harvey . . . do it again": Parry, interview.

155 "This particular night . . . in those days": Ames, interview.

156 "In the long . . . as physical assault": B.R. Crisler, "*Mysterious Mr. Moto of Devil's Island,*" *NYT,* Sept. 19, 1938.

156 "horror, brutality, and murder": California Congress of Parents and Teachers, "*Thank You, Mr. Moto,*" MHL AMPAS.

156 "Peter Lorre was . . . click with audiences": "*Think Fast, Mr. Moto,*" *Variety,* Aug. 18, 1937.

156 "As Mr. Moto . . . for many years": 20th Century–Fox press release, MHL AMPAS.

157 "I'm tired of . . . in the ass": Parry, interview.

157 "Nothing, I make faces": Lenya, interview.

157 "Mr. Moto was . . . good dramatic story": Joe Duncan, "Mr. Moto Roles Childish, Rebellious Mr. Moto Says," *Louisville (KY) Courier-Journal,* Oct. 21, 1944.

157 "He hated the . . . thing he did": Brandt, interview.

157 "found the Mr. . . . I was 'sick,'": Denman Kountze Jr., "Peter Lorre: Typed Actor Is Boring to the Audience," *Omaha (NB) World Herald,* Oct. 1, 1963.

157 "We're like a . . . Want a divorce": Foster, interview.

158 "was very sorry . . . my good will": Dr. Oskar Samek to Eli Leslie, Nov. 11, 1937, Wiener Stadt- und Landesbibliothek, *Karl Kraus contra,* p. 293.

158 "that we can . . . with Dr. Hunter": Eli Leslie to Ivor Montagu, Nov. 19, 1937, Ivor Montagu Collection, BFINL.

158 "for not having . . . a little bronchitis": Peter Lorre to Ivor Montagu, ca. Nov. 1937, ibid.

158 "You must know . . . are forgiving us": Cecile Lorre to Hell Montagu, April 19, 1939, ibid.

159 "sold him up the river": I. Yergin, interview, June 23, 1976.

159 "there was something . . . was just bored": Ames, interview.

159 "Don't Buy Jap Goods": "Rambling Reporter," *HR,* Feb. 2, 1938.

159 "continued solving high . . . heart and soul": Frank Chin, "Confessions of a Number One Son," *Ramparts,* March, 1973.

160 "we would like . . . in the future": Sol M. Wurtzel, memo to E.C. Delavigne, Dec. 4, 1939, TCFLF UCLA.

160 "Peter, apparently, has . . . sink his teeth": Jimmie Fidler, "Movie Medley," *Chicago Sunday Times,* July 10, 1938.

161 "the way he's . . . a deserved reward": Jimmie Fidler, "Fidler in Hollywood," unidentified clipping, PLS.

161 "Peter Lorre, as . . . him in 1939–40": "These Popular Series," *HR,* April 19, 1939.

161 "I had him . . . German in uniform": Dunne, interview.

162 "somewhat mentally disordered . . . of the road": 20th Century–Fox press release, MHL AMPAS.

162 "with a delightful . . . a melodramatic thriller": *Four Men and a Prayer,* Darryl F. Zanuck, script conference, July 11, 1936, TCFC USC.

162 "monk-like, odious character": *Four Men and a Prayer,* draft screenplay by Sonia Levien, cast of characters, July 7, 1936, TCFC USC.

163 "Chaney's results were . . . would be different": 20th Century–Fox publicity release, TCFC USC.

163 "reasonably censorable": Joseph I. Breen to John Hammell, Paramount, Sept. 20, 1934, MPAA PCA.

163 "I think at . . . with pacifistic doctrine": B.P. Schulberg to Joseph I. Breen, Feb. 4, 1937, ibid.

163 "There is a . . . for any reason": Joseph I. Breen, report to B.P. Schulberg, Feb. 5, 1937, ibid.

164 "international political reasons": B.P. Schulberg to Joseph I. Breen, Feb. 22, 1937, ibid.

164 "he has left . . . on another meanie": "'Frankenstein' Plan for New Team Flop," *HR,* Oct. 24, 1938.

164 "go comic": "20-Fox Ends Month's Lull, Three Pix Roll," *Variety,* Jan. 25, 1939.

164 "because of too . . . 'Mr. Moto' series": "Peter Lorre Bids Adieu to 20th for Freelancing," *HR,* July 19, 1939.

165 "very anxious to . . . of the country": Kenneth Thomson to Frank Gillmore, Aug. 12, 1938, Associated Actors and Artistes of America Collection, Robert F. Wagner Labor Archives, Bobst Library, New York Univ., New York.

165 "I hope the . . . in a while": 20th Century–Fox publicity release, MHL AMPAS.

165 "Mr. Peter Lorre . . . piece of acting": "*I Was an Adventuress,*" *Times* (London), Sept. 16, 1940.

166 "Hollywood has used . . . not his talent": Theodore Strauss, "*Island of Doomed Men,*" *NYT,* June 10, 1940.

166 "I think we . . . laughed like hell": C. Barton, interview.

167 "thrown together quickies": unidentified newspaper clipping, PLS.

167 "Meet me in . . . run after him": C. Barton, interview.

168 "fifty-fifty . . . great": Frank Orsatti to Mr. Joe Nolan, RKO Studios, Aug. 19, 1939, RKO Radio Pictures Studio Collection (Collection 3), ALSC UCLA.

168 "After all . . . this young man": Lee Marcus, interdepartment communication to Joe Nolan, Aug. 28, 1939, ibid.

168 "urban nightworld": Ottoson, *American Film Noir,* p. 168.

168 "light-and-shadow . . . on the screen": "Eccentric Camera Work Marks Drama," *Stranger on the Third Floor,* pressbook, 1940.

169 "I remember that . . . same type roles": Margaret Tallichet Wyler to author, May 20, 1975.

170 "This snack . . . agony in itself": ibid.

170 "visual italics": Foster Hirsch, *The Dark Side of the Screen: Film Noir* (New York: A.S. Barnes, 1981), p. 57.

170 "first true film . . . to that time": *Film Noir: An Encyclopedia Reference to the American Style*, ed. Alain Silver and Elizabeth Ward (Woodstock, NY: Overlook, 1979), p. 269.

170 "three notable heavies": Butler, interview.

170 "the script writers . . . devoted to them": Bosley Crowther, "*You'll Find Out,*" *NYT,* Nov. 15, 1940.

171 "charity fracas . . . first-class riot": "Comedians Nip Leading Men," *LAT,* Aug. 9, 1940.

171 "the most hideous . . . in film history": Hull, *Film in the Third Reich,* p. 173.

171 "black masterpiece": Manvell and Fraenkel, *German Cinema,* p. 75.

173 "I put on . . . of a mask": Guernsey, "Peter Lorre, Who Is Nothing like His Roles."

173 "Artist agrees, at . . . opinion of producer": Synopsis of Employment Contract, Nov. 30, 1936, TCFLF UCLA.

174 "He had terrible . . . room with you": Ames, interview.

174 "The role was . . . already been cast": Paul Jarrico to author, May 20, 1975.

174 "eloquent statement on . . . the American dream": James Monaco and the editors of *BASELINE, The Encyclopedia of Film* (New York: Pedigree, 1991), p. 337.

174 "I don't think . . . this particular venture": Don Beddoe to author, Dec. 27, 1979.

174 "didn't keep his . . . not always possible": Robert Florey to Raymond J. Cabana Jr., March 4, 1978, author's collection.

175 "one of his . . . the unforgettable M": Florey, *Hollywood d'hier,* p. 198.

175 "was wicked, frequently . . . in good taste": Don Beddoe to author, Dec. 12, 1979.

175 "His was a . . . glistening-eye approach": Don Beddoe to author, Aug. 6, 1973.

5. BEING SLAPPED AND LIKING IT

Epigraphs: Humphrey Bogart to Peter Lorre, in *The Maltese Falcon* (1941); Lorre, quoted in Don Alpert, "Lorre Laughs When It Hurts," *LAT,* Jan. 20, 1963.

1. The film was retitled *Dangerous Female* for television release.

2. Director Jean Negulesco recalled that he "got the go-ahead from Jack Warner for the remake" of *The Maltese Falcon* and worked on a shooting script "for four hopeful months" before heading east to make an army short. However, when he returned, he learned that Warner had taken the project away from him and given it to John Huston. *Things I Did,* p. 115.

3. In his autobiography, Huston called it "Faustian worldliness." *An Open Book,* p. 79.

4. Lorre pulled the same trick on Judith Anderson in his next film, *All Through the Night.* Not privy to the prank, however, when she learned about it, she chased him with a hairbrush. Huston, interview.

5. This is the most complete telling of one of Lorre's favorite and often-told Bogart anecdotes.

6. According to Thomas Mann biographer Donald Prater, Lorre's "embrace of Katia (Katharina Mann) on one occasion was so violently emotional that he gave her a love-bite on the arm." *Thomas Mann,* p. 281.

7. A restraining order postponed publication of the newspaper articles until December 4, 1938, by which time the spy trials had concluded.

8. On May 14, 1941, Warner Bros. had announced plans to costar George Raft and Olivia de Havilland in *All Through the Night,* whose July 28 starting date, pointed out

Variety, conflicted with Raft's commitment to RKO for *The Mayor of 44th Street* (in which he ultimately did not appear). However, according to an August 4 letter from Sam Jaffe, Bogart's agent, to Steve Trilling, Raft had actually refused the role of Gloves Donahue in *All Through the Night,* preferring to be placed on suspension rather than play a "heel" who "is willing to throw money away in gambling and refuses to assist members of his own family." Edwin Shallert, "Raft Refuses to Play 'Heel' Role at Warners," *LAT,* Aug. 1, 1941. When he stepped down, Bogart, who had "pinch-hitted for Raft and been kicked around from pillar to post," reluctantly stepped in. De Havilland, busy trying to *Hold Back the Dawn* at Paramount, could not stop the clock at Warner Bros. and missed her entrance. Sam Jaffe to Steve Trilling, Aug. 4, 1941, WBA USC, reprinted in Behlmer, *Inside Warner Bros.,* p. 156. By August the studio still had not filled the female lead. Hal Wallis's first choice was Ingrid Bergman, held under very tight contract to David O. Selznick. With shooting under way, he finally settled for Karen Verne.

9. Budgeted at $643,000, nearly twice the budget of *The Maltese Falcon, All Through the Night* proved the exception to the rule and performed well at the box office. William Schaefer Collection, USC Cinema-Television Library, Univ. of Southern California, Los Angeles.

10. Already she had added a second *a* to her first name. Said Barbara: "She liked that. It sounded a little bit Scandinavian, those double 'a's. Then everybody said 'Karen,' so she just gave up and dropped it." Sykes, interview, Sept. 15, 1984.

11. Released as *Missing Ten Days* in the United States.

12. Catharine Lorre, whom Karen and then-husband Jim Powers (an editor for the *Hollywood Reporter*) adopted after her parents' deaths, remembered her stepmother telling of hearing Lorre's distinctive voice. Jim Powers worked as a reporter and critic for *Daily Variety,* as editor for the *Hollywood Reporter,* and later as director of publications for the American Film Institute and West Coast editor of *American Film Magazine.*

13. Capra announced his decision to join the Signal Corps on December 12; he took his army oath on January 29, 1942, at the Southern California Military District Headquarters in Los Angeles. McBride, *Frank Capra,* p. 449.

14. Warner Bros. bought the motion picture rights to Joseph Kesselring's *Bodies in Our Cellar* for $175,000 in April 1941.

15. Reference to the production of *Captain America,* "Minoco to Produce 'Capt. America' in N.Y.," *Variety,* Sept. 30, 1942.

16. Reference to Lorre signing with Music Corporation of America, "Inside Stuff—Pictures," *Variety,* Feb. 10, 1943.

17. In an earlier performance, broadcast January 3, 1943, Lorre had read: "I'm just a little guy trying to get along." A rattled Allen, apparently intending to play off the "ahead" pun, ad-libbed, "Well, I know that. I know that, but you're not getting along in this vein. You're not trying to get a head, you mean, and you're not getting mine, if that's what you had in mind."

18. "Lorre took particular delight in letting Hardwicke finish a lengthy speech," recalled film historian William K. Everson, who visited the set of "The Man Who Lost His Head" (*Climax!*) in 1956, "and then tearing his hair in mock despair. 'They'll need English subtitles if you keep talking in that accent!' he'd scream, 'let's do it over in American!'" "Peter Lorre," p. 16.

19. At this rate, the actor would receive $10,500 per picture the first and second years of his contract, $15,000 the third, $18,000 the fourth, and $21,000 the fifth.

20. When an uncredited actor, whose vocal mannerisms closely resembled those of Peter Lorre, appeared on radio's *I Love a Mystery* in July 1944, the William Morris Agency sent a letter to the program's advertiser asking that the program cease and desist from impersonating its client's voice without his consent. Grams, *I Love a Mystery Companion,* pp. 123–24.

21. "The appearance of Artist at and the rendition of his services . . . without additional compensation" in one radio broadcast with respect to each motion picture in which he appeared for "advertising and exploiting" purposes presumably didn't carry this stipulation. Agreement, June 2, 1943, Peter Lorre legal file, WBA USC.

22. The "exclusive deal" provided for forty out of fifty-two weeks—$1,000 weekly, with a $250 salary increase each of the first five years and $500 thereafter.

23. Paramount did not release a film titled *The Private Eye*.

24. According to a letter in the Paul Kohner Collection at the Stiftung Deutsche Kinemathek in Berlin, the agent had sent Lorre a script of the same title in 1940 and then written to ask how he liked the part. Film historian Tom Weaver disallows the idea it might have been the same film: "Universal's *Chamber of Horrors* would have been an all-star 'monster rally' movie in the wake of *Frankenstein Meets the Wolf Man*—unimaginable in 1940, when such things were years in the future." Tom Weaver to author, Feb. 9, 2000.

25. The *Hollywood Reporter's* "RKO Picture Will Gag Horror Films," June 4, 1943, spared Lorre the promised displacement.

26. Greenstreet received first billing and Lorre fourth, behind Scott and Faye Emerson.

27. David O. Selznick wanted it clearly understood that before bothering to read the story, he was setting Ingrid Bergman's salary for any possibility in *The Conspirators* (originally titled *Give Me This Woman*) at $175,000 for ten weeks. Steve Trilling, interoffice communication to Hal B. Wallis, June 8, 1943, JWC USC.

28. Whereas the studio held Lorre to $1,750 per week with a six-to-eight-week guarantee per picture, Greenstreet's three-year option, as of 1945, included two pictures per year, with a five-to-six-week guarantee and a salary that graduated from $3,500 the first year to $4,166.66 the third. R.J. Orbringer, interoffice communication to J.L. Warner, Feb. 26, 1945, JWC USC.

29. According to *Variety*, the William Morris Agency asked $4,000 per week for Lorre's services. "Morris Office Seeks to Extend Lorre Dates," *Variety*, Aug. 23, 1944.

30. During the 1930s through the 1950s, Wilson did it all, contributing crime stories to *The Bishop and the Gargoyle*, biographies to *These Four Men*, dramas to *Academy Award Theater*, and comedy to *Songs by Sinatra* and *The Big Show*.

31. Lorre's contract stated that "the Artist agrees to conduct himself with due regard to public convention and morals, and agrees that he will not do or commit any act or thing that will tend to degrade himself in society or bring him into public hatred, contempt, scorn or ridicule, or that will tend to shock or offend the community or ridicule public morals or decency or prejudice the Producer or the motion picture industry in general." Agreement, June 2, 1943, Peter Lorre legal file, WBA USC.

32. According to a memo from Henry Blanke to Roy Obringer, dated January 14, 1943, Frank Gruber also worked on the story; "To the characters John Huston had, we have added a private detective on the order of the one portrayed by Humphrey Bogart in *The Maltese Falcon*." WBA USC.

33. Andrea King might well have had Clark Gable's Fletcher Christian in mind, although MGM, not Warner Bros., produced the 1935 classic.

34. In the late 1930s playwright Arch Oboler had scripted *Lights Out*, radio's ultimate horror show, into a late-night institution. Wanting to write, cast, and direct, he put in for his own show. NBC gave him a slot in spring of 1939 and *Arch Oboler's Plays* was airborne.

35. The release cut did not charge Lorre with the murder of the pianist, played by Victor Francen. Rather, it explained his death as an accident. However, the crux of the plot conformed to Siodmak's original premise.

36. An outtake of Lorre included in a documentary history of Warner Bros. shows

him maniacally pounding a nail into a rubber hand. When it accidentally falls off the table, he curses, "You bastard, you," and then breaks up. Robert Guenette, *Here's Looking at You, Warner Bros.,* Warner Studios (1991).

37. According to Florey biographer Brian Taves, the director had "wanted to alter the scene where Lorre nails the menacing hand to one where he stabs his own hand, demonstrating unmistakably that a self-destructive hallucination has taken over his mind." Taves, *Robert Florey,* p. 278.

38. Between 1947 and 1949, Warner Bros.' production of film noir—eleven pictures—ranked second only to RKO and Fox, which both released twelve features in that genre during the three-year period. The Warner Bros. casting department seems to have been oblivious to Lorre's assertion that he and Sydney Greenstreet had finally "decided to split up." Or, in fact, that the actor was leaving the studio altogether. One month after his contract was terminated, Paul Schiller, in his column "Hollywood Diary" for *Aufbau* (July 5, 1946), reported that Lorre and Greenstreet had been cast in featured roles (along with Zachary Scott and Ida Lupino) in *The Apple Orchard,* the story of a utopian community that falls from grace, based on Hans Kafka's novel. Peter Lorre, interview, "Dick Strout with Hollywood Profiles," A Celebrity Fives Presentation: Al Petker-Personality Scope, Beverly Hills, CA, 1963.

39. Lorre's contract with Warner Bros. officially ended on June 14, 1946.

QUOTATION SOURCES BY PAGE NUMBER

176 "The Maltese Falcon": Recollections of Henry Blanke, interviewed by Barry Steinberg, Oral History Program, DSC UCLA.

177 "They liked my . . . and Henry Blanke": Pratley, *Cinema of John Huston,* p. 38.

177 "We'll do the book as it is": Recollections of Henry Blanke, DSC UCLA.

177 "One day [Huston] . . . went there, too": Rivkin, *Hello, Hollywood!* p. 155.

178 "The flight of . . . at his best": Huston, interview.

179 "for some reason . . . o.k. with you": Steve Trilling, interoffice communication to Jack Warner, June 18, 1941, Peter Lorre legal file, WBA USC.

179 "I attempted . . . is the picture": Allan S. Downer, "The Monitor Image," in *Man and the Movies,* ed. W.R. Robinson (Baton Rouge: Louisiana State Univ. Press, 1967), p. 19.

179 "About half the . . . I had drawn": Pratley, *Cinema of John Huston,* p. 40.

179 "that the 'heavy' . . . of his passport": Carl Schaefer, interoffice communication to Henry Blanke, June 4, 1941, WBA USC.

179 "certain objectionable details": Joseph I. Breen to Jack L. Warner, May 23, 1941, WBA USC.

180 "high-pitched thin voice": Dashiell Hammett, *The Maltese Falcon* (New York: Vintage, 1972), p. 38.

180 "gaily colored silk . . . fragrant of *chypre*": ibid., p. 42.

180 "mincing, bobbing steps": ibid., p. 47.

180 "We cannot approve . . . is definitely unacceptable": Breen to Warner, May 23, 1941, WBA USC.

180 "Don't try to . . . with the picture": Hal Wallis, interoffice communication to John Huston, June 20, 1941, WBA USC.

180 "suave form of . . . speaking the lines": Hal Wallis, interoffice communication to Henry Blanke, June 12, 1941, WBA USC.

181 "I would say . . . do you want": Parry, interview.

181 "I'd often shoot . . . were in motion": Huston, interview.

182 "You felt you . . . to good performances": Patrick, interview.

182 "one of my . . . most people can't": Lorre, interview by Glover.

182 "Shock the Tourists . . . fat old fool": Astor, *Life on Film,* p. 162.

183 "Whenever VIPs would . . . to shock people": Huston, interview.

183 "goddam gags . . . and you're in": Astor, *Life on Film,* p. 163.

183 "It was not . . . which was unforgettable": M. Minstrel, "Sein Ruhm begann mit 'M,'" *National Zeitung* (Berlin), Feb. 24, 1962.

184 "if we can . . . a fine actor": Layman and Rivett, *Letters of Dashiell Hammett,* p. 509.

184 "He was a . . . huddled around Peter": Goff, interview, July 31, 1978.

184 "journeymen": Henreid, interview.

184 "Peter was a . . . up-stage about him": Robert Cummings to author, Feb. 23, 1974.

185 "Peter was glad . . . cinema being made": Sperling, interview.

185 "One night Mayo . . . big story conference": Goodman, *Bogey,* pp. 133–34.

186 "I like Bogie . . . with the advantages": Hyams, *Bogie,* p. 120.

186 "Bogie called a . . . did this, too": Seymour, interview.

186 "Colonels were just . . . that Peter was": Garnett, interview.

186 "How dare you . . . 'Kreep,' not 'Creep,'": Goodman, *Bogey,* p. 110.

186 "They used to . . . just a word": Lorre, interview by O'Connell.

186 "Those kreeps that . . . That jerk": Guernsey, "Peter Lorre, Who Is Nothing Like His Roles."

187 "In any case . . . both of them": Lorre, interview by O'Connell.

187 "every actor is a shit": Siegel, *Siegel Film,* p. 77.

187 "a plump little . . and good looks": Warner, *My First Hundred Years,* p. 308.

187 "Listen, you creeps . . . dear old Warners'": Frazier, *The One with the Mustache,* p. 205.

187 "Jesus, it stinks . . . always the same": Garnett, interview.

187 "Peter claimed that . . . Oh, how nice": Kanter, interview.

187 "I can feel it in my urine": R. Shutan, interview.

188 "smoking gag": Goodman, *Bogey,* p. 135.

188 "When he was . . . crazy in advance": ibid.

188 "I noticed today . . . feet of film": Jack Warner to Peter Lorre, Sept. 27, 1943, JWC USC.

188 "the bum true-blue . . . in his part": Capote, *Dog Barks,* p. 374.

188 "Acting's our racket . . . do our best": Willi Frischauer, "Mr. Murder," *Picturegoer,* May 30, 1953.

188 "You're supposed to . . . for the money": A.H. Weiler, "Mild Mannered Villain," *NYT,* June 25, 1944.

188 "As long as . . . we're at it": I. Yergin, interview, June 23, 1976.

189 "Whenever they were . . . old guy seizures": Capra, interview.

189 "Peter was always . . . could draw fun": J. Silverstone, interview.

189 "We'll be ready . . . check your makeup": Crawford, interview.

189 "Peter told me . . . broken his arm": Avalon, interview.

189 "Another night Bogey . . . drag it back": Goodman, *Bogey,* p. 131.

190 "As he was . . . of the cinema": Ernst W. Korngold to author, Feb. 7, 1982.

190 "Everything was looked . . . humor and skepticism": Henreid, interview.

190 "our Warner Brothers . . . him lying there": Warner, *My First Hundred Years,* p. 248.

190 "was the seed . . . good picture making": Sperling and Millner, *Hollywood Be Thy Name,* pp. 18, 245.

190 "stirring warning about . . . German military threat": ibid., p. 61.

191 "a foreign war for whatever idealistic purposes": Shindler, *Hollywood Goes to War,* p. 3.

191 "The Nazis are Coming": "Let the Flag Wave," *Movie Radio Guide,* Dec. 21–27, 1940.

191 "pernicious propaganda poisoning German-American relations": *Los Angeles Examiner,* June 6, 1939.

191 "driving home to . . . proud to wave": "Let the Flag Wave."

191 "a tremendous investment . . . secure that future": "WB's Patriotism Costly, Shorts Lost $1,250,000," *Variety,* March 13, 1940.

192 "threats and pleas . . . of serving America": Sperling and Millner, *Hollywood Be Thy Name,* p. 233.

192 "no propaganda pictures from Warner Brothers": Gordon Sayer, "Hollywood Carries on for Neville," *TAC: A Magazine of Theatre, Film, Radio, Music, Dance,* Oct. 1939, quoted in Dick, *Star-Spangled Screen,* p. 65.

192 "among the country's . . . the Fifth Column": Matthews, *Specter of Sabotage,* dedication page.

192 "Damon Runyan types": Sherman, interview.

192 "He was always . . . of crap once": ibid.

194 "violet-eyed, blonde and vivacious": Robert S. Taplinger, director of publicity, Warner Bros. Studio, "Biography of Kaaren Verne," Karen Verne file, MHL AMPAS.

194 "They lived music . . . she didn't like": Sykes, interviews.

196 "not so that . . . to the company": Katherine Young to Rosalind Martin, Jan. 8, 1939 (Katherine Young letters from author's collection).

196 "under convoy!" Young to Martin, Feb. 20, 1940.

196 "brought on by . . . on a picture": ibid., June 6, 1940.

196 "slated for a . . . first Hollywood picture": "Verne Up for 'Witch,'" *HR,* March 30, 1940.

196 "I have made . . . a start soon": Young to Martin, June 6, 1940.

196 "that once I . . . at the studio": ibid., June 21, 1940.

196 "they liked me . . . talks": ibid., Dec. 16, 1940.

196 "A beautiful German . . . a good actress": Sherman, *Studio Affairs,* p. 93.

197 "would give her whatever aid we could": Steve Trilling, interoffice communication to Roy J. Obringer, Aug. 2, 1941, WBA USC.

197 "that voice": C. Lorre, interviews.

197 "in Germany my . . . were too gruesome": Kirk Crivello, "Kaaren Verne," unidentified clipping, Karen Verne file, MHL AMPAS.

197 "Karen admired him . . . had that down": N. Yergin, interview.

197 "He was like . . . obviously very happy": Sherman, interview.

197 "an active physical . . . arms of steel": Ives, interview.

198 "You thief! Kleptomaniac! . . . initials P.L.": C. Lorre, interview, Oct. 15, 1980.

198 "Anytime they wanted . . . I was ready": Capra, interview.

198 "a cheap film . . . Any hopes": Capra, *Name above the Title,* p. 309.

198 "Jack Warner was . . . than anybody else": Capra, interview.

199 "let the scene . . . a mugger's ball": Capra, *Name above the Title,* p. 311.

199 "word for word . . . before your eyes": Capra, interview.

201 "romantic dream . . . a double meaning": Burnett, interview.

202 "obsession . . . *raison d'être*": Pachter, "On Being an Exile," p. 18.

203 "flagboiler": Haver, "Finally, the Truth about CASABLANCA," p. 12.

203 "mean, sneaky, is generally despised": Warner Bros. Publicity Department, WBA USC.

203 "could be Italian . . . offending Latin America": Carl Shaefer, interoffice communication to Jack Warner and Hal Wallis, May 22, 1942, UAC WCFTR.

204 "'Senior Ugarte' should . . . change his name": Hal Wallis, interoffice communication to Michael Curtiz, May 25, 1942, UAC WCFTR.

204 "an impalpable air of sophistication and intrigue": "*Everybody Comes to Rick's,*" author's collection.

204 "a small thin . . . like a tout": Howard Koch, *Casablanca: Script and Legend* (Woodstock, N.Y.: Overlook, 1973), p.43.

204 "With his round . . . black-market operations": Koch, "Making of Casablanca," p. 21.

204 "Directors didn't direct . . . with the role": Koch, interview.
205 "One of the . . . liked him throughout": ibid.
205 "Peter told me . . . by the reception": Kulik, interview.
205 "none of us . . . anti-hero, Humphrey Bogart": Koch, *Casablanca*, p. 17.
205 "the happiest of happy accidents": Sarris, *American Cinema*, p. 176.
206 "comedy-horror yarn": "Karloff's Clown Scarer Following 'Arsenic,'" *Variety*, March 5, 1941.
206 "The secret of . . . Brooks' 'Young Frankenstein'": Edwin Blum to author, Feb. 26, 1975.
207 "Double Dose of Chills": "Double Dose of Chills," *Variety*, Nov. 12, 1941.
207 "We spent an . . . other, heavier kind": Eric Ambler to author, Aug. 27, 1988.
207 "gave the impression . . . was invariably perfect": Eric Ambler, *Background to Danger* (New York: Ballantine, 1978), pp. 60–61.
207 "putty-faced dummy": Ambler to author.
207 "knock it off": Yablonsky, *George Raft*, p. 154.
208 "Peter was a . . . little helpless guy": Parry, interview.
208 "are working this morning": R.J. Obringer, interoffice communication to Colonel [Jack] Warner, Oct. 21, 1942, Peter Lorre legal file, WBA USC.
210 "a whale of a picture": Garnett, interview.
210 "I knew his . . . slight German tinge": ibid.
211 "a lot of . . . happy coincidences": "Inside Stuff—Pictures," *Variety*, Sept. 15, 1943.
211 "at the soft . . . of the Axis": quoted in Norman Rose, *Churchill: An Unruly Life* (New York: Touchstone Books, 1998), p. 295.
211 "a new ending . . . of the continent": "Keeping Step with War," *Variety*, July 28, 1943.
211 "should have been . . . it is now": Thomas Pryor, "*The Cross of Lorraine*," *NYT*, Dec. 3, 1943.
211 "stark, heavy and unrelieved drama": "*The Cross of Lorraine*," *Variety*, Nov. 10, 1943.
211 "expected masterpiece of . . . a Nazi jailer": *NYT*, Nov. 10, 1943.
211 "to act, pose . . . by the Producer": Agreement between Warner Bros. Pictures Inc. and Peter Lorre, June 2, 1943, Peter Lorre legal file, WBA USC.
211 "Peter was a . . . he was in": Wallis, interview.
211 "the sum of . . . studio services": Agreeement, June 2, 1943, WBA USC.
213 "In a spirit . . . with your request": Ann Rosenthal to Roy J. Obringer, April 13, 1945, WBA USC.
213 "PETER LORRE has . . . to him personally": Steve Trilling to Jack Warner, July 24, 1943, JWC USC.
213 "In such event . . . such directorial work": Phil Friedman, interoffice communication to Roy J. Obringer, Sept. 9, 1943, Peter Lorre legal file, WBA USC.
213 "I know there . . . too many accents": Meredith, interview.
214 "Lorre plans to . . . 'allowable' outside pictures": Roy J. Obringer to Ann Rosenthal, Aug. 17, 1945, Peter Lorre legal file, WBA USC.
214 "physical likeness": Agreement, June 2, 1943, Peter Lorre legal file, WBA USC.
214 "wrote the strip . . . speech markers": Kane and Desris, *Batman Dailies*, pp. 8–9.
215 "They were always . . . an instant way": Fitzgerald, interview.
215 "happily unhappy": Lovsky, interview, May 12, 1977.
215 "goosepimplers . . . all chiller-dillers": "This Will Do It," *Variety*, June 9, 1943.
215 "Casablanca Kids": David Lardner, "*Passage to Marseille*," *New Yorker*, Feb. 19, 1944.
216 "the worst rogue of the lot": Charles Nordhoff and James Norman Hall, "Men without a Country," *Atlantic Monthly*, June 1942, p. 785.
216 "I am very . . . picture with doubles": Eric Stacey, interoffice communication to T.C. Wright, Sept. 18, 1943, WBA USC.
216 "interesting and (pathetic) . . . *Forget it*": Bessie, *Inquisition into Eden*, pp. 108–11.

217 "Take it to . . . page by page": Negulesco, *Things I Did,* p. 116.

217 "respected character actors . . . to it, boys": Negulesco, interview.

217 "I saw the . . . picture proceeded smoothly": Higham and Greenberg, *Celluloid Muse,* pp. 187–88.

218 "It's hard to . . . making better time": "Shadow Threat Puts Actor in New Light," *The Mask of Dimitrios,* pressbook, 1944.

218 "Lorre was the . . . I scare you": Higham and Greenberg, *Celluloid Muse,* p. 188.

218 "had to make . . . sense of heat": Goff, interview, Nov. 16, 1928.

218 "a strange, absorbing . . . intrigue and vengeance": "*The Mask of Dimitrios,*" *HR,* June 6, 1944.

218 "it wasn't that . . . were almost good": Ambler, *Here Lies,* p. 225.

219 "who is so . . . can play anything": Sara Hamilton, "'Mask of Dimitrios' Real Mystery Drama Thriller," *Los Angeles Examiner,* July 1, 1944.

219 "There seemed to . . . from the outset": Peter Lorre, interview, "Dick Strout with Hollywood Profiles."

219 "was that they . . . and opposites attract": Siegel, interview.

219 "So this is the script": ibid.

219 "He used to . . . to the picture": Matheson, interview, Dec. 6, 1994.

220 "It was all . . . had studied it": Siegel, interview.

220 "Fine, then I'll . . . the whole show": Cheatham, "Gruesome Twosome."

220 "Hey, Sydney . . . pair of tits": I. Yergin, interview, June 23, 1976.

220 "Pekingese and a . . . for a romp": *Los Angeles Examiner,* July 1, 1944.

220 "One afternoon . . . all broke up": Astor, *Life on Film,* p. 169.

220 "Sydney Greenstreet was . . . of our time": Peter Lorre, interview, "Dick Strout with Hollywood Profiles."

220 "which sought out . . . same wave-length": Lorring, interview.

220 "It's fun to . . . of his shadow": Cheatham, "Gruesome Twosome."

221 "I have just . . . a straight face": Frederic Prokosch, "Is Hollywood Dying?" *New Republic,* Nov. 13, 1944.

221 "It was a . . . that was enough": Fehr, interview.

221 "What would you be comfortable doing": Daves, interview.

222 "It shall be . . . of the performer": "Warners to Shelve 'H'wood Canteen' if SAG Rules Full Scale for Stars," *Variety,* Dec. 15, 1943.

223 "this very pathetic . . . for more money'": King, interview by Katz.

223 "It's so-o-o-o nice . . . when I'm around": "Peter Lorre Scares Fans in Stage Show at Earle," *Philadelphia Inquirer,* April 23, 1949.

224 "favorite hobby . . . favorite color, black": Boyd Martin, "'Sinister' Peter Lorre Displays New Facet at National—As Comic," *Louisville (KY) Courier-Journal,* Oct. 21, 1944.

224 "What I would . . . in the dark": script, British Broadcasting Corporation, Written Archives Centre, London.

225 "some time figuring . . . do it well": "RKO, Boston," *Variety,* Sept. 13, 1944.

225 "the audience sat . . . and absolutely still": M.O.C., "Lorre, Kenton Head Strong Bill on State Stage," *Hartford (CT) Daily Courant,* Sept. 23, 1944.

225 "demanded Mr. Lorre's continuous curtain calls": "Peter Lorre Makes an Important Debut on the State Stage," *Hartford (CT) Times,* Sept. 23, 1944.

225 "with great dignity . . . or E.H. Southern": Martin, "'Sinister' Peter Lorre Displays New Facet."

225 "hopes to direct . . . whatever he wants": ibid.

225 "like seeing the . . . on their necks": Harrison Carroll, "'Hotel Berlin' Is News-Hot Saga of Nazi Doom," *Los Angeles Evening Herald-Express,* March 10, 1945.

226 "to hit the . . . did with Casablanca": "WB's Berlin Timing," *Variety,* Dec. 13, 1944.

226 "Violently anti-Nazi . . . against the Nazis": "'Hotel Berlin' Cast Violently Anti-Nazi," *Hotel Berlin,* pressbook, 1945.

226 "He always began . . . into a category": Koch, interview.

226 "Hustonesque, somewhat reminiscent . . . twists and turns": Koch, "Reflections on a Golden Boy."

226 "It wasn't my . . . to do it": Koch, interview.

227 "contribution was mostly . . . he had intended ": Koch, "Reflections on a Golden Boy."

227 "his own melancholy . . . of a poet": Negulesco, interview.

227 "I was a . . . going on eleven": Lorring, interview.

227 "The first time . . . to play with": "Joan Lorring and Three Strangers," Ray Nielsen's "Ray's Way," *Classic Images,* no. 159, Sept. 1988.

228 "This comment crushed . . . than I did": Lorring, interview.

228 "was the best . . . have ever done": ibid.

228 "Peter had a . . . running the studio": Koch, interview.

229 "rather sentimentalised": Pratley, *Cinema of John Huston,* p. 37.

229 "a polished, patrician . . . of old age": "Movie Murderer," *Life,* April 2, 1945.

229 "one that is . . . with telling skill": "*Three Strangers,*" *Variety,* Jan. 23, 1946.

229 "under-acting": "Unholy Trio on a Horse," *Cue,* Feb. 23, 1946.

229 "he would go . . . part or another": King, interview by Katz.

229 "Sensation!": advertisement, *NYT,* March 8, 1945.

229 "Chilling on Screen . . . on the Stage": advertisement, *NYT,* March 11, 1945.

229 "the exception to . . . makes a personal": "New Acts: Peter Lorre," *Variety,* March 7, 1945.

230 "probably wind up . . . to mother him": Kilgallen, "Ten Knights in My Date Book."

230 "actually had tremendous . . . into your soul": Court, interview by Katz.

230 "You know . . . make people happy": Vincent, interview.

230 "When you blend . . . saw this happen": J. Silverstone, interview.

230 "Ain't he the . . . better dressing room": I. Yergin, interview, June 23, 1976.

230 "If there is . . . let me know": C. Lorre, interviews.

231 "Peter Lorre and . . . who knew anything": Betsy Jones-Moreland, interview by Tom Weaver, in Weaver, *Attack of the Monster Movie Makers,* p. 193.

231 "Peter was very . . . threatening their idol": J. Silverstone, interview.

231 "That was his . . . touched that closely": C. Lorre, interview, Oct. 15, 1980.

231 "I guess there . . . they got divorced": Falkenberg, interview.

232 "continued the case . . . must be made": "British Actress' Divorce from Soldier Delayed," *LAT,* Nov. 29, 1944.

232 "separate and apart . . . three (3) consecutive years": *Complaint,* Cecile Lorre vs. Peter Lorre, March 13, 1945, Eighth Judicial District Court of the State of Nevada in and for the County of Clark.

232 "failed to introduce . . . of the answer": *Decree of Divorce,* Cecile Lorre vs. Peter Lorre, March 13, 1945, Eighth Judicial District Court of the State of Nevada in and for the County of Clark.

232 "extreme cruelty without . . . of plaintiff's health": *Complaint,* Ingeborg Young vs. Arthur Young, March 13, 1945, Eighth Judicial District Court of the State of Nevada in and for the County of Clark.

232 "Alastair must stay . . . of explanation following": Katherine Young to Rosalind Martin, Dec. 16, 1940.

232 "who is a . . . of this child": *Complaint,* Ingeborg Young vs. Arthur Young, March 13, 1945.

233 "What's the difference . . . none at all": Hyams, *Bogart and Bacall,* p. 103.

233 "Celia didn't have . . . care of her": Miller, interview.

233 "Peter and Karen . . . with the riding": N. Yergin, interview.

234 "During the war . . . of the Gestapo": Lorant, interview.

235 "tops almost all . . . fit of hysteria": "*Confidential Agent,*" *Motion Picture Herald,* Nov. 3, 1945.

235 "which he executed . . . the dirty floor": Herman Shumlin to author, Dec. 16, 1974.

235 "He used to . . . tasted so bad": Seymour, interview.

236 "pocket sized menace man": "Production Notes of The Verdict," WBA USC.

236 "No one could . . . made to seem": Jack D. Grant, "*The Verdict,*" *HR,* Nov. 5, 1946.

236 "Oh, you should . . . can't tell you": "Joan Lorring and Three Strangers," Ray Nielsen's "Ray's Way."

237 "If I had . . . much more difficult": Siegel, interview.

237 "one of the . . . Abbott and Costello": Peter Lorre, interview, "Dick Strout with Hollywood Profiles."

237 "He said he . . . few the number": Conversation between Steve Trilling and Peter Lorre before Don Page and Carrol Sax as witnesses, 4:35 p.m., Oct. 19, 1945, JWC USC.

237 "he had been . . . or any intimation": ibid., 4:55 p.m., Oct. 19, 1945, JWC USC.

237 "timid guys . . . don't go through": Conversation between Steve Trilling and Jack Dales, Oct. 17, 1945, JWC USC.

237 "what I think . . . finish the picture": Statement of Peter Lorre, Feb. 27, 1947, USPHS DHHS.

238 "headaches, hay fever . . . a marked depression": Dr. D.D. Le Grand, Admission Summary, Personal History, March 24, 1947, USPHS DHHS.

238 "gave me at . . . on Sunset Boulevard": Statement of Peter Lorre, Feb. 27, 1947, USPHS DHHS.

238 "You're too effete . . . least a pound": Siegel, *Siegel Film,* pp. 98–100.

238 "You can't make . . . followed the book": Siegel, interview.

239 "heavy-handed . . . sombre monotone": "*The Verdict,*" *Variety,* Nov. 5, 1946.

239 "thrilled": Lorring, interview.

239 "not big enough . . . still my opinion": Curt Siodmak to author, March 26, 1975.

239 "Peter Lorre continues . . . up the old": News and Feature Service, Warner Bros. Studio, Nov. 27, 1945, WBA USC.

239 "I read it . . . as I visualized": Robert Florey to Raymond J. Cabana Jr.

240 "When a writer . . . be the monster": Siodmak to author.

240 "I always had . . . it was Peter": King to author, July 5, 1973.

240 "was really an . . . in your shoe": King, interview by Katz.

241 "would have a . . . got the giggles": King to author.

241 "After all, Peter . . . stop it, please": Andrea King, quoted in McClelland, *Forties Film Talk,* p. 104.

241 "This is just impossible": King, interview by Katz.

241 "The director . . . no close-up": Carradine, interview.

241 "I think it . . . eye on him": Alda, interview.

241 "One night in . . . you, that's all": Crawford, interview.

242 "I think he . . . from inside him": King, interview, March 14, 1979.

242 "inner rhythm": Eisner, *Haunted Screen,* p. 145.

242 "sleepy delirium, like a somnambulist": Taves, *Robert Florey,* p. 275.

243 "Without any explanation . . . Lorre's deranged mind": Mike, "*The Beast with Five Fingers,*" *Variety,* Dec. 25, 1946.

243 "moving quickly in . . . to the whole": Peter Haining, ed., *The Ghouls* (New York: Stein and Day, 1971), p. 220.

243 "Director Robert Florey . . . on being frightened": *Time,* Jan. 13, 1947.

243 "classic . . . with modern audiences": Taves, *Robert Florey,* p. 279.

244 "There has not . . . give a damn": I. Yergin, interview, June 23, 1976.

244 "mutual agreement . . . discharge each other": Agreement, May 13, 1946, Peter Lorre legal file, WBA USC.

244 "We were all . . . a good reason": Fitzgerald, interview.

244 "For the rest . . . a disabused grin": Robert Florey to Raymond J. Cabana Jr.

245 "Any director who . . . wasting his time": Goff, interview, July 31, 1978.

6. INSIDER AS OUTSIDER

Epigraphs: Peter Lorre in *Rope of Sand* (1949); Lang, "He's an INSIDE Actor."

1. Viking Press brought out an American edition under the title *The Pretender* the following year.

2. German actor Fritz Kortner and Dorothy Thompson, writer Sinclair Lewis's wife, financially supported Brecht's entrance into the United States. Émigré director William Dieterle provided an affidavit of support.

When war threatened, German director Rudolph Cartier (Katscher) asked Lorre to arrange a "faked" contract that would allow him to enter the United States. "Lorre was very fond of Vienna poppy-seed cake," recalled Cartier, "but the poppy-seed to make it had to be crushed in a mill [German: *Mohnmühle*] which is unobtainable in the U.S.A. His reply (by cable) became a 'classic': 'You bring Mohnmühle, I arrange contract!' Unfortunately nothing came of this ruse, because war broke out, travel to outside the United Kingdom was stopped, and I spent the war years in England." Rudolph Cartier to author, Dec. 29, 1980.

3. The foul smell of Brecht's cigars left a lasting impression. "Peter invited me one night over to his house when Brecht was there," recalled Burl Ives, "because he wanted to hear me sing and I sang all evening. Peter apologized for Brecht's terrible cigars. He smoked those Italian crook cigars. I'm surprised he didn't smoke good cigars, but he never did." Ives, interview.

4. Born in 1891 of German-American parents, Ferdinand Reyher graduated from the University of Pennsylvania in 1912 and taught English for one year at the Massachusetts Institute of Technology before becoming a newspaper man for the *Boston Post,* which sent him to Europe as a war correspondent in 1915. Over the next fifteen years, he wrote short fiction, serials, and articles for numerous magazines, most notably *Atlantic Monthly, Century Magazine, Collier's, Harper's Magazine, New Republic, Saturday Evening Post, McClure's Magazine,* and *Liberty.* He also penned poems, plays, several novels, and a biography of Admiral David Farragut. Reyher took up screenwriting in 1931, specializing in crime dramas, often based on his own stories. His skills as a writer—an ear for dialogue and the ability to tell a good story—often relegated him to the role of script doctor, improving others' work without screen credit for himself.

Brecht met Reyher first in Berlin in 1931 and again in Copenhagen in late 1938, when he told of plans for a drama based on the life of Galileo. Reyher likely reminded Brecht that the production of a play or film in America might get him into the United States ahead of his quota number. Brecht surprisingly opted for film first, play later, possibly banking on his friend's Hollywood connections and the visual potential— "the moon with its mountains, the phases of Venus, the orbits of the planet Jupiter's four moons"—of a movie version. On December 2 he wrote Reyher that "instead of a film treatment I'm sending you a play" and asked him how to "push" it.

Reyher became "Brecht's closest American friend, and perhaps one of the best male friends in his lifetime." No one more actively solicited help in bringing the writer and his family to America. Brecht, in turn, impressed him as "a great man, the most impressive personality I have ever met." Their compatibility extended to the love of laughter, lively conversation, cheap cigars, chess, and Marxism. With Reyher, Brecht abandoned his customary restraint and let go. "He is a good guide to the states," wrote Brecht, "when . . . he explains the peculiarities of that giant baby, America." Brecht respected Reyher's opinions and treated him as an equal, seeking his input, and often collaboration, on more than one dozen dramas and film stories. Brecht to Reyher, Dec. 2, 1938, in Brecht, *Letters*, p. 294; Lyon, *Brecht in America*, p. 215; Lyon, *Brecht's American Cicerone*, p. 40; Brecht, *Journals*, Feb. 13, 1942, p. 197.

5. It is easy to forget, against the backdrop of failure and frustration, Brecht's profitable collaboration with Fritz Lang and screenwriter John Wexley on the anti-Nazi film *Hangmen Also Die* (1943), which gave him "enough breathing space for three plays. (*The Visions of Simone Machard, The Duchess of Malfi, Schweyk*)." Brecht and Lion Feuchtwanger collaborated on *The Visions of Simone Machard* in late 1942. Feuchtwanger later sold the screen rights to his novel *Simone*, based on the same material, to Sam Goldwyn for $50,000. For his original idea, Brecht received at least $20,000. Brecht, *Journals*, June 24, 1943, p. 280.

6. Elisabeth Hauptmann, Brecht's mistress and collaborator, worked as Peter Lorre's personal secretary during the mid-to-late 1940s.

7. Riker reported that Brecht actually "liked his role very much in *The Maltese Falcon*." Riker, interview, June 21, 1987.

8. At the star-studded premiere, Bentley sat next to Lorre, behind Ingrid Bergman, and in front of Charles and Oona Chaplin. Other celebrities included Charles Boyer, John Garfield, Sydney Greenstreet, and Lewis Milestone, to name just a few.

9. Lorre read six poems from the *Deutschen Satiren*, "Schwierigkeit des Regierens" ("Difficulties of Governing"), "Über die Bezeichnung Emigranten" ("On the Designation 'Emigrants'"), "Legende von der Entstehung des Buches Taoteking auf dem Weg des Laotse in die Emigration" ("Legend of the Origin of the Book Taoteking on Laotse's Journey into Emigration"), "An die Nachgeborenen" ("To Posterity") from the *Svendborger Gedichte* (*Svendborg Poems*), and "An die deutschen Soldaten im Osten" ("To the German Soldier in the East"). He apparently did not read from the "Gesichten" ("Visions") of the Steffinsichen Sammlung (Steffin Collection), as scheduled.

10. Ernest Pascal (1896–1966) wrote more than two hundred short stories and six plays before turning to screenwriting. His movie credits date from 1928 and include *Lloyds of London* (1936), *Kidnapped* (1938), *The Hound of the Baskervilles* (1939), and *Flesh and Fantasy* (1943). Pascal served as president of the Screen Writers Guild from 1935 to 1937.

11. Lorre owned no property at Lake Arrowhead, whose log for August 28, 1943, carried the item that Peter Lorre and Karen Berg [*sic*] had been the summer guests of the Vincent Votres. PL FBI.

12. Although the title page credits the more established Berthold Viertel for the adaptation, it was his son Hans, a native English speaker, to whom writing acknowledgment is due. "When we first started talking about doing this story," said the younger Viertel, "the idea was he'd [Brecht] furnish the story and I'd furnish the English, which didn't mean he wouldn't discuss it with me. He was very, very open to suggestion from anybody and sometimes he'd accept my suggestion that I wasn't sure of much more readily than I really thought he should have." Viertel, interview.

13. Kreymborg had chaired the International Commemoration of the 10th Anniversary of the Burning of the Books, May 10, 1933.

14. After the loss of the child, Ruth Berlau suffered a nervous breakdown in December 1945. Lorre's friend and doctor (Dr. Max Gruenthal), Ferdinand Reyher, and the police escorted her to Bellevue Hospital.

15. Brecht's comment did not carry any political baggage. Rather, it referred to *Schweyk* as being too unorthodox by American standards.

16. In *Brecht's American Cicerone*, p. 96, Lyon acknowledges Barbara Brecht's claim

that she gave her father her copy of Masters's *Spoon River Anthology.*

17. In a "Personal and Confidential" report, dated March 28, 1944, Mrs. Peter Lorre (Celia Lovsky) was reported by various individuals to be an intimate friend of a motion picture director who was allegedly a Communist party member. The name of the filmmaker is blacked out in the unclassified document. PL FBI.

18. Lorre's October 1940 telegram—one of more than a thousand—to the German-American Writers Association, organized by prominent German-American novelists, playwrights, and journalists "to unite all German-American writers, scientists, dramatists, scenario writers and journalists against the propaganda machine of the Nazis in the United States and to preserve true German culture" did not place him far out on a political limb, though his action apparently merited inclusion in his FBI dossier. Given Brecht's almost irrational hatred of Thomas Mann, elected chairman of the association, it is difficult to know whether or not he would have endorsed Lorre's best wishes or, for that matter, the organization itself. *New York Daily Herald,* Oct. 8, 1940.

19. According to a May 4, 1944, Office of Strategic Services interoffice memo, Hanns and Gerhart Eisler's sister, Ruth Fischer, an apostate Communist and FBI and HUAC informant, voluntarily classified thirty-nine organizers and signatories of the Council for a Democratic Germany as Communists, fellow-travelers, or new beginners. Ironically, she identified Lorre as a Communist, along with Oskar Homolka, Fritz Kortner, and Bertolt Brecht, whom she later denounced as "the Minstrel of the GPU" in her book *Stalin and German Communism,* p. 615, while listing Elisabeth Hauptmann, a dedicated Communist, as a fellow-traveler. She did not name her brother Hanns. PL FBI.

20. The mirror maze is curiously and, as it turns out, coincidentally reminiscent of the hall-of-mirrors sequence in Orson Welles's *The Lady from Shanghai* (1948). In December 1945 Charles Laughton read *Galileo* to Welles, who agreed to direct it for presentation by his own Mercury Productions in New York. After seeing his production of Cole Porter's *Around the World,* the following April, Brecht, who felt that "this is the greatest thing I have seen in American theater," wanted no one else for the job of directing the American stage production of *Galileo.* Welles began familiarizing himself with the playwright's theories on "alienated" acting techniques, which set the actors— and spectators—at a critical distance from the characters and story. When producer Mike Todd, who had suddenly withdrawn financial backing from *Around the World,* made Brecht and Laughton an offer they could not refuse, they dropped Welles.

Although circumstances could be said to have alienated Welles from Brecht, the filmmaker subtly applied Brechtian methods to his next film, *The Lady from Shanghai.* With the famous mirror scene, which offered a fresh take on reality, the alienation effects in the Chinese theater sequence, and generally cooled-down performances, Welles aimed for "something off-center, queer, strange." Harry Cohn, however, didn't buy the "'bad dream' aspect" and ordered the film re-edited and rescored. Brecht, quoted in Lyon, *Brecht in America,* p. 179; Orson Welles, memo to Harry Cohn, ca. April 1948, Orson Welles Collection, Manuscripts Department, Lilly Library, Indiana Univ., Bloomington.

QUOTATION SOURCES BY PAGE NUMBER

247 "as a play . . . foreseeable future": Peter Lorre to Lion Feuchtwanger, Jan. 10, 1941, FML USC.
247 "Don't go too . . . shall be back": quoted in Hans Bunge, "Brecht im zweiten Weltkrieg," *Neue deutsche Literatur* 10, no. 3 (1962): 37.
247 "this moribund continent": Bertolt Brecht to Ferdinand Reyher, Dec. 2, 1938, in Brecht, *Letters,* p. 294.
247 "perched on one . . . of breaking loose": Brecht to Henry Peter Matthis, April 11, 1939, in Brecht, *Letters,* p. 300.

247 "Lorre has made . . . owes me money": Elisabeth Hauptmann to Walter Benjamin, Aug. 23, 1934, EHA.
248 "where it is . . . opportunities for earning": Brecht, *Journals*, July 22, 1941, p. 156.
248 "lobster-red": ibid., Aug. 14, 1944, p. 324.
248 "involuntary exile": Lyon, *Brecht in America*, p. 35.
248 "looked like a . . . to humiliate him": Frisch, *Sketchbook*, p. 22.
249 "He hadn't many . . . very unpleasant sight": Lanchester, *Herself*, p. 193.
249 "One doesn't eat such things in Augsburg": Lyon, interview.
249 "no feeling for nature": Berlau, *Living for Brecht*, pp. 89–90.
249 "houses are extensions of garages": Brecht, *Journals*, Sept. 20, 1942, p. 257.
249 "from nowhere and are nowhere bound": "On Thinking about Hell," in Brecht, *Poems*, p. 367.
249 "a universally depraving . . . living with dignity": Brecht, *Journals*, March 23, 1942, p. 210.
249 "Almost nowhere has . . . of easy going": ibid., Aug. 1, 1941, p. 157.
249 "Enmities thrive here . . . another of Germanophilia": Bertolt Brecht to Karl Korsch, end of Sept. 1941, in Brecht, *Letters*, p. 339.
249 "I will not . . . hates Lorre etc": Brecht, *Journals*, Nov. 14, 1941, p. 170.
250 "They would talk . . . own writings, etc": I. Yergin, interview, Dec. 31, 1973.
250 "stink[s] of greed and poverty": "Hollywood Elegies," in Brecht, *Poems*, p. 381.
250 "he was able . . . concern to him": Berlau, *Living for Brecht*, pp. 112–13.
250 "That, unfortunately, was . . . staged nor filmed": ibid., p. 96.
250 "out of the world": Brecht to Karl Korsch, end of Sept. 1941, in Brecht, *Letters*, p. 339.
250 "first priority": Berlau, *Living for Brecht*, p. 112.
250 "a platform for . . . his artistic views": Lyon, "Brecht's Hollywood Years," p. 173.
251 "all-American domestic bliss": Lyon, *Brecht in America*, p. 48.
251 "production, distribution and enjoyment of bread": Reinhardt, *Der Liebhaber*, p. 268.
251 "The industry isn't making costume films": Brecht, *Journals*, April 8, 1942, p. 219.
251 "place among the sellers": "Hollywood," in Brecht, *Poems*, p. 382.
251 "on the main . . . your quota number": Ferdinand Reyher to Brecht, June 13, 1939, reprinted in Lyon, *Bertolt Brecht's American Cicerone*, p. 180.
251 "with few exceptions . . . tackle": Reyher to Brecht, Feb. 14, 1939, ibid., p. 176.
251 "almost every American knows": Brecht to George Pfanzelt, mid-1946, in Brecht, *Letters*, p. 407.
252 "devilish hunchback . . . in details, episodes": Brecht, *Werke, Prosa 5: Geschichten, Filmgeschichten, Drehbücher, 1940–1956* (1997), 20:23–26.
253 "effect change": Berlau, *Living for Brecht*, p. 197.
253 "dream factories of . . . smell of films": "Hollywood Elegies," in Brecht, *Poems*, p. 380.
253 "market where lies are bought": "Hollywood," ibid., p. 382.
253 "The very centre of world drug-trafficking": Brecht, *Journals*, July 27, 1942, p. 249.
253 "laxatives of the soul": quoted in Lyon, *Brecht in America*, p. 56.
253 "cesspool": Brecht to Ruth Berlau, Aug. 31, 1943, in Brecht, *Letters*, p. 366.
253 "spiritual mutilation . . . and moral invalids": Brecht, *Journals*, Jan. 20, 1943, p. 276.
253 "a cult of . . . do with art": ibid., Aug. 9, 1944, p. 323.
253 "Life in the . . . mordant social criticism": Lyon, *Brecht in America*, p. 33.
253 "Brecht's Everyday Vocabulary . . . Words of Condemnation": Berlau, *Living for Brecht*, pp. 239–41.
254 "contradiction between conflicting . . . what is true": Lyon, *Brecht in America*, p. 293.

254 "a person basically . . . hard and rational": Esslin, *Brecht*, p. 32.

254 "the luxury of . . . a consistent framework": Lyon, *Brecht in America*, p. 293.

254 "political compatibility . . . be a disciple": ibid., p. 15.

254 "If he saw . . . things about them": Riker, interview, June 21, 1987.

254 "Peter was undisciplined . . . always apply himself": Greenson, interview.

254 "a certain European . . . with each other": Reisch, interview.

255 "Cream him, daddio": Ives, interview.

255 "Peter immersed himself . . . Real hip": Martin, interview.

256 "ability to resist assimilation": November 18, 1941, Brecht, *Journals*, Nov. 18, 1941, p. 171.

256 "glamorous swamp": Mann and Mann, *Escape to Life*, p. 265.

256 "Just like [Charles] . . . a $50,000 villa": Brecht to Reyher, March 1947, in Brecht, *Letters*, p. 422.

256 "salon socialist": A. Lorre, interview, April 6, 1975.

256 "Peter was not . . . people for fun": Huston, interview.

256 "The circle who . . . the Communist Party": Bentley, interview.

257 "From that time . . . good as dead": Berlau, *Living for Brecht*, pp. 122–23.

257 "He didn't talk . . . any political commitment": Bentley, interview.

257 "an angry nonconformist . . . with limited courage": Lyon, *Brecht in America*, p. 210.

257 "until such time . . . and universal freedom": "Newsreels Record Formal Signing of Declaration," *Hollywood Now*, Dec. 23, 1938.

257 "inhuman bombing of . . . of Loyalist Spain": "Artists Protest Rebel Bombings to President," *Hollywood Now*, Feb. 12, 1938.

258 "imagine reading from . . . generation people didn't": Bentley, interview.

258 "I knew that . . . Joyce and Brecht": Lorre, interview by Gardner.

258 "He worshiped Brecht . . . people like Lorre": St. Joseph, interview.

259 "comfortable intimacy": Berlau, *Living for Brecht*, p. 73.

259 "Bertolt Brecht's actor": Sanford, interview.

259 "the only great friend he ever had": Powers, interview.

259 "[did] not love . . . the few intensely": Hall, "Are You Insane?"

259 "Brecht thought Lorre . . . actor he liked": Viertel, interview.

259 "In our wonderful . . . giving him shit": Riker, interview, May 2, 1987.

259 "a bit possessive . . . be won back": Bentley, interview.

259 "Brecht was very . . . of other people": Riker, interview, June 21, 1987.

260 "sad and inevitable . . . a certain regard": Wurtele, interview.

260 "For Brecht, criticism . . . to aid production": Berlau, *Living for Brecht*, pp. 71–72.

260 "Brecht was very . . . from beneath him": Riker, interview, June 21, 1987.

260 "For a grown . . . really very humiliating": Patrick, interview.

260 "Me act? said . . . you did yesterday": Harold Heffernan, "Lorre 'Mad' in Every Film—Likes It," *Stars and Stripes* (European ed., Darmstadt, Germany), May 4, 1957.

261 "His whole attitude . . . of the story": Garnett, interview.

261 "business, like any . . . stumble-bum years ago": "Face Making a Racket States Screen Madman," *The Beast with Five Fingers*, pressbook, 1946.

261 "I felt a . . . of a freak": Sherman, interview.

261 "jokingly referred to . . . with Bert Brecht": PEM, "Mein Freund, der Versteller."

261 "commercialisation of art": Brecht, *Journals*, Nov. 14, 1941, p. 170.

261 "custom here requires . . . to the urinal": ibid., Jan. 21, 1942, p. 193.

262 "play[ing] both a . . . its own commentary": Heilbut, *Exiled in Paradise*, p. 176.

262 "derives his morality . . . as an actor": Brecht, *Journals*, Oct. 17, 1942, p. 260.

262 "Brecht was very . . . to be recovered": Viertel, interview.

262 "When you heard . . . like to do": Bentley, interview.

262 "When he liked . . . it was his": "Brecht in Hollywood," p. 8.

262 "bright enough to . . . give him resistance": Cook, *Brecht in Exile*, p. 167.

262 "Lorre was talking . . . grasp he had": Bentley, interview.

263 "Talked to LORRE . . . for technical maturity": Brecht, *Journals*, July 11, 1943, p. 284.

263 "was not enthusiastic . . . a great director": Andrew Doe, interview.

263 "I think Brecht . . . to carry out": Ralph Greenson to author, Sept. 10, 1973.

263 "oppositional stance": Lyon, *Brecht in America*, p. 31.

263 "[Brecht] was anti-everything . . . a professional anti-": "Brecht in Hollywood," p. 11.

264 "with dead-pan face . . . had intended it": Lehmann, *Whispering Gallery*, p. 290.

264 "like a piece . . . anyone could speak": Roth, interview.

264 "thankless task of . . . above all, pathos": Henry Marx, "Bert Brecht Abend der Tribüne im Studio Theater," *New Yorker Staats-Zeitung und Herold*, March 8, 1943.

264 "have forgotten nothing . . . remained completely fresh": Brecht, *Journals*, March–April–May 1943, p. 278.

264 "as the finest . . . German poetry alive": Wurtele, interview.

265 "in many of . . . and Schweykish tone": Knust, *Materialien zu Brechts "Schweyk,"* p. 149.

265 "a sly batman . . . scenes, an idiot": Max Brod, quoted in Parrott, *Jaroslav Hasek*, p. 178.

265 "Weill has a . . . plan a Schweyk": Brecht, *Journals*, March-April-May 1943, p. 278.

265 "really went for it": Brecht to Ruth Berlau, June 4, 1944, in Brecht, *Werke, Briefe 2: 1937–1949* (1998), 29:265.

265 "the scene where . . . a dog-dealer": Brecht, *Journals*, May 29, 1943, p. 279.

266 "a pure librettist, without any author's rights": Brecht to Kurt Weill, June 23, 1943, in Brecht, *Letters*, p. 356.

266 "I must have . . . have a say": Brecht to Berlau, June 23, 1943, ibid, p. 358.

266 "largely finished": Brecht, *Journals*, June 24, 1943, p. 280.

266 "make some money soon": Brecht to Berlau, June 30, 1943, in Brecht, *Letters*, p. 358.

266 "something permanent could . . . with United Artists": Brecht to Berlau, June 28, 1943, in Brecht, *Werke*, 29:273.

266 "rides, swims, drives . . . and my student": Brecht, *Journals*, July 3–6, 1943, p. 283.

266 "playground of the . . . a lost century": Brecht to Berlau, July 5, 1943, in Brecht, *Letters*, p. 360.

267 "Brecht had a . . . introduced the character": Viertel, interview.

267 "Marseilles. Autumn 1942 . . . old-fashioned way": "The Fugitive Venus," unpublished treatment, ca. Aug. 1944, PKC AMPAS.

268 "flee the slaughter . . . land of peace": "Children's Crusade," in Brecht, *Poems*, pp. 369.

268 "I wouldn't want . . . against wasting time": Brecht to Berlau, July, 1943, in Brecht, *Letters*, pp. 361–62.

268 "he was ashamed . . . with, of course": Wurtele, interview.

269 "he drew a . . . stay with us": Berlau, *Living for Brecht*, p. 161.

269 "hanger on who . . . was throwing away": N. Yergin, interview.

269 "swinish Brechtian trick": Willett, "Piscator and Brecht," p. 89.

269 "some American writers . . . in the play": Brecht to Berlau, Aug. 12, 1943, in Brecht, *Letters*, p. 364. (Manheim incorrectly dates this letter Aug. 11, 1943).

269 "has as many . . . dog has fleas": ibid., Sept. 14, 1943, p. 368.

269 "seems perfect, simple and powerful": Brecht to Alfred Kreymborg, beginning to middle of Sept. 1943, ibid., p. 369.

269 "In despair about . . . are greatly disappointed": Brecht to Berlau, Sept. 1943, ibid., p. 372.

270 "[He] would solve . . . make a counterproposal": ibid., Sept. 18, 1943, p. 371.

270 "Peter Lorre supported . . . written the music": Berlau, *Living for Brecht,* pp. 161–62.

270 "seems, so far . . . come of it": Brecht to Berlau, April 2, 1944, in Brecht, *Letters,* p. 379.

271 "to the north . . . and home": Ewen, *Bertolt Brecht,* p. 405.

271 "Under no circumstances . . . ground for liberation": Brecht, *Journals,* May 27, 1943, p. 279.

271 "who is boastfully . . . his demoralising influence": Parrott, *Jaroslav Hasek,* p. 187.

271 "recognizes their political . . . to sort out": ibid., p. 184.

271 "help of comedy, humour and parody": F.X. Šalda, quoted ibid., p. 175.

271 "a non-heroic individual . . . only to survive": Lyon, *Brecht in America,* p. 120.

272 "lives-in-death": May Swenson, introduction to Edgar Lee Masters, *Spoon River Anthology* (New York: Macmillan, 1962), p. 9.

272 "national debt . . . shameful charity way": Earl Wilson column, *New York Post,* June 23, 1945.

272 "KORTNER and HOMOLKA . . . sold by speculators": Brecht, *Journals,* Aug. 10, 1944, p. 324.

272 "Commercialism has a . . . of any integrity": John Crockett, "Lorre, Famous Film Villain Less Maniacal in Real Life," *Hartford (CT) Times,* Sept. 22, 1944.

273 "will be to . . . Pan-Germanist movements": "Council for Democratic Germany Formed by Refugee Leaders Here," *NYT,* May 3, 1944.

273 "every outstanding personality . . . and theatrical folk": PL FBI.

273 "Brecht has been . . . a Soviet agent": J. Edgar Hoover, Memorandum for the Attorney General, March 27, 1945, Bertolt Brecht FBI file.

273 "confess my guilt . . . England and America": *Prozess gegen die Leitung,* p. 253.

273 "confidential information": PL FBI.

274 "I don't want . . . with U.S. authorities": Lyon, *Brecht in America,* p. 314.

274 "a revolutionary writer . . . Marxian [sic] thought": Jan. 23, 1945, PL FBI.

274 "a radical and . . . with Communistic tendencies": PL FBI.

274 "express purpose of . . . cooperative publishing house": ibid.

274 "reportedly formed for . . . in this country": ibid.

274 "to spend his . . . writers and actors": Duncan, "Mr. Moto Roles Childish."

275 "desks and trunks . . . his own concoction": "Out in Hollywood, Cherchez Mystery Cherchez M. Lorre," *Mask of Dimitrios,* pressbook, 1944.

275 "a COPY OF . . . Lorre and Reyher": Brecht, *Journals,* Sept. 20, 1945, p. 355.

275 "Maybe I can sell it": Brecht to Berlau, Sept.–Oct. 1945, in Brecht, *Letters,* p. 398.

275 "have chosen to . . . future with it": Brecht, *Werke* (1997), 20:143.

275 "*Be bold in* . . . got a market": ibid., 20:144.

276 "If he makes . . . we'll fool him": ibid., 20:146.

276 "I made him do it": ibid., 20:162.

276 "a distant rumble . . . herd of steers": ibid., 20:183.

276 "quite good": Jerry Wald, interoffice communication to Steve Trilling, Nov. 6, 1945, WBA USC.

276 "RECOMMENDED . . . basic and screenable": Judith Meyers, *Blood Will Have Blood,* Dec. 4, 1945, WBA USC.

276 "pleased with this . . . a little push": Tom Chapman to Ellingwood Kay, Dec. 4, 1945, WBA USC.

276 "It's a grim . . . play to perfection": Ellingwood Kay to Steve Trilling, Dec. 4, 1945. WBA USC.

277 "we weren't interested . . . if he could": Kay, postscript dated Jan. 21, 1945, on memo to Trilling, Dec. 4, 1945, WBA USC.

277 "The kind of . . . it—Peter Lorre": Bentley, interview.

277 "and ensure[s] it is a good likeness": "Wenn Herr K. einen Menschen liebte," in Brecht, *Werke, Prosa 3: Sammlungen und Dialoge* (1995), 18:24.

277 "You have the . . . it is needed": Brock Brower, "The Vulgarization of American Demonology," *Esquire,* June 1964.

277 "mental reserve [to] play a great part": Riker, interview.

277 "dissenter by disposition": Cooke, *Six Men,* p. 194.

278 "againster": Wilson, *Show Business Nobody Knows,* p. 279.

7. THE SWAMP

Epigraphs: Slocum, "The Peter Lorre Nobody Knows"; Lorre, interview by Glover.

1. Columbia-Presbyterian Medical Center included both the New York State Psychiatric Institute and Hospital and the Neurological Institute of New York, where the shock treatments were administered.

2. Two years earlier, *Philco Radio Hall of Fame* had first welcomed "the dark genius of Poe and the even darker genius of Peter Lorre."

3. Director Henry Koster shared the same doctor with Lorre, one of many from whom the actor inveigled both morphine and medical ministration. Because he felt sorry for him and wanted to relieve his suffering, the "warm-hearted" physician risked his license, which he nearly lost after narcotics authorities discovered he was regularly supplying Lorre with opiates. Koster, interview.

4. Harry J. Anslinger's "statutory authority allowed him considerable flexibility in the formulation of drug control policy. The commissioner was empowered to regulate commerce in drugs used for medical and scientific purposes, to enforce federal narcotic laws, and to assist the State Department in conducting antidrug diplomacy." Douglas Clark Kinder and William O. Walker III, "Stable Force in a Storm: Harry J. Anslinger and United States Narcotic Foreign Policy, 1930–1962," *Journal of American History* 72, no. 4 (March 1986): 908.

5. On March 4 Lorre also canceled play dates in Philadelphia and Columbus, along with a March 9 appearance at the Carnegie Chamber Music Hall in New York for a celebration marking the tenth anniversary of Karl Kraus's death. Sponsored by the Austro-American Council to aid Austrian concentration camp victims, the evening also included other members of the Kraus circle: Berthold Viertel, Oskar Homolka, Elisabeth Neumann, and others. Lorre had been scheduled to recite poems and epigrams by the author. The federal government operated two facilities—totaling two thousand beds—for the treatment of narcotic addicts, the larger located in Lexington, Kentucky, and the other in Ft. Worth, Texas, constructed in 1938.

6. Before being admitted to the U.S. Public Health Service Hospital, Lorre was required to deposit $180 in the Inmates' Trust Fund, which he did on March 3, 1947. U.S. Public Health Service Hospital, Fort Worth, USPHS DHHS.

7. According to "Briefs from the Lots," *Variety,* Feb. 26, 1947, Lorre had signed to appear as a heavy in Republic's *Crime Passionelle.* The film was not made.

8. Reference to Karen Verne on Lorre as subject of "The Swamp," Powers, interview.

9. Director Joseph Losey wrote Brecht, "I am doing everything in my power to get a [film] production of GALILEO. . . . The problems with GALILEO have by now become very clear and definite. They are 1) the Johnson Office objections to the theme and you, 2) The universal executive opinion that Laughton is not a sufficient draw to carry the picture." Joseph Losey to Brecht, May 19, 1948, in James Lyon Collection.

10. Lorre's appearance in a television production of *The Overcoat* cannot be confirmed. According to his agent, Lester Salkow, "Peter wanted to make it into a first-rate film. It was the kind of character he felt would be a new emergence for him." Salkow, interview.

11. In an interview for *Der Spiegel*, Sept. 27, 1950, given during his stay at Dr. Wigger's Kurheim in Garmisch-Partenkirchen, Lorre claimed that Nebenzal had asked him to reprise the role of Hans Beckert in the remake of *M* but that he had turned down the offer: "I'm not going to make the same thing twice."

12. In 1945 the Hollywood Democratic Committee and Independent Citizens Committee of the Arts, Sciences, and Professions merged to form HICCASP, described by Larry Ceplair and Steven Englund as "the leading popular front alliance of liberals and radicals in postwar Hollywood." The nonpartisan political organization blocked out a progressive agenda for world peace that included Allied unity, support of the United Nations, the peaceful use of atomic energy, labor and civil rights activism, and opposition to HUAC. *Inquisition in Hollywood*, p. 229.

13. Two potentially promising projects had fallen through in 1948. Lorre had earlier signed for $50,000 with independent producers Harry Joe Brown and Casey Robinson to appear in *Rain before Seven*, with the agreement that he would be paid even if the picture wasn't made. When it wasn't, the actor filed a $54,166 lawsuit for damages. "Lorre Asks for 54G to Make Rain," *Variety*, Feb. 25, 1948. According to the German press in August 1948, Lorre also was scheduled to appear in *Man in the Eiffel Tower* (1949), which featured Charles Laughton as George Simeon's famous sleuth Inspector Maigret. Burgess Meredith, who took over direction from Irving Allen and starred as the sinister knife-grinder, remembered nothing of Lorre's involvement at any stage of production. Meredith, interview.

14. For reference to the troubled production history of *Quicksand*, see "Rooney-King Film Set, Off 'Quicksand,'" *HR*, Feb. 3, 1949; "'Quicksand' to Be Recast If Rooney Fails to Show," *HR*, Feb. 7, 1949; "'Quicksand' Part of Hughes Nass'r Deal," *HR*, Feb. 22, 1949.

15. According to Alastair Young, no show of support was forthcoming.

16. During her marriage to James Powers, Karen made several more attempts to take her life. In 1967 she finally succeeded.

17. Lorre listed his net income at $28,991.64 for 1947 and $18,986.42 for 1948. Petition for leave to file voluntary petition in bankruptcy without schedules, In the Matter of Peter Lorre, Bankrupt, May 20, 1949, Case No. 47613-W, in the District Court of the United States for the Southern District of California, Central Division, p. 1., National Archives and Records Administration, Federal Records Center—Los Angeles, Record Group 21, Records of the U.S. District Court, Central Division, Southern District of California, Bankruptcy Case Files, 1941–1950, box G15, case file 47613.

QUOTATION SOURCES BY PAGE NUMBER

279 "a beefy guy . . . cash there was": Rooney, *Life Is Too Short*, pp. 206, 235.
280 "narcotic . . . gamble on Lorre": Briskin, interview.
280 "Peter had no . . . kind of man": J. Silverstone, interview.
280 "He always had . . . a show-offy way": Ives, interview.
280 "Peter was greatly . . . than he took": J. Silverstone, interview.
280 "There was little . . . to the bellboy": Lester Salkow, interview.
281 "apparently . . . his professional activities": Dr. D.D. Le Grand, Admission Summary, Personal History, March 24, 1947, USPHS DHHS.
281 "When I told . . . was not misplaced": Kirkley, "Theater Notes."
282 "You're crazy to go out there": I. Yergin, interview, Dec. 31, 1973.
282 "pulling in a . . . of the trade": "Roxy, N.Y.," *Variety*, Feb. 19, 1947.
282 "What makes a . . . while he's on": Kountze, "Typed Actor Is Boring."
282 "He knew what . . . could possibly know": Capra, interview.
282 "As his audience . . . following it down": Kanter, interview.
282 "Those kids! . . . times a day": "Bobby Soxer Rush Has Peter Lorre Referring to Freud," *New York Telegram*, March 14, 1945.

282 "heavy declamation . . . a hearty salvo": "Roxy, N.Y."

282 "I was unable . . . was not successful": Statement of Peter Lorre, Feb. 27, 1947, USPHS DHHS.

283 "stay on drugs . . . to justify same": Statement of Colonel Garland H. Williams, district supervisor, Federal Bureau of Narcotics, Feb. 28, 1947, USPHS, DHHS.

283 "a reason to . . . up to him": Anslinger, *Protectors,* p. 181.

284 "Everyone was crying . . . had to be": I. Yergin, interview, Dec. 31, 1973.

284 "movies . . . Protestant . . . work": Inmate's Admission Data Sheet, March 3, 1947, U.S. Public Health Service Hospital, Fort Worth, USPHS DHHS.

284 "FRIEND, Irving YERGIN . . . transmitted to him": Power of Attorney, March 5, 1947, Treasury Department, U.S. Public Health Service, Fort Worth, USPHS DHHS.

284 "The patient . . . for previous addictions": Dr. D.D. Le Grand, Admission Summary, Personal History, March 24, 1947, USPHS DHHS.

284 "pleasant, friendly and . . . over his situation": ibid.

284 "rather disgusted with himself because of depression": Clinical Record, Ward Surgeon's Progress and Treatment Record, Federal Security Agency, U.S. Public Health Service Hospital, Fort Worth, March 16, 1947, USPHS DHHS.

284 "CANNOT UNDERSTAND WHY . . . WEEK LOVE LASLO": Peter Lorre, telephone telegram to Irving Yergin, April 2, 1947, U.S. Public Health Service Hospital, Fort Worth, USPHS DHHS.

284 "negative transference": Dr. Wm. F. Ossenfort, Medical Director in Charge, Admission Summary, April 16, 1947, U.S. Public Health Service Hospital, Fort Worth, USPHS DHHS.

284 "under any other . . . are, nevertheless, real": Dr. D.D. Le Grand, Admission Summary, Personal History, March 24, 1947, USPHS DHHS.

285 "I am satisfied with the . . . defend my rights": Peter Lorre, statement, ca. late March 1947, Federal Security Agency, U.S. Public Health Service Hospital, Fort Worth, USPHS DHHS.

285 "as they have . . . discharged as 'cured'": Dr. D.D. Le Grand, Progress Release Report. U.S. Public Health Service Hospital, Fort Worth, April 15, 1947, USPHS DHHS.

285 "Never in his . . . such a problem": I. Yergin, interview, Dec. 31, 1973.

285 "been treated well . . . be very good": Dr. Wm. F. Ossenfort, Admission Summary, April 16, 1947, USPHS DHHS.

285 "remain off work": Dr. D.D. Le Grand, Progress Release Report, April 15, 1947, USPHS DHHS.

285 "is feeling fine . . . 7 years ago": Karen Lorre to Mr. and Mrs. Cowell(?), Federal Security Agency, U.S. Public Health Service Hospital, Fort Worth, April 20, 1947, USPHS DHHS.

286 "was very unhappy . . . more than justified": I. Yergin to Dr. Wm. F. Ossenfort, April 23, 1947, U.S. Public Health Service Hospital, Fort Worth, USPHS DHHS.

286 "as much radio work as possible": Peter Lorre, interview, May 8, 1947, Federal Bureau of Narcotics, Los Angeles, USPHS DHHS.

286 "Alcohol and narcotics . . . produces mental addiction": Brecht to Dr. Gruenthal, Jan. 2, 1947, in Brecht, *Werke, Briefe 2:* 29:409.

286 "racket": Brecht to Reyher, March, 1947, in Brecht, *Letters,* p. 422.

286 "that his situation . . . at his sickness": Brecht to Gruenthal, Jan. 2, 1947, in Brecht, *Werke,* 29:410.

286 "It might be": quoted in Lyon, *Brecht in America,* p. 213.

287 "I saw many . . . ghastly blissful smile": "The Swamp," in Brecht, *Poems,* p. 381. (Replansky's translation has been published under the title "A Hollywood Elegy" in Bentley, *Brecht-Eisler Song Book,* pp. 47–50.)

287 "For nearly a . . . in his profession": Brecht to Gruenthal, Jan. 2, 1947, in Brecht, *Werke,* 29:409.

287 "the addiction itself . . . to have achieved": Greenson to author, Sept. 10, 1973.

287 "Once again many . . . Lorre's muddled affairs": Brecht to Reyher, March 1947, in Brecht, *Letters,* p. 422.

287 "I need Lorre . . . humans and animals": Brecht to Gruenthal, Jan. 2, 1947, in Brecht, *Werke,* 29:409–10.

288 "Lorre may straighten . . . it too expensive": Reyher to Brecht, March 23, 1947, reprinted in Lyon, *Brecht's American Cicerone,* p. 198.

288 "Naturally, we would . . . in New York": Brecht to Reyher, middle-to-end of March 1947, in Brecht, *Werke,* 29:414.

288 "just came across . . . herewith to you": Paul Kohner to Lorre, July 30, 1952, Paul Kohner Collection, Stiftung Deutsche Kinemathek, Berlin.

289 "finely-shaded and . . . than modest anticipation": "Mystery in the Air," *HR,* July 7, 1947.

289 "For grisliness and . . . in an enclosure": "Poe and Lorre's 'Telltale Heart' Chills Airwaves," *Daily Variety,* July 7, 1947.

289 "I have never . . . way or another": Morgan, interview.

290 "The impressionists had . . . faces at himself": Brandt, interview.

291 "Peter is in . . . do something worthwhile": Elisabeth Hauptmann to Ivor Montagu, Aug. 19, 1947, Ivor Montagu Collection, BFINL.

291 "you can get . . . you'll hate yourself": Crockett, "Lorre Less Maniacal in Real Life."

291 "sex and text": Fuegi, *Brecht and Company,* p. 147.

291 "kick in the . . . with the windmills": Lorre to Montagu, May 12, 1947, Ivor Montagu Collection, BFINL.

291 "who is extremely . . . it in England": Montagu to Lorre, Sept. 22, 1947, ibid.

292 "No prospects for . . . thinking of Switzerland": Brecht, *Journals,* March 24, 1947, p. 365.

292 "it was meant . . . explain to you": Hauptmann to Montagu, Aug. 19, 1947, Ivor Montagu Collection, BFINL.

292 "It would be . . . to the companies": Montagu to Lorre, Sept. 22, 1947, ibid.

292 "Lorre is no . . . 'dated' and distasteful": Joseph Losey to Brecht, May 19, 1948, James Lyon Collection.

293 "touching affection of . . . is completely happy": Brecht, *Texte für Filme,* 2:617–23.

294 "exerted a profound . . . of epic theater": Lyon, *Brecht in America,* p. 84.

294 "very Chaplinesque": Lenya, interview.

294 "even as he . . . of the people": "[Autobiographische Notizen des Clowns Emaël]," in Brecht, *Texte für Filme,* 2:625.

295 "dyed-in-the-wool . . . a few drinks": Martin, interview.

295 "Top honors . . . the previous Slimanes": A.H. Weiler, "CASBAH," *NYT,* May 3, 1948.

295 "Lorre as the . . . among the best": Ruth Waterbury, "'Casbah' Has Everything," *Los Angeles Examiner,* April 15, 1948.

296 "If you want . . . have more names": I. Yergin, interview, June 23, 1976.

296 "bland cherub who . . . tell a lie": Meadow, interview.

296 "local bigots . . . buzz off": Buckley, *Hornes,* p. 160.

296 "They're only tourists . . . desk and left": I. Yergin, interview, June 23, 1976.

297 "That poor Ernst . . . Jews, so what": Frazier, *The One with the Mustache,* p. 216.

297 "not to affiliate . . . more important work": PL FBI.

297 "the most important . . . the 'far left'": "Foreign Nationality Groups in the United States," Memorandum by the Foreign Nationalities Branch to the Director of Strategic Services, no. 187, May 12, 1944, PL FBI.

297 "she was Americanizing . . . worker would seem": Bentley, interview.

298 "that in any . . . freedom of speech": U.S. Congress, House, *Investigation of Un-American Activities,* 75th Cong., 3rd sess., May 26, 1938, *Cong. Rec.,* vol. 83, pt. 7, pp. 7569–70.

298 "not as a . . . on in Washington": Dunne, *Take Two,* p. 193.

299 "American citizens [including . . . of our Constitution": "Hollywood Fights Back!" *HR,* Oct. 28, 1947.

299 "not a fighter": Powers, interview.

300 "solely in the . . . Bill of Rights": Bogart, "I'm No Communist."

300 "found themselves lined . . . frankly, un-American": Hamilton, *Writers in Hollywood,* p. 293.

300 "de facto trials": Dunne, *Take Two,* p. 191.

300 "one of the . . . of glamor Reds": Fagan, *Documentation of the Red Stars in Hollywood,* pp. 100, 72.

300 "the trip was . . . our brains out": "The Bogarts Regret," *Newsweek,* Dec. 15, 1947.

300 "as one of . . . Eugen Friedrich Brecht": PL FBI.

300 "Are you now . . . of any country": Bentley, *Thirty Years of Treason,* p. 209.

301 "get out": Shutan, interview.

301 "When they accused . . . time to leave": Don Ogden Stewart and Ella Winter, interview by James Lyon, Sept. 11, 1972, quoted in Lyon, *Brecht in America,* p. 335.

301 "miasma of fear, hysteria and guilt": Huston, *An Open Book,* p. 129.

301 "a fine tooth . . . Hollywood is vital": Fagan, *Documentation of the Red Stars in Hollywood,* p. 100.

301 "Red Celebrities of . . . machine in America": ibid., p. 5.

301 "TWO hundred of . . . supporters of Marxism": ibid., p. 10.

301 "Stalin's Stars": Fagan, *Red Treason in Hollywood,* p. 61.

301 "to a tremendous PUBLIC DEMAND": Fagan, *Documentation of the Red Stars in Hollywood,* title page.

301 "categorically establish[ed] the . . . Treason in Hollywood'": ibid., p. 9.

301 "organized at the . . . form of Government": ibid., p. 100.

301 "an extension of . . . in New York": ibid., p. 62.

301 "Hollywood Stalinites": ibid., title page.

301 "RED-BAITER": ibid., p. 22.

301 "as soon as . . . have sincerely repented": Fagan, *Documentation of the Red Stars in Hollywood,* p. 105.

302 "suitable . . . internationally-minded Austrian theatre": Hans Kafka, "Hollywood Calling," *Aufbau,* Nov. 9, 1945.

302 "I was attempting . . . be a star": Walter Doniger to author, March 6, 1975.

302 "related in a . . . any societal strictures": Doniger, interview.

302 "reflection of the . . . morality is survival": ibid.

302 "They all acted . . . to that time": Doniger to author.

303 "stand[ing] out . . . fattens his wallet": "*Rope of Sand,*" *HR,* June 28, 1949.

303 "By his voice . . . 'The Telltale Heart'": Gertrude Wolf, "Peter Lorre Enacts Poe's Terror Tale," *Columbus (Ohio) Citizen,* Jan. 11, 1949.

303 "gags": "Paramount, N.Y.," *Variety,* May 18, 1949.

303 "breathless and spellbound": Dick Lowe, "Peter Lorre Brings Real Dramatic Art to Olympia," *Miami Daily News,* Jan. 21, 1949.

303 "Lorre finishes each . . . Barrymore played 'Hamlet'": "Peter Lorre Brings Classic to Life," *Philadelphia Inquirer,* April 25, 1949.

304 "I just felt . . . with the jokes": Cagney, interview.

305 "Be nice to . . . care about her": Riker, interview, May 2, 1987.

306 "I was hanging . . . and nothing helped": Sykes, interview, Sept. 15, 1984.

306 "As soon as . . . me at all": Verne to Martin Soloman, June 4, 1947, author's collection.

306 "customers . . . high class prostitutes": PL FBI.

306 "She always felt . . . the primary relationship": Riker, interview, June 21, 1987.

307 "With my sister . . . the guilty person": Sykes, interview, Sept. 15, 1984.

307 "Brecht was saying . . . welcome to it": Bentley, interview.

308 "first class actors . . . short guest appearances": Brecht, *Arbeitsjournal,* 2:538.

308 "I think it . . . periodic addictive needs": Greenson to author, Sept. 10, 1973.

308 "As middle man . . . times were over": PEM, "Mein Freund, der Versteller."

308 "get Lorre cheap . . . hotel and transportation": Brandt, interview.

308 "when it comes . . . going first class": Ives, interview.

309 "Whatever you do . . . sign your checks": Eden, interview.

309 "He wanted to . . . would have squandered": Wurtele, interview.

309 "Peter considered him . . . not a penny": Eden, interview.

309 In October, 1947 . . . in back pay: Order to Appear before Labor Commission, Department of Industrial Relations, Division of Labor Law Enforcement, Los Angeles, Oct. 29, 1947, EHA.

8. SMOKE GETS IN YOUR EYES

Epigraphs: Zweig, *World of Yesterday,* pp. 354–55; Lorre, quoted in Peters, "Der Mörder mit der sanften Stimme."

1. Reference to Lorre's jaundiced condition, Willy Martin, "Kleines Filmportäts: Peter Lorre," *Neue Film* (Wiesbaden), Jan. 2, 1951. During his nearly two-and-one-half-year stay in Germany, Lorre suffered bouts of what family and friends termed "yellow jaundice."

2. Reference to Lorre's treatment at Wigger's Kurheim, Briskin, interview.

3. Reference to Lorre's tour of veterans' facilities in the Pacific Northwest and California, "Vet Hospital Tours Click, Lorre Tells H'd Committee," *HR,* Oct. 18, 1948. Also among the thirty-one Hollywood personalities were John Hodiak, Ruth Warrick, Edgar Buchanan, Linda Darnell, William Demarest, William Holden, Clifton Webb, and Alan Young.

4. According to Fred Pressburger, Arnold took out a loan to secure further financing. James Powers maintained that Celia Lovsky also mortgaged her home at 1541 Crescent Heights on behalf of the picture. Pressburger, interview, Dec. 1, 1983; Powers, interview.

5. In 1953 the reallocation of surplus German prisoner-of-war funds provided for the construction of six additional America Houses in Berlin, Cologne, Frankfurt, Hannover, Munich, and Stuttgart. U.S. House, Committee on Government Operations, *German Consulate–America House Program,* H. Rpt. 83-168, 83rd Cong., 1st sess., 1953, p. 1.

6. During the casting process, Lorre flew to England and located Johnny Lockwood at the Empire Theater in Chiswick. He told him he had a part for him in his new film and invited the actor to return to Germany with him the next day. "Of course I could not accept his offer and leave the show I was in," said Lockwood. "It was just one of the crazy things Peter would do." Lockwood to author, Oct. 23, 2001.

7. Top-billed as screenwriter, Lorre received no credit as coproducer. However, according to an undated agreement in the Arnold Pressburger Papers, all decisions relating to the production "are to be joint ones between Arnold Pressburger and Peter Lorre."

8. An orchestra conductor at Berlin's UFA Palace, Willy Schmidt-Gentner (1894–1964), "a diligent old man," according to C.O. Bartning, composed more than eighty film scores, beginning with *Der Student von Prag* in 1926. Carl O. Bartning, interview by Corinna Müller, July 30, 1983, author's collection.

9. This document is identified as the "Arbeits—Manuskript des Peter Lorre—Film" (Persönliches Manuskript P.L., 25.4.51.) and was likely reconstructed by C.O. Bartning after the rough-cut copy of the film burned in a lab fire.

10. Perhaps too psychological for Brecht, Lorre's externalizing of an inner reality recalls the whitening of his face to indicate fear in the 1931 production of *Mann ist Mann.*

11. In the only surviving copy of this script, once belonging to set designer Franz Schroedter, the strangulation is prefaced with several pages of what can only be described as sexual foreplay. Inge nervously twists a necklace around her fingers. Rothe grabs it, wraps it around his own fingers, and ties her hands with it. "You're hurting me," she complains before lapsing into submission. The necklace breaks. His face appears tense, his expression lascivious. The "Horla motif" takes musical form. A frightened Inge clutches Rothe, pinning his arms to his sides, then bites the palm of his hand. He reaches for a lock of hair hanging over her forehead and tenderly brushes it over her eyes, then lets his hand slide to her throat. He tightens his grip. A bundle of "passive desire," Inge surrenders with a remote laugh. Rothe stares at her with "a strange, unknown expression." His face goes out of focus. When the scene clears, one sees the gruesome details in the mirror. Inge's lifeless body hangs in Rothe's hands, which hold tightly around her throat. She glides to the ground. His hand restlessly sweeps over his face as he looks in the mirror, a scene intentionally reminiscent of that in the laboratory basement.

12. The use of the word *Totmacher* dates back at least to the Schroedter script, which includes the same scene.

13. In the Schroedter script, Helene tells Rothe, "It is so seldom that one finds today a good looking man your age who hasn't been drafted."

14. With the eternally transient Lorre, it is hard to know whether the *Wohnungsamt* (Housing Office) frequently reassigned him to new living quarters or whether he importuned the authorities to relocate him as opportunities opened up and insolvency closed in. During production, he lived on the Elbchaussee, where he joked about buying a cannon and shooting across the bows of the outgoing ships; in a house on the grounds of a margarine factory in Barmbeck; in "noble quarters" in Harvestehude; and in an apartment at the corner of Magdalenenstrasse and Böttgerstrasse. Eggebrecht to author, July 12, 1985.

15. The Schroedter script gives more attention to the individual murders, both contemplated and committed, in one long flashback, opening with Rothe walking the railway tracks outside the refugee camp (once a prison) remembering things that happened four years earlier. "Fear . . . fear . . . ," he says again and again, "each time with a new emphasis," a script note indicates, "in one case with horror, in another with irony, indifference, cynicism, and finally with the emphasis of liberation." He resumes, "But where did it begin, if it is now at an end?" A gap of fifty script pages (which must have included the second-billed Elfe Gerhart as "Christa Feldt," who does not appear in pages 55–205) finds Dr. Rothe at the bacteriological department of the Tropical Institute: "I was never what one would call a happy person—however, I was never painfully aware of it. I knew no strong emotions at all." The story proceeds linearly, without the political conspiracy, to Rothe's falsified death. The story then returns to the refugee camp and what would become the opening and closing scenes of the film. "Fear—? Fear—?" Rothe repeats the word (his last) "with the clear impression of freedom" before meeting his death. The lifting of the railway gate visually underlines the idea, acknowledged by few contemporary reviewers, that the doctor dies a free man.

16. Lorre later claimed to hold all distribution rights to *Der Verlorene* outside Germany. "Lorre Offers 'Team' Idea for Production," *Variety*, July 11, 1952.

17. For his role as actor, Lorre received twenty thousand deutsche marks. Arnold Pressburger Papers, author's collection.

18. Though he would have been loath to admit it, Brecht, at least on one occasion, crossed over to Mann's camp. After listening to German students belt out some tradi-

tional anti-Semitic tunes, including "Saujud" ("Jewish Swine") at the 1950 Munich Oktoberfest, Brecht kicked over the bench that he, Eric Bentley, and Ruth Berlau were sitting on and stomped out. "And they say these people have changed! Good liberals now, are they? I know this sort! They will never change!" Eric Bentley, "The Last of Brecht," *London Magazine* 24 (Nov. 1984): 42.

19. According to Bartning, the resistance story evolved out of Eggebrecht's influence.

20. Green Thursday is also known as Maundy Thursday.

21. The first page of the Schroedter script warns: "It is the obvious, decent duty of every co-worker that he should keep the production secret, that he will not give this book to others, and that he will not publish anything from it.... Any misuse of this text can lead to civil and criminal penalties."

22. This is possibly a reference to the Bonner Bundeshaus (Committee for the Movies at the Home-Department), which awarded film prizes and supporting premiums for films that not only entertained but "serve[d] the cultural advancement and development of taste." "Verleihung der deutschen Filmpreise," *Der neue Film*, April 28, 1952.

23. The trailer, however, was approved for children over ten years of age.

24. Reference to Egon Jameson's authorship of the serialization for *Münchner Illustrierte* in *Film Press* (Hamburg), Aug. 15, 1951. In 1996 Belleville Verlag (Munich) published a trade edition of the serialized story and credited Lorre as author, again at Egon Jameson's expense.

25. Stamps on Lorre's passport would seem to confirm a note in the *Frankfurter Allgemeine*, Sept. 6, 1951, reporting that after rumored rejection by the Biennale committee, Lorre planned to arrange a private premiere of *Der Verlorene* in London. Failure to clear the film with British customs, however, forced cancellation of the showing.

26. Film historian Marta Mierendorff believed that contemporary reviewers
"put the lust murder in the center of the film, making it a psychiatric case which could play in *all* societies. This approach allowed them to minimize the Third Reich events, to neutralize it completely. They did not understand or did not want to understand that Lorre worked with a contrast: The murderous state politics, 'legal killings' against a private killing. What happened to Lorre in this story could not happen in a democratic society. The background of the murder had something to do with *Schuld* und *Sühne* [guilt and atonement]. Lorre was a private murderer, but contrary to the sanctioned murders he WANTED to be punished and was betrayed of punishment because in this political surrounding, a murder meant nothing. He was a murderer with a conscience. Er sühnte! [He atoned!]."
Marta Mierendorff to author, Feb. 2, 1988.

27. From September 1, 1951, to March 22, 1952, the FBL reviewed 306 *Kulturfilme*, of which 189 received the *Prädikat* "valuable" and 16 the *Prädikat* "especially valuable." *Filmblätter* (East Berlin), March 28, 1952.

28. According to *Der Grosse Duden: Etymologie* (Mannheim: Bibliographisches Institut, Dudenverlag, 1963), p. 618, in 1948 an orchestra leader for the NW German Rundfunk coined the malapropism when he referred to sentimental film and theater productions as "*schnulzig*" instead of "*schmalzig.*"

29. *Robert Koch* (1939) was based on the life of a German doctor who advanced the theory that infectious diseases were caused by bacterial organisms; *Germanin* (1943) told the story of a German physician who discovers a cure for sleeping sickness, in effect challenging the loss of rights to colonies in Africa after World War I.

30. In the Schroedter script, scenes of destruction play a greater part in visually documenting the postwar setting.

31. In a "Notice of Sale of Personal Property at Private Sale," Robert Shutan and

Alan S. Pitt, attorneys for the Administratrix (Annemarie) of the Estate of Peter Lorre, offered to sell "an undivided forty percent (40%) interest in 'Der Verlorene,' a film produced in 1952 in which decedent owned a forty percent (40%) interest in said film with respect to net proceeds from English speaking countries. Location of the negative is unknown. Said film never has been distributed in English speaking countries nor is it contemplated that it ever will be so distributed." No. P 481, 356, Nov. 21, 1967, Superior Court of the State of California for the County of Los Angeles.

32. Rudolf Katscher changed his name to Rudolph Cartier in 1942.

33. Reference to the proposed film production of Alfred Neumann's *The Patriot,* Neumann to William Dieterle, March 20, 1951, Forschungsarchiv Marta Mierendorff, Max Kade Institute for Austrian-German-Swiss Studies, Univ. of Southern California, Los Angeles.

34. Reference to foreign press reports of European offers, "Augen sehen dich an," *Der Spiegel* (Hannover), July 4, 1951; Rolf Thoel, "Unter dem Vulkan," *Die Welt* (Hamburg), Feb. 24, 1952; P, "Welt im Ausschnitt," *Das grüne Blatt* (Dortmund), Feb. 24, 1952.

35. A film poster from Lorre's *Las Manos de Orlac* (*Mad Love*) picturing a murderer's hands "laced with blood" also reinforces the recurring motif of what Ken Moon terms "unwilled impulsion" that will end in death: "I think I've seen the Peter Lorre movie somewhere," says Hugh, the Consul's brother. Malcolm Lowry commented, "He's a great actor but it's a lousy picture. . . . It's all about a pianist who has a sense of guilt because he thinks his hands are a murderer's or something and keeps washing the blood off them." Perhaps not so coincidentally, as in *Mad Love,* the female side of a love triangle involving the Consul and Hugh is named Yvonne, a one-time movie actress. Ken Moon, "Lowry's *Under the Volcano,*" *Explicator* 46, no. 3 (Spring 1988): 38; Malcolm Lowry, *Under the Volcano* (New York: New American Library), p. 110.

36. Why Lowry established a connection between Lorre and the Hungarian director is unknown. In the 1920s, Fejos emigrated to the United States, where he worked for Universal before going back to Europe and directing both documentaries and feature films. After returning to America in the late 1930s, he devoted himself to anthropological research. Perhaps Lowry confused Fejos's 1933 Austrian production *Frühlingsstimmen* (*Spring's Voices*) with *Frühlings Erwachen.*

37. Reference to his contractual agreement with the Plymouth Theater for a stage production of Pierre La Mure's *Moulin Rouge,* Walter Anatole Perisch, "Lorre geht zum Broadway," *Der Mittag* (Düsseldorf), Dec. 30, 1951.

QUOTATION SOURCES BY PAGE NUMBER

311 "I removed myself . . . experience on occasions": Frischauer, "Mr. Murder."

311 "making faces": "Lorre's 'Lost One,'" *NYT,* July 20, 1952.

311 "rapturous acclamation": C.T., "Hippodrome," *Manchester Guardian,* July 26, 1949.

311 "The Brits were . . . funny he was": Johnny Lockwood to author, Oct. 23, 2001.

312 "Mr. Lorre will . . . go to bed": "London Parents Warned about Lorre Video Show," *NYT,* Aug. 18, 1949.

312 "ruin his image": Lockwood to author.

313 "a clinically let . . . under certain conditions": Promotional literature for Wigger's Kurheim, undated, author's collection.

313 "She was very . . . stay off morphine": Sykes, interview, Sept. 15, 1984.

314 "We were sitting . . . edge of going": ibid.

314 "the Peter Lorre stamp": Elmo Williams to author, June 9, 1975.

315 "Peter Lorre taught . . . captivated by him": Ken Annakin to author, July 24, 1975.

315 "Lorre is so . . . and mutual admirers": *Double Confession,* pressbook, 1950.

315 "It was the . . . a convenient hotel": Sykes to author, July 8, 1985.

315 "a penny . . . very highly intelligent": Sykes, interview, Sept. 15, 1984.

316 "for your eyes . . . an enormous effort": Peter Lorre to Elisabeth Hauptmann, EHA.

317 "During the war . . . This is important": Eileen Creelman, Picture Plays and Players: "Peter Lorre Discusses 'Rope of Sand,'" *New York Sun*, May 18, 1949.

317 "we who are . . . among these unfortunates": Jack Cosgrove, "Lorre in 'Toils'—At Vet Hospital," *Baltimore News-Post*, March 5, 1949.

317 "They tell me . . . the script demands": "Peter Lorre Worries: Is He Bad Enough?" *Quicksand*, pressbook, 1949.

317 "I would find . . . hands with me": "Actor Praises Men in Hospitals," *New Orleans Times-Picayune*, Oct. 11, 1944.

317 "I don't sing . . . dance, you know": "Peter Lorre Worries."

317 "In the United . . . also in Germany": "Kein Platz für zwei Mörder."

317 "Such visits . . . very humble man": "Peter Lorre Worries."

317 "Lorre has returned . . . totally forgotten one": Kilian Karg, "Das Untier vor den Toren," *Münchner Merkur*, March 3–4, 1951.

317 "psychological task": "Kein Platz für zwei Mörder."

317 "a land of . . . means of existence": Botting, *From the Ruins of the Reich*, p. 123.

318 "great wilderness of debris": Shirer, *End of a Berlin Diary*, p. 132.

318 "sordid caricature of humanity": Gollanz, *In Darkest Germany*, p. 90.

318 "like wild animals . . . seven or so": Botting, *From the Ruins of the Reich*, p. 130.

318 "godless destruction . . . nihilistic contempt": Gollanz, *In Darkest Germany*, pp. 184, 37, 232, 230.

318 "What would you . . . work of art": Kirkley, "Theater Notes."

319 "a psychological study . . . women he meets": "Das 'Untier' antwortet," *Münchner Merkur*, April 28, 1951.

319 "The original idea . . . compulsion to kill": Bartning, interview.

319 "In refugee camp . . . my new film": "Kein frei erfundener Film," *Der Verlorene*, pressbook, 1951.

320 "Movies that are . . . come about again": Fr. Porges, "Film ist Gemeinschaftswerk: Peter Lorre über Filmarbeit und Zukunftspläne," *Abendpost* (Frankfurt am Main), March 10, 1954.

320 "I had promised . . . make this film": Peter Lorre, interview by Martin Jente von Lossow, "Interview with Peter Lorre and Egon Jameson at the premiere of *Der Verlorene* in Frankfurt," *Dokumentationsband Zeitfunk*, Hessischer Rundfunk (Frankfurt), Sept. 18, 1951.

320 "If my film . . . made for nothing": "Kein frei erfundener Film."

320 "Lorre was a . . . the Vidocq part": Halliday, *Sirk on Sirk*, p. 68.

320 "risk-happy": Gerhard Midding, "Arnold Pressburger," *Filmexil/Exilfilm*, Pr 5, June 21, 1995.

320 "Desperate to make . . . as an actor": Pressburger, interview, Dec. 1, 1983.

320 "a production team . . . or a play": "Peter Lorre Seems Stuck with a Hit, and the Idea Really Appalls Him," *York (PA) Gazette and Daily*, Sept. 19, 1952.

320 "the responsibility to . . . of departmental overheads": "Archer Winsten's Reviewing Stand: Peter Lorre, Shadow & Substance," *New York Post*, April 5, 1955.

320 "In making frequent . . . weak": "Kein Platz für zwei Mörder."

320 "a truly good and remarkable film": Porges, "Film ist Gemeinschaftswerk."

322 "is going to . . . women this time": gdt., "Bestie Mensch," *Hamburger Echo*, July 22, 1950.

322 "Lorre wanted to . . . cannot be disputed": Axel Eggebrecht to author, May 26, 1983.

322 "it was completely . . . have denied it": Bartning, interview.

322 "it was just . . . of Hitler Germany": *NYT*, Sept. 23, 1951.

322 "Germany of the . . . meaning of *M*": Peter Lorre, quoted in Tom Granich, "Le

intervisté di 'Cinema'–Lorre: *M torna con Lo sperduto*," *Cinema*, n.s. (Mailand), no. 71, Oct. 1, 1951.

322 "was afraid of . . . was known for": C. Lorre, interview, Oct. 15, 1980.

322 "I do not . . . of creative effort": Kirkley, "Theater Notes."

323 "radiantly fascinating": HA, "Lorre herzlich begrüsst," *Hamburger Abendblatt*, Aug. 11, 1950.

323 "as fresh as ever": Brecht to Hauptmann, Sept. 1950, in Brecht, *Werke, Briefe 3: 1950–1956* (1998), 30:38.

323 "Listen, we are . . . And come": "To the Actor P.L. in Exile," in Brecht, *Poems*, p. 418.

324 "that he has . . . with Peter Lorre": contract, Arnold Pressburger Papers.

325 "he walked up . . . radiation, this aura": Trowe, interview.

325 "Yes, make it . . . or the actress": "Filmregie mit den Augen," *Der Verlorene*, pressbook, 1951.

326 "I knew in . . . and overcoming it": Renate Mannhardt, "Peter Lorre war mein Regisseur!" *Der Verlorene*, pressbook, 1951.

326 "She wasn't really . . . devoted to Peter": Pressburger, interview, Dec. 1, 1983.

326 "How is it . . . for women's tastes": Meadow, interview.

326 "Peter loved women . . . beck and call": B. Silverstone, interview.

326 "I'd be a . . . live without acting": "Biography of Peter Lorre," Paramount Pictures, May 16, 1947, MHL AMPAS.

327 "the morale of the enemy civilian population": Middlebrook, *Battle of Hamburg*, p. 74.

327 "a dark period in November": Bartning, interview.

327 "palpable actuality . . . picture without retouching": "Peter Lorres Reportage-Stil," *Der Verlorene*, pressbook, 1951.

327 "Lorrealismus": Gunter Groll, "Der Verlorene," *Süddeutsche Zeitung* (Munich), Oct. 20, 1951.

327 "It shall be . . . a new realism": "Plauderei aus dem Paradies," *Die Welt* (Hamburg ed.), Jan. 29, 1951.

327 "film beauties . . . was naturally correct": Johanna Hofer Kortner to author, April 6, 1976.

327 "comprehending the human . . . and clear detail": "Ein Künstler an der Kamera," *Der Verlorene*, pressbook, 1951.

328 "Everyone was more . . . convinced of this": Bartning, interview.

328 "a fantastic constructor . . . testing new starts": Eggebrecht to author, May 26, 1983.

328 "talked about the . . . their own words": "Peter Says He's Very Well," *Mansfield (Ohio) News-Journal*, Feb. 24, 1960.

328 "A formulation in . . . degree of authenticity": "Peter Lorres Reportage-Stil."

328 "I won't tell . . . I'll be murdered": Eismann, "Weltberühmter 'Mörder.'"

328 "the kind of . . . a jam session": "Peter Lorre—Between Chimp & Art: Veteran Performer Projects Own Prod. Team While Touring with Simian Co-Star," *Variety*, Sept. 5, 1962.

328 "This was different . . . have ever seen": Eggebrecht to author, Aug. 10, 1983.

328 "well kept corner . . . sorts of things": Bartning, interview.

331 "played around with this scene terribly": ibid.

332 "Lorre said to . . . mysterious after all": Trowe, interview.

334 "pinching something from . . . is empty again": Bartning, interview.

335 "Then during the . . . a crazy moment": ibid.

335 "There were several . . . believability in it": Daniel Haller, interview.

335 "was very rare . . . well into expression": Lotte Rausch to author, Jan. 12, 1978.

336 "I never heard . . . him at once": Bartning, interview.

336 "Because he knew . . . them as friends": Rausch to author.

336 "unity of spirit": Porges, "Film ist Gemeinschaftswerk."
336 "He loved his ... of an echo": Rausch to author.
336 "loosened self-consciousness ... able to lie": Trowe, interview.
336 "working under Peter ... as his partner": Mannhardt, "Peter Lorre war mein Regisseur!"
337 "Everything that could ... resorting to drugs": Pressburger, interview, Dec. 1, 1983.
337 "a worried, troubled, and harried individual": Lindesmith, *Addiction and Opiates*, p. 41.
337 "a poor self-image ... of, and disrespected": Pradan, *Drug Abuse*, p. 202.
337 "a state of ... flow of ideas": Lindesmith, *Addiction and Opiates*, p. 27.
337 "He would suddenly ... just be lost": Pressburger, interview, Dec. 1, 1983.
338 "Although he never ... hidden from us": Rausch to author.
338 "He didn't want ... at Lorre's feet": Bartning, interview.
338 "Oh, yes ... one before me": Inge Landgut to author, May 6, 1985.
338 "He wanted money ... to get it": Pressburger, interview, Jan. 1, 1983.
338 "I remember still ... him 200 marks": Bartning, interview.
338 "Look, you have ... am a partner": Pressburger, interview, Dec. 1, 1983.
338 "How he did ... other people down": Bartning, interview.
339 "on condition that ... of the film": Arnold Pressburger Papers.
339 "He had, I ... was always gone": Bartning, interview.
339 "Without it, he ... take my cigarette'": Steven Gaydos, "Eurotrak: The Euro-Hollywood Axis," *Variety*, June 14, 2004.
339 "He didn't just ... the next dawn": Cummings to author.
339 "timely nervousness": Manes Kadow, "Das Unheimliche Gesicht," *Frankfurter Neue Presse*, Sept. 20, 1951.
339 "the tired sadness ... the seemingly unimportant": Herbert Timm, "'Der Verlorene'—ein revolutionierender Film," *Weser Kurier* (Bremen), Nov. 17, 1951.
340 "The main problem ... to be about": Pressburger, interview, Dec. 1, 1983.
340 "Lorre wanted just ... to be included": Bartning, interview.
340 "stress of circumstances": Friedrich Schiller, *Sämtliche Werke* (Stuttgart: JG. Cotta Nachf., 1904–5), 11:163, quoted in Stahl, *Friedrich Schiller's Drama*, p. 82.
340 "psychopathic hero": *NYT*, Sept. 23, 1951.
340 "Peter was until ... his political views": Eggebrecht to author, June 10, 1987.
340 "any kind of ... must have been": Halliday, *Sirk on Sirk*, p. 145.
340 "It will not ... foreground, but people": *Welt am Sonntag* (Berlin ed.), Jan. 28, 1951.
341 "Five or six ... the necessary reckoning": Eggebrecht to author, March 17, 1985.
341 "feels naked without ... for being German": Orson Welles, "Thoughts on Germany," *Fortnightly*, March, 1951, p. 145.
341 "Let the hour ... our unrevolutionary people": Thomas Mann to Brecht, in Mann, *Briefe*, vol. 2, *1937–1947* (Frankfurt am Main: S. Fischer, 1963), p. 341.
341 "a bad and ... cunning into evil": Mann, "Deutschland und die Deutschen," p. 1146.
341 "escape from reality ... what really happened": Arendt, "Aftermath of Nazi Rule," pp. 343, 342.
341 "No one ever ... a 'new' beginning": Pachter, "On Being an Exile, p. 37.
342 "crimes have been ... help to excuse": Mann, "Deutschland und die Deutschen," p. 1140.
342 "murderer because the ... destroyed his equilibrium": Peter Lorre, quoted in Granich, "Lorre: *M* torna con *Lo sperduto*."
342 "learned nothing, understand nothing, regret nothing": Thomas Mann to Erich von Kahler, Oct. 20, 1944, in Mann, *Briefe*, p. 397.
342 "Peter had a ... became a pleasure": Pressburger, interview, Dec. 1, 1983.

342 "the rupture between . . . back is dead": Marcuse, *Mein zwanzigstes Jahrhundert,* p. 178.

343 "corporate cover": Pressburger, interview, Dec. 1, 1983.

343 "terrific fight . . . accepted with joy": Hans Grimm to Arnold Pressburger, Jan. 12, 1951, Arnold Pressburger Papers.

343 "assist Mr. Lorre . . . Lorre became impossible": Grimm to Arnold Pressburger, March 18, 1951, ibid.

343 "*Gott führt uns . . . Pfui*": "Augen sehen dich an."

344 "Naturally this theme . . . totally depressed situation": Axel Eggebrecht to author, Dec. 31, 1975.

344 "We had always . . . after his ass": Bartning, interview.

345 "because he tried like crazy": Pressburger, interview, Oct. 1, 1985.

345 "Pressburger sat down . . . everything completely differently": Bartning, interview.

345 "My suggestions were . . . certain things shorter": Pressburger, interview, Oct. 1, 1985.

345 "murder and violence . . . and unbridled longings": *Graubuch,* Staatsverlag DDR, Berlin, March 1967, p. 273.

345 "numerous . . . here continuously psychopathically": Karg, "Das Untier vor den Toren."

345 "The fact is . . . be a *Lustmörder*": "Das 'Untier' antwortet."

346 "censors did not . . . you of that": Eggebrecht to the author, March 27, 1977.

346 "already suspicious": Klaus Hebecker, "Psychologische Studie über die Diktatur," *Westfalenpost* (Hagan), Sept. 11, 1951.

348 "enlightened explanation": "Der Unaufgeklärte Mord—ein Zeitproblem!" *Der Verlorene,* pressbook, 1951.

348 "indictment and admonition raised to humanity": "Zeitbericht und Lebensbeichte," *Der Verlorene,* pressbook, 1951.

348 "essentially a showcase . . . Italian film industry": Kotsilibas-Davis and Loy, *Myrna Loy,* p. 238.

348 "We were both . . . only help Lorre": Pressburger, interview, Oct. 1, 1985.

348 "Rumor-mongers": Hawkins, "This Year the Good Films," p. 8.

348 "those films which . . . brotherhood of Nations": "Some Aspects of the Twelfth International Exhibition of Art," unidentified publication, BFINL.

348 "a great deal . . . semi-official sources": Pressburger, interview, Dec. 1, 1983.

348 "was not included . . . enter the competition": La Biennale di Venezia, press release, Sept. 8, 1951.

349 "*Der Verlorene,* seen . . . the Hitler regime": Hawkins, "This Year the Good Films."

349 "mad and disappointed . . . simply went out": Bartning, interview.

349 "the hottest iron . . . of their minds": Hans Hellmut Kirst, "'Der Verlorene'—eine Fundgrube," *Münchner Merkur,* Oct. 20, 1951.

349 "not large sums . . . poets—film poets": Alexandre Alexandre, "Ansatz zum Wiederaufstieg des deutschen Films?" *Der Mittag* (Düsseldorf), June 30–July 1, 1951.

349 "possible to escape . . . German postwar movie": W.M., Neue Filme: "Der Verlorene," *Südkurier* (Konstanz), March 1, 1952.

350 "regime of inhumanity . . . human and beast": St-e, "Filmreportage aus unserer Zeit," *Hamburger Echo,* Nov. 14, 1951.

350 "cannot mix a . . . a political system": G-z, "Lustmord und Politik," *Stuttgarter Zeitung,* March 1, 1952.

350 "how a man . . . universal and symbolic": Groll, "Der Verlorene."

350 "one cannot touch . . . with other crimes": G-z, "Lustmord und Politik."

350 "long and intensive . . . state can lead": "*Der Verlorene,*" Filmbewertungsstelle Wiesbaden (FBW), Sept. 7, 1951.

351 "Etched black on black": Walter Bitterman, "Der Verlorene," *Rheinischer Merkur* (Koblenz), Sept. 28, 1951.

351 "nihilistic fog": Groll, "Der Verlorene."

351 "burdens the senses . . . We need more": Kadow, "Das Unheimliche Gesicht."

351 "hopeless hero": Karl Sabel, "In manischer Gier verloren," *Westdeutsche Allgemeine—Bochumer Anzeiger* (Darmstadt), March 22, 1952.

351 "not worth pitying . . . soft drifting away": W.M., "Der Verlorene."

351 "jungle of art . . . zone of life": Felix Hanseleit, "Grenzfall des Lebens—und der Kunst," *Kurier* (Berlin), Nov. 17, 1951.

351 "the devilish workings . . . of our epoch": Alexandre Alexandre, "Lorre 'Der Verlorene' von internationalem Format," *Abendpost* (Frankfurt am Main), July 14, 1951.

351 "small boy's picture of the resistance": b.m., Der Verlorene," Dü, Oct. 20, 1951, Stiftung Deutsche Kinemathek, Berlin.

351 "He alone convinces . . . a great actor": Christian Ferber, "Verhängnisvolle Trinität," *Die neue Zeitung* (Munich), Oct. 21, 1951.

351 "brilliantly moderated": "Der Verlorene," Mosk, *Variety,* Sept. 5, 1951.

351 "etches the hell . . . into our consciousness": St. H., "Der sehr sympathische Massenmörder," *Lüdenscheider Nachrichten* (Lüdenscheid), June 26, 1954.

351 "painful impressiveness": Timm, "'Der Verlorene,'"

352 "because barely before . . . suggestive in effect": Groll, "Der Verlorene."

352 "the lostness of . . . has ever shown": Kirst, "'Der Verlorene'—eine Fundgrube."

352 "face doesn't let go": Timm, "'Der Verlorene.'"

352 "Even the most . . . his own stereotype": Gerd Schulte, "Der Verlorene," *Hannoversche Allgemeine Zeitung* (Hannover), March 15, 1952.

352 "the cultural advancement . . . development of taste": "Verleihung der deutschen Filmpreise," *Der neue Film* (Wiesbaden), April 28, 1952.

352 "lobende Anerkennun . . . the recent past": L.W., "Der verlorene 'Verlorene': Ein Wort über den 'Deutschen Filmpreis 1952,'" *Oberhessiche Presse* (Marburg), April 2, 1952.

352 "accusatory": Eisner, "A la seconde vision."

352 "idealized pleasures of country life": Manvell and Fraenkel, *German Cinema,* p. 115.

352 "heather and heartache": Bernd Lubowski, "Wiedersehen mit Peter Lorres einziger Regie," *Berliner Morgenpost,* Nov. 25, 1988.

353 "hard-boiled melancholy": Werremeier, "Alle Tot," p. 263.

353 "They didn't misunderstand . . . out of step": Pressburger, interview, Dec. 1, 1983.

353 "The Germans must . . . into the future": Erich Pommer, quoted in Manvell and Fraenkel, *German Cinema,* p. 108.

353 "a sensational thriller with political shading": Eggebrecht, interview.

354 "The 'lost one' . . . could be understood": Eisner, "A la seconde vision."

354 "Lorre gives evidence . . . hopes of renewal": Eisner, *Haunted Screen,* pp. 339–40.

355 "simply treated as . . . times without law": "Peter Lorre Says He's Very Well."

355 "I must be . . . 60% of it": "Peter Lorre—Between Chimp & Art."

355 "not ever bring . . . other country's politics": Irene Thirer, "Movie Spotlight: Lorre: 'Time Not to Make Money,'" *New York Post,* Aug. 28, 1962.

355 "He reached new . . . and significant silences": Prairie Farkus, "Lorre's Talents Shine in This Film," *New York Daily World,* Aug. 3, 1984.

355 "an interesting expression . . . Lorre's creative personality": Vincent Canby, "Film: 1951 'Lost One,' Directed by Peter Lorre," *NYT,* Aug. 1, 1984.

355 "with an almost palpable weariness and despair": "*The Lost One,*" *Los Angeles Herald-Examiner,* April 19, 1983.

355 "looks tired, weary . . . chain smoked cigarettes": Shawn Cunningham, "Peter Lorre as Actor/Director," *Villager* (New York), Aug. 2, 1984.

355 "authentic note of . . . cannot be questioned": Archer Winsten, "Lorre's 'The Lost One' Has Been Found Again," *New York Post,* Aug. 1, 1984.

355 "carefully controlled, intense performance": *NYT,* Aug. 1, 1984.

355 "evocative": William Wolf, "The Lost One," Gannett News Services, ca. July 1984.

355 "platitudinous": Ernest Leogrande, "Peter Lorre's 'Lost' Movie," *New York Daily News,* Aug. 1, 1984.

355 "natural . . . deal of restraint": Cunningham, "Peter Lorre as Actor/Director."

355 "inwardly tortured psychotic . . . guy at heart": Sy Syna, "Lorre's 'Lost One' for Fans Only," *New York Tribune,* Aug. 1, 1984.

355 "We sat in . . . No one called": Manfred George, "Der unheimliche Peter Lorre," *Aufbau* (New York), March 27, 1964.

355 "an outsider and . . . in the side": L.W., "Der verlorene 'Verlorene.'"

355 "The defeat of . . . energy was gone": C. Lorre, interview Oct. 17, 1980.

356 "the winter sleep . . . grateful to you": Lorre to Hauptmann, undated, EHA.

356 "just as every . . . a human being": Granich, "Lorre: *M* torna con *Lo sperduto.*"

357 "for fear of censorship": Malcolm Lowry to Clemens ten Holder, Oct. 31, 1951, in Grace, *Sursum Corda,* p. 448.

357 "would rather have . . . in the world": Lowry to Ernst Klett, Oct. 31, 1951, ibid., p. 450.

357 "a complete dither of excitement": Lowry to ten Holder, Oct. 31, 1951, ibid., p. 448.

357 "many excellent ideas . . . would be valuable": Lowry to Klett, Oct. 31, 1951, ibid., p. 450.

357 "a great hash": Day, *Malcolm Lowry,* p. 139.

357 "concerned with the . . . with his doom": Breit and Bonner, *Letters of Malcolm Lowry,* p. 66.

357 "the part [of . . . for him [Lorre]": Lowry to Harold Matson, Dec. 8, 1951, in Grace, *Sursum Corda,* p. 474.

358 "the present cannot . . . of his past": Tiessen, "Cinema of Malcolm Lowry," p. 45.

358 "expressive emphasis and distortion": Willett, *Expressionism,* p. 8, quoted in Grace, "Lowry and the Expressionist Vision," p. 94.

358 "stifling, doom-laden . . . and self-destructiveness": Joy Gould Boyum, "*Under the Volcano:* Looking Outward," in Boyum, *Double Exposure,* p. 207.

358 "the autobiographic consciousness": Spender, introduction to *Under the Volcano,* p. xvi.

358 "God knows what . . . lead to eventually": Lowry to Matson, Nov. 23, 1951, in Grace, *Sursum Corda,* p. 452.

358 "one of the . . . has ever lived": Lowry to Matson, Dec. 8, 1951, ibid., p. 474.

358 "a real regard . . . him, or himself": ibid., pp. 474–75.

358 "fascinated . . . go around": ten Holder to Lowry, Nov. 30, 1951, in Wehr, *Schreibheft,* p. 92.

358 "say in the treatment and scenario": Lowry to Matson, Dec. 8, 1951, in Grace, *Sursum Corda,* p. 476

359 "interest hot": ibid., p. 474.

359 "whole tangle . . . forthcoming from Klett": Matson to Lowry, Jan. 14, 1952, in Breit and Bonner, *Letters of Malcolm Lowry,* p. 447.

359 "Strange to say . . . as a play": José Ferrer to author, May 7, 1984.

9. ELEPHANT DROPPINGS

Epigraphs: Lorre, interview by Gardner; Lorre, quoted in Peters, "Der Mörder mit der sanften Stimme."

1. After completing its Norwich run on August 23, the production played at the Boston Summer Theater August 25–30 before moving on to the Grist Mill Playhouse

in Andover, New Jersey, September 1–6; the Kenley Theater in Barnesville, Pennsylvania, September 8–14; and Kenley Players in York, Pennsylvania, September 15–20.

2. Lee, Sam, and Jacob Shubert were America's biggest theater owners and producers.

3. Reference to Lorre's plans, "Lorre Offers 'Team' Idea for Production," *Film Daily*, July 11, 1952. Fellow Austrian émigré Oscar Karlweis also expressed interest in starring in *The Happy Ant Hill*. Repeatedly deferred, the play never reached Broadway and saw the stage only in a two-day trial run—without Lorre—at the White Barn Theatre in Westport, Connecticut, July 17–18, 1954.

4. What Karen did not list in her complaint was an incident mentioned almost forty years later by Lon Chaney Jr.'s widow, Patsy. In an interview for *Filmfax* (May 1990), she said that "one time I saw him [Lorre] at a restaurant in New York, and he put a cigarette out on his wife's face." This allegation of behavior, more in keeping with Lorre's persona than his person, still warrants discussion if only to debunk it. Nearly six decades after its supposed occurrence, all of the principals in Lorre's life are deceased. Their silence during their lifetimes, however, would seem to refute rather than corroborate the account. Karen Verne's sister, Barbara, visited her in California during the late 1940s (the likely time of the alleged episode, as it was at this point that Chaney and Lorre were working together on *My Favorite Brunette*) and kept in close contact from abroad. She had no love for Lorre, hence no reason to protect his reputation. Indeed, had the incident occurred, she would likely have mentioned a scar or the story behind it. In neither letter nor interview did she touch upon it. Nor did Karen's third husband, James Powers, later a good friend to Lorre, the alleged attacker of his wife. Celia Lovksy was both friend and confidant to Karen. Protective as she was of Peter, it is unlikely that their friendship would have survived reports of such a violent incident. Nor did close friend Rhoda Riker, who saw Karen often during this period and had no special feeling for Lorre, remember hearing her talk about an episode of physical abuse.

5. Santana Picture Corp. paid Huston's, Bogart's, Lorre's, and Jennifer Jones's salaries.

6. Overstating its "all-star cast," United Artists peddled the picture as an adventure-melodrama in the tradition of *The Maltese Falcon*.

7. Selma Lagerlöf was a Swedish writer of children's stories.

8. Before accepting the assignment, Fleischer cleared the idea with his father, Max Fleischer, an animator and one-time rival of Disney. Fleischer, interview.

9. While "Young Couples Only" was copyrighted September 3, 1955, contemporary television indexes and guides do not cite an air date, causing some media historians to question whether the episode actually appeared on the small screen.

10. For his performance in *Congo Crossing*, Lorre earned six thousand dollars for four weeks' work, well below his standard rate of pay.

11. Advertised in the trades as "mystery telefilms," his thirty-nine scripts were, according to Trayne, "straight stories with O'Henry endings." Trayne, interview.

12. Phil Tucker directed *Robot Monster* (1953), considered by many to be the worst movie ever made. In his *Movie and Video Guide* (1992), film critic and historian Leonard Maltin describes it as "one of the genuine legends of Hollywood: embarrassingly, hilariously awful."

13. A Ukrainian folk-dance step featuring the execution of a squat kick.

14. Lorre's commitment to MGM possibly interfered with his plans to tackle Broadway. On January 23, 1956, the *New York Times* announced that the actor would costar with Estelle Winwood in Marcel Aymé's comedy *Clèrambard*, scheduled for the fall season. Arthur Gelb, "Magazine Story Will Be Staged," *NYT*, Jan. 23, 1956.

15. The Adjustment Committee reduced Lorre's debt to roughly forty dollars.

16. Having "approached *every*one," said coproducer Aubrey Schenck, "we got what

we could get." In the end, he got Akim Tamiroff for the part of Odo. Aubrey Schenck, interview by Tom Weaver, quoted in *It Came from Weaver Five: Interviews with 20 Zany, Glib, and Earnest Moviemakers in the SF and Horror Traditions of the Thirties, Forties, Fifties, and Sixties,* by Tom Weaver (Jefferson, NC: McFarland, 1996), p. 276.

17. John Carradine, claiming he had retired from monster pictures to play Shakespeare, also turned down the part. Gordon finally settled on Chester Morris, whom *Variety,* Aug. 29, 1956, judged "too able an actor to be entirely submerged in this shoddy material."

18. Lorre's commitment to Irwin Allen very possibly ruled out an offer to appear in a television production of *Aladdin* written by S.J. Perelman with music and lyrics by Cole Porter, which aired February 21, 1958.

19. Mike Todd Sr. died in a plane crash in March 1958.

20. In "100 Greatest Episodes of Our Time," *TV Guide* (June 28–July 4, 1997) ranked "Man from the South" number forty-one.

21. AIP productions were typically shot in ten days or fewer and budgeted under one hundred thousand dollars.

22. AIP staff composer Les Baxter felt that "they could have used his comic talent very much more than they did. He was used in horror films, I guess, because he looked a little strange, and had a strange way of pronouncing his speeches, but he had a very pixie sense of humor that went along with it." Weaver, *It Came from Weaver Five,* p. 33.

23. Reference to divorce settlement, "Divorce Asked by Wife of Actor Peter Lorre," *LAT,* Aug. 16, 1963.

24. Reference to no money sums being mentioned in divorce settlement, Shutan, interview.

25. Reference to AIP signing Lorre, "AIP Pacts Karloff," *HR,* March 4, 1963.

26. At one point, Gillie and Trumbull creep up a staircase. When Waldo steps on Felix's hand, Lorre cries out, "My foot—uh—*your* foot, my hand!" The flubbed line remains in the finished film.

27. Available medical records indicate that Lorre confined himself to morphine.

QUOTATION SOURCES BY PAGE NUMBER

362 "He didn't say . . . the southern politician": Sawyer, interview.

362 "You can stay . . . all over again": Lorre, interview by Glover.

363 "Broadway could do . . . can be it": Vernon Rice, "Strawhat Reviews: Night at Mme. Tussaud's," *Variety,* Aug. 20, 1952.

363 "Somebody will have . . . comedy that's stressed": Vernon Rice, "Summer Theater: A Slight Change in Billing Suggested," *New York Post* (evening ed.), Aug. 20, 1952.

363 "a great man . . . a great patriot": Alta Maloney, "Hopkins, Lorre at Boston," *Boston Traveler,* Aug. 26, 1952.

363 "crime for the fun of it": Rice, "A Slight Change in Billing Suggested."

363 "The reason I . . . at any moment": Alpert, "Lorre Laughs When It Hurts."

363 "ghoulish mélange of . . . blood and paranoia": "Critic's Corner: Lorre, Hopkins Pace Excellent Cast in Horror 'A Night at Mme. Tussaud's,'" *York (PA) Gazette and Daily,* Sept. 16, 1962.

363 "the play needs . . . response so far": Ken Crotty, "Lorre Affable despite Sinister Movie Roles," *Boston Post,* Aug. 29, 1952.

364 "Lorre and Hopkins . . . top dog": Mayer, interview by Bigwood.

364 "you could hear . . . as a cob": Warren, interview.

364 "Hopkins got so . . . have enjoyed that": Mayer, interview by Bigwood.

364 "Hopkins held the . . . to fall apart": Mayer, interview by author.

364 "It was not . . . an audience-pleaser": Mayer, interview by Bigwood.

364 "the master scarer . . . for curiosity value": Rice, "A Slight Change in Billing Suggested."

365 "You know, John . . . heard that one": St. Joseph, interview.
365 "he looked like . . . world at all": King, interview by Katz.
365 "Peter was upset . . . attractive physiological being": J. Silverstone, interview.
365 "outstanding and successful . . . in principle, interested": Paul Kohner to Lorre, April 9, 1952, Paul Kohner Collection, Stiftung Deutsche Kinemathek, Berlin.
366 "sultry, shapely . . . and spends lavishly": Alfred Albelli, "Hungry Mrs. Lorre Seeks Alimony," *New York News,* Dec. 16, 1952.
366 "fragrant with imperial . . . the distant future": Cockburn, introduction to *Beat the Devil.*
366 "good luck token": Benchley, *Humphrey Bogart,* p. 218.
366 "We are trying . . . you want him": Humphrey Bogart to John Huston, Nov. 26, 1952, JHC.
366 "It stinks": Benchley, *Humphrey Bogart,* p. 218.
367 "a certain lightness of touch": Jack Clayton to author, Aug. 3, 1981.
367 "My brother and . . . was a mistake": John Woolf to author, Nov. 11, 1987.
367 "this is a . . . fine by me": Huston to Bogart, Nov. 19, 1952, JHC.
367 "the brains": Bogart to Huston, Nov. 26, 1952, JHC.
367 "unacceptable under the . . . in the story": Joseph I. Breen to Jesse S. Morgan, MPAA PCA.
367 "brand new . . . a walking stick": Huston to Bogart, Nov. 19, 1952, JHC.
367 "And now we . . . do with THAT": Bogart to Huston, Nov. 26, 1952, JHC.
368 "Hell, it's only . . . best we could": Huston, *An Open Book,* p. 246.
368 "next-door to penniless": Truman Capote to Cecil Beaton, quoted in Gerald Clarke, *Capote: A Biography* (New York: Simon and Schuster, 1988), p. 233.
368 "even if it . . . least I think": David O. Selznick to Huston, Jan. 30, 1953, in Behlmer, *Memo from Selznick,* p. 415.
368 "When I got . . . the following week": Knight, "With Huston in Italy."
368 "We usually have . . . movie on Monday": Morris, interview.
368 "Was it really . . . game to you": quoted in Clarke, *Capote,* p. 239.
368 "changed the whole . . . what was happening": J.G. Barton, interview.
369 "We enjoyed the . . . went with it": Pratley, *Cinema of John Huston,* pp. 99–100.
369 "long before the . . . that went on": Morris, interview.
369 "the unholy three": Lovsky, interviews.
369 "He was a delight . . . in his body": Huston, interview.
370 "Truman had that . . . play my son": J.G. Barton, interview.
370 "He had a . . . It never failed": Morris, interview.
370 "seemed to be . . . having a ball": J.G. Barton, interview.
370 "If anyone had . . . in his body": ibid.
371 "I have always . . . to listen to": Robert Morley to author, May 25, 1973.
371 "Ernest Hemingway words": Mike Wallace, interview with Peter Lorre, pre-interview notes.
371 "I remember an . . . do much good": Morley to author.
371 "I get a . . . them into it": Huston, interview.
371 "John would let . . . could tell him": J.G. Barton, interview.
371 "veered off more . . . of Peter himself": Morris, interview.
371 "a nimble creature . . . and also supple": Huston, interview.
371 "the crooks, ostensibly . . . virtue, become absurd": Pratley, *Cinema of John Huston,* p. 102.
372 "a little vignette . . . a delightful interlude": Huston, interview.
372 "healthy departure from my Hollywood roles": Bob Thomas, "Peter Lorre Back in Hollywood, No Longer in Type Pigeonhole," *Newport (RI) News,* Feb. 9, 1954.
372 "Peter Lorre has . . . old evil stand": "Lorre Ditches Virtue at Last," *Beat the Devil,* pressbook, 1954.

372 "it is hard . . . an action picture": Huston to Bogart, Nov. 19, 1952, JHC.

372 "a sort of . . . private detective": M.A. Schmidt, "Battling Bogart's Saga," *NYT,* Sept. 6, 1953.

372 "more a lark . . . very good time": Pratley, *Cinema of John Huston,* pp. 99, 101–2.

372 "It was a . . . didn't get it": Thirer, "Lorre: 'Time Not to Make Money.'"

373 "a mess": Axel Madsen, *John Huston* (Garden City, NY: Doubleday, 1978), p. 141.

373 "the air of . . . justify public performance": Lindsay Anderson, "In Brief: *Beat the Devil,*" *Sight and Sound,* Jan.-March 1954, pp. 147–48.

373 "lived separate and . . . since March 8, 1950": Complaint, Ingeborg Karen Lorre vs. Peter Lorre, June 20, 1953, In the Eighth Judicial District Court of the State of Nevada in and for the County of Clark.

373 "miracle child . . . to do it": Annemarie Lorre to PEM (Paul E. Marcus), March 22, 1954, author's collection.

373 "horseyback . . . it looks good": C. Lorre, interview.

374 "an ideal *cafehaus* . . . and garbage disposal": Annemarie Lorre to PEM.

374 "momentary fits of . . . care what happens": "The Human Beast," undated treatment/synopsis, Jerry Wald Collection, Cinema-Television Library, Univ. of Southern California, Los Angeles.

374 "*everybody* is bad": Bogdanovich, *Fritz Lang in America,* p. 95.

374 "present-day American": Fritz Lang, interoffice communication to Jerry Wald, Feb. 17, 1953, FLC USC.

375 "ballet inserts . . . and drawn him": Goff, interview, July 31, 1978.

376 "empirical script": ibid.

376 "fit for any . . . but no nerves": Jules Verne, *20,000 Leagues under the Sea,* translated by Anthony Bonner (New York: Bantam, 1981), pp. 24–25.

376 "I always had . . . been ad-libbing it": Goff, interview, July 31, 1978.

376 "Even things offered . . . carefully and deeply": Fleischer, interview.

376 "His screen image . . . trying new things": Richard Fleischer to author, May 30, 1975.

377 "After all these . . . was a mistake": Joe Reddy, "Peter Lorre Proves He's Funny in Disney 20,000 Leagues," Walt Disney Productions, Peter Lorre file, BFINL.

377 "high hopes": Fleischer, interview.

377 "I thought that . . . thing that will": Goff, interview, July 31, 1978.

377 "That I was . . . I usually play": Reddy, "Peter Lorre Proves He's Funny."

377 "There could be . . . he could find": Fleischer to author.

377 "cohesive factor": ibid.

377 "A discussion took . . . any further distress": James Mason to author, Oct. 3, 1975.

378 "Peter defied him . . . pay the bill'": Goff, interview, July 31, 1978.

378 "Peter wasn't sure . . . *Under the Sea*": ibid.

378 "has always been . . . parts I play": Reddy, "Peter Lorre Proves He's Funny."

378 "a giant agitation . . . when he wants": Annemarie Lorre to PEM.

379 "There are some . . . a boyish face.": ibid.

380 "mutual exchange of . . . on both sides": Porges, "Film ist Gemeinschaftswerk."

380 "every day I . . . without being called": kfj, "Ist Peter Lorre vergessen?" *Hamburger Anzeiger,* March 10, 1954.

380 "went to bat . . . can kill you": Barry Nelson, Q & A session, *Casino Royale* screening, Univ. of Southern California, May 8, 1982.

380 "Peter expired as . . . thirty million viewers": Charles Bennett, "Peter Lorre: Gentlest Murderer," in Peary, *Close-Ups,* p. 334.

381 "was appalled, so . . . what had happened": Charles Bennett to author, April 19, 1975.

381 "the morticians": Swope, interview.

381 "made the perfect . . . them out beautifully": Chan, "Arsenic and Old Lace," *Variety,* Jan. 12, 1955.

381 "The movie actor . . . buyin' a newspaper": J.D. Salinger, *The Catcher in the Rye* (Boston: Little, Brown, 1951), p. 93.

381 "The man is . . . him a break": Richard Matheson, "Shipshape Home," in *Richard Matheson: Collected Stories* (Los Angeles: Dream/Press, 1989), p. 151.

382 "I tried . . . never got made": Matheson, interview, Dec. 6, 1994.

382 "for a welcome . . . is the law": Peter Lorre, introduction to "The Blue Landscape," NBC, Dec. 10, 1955.

384 "lowbrow bonanzas": Gow, *Hollywood in the Fifties,* p. 195.

384 "Peter Lorre played . . . a word, great": Jack O'Brian's TViews, "Cantor Tops in Real Gem," *New York Journal-American,* Oct. 19, 1956.

385 "The ultra-reliable . . . most brooding works": "The Last Tycoon," *Variety,* March 20, 1957.

385 "I'm grateful you . . . him in dismay": St. Joseph, interview.

385 "television came into . . . think about it": "He's Only Human."

385 "a chance to . . . he could say": St. Joseph, interview.

386 "They were laughing . . . of some kind": Meadow, interview.

386 "I think he . . . off his back": Robertson, interview.

386 "Almost all of . . . do our best": Meadow, interview.

387 "It had a . . . wasting their money": Price, interview, Jan. 30, 1974.

388 "One criticism that . . . we still do": Lorre, interview by Glover.

388 "in spite of . . . he was right": Robertson, interview.

388 "Just be Peter Lorre": Haller, interview.

388 "It is horrible . . . sure of that": Peter Lorre, "Bin ich noch ein Mensch?" unidentified clipping, Aug. 13, 1957, Deutsches Institut für Filmkunde, Wiesbaden, Germany.

389 "I don't want . . . do a role": "New Formula for Lorre," *New York Morning Telegraph,* Oct. 18, 1962.

389 "Let us say . . . whatever is human": "He's Only Human."

389 "Character actors . . . much like him": Mamoulian, interview.

392 "I'm not a . . . it was wonderful": Pan, interview.

392 "I am a very sick man": Buloff, interview.

392 "he was taking . . . across the stage": "Charisse Still Puts On a Nice Spin," *San Francisco Chronicle,* March 19, 2004.

393 "During Silk Stockings . . . out of him": Mamoulian, interview.

393 "Peter didn't want . . . of his talents": Lester Salkow, interview.

393 "I can do . . . for no money": Lorre, interview by Paar.

393 "European kind of fatalistic view": Sanford, interview.

393 "That would have . . . it was shit": Wynn, interview.

394 "the perennial bad man Peter Lorre": listing for *The Red Skelton Show, TV Guide,* Jan. 18, 1955.

394 "I am without . . . man in nightclubs": Joseph Finnigan, "Defends Bad Name," *Newark (NJ) Evening News,* Nov. 19, 1963.

394 "Once when I . . . like Peter Lorre": "He's Only Human."

394 "Let me assure . . . for an adjustment": Peter Lorre to Pat Somerset, Feb. 17, 1954, Lorre member file, Screen Actors Guild, Los Angeles.

394 "We have to . . . her very much": Peter Lorre to Otto Andreas and Käethe Brenning, ca. June 1956, author's collection.

395 "nerves shot up": Lovsky, interview, May 12, 1977.

395 "dinner at Peter's . . . won't be abused": Lovsky, diary, Dec. 8, 1956.

395 "If the theater . . . famous psychoanalyst today": "He's Only Human."

395 "was supposed to . . . the part up": Reginald LeBorg, interview by Tom Weaver, in Weaver, *Interviews with B Science Fiction and Horror Movie Makers,* p. 243.

395 "a piece of junk": Gordon, interview.

395 "He hated it . . . a cheap film": Alex Gordon, quoted in John Hoxley, "Alex Gordon: The Deadly 'B's,'" *Fangoria*, Aug. 1979.

396 "If they'll pay . . . you'll do it": Gordon, interview by Tom Weaver.

396 "This is what . . . were your agent": Laura Salkow, interview.

396 "one of the . . . filmed science fiction": Bill Warren, *Keep Watching the Skies! American Science Fiction Movies of the Fifties*, vol. 2, *1958–1962* (Jefferson, NC: McFarland, 1986), p. 602.

396 "cinema genius": I. Allen, interview.

397 "Playing a clown . . . definition of acting": Price, interview, Jan. 30, 1974.

397 "Hey, this is . . . time to me": I. Allen, interview.

398 "had 10% of . . . to do it": Mature, interview.

398 "Could I have a little yellow bird": Zastupnevich, interview.

398 "To me he . . . with Peter's part": Bennett to author, April 19, 1975.

399 "It is an . . . of the show": Bosley Crowther, "*Scent of Mystery*," *NYT*, Feb. 19, 1960.

399 "an intentional light-hearted . . . maintain an image": Michael Todd Jr. to author, Sept. 13, 1976.

400 "Fifteen years ago . . . the small one": *Scent of Mystery*, draft screenplay, June 1959, author's collection.

400 "very jokey, very . . . Oh, no, Monsieur": Elliott, interview.

400 "One evening in . . . like colossal hiccups": Cardiff, *Magic Hour*, pp. 236–37.

401 "No one . . . doctor proved right": Todd to author, Nov. 10, 1976.

401 "Of course, he . . . running for him": Cardiff, *Magic Hour*, p. 237.

401 "I didn't die . . . change my outlook": Lorre, interview by Wallace.

401 "I play a . . . like many pictures": Slocum, "The Peter Lorre Nobody Knows."

401 "Except for the . . . is downright atrocious": *NYT*, Feb. 19, 1960.

401 "Whiff gags": Philip K. Scheuer, "Movies Square Off in Battle of Odors," *LAT*, Jan. 10, 1960.

401 "the Muzak of . . . an undertaking parlor": Margaret Harford, "A Whiff of Showmanship," *Los Angeles Mirror-News*, Jan. 26, 1960.

403 "It was just . . . was his fun": Avalon, interview.

403 "The hell with realism": Colliver, *Seaview*, p. 27.

403 "Mr. Lorre, as . . . the most sense": Howard Thompson, "*Voyage to the Bottom of the Sea*," *NYT*, July 20, 1961.

403 "I get to . . . she's all mine": "Vital Statistics on Irwin Allen's *Voyage to the Bottom of the Sea*," 20th Century–Fox publicity release, MHL AMPAS.

404 "He had a . . . delightful utterance": Joseph Newman to author, Dec. 12, 1974.

404 "He had a . . . every round inch": Eden, interview.

404 "a director's actor": Newman to author.

404 "Goldner . . . that PARTICULAR character": Joseph Newman Oral History, MHL AMPAS.

404 "Peter believed in . . . with open heart": I. Allen, interview.

404 "And I think . . . mean a thing": Lorre, interview by Wallace.

405 "Before Peter shoots . . . for his lines": Veigel, interview.

405 "I'll grab a . . . me at all": Lorre, interview by Wallace.

405 "caricature of a . . . is simply tired": A.H. Weiler, "*Five Weeks in a Balloon*," *NYT*, Aug. 27, 1962.

405 "I know my . . . a little vest": Zastupnevich, interview.

405 "From an actor's . . . it that way": Bennet, in Peary, *Close-Ups*, pp. 334–35.

405 "There was a . . . doubt about it": Buttons, interview.

406 "Just the mere . . . thousand, or more": Arkoff, interview, Jan. 29, 1981.

406 "In one of . . . pseudointellectual": Arkoff, *Flying through Hollywood*, p. 110.

407 "Pepsi Cola Gothic": Vincent Canby, "Bye, Bye, Beach Bunnies," *NYT,* March 2, 1969.

407 "lighten up . . . an extra factor": Arkoff, interview, Jan. 29, 1981.

407 "to be consistently down-beat": Matheson, interview, Jan. 3, 1975.

407 "Even though there . . . of the past": Moritz, interview.

408 "I wanted to . . . the creative process": Corman, interview.

408 "all of the . . . their own characters": Jameson, interview.

408 "more of a . . . fashioned their roles": Matheson, interview, Jan. 3, 1975.

408 "most spontaneous and . . . the three actors": Corman, interview.

408 "lots of independence to improvise": Price, interview, Jan. 30, 1974.

408 "Peter abhorred dullness . . . away with it": Lester Salkow, interview.

408 "Peter said he . . . back to it": Corman, interview.

408 "Poe type of sardonic humor": *New York Morning Telegraph,* Oct. 18, 1962.

408 "But don't think . . . then be terrified": "Top Terror Actor, Real-Life Prankster, Gets to Be Self in Hilarious Terror Comedy," *Comedy of Terrors,* pressbook, 1964.

408 "Cast as a . . . the character human": Rose Pelswick, "Mr. Lorre's an Amiable Menace," *New York Journal-American,* Sept. 2, 1962.

408 "Peter took a . . . fit him better": Price, interview, Jan. 30, 1974.

408 "elfin Thurber touch to the murderous tale": James Powers, "'Poe's Tales of Terror' A Class Horror Picture," *HR,* June 4, 1962.

408 "There was so . . . out of them": Matheson, interview, Jan. 3, 1975.

409 "Peter's mad background": ibid.

409 "into a mask . . . do something nasty, Tales of Terror": draft screenplay, undated, author's collection.

409 "I don't eat . . . not a cow": Sanford, interview.

409 "He ate everything . . . funny little confession": Meadow, interview.

410 "I'm very little, but I'm solid": "Peter Lorre, Shadow & Substance."

410 "a rather rude . . . that feels good": Lorre, interview by Wallace.

410 "I have to . . . for my child": Ebinger, *Blandine—,* p. 169.

410 "Do I look . . . you're pretty fat": Parry, interview.

410 "How long have . . . pieces of wood": Kanter, interview.

411 "his poems, songs . . . questions and answers": Louis Calta, "Theatre: 'Brecht on Brecht' Offered," *NYT,* Nov. 15, 1961.

411 "For instance, the . . . meaning was lost": P.K., "Peter Lorre—Fan of Brecht."

411 "had a wonderful . . . union was over": Bentley, interview.

411 "Now I'm doing . . . that you're there": Lovsky, diary, June 9, 1956.

412 "We voted—for . . . you are. Peter": ibid., June 5, 1956.

412 "Annemarie was very . . . her his hand": ibid., May 2, 1956.

412 "opposing counsel": R. Shutan, interview

412 "Peter was very . . . the office once": Kennard, interview.

413 "all over the . . . in your blood": Lorre, interview by Wallace.

413 "He read from . . . drama and comedy": C. Lorre, interview, Oct. 15, 1980.

413 "I felt that . . . he'd get revengeful": Parry, interview.

414 "all of which . . . squandered or secreted": Annemarie Lorre vs. Peter Lorre: Complaint for Divorce, Superior Court of the State of California for the County of Los Angeles, Aug. 15, 1963.

414 "multiple deals . . . at a time": Lester Salkow, interview.

414 "It was tongue-in-cheek from the very beginning": Matheson, interview, Jan. 3, 1975.

414 "step through the . . . box office receipts": AIP promotional recording for *The Raven,* author's collection.

415 "Roger just let . . . have a go": Hazel Court, interview, March 12, 1979.

415 "He's the only . . . feel like it": Matheson, interview, May 31, 2001.

415 "didn't spend much . . . to his scenes": Corman, *How I Made a Hundred Movies*, p. 85.

415 "I felt that . . . a joyous thing": Court, interview by Katz.

416 "Peter loved to . . . technique was improvisation": Price, interview, Jan. 30, 1974.

416 "Often on a . . . works out well": P.K., "Peter Lorre—Fan of Brecht."

416 "enough blank space either side": Brock Brower, "The Vulgarization of American Demonology," *Esquire*, June 1964.

416 "With Boris and . . . scenes with Peter": Corman, *How I Made a Hundred Movies*, p. 85.

416 "For Christsake, Peter . . . on with it": Price, interview, April 26, 1984.

416 "You would do . . . he always did": Court, interview, March 12, 1979.

416 "was always pinching . . . of course not": Court, interview by Williams.

417 "one of the . . . I ever knew": Richard Apt, "Jack Nicholson Talks about Making Movies and People in Them," *Atlantic City (NJ) Sunday Press*, Jan. 30, 1972.

417 "more grotesquely droll . . . to my life": *The Raven*, draft screenplay, undated, author's collection.

417 "There was something . . . he was in": "Richard Matheson, Storyteller: *The Comedy of Terrors*," MGM Presents Midnite Movies Double Feature: *The Comedy of Terrors / The Raven*, produced and directed by Greg Carson, MGM Home Entertainment LLC, 2003.

417 "As a serious actor . . . quickies": Price, interview, Jan. 30, 1974.

417 "awful . . . with the ladies": Sanford, interview.

417 "used to be . . . cost too much": Arkoff, interview, Feb. 1, 1995.

418 "Strictly a picture . . . quote the critic": Bosley Crowther, "Peter Lorre Heads Cast in 'The Raven,'" *NYT* (Western ed.), Jan. 26, 1963.

418 "low grade": Bosley Crowther, "Four New Films Are Imitations," *NYT*, Feb. 6, 1963.

418 "Price, Lorre and . . . that are virtuoso": James Powers, "*The Raven*," *HR*, Jan. 30, 1963.

418 "production values and . . . chill-and-thrill entertainment": "Nicholson-Arkoff Company Easing Off Imported Pix; Planning 18 to 24 in Year," *HR*, Sept. 3, 1963.

418 "we were always ready to shift gears": Arkoff, interview, Feb. 1, 1995.

418 "so bad at . . . them off himself": Matheson, interview, May 31, 2001.

419 "it took Peter . . . as a menace": *Comedy of Terrors*, pressbook, 1964.

419 "fierce and dogmatic": David DelValle, "Joyce Jameson Interview," *Cult Movies* 28 (1999): 63.

419 "Laurel and Hardy": Matheson, interview, Jan. 3, 1975.

419 "just sort of . . . could you do": Matheson, interview, Dec. 6, 1994.

420 "tremendous sense of comedy timing": ibid., Jan. 3, 1975.

420 "chillerdiller—dill as . . . horroromp": Howard Thompson, "*The Comedy of Terrors*," *NYT*, Jan. 23, 1964.

420 "ashamed to watch . . . their poor images": "*Comedy of Terrors*: Film Monstrosity," Philip K. Scheuer, *LAT*, Jan. 23, 1964.

420 "The world isn't . . . the next toy": Campbell, interview.

420 "this is a . . . sense of humor": Arkoff, interview, Jan. 29, 1981.

420 "Peter was very . . . you feel good": Court, interview, March 12, 1979.

421 "he was a . . . to be with": Price, interview, Jan. 30, 1974.

421 "Peter always threw . . . rest in peace": Lester Salkow, interview.

421 "It was kind . . . egotistical about them": Matheson, interview, Jan. 3, 1975.

421 "How do I . . . feed a daughter": Lorre, interview by Gardner.

421 "opening-night bit": Slocum, "The Peter Lorre Nobody Knows."

421 "because I only . . . looking at them": Lorre, interview by Wallace.

421 "I don't like . . . people watch it": Lorre, interview by Gardner.

422 "I hate to . . . dragged me there": Lorre, interview by Wallace.

422 "This is one . . . you don't age": Lorre, interview by Glover.

422 "Peter was very . . . of being ill": Court, interview by Katz.

422 "he wasn't feeling . . . did the scene": Post, interview by Weaver.

423 "It was all . . . to go near": Kennard, interview.

423 "after every scene . . . for several minutes": McGee, *Faster and Furiouser,* p. 205.

423 "with his head . . . to go home": Burns, interview by Weaver.

423 "I had a . . . of the picture": Jameson, interview.

424 "It was a . . . ill he was": Sanford, interview.

10. THE MASK BEHIND THE FACE

Epigraphs: Lorre, unidentified clipping, PLS; Sanford, interview.

1. On March 3, 1963, Lorre admitted to interviewer Hy Gardner that he had not been a student of Sigmund Freud's: "I want to correct you on this. . . . He was lecturing at that time and I heard many a lecture of his, but I did study with Dr. [Alexander] Neuer," an Adlerian psychiatrist. *The Hy Gardner Show,* March 3, 1963.

2. As the "regularly appointed administratrix of his estate," Annemarie "was duly substituted by order of court as objector in the written proceeding." *Weingand v. Lorre,* 231 Cal. App. 2d 289, 41 Cal. Rptr. 778 (Dist. Ct. App. 1964), p. 290.

3. Sam Arkoff labeled it a "horror-love story; it was going to be sort of a wistful picture with a certain mood in it." Arkoff, interview, Jan. 29, 1981.

4. Reference to Lorre's plans in the *Berliner Tageblatt,* Dec. 29, 1963.

5. Reference to the actor's estate, "Peter Lorre Estate Set at $13,000," *LAT,* May 7, 1964.

QUOTATION SOURCES BY PAGE NUMBER

425 "Facial expression . . . manifestation of man": Béla Balázs, *Theory of the Film: Character and Growth of a New Art* (New York: Dover, 1970), p. 60.

425 "multiplicity of the human soul": ibid., p. 64.

426 "It's an amazing . . . to the ideal": "Peter Lorre, Shadow & Substance."

426 "do what you . . . always branch out": Haller, interview.

426 "There comes a . . . in my life": "He's Only Human."

426 "after a certain . . . start something else": Lorre, interview by Glover.

426 "For a lazy . . . work awfully hard": *LAT,* Jan. 20, 1963.

426 "on top of . . . 'Mr. Moto' series": Lorre, interview by Glover.

427 "People say if . . . I've worked with": Zastupnevich, interview.

427 "good old days . . . has done it": Bob Thomas, "Peter Lorre Talks of the Good Old Daze," *New York Post,* April 13, 1962.

427 "I guess I'm . . . left me alone": "Screen Villain Peter Lorre's Fabulous Career Recalled," *Los Angeles Herald-Examiner,* March 24, 1964.

427 "The movies are . . . cold-hearted business": Bob Thomas, "Cold-Hearted Industry: No Loyalty to Employees, Claims Lorre," *Newark Evening News,* Feb. 20, 1960.

427 "showed up, did . . . and went home": Kanter, interview.

427 "I hate to . . . me a star": Transcript, Oct. 3, 1963, In the Matter of the application of Eugene Weingand for Change of Name, Case No. 819718, Superior Court of the State of California for the County of Los Angeles, p. 54.

427 "He loved to . . . in his mind": Avalon, interview.

427 "In Europe . . . a good part": Amsterdam, interview.

428 "Peter said that . . . against the government": Jameson, interview.

428 "First picture I . . . that comes along": Transcript, p. 54

428 "Is that a . . . at American-International": Everson, "Peter Lorre," p. 16.

428 "playful, pixieish, rebellious . . . the same bores": Lorre, interview by Wallace, pre-interview notes.

428 "I have very . . . Bogey so much": *LAT,* Jan. 20, 1963.

428 "was my dearest . . . Joe E. Lewis": Lorre, interview by Wallace.

428 "without chasing [him] out of the window": Lorre, interview by Paar.

428 "an incongruous bunch of creeps": *LAT,* Jan. 20, 1963.

429 "I think he . . . most people realized": Lorre, interview by Wallace.

429 "whatever Bogie played . . . a great actor": Lorre, interview, "Dick Strout with Hollywood Profiles."

429 "the relief of . . . perpetuation of independence": Hyams, *Bogart and Bacall,* p. 205.

429 "Toward the end . . . ever gone through": Lorre, interview by Wallace.

430 "My dearest pal . . . feel the void": Thirer, "Lorre: 'Time Not to Make Money.'"

430 "Brecht is dead": Lovksy, diary, Aug. 17, 1956.

430 "I would like . . . signs his name": Ives, interview.

431 "Peter was a . . . practically bleeding inside": Veigel, interview.

432 "Don't you think . . . in his heart": Goff, interview, July 31, 1978.

432 "I think we . . . form of compensation": Joseph Pevney to author, Aug. 21, 1975.

432 "In *The Big* . . . could be helpful": Zastupnevich, interview.

432 "He said that . . . the right spot": Fitzgerald, interview.

433 "He had a . . . he had done": Vincent, interview.

433 "had an accident . . . Especially a monkey": "Peter Lorre—Between Chimp & Art."

433 "Tell those undertakers . . . you right up": Sanford, interview.

434 "some of the . . . horror sans makeup": CBS publicity material, Oct. 26, 1962, CBS Entertainment, New York.

434 "There was a . . . me for him": Andrew Lorre to author, June 4, 1981.

434 "Aren't you Peter . . . telling people that": Shutan, interview.

435 "In my first . . . graduated to grownups": Alpert, "Lorre Laughs When It Hurts."

435 "I have no . . . All degenerates are": "Peter Lorre—Between Chimp & Art."

435 "But he didn't . . . hurts the most": Slocum, "The Peter Lorre Nobody Knows."

435 "I think he . . . to the piper": Sanford, interview.

435 "What you want . . . Lorre, don't you": Haller, interview.

435 "I've played mostly . . . away with murder": Alpert, "Lorre Laughs When It Hurts."

436 "I had never . . . cared about them": Sanford, interview.

436 "If autograph people . . . that important now": Zastupnevich, interview.

436 "I come here . . . for my autograph": Greenfield, interview.

436 "the gang . . . the psychotic killer": Blum to author, Feb. 26, 1975.

437 "I look at . . . I've seen him": Maude Cheatham, "Gruesome Twosome," *Movie Show,* March 1946.

437 "He trusted me . . . to everyone else": Sanford, interview.

438 "I think he . . . without being intimate": ibid.

438 "Peter wanted to . . . the sad things": Veigel, interview.

438 "He thought of . . . of options diminished": Powers, interview.

438 "When I met . . . make a living": Kirk Douglas to author, Jan. 14, 1974.

439 "goodly amount of cynicism": Kulik, interview.

439 "strange, tired, sensual-mysterious . . . You bore me": Ebinger, *"Blandine—,"* p. 169.

439 "I think he . . . again after that": Sanford, interview.

439 "I don't sign . . . make the deals": Kennard, interview.

439 "I have to return to latrine duty": A. Lorre, interview, June 19, 1973.

439 "It's always the . . . I am stamped": Ebinger, *"Blandine—,"* p. 169.

439 "I think toward . . . to do more": Sanford, interview.

439 "There was a . . . himself much earlier": Kanter, interview.

440 "Because everybody calls . . . hard to pronounce": Transcript, pp. 4–5.

440 "I am without . . . relationship to others": Joseph Finnigan, "Defends Bad Name: Lorre Protected from Pseudo-Lorre," *Newark Evening News,* Nov. 19, 1963.

440 "Have you any . . . to believe that": Deposition, Sept. 10, 1963, In the Matter of the Application of Eugene Weingand, for Change of Name, Petitioner, Case No. 819718, Superior Court of the State of California for the County of Los Angeles, pp. 14, 16–17.

441 "Well, I want . . . Perhaps": ibid., pp. 26–27.

442 "Anyone ever call . . . (No response)": Transcript, pp. 4–5.

442 "Be seated, please . . . it to somebody": ibid., 53, 57.

442 "considered box-office value": ibid., p. 35.

442 "exclusive": ibid., p. 49.

442 "to cash in . . . by Peter Lorre": ibid., p. 69.

443 "in permanently restraining . . . of Peter Lorre": *Weingand v. Lorre,* 231 Cal. App. 2d 289, 41 Cal. Rptr. 778 (Dist. Ct. App. 1964), p. 294.

443 "No, he has . . . Alcohol": Transcript, p. 27.

443 "the surviving son . . . of the petitioner": Petition, Nov. 23, 1971, In the Matter of the Application of Eugene Weingand, aka Peter Lorre, Jr. for Change of Name, Case No. 16990, Superior Court of the State of California for the County of Los Angeles, pp. 1–2.

444 "One of the . . . an adult picture": Arkoff, interview, Jan. 29, 1981.

444 "younger edition of Winston Churchill": Hy Gardner, interview with Peter Lorre.

444 "but I would . . . can't speak English": Lorre, interview by Gardner.

444 "servant in the . . . the Transylvanian navy": Richard Matheson, quoted in McGee, *Faster and Furiouser,* p. 215.

444 "all four of them": Matheson, interview, Dec. 6, 1994.

444 "They're all called . . . very funny script": Richard Matheson, quoted in Weaver, *Science Fiction Stars,* p. 312.

445 "popping off": Matheson, interview, Dec. 6, 1994.

445 "It was a . . . a pleasant murderer": Haller, interview.

445 "in which Peter . . . take Peter's place": Bennett to author, April 20, 1982.

445 "To be really . . . interpreted it right": Thirer, "Lorre: 'Time Not to Make Money.'"

446 "For Peter . . . there was nothing": Jameson, interview.

446 "There was no . . . attention to Jerry": Wynn, interview.

446 "a scene thief beyond compare": Jerry Lewis, *The Total Film-Maker* (New York: Random House, 1971), p. 121.

446 "If he could . . . of the film": C. Lorre, interview, Oct. 17, 1980.

446 "Peter was afraid . . . his fellow actors": Zastupnevich, interview.

447 "He just couldn't . . . sorry for him": Kerschner, interview.

447 "His health was . . . very troubled way": Meadow, interview.

447 "Basically, Peter was . . . aware of it": J. Silverstone, interview.

447 "of someone utterly . . . a long time": Greenberg, "Peter Lorre."

447 "He didn't like . . . wall and die": Meadow, interview.

448 "Peter got more . . . into the ground": Parry, interview.

448 "A great actor . . . of the man": Peter Lorre file, MHL AMPAS.

450 "I guess that's . . . you for coming": Price, interview, Jan. 30, 1974.

450 "Peter never got . . . career and life": Haller, interview.

450 "He always had . . . real artistic film": Lester Salkow, interview.

EPILOGUE

Epigraph: Otto Fenichel, "On Acting," *Psychoanalytic Quarterly* 15 (1946): 150.

BIBLIOGRAPHY

PRINT SOURCES

Adam, Peter. "Lotte Lenya: September Song." *Listener* (London), May 24, 1979.

Ambler, Eric. *Here Lies: An Autobiography.* New York: Farrar, Straus, 1986.

Anslinger, Harry J. *The Protectors: Narcotic Agents, Citizens, and Officials against Organized Crime in America.* New York: Farrar, Straus and Giroux, 1964.

Arendt, Hannah. "The Aftermath of Nazi Rule: Report from Germany." *Commentary,* Oct. 1950.

Arkoff, Sam. *Flying through Hollywood by the Seat of My Pants.* Secaucus, NJ: Carol, 1992.

Armour, Robert A. *Fritz Lang.* Boston: Twayne, 1977.

Arnold, Edward. *Lorenzo Goes to Hollywood: The Autobiography of Edward Arnold.* New York: Liveright, 1940.

Astor, Mary. *A Life on Film.* Garden City, NY: Doubleday, 1959.

Aufricht, Ernst Josef. *Erzähle damit du dein Recht erweist.* Berlin: Propyläen, 1966.

Aurich, Rolf, Wolfgang Jacobsen, and Cornelius Schnauber, eds. *Fritz Lang: His Life and Work: Photographs and Documents.* Berlin: Jovis, 2001.

Bacall, Lauren. *Lauren Bacall by Myself.* New York: Knopf, 1979.

Bartram, Graham, and Anthony Waine, eds. *Brecht in Perspective.* London: Longman, 1982.

Bauer, Alfred. *Deutscher Spielfilm-Almanach 1929–1950.* Berlin: Filmblätter, 1950.

Baxter, John. *The Hollywood Exiles.* New York: Taplinger, 1976.

———. "The Sternberg Style." In *Great Film Directors,* ed. Leo Braudy and Morris Dickstein. New York: Oxford Univ. Press, 1978.

Baynes, Norman H., ed. *The Speeches of Adolf Hitler, 1922–1939.* Oxford: Oxford Univ. Press, 1942.

Behlmer, Rudy. *America's Favorite Movies: Behind the Scenes.* New York: Frederick Ungar, 1982.

———, ed. *Inside Warner Bros, 1935–1951.* New York: Viking, 1985.

———. *Memo from David O. Selznick.* New York: Viking, 1972.

Benchley, Nathaniel. *Humphrey Bogart.* Boston: Little, Brown, 1975.

Benjamin, Walter. *Understanding Brecht.* Translated by Anna Bostock. London: NLB, 1973.

Bentley, Eric. *The Brecht Commentaries, 1943–1980.* New York: Grove, 1981.

———. *The Brecht Memoir.* New York: PAJ Publications, 1985.

———, ed. *The Brecht-Eisler Song Book.* New York: Oak, 1967.

————. *Thirty Years of Treason: Excerpts from Hearings before the House Committee on Un-American Affairs, 1938–1968.* New York: Viking, 1971.

Berlau, Ruth. *Living for Brecht: The Memoirs of Ruth Berlau.* Edited by Hans Bunge. Translated by Geoffrey Skelton. New York: Fromm, 1987.

Bessie, Alvah. *Inquisition into Eden.* New York: Macmillan, 1965.

Binns, Ronald. "Malcolm Lowry." In *Dictionary of Literary Biography,* part 1, edited by Bernard Oldsey. Detroit: Gale Research, 1983.

Birdwell, Michael E. *Celluloid Soldiers: The Warner Bros. Campaign against Nazism.* New York: New York Univ. Press, 1999.

Bogart, Humphrey. "I'm No Communist." *Photoplay,* March 1948.

————. "Why Hollywood Hates Me." *Screen Book,* Jan. 1940.

Bogdanovich, Peter. *Fritz Lang in America.* New York: Praeger, 1967.

————. *Who the Devil Made It.* New York: Knopf, 1997.

Botting, Douglas. *From the Ruins of the Reich: Germany, 1945–1949.* New York: Crown, 1985.

Boyers, Robert., ed. *Legacy of the German Refugee Intellectuals.* New York: Schocken, 1969.

Boyle, Kay. *The Smoking Mountain: Stories of Postwar Germany.* New York: McGraw-Hill, 1950.

Boyum, Joy Gould. *Double Exposure: Fiction into Film.* New York: Universe, 1985.

Brecht, Bertolt. *Arbeitsjournal 1938–1955.* 2 vols. Edited by Werner Hecht. Frankfurt am Main: Suhrkamp, 1973.

————. *Collected Plays.* Edited by Ralph Manheim and John Willett. 7 vols. New York: Vintage, 1971.

————. *Happy End.* Translated, adapted, and introduced by Michael Feingold. London: Methuen, 1972.

————. *The Jewish Wife and Other Short Plays.* English versions by Eric Bentley. New York: Grove, 1978.

————. *Journals, 1934–1955.* Translated by Hugh Rorrison. Edited by John Willett. New York: Routledge, 1993.

————. *Letters, 1913–1956.* Translated by Ralph Manheim. Edited by John Willett. New York: Routledge, 1990.

————. *Poems, 1913–1956.* Edited by John Willett and Ralph Manheim. New York: Methuen, 1979.

————. *Texte für Filme.* Edited by Wolfgang Gersch and Werner Hecht. 2 vols. Frankfurt am Main: Suhrkamp, 1969.

————. *Werke: Grosse kommentierte Berliner und Frankfurter Ausgabe.* Edited by Werner Hecht, Jan Knopf, Werner Mittenzwei, and Klaus-Detlef Müller. 30 vols. Frankfurt am Main: Suhrkamp, 1988–2000.

"Brecht in Hollywood." In *Annual Annual.* Berkeley: Pacifica Foundation, 1965.

Breit, Harvey, and Margerie Bonner Lowry. *Selected Letters of Malcolm Lowry.* New York: Capricorn, 1969.

Breuer, William. *Hitler's Undercover War: The Nazi Espionage Invasion of the U.S.A.* New York: St. Martin's, 1989.

Bronnen, Arnolt. *Tage mit Bertolt Brecht: Geschichte einer unvollendeten Freundschaft.* Munich: Kurt Desch, 1960.

Brook, Peter. *The Empty Space.* New York: Athenaeum, 1978.

Brosnan, John. *The Horror People.* New York: New American Library, 1976.

Buchanan, Barbara. "REAL and UNREAL Horror." *Film Weekly* (London), Dec. 14, 1935.

Buchanan, Joan. "Horror Is Hard Work." *Radio Life,* Aug. 24, 1947.

Buckley, Gail Lumet. *The Hornes: An American Family.* New York: New American Library, 1986.

Capote, Truman. *The Dog Barks: Public People and Private Places.* New York: Random House, 1973.

Capra, Frank. *The Name above the Title: An Autobiography.* New York: Macmillan, 1971.

Cardiff, Jack. *Magic Hour: The Life of a Cameraman.* London: Faber and Faber, 1996.

Cargnelli, Christian, and Michael Omasta, eds. *Aufbruch ins Ungewisse.* Vol. 2, *Lexicon. Tributes. Selbszeugnisse.* Vienna: Wespennest, 1993.

Ceplair, Larry, and Steven Englund. *The Inquisition in Hollywood: Politics in the Film Community, 1930–1960.* Garden City, NY: Anchor Press / Doubleday, 1980.

Cheatham, Maude. "Gruesome Twosome." *Movie Show,* March 1946.

Cockburn, Claud. *Beat the Devil.* London: Hogarth, 1985.

Cogley, John. *Report on Blacklisting.* Vol. 1, *The Movies.* New York: Fund for the Republic, 1956.

Colgan, Ann Christine. "Warner Brothers' Crusade against the Third Reich: A Study of Anti-Nazi Activism and Film Production, 1933 to 1941." Ph.D. diss., Univ. of Southern California, 1985.

Colliver, Timothy L. *Seaview: The Making of Voyage to the Bottom of the Sea.* Dunlap, TN: Star Tech, 1992.

Cook, Bruce. *Brecht in Exile.* New York: Holt, Rinehart, and Winston, 1982.

Cooke, Alistair. *Six Men.* New York: Knopf, 1977.

Corman, Roger. *How I Made a Hundred Movies in Hollywood and Never Lost a Dime.* New York: Random House, 1990.

Csokor, Franz Theodor. *Zeuge einer Zeit: Briefe aus dem Exil, 1933–1950.* Munich: Albert Langen, Georg Müller, 1964.

Dalton, Elizabeth. "'Old Glory': Notes on Warners Shorts." *Velvet Light Trap* 8 (1973).

Daviau, Donald G., ed. *Major Figures of Turn-of-the-Century Austrian Literature.* Riverside, CA: Ariadne Press, 1991.

Davie, Maurice R. *Refugees in America: Report of the Committee for the Study of Recent Immigration from Europe.* New York: Harper, 1947.

Dawidowicz, Lucy S. *The War against the Jews, 1933–1945.* New York: Holt, Rinehart, and Winston, 1975.

Day, Douglas. *Malcolm Lowry: A Biography.* New York: Oxford Univ. Press, 1984.

Deutsches Bühnen-Jahrbuch: Theatergeschichtliches Jahr- und Adressenbuch. Berlin: Genossenshcaft Deutscher Bühnen-Angehöriger, 1920–33.

Dick, Bernard F. *The Star-Spangled Screen: The American World War II Film.* Lexington: Univ. Press of Kentucky, 1985.

Dillman, Michael. *Heinz Hilpert: Leben und Werk.* Berlin: Akademie der Künste, 1990.

Dubrovic, Milan. *Veruntreute Geschichte.* Vienna: Paul Zsolnay, 1985.

Dunne, Philip. *Take Two: A Life in Movies and Politics.* New York: McGraw-Hill, 1980.

Durgnat, Raymond. *The Strange Case of Alfred Hitchcock: or, The Plain Man's Hitchcock.* Cambridge, MA: MIT Press, 1974.

Ebinger, Blandine. *"Blandine—": Von und mit Blandine Ebinger, der grossen Diseuse der Zwanziger Jahre, der kongenialen Muse von Friedrich Hollaender.* Zürich: Arche, 1985.

Eggebrecht, Axel. *Der halbe Weg: Zwischenbilanz einer Epoche.* Hamburg: Rowohlt, 1975.

Eisner, Lotte H. "A la seconde vision." *Cahiers du Cinema,* Feb. 1953.

———. *Fritz Lang.* New York: Oxford Univ. Press, 1977.

———. *The Haunted Screen: Expressionism in the German Cinema and the Influence of Max Reinhardt.* Berkeley: Univ. of California Press, 1969.

———. "Peter Lorre le Meurtrier." *Cinématographe* 2 (May 1937).

Esslin, Martin. *Brecht: The Man and His Work.* Garden City, NY: Doubleday, 1960.

Everett, Susanne. *Lost Berlin.* New York: St. Martins, 1979.

Everson, William K. "Peter Lorre: A Personal Reminiscence." *Castle of Frankenstein,* #5, vol. 2, no. 1, 1964.

Ewen, Frederic. *Bertolt Brecht: His Life, His Art, and His Times.* New York: Citadel, 1969.

Eyck, Erich. *A History of the Weimar Republic.* Translated by Harlan P. Hanson and G.L. Waite. 2 vols. Cambridge, MA: Harvard Univ. Press, 1962–63.

Fagan, Myron C. *Documentation of the Red Stars in Hollywood.* Hollywood, CA: Cinema Educational Guild, 1950.

————. *Red Treason in Hollywood!!* Hollywood, CA: Cinema Educational Guild, 1949.

Fehrenbach, Heide. *Cinema in Democratizing Germany: Reconstructing National Identity after Hitler.* Chapel Hill: Univ. of North Carolina Press, 1995.

Field, Frank. *The Last Days of Mankind: Karl Kraus and His Vienna.* New York: St. Martin's, 1967.

Fischer, Ruth. *Stalin and German Communism: A Study in the Origins of the State Party.* Cambridge, MA: Harvard Univ. Press, 1948.

Fleisser, Marieluise. "Avantgarde." In *Gesammelte Werke,* edited by Günther Rühle, vol. 3. Frankfurt am Main: Suhrkamp, 1972.

Florey, Robert. *Hollywood d'hier et d'aujourd'hui.* Paris: Editions Prisma, 1948.

Foster, Robert Anthony. "Hollywood by Roller Coaster: A Personal Remembrance." *Filmfax,* Jan.–Feb. 1995.

Frank, Rudolph. *Spielzeit meines Lebens.* Heidelberg: Lambert Schneider, 1960.

Frazier, George. *The One with the Mustache Is Costello.* New York: Random House, 1947.

Freedland, Michael. *The Warner Brothers.* New York: St. Martin's, 1983.

Friedrich, Otto. *Before the Deluge: A Portrait of Berlin in the 1920s.* New York: Harper and Row, 1972.

Friedrich, Thomas. *Berlin between the Wars.* New York: Vendome, 1991.

Frisch, Max. *Sketchbook, 1966–1971.* Translated by Geoffrey Skelton. New York: Harcourt Brace Jovanovich, 1974.

Frischauer, Willi. "Mild Mannered Villain." *Picturegoer,* May 1953.

"Fritz Lang Seminar." *Dialogue on Film,* April 1974.

Fuegi, John. *Brecht and Company: Sex, Politics, and the Making of the Modern Drama.* New York: Grove, 1994.

————. "Chaos, according to Plan." In *The Cambridge Companion to Brecht,* edited by Peter Thomson. Cambridge: Cambridge Univ. Press, 1994.

Gandert, Gero. "Fritz Lang über 'M': Ein Interview." In *M: Protokoll,* Cinemathek, 3, *Ausgewählte Filmtexte.* Hamburg: Marion von Schröder, 1963.

Gay, Peter. *Weimar Culture: The Outsider as Insider.* New York: Harper and Row, 1968.

Gersch, Wolfgang. *Film bei Brecht.* Berlin: Henschel, 1975.

Gittleman, Sol. *Frank Wedekind.* New York: Twayne, 1969.

Gollanz, Victor. *In Darkest Germany.* Hinsdale, IL: Henry Regnery, 1947.

Goodman, Ezra. *Bogey: The Good-Bad Guy.* New York: Lyle Stuart, 1965.

Gorelik, Mordecai. "On Brechtian Acting." *Quarterly Journal of Speech,* Oct. 1974.

Gottlieb, Sidney, ed. *Hitchcock on Hitchcock: Selected Writings and Interviews.* Berkeley: Univ. of California Press, 1995.

Gow, Gordon. *Hollywood in the Fifties.* New York: A.S. Barnes, 1971.

Grace, Sherill E. "Malcolm Lowry and the Expressionist Vision." In *The Art of Malcolm Lowry,* edited by Anne Smith. London: Vision, 1978.

————, ed. *Sursum Corda! The Collected Letters of Malcolm Lowry.* Vol. 2, *1947–1957.* Toronto: Univ. of Toronto Press, 1995.

Grams, Martin, Jr. *The I Love a Mystery Companion.* Churchville, MD: OTR Publishing, 2003.

Grant, Keith, ed. *Fritz Lang Interviews.* Translated by Glenwood Irons. Jackson: Univ. Press of Mississippi, 2003.

Greenberg, Joel. "Peter Lorre: An Appreciation." *International Press Bulletin* 2, no. 1 (1964).

Greene, Graham. "The Genius of Peter Lorre." *World Film News* (London), July 1936.

Gregor, John. *Der Schauspielerführer.* Vol. 7. Stuttgart: Anton Hiersemann, 1964.

Grimstad, Kari. *Masks of the Prophet: The Theatrical World of Karl Kraus.* Toronto: Univ. of Toronto Press, 1982.

Grobel, Lawrence. *The Hustons.* New York: Scribner's, 1989.

Hall, Gladys. "Are You Insane?" *Screenland,* Jan. 1939.

Halliday, Jon. *Sirk on Sirk: Conversations with Jon Halliday.* London: Faber and Faber, 1997.

Hamilton, Ian. *Writers in Hollywood, 1915–1951.* New York: Harper and Row, 1990.

Hardwicke, Cedric. *A Victorian in Orbit.* New York: Metheun, 1961.

Hardy, Forsyth, ed. *Grierson on the Movies.* London: Faber and Faber, 1981.

Harmetz, Aljean. *Round Up the Usual Suspects: The Making of Casablanca: Bogart, Bergman, and World War II.* New York: Hyperion, 1992.

Harvey, William F. "The Beast with Five Fingers." In *The Ghouls,* ed. Peter Haining. New York: Stein and Day, 1971.

Hasek, Jaroslav. *The Good Soldier: Schweik.* Translated by Paul Selver. New York: Signet Classic, 1963.

———. *The Good Soldier Švejk and His Fortunes in the World War.* Translated by Cecil Parrott. New York: Knopf, 1993.

Haver, Ron. "Finally, the Truth about Casablanca." *American Film,* June 1976.

Hawkins, Robert F. "This Year the Good Films Were Surprisingly Numerous." *Films in Review,* Oct. 1951.

Hayman, Ronald. *Brecht: A Biography.* London: Weidenfeld and Nicolson, 1983.

———. *Thomas Mann: A Biography.* New York: Scribner's, 1995.

Heilbut, Anthony. *Exiled in Paradise: German Refugee Artists and Intellectuals in America, from the 1930s to the Present.* New York: Viking, 1983.

Henreid, Paul. *Ladies Man: An Autobiography.* New York: St. Martin's, 1984.

"He's Only Human." *TV Guide,* Nov. 2–8, 1957.

Higham, Charles. *Orson Welles: The Rise and Fall of an American Genius.* New York: St. Martin's, 1985.

Higham, Charles, and Joel Greenberg. *The Celluloid Muse: Hollywood Directors Speak.* London: Angus and Robertson, 1969.

Hochman, Stanley, ed. *From Quasimodo to Scarlett O'Hara: A National Board of Review Anthology, 1920–40.* New York: Frederick Ungar, 1982.

Hollaender, Friedrich. *Von Kopf bis Fuss: Mein Leben mit Text und Musik.* Munich: Kindler, 1965.

Hollander, Frederick. *Those Torn from Earth.* New York: Liveright, 1941.

Hollstein, Dorothea. *Antisemitische Filmpropaganda.* Munich: Pullach, Dokumentation, 1971.

"Hollywood By-The-Way: Lorre Lore." *Family Circle,* July 8, 1937.

Horst, Astrid. *Prima inter pares: Elisabeth Hauptmann, die Mitarbeiterin Bertolt Brecht.* Würzburg: Königshausen und Newmann, 1992.

Houseman, John. *Run-Through: A Memoir.* New York: Simon and Schuster, 1972.

Huesmann, Heinrich. *Welt Theater Reinhardt: Bauten Spielstätten Inszenierungen.* Munich: Prestel, 1983.

Hull, David Stewart. *Film in the Third Reich: A Study of the German Cinema 1933–1945.* Berkeley: Univ. of California Press, 1969.

Huston, John. *An Open Book.* New York: Knopf, 1980.

Hyams, Joe. *Bogart and Bacall: A Love Story.* New York: David McKay, 1975.

———. *Bogie: The Biography of Humphrey Bogart.* New York: New American Library, 1966.

Jameson, Egon. *Wenn ich mich recht errinere: Das Leben eines Optimisten in der besten aller Welten.* Bern: Scherz, 1963.

Janik, Allan, and Stephen Toulmin. *Wittenstein's Vienna.* New York: Simon and Schuster, 1973.

Jensen, Paul M. *The Cinema of Fritz Lang,* New York: A.F. Barnes, 1969.

Jhering, Herbert. "Kritiken aus den zwanziger Jahren: Der Dramatiker Bert Brecht." In *Sinn und Form,* Zweites Sonderheft Bertolt Brecht. Berlin: Rütten und Loening, 1957. Originally published in *Berliner Börsen Courier,* Oct. 5, 1922.

———. "Peter Lorre zum Gedächtnis." *Theater heute,* May 1964.

———. *Von Reinhardt bis Brecht: Vier Jahrzehnte Theater und Film.* 3 vols. Berlin: Aufbau, 1959.

Kaes, Anton. *M.* London: BFI, 2001.

Kaminsky, Stuart M. *Don Siegel: Director.* New York: Curtis, 1974.

———. *John Huston: Maker of Magic.* Boston: Houghton Mifflin, 1978.

Kane, Bob, and Joe Desris. *Batman Dailies.* Vol. 2, *1944–1945.* Princeton, WI: Kitchen Sink, 1991.

Kapczynski, Jennifer M. "Homeward Bound? Peter Lorre's *The Lost Man* and the End of Exile" *New German Critique* 89 (Spring–Summer 2003).

Kaplan, E. Ann. *Fritz Lang: A Guide to References and Resources.* Boston: G.K. Hall, 1981.

Kebir, Sabine. *Ich fragte nicht nach mein Anteil: Elisabeth Hauptmanns Arbeit mit Bertolt Brecht.* Berlin: Aufbau, 1997.

"Kein Platz für zwei Mörder." *Der Spiegel* (Hamburg), Sept. 27, 1950.

Keiner, Reinhold. *Thea von Harbou und der Deutsche Film bis 1933.* Hildesheim, Germany: Georg Olms, 1984.

Kennedy, Tom. "Monarch of Menace." *Screenland,* Aug. 1936.

Kenworthy, Brian J. *Georg Kaiser.* Oxford: Blackwell, 1957.

Kessler, Harry Graf. *Tagebücher 1918–1937.* Frankfurt am Main: Insel, 1961.

Kilgallen, Dorothy. "Ten Knights in My Date Book." *Photoplay,* June 1943.

Knight, Arthur. "With Huston in Italy." *Saturday Review,* March 13, 1954.

Knopf, Jan. *Brecht-Handbuch: Eine Ästhetik der Widersprüche.* 2 vols. Stuttgart: J.B. Metzler, 1980.

Knust, Herbert. *Materialien zu Bertolt Brechts "Schweyk im zweiten Weltkrieg."* Frankfurt am Main: Suhrkamp, 1974.

Koch, Howard. "The Making of Casablanca." In *Casablanca: Script and Legend.* Woodstock, NY: Overlook, 1973.

———. "Reflections on a Golden Boy: Howard Koch on the Young John Huston." *Film Comment,* May 1973.

Kortner, Fritz. *Aller Tage Abend.* Munich: Deutscher Taschenbuch, 1969.

Kosch, Wilhelm. *Deutsches Theater-Lexikon.* 2 vols. Klagenfurt, Austria: F. Kleinmayr, 1960.

Kotsilibas-Davis, James, and Myrna Loy. *Myrna Loy: Being and Becoming.* New York: Knopf, 1987.

Kracauer, Siegfried. *From Caligari to Hitler: A Psychological History of the German Film.* Princeton, NJ: Princeton Univ. Press, 1947.

Kraus, Karl. *Drama,* vol. 14 of *Werke.* 14 vols. Munich: Albert Langen–Georg Müller, 1967.

Kraus, René. *Winston Churchill: A Biography.* New York: Literary Guild of America, 1941.

Kreimeier, Klaus. *The Ufa Story: A History of Germany's Greatest Film Company, 1918–1945.* Berkeley: Univ. of California Press, 1996.

Lanchester, Elsa. *Herself.* New York: St. Martin's, 1983.

Lang, Harry. "He's an INSIDE Actor." *Screen Book,* Dec. 1937.

Layman, Richard, and Julie M. Rivett, eds. *Selected Letters of Dashiell Hammett.* Washington, DC: Counterpoint, 2001.

Leaming, Barbara. *Orson Welles: A Biography.* New York: Penguin, 1985.

Lehmann, John. *The Whispering Gallery: Autobiography I.* New York: Harcourt, Brace, 1955.

Lenk, Elisabeth, and Roswitha Kaever, eds. *Leben und Wirken des Peter Kürten, genannt der Vampir von Düsseldorf.* Munich: Rogner und Bernhard, 1974.

Lenya, Lotte. "August 28, 1928." Originally published as "That Was a Time!" in *Theatre Arts,* May 1956. Reprinted in *The Threepenny Opera,* by Bertolt Brecht. New York: Grove, 1964.

Lindesmith, Alfred R. *Addiction and Opiates.* Chicago: Aldine, 1968.

Lingen, Theo. *Ich über mich: Interview eines Schauspielers mit sich selbst.* Velber bei Hannover: Friedrich, 1963.

Lorre, Peter. "Auf vier Jahre Rückblick und eine Vorshau." *Mein Film* (Vienna), March 17, 1933.

Lothar, Ernst. *Das Wunder des Überlebens: Erinnerungen und Ergebnisse.* Hamburg: Paul Zsolnay, 1961.

Luft, Herbert G. "Peter Lorre." *Films in Review,* May 1960.

Lynn, Hilary. "He'd Rather Act Than Eat." *Modern Screen,* Jan. 1936.

Lyon, James. *Bertolt Brecht in America.* Princeton, NJ: Princeton Univ. Press, 1980.

———. *Bertolt Brecht's American Cicerone: With an Appendix Containing the Complete Correspondence between Bertolt Brecht and Ferdinand Reyher.* Bonn: Bouvier Verlag Hebert Grundmann, 1978.

———. "Bertolt Brecht's Hollywood Years: The Dramatist as Film Writer." *Oxford German Studies* 6 (1971–72).

Malmberg, Helga. *Widerhall des Herzen: Ein Peter Altenberg-Buch.* Munich: Albert Langen, Georg Müller, 1961.

Mann, Erika, and Klaus Mann. *Escape to Life.* Boston: Houghton Mifflin, 1939.

Mann, Thomas. *Briefe 1948–1955.* Ed. Erika Mann. Frankfurt am Main: S. Fischer, 1965.

———. *Briefwechsel mit Agnes E. Meyer 1937–1955.* Frankfurt am Main: S. Fischer, 1992.

———. "Deutschland und die Deutschen." In *Gesammelte Werke,* vol. 11, *Reden und Aufsätze* 3. Frankfurt am Main: S. Fischer, 1960.

Manvell, Roger, and Heinrich Fraenkel. *The German Cinema.* New York: Praeger, 1971.

Marcuse, Ludwig. *Mein zwanzigstes Jahrhundert: Auf dem Weg zu einer Autobiographie.* Munich: Paul List, 1960.

Matthews, Blayney F. *The Specter of Sabotage.* Los Angeles: Lymanhouse, 1941.

McBride, Joseph. *Frank Capra: The Catastrophe of Success.* New York: Simon and Schuster, 1992.

McClelland, Doug. *Forties Film Talk: Oral Histories of Hollywood, with 120 Lobby Posters.* Jefferson, NC: McFarland, 1992.

McGee, Mark Thomas. *Fast and Furious: The Story of American International Pictures.* Jefferson, NC: McFarland, 1984.

———. *Faster and Furiouser: The Revised and Fattened Fable of AIP.* Jefferson, NC: McFarland, 1996.

McGilligan, Patrick. *Fritz Lang: Nature of the Beast.* New York: St. Martin's, 1997.

Meyers, Jeffrey. *Bogart: A Life in Hollywood.* Boston: Houghton Mifflin, 1997.

Middlebrook, Martin. *The Battle of Hamburg: Allied Bomber Forces against a German City in 1943.* New York: Scribner's, 1981.

Mierendorff, Marta. *William Dieterle: The Plutarch von Hollywood.* Berlin: Henschel, 1993.

Montagu, Ivor. "Working with Hitchcock." *Sight and Sound,* Summer 1960.

Moore, Sonia. *The Stanislavski System: The Professional Training of an Actor.* New York: Penguin, 1984.

Moorehead, Caroline. *Sidney Bernstein: A Biography.* London: Jonathan Cape, 1984.

Moreno, Jacob Levy. *Psychodrama.* 2 vols. New York: Beacon House, 1946.

———. *Das Stegreiftheater.* Potsdam, Germany: Gustav Kipenheuer, 1923.

Moreno, Zerka. "Escape Me Never." *Group Psychotherapy, Psychodrama, and Sociometry* 32 (1979).

Morse, Arthur D. *While Six Million Died: A Chronicle of American Apathy.* New York: Random House, 1967.

Navasky, Victor S. *Naming Names.* New York: Penguin, 1981.

Needle, Jan, and Peter Thomson. *Brecht.* Chicago: Univ. of Chicago Press, 1981.

Negulesco, Jean. *Things I Did . . . and Things I Think I Did.* New York: Simon and Schuster, 1984.

Der Neuer Theater-Almanach: Theatergeschichtliches Jahr- und Adressenbuch. Berlin: Genossenshcaft Deutscher Bühnen-Angehöriger, 1911.

Omasta, Michael, Brigitte Mayr, and Elisabeth Streit, eds. *Peter Lorre: Ein Fremder im Paradies.* Vienna: Paul Zsolnay, 2004.

Ophüls, Max. *Spiel im Dasein: Eine Rückblende.* Stuttgart: Henry Goverts, 1959.

Ott, Frederick. *The Films of Fritz Lang.* Secaucus, NJ; Citadel, 1979.

———. *The Great German Films: From before World War I to the Present.* Secaucus, NJ: Citadel, 1979.

Ottoson, Robert. *A Reference Guide to the American Film Noir: 1940–1958.* Metuchen, NJ: Scarecrow, 1981.

Pachter, Henry. "On Being an Exile: An Old-Timer's Personal and Political Memoir." *Salmagundi* (Fall 1969–Winter 1970).

Parrott, Cecil. *Jaroslav Hasek: A Study of Švejk and the Short Stories.* Cambridge: Cambridge Univ. Press, 1982.

Patterson, Michael. "Brecht's Legacy." In *The Cambridge Companion to Brecht,* ed. Peter Thomson. Cambridge: Cambridge Univ. Press, 1994.

———. *The Revolution in German Theatre, 1900–1933.* Boston: Routledge and Kegan Paul, 1981.

Peary, Danny, ed. *Close-Ups: Intimate Profiles of Movie Stars by Their Co-Stars, Directors, Screenwriters, and Friends.* New York: Workman, 1978.

PEM [Paul E. Marcus]. *Heimweh nach dem Kurfürstendamm: Aus Berlins glanzvollsten Tagen und Nächten.* Berlin: Lothar Blanvalet, 1952.

———. *Strangers Everywhere.* London: John Lane, Bodley Head, 1939.

Peterson, Donald Kent. *The Refugee Intellectual: The Americanization of the Immigrants of 1933–1941.* New York: Columbia Univ. Press, 1953.

Pradan, Sachindra N. *Drug Abuse: Clinical and Basic Aspects.* St. Louis: C.V. Mosby, 1977.

Prater, Donald. *Thomas Mann: A Life.* New York: Oxford Univ. Press, 1995.

Pratley, Gerald. *The Cinema of John Huston.* South Brunswick, NJ: A.S. Barnes, 1977.

Prozess gegen die Leitung des staatsfeindlichen Verschwörerzentrums mit Rudolf Slánský an der Spitze. Prague: Justizministerium, 1953.

Rachlis, Eugene. *They Came to Kill: The Story of Eight Nazi Saboteurs in America.* New York: Random House, 1961.

Rank, Otto. *The Double: A Psychoanalytic Study.* Chapel Hill, NC: Univ. of North Carolina Press, 1971.

Reinhardt, Gottfried. *Der Liebhaber: Errinerungen seines Sohnes Gottfried Reinhardt an Max Reinhardt.* Munich: Droemer Knaur, 1973.

Rentschler, Eric, ed. *The Films of G.W. Pabst: An Extraterritorial Cinema.* New Brunswick, NJ: Rutgers Univ. Press, 1990.

Reuth, Ralf Georg, ed. *Joseph Goebbels Tagebücher 1924–1945.* Vol. 2. Munich: Piper, 1992.

Reynolds, Quentin. "Reluctant Menace." *Collier's*, Jan. 18, 1936.

Riess, Curt. *Das gab's nur einmal: Das Buch der schönsten Filme unseres Lebens*. Hamburg: Sternbücher, 1956.

Rivkin, Allen. *Hello, Hollywood!* New York: Doubleday, 1962.

Robinson, W.R. "The Monitor Image." In *Man and the Movies*, edited by W.R. Robinson. Baton Rouge: Louisiana State Univ. Press, 1967.

Roeber, Georg, and Gerhard Jacoby. *Handbuch der filmwirtschaftlichen Medienbereiche*. Munich: Verlag Dokumentation, 1973.

Rooney, Micky. *Life Is Too Short*. New York: Villard, 1991.

Roters, Eberhard. *Berlin, 1913–1933*. New York: Rizzoli, 1982.

Rothenberg, Gunther E. *The Army of Francis Joseph*. West Lafayette, IN: Purdue Univ. Press, 1976.

Roy, Frederick Hampton. *Ocular Differential Diagnosis*. Philadelphia: Lea and Febiger, 1993.

Rühle, Günther. *Theater für die Republik: 1917–1933 im Spiegel der Kritik*. Frankfurt am Main: S. Fischer, 1967.

———, ed. *Materialien zum Leben und Schreiben der Marieluise Fleisser*. Frankurt am Main: Suhrkamp, 1973.

Rühmann, Heinz. *Das War's: Erinnerungen*. Frankfurt am Main: Ullstein, 1982.

Ryall, Tom. *Alfred Hitchcock and the British Cinema*. Urbana: Univ. of Illinois Press, 1986.

Sahl, Hans. *Memoiren eines Moralisten: Errinerungen*. Zürich: Ammann, 1983.

Sakall, S.Z. *The Story of Cuddles: My Life under the Emperor Francis Joseph, Adolf Hitler, and the Warner Brothers*. London: Cassell, 1954.

Sarris, Andrew. *The American Cinema: Directors and Directions 1929–1968*. New York: E.P. Dutton, 1968.

Schleunes, Karl A. *A Twisted Road to Auschwitz: Nazi Policy toward German Jews, 1933–1939*. Urbana: Univ. of Illinois Press, 1970.

Schoeps, Karl H. *Bertolt Brecht*. New York: Frederick Ungar, 1977.

Schürer, Ernst. *Georg Kaiser*. New York: Twayne, 1971.

Segel, Harold B., ed. and trans. *The Vienna Coffeehouse Wits, 1890–1938*. West Lafayette, IN: Purdue Univ. Press, 1993.

Service, Faith. "Women Scream at the Sight of Him." *Motion Picture*, Feb. 1935.

Sheridan, Michael. "Merchant of Menace." *Modern Screen*, Feb. 1945.

Sherman, Vincent. *Studio Affairs: My Life as a Film Director*. Lexington: Univ. Press of Kentucky, 1996.

Shindler, Colin. *Hollywood Goes to War: Films and American Society, 1939–1952*. London: Routledge and Kegan Paul, 1979.

Shirer, William L. *End of a Berlin Diary*. New York: A Knopf, 1947.

Siebig, Karl. "Ich geh' mit dem Jahrhundert mit." In *Ernst Busch: Eine Dokumentation*. Reinbeck bei Hamburg: Rowohlt, 1980.

Siegel, Don. *A Siegel Film: An Autobiography*. London: Faber and Faber, 1993.

Silke, James R. *Here's Looking at You, Kid: 50 Years of Fighting, Working, and Dreaming at Warner Bros*. Boston: Little, Brown, 1976.

Sklar, Robert. *Movie-Made America: A Social History of American Movies*. New York: Random House, 1975.

Slezak, Walter. *What Time's the Next Swan? By Walter Slezak as Told to Smith-Corona Model 88E*. Garden City, NY: Doubleday, 1962.

Spalek, John, and Joseph Strelka, eds. *Deutsche Exilliteratur seit 1933*. Vol. 1, *Kalifornien*. Bern: Francke, 1976.

Spender, Stephen. Introduction to *Under the Volcano*, by Malcolm Lowry. New York: Plume, 1971.

Sperber, Ann, and Eric Lax. *Bogart.* New York: William Morrow, 1997.

Sperling, Cass Warner, and Cork Millner, with Jack Warner Jr. *Hollywood Be Thy Name: The Warner Bros. Story.* Rockling, CA: Prima, 1994.

Spoto, Donald. *The Art of Alfred Hitchcock: Fifty Years of Motion Pictures.* New York: Hopkinson and Blake, 1976.

———. *The Dark Side of Genius: The Life of Alfred Hitchcock.* Boston: Little, Brown, 1983.

Stahl, E.L. *Friedrich Schiller's Drama: Theory and Practice.* Oxford: Clarendon, 1954.

Steinweis, Alan E. *Art, Ideology, and Economics in Nazi Germany.* Chapel Hill: Univ. of North Carolina Press, 1993.

Sternberg, Josef von. *Fun in a Chinese Laundry: An Autobiography.* New York: Collier, 1965.

Straker, Jean. "Such a Modest Murderer." *Film Pictorial,* May 9, 1936.

Strauss, Herbert A., ed. *Jewish Immigrants of the Nazi Period in the USA.* Vol. 1. New York: K.G. Saur, 1978.

Surmelian, Leon. "*Sh!* Meet PETER LORRE—the *Menacing* Man!" *Motion Picture,* June 1936.

Szczesny, Gerhard. *The Case against Bertolt Brecht.* Translated by Alexander Gode. New York: Frederick Ungar, 1969.

Tatar, Maria. *Lustmord: Sexual Murder in Weimar Germany.* Princeton, NJ: Princeton Univ. Press, 1995.

Taves, Brian. *Robert Florey, the French Expressionist.* Metuchen, NJ: Scarecrow, 1987.

Tax, Sissi. *Marieluise Fleisser, Schreiben, Überleben: Ein Biographischer Versuch.* Frankfurt am Main: Stroemfeld / Roter Stern, 1984.

Taylor, John Russell. *Hitch: The Life and Times of Alfred Hitchcock.* New York: Berkeley, 1980.

———. *Strangers in Paradise: The Hollywood Émigrés, 1933–1950.* New York: Holt, Rinehart, and Winston, 1983.

Tessitore, John A. "The German Film 1: Expressionism in 'M.' *Bright Lights* (UK) 1, no. 3 (Summer 1975).

Tiessen, Paul. "The Cinema of Malcolm Lowry." *Canadian Literature* 44 (Spring 1970).

Truffaut, François. *Hitchcock.* New York: Simon and Schuster, 1967.

Ulrich, Klaus J. *Deutsche Tonfilme: Filmlexikon der abendfüllenden deutschen und deutschsprachigen Tonfilme nach ihren deutschen Uraufführungen.* Berlin: Ulrich J. Klaus-Verlag, 1992.

Viertel, Salka. *The Kindness of Strangers.* New York: Holt, Rinehart, and Winston, 1969.

Völker, Klaus. *Brecht: A Biography.* Translated by John Nowell. New York: Seabury, 1978.

Wächter, Hans-Christof. *Theater im Exil: Sozialgeschichte des deutschen Exil-theaters 1933–1945.* Munich: Carl Hanser, 1973.

Wallace, A.H. *Guy de Maupassant.* New York: Twayne, 1973.

Warner, Jack. *My First Hundred Years in Hollywood.* New York: Random House, 1965.

Weaver, Tom. *Attack of the Monster Movie Makers: Interviews with 20 Genre Giants.* Jefferson, NC: McFarland, 1994.

———. *Interviews with B Science Fiction and Horror Movie Makers: Writers, Producers, Directors, Actors, Moguls, and Makeup.* Jefferson, NC: McFarland, 1988.

———. *Science Fiction Stars and Horror Heroes: Interviews with Actors, Directors, Producers, and Writers of the 1940s through 1960s.* Jefferson, NC: McFarland, 1991.

Wehr, Norbert, ed. *Schreibheft, Zeitschrift für Literatur 23: Malcolm Lowry.* Essen: Rigodon-Verlag, 1984.

Weinberg, Herman G. *Josef von Sternberg: A Critical Study of the Great Film Director.* New York: E.P. Dutton, 1967.

Welles, Orson. "Thoughts on Germany." *Fortnightly* (London), March 1951.

Werfel, Franz. *The Pure at Heart.* New York: Simon and Schuster, 1931.

Werremeier, Friedhelm. "Alle Tot." In *Der Verlorene,* by Peter Lorre. Munich: Belleville, 1996.

Wiener Stadt- und Landesbibliothek. *Karl Kraus contra . . . : Die Prozessakten der Kanzlei Oskar Samek in der Wiener Stadt- und Landesibliothek.* Vol. 3, *1930–1933,* edited by Herwig Würtz. Vienna: Wiener Stadt- und Landesbibliothek, 1996.

Willett, John. *Expressionism.* New York: McGraw-Hill, 1970.

———. "Piscator and Brecht: Closeness through Distance." *ICarbS,* Spring–Summer 1974.

———. *The Theatre of the Weimar Republic.* New York: Holmes and Meier, 1988.

———, ed. and trans. *Brecht on Theatre: The Development of an Aesthetic.* New York: Hill and Wang, 1964.

Williams, Lucy Chase, *The Complete Films of Vincent Price.* Secaucus, NJ: Citadel, 1995.

Williams, Whitney. "PETER LORRE Acclaimed the WORLD'S GREATEST ACTOR." *Silver Screen,* Aug. 1935.

Wilson, Earl. *The Show Business Nobody Knows.* Chicago: Cowles, 1971.

Witt, Hubert, comp. *Brecht as They Knew Him.* New York: International, 1974.

Wollenberg, H.H. *Fifty Years of German Film.* New York: Arno Press and *New York Times,* 1972.

Wysling, Hans, and Marianne Fischer, eds. *Dichter über ihre Dichtungen.* Vol. 14, *Thomas Mann,* part 3, *1944–1955.* Munich: Heimeran / S. Fischer, 1981.

Wyss, Monika. *Brecht in der Kritik: Rezensionen aller Brecht-Uraufführung.* Munich: Kindler, 1977.

Yablonsky, Lewis. *George Raft.* New York: McGraw-Hill, 1974.

Youngkin, Stephen. "M—wie Morphium." In *Der Verlorene,* by Peter Lorre. Munich: Belleville, 1996.

Youngkin, Stephen, James Bigwood, and Raymond J Cabana Jr. *The Films of Peter Lorre.* Secaucus, NJ: Citadel, 1982.

Youngkin, Stephen, and Felix Hofmann. *Peter Lorre: Portrait des Schauspielers auf der Flucht.* Munich: Belleville, 1998.

Zohn, Harry. "John Kafka." In *Deutsche Exilliteratur seit 1933,* edited by John M. Spalek and Joseph Strelka, vol. 1, *Kalifornien,* part 1. Bern: Francke, 1976.

———. *Karl Kraus.* New York: Twayne, 1971.

Zuckmayer, Carl. *A Part of Myself.* Translated by Richard Winston and Clara Winston. New York: Harcourt Brace Jovanovich, 1970.

Zweig, Stefan. *The World of Yesterday: An Autobiography.* New York: Viking, 1943.

INTERVIEWS

Unless otherwise noted, interviews were conducted by the author.

Alda, Robert	Aug. 22, 1988
Allen, Irwin	Oct. 9, 1980
Allen, Robert	Aug. 28, 1978
Alten, Jürgen von	March 24, 1984
Alvin, John	June 30, 2000 (interview by Tom Weaver)
Ames, Leon	Jan. 23, 1979
Amsterdam, Morey	Sept. 25, 1980
Arkoff, Sam	Jan. 29, 1981; Feb. 1, 1995
Avalon, Frankie	Dec. 30, 1974
Bartning, Carl O.	July 30, 1983 (interview by Corinna Müller)

Barton, Charles Jan. 18, 1975
Barton, Julie Gibson Jan. 18, 1975
Beck, Thomas Dec. 17, 1993
Bennett, Charles Jan. 28, 1995
Bentley, Eric Aug. 10, 1973
Bienert, Gerhard March 27, 1984
Blanke, Henry March 14, 1979
Brandt, Eddie May 31, 2001
Briskin, Mort March 12, 1979
Buloff, Joseph March 4, 1983
Burnett, Murray July 7, 1983
Burns, Bob Feb. 7, 2002 (interview by Tom Weaver)
Butler, David Oct. 15, 1973
Buttons, Red Nov. 15, 1978
Cagney, Jeanne Dec. 19, 1978
Calvet, Corinne Aug. 19, 1980
Campbell, William July 9, 1999
Capra, Frank Sept. 11, 1978
Carradine, John Jan. 3, 1975
Chandler, Chick Feb. 14, 1975
Corman, Roger July 9, 1974
Court, Hazel March 12, 1979
——— March 22, 1996 (interview by Bill Katz)
——— Dec. 12, 1994 (interview by Lucy Chase Williams)
Crawford, Broderick Aug. 23, 1980
Daves, Delmer June 30, 1976
Doe, Andrew Jan. 14, 1982
Doniger, Walter Sept. 30, 1975
Drake, Frances Oct. 15, 1983
Duff, Amanda Nov. 23, 1987
Dunne, Philip Nov. 23, 1987
Eden, Barbara Oct. 9, 1980
Eggebrecht, Axel April 24, 1988 (interview by Corinna Müller)
Elliott, Denholm July 14, 1980
Epstein, Julius Nov. 19, 1980
Falkenberg, Paul July 20, 1983
Fehr, Rudi Feb. 2, 1981
Feld, Fritz Nov. 14, 1978
Feuchtwanger, Marta Oct. 16, 1973
Fitzgerald, Geraldine Jan. 31, 1976
Fleischer, Richard July 14, 1975
Florey, Robert June 11, 1975
Foster, Norman July 2, 1974
Fraenkel, Heinrich June 26, 1973
Freeman, Kathleen March 11, 1981
Garnett, Tay May 20, 1975
Gershe, Leonard May 21, 1975
Goff, Harper July 31, Nov. 16, 1978
Gordon, Alex March 11, 2000 (interview by Tom Weaver)
Greenfield, Ted Aug. 24, 1998
Greenson, Ralph Jan. 3, 1975
Haller, Daniel Dec. 6, 1984

Hayman, Irene	Aug. 7, 1982
Henreid, Paul	July 4, 1974
Hitchcock, Alfred	Oct. 17, 1973
Houseman, John	Feb. 8, 1988
Huston, John	Oct. 20, 1974
Ives, Burl	June 22, 1976
Jacobi, Lotte	Sept. 15, 1984
Jaffe, Sam	May 31, 1980
Jameson, Joyce	Oct. 15, 1973
Joseph, Rudolph	March 4, 1990
Kanter, Hal	Aug. 24, 1998
Kennard, Arthur	March 22, 1996
Kerschner, Irvin	July 21, 1980
King, Andrea	March 14, 1979; July 24, 1997
———	March 20, 1996 (interview by Bill Katz)
Kingsley, Sidney	Nov. 14, 1974
Koch, Howard	Jan. 4, 1975
Koster, Henry	May 30, 1985
Kulik, Buzz	Dec. 15, 1977
Lahn, Ilse	Oct. 10, 1982
Lang, Fritz	Oct. 14, 1973
Lenya, Lotte	Oct. 7, 1979
Link, William C.	Nov. 16, 1985
Lockwood, Johnny	Nov. 7, 2001
Lorant, Francis	Oct. 10, 1979
Lorre, Andrew	June 19, 1973; April 6, 1975; March 21, 1980
———	Oct. 7, 1978 (interview by James Bigwood)
Lorre, Catharine	Oct. 15, 17, 1980
Lorre, Zelma	Feb. 15, 1988
Lorring, Joan	Oct. 25, 1980
Lovsky, Celia	Oct. 14, 1973; May 12, 1977
Lyon, James	Aug. 12, 1975
Mamoulian, Rouben	March 15, 1979
Marsh, Marian	July 14, 1987
Martin, Tony	June 26, 1979
Matheson, Richard	Jan. 3, 1975; Dec. 6, 1994; May 31, 2001
Mature, Victor	July 20, 1980
Mayer, Paul	April 13, 1983
———	March 22, 1983 (interview by James Bigwood)
Meadow, Herb	June 17, 1978
Meredith, Burgess	March 21, 1986
Miller, Romaine	March 5, 1998
Morgan, Harry	March 14, 1979
Moritz, Milton	Dec. 2, 1980
Morris, Oswald "Ossie"	May 10, 1988
Nebenzal, Harold	Aug. 21, 1980
Negulesco, Jean	May 31, 1985
Oser, Jan	Jan. 7, 1983
Pan, Hermes	April 1, 1986
Parry, Harvey	Oct. 16, 1978
Patrick, Lee	March 12, 1979
Post, Ted	Aug. 29, 2001 (interview by Tom Weaver)

Powers, James	Jan. 2, 1975
Pressburger, Fred	Dec. 1, 1983; Oct. 1, 1985
Price, Vincent	Jan. 30, 1974; April 26, 1984
Reisch, Walter	Oct. 15, 1978
Riker, Rhoda	May 2, June 21, 1987
Rivkin, Allen	Nov. 17, 1982
Robertson, Cliff	Feb. 24, 1980
Roth, Wolfgang	April 5, 1984
Sahl, Hans	Jan. 27, 1985
Salkow, Laura	Feb. 12, 1980
Salkow, Lester	Oct. 16, 1973
Sanford, Wendy	April 17, 1988
Sawyer, Tom	Sept. 21, 1985
Seymour, Dan	Sept. 2, 1975
Sheldon, Sidney	Jan. 3, 1975
Sherman, Vincent	Aug. 22, 1980
Shutan, Jan	Oct. 17, 1980
Shutan, Robert	Oct. 17, 1980
Siegel, Don	June 25, 1976
Silverstone, Beatrice	Aug. 10, 1973
Silverstone, Jonas	Aug. 10, 1973
Sperling, Milton	May 29, 1985
Spiegel, Sam	Jan. 31, 1979
St. Joseph, Ellis	Jan. 4, 1975
Swope, Herbert	March 12, 1984
Sykes, Barbara	May 8, Sept. 15, 1984; March 27, 1995
Trayne, John	Dec. 31, 2001
Trowe, Gisela	March 1, 1984 (interview by Felix Hofmann)
Veigel, Ludwig	June 24, 1976
Vern-Barnett, Kathy	July 1, 1988
Viertel, Hans	May 27, 1986
Vincent, June	March 14, 1979
Wallis, Hal	March 15, 1979
Warren, Joseph	Oct. 12, 1982 (interview by James Bigwood)
Wilder, Billy	March 14, 1979; March 31, 1986
Wood, Bob	Jan. 27, 1979
Wood, Thomas	March 12, 1979
Wurtele, Morton	Nov. 18, 1986
Wynn, Keenan	Aug. 19, 1980
Yergin, Irving	Dec. 31, 1973; June 23, 1976
Yergin, Naomi	March 3, 1987
Zastupnevich, Paul	Feb. 12, 1981

INDEX

Illustration galleries A, B, and C follow pages 106, 266, and 426 respectively. References to illustrations are in italic and cited by page within the gallery (for example, *A3*).

Beat the Devil (Cockburn), 366
Beat the Devil (1953), 188, 366–73, 555n.
    5, C12; color vs. black and white, 367;
    improvised script, 369; Italy, setting for,
    368, 370; Production Code troubles,
    367; release, 372–73, 555n. 6
Beaverbrook, Max, 163
Bechstein piano company, 194, 305. See
    also Verne, Karen
Beck, Thomas, 149
Beddoe, Don, 174, 175
Beer, Rudolf, A5
Beery, Wallace, 145
Beggar's Opera, The (Gay), 28
Bein, Albert, 265
Békessy, Irme, 39–40
Bel-Air Productions, 395
Belloc-Lowndes, Marie, 289
"Bells, The" (Poe), 312
Benjamin, Walter, 36, 99, 248, 259
Bennett, Charles, 27, 92, 93, 133, 380–81,
    397, 398, 405, 445, 509n. 3
Benny, Jack, 170–71, 221, 433–34
Bentley, Eric, 42–45, 50–51, 256–58, 262–
    63, 277, 291, 297, 307–8, 496n. 35,
    534n. 8, 546n. 18
Berg, Gretchen, 54
Berges, Max, 106
Bergman, Ingrid, 203, 205, 255, 302, 370,
    379, 453, 523–24n. 8, 525n. 27
Bergner, Elisabeth, 32, 33, 37, 264
Berlau, Ruth, 323, 546n. 18; and Brecht, in
    America, 247–60, 266, 268–70, 275;
    giving birth to Brecht's child, 269,
    534n. 14
Berle, Milton, 171, 255, 383, 394
Berlin: in late 1920s, 24–25; Lorre, acting
    in, 25–37, 39–42, 45–51, 67, 68–72,
    495n. 22; Lorre, flight from, 77, 80, 84;
    Reichstag Fire Trial, 1933, 37, 90, 247;
    World War II, fall of, 226
Berliner, Trudy, 226
Berliner Ensemble, 25, 308, 323
Berliner Volksbühne (People's Theater),
    21, 48
Bermuda Troubles (film story, Brecht), 251
Bernfeld, Siegfried, 15
Bernhardt, Kurt (Curtis), 78
Bernstein, Sidney, 90–91, 98, 252
Berry, John, 295
Bertolt Brecht in America (Lyon), 250
Bessie, Alvah, 216–17

Bestie Mensch (The Human Beast). See
    Verlorene, Der (1951)
Best of Broadway, The (television series):
    "Arsenic and Old Lace," 381
Bête Humaine, La (1938), 374
Bête Humaine, La (Zola), 374
Bianchi, Kenneth A., 2
Biedryznski, Richard, 30
Bienert, Gerhard, 44, 45, 59, 61, 71
Big Bow Mystery, The (Zangwill), 235
Big Circus, The (1959), 397–98, 404, 432,
    C14
Biggers, Earl Derr, 145
Big Heat, The (1953), 374–75
Big Show, The (radio show): "Cask of
    Amontillado, The" (Poe)/Who Did
    What to Fadalia, 360–61
"Birth of a Notion, The" (Daffy Duck
    animation), 214
Bitte, wer war zuerst da? (Please, Who Was
    Here First?, stage production), 23
Bitter Sweet (1940), 196
Black Angel (1946), 230, 244, 433
"Black Cat, The" (Poe), 407
Blackmail (1929), 74
Black Sleep, The (1956), 395, 555n. 16
Blanchar, Pierre, 128
Blanke, Henry, 176, 177, 178, 190, 217–18
Blevin, Bruce, 64
Blood on the Sun (1945), 213
Blood Will Have Blood. See Lady Macbeth
    of the Yards (Brecht and Reyher)
Blum, Edwin, 126, 206, 436–37
Blumenthal, Oskar, 32
Bodies in Our Cellar (Kesselring), 206,
    524n. 14
Bogart, Humphrey, 147, 220, 227, 235, 302,
    379, 402, 421–22, 452; All Through the
    Night (1942), 192, 194, 523–24n. 8;
    Beat the Devil (1953), 188, 366–73,
    555n. 5; Casablanca (1942), 203, 204,
    205, 366; death, 428–30; and Lorre, 10,
    185–89, 193, 216, 231–33, 241, 246,
    260, 277–78, 305, 306, 427–30, 523n. 5,
    B15, C5, C12; Maltese Falcon, The
    (1941), 176, 178, 180, 182–84; Passage
    to Marseille (1944), 216; political
    troubles, 296, 298, 299–300, 301
Bogdanovich, Peter, 37
Bois, Curt, 130, 171, 178, 308
Bomben auf Monte Carlo (Bombs on Monte
    Carlo) (1931), 67–68, 266

Bonaparte, Napoleon: portrayals, stage and screen, 22, 140–41, 143–45, 397

Bond, James. *See* Fleming, Ian

Bond, Ward, 182

Bonner Bundeshaus, 348, 546n. 22

Boogie Man Will Get You, The (Andrews), 206

Boogie Man Will Get You, The (1942), 206–7

Borodin, Elfriede, *A10*

Bourvil, 446

Boyer, Charles, 73, 140, 235, 251, 294

Brăila, Romania, 7

Brand, Harry, 152, 163

Brando, Marlon, 94

Brandt, Eddie, 157, 290, 308

Bread King, The (film story, Brecht), 251

Brecht, Barbara, 247, 534n. 16

Brecht, Bertolt, 24, 77, 83, 98, 129, 305, 309, 316, 328, 336, 509n. 1; in America, political activities, 272–74, 297–98, 300–301, 534n. 18, 535n. 19; American visa, trying to obtain, 247, 251; and Chaplin, 43, 294; death, 257, 430; *Dreigroschenoper, Die (The Threepenny Opera)*, 26, 28, 33, 56, 251, 265, 307, 496n. 27; *Fugitive Venus, The*, 267–68, 269, 534n. 12; *Galileo*, 262, 275, 291, 308, 533n. 4, 534n. 8, 535n. 20, 540n. 9; and Germany, flight from, 247–48, 532–33n. 2; and Germany, planning return to, 287–88, 292, 300; and Germany, return to, 307–8; and Germany, views of after war, 341–42, 546n. 18; *Grosse Clown Emaël, Der (The Great Clown Emaël)*, 293–94, 307; *Happy End*, 33–34, 496n. 29; in Hollywood, 104, 248–50, 253–54, 266–67, 533n. 3; in Hollywood, writing, 250–53, 264–68, 269–73, 275–77, 286–88, 292–93, 533nn. 4–5, 534n. 16, 535n. 20; *Lady Macbeth of the Yards*, 275–77, 288, 414, 535n. 20; and Lorre, during 1960s, 411, 413, 416, 426; and Lorre, friendship in America, 244, 247–48, 250, 254, 255–60, 277–78, 281, 286–88, 297–98, 504n. 10, 533n. 3, 534nn. 6–7; and Lorre, in America, trying to work with, 250–53, 261–75, 291–94; and Lorre, in Berlin, 25–26, 27, 31, 45–51, 61, 65, 81, 93, 439, 495–96n.23, 496n. 35; and Lorre, on return to Germany,

287–88, 307–8, 323–24, 356; *Mann ist Mann (Man Equals Man)*, 48–51, 130, 263, 264, 307, 545n. 10; *Mutter, Die (The Mother)*, 44, 45, 71, 78; and Nazism, dramas against, 268, 271–72; *Pioniere in Ingolstadt (Engineers in Ingolstadt)* (Fleisser), 26, 28–31; poetry, 264, 268, 286–87, 356, 534n. 9; *Schweyk im zweiten Weltkrieg (Schweyk in the Second World War)*, 264–66, 269–72, 307, 534n. 15; and Shakespeare, 293; theater/writing theories/style, 18, 28, 43–51, 57, 173, 438, 511n. 24

Brecht, Michel, 269

Brecht, Stefan, 247, 254, 269

"Brecht on Brecht: An Improvisation" (stage production), 411

Brecht on Theatre (Willett), 46–47

Breen, Joseph I., 163, 179–80, 191, 367

Bremer Stadtmusikanten, Die (The Bremen Town Musicians, Grimm), 20

Brennan, Walter, 157

Brenning, Annemarie Hanna, 359, 361, 562n. 2, *C7*; early life, 326; birth of daughter, Lorre, Catharine, 373; and Lorre, filing for divorce from, 414, 450; and Lorre, life with in Hollywood, 378–79, 394–95, 397, 401, 405, 411–12, 448; and Lorre, marriage, 373–74; and Lorre, separation from, 412; miscarriage, 394–95, 411

Briskin, Irving, 166, 206

Briskin, Mort, 279, 280, 314

British Board of Film Censors, 134, 163

British Broadcasting Corporation (BBC), 312

British International Pictures (B.I.P.), 92, 93

Broadway "An American Time-Picture in Three Acts," 362

Bronnen, Arnolt, 27

Brooks, Clive, 99

Brown, Joe E., 402

Browning, Tod, 115

Bruckner, Ferdinand, 81, 140–41, 144

Brueghel, Pieter, the Elder, 50

Buchman, Sidney, 272

Büchner, Georg, 34

Bucket of Blood, A (1959), 444

Bud Abbott and Lou Costello Show, The (radio show), 288

Budapest, Hungary, 36, 138, 234–35

Bugs Bunny, 214, 453

Bühnengenossenschaft (Society of German Theater Employees), 25

Buloff, Joseph, 390, 392, *C12*

Bunge, Hans, 253

Buono, Angelo, Jr., 2

Burgtheater, Vienna, 14, 18, 24, 33

Burnett, Murray, 201–2, 203

Burns, Bob, 423

Burri, Emil, 323

Busch, Ernst, 45, 47, 69, 72, 308

Buster Keaton Story, The (1957), 384

Butler, David, 170

Buttons, Red, 405–6

Caesar's Last Days (film story, Brecht), 251

Café Central, Vienna, 15, 38, 495n. 16

Café Herrenhof, Vienna, 15, 18, 495n. 11

Café Kosmos, Vienna, 38

Café Siller, Vienna, 38

Cagney, James, 147, 257, 452

Cagney, Jeanne, 304

Cahn, Edward L., 395

Calleia, Joseph, 295

Calthrop, Donald, 74

Calvet, Corinne, 129, 302, 303

Cambridge Productions, 396

Cameron, Kate, 120

Campbell, William, 420

Canadian Broadcasting Corporation (CBC), 387, 426

Canby, Vincent, 355, 407

Cantor, Eddie, 301, 381

Capone, Amadeo "Mimi," 230

Capote, Truman, 188, 368, 370, 372

Capra, Frank, 152, 162, 189, 524n. 13; *Arsenic and Old Lace* (1944), 189, 198–200; and Lorre, 199–200, 282

Captain America (1942), 207

Cardiff, Jack, 399, 400–401

Carradine, John, 13, 152, 162, 241, 395, 555n. 17

Carroll, Harrison, 225

Carroll, Madeleine, 132–33

Carrotblanca (1995), 453

Carson, Charles, 133

Carson, Johnny, 95

Carter, Nick, 196

Cartier, Rudolph, 72, 73, 78, 80, 356, 532–33n. 2, 547n. 32

Casablanca (1942), 74, 211, 212, 215, 221, 223, 226, 236, 239, 268, 302, 366; and

émigré actors in Hollywood, 202–3; making of, 203–5; spoofs of, 451, 453; surprising success of, 205; true-life story for, 201–2

Casbah (1948), 294–96

Case Against Bertolt Brecht, The (Szczesny), 44

"Cask of Amontillado, The" (Poe), 209, 407; *Big Show, The* (radio show), Lorre performance of, 361

Caspar Hauser (story), 77, 83, 84–85, 356. *See also Kaspar Hauser von Heute, Ein (A Caspar Hauser of Today)* (Lorre and Eggebrecht)

Caspar Hauser (Wassermann), 110

Castlerosse, Valentine, 163

Catcher in the Rye (Salinger), 381

Cat Creature, The (1973), 443

Cat on a Hot Tin Roof (1958), 431

Cat People (1942), 419

Caucasian Chalk Circle, The (Brecht), 308

Centre Nationale de la Cinematographie, 62

Chamber of Horrors (projected, 1944), 215, 524–25n. 24

Champion (1949), 375

Chan, Charlie. *See* Charlie Chan films

Chandler, Chick, 150, 152

Chaney, Lon, Jr., 163, 215, 231, 395, 423, 434, 554–55n. 4

Chaplin, Charles, 104, 140, 250, 301, 312; and Brecht, 43, 294; and Lorre, 99–100, 101, 358

Chapman, Tom, 276

Charisse, Cyd, 390, 391

Charlie Chan at the Fights. See Mr. Moto's Gamble (1938)

Charlie Chan at the Ringside. See Mr. Moto's Gamble (1938)

Charlie Chan films, 147, 148, 149, 150, 151–52, 153, 157, 159, 160, 162, 518n. 9, 519n. 16; *Chinese Parrot, The* (1927), 145; *House without a Key, The* (1926), 145

Chase, The (1946), 184, 244, 327, 378

Chase, William James Hadley, 404

Chatterton, Ruth, 144

Cheap Detective, The (1978), 452

Chester the chimp, 433, 435

"Children's Crusade" (poem, Brecht), 268

Chinese Parrot, The (1927), 145

Christie, Agatha, 413

409–11, 422–23, 545n. 1; health issues, in 1920s, 21, 22, 24, 25, 39, 40–41; and Hitler, joking about, 84–85, 203, 413, 421; Hollywood, arrival, 99, 105–9; Hollywood, political involvement, lack of, 257; Hollywood, political trouble, 244, 273–74, 296–302, 534n. 18, 535n. 19; Hollywood, railing against, 263–64; and the Hollywood Canteen, 221; infidelity, 306; and Ives, Burl, friendship, 198, 373, 428, 430–32, 448, 533n. 3; at Lake Arrowhead, 266, 268, 534n. 11; and Lovsky, Celia, *B4, B11*; and Lovsky, Celia, early relationship, 31–32, 33, 41, *B1–2*; and Lovsky, Celia, marriage, 96–97, 496n. 32; and Lovsky, Celia, separation from, 184, 193–94; modesty, 3; name change, 19, 197; and Nazi crackdown on Jews, 79–80; office materials, love of, 329, 379; Paris, emigration to, 70, 83–88, 504n. 19; personal popularity of, 229–31, 282; pet St. Bernard, 281, 305–6, 316; and Ping-Pong, 74, 99, 371; politics of, 296, 340–41, 361–62, 437–38; and practical jokes, 182–83, 190, 216, 235, 240–41, 369, 377–78, 390, 391–92, 396, 523nn. 4, 6; as "psychiatrist," 370–71, 386–87, 420–21, 426, 432–33, 562n. 1; reading, love of, 413; retelling of past, 425–28, 437, 447; and Sanford, Wendy, 437; sense of humor, 26–27, 47–48, 60, 73, 96, 125, 136–37, 154, 175, 210, 417, 495n. 21, 510n. 11, 524n. 17, 525n. 36; sense of humor, with Bogart, 186–89, 216, 369–70; sense of humor, with Greenstreet, 219–20; and smoking, 235, 242, 313, 339, 403, 452; and tennis, 197–98; touring Displaced Person (DP) camps, 316; United States, arrival, 98–99; and Verne, divorce, 366, 373; and Verne, failing marraige, 304–7, 316, 554–55n. 4; and Verne, friendship with after divorce, 411, 412; and Verne, life with in Hollywood, 250, 262, 266, 284, 292, 309, 554–55n. 4, *C4*; and Verne, marriage, 225, 232–33; and Verne, on the road with, 229, 230; and Verne, meeting and romance, 197, 524n. 12, *B15*; veteran tours, 316–18, 361, 545n. 3; Vienna, flight from to Czechoslovakia, 83; Viennese coffeehouse life,

15–16, 18, 38–39; voice, distinctive, 138, 197, 290, 404, 420, 434–35, 451, 453, 524n. 12; wartime activities, 209, 221; and wives, friendships with, 411–12, 448

Lorre Inc., 280, 294, 304

Lorre, Peter: Stage and Screen Career: *Abend der Überraschungen, Ein (An Evening of Surprises)*, *A5*; acting, American stage, 223–25, 229, 264, 281–82, 283, 303–4, 362–64, 433, 525n. 29, 534n. 9, 554n. 1; acting, beginnings, 10–12; acting, Berlin, 25–37, 39–42, 45–51, 67, 68–72, 495n. 22; acting, Brecht, in Berlin, 25–26, 27, 31, 45–51, 61, 65, 81, 93, 439, 495–96n.23, 496n. 35; acting, Breslau, 19–21, 138; acting, Broadway, possibilities, 143–45, 162, 212, 268–69, 359, 362–65, 554n. 3, 555n. 14; acting, duality of, 45–46, 143, 166, 178–79, 384, 425–26, 433–35; acting, England, film work, 89–97; acting, England, theatre, 309, 311–12; acting, Greenstreet, work with, 219–20, 221–23, 236–37, 244, 245, 295, 525n. 28, 525–26n. 38, *C1*; acting, Hitchcock, work with, 91, 93–94, 95–98, 133, 136, 401–2, 504n. 9, 511n. 30; acting, impersonators, 394, 439–43, 451–53, 562n. 2; acting, improvising lines, 227, 315, 335, 343, 373, 377, 408, 416, 419; acting, Lang, work with, 37, 58, 59–61, 66–67, 504n. 10, *B3*; acting, leading man, 227, 229, 239, 245, 361; acting, Napoleon, as role, 140–41, 163, *B10*; acting, Nero, as role, 247, 397; acting, Paris, lack of, 86–88, 505n. 21; acting, projects, 1948, fallen through, 540–41n. 13; acting, Quasimodo, as role, 163; acting, scene-stealing, 241–42, 314–15, 446; acting, screen career after *M*, 67–68, 72–78, 80–81; acting, screen debut, 37–38; acting, screen villainy, 1–2, 510nn. 11, 19; acting, screen villainy, expertise, 91–92, 115–16, 119–20, 126, 129, 165, 166, 314–15; acting, screen villainy, typecasting, 86–87, 109–10, 156, 311, 381–82; acting, Shakespeare, 20, 21, 62, 82–83, 277, 356; acting, smoking, use of, 22, 91, 204–5, 208, 214, 333, 339; acting, Star on Walk of Fame, 413; acting, Stegreiftheater

(Theater of Spontaneity), 16–18; acting, Stiefel as manager, 279–80; acting, style, 45–48, 50–51, 61–62, 116–17, 119–20, 124–25, 129, 130, 242; acting, thoughts on, 17, 147, 163, 246, 260–61, 272, 404–5, 408, 425; acting, thoughts on being typecast, 67, 76, 311, 322, 361, 377, 388–89, 393, 426, 510nn. 17–18; acting, thoughts on, in movies, 421–22, 426, 432, 439; acting, union involvement, 21, 23, 164–65, 237–38; acting, unrealized projects, AIP, 443–46; acting, unrealized projects at death, 446; acting, Vienna, 11, 23–24, 38, 81–83, 362, A3–5; acting, Zurich, 21–22; *Alles verkehrt! (Everything Upside Down!)* (cabaret piece), 23; *All Through the Night* (1942), 153, 192–93, 194, 197, 212, 523n. 4; *Amazing Dr. Clitterhouse, The* (projected remake, 1943), 216–17; animated appearances of, 214–15, 453; *Around the World in Eighty Days* (1956), 384; *Arsenic and Old Lace* (1944), 189, 199–200; *Background to Danger* (1943), 207–8; *Beast with Five Fingers, The* (1946), 239–44, 510n. 18, 525nn. 35–37; *Beat the Devil* (1953), 188, 366–73, 555n. 5, C12; *Bertolt Brecht Evening* (Studio Theater of the New School for Social Research, New York), 264, 534n. 9; *Big Circus, The* (1959), 397–98, 404, 432, C14; *Bitte, wer war zuerst da? (Please, Who Was Here First?*, stage production*)*, 23; *Black Angel* (1946), 230, 244, 433; *Bomben auf Monte Carlo (Bombs on Monte Carlo)* (1931), 67–68, 266; *Boogie Man Will Get You, The* (1942), 206–7; *Bremer Stadtmusikanten, Die (The Bremen Town Musicians,* Grimm), 20; Broadway "An American Time-Picture in Three Acts," 362; *Buster Keaton Story, The* (1957), 384; *Captain America* (1942), projected for, 207; *Casablanca* (1942), 203–5, 211, 212, 215, 221, 223, 226, 302, 366; *Casbah* (1948), 294–96; and *Caspar Hauser* story, 77–78, 83, 84–85, 110, 356; *Chase, The* (1946), 184, 244, 327, 378; *Comedy of Terrors, The* (1964), 410, 418–21, 423, 438, 444, 556n. 26; *Confidential Agent* (1945), 235, 275, C5; *Congo Crossing* (1956),

384, 555n. 10; *Conspirators, The* (1944), 220, 221; *Constant Nymph, The* (1943), 199, 200, 212; *Crack-Up* (1937), 142–43, 157, 518n. 2; *Crime and Punishment* (1935), 113–14, 121–28, 131, 178, 227, 242, 395, 426, 510n. 13, 511n. 21, B5; *Cross of Lorraine, The* (1943), 186, 210–11, 215, 524n. 18; *Danger Island* (1939), 148, 151, 152, 157, 159; *Dantons Tod (Danton's Death)* (Büchner), 34–35; as director, 335–37, 363; as director, aspiring, 213, 321; Döblin, Alfred, 65th birthday celebration, 269; *Dompteur, Der (The Lion Tamer,* Savoir), 67, 397; *Double Confession* (1950), 314–15; *Du haut en bas (From Top to Bottom,* 1933), 86–87; *Face behind the Mask, The* (1941), 172–75, 242, 378, B13; *Faust* (Goethe), 22; *Faust* (Lenau), 23; *Five Weeks in a Balloon* (1962), 405–6, 410, 433; *fleissige Leserin, Die (The Diligent Reader),* 23, A3; *F.P.1 antwortet nicht (Floating Platform 1 Doesn't Answer,* 1932), 73–75, 504n. 14, A16; *Frühlings Erwachen (Spring's Awakening,* Wedekind), 35–37, 39, 72, A7; *Fünf von der Jazzband (The Jazz Band Five,* 1932), 71–72; *Geschichten aus dem Wiener Wald: Volksstück in Drei Teilen (Tales from the Vienna Woods: Folk Piece in Three Acts,* Horváth), 70; *Gesellschaft (Loyalties,* Galsworthy), 21; *Golgotha* (Ludwig), 81, B2; and *Good Soldier Švejk, The,* 100–101, 140, 162, 186, 265–66, 270–71, 400, 439; *Happy End* (Brecht), 33–34, 496n. 29; *heilige Johanna, Die (St. Joan,* Shaw), 22; *Heinrich IV* (Pirandello), 22; *Hell Ship Mutiny* (1957), 396; *Hermannsschlacht, Die (Hermann's Battle,* Kleist), 20; Hollywood, Columbia, first contract, 92, 98, 105, 137–38, 139–41, 199, 509n. 4; Hollywood, Columbia, later contract, 166–68, 172; Hollywood, Columbia, waiting at, 110–14; Hollywood, comedy, 142–43, 162, 165–66, 199–200, 280–81, 294, 372, 377, 393, 405–6, 408, 555nn. 14, 22; Hollywood, dissatisfaction with, 246–47, 261–62, 292–93, 384, 427–28; Hollywood, hiatus from films, mid-fifties, 379–80; Hollywood, image making, 111–13, 152, 274–75, B6–8; Hollywood, integration into, 130–31, 436–37; Hollywood, RKO contract, 168; Hollywood, 20th Century–Fox, contract, 141, 142–45, 157, 159, 164, 173–74, 518n. 2, 518–19n. 10, 519n. 13; Hollywood, Warner Bros., contract, 179, 211–14, 225, 253, 524nn. 19, 21, 525n. 31; Hollywood, Warner Bros., contract, end of, 244, 280, 281, 297; Hollywood, Warner Bros., dissatisfaction with, 226, 240–41, 244–45, 278; Hollywood, Warner Bros., drug addiction during time at, 337; Hollywood, Warner Bros., and Greenstreet, better payment of, 222–23, 525n. 28; Hollywood, Warner Bros., life at, 184–87, 215, 244–45, 246, 252, 525n. 36; Hollywood, Warner Bros., remembering, 365, 427; Hollywood Canteen (1944), 221–22; Hotel Berlin (1945), 225–26, 229, 241, 341; I'll Give a Million (1938), 13, 161–62, 241; Invisible Agent (1942), 201, 203; I Play the Devil (Pascal), 212; Island of Doomed Men (1940), 62, 166–67; I Was an Adventuress (1940), 165–66; Journalisten, Die (The Journalists, Freytag), 20; Kandidat, Der (The Candidate) (Sternheim), 41; Koffer des Herrn O.F., Die (The Luggage of Mr. O.F., 1931), 68, A15; Lancer Spy (1937), 161, 208, 519n. 18; lustigen Weiber von Windsor, Die (The Merry Wives of Windsor, Shakespeare), 20; M (1931), 38, 52–62, 64–66, 90, 99, 139, 178, 229, 428, 435, 436, 443–44, 540n. 11, A11–14; Mädchen auf dem Diwan, Die (The Girls on the Couch), 23; Mad Love (1935), 114, 115–19, 121, 124, 227, 510n. 15, 547–48n. 35, B3; Maltese Falcon, The (1941), 176, 178–84, 185, 197, 211, 222, 247, 327, 366, 534n. 7; Mann, das Tier und die Tugend, Der (The Man, the Animal, and Virtue, Pirandello), 21; Mann ist Mann (Man Equals Man, Brecht), 48–51, 263, 264, 282, 307, 411, 545n. 10, A9–10; Man Who Knew Too Much, The (1934), 91–95, 96, 105, 132, 133; Man with the Head of Glass, The (Wilson) (monologue), 224–25, 229, 230; Marlborough

zieht in den Krieg (Marlborough Goes to War), A4; Mask of Dimitrios, The (1944), 187, 217–19, 220, 274, 327, 525n. 26, C1–2; Meet Me in Las Vegas (1956), 382; Mr. District Attorney (1941), 175; Mr. Moto movies, 146–61, 201, 426, 518n. 9, 518–19n. 10, 519nn. 11, 14, B11; Mr. Moto movies, projects missed during, 162–64; Mr. Moto's Gamble (1938), 148, 151–52, 162; Mr. Moto's Last Warning (1939), 148, 149, 150, 155, 519n. 12; Mr. Moto Takes a Chance (1938), 148, 149, 150, 161; Mr. Moto Takes a Vacation (1939), 148, 156; Muscle Beach Party (1964), 189, 444; My Favorite Brunette (1947), 280–81, C6; Mysterious Mr. Moto (1938), 148, 150, 151, 154, 155, 398; Nacht der Prominenten (Night of Prominent People, Kabarett der Komiker), 283; Nancy Steele Is Missing (1937), 144, 145, 208; Napoleon oder die hundert Tage (Napoleon or the Hundred Days) (Grabbe), 22; Nebeneinander: Volksstück in fünf Akten (Side by Side: Popular Play in Five Acts, Kaiser), 68–69; Nemo Bank, Die (Verneuil), 70–71; Night at Madame Tussaud's, A: A Shocker in the Grand Guignol Manner (Mayer), 362–65, 554n. 1; Passage to Marseille (1944), 185, 188, 215–16, 237; Patsy, The (1964), 339, 446; Peer Gynt (Ibsen), 22; Pioniere in Ingolstadt (Engineers in Ingolstadt) (Fleisser), 26, 28–31, 35, 36, 37, 71, 72, A6; Quadratur des Kreises, Die (Squaring the Circle, Katayev), 26–27, 42, 55; Quicksand (1950), 304; Raven, The (1963), 120, 414–18, 422, 428, 436; Romeo und Julia (Romeo and Juliet) (Shakespeare), 20; Rope of Sand (1949), 129, 302–3; Sad Sack, The (1957), 396; Scent of Mystery (1960), 399–401, 428; schlimmen Buben in der Schule, Die (The Bad Boys in the School, Nestroy), 21; Schuss im Morgengrauen (A Shot at Dawn, 1932), 72–73, 78, 97; Secret Agent (1936), 66, 124, 131–37, B9; Silk Stockings (1957), 257, 390–93, C12; Story of Mankind, The (1957), 396–97; Strange Cargo (1940), 165; Stranger on the Third Floor (1940), 168–70, 327, 520nn. 23–24;

231, 423, 434; *Royal Gelatin Hour, The* (radio show), 160, 208; *Spotlight Revue* (radio show), 157, 290, 308; *Stage Door Canteen* (radio show), 209; *Stars for Humanity* (radio show), 209; *Studio 57* (television series), 382, 555n. 9; *Suspense* (radio show), 208–9, 212, 213–14, *C2*; *Tell It to Groucho* (television series), 410; "Tell-Tale Heart, The" (Poe), radio performance of, 289; *Texaco Star Theater, The* (radio show), 160, 209–10, 524n. 17; *Texaco Star Theater, The* (television series), 304; *Treasury of Terror* (pilot radio episode), 445–46; *Treasury Star Parade* (radio show), 209; *Variety* (BBC television series), "Man with the Head of Glass, The," 312

Lorring, Joan, 220, 227–28, 236, 239

Losey, Joseph, 292, 540n. 9

Lost Horizon (1937), 162

Love Me Tonight (1933), 389

Love under Fire (1937), 162

Lovsky, Celia (first wife), 6, 14, 60, 215, 309, 496n. 28, 534n. 17, 545n. 4, *A6*; acting career, 32–33, 39, 41, 67, 70, 81, 98, 252, 382, 411, 496nn. 26, 27, 34; and Brecht, 258–59, 430; and Lorre, aiding career of, 33, 36–37, 38–39; and Lorre, aiding him in second marriage, 231–32, 233, 554–55n. 4; and Lorre, death, 448; and Lorre, drug addiction, 131–32; and Lorre, early relationship, 26, 31–32, 33, 41, 83–84, *B1–2*; and Lorre, financial manager, 87, 92, 111, 114–15, 137–38, 158–59; and Lorre, friendship after divorce, 307, 395, 411–12, 413, 438; and Lorre, life with in Hollywood, 99, 106–7, 125, *B3–4*, *B11*; and Lorre, marriage, 96–97, 496n. 32; and Lorre, quality of relationship, 231–32; and Lorre, separation from, 184, 193–94

Lowry, Malcolm, 357–58, 547–48n. 35, 548n. 36

Loy, Myrna, 348, 389

Lubitsch, Ernst, 97, 99, 141, 144, 255, 257, 390

Lucky Nick Cain (1951), 404

Lucretia Borgia (Bruckner), 144

Ludwig, Emil, 140, 141

Ludwig, V.O., 81

Lugosi, Bela, 164, 170, 215, 395, 451, 453

Lukas, Paul, 197, 198, 376

Luke, Hanna, 84, 86

Luke, Keye, 116

Lumière Project (European Union), 38

Lustig, Hans G. "Jan," 84, 85, 110

Lustigen Weiber von Windsor, Die (The Merry Wives of Windsor, Shakespeare), 20

Lux Radio Theater (radio show), 208

Lux Video Theatre (television series): "Taste," 361

Lvovsky, Bratislav Emil, 32, 496nn. 25–26

Lvovsky, Cäcilie Josephine. *See* Lovsky, Celia (first wife)

Lye, Len, 134–35

Lyndon, Barre, 385

Lyon, James, 250, 253, 286, 294

M (1931), 1, 2, 78, 130, 175, 252, 264, 321, 338, 503n. 2, *A14*; acclaim for Lorre, 64–65, 90, 99, 178, 436; beginnings, 52–55; English version, 504n. 9, *A12*; Lang's working style, 59–62; Lorre, playing similar roles, 115–16, 133, 169–70, 242; as Lorre's "first" film, 38, 428, 435; Lorre typecasting from, 76, 80, 86–87, 89, 109–10, 164, 245, 426, 435; *M le maudit (M the Damned One)* (French language version), 62–63, 83, 504n. 9, *A13*; music, 57, 58; Nazi view of, 84–85, 172; posters, *A11–13*; premiere and impact, 63–66; radio monologue from, 139; remake, 292; remake, and Lorre, 292, 443–44, 540n. 11; story, 55–59; United States showings, 97–98, 509n. 5; and *Verlorene, Der* (1951), comparison, 322, 330, 333, 334, 346–47, 355

M (1951), 292

MacArthur, Charles, 139

Macbeth (Shakespeare), 275

MacDonald, Jeanette, 196, 316

MacDonald, Philip, 150

MacDonald, Wallace, 166

Macgowan, Kenneth, 146

MacKenzie, Aeneas, 121

MacMurray, Fred, 184

Mädchen auf dem Diwan, Die (The Girls on the Couch), 23

Mad Doctor (Thwaites), 139

Mad Love (1935), 114, 115–19, 121, 124, 141, 227, 242, 510n. 15, 547–48n. 35, *B3*

Nolan, Lloyd, 160
Norddeutscher Rundfunk, Hamburg, 328
Nordhoff, Charles, 215–16
Notes from the Underground
(Dostoyevsky), 113
Not Too Narrow...Not Too Deep (Sale), 165
Nyiregyhazi, Erwin, 243

Oboler, Arch, 233–34, 250, 525n. 34
O'Brian, Jack, 384
O'Brien, Pat, 146, 184, 402
Obringer, Roy J., 208, 213
O'Connell, Helen, 3, 13, 20, 413
O'Connell, Thomas Edward, 172
Odets, Clifford, 250, 251
Offenbach, Jacques, 41, 67, 70, 71
O'Hara, John, 186
Oh My Nerves (1935), 127
Oland, Warner, 148, 153, 157
Olivier, Laurence, 136
One in a Million (1936), 141
Open Book, An (Huston), 368
Ophüls, Max, 22, 27, 113
Orsatti, Frank, 168, 196, 217
Orska, Maria, 32
Ossenfort, William F., 284, 285, 286
Österreichische Musik und Theaterzeitung, 32
Österreichischen Bühnenvereins (Austrian
Theater Union), 23
Österreichisches Filmindustrie, 38
Oswald, Richard, 37, 52
Othello (Shakespeare), 32
Outsider, The (1940), 196

Pabst, G.W., 86, 99, 496n. 28, *B3*
Pachter, Henry, 104, 109, 202, 341
Palance, Jack, 385
Pallenberg, Max, 265
Pan, Hermes, 392
Pan-Film, Austria, 114
Panski, Waclaw, 163, 519n. 21
Parables for the Theater (Bentley), 258
Paramount Pictures, 139, 141, 163–64,
202, 213, 215, 248, 302, 384, 387, 389,
524n. 23; the *Paramount* case, 382;
Patsy, The (1964), 446; *Rope of Sand*
(1949), 302–3
Paramount Theatre, New York, 303
Parker, Eleanor, 235
Parrott, Cecil, 100–101, 271
Parry, Harvey, 147–48, 153–57, 181, 207–8,
410, 413, 423, 448

Parsons, Louella, 141, 163
Partos, Frank, 168, 169, 170
Pascal, Ernest, 212, 266, 286, 534n. 10
Passage to Marseille (1944), 185, 188, 215–
16, 221, 236, 237
Pathé Studios, 145
Patrick, Lee, 180, 182, 260
Patriot, Der (The Patriot, Neumann), 356
Patsy, The (1964), 339, 446
Paul Kohner Agency, 268
Peary, Harold, 402
Peer Gynt (Ibsen), 22
Peer Gynt Suite "Hall of the Mountain
King" (Grieg), 57, 58, 452
Pelswick, Rose, 408
Penelope the cat, 453
Pepe Le Moko (Ashelbe), 294
Peppler, Hans, 20, 21, 23, 39, 504n. 5
Pepsodent Show, The (NBC radio show), 138
Perfect Crime, The (1928), 236
Persecution of the Jews in Germany, The
(Bernstein), 90
Peter Lorre Playhouse (pilot television
series), 387, 555n. 11
"Peter Lorre" (song, The Jazz Butcher), 453
Peterson, Donald Kent, 108
Petrucci, Antonio, 348
Pevney, Joseph, 47, 432
Phantom from 10,000 Leagues, The (1956),
406
Philco Radio Time (radio show), 290
Philip Morris Playhouse, The (radio show),
208
Phillips, Gene, 58
Pichel, Irving, 304, 389
Pidgeon, Walter, 403, 404
Pinthus, Kurt, 30, 40
*Pioniere in Ingolstadt (Engineers in
Ingolstadt)* (Fleisser), 26, 28–31, 35, 36,
37, 71, 72, *A6*
Pirandello, Luigi, 21, 22
Piscator, Erwin, 265, 269, 270
Planer, Franz, 378
Playhouse 90 (television series): "Cruel
Day, The," 386; "Last Tycoon, The," 385;
"Sizeman and Son," 384
Playwrights Company, 364
Plummer, Christopher, 452
Poe, Edgar Allen, 111, 120, 209, 268, 281,
289, 303, 312, 322–23, 360–61, 362; AIP
horror-comedies of stories of, 406–8,
413–21, 444

Vern-Barnett, Kathy, 6, 8, 10, 11
Verne, Jules, 375, 376
Verne, Karen, 362, 448, 524n. 10, *B14*;
    acting career, 195–97, 294, 305–6, 316,
    523–24n. 8; death, 541n. 16; early life,
    194–95; England and Germany, return
    to, 310, 311–13; and Lorre, divorce,
    366, 373; and Lorre, drug addiction,
    285–86, 313–14, 315; and Lorre, failing
    marriage, 304–7, 316, 554–55n. 4; and
    Lorre, friendship with after divorce,
    411, 412; and Lorre, life with in
    Hollywood, 250, 262, 266, 284, 292,
    309, 554–55n. 4, *C4*; and Lorre,
    marriage, 225, 232–33; and Lorre, on
    the road with, 229, 230; and Lorre,
    meeting and romance, 197, 524n. 12,
    B15; and Lovsky, Celia, friendship with,
    233, 412; low self-esteem, 305–7, 316;
    MGM, contract with, 196; and Powers,
    James, 418, 524n. 12, 541n. 16, 554–
    55n. 4; and son, Young, Alastair, 195,
    232, 306, 307, 313, 541n. 15; 20th
    Century–Fox, contract with, 196;
    Warner Bros., contract with, 196–97;
    and Young, Arthur, 195, 232, 306
Verneuil, Louis, 70
*verschwundene Frau, Die (The Missing
    Wife,* 1929), 37–38, *A8*
Via Mala (1948), 324
Vich, Vaclav, 324, 325, *C11*
Vidocq. See Scandal in Paris, A (1945)
Vidocq, François Eugène, 320
Vidor, King, 99
Vienna, Austria, 7–8; coffeehouse life, 15–
    16, 18, 38–39
Viertel, Berthold, 69, 248, 262, 534n. 12,
    540n. 5
Viertel, Hans, 259, 262, 267, 269, 534n. 12
Viertel, Peter, 366–67, 372
Viertel, Salka, 104, 107, 248, 250, 262
Vigny, Benno, 319, 321, 322, 324
Vincent, Allen, 174
Vincent, June, 230, 433
Volksbühne, Berlin, 34, 39, 40, 48, 68–69
von Harbou, Thea, 53–55, 57, 58, 59, 60, 322
von Sternberg, Josef, 80, 99, 114, 141;
    Crime and Punishment (1935), 121–24,
    126, 127, 131, 510n. 13, *B5*
Voodoo Woman (1956), 406
*Voruntersuchung (Preliminary Investiga-
    tion,* Alsberg and Hesse), 41–42

Voyage to the Bottom of the Sea (1961),
    309, 402–4

Wachsmann, Franz. *See* Waxman, Franz
Wald, Jerry, 276, 374
Walker, Alexander, 61
Walker, Theodore J., 21, 238, 283
Walker, Vernon L., 170
Wall, Hilde, 22
Wallace, Mike, 109, 404, 410, 422, 428, 429
Wallensteins Tod (Wallenstein's Death)
    (Schiller), 22
Wallis, Hal, 177, 180, 191, 211, 221, 302–3,
    523–24n. 8; *Casablanca* (1942), 202,
    203–4; *Conspirators, The* (1944), 221
Walsh, Bill, 376
Walsh, Raoul, 207–8
Walton, William, 93
Waltzes from Vienna (1933), 93
War Is Declared (Panski), 163, 519n. 21
Warner, Albert, 190
Warner, Harry, 187, 190, 191–92
Warner, Jack L., 190, 192, 208, 213, 217,
    239, 257, 276, 297; *Arsenic and Old Lace*
    (1944), 198–99; *Casablanca* (1942),
    203–4; *Hotel Berlin* (1945), 226; called
    "kreep" by Bogart/Lorre, 186–87; and
    Lorre, 179, 188, 211, 220, 223, 227, 238,
    244, 253; *Maltese Falcon, The* (1941),
    177, 180, 523n. 2; *Verdict, The* (1946),
    236, 238
Warner, Sam, 190
Warner Bros. Pictures, 140, 141, 148, 164,
    200, 272, 302, 372, 375, 382, 396, 437,
    453; *All Through the Night* (1942), 153,
    192, 194, 523–24n. 8; anti-Nazi stance
    of, 190–93, 215–16; *Arsenic and Old
    Lace* (1944), 198, 524n. 14; *Background
    to Danger* (1943), 207–8; *Beast with
    Five Fingers, The* (1946), 239–44,
    525nn. 35–37; *Casablanca* (1942), 202–
    5; and film noir, 525–26n. 38; *Hotel
    Berlin* (1945), 225–26; Lorre, contract
    with, 179, 211–14, 225, 253, 524nn. 19–
    21, 525n. 31; Lorre, contract with, end
    of, 244, 280, 281, 297; Lorre, dissatis-
    faction with, 226, 240–41, 244–45, 278;
    Lorre, drug addiction, during time at,
    337; Lorre, life at, 184–87, 215, 244–45,
    246, 252, 525n. 36; Lorre, remember-
    ing, 365, 427; Lorre vs. Greenstreet,
    payment of, 222–23, 525n. 28; *Maltese*

448; as publicist, during Lorre's drug investigation, 283–86